SLAUGHTERHOUSE

SLAUGHTERHOUSE

THE HANDBOOK
OF THE EASTERN FRONT

THE ABERJONA PRESS
BEDFORD, PA

German Army and *Luftwaffe* Order of Battle Information: *Steve Myers,*
   Hugh Foster, Keith E. Bonn
Waffen-SS Order of Battle Information: *Mark Rikmenspoel*
Soviet Order of Battle Information: *Scott McMichael, and Yuri and Natalya*
   Khonko
German Biographical Sketches: *Keith E. Bonn, Steve Myers, and Hugh Foster*
Soviet Biographical Sketches: *Scott McMichael*
Chronology and Forgotten Battles Chapters: *David Glantz*
Finnish, Hungarian, Romanian, and Italian Unit Histories: *Keith E. Bonn*
Weapons Tables: *Hugh Foster and Keith E. Bonn*

Acknowledgements
In addition to graciously giving permission to use edited versions of some
of his privately published work, David Glantz contributed much of the
material used in the chapter about the Soviet WWII order of battle.

Special thanks to George Nafziger for his information about the Hungarian and Romanian orders of battle.

Special thanks to Mikko Härmeinen for his contributions about the Finns.

Editor: Keith E. Bonn
Production: Aegis Consulting Group, Inc.
Printer: Mercersburg Printing

The Aberjona Press is an imprint of Aegis Consulting Group, Inc.,
    Bedford, Pennsylvania 15522

ISBN: 0-9717650-9-X

Originally published by The Military Book Club as *Slaughterhouse: The
Encyclopedia of the Eastern Front*
Visit us at www.militarybookclub.com
This edition published in cooperation with BOOKSPAN

All photos are from the National Archives, College Park, Maryland (NA),
or from the Military History Institute, Carlisle, Pennsylvania (MHI).

Contents

German Rank Abbreviations

Deutsche Heer	Abbreviation
Generalfeldmarschall	Gen.Feldm.
Generaloberst	Gen.Oberst
General der . . .	
Artillerie	Gen.d.Art.
Gebirgstruppen	Gen.d.Geb.
Infanterie	Gen.d.Inf.
Kavallerie	Gen.d.Kav.
Luftwaffe	Gen.d.Luft.
Panzertruppen	Gen.d.Pz.Tr.
Pionerie	Gen.d.Pio.
Generalleutnant	Gen.Lt.
Generalmajor	Gen.Major
Oberst	Oberst
Oberstleutnant	Obstlt.
Major	Major
Rittmeister (cav)	Rittm.
Hauptmann	Hptm.
Oberleutnant	Oblt.
Leutnant	Lt.

SS	
Reichsführer-SS	
SS-Oberstgruppenfuhrer	SS-Oberstgruf.
SS-Obergruppenführer	SS-Ogruf.
SS-Gruppenführer	SS-Gruf.
SS-Brigadeführer	SS-Brif.
SS-Oberführer	SS-Oberf.
SS-Standartenführer	SS-Staf.
SS-Obersturmbannführer	SS-Ostubaf.
SS-Sturmbannführer	SS-Stubaf.
SS-Hauptsturmführer	SS-Hstuf.
SS-Obersturmführer	SS-Ostuf.
SS-Untersturmführer	SS-Ustuf.

Rank Equivalents

US Army	Soviet Army	German Army	Waffen-SS
—	Generalissimus	—	
General of the Army	Marshal Sovetskogo Soyuza	Generalfeldmarschall	
General	General Armiyi	Generaloberst	SS-Oberstgruppenführer
Lieutenant General	General Polkovnik	General (der Infanterie, der Artillerie, etc.)	SS-Obergruppenführer
Major General	General Leytenant	Generalleutnant	SS-Gruppenführer
Brigadier General	General Major	Generalmajor	SS-Brigadeführer
—	—	—	SS-Oberführer
Colonel	Polkovnik	Oberst	SS-Standartenführer
Lieutenant Colonel	Podpolkovnik	Oberstleutnant	SS-Obersturmbannführer
Major	Major	Major	SS-Sturmbannführer
Captain	Kapetan	Hauptmann	SS-Hauptsturmführer
1st Lieutenant	Starshiy Leytenant	Oberleutnant	SS-Obersturmführer
—	Leytenant	—	—
2nd Lieutenant	Mladshiy Leytenant	Leutnant	SS-Untersturmführer
Sergeant Major*	—	Stabsfeldwebel	SS-Sturmscharführer
Master Sergeant/ First Sergeant	Starshina	Oberfeldwebel	SS-Hauptscharführer
Technical Sergeant	Starshiy Serzhant	Feldwebel	SS-Oberscharführer
Staff Sergeant	—	Unterfeldwebel	SS-Scharführer
Sergeant	Serzhant	Unteroffizier	SS-Unterscharführer
Corporal	Mladshiy Serzhant	—	—
Private First Class	Yefreytor	Hauptgefreiter Obergefreiter Gefreiter	SS-Rottenführer
—	—	Obersoldat (Obergrenadier, Oberkanonier, etc.)	SS-Sturmmann
Private	Krasnoarmeyets	Soldat (Grenadier, Kanonier, etc.)	SS-Mann

*Not a rank in the US Army during WWII. NCOs serving as sergeants major during that era were usually Master Sergeants.

Introduction

by David M. Glantz

Suddenly and without warning, early on the morning of 22 June 1941, over three million German and German-allied soldiers lunged across the Soviet state border and commenced Operation BARBAROSSA. Spearheaded by four powerful panzer groups and protected by an impenetrable curtain of air support, the seemingly invincible *Wehrmacht* advanced from the Soviet Union's western borders to the immediate outskirts of Leningrad, Moscow, and Rostov in the shockingly brief period of less than six months. Faced with this sudden, deep, and relentless German advance, the Soviet Army and state were forced to fight desperately for their very survival.

The ensuing struggle, which encompassed a region totaling roughly 600,000 square miles, lasted for almost four years before the Soviet Army triumphantly raised the Soviet flag over the ruins of Hitler's *Reich*'s Chancellery in Berlin in late April 1945. The war on the Eastern Front — the Soviet Union's self-proclaimed "Great Patriotic War" — was one of unprecedented brutality. It was a war to the death between two cultures, which killed as many as 35 million Russian soldiers and civilians; almost 4 million German soldiers and countless German civilians; and inflicted unimaginable destruction and damage to the population and institutional infrastructure of most of central and eastern Europe.

By the time this deadly conflict ended on 9 May 1945, the Soviet Union and its army had occupied and dominated the bulk of central and eastern Europe. Less than three years after victory, an Iron Curtain descended across Europe that divided the continent into opposing camps for over four decades. More important still, the searing effect of this terrible war on the Russian soul endured for generations, shaping the development of the postwar Soviet Union and, ultimately, contributing to its demise in 1991.

Despite its massive scale, scope, cost, and global impact, it is indeed ironic that much of the war on the Eastern Front remains

Based on the first two chapters of *The Soviet-German War, 1941–1945: Myths and Realities, A Survey Essay*, © David M. Glantz. Self-published. Used by permission.

1

obscure and imperfectly understood by Westerners and Russians alike. Worse still, this obscurity and misunderstanding has perverted the history of World War II overall by masking the Soviet Army's and State's contributions to ultimate Allied victory.

Those in the West who understand anything at all about the Eastern Front regard it as a mysterious, brutal four-year struggle between Europe's most bitter political enemies and its largest and most formidable armies. During this struggle, the *Wehrmacht* and Soviet Army waged war over an incredibly wide expanse of territory; the sheer size, physical complexity, and severe climatic conditions in the theater of war made the conflict appear to consist of a series of successive and seamless offensives punctuated by months of stagnant combat and periodic dramatic battles of immense scale such as the Battles of Moscow, Stalingrad, Kursk, Belorussia, and Berlin. The paucity of detailed information on the war available in the English language reinforces the natural American (and Western) penchant for viewing the Soviet-German War as a mere backdrop for more dramatic and significant battles in western theaters, such as El Alamein, Salerno, Anzio, Normandy, and the Ardennes Offensive.

This distorted layman's view of the war so prevalent in the West is understandable since most histories of the conflict have been, and continue to be, based largely on German sources, sources which routinely describe the war as a struggle against a faceless and formless enemy whose chief attributes were the immense size of its Army and the limitless supply of expendable human resources. Therefore, only truly sensational events stand out from the pale mosaic of four years of combat.

Even those who are better informed about the details of the war on the Eastern Front share in these common misperceptions. While they know more about the major battles that occurred during the war and have read about others — such as Manstein's counterstroke in the Donbas and at Kharkov; the fights in the Cherkassy Pocket and at Kamenets-Podolsk; the collapse of *Army Group Center*; and Soviet perfidy at the gates of Warsaw — the very terminology they use to describe these struggles is indicative of an understanding based primarily on German sources. More important, most laymen readers and historians alike lack sufficient knowledge and understanding of the Soviet-German War to fit it into the larger context of World War II and to understand its relative importance and regional and global significance.

Who, then, is at fault for promoting this unbalanced view of the war? Certainly, Western historians who wrote about the war from only the German perspective share part of the blame. They argue with considerable justification, however, that they did so because only German sources were available to them. Ethnocentrism, a force that conditions a people to appreciate only that which they have themselves experienced, has also helped produce this unbalanced view of the war; in fact, it has done so on both sides. Aside from these influences, the most important factor in the creation of the existing perverted view of the war is the collective failure of Soviet historians to provide Western (and Russian) readers and scholars with a credible account of the war. Ideology, political motivation, and shibboleths born of the Cold War have combined to inhibit the work and warp the perceptions of many Soviet historians.

While many Soviet studies of the war and wartime battles and operations are detailed, scholarly, and accurate as far as they go, they cover only what State officials permit them to cover and either skirt or ignore those facts and events considered embarrassing by the State. Unfortunately, the most general works and those most accessible to Western audiences tend to be the most biased, the most highly politicized, and the least accurate. Until quite recently, official State organs routinely vetted even the most scholarly of these books for political and ideological correctness. Even now, eleven years after the fall of the Soviet Union, political pressure and limited archival access prevents Russian historians from researching or revealing many events subject to censorship in the past.

These sad realities have undercut the credibility of Soviet (Russian) historical works (fairly or unfairly); permitted German historiography and interpretation to prevail; and, coincidentally, damaged the credibility of those few Western writers who have incorporated Soviet historical materials into their accounts of the war. These stark historiographical realities also explain why today sensational, unfair, and wildly inaccurate accounts of certain aspects of the war so attract the Western reading public and why debates still rage concerning the war's direction and conduct.

Today, several formidable barriers continue to inhibit the exploitation of Soviet (Russian) sources and make a fundamental reassessment of the war on the Eastern Front more difficult. These barriers include an ignorance of the scope of Soviet writing on the war, an inability to obtain and read what Soviet historians have written (the language barrier), and an unwillingness to accept what those historians have written. Of late, however, Western historians have begun to overcome first two barriers by publishing an increasing number of books that critically exploit the best Russian sources and test them against German archival sources. By doing so, they have lifted the veil on Soviet historiography, and candidly and credibly displayed both its vast scope and its inherent strengths and weaknesses.

The third barrier, that of credibility, is far more formidable, however, and, hence, more difficult to overcome. To do so will require the combined efforts of both Western and Russian historians accompanied by an unfettering of the binds on Russian archival materials, a process that has only just begun. In short, the blinders and restrictions that inhibited the work of Soviet and Russian military historians must be recognized and eliminated. Only then can historians produce credible and sound histories of the war that accord the Soviet Union and the Soviet Army the credit they so richly deserve.

The Parameters
of the Soviet-German War

Scale

The scale of combat on the Eastern Front was unprecedented in modem warfare, both in terms of the width of the operational front and the depth of military operations (see Figure 1).

The objectives of Operation BARBAROSSA were of gigantic proportion. Plan BARBAROSSA required *Wehrmacht* forces to advance about

---

The Combat Front

 Initial BARBAROSSA front (total)—1,720 miles (2,768 kilometers)
 Initial BARBAROSSA front (main)—820 miles (1,320 kilometers)
 Maximum extent in 1942 (total)—1,900 miles (3,058 kilometers)
 Maximum extent in 1942 (main)—1,275 miles (2,052 kilometers)

The Depth of German Advance

 BARBAROSSA objectives (1941)—1,050 miles (1,690 kilometers)
 Maximum extent (1941)—760 miles (1,223 kilometers)
 Maximum extent (1942)—1,075 miles (1,730 kilometers)

Figure 1. Scale of Operations
These figures indicate length as the "crow flies." Actual length was about half again as long.

1,050 miles (1,690 kilometers) to secure objectives just short of the Ural Mountains, a depth equivalent in U.S. terms to the distance from the east coast to Kansas City, Missouri. To do so, in June 1941, the *Wehrmacht* deployed its forces for the attack against the Soviet Union along a 1,720-mile (2,768-kilometer) front extending from the Barents Sea in the north to the Black Sea in the south. In U.S. terms, this was equivalent to the distance along its eastern coast from the northern border of Maine to the southern tip of Florida. Initially, the *Wehrmacht* concentrated its main thrusts in an 820-mile (1,320-kilometer) sector extending from the Baltic Sea to the Black Sea, which was equivalent to the distance from New York City to Jacksonville, Florida.

Even though the *Wehrmacht*'s 1939 and 1940 campaigns in Poland and Western Europe in no way prepared it to cope with combat in the vast Eastern theater, German forces still performed prodigious feats during the first two years of the war. During its initial BARBAROSSA advance, for example, by early December 1941, *Wehrmacht* forces had advanced to the gates of Leningrad, Moscow, and Rostov, a distance of 760 miles (1,223 kilometers), which was equivalent to the distance from New York City to Springfield, Illinois. During Operation *BLAU* [BLUE], Hitler's offensive in the summer and fall of 1942, German forces reached the Stalingrad and Caucasus region by October, a total depth of 1,075 miles (1,730 kilometers) into the Soviet Union. This was equivalent to the distance from the U.S. east coast to Topeka, Kansas.

By this time, Germany's entire eastern front extended from the Barents Sea to the Caucasus Mountains, a distance of 1,900 miles (3,058 kilometers), which was equivalent to the distance from the mouth of the St. Lawrence River to the southern tip of Florida. At this time, the Germans and their Axis allies occupied contiguous positions along a front which extended 1,275 miles (2,052 kilometers) from the Gulf of Finland west of Leningrad to the Caucasus Mountains, equivalent to the distance from Austin, Texas to the Canadian border.

At its greatest extent, the German advance in the Soviet Union (1,075 miles) was over three times greater than its 1939 advance in Poland (300 miles) and over twice as deep as its advance in the Low Countries and France during the 1940 campaign (500 miles).

At the same time, the *Wehrmacht*'s operational front in the East (1,900 miles) was over 6 times as large as its 1939 front in Poland (300 miles) and over 5 times larger than its 1940 front in the West (390 miles).

Scope

Throughout the entire period from 22 June 1941 through 6 June 1944, Germany devoted its greatest strategic attention and the bulk of its military resources to action on its Eastern Front. During this period, Hitler maintained a force of almost four million German and other Axis troops in the East fighting against a Soviet force that rose in strength from under three million men in June 1941 to over six million in the summer of 1944. While over eighty percent of the *Wehrmacht* fought in the East during 1941 and 1942, over sixty percent continued to do so in 1943 and 1944 (see Figure 2).

In January 1945, the Axis fielded over 2.3 million men, including sixty percent of the *Wehrmacht's* forces and the forces of virtually all of its remaining allies, against the Soviet Army, which had a field-strength of 6.5 million soldiers. In the course of the ensuing winter campaign, the *Wehrmacht* suffered 500,000 losses in the East against 325,000 in the West. By April 1945, 1,960,000 German troops faced the 6.4 million Soviet troops at the gates of Berlin, in Czechoslovakia, and in numerous isolated pockets to the east, while four million Allied forces in western Germany faced under one million *Wehrmacht* soldiers. In May 1945, the Soviets accepted the surrender of almost 1.5 million German soldiers, while almost one million more

	Axis Forces	Soviet Army Forces
June 1941	3,767,000	2,680,000 (in theater)
	3,117,000 (German)	5,500,000 (overall)
	900,000 (in the West)	
June 1942	3,720,000	5,313,000
	2,690,000 (German)	
	80% in the East	
July 1943	3,933,000	6,724,000
	3,483,000 (German)	
	63% in the East	
June 1944	3,370,000	6,425,000
	2,520,000 (German)	
	62% in the East	
January 1945	2,330,000	6,532,000
	2,230,000 (German)	
	60% in the East	
April 1945	1,960,000	6,410,000

Figure 2. Scope of Operations

fortunate Germans soldiers surrendered to the British and Americans, including many who fled west to escape the dreaded Soviet Army.

Course

The war on the Eastern Front lasted from 22 June 1941 through 9 May 1945, a period slightly less than four years. On the basis of postwar study and analysis of the war, Soviet (Russian) military theorists and historians have subdivided the overall conflict into three distinct periods, each distinguished from one another by the strategic nature of military operations and the fortunes of war. This construct is valid for studying the course of the war on the Eastern Front from any military perspective, not just Soviet. In turn, these periods can be usefully subdivided each wartime period into several campaigns, each of which occurred during one or more seasons of the year (see Figure 3).

According to this construct, the 1st Period of the War lasted from Hitler's BARBAROSSA invasion on 22 June 1941 through 18 November 1942, when German offensive operations toward Stalingrad ended. This period encompasses Hitler's two most famous and spectacular strategic offensives, Operation BARBAROSSA (1941) and Operation

---

The 1st Period of the War (22 Jun 1941–18 Nov 1942)—Germany Holds the Strategic Initiative

    The Summer-Fall Campaign (22 June–December 1941)
    The Winter Campaign (December 1941–April 1942)
    The Summer-Fall Campaign (May–October 1942)

The 2d Period of the War (19 Nov 1942–31 Dec 1943)—A Period of Transition

    The Winter Campaign (November 1942–March 1943)
    The Summer-Fall Campaign (June–December 1943)

The 3d Period of the War (1944–1945)—The Soviet Union Holds the Strategic Initiative)

    The Winter Campaign (December 1943–April 1944)
    The Summer-Fall Campaign (June–December 1944)
    The Winter Campaign (January–March 1945)
    The Spring Campaign (April–May 1945)

Figure 3. Periods of War

BLAU (BLUE) (1942). Although the Soviet Army halted the German advances on Moscow and Leningrad in December 1941, and conducted its own major offensives in the winter of 1942/43, throughout this period the strategic initiative remained predominantly in German hands. During this period, the *Wehrmacht*'s tactical and operational military skills far exceeded those of the Soviet Army, and the rigors of incessant combat, the vastness of the theater of military operations, and the harshness of the climate had not yet significantly dulled the cutting edge of German military power.

During the first period of the war, the virtual destruction of its pre-war army and military force structure forced the Soviets to resort to a simpler and more fragile force structure while it educated its military leaders and developed a new force structure that could compete effectively with its more experienced foe. Despite the Soviet Army's travails, during this period it was able to produce one of the first turning points of the war in the winter of 1941 and 1942. In short, the Soviet Army's Moscow counteroffensive in December 1941 and its subsequent winter offensive in January and February 1942 defeated Operation BARBAROSSA and insured that Germany could no longer win the war.

The second period of the war lasted from the commencement of the Soviet Army's Stalingrad counteroffensive on 19 November 1942 to the Soviet Army's penetration of German defenses along the Dnepr River and invasion of Belorussia and the Ukraine in December 1943. Defined as a transitional period during which the strategic initiative shifted inexorably and irrevocably into the Soviet Army's hands, this was the most important period of the war in terms of the struggle's ultimate outcome. During this period and in nearly constant combat, the Soviet Army restructured itself into a modem army that could more effectively engage and, ultimately, defeat *Wehrmacht* forces.

The winter campaign began with the Soviet Army's massive offensives at Rzhev (Operation MARS) and Stalingrad (Operation URANUS) in mid-November 1942, and ended with the surrender of *6th Army* at Stalingrad and massive Soviet Army offensives along virtually the entire expanse of the German Eastern Front. Although the Soviet Army fell short of fulfilling Stalin's ambitious objectives, the winter campaign represented the second and most important turning point in the war. After its Stalingrad defeat, it was clear that Germany would lose the war. Only the scope and terms of that defeat still remained to be determined.

The Soviet Army's ensuing summer-fall campaign of 1943 produced the third major turning point of the war. After its defeat at Kursk, it was clear that German defeat would be total. Only the time and costs necessary to effect that defeat remained to be determined.

During the third period of the war (1944-45), the Soviet Union held the strategic initiative. The ensuing campaigns from December 1943 through May 1945 were almost continuous, punctuated only by brief pauses while the Soviet war machine gathered itself for another major offensive. This period witnessed an unalterable decline in German military strength and fortunes and the final maturity of the Soviet Army in terms of structure and combat techniques. After Kursk, the strength and combat effectiveness of the German armies in the East entered a period of almost constant decline. Although periodic influxes of new conscripts and equipment accorded the defending Germans the means to conduct local counterattacks and counterstrokes, these attacks were steadily less effective, both because of the growing sophistication of the Soviet troops and because of the steady decay in the level of German training and effectiveness.

Conversely, the sophistication of Soviet Army offensive operations grew as it undertook simultaneous and often consecutive offensive across the entire combat front. During the winter campaign of 1943-44, Soviet Army forces launched major offensives simultaneously in the Leningrad region, Belorussia, the Ukraine, and the Crimea.

Although the Belorussian offensive faltered short of its goals, Soviet Army forces cleared German defenders from most of the southern Leningrad region, from the Ukraine westward to the Polish and Rumanian borders, and from the Crimean peninsula.

During the summer-fall campaign of 1944, the Soviet Army conducted strategic offensives successively against German army groups defending Belorussia, southern Poland, Rumania, and the Balkans. By early December 1944, these offensives encompassed the entire combat front from the Baltic region to Budapest, Hungary and Belgrade, Yugoslavia. During the ensuing winter campaign of 1945, Soviet Army forces smashed German defenses in Poland and western Hungary and reached the Oder River, only 36 miles from Berlin, and Vienna, Austria. The Soviet Army capped its successes in this final period of war by mounting its Berlin and Prague offensives, which marked the destruction of the *Third Reich,* in April and May 1945.

Cost

Although exact numbers can never be established, World War II cost the Soviet Union about 14.7 million military dead, half again as many men as the United States fielded in the entire war effort and more than 30 times the 375,000 dead the United States suffered in the war. Overall, the Soviet Army, Navy, and NKVD suffered at least 29 million and perhaps as many as 35 million military casualties (see Figure 4).

Although incalculable, the civilian death toll was even more staggering, probably reaching the grim figure of another twenty million souls. In addition, the dislocation of the Soviet Union's wartime population was catastrophic, comparable to enemy occupation of the United States from the Atlantic coast to well beyond the Mississippi River. While countless millions of Soviet soldiers and civilians disappeared into German detention camps and slave labor factories, millions more suffered permanent physical and mental damage. As unimaginable as it may be, the total Soviet human losses amounted to as many as thirty-five million dead and an equal number of maimed.

Economic dislocation was equally severe. Despite the prodigious feats the Soviets accomplished in moving their productive capability deep within the Soviet Union and east of the Urals and building a new industrial base in the Urals region and Siberia, the losses in resources and manufacturing capacity in western Russia and Ukraine were catastrophic. The heavy industry of the Donbas, Kiev, Leningrad, Kharkov, and a host of regions fell under German control along with key mineral resource deposits and most of the Soviet Union's prime agricultural regions. The degree of damage to the

	Total Killed	Missing or Captured
1941	4,308,094	2,993,803
1942	7,080,801	2,993,536
1943	7,483,647	1,977,127
1944	6,503,204	1,412,335
1945	2,823,381	631,633
Official Total	28,199,127	10,008,434
Armed Forces	29,629,205	1,285,057 (38.1% of the total)
Actual	35,000,000	14,700,000 (42%) of the total

Figure 4. Soviet Army Wartime Casualties

Soviet Union's economy and military productive capability caused by the German invasion was equivalent to the amount of damage the United States would have suffered if an invading power conquered the entire region from the east coast across the Mississippi River into the eastern Great Plains. This stark context underscores the importance of Lend-Lease shipments and explains why the words "Villies," "Studabaker," "Duglass," and "Spam" remain familiar terms to middle-aged and older Russians.

Germany did not escape the carnage it wrought by initiating the war in the east (see Figure 5).

September 1939–1 September 1942	922,000 (over 90% in the East)
1 September 1942–20 November 1943	2,077,000 (over 90% in the East)
20 November 1943–June 1944	1,500,000 est. (80% in the East)
June–November 1944	1,457,000 (903,000 or 62% in the East)
30 December 1944–30 April 1945	2,000,000 (67% in the East)
Total Losses to 30 April 1945	11,135,500
	3,888,000 dead
	3,035,700 captured
Total Armed Forces Losses	13,488,000
	10,758,000 (80% in the East)

Figure 5. German Permanent Losses in the East (Dead, missing, or disabled)

From September 1939 to September 1942, the bulk of the German Army's 922,000 dead, missing, and disabled (14 percent of Germany's total armed force) could be credited to combat in the East. Between 1 September 1942 and 20 November 1943, this grim toll rose to 2,077,000 (30 percent of Germany's total armed force), again primarily in the East.

After the opening of the "second front" in Normandy, the *Wehrmacht* suffered another 1,457,000 irrevocable losses (dead, missing, or captured) from June through November 1944. Of this number, it suffered 903,000 (62 percent of the total losses) of these losses in the East. Finally, after losing 120,000 men to the Allies in the Battle of the Bulge, from 1 January to 30 April 1945, the *Wehrmacht* suffered another two million losses, two-thirds of which fell victim to the Soviet Army. Today, the stark inscriptions "Died in the East," which are carved on countless thousands of headstones in scores of German cemeteries bear mute witness to the carnage in the East, where the will and strength of the *Wehrmacht* perished.

In addition, Germany's allies also suffered mightily, losing almost 2 million men in less than four years of war (see Figure 6).

The Losses of Other Axis Countries			
	Dead & Missing	POWs	Total
Hungary	350,000	513,700	863,700
Italy	45,000	48,900	93,900
Rumania	480,000	210,800	681,800
Finland	84,000	2,400	86,400
Total	959,000	766,800	1,725,000

This grim toll brought total Axis losses in the Soviet-German War to the gruesome figure of 12,483,000 soldiers killed, missing, captured, or permanently disabled.

Figure 6. The Wartime Losses of Germany's Axis Allies

Impact

During its Great Patriotic War, the Soviet Army defeated the twentieth century's most formidable armed force after suffering the equivalent of what the Soviets later described as the effects of an atomic war. The Soviet Army's four-year struggle made the largest contribution to the destruction of Hitler's Third Reich and ended German domination of Europe. German power was eviscerated, and Germany itself was ripped into several pieces: these included not only the German Federal and "Democratic" republics, but the very large parts that were sliced off entirely and awarded to Poland or consumed by the Soviet Union. [The Soviets retained the approximately 30 percent of Poland they had occupied in 1939, and "compensated" post-war Poland by appropriating to it, with Allied concurrence, an almost equal land mass consisting of territory that had been German for the better part of two centuries or more.]

German culture was severely suppressed in the new Soviet and Polish zones, and fundamentally altered in the Soviet-dominated "Democratic" Republic. The threat of an independent German military resurgence was annihilated.

The Soviet Army emerged as the world's premier killing machine. Tragically, however, this killing machine proved as deadly for its own soldiers as it did for those serving the Axis powers. After war's end and by virtue of its performance in the war, the Soviet Union quickly emerged as the dominant power in Eurasia and one of the world's two superpowers. It absolutely dominated eastern and much of central Europe as well.

The erroneously sophisticated warfighting capability that the Soviets forged in war and the international stature the Soviet Union achieved after war's end redounded to the credit not only of Stalin but also of his entire government. The German invasion gave the Communist regime an unprecedented legitimacy as the organizer of victory. Men and women who had been apathetic about that regime could not avoid physical and emotional involvement in the struggle against the invader. By emphasizing patriotism rather than Marxist purity, the Communists identified themselves with the survival of the entire nation. In the process, soldiers found it much easier to obtain membership in the Communist Party and in the *Komsomol* (Young Communist League), giving the Communists a more pervasive, if less obtrusive, hold on the Army and the entire country. During and even after the war, virtually the entire Soviet population was united by the drive to expel the Germans and the determination to prevent any repetition of the horrors of 1941–42.

Yet after the war ended, in some sense, the Soviets became prisoners of their own success and hostage to present and future fears generated by their past horrors, trials, and tribulations. Clearly the war had a searing effect on the Russian psyche, an effect that ultimately contributed to the demise of the Soviet State. Shortly after war's end, a new slogan emerged that dominated the Soviet psyche for over 40 years. It declared:

"NO ONE IS FORGETTEN, NOTHING IS FORGOTTEN"

Although the Soviet Army was scaled back after war's end, it still occupied pride of place in the Soviet government, and all postwar Soviet leaders struggled to limit both the political and the budgetary impact of the defense forces. The Soviet economy, already stunted by its wartime experiences, was forced to allocate its most valuable resources to defense.

The Great Patriotic War, with its devastation and suffering, colored the strategic thinking of an entire generation of Soviet leaders. Postwar Soviet governments created an elaborate system of buffer and client states, designed to not only expand Soviet influence, but to insulate the Soviet Union from attack. Although the Warsaw Pact countries contributed to Soviet defense and to the Soviet economy, their rebellious populations were a recurring threat to the regime's sense of security. Outposts such as Cuba and Vietnam might appear to be useful gambits in the Cold War struggle with the West, but these outposts represented further drains on the Soviet economy. In the long run, the Soviet government probably lost as much as it gained from the buffer and client states.

In retrospect, therefore, the determination to preserve the fruits of victory and preclude future attacks was a dangerous burden for the Moscow government. This determination, accompanied by huge military spending and ill-conceived foreign commitments, was a permanent handicap that helped doom the Soviet economy and with it, the Soviet state.

An Annotated Chronology of the War on the Eastern Front

by David M. Glantz

Events Leading Up to the War

Date	Event
16 Apr 22	International pariah states Germany and USSR conclude the Treaty of Rapallo. Related secret military protocols arrange German/Soviet military cooperation in the development of ordnance and tactical doctrine, especially armor and aircraft, which Germany is forbidden to develop by the Treaty of Versailles.
1929	Josef Stalin (Stalin was an alias meaning "Man of Steel," he was born Josef Dzugashvili) assumed sole dictatorial power in the USSR after five years of rule as a member of the "troika" which took over in 1924.
30 Jan 33	Adolf Hitler becomes Chancellor of Germany. Shortly thereafter, he unilaterally repudiates the

Based on chapters 3–6 of *The Soviet-German War, 1941–1945: Myths and Realities, A Survey Essay,* © David M. Glantz. Self-published. Used by permission.

terms of the Treaty of Rapallo, as well as those of Versailles.

27–28 Feb 33   Nazis burn the *Reichstag* (National Legislature), blame it on Communists; Hitler declares a "state of emergency" and is legally awarded practically dictatorial powers. The Enabling Act of 24 March confirms these powers for four more years. All parties but the National Socialist German Worker Party are abolished by July.

Oct 36   Rome-Berlin Axis formed.

1936–39   Spanish Civil War. In addition to the belligerent participation by both German and Soviet "volunteers," major weapons systems — especially aircraft and some armored vehicles — are "tested" in combat. Many of the results are misinterpreted.

1937–38   Stalin purges his senior military leadership, executing chief military reformer Marshal Tukhachevsky, and 17 other top commanders, as well as about 35,000 other officers, wiping out approximately 50 percent of the officer corps. The Soviet Army is effectively decapitated.

23 Aug 39   Germany and the USSR sign the Non-Aggression Pact.

1 Sep 39   Germany invades Poland.

17 Sep 39   The USSR invades Poland.

6 Oct 39   Poland surrenders; its territory is divided between the victors. Germany and the USSR now share a common border.

Nov 39–Mar 40   The USSR invades Finland. The "Winter War" follows.

                When the USSR and Finland conclude an armistice, Finland has to cede some frontier territory, but by holding out in the face of overwhelming odds, has humiliated the Soviet Union and made her Army appear undertrained, badly led, and poorly motivated. The Soviet Army loses 200,000 men, 1,500 tanks, 700 aircraft.

9 Apr 40   Germany invades Denmark and Norway, meeting significant resistance only in Norway.

10 May 40	Germany invades France and the Low Countries.
25 Jun 40	France capitulates, although a few Maginot garrisons hold out until 2 July. Belgium, the Netherlands, France, Luxembourg, Norway, and Denmark are now all under German control. Only Great Britain refuses to surrender.
May–Sep 40	German air campaign against Great Britain as preparation for the invasion of the British Isles.
17 Sep 40	Operation SEALION is indefinitely postponed. Great Britain remains independent and actively at war with Germany. Western Europe remains at risk of invasion and must be manned with forces not only for occupation, but increasingly for defense as Allied capabilities eventually mount.
20 Nov 40	Hungary joins the Axis.
23 Nov 40	Romania joins the Axis.
	Slovakia joins the Axis.
1 Mar 41	Bulgaria joins the Axis.
6 Apr 41	Germany invades Yugoslavia and Greece.
13 Apr 41	USSR and the Empire of Japan conclude a Non-Aggression Pact.
	German forces move into Finland.
	German forces deployed in Hungary, Romania, poised to attack the USSR.

BARBAROSSA
22 June–31 December 1941

22 Jun 41	The invasion of the USSR, Operation BARBAROSSA, begins. An Axis (overwhelmingly German) force of over 3 million men crushes Soviet Army forces in the frontier regions and races inexorably forward toward Leningrad, Moscow, and Kiev, leaving a shattered Soviet Army in its wake.
1 Oct 41	The 5.5-million-man Soviet Army has lost at least 2.8 million men.

Oct 41	Stalin evacuates the bulk of the Soviet government to Kuibyshev.
Nov 41	By 1 November, German forces in the USSR had lost fully 20 percent of their committed strength (686,000 men); as many as 330,000 of its 500,000 vehicles; and 65 percent of its tanks. The German Army High Command (*Oberkommando des Heeres,* or *OKH*) rated its 136 divisions in the east as equivalent to 83 full-strength divisions. Logistics were strained to the breaking point, and, as the success of the Soviet Army's counteroffensive indicated, the Germans were clearly not prepared for combat in winter conditions.
	Axis forces launch the final advance on Moscow.
	US Lend-Lease aid ($1 billion) to the USSR begins.
7 Dec 41	Japan attacks the United States and declares war.
8 Dec 41	The US declares war on Japan.
11 Dec 41	Germany and Italy declare war on the US. Congress declares war on them the same day.
13 Dec 41	Bulgaria, Hungary, Croatia, Slovakia, and Romania declare war on US.
31 Dec 41	The Soviets have lost about 1.6 million more men by this date. From the invasion to this point, the Soviets have raised 821 division equivalents and lost a total of 229 division equivalents.
	Soviet Army strength reaches 4.2 million, organized into 43 armies.

Operations Summary,
22 June–31 December 1941

The *Wehrmacht's* advance during Operation BARBAROSSA was a veritable juggernaut, a series of four successive offensives, culminating in December 1941 with the dramatic, but ill-fated, attempt to capture Moscow (See Map 1). In summary, these successive stages included:

   ❏ The Border Battles (June–July 1941)
   ❏ The German Advance on Leningrad (July–September 1941)

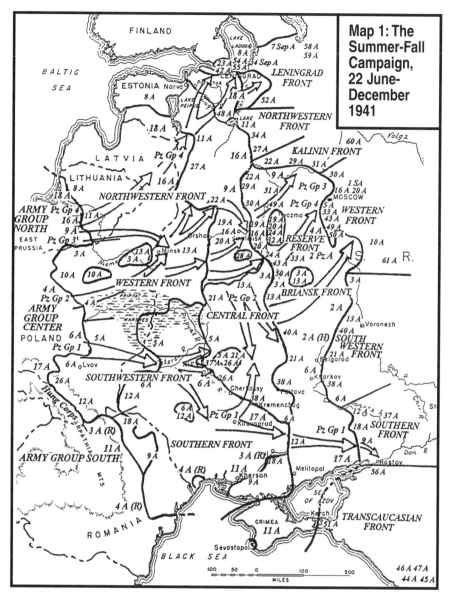

Map 1: The Summer-Fall Campaign, 22 June–December 1941

- ❏ The Battle of Smolensk (July–August 1941)
- ❏ The Uman and Kiev Encirclements (August–September 1941)
- ❏ German Operation TYPHOON and the Viazma and Briansk Encirclements (30 September–5 November 1941)
- ❏ The German Advance on Moscow (7 November–4 December 1941)
- ❏ The German Tikhvin Offensive (16 October–18 November 1941)

❐ The German Advance on Kharkov, the Crimea, and Rostov (18 October–16 November 1941)

❐ The Soviet Rostov Counterstroke (17 November–2 December 1941)

During the first stage of Operation BARBAROSSA, the border battles of June and early July, the *Wehrmacht* smashed the Soviet Army's strategic defenses along the USSR's western frontiers and advanced rapidly along the northwestern, western, and southwestern strategic axes. *Army Groups North* and *Center* shattered the forward defenses of the Soviet Army's **Northwestern** and **Western Fronts,*** encircled the bulk of three Soviet armies (the **3d, 4th,** and **10th**) west of Minsk, and thrust eastward across the Western Dvina and Dnepr Rivers, the Soviet Army's second strategic defense line. Once across those two key river barriers, the two army groups lunged toward Leningrad and the key city of Smolensk. To the south, *Army Group South* advanced inexorably eastward toward Kiev against stronger resistance by the **Southwestern Front,** while other German and Romanian forces invaded Moldavia, penetrated the **Southern Front'**s defenses, and threatened the Soviet Black Sea port of Odessa.

During BARBAROSSA's second stage in July and August, Leeb's *Army Group North* captured Riga and Pskov and advanced north toward Luga and Novgorod. Bock's *Army Group Center* began a month-long struggle for Smolensk, in the process partially encircling three Soviet armies (the **16th, 19th,** and **20th**) in Smolensk proper, and fending off increasingly strong and desperate Soviet counterattacks to relieve their forces nearly isolated around the city. Rundstedt's *Army Group South* drove eastward toward Kiev; encircled and destroyed two Soviet armies (the **6th** and **12th**) in the Uman region; and blockaded Soviet forces in Odessa. This stage ended in late August when Hitler decided to halt temporarily his direct thrusts on Leningrad and Moscow and, instead, to attack to eliminate Soviet forces stubbornly defending Kiev and the central Ukraine.

In BARBAROSSA's third stage during late August and September, *Army Group North* besieged but failed to capture Leningrad, while *Army Groups Center* and *South* jointly attacked and encircled the bulk of the Soviet Army's **Southwestern Front,** which was defending the Kiev region. In the process, *Wehrmacht* forces encircled and

---

*While the Germans employed army groups as their premier strategic force, the Soviet Army employed *fronts,* which, initially, were roughly equivalent in size and mission to army groups. After the 1941 campaign, the Soviets reduced the size and increased the number of *fronts,* making them roughly equivalent to German armies.

destroyed four Soviet armies (the **5th, 21st, 26th,** and **37th**) in the Kiev region, bringing the total Soviet force eliminated in the Ukraine to the awesome figure of over one million men.

The *Wehrmacht* began its culminating offensive on Moscow (Operation TYPHOON) in early October 1941. While *Army Groups North* and *South* continued their advances on Leningrad in the north and toward Kharkov and the Donets Basin [Donbas] in the south, *Army Group Center,* spearheaded by three of the *Wehrmacht*'s four panzer groups, mounted a concerted offensive to capture Moscow. The attacking German forces tore through Soviet Army defenses, routed three Soviet Army fronts, and quickly encircled and destroyed five Soviet armies (the **16th, 19th, 20th, 24th,** and **32d**) around Viazma and three more Soviet armies (the **3d, 13th,** and **50th**) north and south of Briansk. After a short delay prompted by deteriorating weather and sharply increasing Soviet resistance, Operation TYPHOON culminated in mid-November when *Army Group Center* attempted to envelop Soviet forces defending Moscow by dramatic armored thrusts from the north and south.

In early December 1941, however, the effects of time, space, attrition, desperate Soviet Army resistance, and sheer fate combined to deny the *Wehrmacht* a triumphant climax to its six months of near-constant victories. Weakened by months of heavy combat in a theater of war they never really understood, the vaunted *Wehrmacht* finally succumbed to the multiple foes of harsh weather, alien terrain, and a fiercely resisting enemy. Amassing its reserve armies, in early December, the *Stavka* (Soviet High Command) halted the German drive within sight of the Kremlin's spires in Moscow and unleashed a counteroffensive of its own that inflicted an unprecedented defeat on the Axis forces. Simultaneously, the Soviet forces struck back at German forces on the northern and southern flanks. Soviet Army offensives at Tikhvin, east of Leningrad, and at Rostov in the south, drove German forces back, denying them victory along any of the three principal strategic axes.

While the *Wehrmacht* was conducting Operation TYPHOON, the *Stavka* was frantically raising and deploying fresh reserves to counter the German onslaught. Straining every available resource, it fielded ten additional field armies during November and December 1941, six of which it committed to combat in or adjacent to the Moscow region (the **1st Shock, 10th, 26th, 39th, 60th,** and **61st**) during its November defensive or during its December 1941 and January 1942 counteroffensives. Even though these fresh armies were only pale reflections of what Soviet military theory required them to be, their presence would prove that adage that "quantity has a quality of its own." These hastily-assembled reserves were especially valuable, given the attrition that afflicted the *Wehrmacht* during its final thrust toward Moscow.

At this juncture, to the Germans' surprise, on 5 December, the Soviet Army struck back with the first in what became a long series of counterstrokes, which ultimately grew into a full-fledged counteroffensive (See Map 2). In reality, the counteroffensive of December 1941, which ended in early January 1942, consisted of a series of consecutive, and then simultaneous, multi-army operations whose cumulative effect was to drive German forces back from the immediate approaches to Moscow.

During the initial phase of this counteroffensive, the right wing and center of Zhukov's **Western Front** (spearheaded by the new **1st Shock Army** and a cavalry corps) drove *Army Group Center's Third* and *4th Panzer Groups* westward from the northern outskirts of Moscow through Klin to the Volokolamsk region. Soon after, General Konev's **Kalinin Front** seized Kalinin and advanced to the northern outskirts of Rzhev. To the south, the **Western Front's** left wing (including the new **10th Army** and a cavalry group commanded by General P. A. Belov) sent Guderian's *2d Panzer Army* reeling westward in disorder from Tula. Subsequently, the **Western** and **Southwestern Fronts** (including the new **61st Army**) nearly encircled major elements of *Army Group Center's 4th Army* near Kaluga, split this army away from *2d Panzer Army* by a deep thrust to Mosalsk and Sukhinichi, and pushed *2d Army* southward toward Orel. The ferocity and relentlessness of the Soviet Army's assaults sorely tested the *Wehrmacht's* staying power and prompted Hitler to issue his "stand fast" order, which may have forestalled complete German rout.

January–April 1942

Date	Event
Jan–Feb 42	Nine Soviet fronts with 37 armies, including over 350 divisions, smash German defenses along a 600-mile frontage, from Staraia-Russa to Belgorod. They drive German forces back 80–120 miles before the Germans stabilize their lines in March.

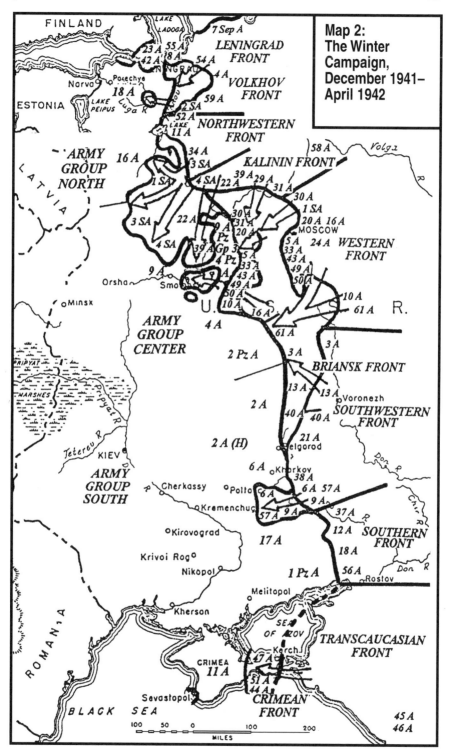

Map 2:
The Winter
Campaign,
December 1941–
April 1942

Operations Summary, January–April 1942

The winter campaign of 1941–42 includes the following major operations:

- ❑ The Soviet Moscow Counteroffensive (5 December 1941–7 January 1942)
- ❑ The Soviet Moscow Offensive (The Battle for Moscow) (8 January–20 April 1942)
- ❑ The Soviet Tikhvin Offensive (10 November–30 December 1941)
- ❑ The Soviet Demiansk Offensive (7 January–25 February 1942)
- ❑ The Soviet Toropets-Kholm Offensive (9 January–6 February 1942)
- ❑ The Soviet Barvenkovo-Lozovaia Offensive (18–31 January 1942)
- ❑ The Soviet Kerch-Feodosiia Offensive (25 December 1941–2 January 1942)

Swept away by a burst of optimism born of his army's sudden and unexpected success, in early January 1942, Stalin ordered the Soviet Army to commence a general offensive along the entire front from the Leningrad region to the Black Sea. The second stage of the Soviet Army's Moscow counteroffensive, which began on 8 January, consisted of several distinct front offensive operations whose overall aim was the complete destruction of *Army Group Center*. The almost-frenzied Soviet counteroffensives in the Moscow region placed enormous pressure on defending German forces as they sought to regain their equilibrium. The counteroffensive also resulted in immense losses among Soviet forces which, by late February, had lost much of their offensive punch. By this time, Soviet Army forces had reached the approaches to Vitebsk, Smolensk, Viazma, Briansk, and Orel, and had carved huge gaps in the *Wehrmacht*'s defenses west of Moscow.

While the Soviet Army's **Kalinin** and **Western Fronts** were savaging *Army Group Center* west of Moscow, other Soviet Army fronts were conducting major offensives southeast of Leningrad and south of Kharkov in the Ukraine. They managed to penetrate the *Wehrmacht*'s defenses and lunge deep into its rear area. Even though the advancing Soviet forces seized huge swathes of open countryside across the entire front, the Germans held firmly to the cities, towns, and major roads. By late February, the front was a patchwork quilt of overlapping Soviet and German forces, and neither side was able to overcome the other. In fact, the Soviet offensive had stalled, and, despite his exhortations, entreaties, and threats, Stalin could not rekindle the offensive flame. Although the local counterstrokes in the immediate vicinity of Moscow had grown into a full-fledged counteroffensive and then into a general strategic offensive that formed the centerpiece of a full-fledged Soviet Army winter campaign, both the Moscow offensive and the winter campaign expired in utter exhaustion in late April 1942.

The Battle of Moscow as a "Turning Point"

For years, debates have raged among historians over "turning points" on the Eastern Front, specifically, regarding precisely when the fortunes of war turned in the Soviet Army's favor and why. These debates have surfaced three leading candidates for the honor of being designated "turning points": the Battles of Moscow, Stalingrad, and Kursk; and, more recently, a fourth, Guderian's southward turn to Kiev. Two of these battles occurred during the first period of the war, throughout which the *Wehrmacht* maintained the strategic initiative with exception of the five-month period from December 1941 through April 1942 during the Soviet Army's winter campaign. By definition, therefore, Russian historians identify the Battle of Stalingrad as the most important "turning point" since the Germans lost the strategic initiative irrevocably only after that battle.

In fact, the Battle of Moscow represents one of three "turning points" in the war, but by no means was it the most decisive. At Moscow, the Soviet Army inflicted an unprecedented defeat on the *Wehrmacht* and prevented Hitler from achieving the objectives of Operation BARBAROSSA. In short, after the Battle of Moscow, Germany could no longer defeat the Soviet Union or win the war on the terms set forth by Hitler.

Finally, Guderian's southward turn and the ensuing delay in Hitler's offensive to capture Moscow cannot qualify as a crucial "turning point." In fact, it may have improved the *Wehrmacht*'s chances for victory over the Soviet Army at Moscow by eliminating the Soviet Army's massive **Southwestern Front** as a key player in the fall portion of the campaign and by setting up the **Western**, **Reserve**, and **Briansk Fronts** for their equally decisive October defeats. Furthermore, at the time, few, if any, figures in the *Wehrmacht*'s senior strategic leadership either opposed Guderian's "turn" or anticipated the subsequent German defeat at Moscow.

April–October 1942

Date	Event
28 Jun 42	The Germans launch Operation *BLAU* (BLUE) with roughly 2,000,000 troops toward Stalingrad and the Caucasus, smashing the defenses of about 1.8 million Soviet Army troops in southern Russia.
Sep 42	German forces have advanced to a depth equivalent—in US geographical terms—to the entire region from the Atlantic coast to Topeka, Kansas.
	German forces reach Stalingrad and the foothills of the Caucasus Mountains.
Late Oct 42	The Germans halted operations to destroy Soviet forces in Stalingrad.

Operations Summary, April–October 1942

The summer-fall campaign consists of the following major military operations:

- ❐ The Soviet Kharkov Offensive (12–29 May 1942)
- ❐ The Soviet Crimean Debacle (8–19 May 1942)
- ❐ German Operation *BLAU*: The Advance to Stalingrad and the Caucasus (28 June–3 September 1942)
- ❐ The Soviet Siniavino Offensive (19 August–10 October 1942)
- ❐ The Battle of Stalingrad (3 September–18 November 1942)

After the Soviet Army's winter offensive collapsed in late April 1942, a period of relative calm descended over the Soviet-German front while both sides reorganized and refitted their forces and sought ways to regain the strategic initiative. Eager to accomplish the objectives that had eluded him during the winter, Stalin preferred that the Soviet Army resume its general offensive in the summer of 1942. After prolonged debate, however, other *Stavka* members convinced the dictator that Hitler was sure to renew his offensive toward Moscow in the summer to accomplish the most important goal of Operation BARBAROSSA. Although Stalin finally agreed to conduct a deliberate strategic defense along the Moscow axis, he insisted that the Soviet Army conduct offensive operations in other sectors at least to weaken the German blow toward Moscow and to possibly to regain the strategic initiative as well. Consequently, Stalin ordered his forces to mount two offensives, the first in the Kharkov region and the second in the Crimea.

Nor was Hitler chastened by the *Wehrmacht*'s winter setbacks. Confident that his forces could still achieve many of Operation BARBAROSSA's original aims, Hitler and his High Command planned a new campaign designed to erase sad memories and fulfill the *Third Reich*'s most ambitious strategic objectives. On 5 April 1942, Hitler issued *Führer* Directive No. 41, which ordered the *Wehrmacht* to conduct Operation *BLAU*, a massive offensive in the summer of 1942 designed to capture Stalingrad and the oil-rich Caucasus region, and then Leningrad. Ultimately, the *Wehrmacht* began Operation *BLAU* on 28 June, after delaying the offensive for several weeks to defeat the Soviet Army offensives.

The first of Stalin's "spoiling" offensives began on 12 May 1942, when Timoshenko's **Southwestern Front** struck Bock's *Army Group South* defenses north and south of Kharkov (See Map 3). Predictably, the Soviet offensive faltered after only limited gains, and German panzer forces assembled to conduct Operation *BLAU,* then counterattacked and crushed Timoshenko's assault force, killing or capturing over 270,000 Soviet troops. Days before, the *11th Army* in the Crimea defeated a feeble offensive launched by the **Crimean Front** and then drove its remnants into the sea, killing or capturing another 150,000 Soviet soldiers. Although the twin Soviet offensives did succeed in delaying the initiation of Operation *BLAU,* they also severely weakened Soviet Army forces in southern Russia and postured them for even greater defeat when *BLAU* finally began.

On 28 June, the massed forces of *Army Group South*'s left wing (the *4th Panzer, 2d* and *6th Armies,* and *2d Hungarian Army*) struck and utterly shattered the **Briansk** and **Southwestern Fronts**' defenses along a 280-mile front from the Kursk region to the Northern Donets River. While the army group's left wing thrust rapidly eastward toward Voronezh on the Don River and then swung southward along the south bank of the Don, the remainder of the army group (*1st Panzer* and *17th Armies;* and *Romanian 3d* and *4th Armies*) joined the offensive on 7 July, pushing eastward across a 170-mile front and then wheeling south across the open steppes toward Rostov. Within two weeks, the *Wehrmacht*'s offensive demolished the Soviet Army's entire defense in southern Russia, as the *Stavka* tried frantically to repair the damage and slow the German juggernaut.

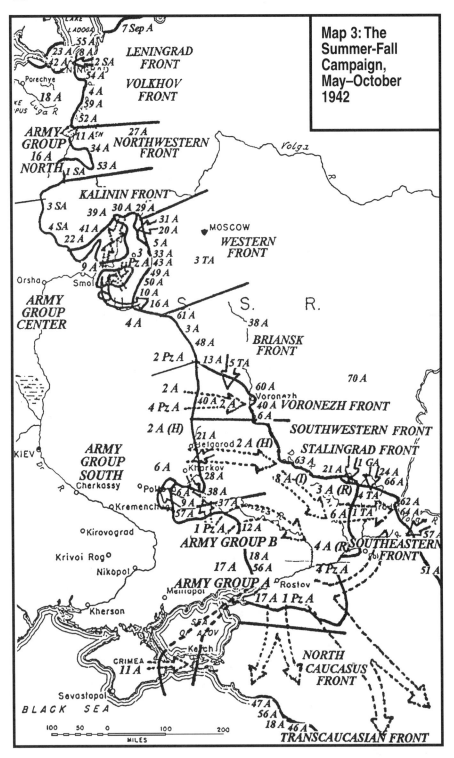

Map 3: The Summer-Fall Campaign, May–October 1942

A week after Operation *BLAU* began, Stalin reluctantly accepted the reality that the German summer offensive was actually taking place in southern Russia and altered his strategy accordingly by ordering his stricken forces to withdraw eastward. At the same time, the *Stavka* began raising ten fresh reserve armies and deployed the first of these armies to slow and contain the German advance. All the while, it began planning for future counterstrokes and counteroffensives at places and times of its own choosing.

Throughout July and August 1942, *Army Group South*, now reorganized into *Army Groups A* and *B* so that Axis forces could be controlled more effectively in so vast a theater, advanced eastward toward the "great bend" in the Don River and Stalingrad and through Rostov into the Caucasus region. After *Army Group B's 2d Army* captured Voronezh on 6 July and dug in along the Don, its *4th Panzer* and *6th Armies* swung southeastward through Millerovo toward Kalach on the Don, encircling the bulk of three Soviet armies in the process (the **9th, 28th,** and **38th**). At the same time, *Army Group A's 1st Panzer* and *17th Armies* cleared Soviet troops from the Voroshilvgrad region and then wheeled southward toward Rostov on the Don without encountering heavy resistance and without destroying major Soviet troop concentrations. By 24 July, *Army Group B's* spearheads were approaching Kalach on the Don, less than 50 miles west of Stalingrad, and *Army Group A's* forces captured Rostov and were preparing to cross the Don River into the Caucasus region.

At this juncture, however, an excessively optimistic Hitler altered his plans. Instead of attacking toward Stalingrad with *Army Group B's 6th* and *4th Panzer Armies*, he shifted the latter's advance axis southward toward the Don River east of Rostov to cut off Soviet forces before they crossed the river. This left the *6th Army* with the arduous task of forcing the Don and advancing on Stalingrad alone. Deprived of its support, the *6th Army's* advance slowed significantly in late July and early August against determined Soviet resistance and incessant counterattacks.

So slow was *6th Army's* progress that in mid-August Hitler once again altered his plan by ordering *4th Panzer Army* to reverse course and advance on Stalingrad from the southwest. Subsequently, the two German armies encountered significantly increased Soviet resistance and heavy fighting that severely sapped their strength as they fought their way into Stalingrad's suburbs.

On 23 August, the *6th Army's XIV Panzer Corps* finally reached the Volga River in a narrow corridor north of the city. Three days later,

4th Panzer Army's forces reached within artillery range of the Volga south of Stalingrad. This marked the commencement of two months of desperate and intense fighting for possession of Stalingrad proper, during which German forces fought to the point of utter exhaustion against fanatical Soviet Army resistance.

Meanwhile, *Army Group A* advanced deep into the Caucasus region, leaving only three Axis armies (*Romanian 3d* and *4th,* and Italian *8th*) in *Army Group B's* reserve. The heavy fighting in Stalingrad, which decisively engaged both the *6th* and *4th Panzer Armies*, forced *Army Group B* to commit these German allies' armies into frontline positions north and south of Stalingrad in late August and September.

Throughout the German advance to Stalingrad, Stalin and the *Stavka* conducted a deliberate withdrawal to save their defending forces, wear down the advancing Germans, and buy time necessary to assemble fresh strategic reserves with which to mount a new counteroffensive. The **Briansk, Southwestern,** and **Southern Fronts** withdrew to the Don River from Voronezh to Stalingrad, and the **Southern Front** withdrew through Rostov to the northern Caucasus region, where it became the **North Caucasus Front.** Soon the *Stavka* formed the **Voronezh, Stalingrad,** and **Southeastern Fronts,** the first to defend the Voronezh sector and other two to defend the approaches to Stalingrad. During the fierce fighting for Stalingrad, Stalin committed just enough forces to the battle in the city's rubble to keep the conflagration raging and distract the Germans while the *Stavka* prepared for the inevitable counteroffensive.

Throughout this planned Soviet Army withdrawal, the various defending fronts mounted limited counterattacks in order to wear the advancing Germans down and influence the German strategic penetration.

The most noteworthy of these counteractions took place at and around Voronezh in early July, along the Don River near Kalach in late July, and, thereafter, along the immediate approaches to and within Stalingrad. As had been the case at Moscow the year before, Stalin committed the first of his new ten reserve armies in July and August to halt the German drive and retained control over the remainder for use in his future counteroffensive.

Finally, during August and September, the *Stavka* ordered its forces in the Leningrad region (Siniavino) and west of Moscow (Rzhev) to conduct limited objective offensives to tie down German forces in those regions.

November 1942–April 1943

Date	Event
Nov–Dec 42	Seven Soviet armies with 83 divisions, 817,000 men, and 2,352 tanks strike *9th Army* at Rzhev in Operation MARS. The 23 defending German divisions barely manage to repel the assaults, but inflict almost 250,000 casualties on the Soviets (including almost 100,000 dead) and destroy roughly 1,700 tanks.
Nov 42–Feb 43	At Stalingrad and along the Don River, 17 Soviet armies (with 1,143,000 men, over 160 divisions, and 3,500 tanks) destroy or badly damaged five Axis armies (including two German, totaling more than 50 divisions) and kill or capture more than 600,000 Axis troops.
Jan–Mar 43	Eleven Soviet Army fronts, including 44 armies, over 4.5 million men, and over 250 divisions conduct massive offensives along a 1,000-mile front before being halted by German counterstrokes.

Operations Summary, November 1942–April 1943

The winter campaign of 1942–43 includes the following major military operations:

- ❏ The Soviet Stalingrad Offensive, Operation URANUS (19 November 1942–2 February 1943)
- ❏ Soviet Operation MARS: The Rzhev-Sychevka Offensive (25 November–20 December 1942)
- ❏ The Soviet Kotelnikovskii Defense and Offensive (12–30 December 1942)
- ❏ Soviet Operation LITTLE SATURN (16–30 December 1942)
- ❏ The Soviet Rostov Offensive (1 January–18 February 1943)
- ❏ The Krasnodar-Novorossiisk Offensive (11 January–24 May 1943)
- ❏ The Soviet Siniavino Offensive, Operation SPARK (12–30 January 1943)

❑ The Soviet Ostrogozhsk-Rossosh Offensive (13–27 January 1943)
❑ The Soviet Voronezh-Kastornoe Offensive (24 January–5 February 1943)
❑ The Soviet Donbas Offensive (1–20 February 1943)
❑ The Soviet Kharkov Offensive (2–26 February 1943)
❑ The Demiansk Offensive (15 February–1 March 1943)
❑ Manstein's Donbas and Kharkov Counterstrokes (20 February–23 March 1943)
❑ The Rzhev-Viazma Offensive (2 March–1 April 1943)

The Soviet Army's counteroffensive at Stalingrad and the ensuing winter campaign of 1942–43 were critical moments in the war on the Eastern Front. For the second time in the war, at Stalingrad, the Soviet Army succeeded in halting a major German offensive and in mounting a successful counteroffensive of its own. For the first time in the war, large Soviet Army tank and mechanized forces were able to exploit deep into the enemy's rear area, encircle, and subsequently destroy more than a full enemy army. For this reason, Stalingrad became one of three "turning points" in the war. The year before, the defeat at Moscow indicated that Operation BARBAROSSA had failed and Germany could not win the war on terms Hitler expected. The Soviet Army's victory at Stalingrad proved that Germany could not win the war on *any* terms. Later, in the summer of 1943, the immense Battle of Kursk would confirm that Germany would indeed lose the war. The only issues remaining after Kursk were how long that process take, and how much it would cost.

The Soviet Army's Stalingrad counteroffensive, Operation URANUS, began on 19 November 1942, and its ensuing winter campaign lasted from the end of this offensive until late March 1943 (See Map 4). In mid-November, the bulk of *Army Group B's 6th* and *4th Panzer Armies* were bogged down fighting in the city. Within days after attacking and routing Romanian forces defending north and south of the city, the mobile forces of the **Southwestern, Don,** and **Stalingrad Fronts** exploited deeply and linked up west of Stalingrad, encircling 300,000 German and Romanian soldiers in the infamous Stalingrad pocket.

In addition to Operation URANUS at Stalingrad, the Soviet Army's **Kalinin** and **Western Fronts,** operating under Zhukov's direct control, struck hard at *Army Group Center's* defenses along the equally vital western axis in Operation MARS. On 24 November, the **Kalinin Front's 3d Shock Army** attacked the defenses of *Army Group Center's*

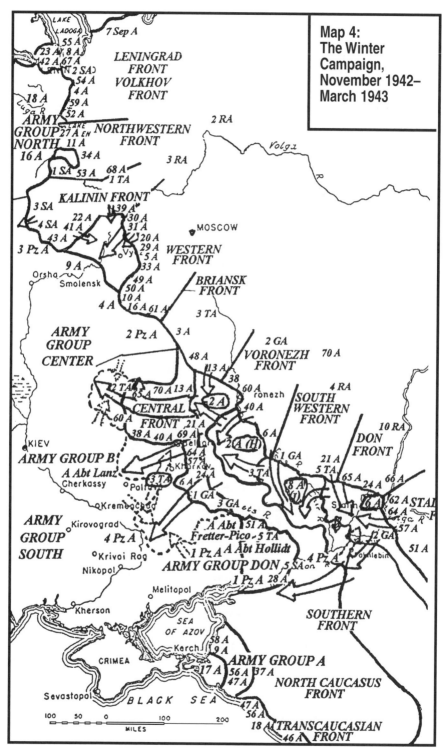

Map 4:
The Winter
Campaign,
November 1942–
March 1943

Third Panzer Army at Velikie Luki and, the next day, six more of Zhukov's armies (the **20th, 22d, 29th, 31st, 39th,** and **41st**) attacked the defenses of *Army Group Center's 9th Army* around the entire periphery of the Rzhev salient, which Germans and Soviets still recognized as "a dagger aimed at Moscow." Finally, on 28 November, the **Northwestern Front'**s forces assaulted the defenses of *Army Group North's Sixteenth Army* around the infamous Demiansk salient.

While the **Don** and **Stalingrad Fronts'** forces prepared to reduce the encircled Germans, Hitler appointed Manstein to command *Army Group B* (soon renamed *Army Group Don*) and ordered him to restore the situation in southern Russia. Manstein's orders were to relieve the German forces encircled at Stalingrad, while the German High Command extracted *Army Group A's* overextended forces from the Caucasus region. To do so, Manstein planned two operations in mid-December designed to rescue the encircled Stalingrad force, a thrust by the *LVII Panzer Corps* northeastward toward Stalingrad and an advance by *XLVIII Panzer Corps* directly eastward toward Stalingrad. However, the latter never materialized, and the former faltered in heavy and frustrating winter fighting. Subsequently, after a long and terrible siege, on 2 February 1943, the German forces in Stalingrad surrendered. Manstein's relief efforts failed for two reasons. First, in mid-December, the **Southwestern Front,** supported by the **Voronezh Front'**s left wing, launched a massive offensive (Operation LITTLE SATURN) across the Don River against the *Italian 8th Army* that destroyed that army and preempted the *XLVIII Panzer Corps'* relief effort.

Second, in mid-December, a strong Soviet defense and counterstroke by the powerful **2d Guards Army** halted, then drove back the *LVII Panzer Corps'* relief effort after the corps reached to within 35 miles of its objective. While some historians argue that *6th Army's* refusal to break out condemned the rescue effort to failure, others say that the severe winter conditions simply made relief impossible.

After defeating the two German relief attempts, in early January the **Southwestern** and **Stalingrad Fronts** drove German forces from the Don River bend toward Millerovo and Rostov. Then, on 13 January 1943, the **Southwestern** and **Voronezh Fronts** struck, encircled, and defeated Hungarian and Italian forces defending further north along the Don River, tearing an immense gap in German defenses and threatening the *2d Army* defending in the Voronezh region (the Ostrogozhsk-Rossosh Offensive). Before the Germans could restore their front, on 24 January 1943, the **Briansk** and **Voronezh Fronts** attacked and nearly encircled *Army Group B's 2d Army* west of Voronezh and forced the Germans to withdraw westward in disorder toward Kursk and Belgorod (the Voronezh-Kastornoe operation). Simultaneously, the **Southwestern** and **Southern Fronts** drove German forces away from the approaches to Stalingrad back to the Northern Donets River and Voroshilovgrad, while the **Southern** (formerly **Stalingrad) Front** captured Rostov on 14 February and reached the Mius River by 18 February (the Rostov operation).

In late January, the *Stavka* exploited its successes by ordering the **Southwestern** and **Voronezh Fronts** to mount two new offensives toward Kharkov and into the Donbas region, and to capture Kursk as well. Initially, the two fronts achieved spectacular success. The **Southwestern Front's** forces crossed the Northern Donets River in early February, captured Voroshilovgrad on 14 February, and approached Zaporozhe on the Dnepr River by 18 February (the Donbas operation), The **Voronezh Front's** forces captured Kursk and Belgorod on 8 and 9 February and Kharkov on 16 February (the Kharkov operation). Swept away by a wave of unbridled optimism, and assuming that the Germans were about to abandon the Donbas region, the *Stavka* assigned its forces ever-deeper objectives, even though Soviet Army forces were clearly outrunning their logistical support, becoming ragged and overextended.

In the midst of these Soviet Army offensives, Manstein orchestrated a miraculous feat that preserved German fortunes in the region. Employing forces which had been withdrawn from the Caucasus and fresh forces from the West, on 20 February, he struck the flanks of the exploiting **Southwestern Front's** forces as they neared the Dnepr River. Within days, the entire Soviet force collapsed, and the Germans drove Soviet forces back to the Northern Donets River in disorder. In early March, Manstein's army group then struck the **Voronezh Front's** forces and recaptured Kharkov and Belgorod on 16 and 18 March.

In addition to thwarting the Soviet's ambitious offensive, Manstein's counterstroke produced utter consternation within the *Stavka*. To forestall further defeat, the *Stavka* transferred fresh forces into the Kursk and Belgorod regions, which, with deteriorating weather, forced the Germans to postpone further action. During this period, the Germans also abandoned their Demiansk and Rzhev salients to create a more defensible front. The legacy of combat during this period was the infamous Kursk Salient, which protruded westward into German defenses in the central sector of the Soviet-German front.

The Battle of Stalingrad as a "Turning Point"

In comparison with the Battles of Moscow and Kursk, the Battle of Stalingrad was indeed the most important "turning point" on the Eastern Front. The Soviet Army's success in the counteroffensive and during the ensuing winter offensive clearly indicated that Germany could no longer win the war on any terms.

This fact was underscored by the grim reality that, at Stalingrad and during its subsequent offensives, the Soviet Army accomplished the unprecedented feat of encircling and destroying the bulk of two German armies (the *6th* and *4th Panzer*), and destroying or severely damaging one more German army (*2d*) and four Allied armies (the *3d* and *4th Romanian*, *8th Italian*, and *2d Hungarian*). In the future, the Axis could neither replace these armies nor conduct successful offensive without them.

May–December 1943

Date	Event
Jul–Aug 43	Using 1,000,000 men, Germans launch Operation ZITADELLE (CITADEL) against 2.5 million Soviet Army troops in the Kursk Salient.
	After defeating Operation ZITADELLE, Soviets launch offensives with 6,000,000 soldiers against 2.5 million Germans along a front of over 1,500 miles and advance toward the Dnepr River.
Oct–Nov 43	Six Soviet Army fronts with 37 armies (over 300 divisions) including over 4 million soldiers, assault German defenses in a 770-mile sector in Belorussia, at Kiev, and along the lower Dnepr River, piercing the German Eastern Wall in four regions.

Operations Summary, May–December 1943

The summer-fall campaign of 1943 includes the following major military operations:

❑ German Operation ZITADELLE and the Battle of Kursk (5–23 July 1943)

❐ The Soviet Orel Offensive (Operation KUTUZOV) (12 July–18 August 1943)

❐ The Soviet Belgorod-Kharkov Offensive (Operation RUMIANT-SEV) (3–23 August 1943)

❐ The Soviet Smolensk Offensive (Operation SUVOROV) (7 August–2 October 1943)

❐ The Soviet Briansk Offensive (1 September–3 October 1943)

❐ The Soviet Chernigov-Poltava Offensive (The Soviet Army Advance to the Dnepr River) (26 August–30 September 1943)

❐ The Soviet Donbas Offensive (13 August–22 September 1943)

❐ The Soviet Melitopol Offensive (26 September–5 November 1943)

❐ The Soviet Novorossiisk-Taman Offensive (10 September–9 October 1943)

❐ The Soviet Nevel-Gorodok Offensive (6 October–31 December 1943)

❐ The Soviet Gomel-Rechitsa Offensive (10–30 November 1943)

❐ The Soviet Kiev Offensive (3–13 November 1943)

❐ The Soviet Lower Dnepr Offensive (26 September–20 December 1943)

❐ Manstein's Kiev Counterstrokes (13 November–22 December 1943)

❐ The Soviet Zhitomir-Berdichev Offensive (24 December 1943–14 January 1944)

The summer of 1943 was a pivotal period for both the *Wehrmacht* and the Soviet Army. By this time, operations on the Eastern Front had evolved into a clear pattern of alternating, but qualified, strategic successes by both sides. While the *Wehrmacht* proved its offensive prowess in Operations BARBAROSSA and *BLAU*, at the culminating point of each of these offensives, it faltered in the face of unanticipated Soviet Army strength and tenacity, the rigors of Russian weather, and the deterioration of their own forces and logistical support.

Similarly, the Soviet Army successfully halted both German offensives short of their objectives, mounted effective counteroffensives, and was then able to expand these counteroffensives into massive winter campaigns that stretched German strategic defenses to the breaking point. In both cases, however, the *Wehrmacht's* defenses bent but did not break. The Germans ultimately frustrated the *Stavka's* strategic offensive ambitions through a combination of their own over-optimism, the unanticipated tenacity of *Wehrmacht* troops, and vexing spring thaws.

By the summer of 1943, two years of war experience indicated that the German "owned" the summers and the Soviets the winters. By this time, both sides realized that this strategic pattern was a prescription for stalemate, a situation that frustrated the strategic aspirations of both sides. German frustration was the greatest for good reason, since by mid-1943, Germany was waging a world war in an increasing number of continental and oceanic theaters. Not only was it bogged down in Russia, but it was also waging a U-boat war in the Atlantic, countering an Allied air offensive over the German homeland, losing a ground war in North Africa, and defending the French and Norwegian coasts against the threat of a "second front." Therefore, circumstances indicated that Germany's success in the war, if not her overall fate, depended on the course of the war in the East and dictated that the *Wehrmacht* achieve the sort of victory in the East that would exhaust the Soviets and prompt them to negotiate a separate peace on whatever terms possible. To do so, Hitler decided to launch his third major strategic offensive of the war, code-named Operation ZITADELLE, in the more restricted sector at Kursk.

Stalin and the *Stavka* also faced serious, though less daunting, challenges in the summer of 1943. Even though the Soviet Army had inflicted unprecedented defeats on the *Wehrmacht* and its allies during the previous winter, German forces ultimately managed to stabilize the front. To achieve more — that is, to defeat the *Wehrmacht* and drive it from Russian soil — the Soviet Army had to prove it could defeat the *Wehrmacht* in the summer as well as the winter. To do so, Stalin and the *Stavka* resolved to begin the summer-fall campaign by conducting a deliberate defense of the Kursk Salient, where the German attack was most likely to occur. Once the Germans were halted, it decided to launch a series of counterstrokes in the Kursk region and, subsequently, expand the offensive to the flanks. The *Stavka's* ultimate aim was to project Soviet Army forces to the Dnepr River and, if possible, to expand the offensive into Belorussia and the Ukraine.

Subsequently, the summer-fall campaign developed in three distinct stages: the Battle of Kursk, the advance to the Dnepr River; and the struggle for possession of bridgeheads across the Dnepr (See Map 5). During the first stage, which lasted from 5 to 23 July, the Soviet Army's **Central** and **Voronezh Front**s, supported by elements of the **Steppe Front,** defeated *Army Groups Center's* and *South's 9th* and *4th Panzer Armies* and *Army Detachment Kempf,* which were attacking the flanks of the Kursk salient in Operation ZITADELLE. Before the fighting at Kursk ended, on 12 July the **Western, Briansk,**

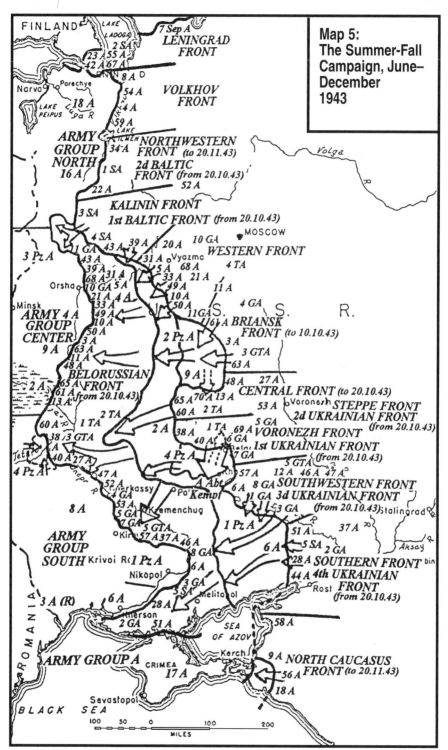

Map 5:
The Summer-Fall
Campaign, June–
December
1943

and **Central Fronts** attacked and defeated *Army Group Center's 2d Panzer Army,* whose forces were defending the Orel salient, in Operation KUTUZOV.

Before the fighting at Orel ended on 18 August, on 3 August the **Voronezh** and **Steppe Fronts** assaulted and defeated *Army Group South's 4th Panzer Army* and *Army Detachment Kempf,* which were defending south of the Kursk Bulge, in Operation RUMIANTSEV and liberated Belgorod and Kharkov by 23 August.

On the flanks of this massive offensive, 2 August through 2 October, the **Kalinin** and **Western Fronts** drove *Army Group Center's 3d Panzer* and *4th Armies* westward and, in stages, liberated Spas-Demensk, Yelnya, Roslavl, and Smolensk in Operation SUVOROV. While the Smolensk offensive was still unfolding, from 17–26 August, the **Briansk Front** defeated *Army Group Center's 9th Army* in the Briansk region in the Briansk operation. To the south, from 13 August through 22 September, the **Southwestern** and **Southern Fronts** defeated *Army Group South* defending the Donbas region in the Donbas operation and advanced to the outskirts of Zaporozhe and Melitopol. Simultaneously, the **North Caucasus Front's** forces drove German troops from the Krasnodar region in the northern Caucasus into the Taman Peninsula during the Novorossiisk-Taman operation.

Once it became apparent to the *Stavka* that victory was at hand at Kursk, it ordered the Soviet Army to continue its offensive toward the Dnepr River along the Kursk-Kiev and Kursk-Kremenchug axes. Beginning on 26 August, the **Central, Voronezh,** and **Steppe Fronts** commenced multiple offensives, known collectively as the Chernigov-Poltava operation, which drove *Army Group South's 2d, 4th Panzer,* and *8th Armies* back to the line of the Dnepr River by late September. By 30 September, the Soviet Army's forces had reached the banks of the Dnepr River on a broad front from north of Kiev to the approaches to Dnepropetrovosk in the south. During the final stages of this advance, Soviet forces captured small, but vital, bridgeheads over the river south of Gomel, near Chernobyl and Liutezh north of Kiev, at Bukrina south of Kiev, and south of Kremenchug.

During the second half of October, the **Belorussian** (formerly **Central**) and **1st Ukrainian** (formerly **Voronezh**) **Fronts** consolidated their footholds over the Dnepr River, and the **2d** and **3d Ukrainian** (formerly **Steppe** and **Southwestern**) **Fronts** cleared *Wehrmacht* forces from the eastern bank of the Dnepr; captured the cities of Dnepropetrovosk and Zaporozhe; and established bridgeheads on the river's western bank. Meanwhile, the **4th Ukrainian** (formerly Southern) **Front** seized Melitopol and the territory between the Dnepr River and the approaches to the Crimea.

According to most accounts, the third stage of the Soviet Army's summer-fall offensive commenced in early November when the **1st, 2d,** and **3d Ukrainian Fronts** attacked from their bridgeheads across the Dnepr. From 3 through 13 November, the **1st Ukrainian Front** struck from the Liutezh bridgehead north of Kiev, captured Kiev, Fastov, and Zhitomir from *Army Group South's 4th Panzer Army*, and secured a strategic-scale bridgehead west of the Ukrainian capital. Thereafter, from 13 November through 23 December, it defended this bridgehead against fierce German counterstrokes orchestrated by Manstein and his *Army Group South.*

At the same time, the **2d** and **3d Ukrainian Fronts** assaulted across the Dnepr River south of Kremenchug and Dnepropetrovosk but failed to capture their objective of Krivoi Rog from *Army Group South's 8th* and *1st Panzer Armies*. For the next two months, the two fronts managed to expand their bridgehead, primarily to the west, while the **4th Ukrainian Front** besieged elements of the new *6th Army* in the Nikopol bridgehead east of the Dnepr River. Finally, in late December the reinforced **1st Ukrainian Front** attacked toward Berdichev and Vinnitsa in the Zhitomir-Berdichev operation, an offensive against *Army Group South's 4th Panzer Army* that continued well into the New Year.

The Battle of Kursk as a "Turning Point"

While the Battle of Stalingrad was the most important "turning point" in the war, the Battle of Kursk also represented a vital turn in German fortunes. In addition to being the last major offensive that offered the Germans any prospect for strategic success, the battle's outcome proved conclusively that Germany would lose the war. After Kursk, the only question that remained regarded the duration and final cost of the Soviet Army's inevitable victory.

January–April 1944

Date	Event
Jan–Mar 1944	The Soviet Army launches massive offensives with 10 fronts; 55 armies, which include over 300

divisions; and over 4.5 million men. Soviet forces liberate the Leningrad region, penetrate Belorussia, and reach the Polish and Romanian borders. The assaults badly damage three German army groups and inflict over one million casualties on Axis forces.

Operations Summary, January–April 1944

Major military operations constituting the winter campaign of 1943–44 include:

- ❐ The Soviet Leningrad-Novgorod Offensive (14 January–1 March 1944)
- ❐ The Soviet Zhitomir-Berdichev Offensive (24 December 1943–14 January 1944)
- ❐ The Soviet Kirovograd Offensive (5–16 January 1944)
- ❐ The Soviet Korsun-Shevchenkovskii Offensive (Cherkassy) (24 January–17 February 1944)
- ❐ The Soviet Rovno-Lutsk Offensive (27 January–11 February 1944)
- ❐ The Soviet Vitebsk Offensive (3 February–13 March 1944)
- ❐ The Soviet Rogachev-Zhlobin Offensive (21–26 February 1944)
- ❐ The Soviet Proskurov-Chernovits Offensive (Kamenets-Podolsk) (4 March–17 April 1944)
- ❐ The Soviet Uman-Botoshany Offensive (5 March–17 April 1944)
- ❐ The Soviet Bereznegovatoe-Snigirovka Offensive (6–18 March 1944)
- ❐ The Soviet Odessa Offensive (26 March–14 April 1944)
- ❐ The Soviet Crimean Offensive (8 April–12 May 1944)

In early December 1943, the *Stavka* formulated strategic plans for the conduct of its third winter campaign. These required the Soviet Army to drive Küchler's *Army Group North* from the Leningrad region and Manstein's *Army Group South* from the Ukraine and the Crimea and to create favorable conditions for the subsequent destruction of *Army Group Center's* forces in Belorussia. The Soviet Army's **1st, 2d, 3d,** and **4th Ukrainian Fronts** were to conduct the main effort in the Ukraine first by attacking successively and later simultaneously. This permitted the *Stavka* to switch key artillery and mechanized resources from front to *front,* while concealing the true scope and intent of the offensive.

The first phase of the Soviet Army's offensive in the Ukraine, which began in late December 1943 and lasted through late February 1944, consisted of five major offensive operations, each conducted by one or two fronts against *Army Group South* (See Map 6). The first two operations, which the **1st** and **2d Ukrainian Fronts** conducted, were continuations of the earlier operations designed to expand the Soviet Army's bridgeheads across the Dnepr River. On 24 December 1943, Vatutin's **1st Ukrainian Front** attacked from its bridgehead at Kiev toward Zhitomir, Berdichev, and Vinnitsa in the Zhitomir-Berdichev offensive. Although *Army Group South's 1st* and *4th Panzer Armies* (the former was transferred to this region on 1 January) were hard-pressed to contain the offensive, a counterstroke by Manstein's panzer corps (the *III, XLVI,* and *XLVIII*) halted the front's two exploiting tank armies (the **1st** and **3d Guards**) just short of their objective, Vinnitsa. Meanwhile, from 5–16 January, Konev's **2d Ukrainian Front** wheeled westward from its previous objective, Krivoi Rog, and its tank army (the **5th Guards**) seized Kirovograd from *Army Group South's 8th Army*. The twin Soviet Army offensives pinned two of *8th Army's* corps into a large salient along the Dnepr River north of Korsun-Shevchenkovskii.

After these initial offensive successes, from 24 January through 17 February, the **1st** and **2d Ukrainian Fronts** struck the flanks of *8th Army's* defenses at the base of the Korsun-Shevchenkovskii salient, and two exploiting tank armies (the new **6th** and **5th Guards**) encircled the defending German corps. In several weeks of heavy fighting, Soviet Army troops destroyed up to 30,000 *Wehrmacht* troops while fending off fierce German counterstrokes before *Army Group South* was able to once again stabilize its defenses.

While German attention was riveted on the fierce fighting at Korsun-Shevchenkovskii, the *Stavka* ordered Soviet Army forces to strike both flanks of *Army Group South* to capitalize of the fact that the bulk of the army group's panzer reserves were decisively engaged in the Korsun-Shevchenkovskii region. On the **1st Ukrainian Front's** right flank, from 27 January through 11 February, the **13th** and **60th Armies** and the **1st Guards** and **6th Guards Cavalry Corps** attacked Manstein's overextended left flank south of the Pripet Marshes, unhinged German defenses, and seized Rovno and Lutsk, creating favorable positions from which to conduct future operations into *Army Group South's* rear. Further south, from 30 January to 29 February Malinovsky's **3d** and Tolbukhin's **4th**

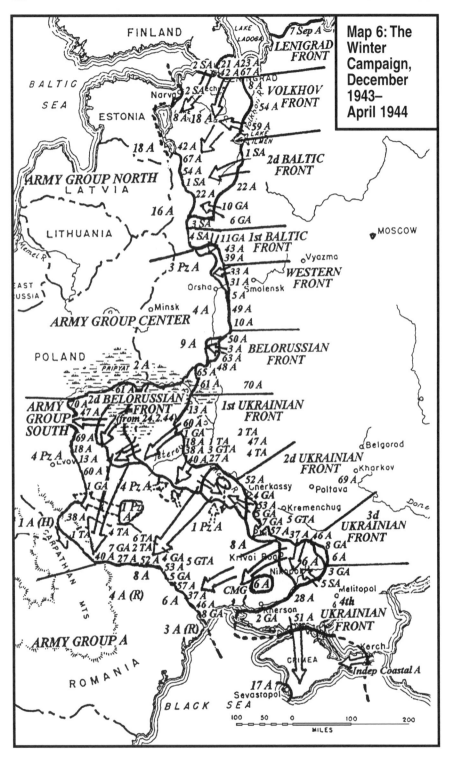

Map 6: The Winter Campaign, December 1943–April 1944

Ukrainian Fronts launched concentric blows against the defenses of *Army Group South's 6th Army* anchored in the "great bend" of the Dnepr River, collapsed German defenss in the Nikopol bridgehead on the Dnepr's south bank, seized the salient in the river's "great bend," and captured Krivoi Rog.

By the end of February, Soviet forces had cleared German defenders from the entire Dnepr River line. Deprived of their river defenses, Manstein's forces were now vulnerable to defeat in detail in the vast interior plains of Ukraine. During this period, General L. A. Govorov's **Leningrad Front** and Meretskov's **Volkhov Front,** soon joined by General M. M. Popov's **2d Baltic Front,** conducted the massive Leningrad-Novgorod offensive in the Leningrad region, a painfully slow advance that began on 14 January and endured through February, driving the *Eighteenth* and *Sixteenth Armies* of Model's *Army Group North* back to their "Panther Line" defenses. At the same time, the **1st Baltic, Western,** and **Belorussian Fronts** conducted limited diversionary operations against *Army Group Center's* forces in eastern Belorussia.

The Soviet Army's offensive operations along the main strategic axis in the Ukraine continued virtually without a halt in early March despite miserable terrain conditions created by the spring thaw. During the second phase of this offensive, which began on 4 March and lasted through late April, five additional Soviet Army offensives, which involved all six of the Soviet Army's tank armies, cleared *Wehrmacht* forces from the Ukraine and the Crimea. The *Stavka's* strategic objective was to separate *Army Groups Center* and *South* from one another and destroy the latter by pinning it against the Black Sea or Carpathian Mountains.

On 4 March, the **1st Ukrainian Front,** now personally commanded by Zhukov (after Vatutin's death at the hands of Ukrainian partisans), attacked southwestward from the Shepetovka and Dubno regions toward Chernovits near the Romanian border. Two of Zhukov's tank armies (the **3d Guards** and **4th**) tore a gaping hole in the defenses of *Army Group South's 4th Panzer Army* and by 7 March, approached Proskurov, where Manstein's panzer reserves (the *III* and *XLVIII Panzer Corps*) halted their advance.

Soon after, however, the **1st Tank Army** joined the offensive, and on 21 March, the **1st** and **4th Tank Armies** once again burst into operational depth in Manstein's army group's rear area. By 27 March, the two tank armies reached and crossed the Dnestr River, encircling the bulk of *1st Panzer Army* in the Kamenets-Podolsk region. By 17 April, the **1st Tank Army** had reached the Carpathian

Mountains, effectively cutting off Manstein's army group (which had been re-named *Army Group North Ukraine*) from contact with Schörner's *Army Group South Ukraine*, which was operating to the south in northern Romania. However, Manstein successfully withdrew the encircled *1st Panzer Army* to safety in southern Poland in several weeks of intense and complex fighting.

One day after Zhukov's **1st Ukrainian Front** began its offensive on Proskurov, on 5 March, Konev's **2d Ukrainian Front** attacked toward Uman, spearheaded by three more tank armies (the **2d, 5th Guards,** and **6th**). The front's exploiting tank forces captured Uman and Vinnitsa on 10 March, and on 17 March, the **5th Guards Tank Army** reached and crossed the Dnestr River, effectively separating Hube's *1st Panzer Army* of *Army Group North Ukraine* from Wöhler's *8th Army* of *Army Group South Ukraine*. While the six tank armies were setting the offensive pace for the **1st** and **2d Ukrainian Fronts**, on 6 March, Malinovsky's **3d Ukrainian Front** launched its own offensive (the Bereznegovatoe-Snigirevka operation) along the Black Sea coast against Kleist's *Army Group A*.

By 18 March, the **3d Ukrainian Front** had encircled but failed to destroy *Army Group A's 6th Army* and created conditions conducive to a subsequent advance on Odessa. Simultaneously, Tolbukhin's **4th Ukrainian Front** assaulted Jaenecke's *17th Army's* defenses in the Crimea on 8 April, bottled German forces up in Sevastopol by 16 April, and forced the Germans to evacuate the city by 10 May.

As far as Soviet Army operations in Belorussia were concerned, Russian official histories recognize only two offensive operations in the region. First, between 3 February and 13 March, Bagramian's **1st Baltic Front** and Sokolovksy's **Western Front** pounded the defenses of *Army Group Center's 3d Panzer* and *4th Armies* around Vitebsk, but to no avail. Second, from 21–26 February, Rokossovsky's **Belorussian Front** struck the defenses of *Army Group Center's 9th Army* at Rogachev and Zhlobin, driving the Germans back but capturing only Rogachev. Russian historians, however, label the two offensives as diversionary in nature.

During the course of four months of nearly continuous combat, the Soviet Army liberated Leningrad, the Ukraine, and the Crimea, and made slight inroads into Belorussia. In the process, the Soviet Army eliminated 16 German divisions and at least 50,000 troops from the *Wehrmacht's* order of battle by means of encirclements and sheer attrition, and reduced another 60 German divisions to skeletal strength. Whereas the late winter/spring of 1942/43 had been periods of rest and refitting for the Germans, the corresponding period of 1944 was one unremitting struggle for survival. By the time the winter campaign ended, *Army Group Center*, the one area of relative stability during this period, had become a huge salient jutting to the east, denuded of most of its reserves.

By May 1944, the Soviet Army had taken back virtually all Soviet territory in the south and, in the process, shattered large portions of the *1st Panzer*, *6th*, *8th*, and *17th Armies*. In the north, Soviet forces had liberated most of the southern Leningrad region, and its unceasing assaults on Busch's *Army Group Center* in Belorussia had seriously weakened that force, which had already lost reserves to shore up sagging German defenses to the north and south. After the collapse of Germany's defenses on the northern and southern flanks, the strategic attention of Hitler and the German High Command was now riveted on the southern region. The presence of all six Soviet tank armies in that region led them to conclude that it would be the focus of the Soviet Army's summer offensive. This preoccupation explains the German's surprise when the *Stavka's* next great offensive was aimed at *Army Group Center*.

The Soviet Army's victories during the winter and spring of 1944 had political and well as military implications. In short, Romanian support of the German war effort weakened in light of Romania's already catastrophic military losses and the loss of its northern regions (Bessarabia and Moldavia) in April and May 1944. Then, on 19 March German troops occupied Hungary to prevent its possible defection to the Allied camp.

In late spring 1944, while the Germans focused their political and strategic attention on the Balkans, Stalin and the *Stavka* prepared to deal, once and for all, with *Army Group Center*.

May–December 1944

Date	Event
Jun–Aug 1944	Eight Soviet fronts with 52 armies including 5.5 million men, and about 300 divisions defeat and destroy three German army groups totaling about 1.5 million men and over 100 divisions, inflicting over 800,000 casualties on the Germans, and reach East Prussia, the Vistula River south of Warsaw, Hungary, and Bulgaria.
Oct–Dec 1944	Seven Soviet Army fronts — 30 armies, 3 million men and over 200 divisions — conquer the Baltic region, besiege Budapest, and capture Belgrade.

Operations Summary, May–December 1944

Military operations during the summer-fall campaign of 1944 include the following major operations:

❐ The Soviet Karelian Offensive (10–20 June 1944)
❐ The Soviet Belorussian Offensive (Operation BAGRATION) (23 June–29 August 1944)
❐ The Soviet Lublin-Brest Offensive (18 July–2 August 1944)
❐ The Soviet Lvov-Sandomir Offensive (13 July–29 August 1944)
❐ The Soviet Iassy-Kishinev Offensive (20 August–25 September 1944)
❐ The Soviet Baltic Offensive (14 September–20 October 1944)
❐ The Soviet Memel Offensive (5–22 October 1944)
❐ The Soviet Petsamo-Kirkenes Offensive (7–29 October 1944)
❐ The Soviet Debrecen Offensive (6–28 October 1944)
❐ The Soviet Belgrade Offensive (28 September–20 October 1944)
❐ The Soviet Budapest Offensive (29 October 1944–13 February 1945)

Largely for logistical and operational reasons, the *Stavka* planned to conduct five major strategic offensive operations in staggered sequence during the summer of 1944, beginning in the north and working successively to the south. After commencing with an operation against Finnish forces on the Karelian Isthmus in early June, subsequently, the offensives would expand to encompass Belorussia in late June, central and southern Poland in mid-July, and Romania in late August. The *Stavka*'s intent in launching these offensives was to encircle and destroy *Army Group Center*, smash *Army Groups North* and *South Ukraine*, and capture Riga, Minsk, Lvov, and Bucharest by the end of August 1944.

Govorov's **Leningrad Front** conducted the first of these strategic offensives (See Map 7). After prolonged but fruitless political negotiations with the Finnish government regarding its withdrawal from the war, the **Leningrad Front**'s **21st** and **23d Armies** struck by surprise on 10 June 1944, penetrated three Finnish defense lines, and captured Vyborg on 20 June. In September, Finland signed a separate armistice with the USSR. The German forces in north Karelia and opposite Murmansk were forced to withdraw, mostly on foot, to Norway. Under extreme pressure from the Soviets—who occupied several Finnish border cities as "hostages"—the Finns were forced to turn on their erstwhile German allies and hound them to the Norwegian frontier.

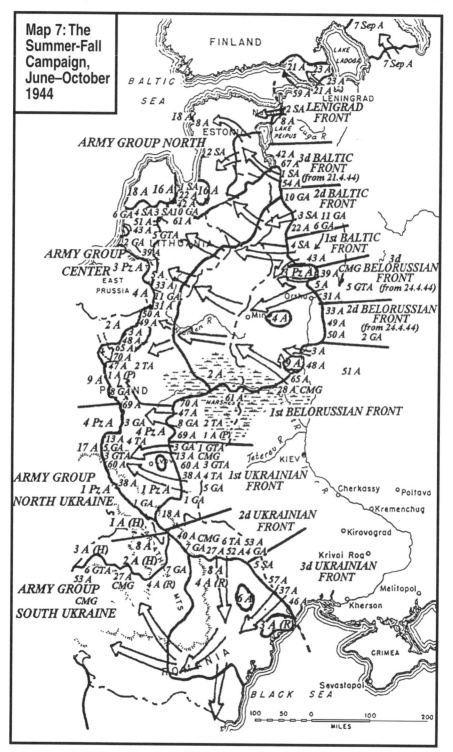

Map 7: The Summer-Fall Campaign, June–October 1944

Only days after the fall of Vyborg, the Soviet Army began its massive offensive against *Army Group Center* in Belorussia. Striking on 22 and 23 June, three Soviet Army fronts began two tactical encirclement operations to eliminate the German anchor positions on the northern and southern flanks of the Belorussian salient. While three armies of the Bagramian's **1st Baltic Front** and Cherniakhovsky's **3d Belorussian Front** encircled two corps of *Army Group Center's Third Panzer Army* in Vitebsk, four armies on the right wing of Rokossovsky's **1st Belorussian Front** encircled two corps of the army group's *9th Army* in Bobruisk. The **5th Guards Tank Army** and a cavalry-mechanized group, cooperating with the **3d Belorussian Front** in the north and a collection of mobile corps and cavalry-mechanized group from the **1st Belorussian Front** in the south, then conducted a deep envelopment off all of *Army Group Center's 4th Army* east of Minsk. By early August, the four attacking Soviet Army fronts had virtually destroyed *Army Group Center* and occupied much of Belorussia.

After achieving striking success in the initial stage of the Belorussian operation, the *Stavka* expanded the offensive to the northern and southern flanks. In the north, the **1st Baltic Front** attacked westward along the banks of the Western Dvina River through Polotsk in the direction of East Prussia to protect the northern flank of the Soviet Army's main attack force in Belorussia and to create favorable conditions for a subsequent exploitation toward Riga.

Then, on 18 July five armies (including one Polish army) deployed on the **1st Belorussian Front**'s left wing south of the Pripet Marshes, struck and shattered the defenses of Balck's *4th Panzer Army* of *Army Group North Ukraine* west of Kovel. Within hours, the front's **2d Tank Army** and several mobile corps began exploiting success to the west with the infantry in their wake. On 24 July Rokossovsky's forces captured Lublin and pushed on westward towards the Vistula River south of Warsaw. By 2 August, the **1st Belorussian Front**'s left wing armies seized bridgeheads over the Vistula River at Magnuszew and Pulavy and commenced an almost two-month struggle with counterattacking *Wehrmacht* forces to retain these vital bridgeheads as staging areas for future, even larger-scale offensives into heart of central Poland toward Berlin.

During the advance by the **1st Belorussian Front**'s left wing to the Vistula River, the **Polish Home Army** staged an insurrection in Warsaw. Only days before, the *Stavka* had ordered Rokossovsky to dispatch his **2d Tank Army** in a dash toward Warsaw's eastern suburbs, protected on the right by a cavalry corps (the **2d Guards**) and the **47th Army**. The tank army reached the region east of Warsaw on 29 July, but before the **47th Army** could arrive, from 30 July through 5 August, two panzer corps (*XXXIX* and *IV SS*) counterattacked the tank army and forced it to withdraw with heavy losses. At the time, the bulk of the **1st Belorussian Front**'s center and right wing were struggling to overcome German defenses north of Siedlice on the approaches to the Narew River and, according to Soviet accounts, were unable to support the dash to Warsaw. Western accounts claim that Stalin deliberately withheld support for the **Polish Home Army** until it was totally destroyed.

Compounding the Germans' difficulties, Konev's **1st Ukrainian Front** began its offensive toward Lvov on 13 July with the mission of encircling and destroying *Army Group North Ukraine*'s *4th Panzer Army* and its panzer reserves east of Lvov and capturing the vital Polish city. After penetrating German defenses east and northeast of Lvov, Konev committed his **1st, 3d Guards,** and **4th Tank Armies** to combat, encircled and destroyed *4th Panzer Army's XIII Army Corps* in the Brody region, partially encircled *Wehrmacht* forces at Lvov, and launched his **3d Guards** and **4th Tank Armies** on a deep exploitation northwestward toward the Vistula River in the vicinity of Sandomir in southern Poland. In early August, Konev's exploiting forces seized a bridgehead over the Vistula River at and south of Sandomir and commenced a two-month struggle against German reserves for possession of the vital gateway for future operations across southern Poland. The twin offensives across central and southern Poland projected Soviet Army forces forward to the Vistula River and severely damaged *Army Group North Ukraine.*

The climax of the Soviet Army's summer offensive occurred on 20 August 1944 when Malinovsky's **2d** and Tolbukhin's **3d Ukrainian Fronts** commenced operations to destroy *Wehrmacht* and Romanian forces assigned to *Army Group South Ukraine* in Romania. Attacking north of Iassy and east of Kishinev, the two fronts smashed German defenses, forced the surrender of the *Romanian 3d* and *4th Armies*, and committed the **6th Tank Army** and multiple mobile corps to an exploitation operation deep into Romania. The attacking force occupied Bucharest on 31 August and then swept westward across the Carpathian Mountains into Hungary and southward into Bulgaria. In the process, the Soviet forces encircled and destroyed the German *6th Army* (for the second time) and forced *Army Group South Ukraine*'s shattered *8th Army* to withdraw westward into Hungary.

The Soviet Army completed this vast mosaic of successful operations in the fall. As it did so, its forces in the far north defeated German forces west of Murmansk and seized the Petsamo region. At the same time, while the **Leningrad, 2d** and **3d Baltic Fronts** overcame *Army Group North*'s strong "Panther Line" defenses and liberated the bulk of the Baltic region in September and October, from October through December the **2d, 3d,** and **4th Ukrainian Fronts** advanced into Hungary, besieged Budapest, and occupied Belgrade in cooperation with Tito's partisan forces.

Overall, the Soviet Army's summer and fall campaign of 1944 constituted a long series of unmitigated disasters for Axis armies and fortunes in the East. The Soviet Army's summer offensives alone cost Axis forces an estimated 465,000 soldiers killed or captured. Between 1 June and 30 November 1944, total German losses on all fronts were 1,457,000, of which 903,000 were lost on the Eastern Front. By the end of 1944, only Hungary remained as a German ally, and Germany felt increasingly besieged and isolated, with the Soviet Army lodged in East Prussia in the north, along the Vistula River in Poland, and across the Danube in Hungary, and with Allied armies within striking distance of Germany's western borders.

The Soviet Union also suffered heavily during this period, coming ever closer to the bottom of its once-limitless barrel of manpower. In an effort to compensate for this, Soviet plans used steadily increasing amounts of artillery, armor, and airpower to reduce manpower losses. In the process, moreover, the Soviet commanders had the opportunity to test out their operational theories under a variety of different tactical and terrain considerations. These commanders still made occasional mistakes, but they entered 1945 at the top of their form.

By the end of 1944, the Soviet Army was strategically positioned to conquer the remainder of Poland, Hungary, and Austria in a single campaign. The only question that remained was whether this last strategic thrust would propel Soviet forces to Berlin as well, and, if so, where the Allied armies would complete their operations. Shadow Soviet-style governments had accompanied the Soviet Army into eastern Europe, and the Yalta Conference, to be held in February 1945, would tacitly legitimize these regimes. Where the contending armies advanced in 1945 would have a decisive influence over the political complexion of postwar Europe. This stark fact underscored the importance of subsequent operations during the race for Berlin and, coincidentally, generated more than a little suspicion in the respective Allied camps.

January–4 April 1945

Date	Event
Jan 1945	Five Soviet fronts with 35 armies, 250 divisions, and almost 4 million men smash two German army groups defending East Prussia and Poland and advance to Königsberg and the Oder River, inflicting 500,000 casualties on German forces.
By 1 Feb 1945	Soviet troops occupy bridgeheads across the Oder, 36 miles from Berlin.
	Allied armies are arrayed along the Rhine, from Switzerland to the Netherlands: the closest is 300 miles from Berlin.
Feb–4 Apr 1945	Allied troops attack in the Rhineland. In March, they cross the Rhine, encircle most of Army Group B in the Ruhr Pocket, and by 4 April, reach the Weser River, 170 miles from Berlin.
	Soviet Army conquers East Prussia, Pomerania, and Silesia, repels the last *Wehrmacht* offensive of the war (Operation SPRING AWAKENING) near Lake Balaton in Hungary, and advances to Vienna.

Operations Summary, January–4 April 1945

Military operations during the winter campaign of 1945 includes the following major operations:

- ❐ The Soviet Vistula-Oder Offensive (12 January–3 February 1945)
- ❐ The Soviet East Prussian Offensive (13 January–25 April 1945)
- ❐ The Soviet Lower Silesian Offensive (8–24 February 1945)
- ❐ The Soviet East Pomeranian Offensive (10 February–4 April 1945)
- ❐ The Soviet Upper Silesian Offensive (15–31 March 1945)
- ❐ The Morava-Ostravka Offensives (10 March–5 May 1945)
- ❐ The Banska-Bystrica Offensive (10–30 March 1945)
- ❐ The German Balaton Offensive (6–15 March 1945)
- ❐ The Soviet Vienna Offensive (16 March–15 April 1945)
- ❐ The Bratislava-Brno Offensive (25 March–5 May 1945)

After reviewing all of its strategic options, the *Stavka* began planning the Soviet Army's winter campaign in late October 1944. The victories of the summer and fall had created a much more favorable situation for Soviet Army offensive action; the overall length of the main front shortened from over 1,000 miles to 780 miles, significant German forces uselessly isolated in Kurland and Budapest, and the Soviet Union clearly held the strategic initiative. Soviet intelligence estimates indicated that, during 1944, 96 German divisions had been captured or destroyed, and another 33 so weakened that they were disbanded. Still, even the seemingly inexhaustible strength of the Soviet Union had its limits, and the planners sought a means for rapid and relatively bloodless victory. The shortened front meant that the Soviet Army could conduct fewer but far more powerful offensives to accomplish its objectives of seizing Berlin and destroying Nazi Germany. This was necessary since German defenses thickened as Soviet Army forces advanced west.

In addition, Stalin restructured his command and control methods to insure greater efficiency. In late October, he decided to control the Soviet Army's operating fronts directly from Moscow, dispensing with the *Stavka* representatives and coordinators who had represented it in the field during the previous three years. Instead, he restructured his forces for the new offensives into a smaller number of extremely powerful fronts and reshuffled his front commanders. The **1st Belorussian Front**, now personally commanded by Zhukov, was to advance directly on Berlin with Konev' s **1st Ukrainian Front** advancing on a parallel course just to its south. The **2d Belorussian Front**, now under Rokossovsky's command, was to advance westward north of the Vistula River toward Danzig and Pomerania to protect the **1st Belorussian Front's** right flank.

Based upon the plan formulated by the *Stavka*, the Soviet Army conducted a two-stage operation to destroy the *Third Reich* (See Map 8). First, as described above, Malinovsky's **2d** and Tolbukhin's **3d Ukrainian Fronts** continued their advance in Hungary during November and December to draw German reserves away from the Warsaw-Berlin axis. Then the main offensive, which was tentatively scheduled to begin between 15 and 20 January 1945, but began on 13 January to relieve German pressure on the Allies in the Battle of the Bulge, shattered the Germans' Vistula and East Prussian defenses in two large-scale operations. The lesser of these attacks, conducted by Cherniakhovsky's **3d** and Rokossovsky's **2d Belorussian Fronts**, performed the difficult task of clearing *Army Group Center* from East Prussia. While the former bulled its way westward through the

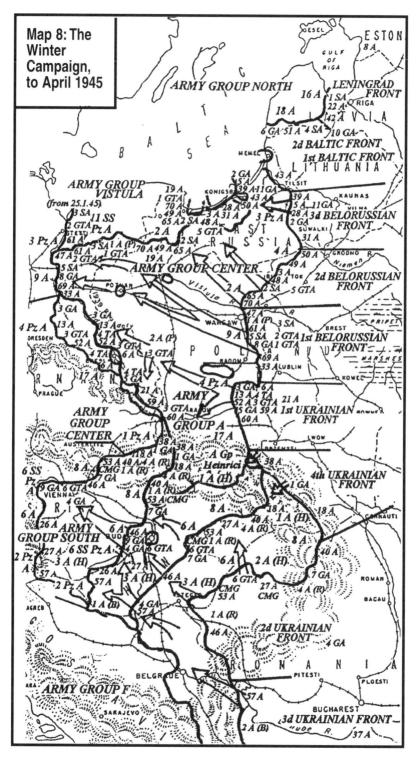

Map 8: The Winter Campaign, to April 1945

German defenses toward Königsberg, the latter, with a single tank army (the **5th Guards**), enveloped East Prussia from the south and protected the **1st Belorussian Front**'s right flank. At the same time, Zhukov's **1st Belorussian** and Konev's **1st Ukrainian Fronts**, each spearheaded by two tank armies (the **1st** and **2d Guards** and the **3d** and **4th Guards**, respectively), conducted the main offensive across Poland against *Army Group A*, to which Hitler had assigned responsibility for defending the vital Warsaw-Berlin axis.

Both offensives achieved immediate and spectacular success. After shattering *Army Group A*'s defenses opposite their bridgeheads, the **1st Belorussian** and **1st Ukrainian Fronts** forces pushed aside German panzer reserves and raced westward with their four tank armies far in advance. The *Wehrmacht's* front in Poland vaporized, and by 1 February, the lead elements of the **1st** and **2d Guards Tank Armies** captured bridgeheads over the Oder River only 36 miles from Berlin. To the south, the **1st Ukrainian Front** kept pace, reaching and crossing the Oder north and south of Breslau. In their wake, thousands of *Wehrmacht* troops remained helplessly encircled in numerous pockets and bypassed cities and towns.

To the north, the **2d** and **3d Belorussian Fronts** smashed *Army Group Center*'s defenses in East Prussia and, by the end of January, isolated the remnants of the army group in a pocket around the city of Königsberg. However, the **2d Belorussian Front** was not able to smash totally German defenses in the Danzig area, leaving a sizable German force hanging threateningly over the **1st Belorussian Front**'s left flank. Given the twin threats posed to the **1st Belorussian Front** by *Wehrmacht* forces in Pomerania and in Silesia to the south, on 2 February, Stalin ordered Zhukov and Konev to halt their offensives until their flanks could be secured. Subsequently, the Soviet Army mounted four major and several minor offensives in February and March designed to clear *Wehrmacht* forces from Pomerania and Silesia. During this period, the **1st** and **2d Belorussian Fronts** eliminated the threat in Silesia, and the **1st Ukrainian Front** did the same in Silesia.

To the south in Hungary, from 6 to 15 March, Hitler conducted his final offensive of the war by launching Dietrich's *6th SS Panzer Army* in a dramatic, but futile, attempt to crush Soviet defenses west of Budapest and protect the vital Balaton oilfields. Just as this offensive faltered in mid-March, the **2d** and **3d Ukrainian Fronts** launched another major offensive and several minor offensives against the depleted forces of *Army Group South*, driving them from Hungary and Slovakia and liberating Vienna on 13 April, only three days before the Soviet Army began its onslaught against Berlin.

These catastrophic defeats cost Germany much of the industry that had been dispersed in Poland to shield it from allied bombing. Soviet estimates that Germany lost 60 divisions, 1,300 tanks, and a similar number of aircraft are undoubtedly simplistic, since many small units survived and infiltrated elsewhere. Moreover, although German personnel losses in these operations were high (in excess of 660,000), replacements and transfers from other theaters caused German troop strength in the East to decline from 2,030,000 (with 190,000 allies) to just under 2,000,000 men at the end of March. However, 556,000 of these troops were isolated in Kurland and East Prussia and virtually irrelevant to future operations. To make matters worse, the Soviets could now concentrate the bulk of its 6,461,000 troops on the most critical axis. For over a third of these forces, the next stop would be Berlin.

4 April–8 May 1945

Date	Event
18 Apr 1945	Allied forces reach the Elbe River, 60 miles from Berlin, and halt in accordance with Allied agreements.
16 Apr– 7 May 1945	Over two million Soviet troops conduct the Berlin and Prague offensives at a cost of 413,865 casualties, including 93,113 dead or missing. These losses equal 25 percent of the United States' entire wartime death toll.
8 May 1945	Out of the 13.5 million men fielded by the *Wehrmacht* during the war, 10.8 million had perished or been captured on the Eastern Front.
	Soviet Army strength in Europe totals roughly 6.4 million soldiers and 500 divisions.

Operations Summary,
4 April–8 May 1945

Major operations during the spring campaign include:

- ❐ The Battle for Kurland (16 February–8 May 1945)
- ❐ The Siege of Königsberg and adjacent pockets (13 March–9 April 1945)

❏ The Battle for Berlin (16 April–8 May 1945)
❏ The Prague Offensive (6–11 May 1945)

After more than three years of enormous destruction and unimaginable casualties, the *Stavka* was determined to destroy the Nazi regime and end the terrible war in the spring of 1945. Furthermore, after expending so much blood and energy to defeat the *Wehrmacht* in the field, Stalin was unwilling to permit the western allies to seize the final victory. Quite apart from his desire to dominate postwar Central Europe and the Allied agreement that the Soviets should seize the city, this emotional preoccupation drove the Soviet Army forward toward Berlin (See Map 9).

During the war's final campaign, the Soviet Army faced the equally determined and desperate remnants of the once proud but now decimated *Wehrmacht*. This force of about 1.6 million men under Himmler's (later Heinrici's) *Army Group Vistula* and *Army Group Center* manned deeper than usual defenses along the Oder and Neisse Rivers and the Czech border. Leaving only limited forces to face the British, Americans, Canadians, and French in the West, Hitler's High Command assembled roughly 85 divisions and numerous smaller, separate units totaling as many as one million men and boys and 850 tanks to wage the final struggle along the Oder River. An even greater challenge to the Soviet Army during the spring campaign was the fact that, for the first time in the war, it had only limited room to maneuver. With the large city of Berlin only 36 miles to their front and with the forward lines of their Allies only 62 miles beyond, the Soviets faced the unwelcome prospect of having to conduct repeated penetration attacks against successive, fully-manned, defensive lines anchored on increasingly urbanized terrain.

Therefore, the *Stavka* prepared and conducted its spring campaign with immense care. Deep down, Stalin was also unsure of how many Germans in the West would join their comrades along the Oder to face the more dreaded and feared Soviet Army.

Experience had demonstrated that a force of up to one million men could offer credible resistance along a formidable river barrier, even against a force more than twice its size. Thus, the Soviets prepared an offensive fitting to the task — an offensive whose conduct would warrant credit in the eyes of her Allies who were approaching Berlin from the west.

In accordance with the *Stavka's* strategic plan for the spring campaign, the Soviet Army dealt first with *Army Group Vistula* defending Berlin, and only then engaged *Army Group Center* in

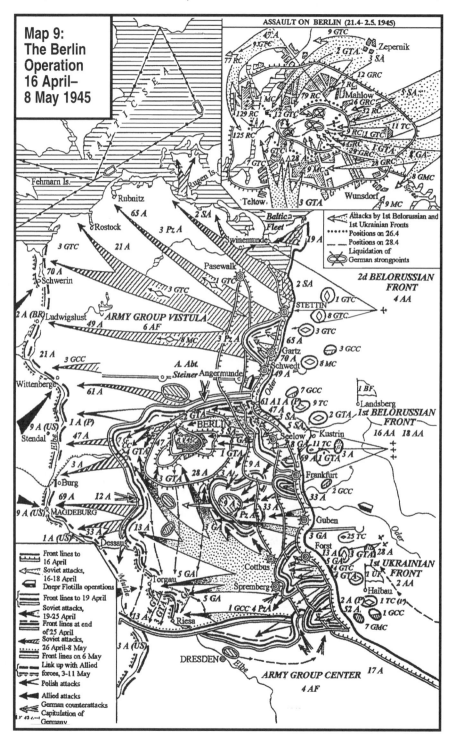

**Map 9:
The Berlin
Operation
16 April–
8 May 1945**

ASSAULT ON BERLIN (21.4–2.5. 1945)

Czechoslovakia. The Soviet Army's objectives were limited to those boundaries that had already been mutually agreed upon with the Allies. Three reinforced fronts took part in the Berlin offensive (See Map 9). Zhukov's **1st Belorussian Front** attacked directly toward Berlin from the Küstrin bridgehead on the western bank of the Oder River to envelop the city from the north; Konev's **1st Ukrainian Front** thrust across the Oder to the south to envelop Berlin from the southwest; and, to the north, Rokossovsky's **3d Belorussian Front** attacked across the Oder several days later to destroy German forces in the coastal plain north of Berlin and link up with Allied forces along the Elbe River. The ensuing struggle, and in particular, the advance by Zhukov's front into Berlin proper, was prolonged and bloody. It only ended on 7 and 8 May when Soviet Army forces linked up with Allied forces along the Elbe River and *Wehrmacht* forces in Germany capitulated. During the course of the Berlin operation, Soviet Army forces crushed the remnants of *Army Group Vistula* and captured 480,000 German troops. The cost, however, had been great as 361,367 Soviet and Polish soldiers fell in the effort.

The Soviet Army's **1st** and **2d Baltic Fronts,** which had isolated a large portion of *Army Group North* in the Kurland Peninsula in October 1944, continued to besiege this German force until its surrender on 9 May 1945.

While these fronts bottled up over 500,000 *Wehrmacht* troops and three other Soviet Army fronts conducted the climactic Berlin offensive, other Soviet Army forces completed the conquest of Austria and liquidated resisting pockets of German forces inKurland and on the Samland Peninsula, west of Königsberg. The **2d** and **3d Ukrainian Fronts** seized Vienna from Wöhler's *Army Group South*, captured Brno, Czechoslovakia, and approached Graz, Austria. The **1st** and **2d Baltic Fronts** destroyed the remnants of *Army Group North* (renamed *Army Group Kurland* on 26 January) in Kurland, seizing up to 100,000 prisoners. Finally, the **3d Belorussian Front** liquidated the remaining forces of former *Army Group Center* (renamed *Operational Group Samland*) in the Samland pocket west of Königsberg, taking another 189,000 pnsoners.

As early as 1 May, the *Stavka* ordered Zhukov's **1st Belorussian Front** to relieve all elements of the **1st Ukrainian Front** engaged in mopping up in Berlin so that Konev's forces could turn southwestward and, in conjunction with the Malinovsky's **2d** and Eremenko's **4th Ukrainian Fronts**, advance on Prague against the Soviet Army's old nemesis, *Army Group Center*, whose 600,000 men awaited inevitable destruction, ironically, not in Germany, but in Czechoslovakia, which had been one of Hitler's initial victims.

While the *Reichstag* was still under assault, between 1 and 6 May, the **1st, 4th,** and **2d Ukrainian Fronts** regrouped their forces and began their rapid advance toward Prague. The combined force of over 2 million Soviet and Polish soldiers relied heavily on tank forces, including three tank armies and a cavalry-mechanized group, to spearhead a rapid thrust directly on the Czech capital. According to the hastily-formulated plan, the **1st Ukrainian Front** attacked west of Dresden, penetrated the Erzgeberg Mountain passes in southern east Germany, and committed two tank armies (the **3d Guards** and **4th Guards**) in the rapid dash to Prague. Polish and Soviet forces under the **1st Ukrainian Front**'s control launched a supporting attack in the Görlitz zone, and simultaneously, the **2d** and **4th Ukrainian Fronts** launched tank-heavy offensives toward Prague in a wide arc spanning the eastern and southern frontiers of Czechoslovakia.

The forward detachments of the **1st Ukrainian Front**'s **3d** and **4th Guards Tank Armies** liberated Prague on 9 May. During the following two days, Soviet Army forces accepted the surrender of more than 600,000 German troops of Reinhardt's *Army Group Center*. On 11 May, the lead elements of the **4th Guards Tank Army** linked up with the **US Third Army** east of Pilsen, ending the major wartime field operations of the Soviet Army.

The military consequences of operations in the spring of 1945 were clear. The remaining forces of the once proud and seemingly indestructible armies of Germany were crushed by the combined efforts of Allied forces assaulting from east and west. National Socialist Germany, which had based its power and built its empire on the foundations of warfare of unprecedented violence and destructiveness, was felled in equally violent and decisive fashion. The colossal scope and scale of the Berlin operation, with the appalling Soviet casualties and equally massive destruction of the German capital, was a fitting end to a war which was so unlike previous wars. As more than one German veteran observed, the war in the West was conducted in a relatively civilized fashion, while the war in the East was unmitigated savagery and horror. This final horror eliminated the remaining two million men of the *Wehrmacht* and reduced Germany to ashes.

The political consequences of these last operations reflected a process which had been going on for over a year, which the Soviet Union's allies had largely overlooked or tolerated in their search for victory. That process now became crystal clear during the peace that followed. In the baggage of the victorious Soviet Army came political power in the guise of newly-formed national armies for

Soviet-controlled states and governments to go with those armies. Two Polish, three Romanian, and two Bulgarian armies fought and bled alongside the Soviet Army, together with a Czech corps and other smaller national formations. Once returned to their native lands, these units cooperated with local partisan formations, many also sponsored and equipped by the Soviet Union. Under the protection of the Soviet Army, these armed forces and the governments-in-exile that accompanied them, quickly transformed military into political power.

   Slowly, in mid-May 1945, the firing died out and the war in Europe gradually came to an end. Having captured Bucharest, Belgrade, Warsaw, Budapest, Vienna, Berlin, and Prague from the shattered *Wehrmacht*, the Soviet Army, by rights, had undisputed claim to the lion's share of fighting and bleeding for this victory over Nazi Germany. In Western perceptions, however, the political consequences of that victory soon deprived them of that right. Within a few short years, the horrors of war were replaced by the menace of the Cold War, and Cold War suspicions soon obscured the unprecedented suffering and triumph of the Soviet peoples.

Conclusions

Beyond the issues covered in this chronology, three over-arching matters remain to be treated. In brief, these issues regard the relative contributions of the United States, Great Britain, and the Soviet Union to Allied victory in Europe, the role of the "second front" in achieving that victory, and the impact of Allied Lend-Lease on the ability of the Soviet Army to wage war. All three of these issues were important during the course of the war, all three have remained contentious since war's end, and the continuing debates over all three will likely effect U.S.-Russian relations far into the future. This alone makes a brief discussion of these issues essential.

Relative Contributions to Victory

Generally, the Soviet Army and the Soviet citizenry of many nationalities bore the lion's share of the struggle against Germany from 1941 to 1945. Only China, which suffered almost continuous Japanese attack from 1931 onward, matched the level of Soviet suffering and effort. In military terms, moreover, the Chinese participation in the war was almost insignificant in comparison with the Soviet war, which constantly engaged more than half of all German forces.

From June through December 1941, only Britain shared with the Soviet Union the trials of war against the Germans. Over three million German troops fought in the East, while 900,000 struggled elsewhere, attended to occupied Europe, or rested in the homeland. From December 1941 through November 1942, while over 9,000,000 troops on both sides struggled in the East, the only significant ground action in the Western Theater took place in North Africa, where relatively small British forces engaged Rommel's *Afrika Korps* and its Italian allies.

In October and November 1942, the British celebrated victory over the Germans at El Alamein, defeating four German divisions and a somewhat larger Italian force, and inflicting 60,000 Axis losses. The same month, at Stalingrad, the Soviets defeated and encircled the German *6th Army*, damaged *4th Panzer Army*, and smashed the *Romanian 3d* and *4th Armies*, eradicating over 50 divisions and over 300,000 men from the Axis order of battle. By May 1943, the Allies pursued the *Afrika Korps* across northern Africa and into Tunisia, where after heavy fighting, the German and Italian force of 250,000 surrendered. Meanwhile, in the East, another German army (the *2d*) was severely mauled, and the *Italian 8th* and *Hungarian 2d Armies* were utterly destroyed, exceeding Axis losses in Tunisia.

While over 3.5 million German and Soviet troops struggled at Kursk and 8.5 million later fought on a 1,500-mile front from the Leningrad region to the Black Sea coast, in July 1943, Allied forces invaded Sicily, and drove 60,000 Germans from the island. In August, the Allies landed on the Italian peninsula. By October, when 2.5 million men of the *Wehrmacht* faced 6.6 million Soviets, the frontlines had stabilized in Italy south of Rome as the Germans deployed a much smaller, although significant, number of troops to halt the Allied advance.

By 1 October 1943, 2,565,000 men (63 percent) of the *Wehrmacht*'s 4,090,000-man force struggled in the East, together with the bulk of the 300,000 *Waffen-SS* troops. On 1 June 1944, 239 (62 percent) of the German Army's 386 division equivalents fought in the East. With operations in Italy at a stalemate, until June 1944, in fact, the *Wehrmacht* still considered the west as a semi-reserve. In August 1944, after the opening of the second front, while 2.1 million Germans fought in the East, one million opposed Allied operations in France.

Casualty figures underscore this reality. From September 1939 to September 1942, the bulk of the German Army's 922,000 dead, missing, and disabled (14 percent of the total force) could be credited to combat in the East. Between 1 September 1942 and 20

November 1943, this grim count rose to 2,077,000 (30 percent of the total force), again primarily in the East. From June through November 1944, after the opening of the second front, the German Army suffered another 1,457,000 irrevocable losses. Of this number, 903,000 (62 percent) were lost in the East. Finally, after losing 120,000 men to the Allies in the Battle of the Bulge, from 1 January to 30 April 1945, the Germans suffered another 2 million losses, two-thirds at Soviet hands. Today, the stark inscription, "died in the East," that is carved on countless thousands of headstones in scores of German cemeteries bear mute witness to the carnage in the East, where the will and strength of the *Wehrmacht* perished.

The Role of the "Second Front" in Allied Victory

During the war and since war's end, the Soviets have bitterly complained about the absence of a real "second front" before June 1944, and that issue remains a source of suspicion even in post-Cold-War Russia. Yet, Allied reasons for deferring a second front until 1944 were valid, and Allied contributions to victories were significant. As the Anglo/Canadian performance at Dieppe indicated in August 1942, and as the American debacle at the Kasserine Pass in December 1942 indicated, Allied armies were not ready to operate in France in 1943, even had a sufficient number of landing craft been available for the invasion, which they were not. Even in the late spring of 1944, Allied success at Normandy was initially tenuous. Once in France, after the breakout from the Normandy beachhead in August, the 2 million Allied troops in France inflicted grievous losses on the 1 million defending Germans, 100,000 at Falaise, and a total of 400,000 by December 1944. In the subsequent winter battles in the Ardennes, Alsace, and eastern Lorraine, the Germans lost another 120,000 men. These losses in the West, combined with the over 1.2 million lost in the East during the same period, broke the back of the *Wehrmacht* and set the context for the final destruction of Germany in 1945.

In addition to its ground combat contribution, the Allies conducted a major strategic bombing campaign against Germany (which the Soviets could not mount) and in 1944 drew against themselves the bulk of German operational and tactical airpower. The strategic bombing campaign wreaked significant damage on German industrial targets; struck hard at the well-being and morale of the German civil population; and sucked into its vortex and destroyed a large part of the German fighter force, which had earlier been used effectively in a ground role in the East. Although airpower did not prove to be a war-winning weapon, and German industrial mobilization and weapons production peaked in late 1944, the air campaign seriously hindered the German war effort.

Equally disastrous for the Germans were the losses of tactical fighters in that campaign and in combat in France in 1944. So devastating were these losses that after mid-1944, the German air force was no longer a factor on the Eastern Front.

The Role of Lend-Lease in Allied Victory

Another controversial Allied contribution to the war effort was the Lend-Lease program of aid to the Soviet Union. Although Soviet accounts have routinely belittled the significance of Lend-Lease in sustaining the Soviet war effort, the overall importance of this assistance cannot be understated. Lend-Lease aid did not arrive in sufficient quantities to make the difference between defeat and victory

	Lend-Lease	Domestic Production
Armored vehicles	12,161 (12%)	98,300
	(7,056 US)	
Guns and mortars	9,600 (2%)	525,200
Machine guns	131,600	
Combat aircraft	18,303 (15%)	122,100
Fighters	13,857	
Bombers	3,633	
Transport	710	
Reconnaissance	19	
Training	84	
Aircraft engines	14,902 (6.7%)	222,418
Trucks and Jeeps	409,526 (55%)	744,400
(reached Russia)	312,600 (42%)	
Explosives (tons)	325,784	
Locomotives	1,860 (6.3%)	29,524
Rail cars	11,181	
Field telephones	422,000	
Foodstuffs (tons)	4,281,910 (25%)	17,127,640
Oil (POL) (tons)	2,599,000	
Boots (pairs)	15,000,000	

Figure 7. Lend-Lease Assistance to the Soviet Union

Soviet troops descend from a US vehicle provided by Lend-Lease.

in 1941–42; that achievement must be attributed solely to the Soviet people and to the iron nerve of Stalin, Zhukov, Shaposhnikov, Vasilevsky, and their subordinates. As the war continued, however, the United States and Great Britain provided many of the implements of war and strategic raw materials needed for Soviet victory.

Without Lend-Lease food, clothing, and raw materials (especially metals), the Soviet economy would have been even more heavily burdened by the war effort. Perhaps most directly, without Lend-Lease trucks, rail engines, and railroad cars, every Soviet offensive would have stalled at an earlier stage, outrunning its logistical tail in a matter of days. In turn, this would have allowed the German commanders to escape at least some encirclements, while forcing the Soviet Army to prepare and conduct many more deliberate penetration attacks in order to advance the same distance.

Left to their own devices, the Soviets might have taken 12 to 18 months longer to defeat the *Wehrmacht;* the ultimate result would probably have been the same, except that Soviet soldiers could have waded at France's Atlantic beaches. Thus, while the Soviet Army shed the bulk of Allied blood, it would have shed more blood for longer without Allied assistance.

Biographies of Important Germans and Their Allies

Fedor von Bock was born into an old military family on 3 December 1880 in Küstrin, Brandenburg, and was commissioned in 1898. During the Great War, he earned Germany's highest award for valor, the *Pour le Merité,* while commanding a battalion. Remaining in the Army after the war, he rose to command of *Wehrkreis* (Military District) *II* (Pomerania) by the time of Hitler's rise to power in 1933. Bock commanded *Army Group North* in the invasion of Poland in 1939, and was awarded the Knight's Cross for his service in that operation. Later, he commanded *Army Group B* in the invasion of western Europe in 1940. Promoted to *Generalfeldmarschall* in July 1940, Bock was assigned to command *Army Group Center* in Operation BARBAROSSA.

Bock's armies achieved successes unprecedented in modern warfare during the first four months of combat in the USSR. Including those in which it played a part in coordination with the adjacent *Army Groups North* and *South*, as well as those it achieved by itself, *Army Group Center* encircled and destroyed no less than eighteen Soviet field armies in less than four months. However, between the onset of a particularly ferocious Russian winter, the sheer size of the Soviet Union, and, most of all, the unrelenting tenacity of Soviet forces, *Army Group Center* came to a halt just shy of Moscow in December 1941. On 19 December 1941, Bock was too ill to continue his duties, and was replaced by Kluge.

Thirty days later, Bock was ordered to assume command of *Army Group South*, following the death of its former commander, Reichenau. While in command, he and his armies sustained the impact of two major Soviet offensives; the second one, in May 1942, threatened to encircle German forces around Kharkov, but Bock's counterattack blunted the attempt and inflicted about 270,000 casualties on Timoshenko's **Southwestern Front** in the process.

Fedor von Bock

As the entire German military machine in the east went over to the offensive a few weeks later, launching Operation *BLAU*, Bock's armies achieved stunning successes. They utterly shattered the **Briansk** and **Southwestern Fronts'** defenses along a 280-mile zone from the Kursk region to the Northern Donets River, and within two weeks, demolished the Soviet Army's entire defense in southern Russia. Bock's men accomplished this, however, by deviating from Hitler's prescribed plan, and in mid-July 1942, Bock accepted strong suggestions that he retire "for reasons related to his health."

An extraordinarily successful commander of large units in combat, Bock spent the rest of the war in retirement. He and his wife were killed in an air raid in Lensahn, Holstein, five days before the end of the war.

Eduard Dietl was born 21 June 1890 in Bad Aibling, Bavaria. He joined the *Bavarian 5th Infantry Regiment* in 1909 and was commissioned in 1911. Dietl saw extensive action as a company commander during the Great War; in 1918 and 1919, he joined the *Ritter* von Epp's *Freikorps* and fought in the suppression of the Bavarian Soviet Republic.

In 1919, Dietl joined the German Worker's Party, which in 1920 became the National Socialist German Worker's — or Nazi — Party. In

1920, Dietl was commissioned in the *Reichswehr* as a *Hauptmann*, and in 1921, when political activity among *Reichswehr* officers was banned, he renounced his party membership. He remained, however, a devoted adherent to the Nazi cause, and eventually became an ardent follower of Hitler.

Dietl assumed command of a mountain infantry battalion in Bavaria in 1931 and ascended to command of a mountain infantry regiment in 1935. As a *Generalmajor,* he commanded the *3d Mountain Division* in the invasion of Poland, and was promoted to Gener-

Eduard Dietl

alleutnant just before the invasion of Norway in April 1940. In that campaign, Dietl commanded the Narvik expedition and became a national hero through the efforts of the Propaganda Ministry. For his exploits, Dietl was awarded not only the Knight's Cross, but the first Oakleaves awarded as well. He was also simultaneously promoted to *General* of Mountain Troops.

Dietl was next assigned to command *Mountain Corps Norway* (of the German "*Army of Norway*") in the offensive toward Murmansk [Operation PLATINFUCHS (PLATINUM FOX)], which commenced 29 June 1941. The offensive fell well short of its important strategic objective, and control of German forces attacking from Finland was turned over to a new headquarters — the *Army of Lapland* — command of which was assigned to Dietl. Later renamed *20th Mountain Army,* it remained under Dietl's command throughout its largely fruitless operations during the next two and a half years.

Throughout his service to the Third Reich, Dietl remained a passionate and involved supporter of the regime. On the tenth anniversary of the Nazi accession to national power, 30 January 1943, Dietl was awarded the Golden Party Badge; on the twentieth anniversary of the Beer Hall Putsch later that year, he delivered an impassioned speech on the steps of the Feldherrnhalle.

In June 1944, after attending a strategic conference in Germany, Dietl and his corps commanders were killed when their transport crashed en route to Finland.

Dietl was a physically tough, charismatic commander who elicited fierce loyalty from his subordinates across his entire field army, especially those assigned to mountain units under his command. After the war, a *Bundeswehr* barracks in Bavaria was named in his honor. Long afterwards, in 1995, upon the vehement insistence of the German political Left that having a government edifice named for an ardent Nazi was unacceptable, Christian Democrat Defense Minister Volker Rühe decided to rename the edifice.

Nikolaus von Falkenhorst was born in Breslau, Silesia, on 17 January 1885, the son of an old military family. He joined the Army in 1907 and served in various regimental and staff assignments during the First World War. In 1918, he served in a staff position with the German forces in Finland.

After service with a *Freikorps* after the war, Falkenhorst entered the *Reichswehr* and served in a variety of command, staff, and foreign embassy positions. Promoted to *Generalleutnant*, he commanded a corps of *3d Army* in the invasion of Poland in 1939. A few months after the Polish campaign, Falkenhorst was assigned to command German forces in the invasion of Norway. He was awarded the Knight's Cross for his service in that operation, and as recognition of the potential he showed in the swift and devastating conquest of Norway, Falkenhorst was promoted to Generaloberst on 19 July 1940. He remained in command of German forces in Norway and, as such, he commanded the German *"Army of Norway"* in the invasion of northern Karelia in July 1941. In Operation PLATINFUCHS, his *Mountain Corps Norway* thrust toward Murmansk on the Arctic

Nikolaus von Falkenhorst

Ocean commencing 29 June; in Operation *SILBERFUCHS* (SILVER FOX) his *XXXVI Corps* attacked toward Kandalaksha on the White Sea. Neither corps achieved its objective, and German forces on the northern front eventually settled into essentially static situations until the Finnish-Soviet armistice of September 1944.

Falkenhorst retained command of the *Army of Norway*, but by Hitler's directive, in November 1941, these forces consisted only of German forces actually in Norway; the forces employed in combat in Karelia became subordinated to the newly created *Army of Lapland*, under Dietl.

Even after the Germans withdrew their forces from northern Karelia through Finland in September 1944, Falkenhorst remained in command of the *Army of Norway*. However, after multiple disagreements with the German proconsul in Norway, Falkenhorst was recalled to Berlin in December.

Condemned to death for allowing the execution of British commandos in Norway (the so-called "Commando Order"), Falkenhorst's sentence was commuted, and he was released even earlier than scheduled, in 1953, in consideration of his poor health. He died in Holzminden, Lower Saxony, 15 years later, on 18 June 1968.

Heinz Wilhelm Guderian was born 17 June 1888 in Kulm an der-Weichsel, West Prussia. An infantry officer, he was also trained in communications before the Great War, and gained extensive experience with radio operations during the war. He also earned both classes of the Iron Cross during the Great War, as well as Württemberg's Order of Frederick with Swords.

Remaining in the Army after the war, Guderian became the leading proponent of mechanization and the development and implementation of combined arms mobility tactics in the *Reichswehr*. Fluent in English and French, he translated the writings of Lidell-Hart, Fuller, and DeGaulle, and wrote many influential articles and even a book about the subject. His technical expertise served him well during a visit to the Soviet Union where, under secret protocols to the Rapallo Treaty of 1922, Guderian observed tactical experimentation with tanks that was forbidden in Germany under the Versailles restrictions.

Appointed to command "transportation" units—which were, in fact, testbeds for experiments with tactical vehicles and mobile formations—Guderian caught Hitler's eye as a visionary. In the war that Hitler had been planning since he wrote *Mein Kampf*, he knew that an army equipped and trained for a reprise of the Great War, as the *Reichswehr* was in the middle 1930s, was an army doomed to failure. When Hitler saw a demonstration by an armored test force under Guderian's leadership, he knew he had found the man who could help him build an army capable of rapid, relatively short and "low-cost" victories. From this point, Guderian's star rose quickly.

In January 1935, Hitler gave Guderian command of the new *2d Panzer Division* while he was still an *Oberst*. Promoted a year later to *Generalmajor,* Guderian retained command of this elite formation until January 1938, when he was promoted to *Generalleutnant*

Heinz Wilhelm Guderian

(and nine days thereafter to *General* of Panzer Troops) and assigned to command *XVI Corps* in Berlin. Less than a year later, he was made Chief of Mobile Troops, a position from which he influenced the formation of all German Army panzer and motorized infantry formations, as well as development of tanks and armored vehicles.

Just before the invasion of Poland, Guderian was assigned to command *XIX Panzer Corps,* which, as part of Bock's *Army Group North*, slashed across the Danzig Corridor, through East Prussia, and strategically enveloped the entire Polish Army. For this spectacular performance, Guderian was awarded the Knight's Cross. He continued in command of *XIX Panzer Corps* through the invasion of western Europe, in which the corps was assigned to *Panzer Group Kleist* in Rundstedt's *Army Group A*. It was Guderian's corps which broke the back of the French Army at Sedan and led the race to the coast at Abbéville. Although he bickered seriously with Kleist in May— Guderian actually offered his resignation— he was promoted to *Generaloberst* after the campaign. Belatedly (in July 1941), he was awarded the Oakleaves to the Knight's Cross for his achievements in France.

During Operation BARBAROSSA, Guderian commanded the *2d Panzer Group* (later redesignated *2d Panzer Army*) in Bock's *Army*

Group Center. His divisions played a pivotal role in the great encirclements of whole Soviet armies at Minsk, Smolensk, Kiev, and Briansk, although they brought Guderian into conflict with Kluge, his superior at *4th Army.* As the autumn mud appeared, Guderian's panzer group attempted another great envelopment of Moscow. The operation failed, and Guderian had more trouble with Kluge, who had succeeded Bock as commander of *Army Group Center.*

In December, Guderian confronted Hitler about his conduct of the war on the Eastern Front. He failed to sway Hitler appreciably, and between his differences with the him and with Kluge, Guderian was relieved on the day after Christmas. He spent the next fourteen months in the oblivion of the "Leader Reserve," in which he had no responsibilities or opportunities to contribute to the war effort. During his hiatus from command, he suffered a serious heart attack.

After the German debacles at Stalingrad in early 1943, Guderian was assigned as Inspector of Panzer Troops, with responsibilities for improving the effectiveness of the German Army's armored units on all fronts. Although still not fully recovered from his coronary condition, he performed his duties well and, despite a certain amount of bickering, generally pleased Hitler greatly. After the 20 July attempt on Hitler's life, Guderian was appointed Chief of the General Staff. He was a sharp critic of the conspirators, and sat on the "Honor Court" with Keitel and Jodl that dismissed hundreds of innocent officers from the service, leaving them at the mercy of the kangaroo "People's Courts."

Guderian continued as Chief of Staff until March 1945, when his frequent professional disagreements with Hitler made it impossible to continue. Hitler ordered him on "temporary sick leave" on 28 March 1945, but the war ended before he could return to his duties.

Guderian was in every way the father of the German armored corps, a man who truly revolutionized warfare. Although not universally respected by his superiors, who often found him overly willing to take tactical and operational risks, he was a visionary who was as adept at theory as he was at practice. Guderian passed away in Schwangau bei Füssen, Bavaria, on 17 May 1954.

Franz Halder was born 30 June 1884 in Würzburg, Bavaria, to an ancient Bavarian military family. Commissioned into the field artillery in 1904, Halder served as a staff officer at several levels during the Great War, including service on the staff of Crown Prince Rupprecht. An outstanding staff officer, Halder also developed an excellent reputation as a fine trainer of troops.

Halder remained in the Army after the war, and rose fairly quickly through a succession of staff assignments. From Chief of Staff of *Wehrkreis VI* (Westphalia), he was promoted to *Generalmajor* and assumed command of the *Wehrmacht*'s *7th Infantry Division* in 1935. Later, he helped stage the infamous 1937 *Wehrmacht* maneuvers, designed to demonstrate to the world the resurgence of German arms. In 1938, he was promoted to *Generalleutnant* and assigned to training and operations staff positions in Berlin. It was here that his rise became meteoric. With Hitler's approval, the Commander in Chief of the Army, Brauchitsch, appointed Halder to be the Chief of the General Staff upon the resignation of the anti-Nazi Beck in 1938. Halder, now a *Generaloberst,* thus became the first Bavarian to ascend to that lofty position.

Franz Halder

Halder loathed Hitler and recognized the dangers inherent to his war aims from 1938 forward. He actually planned *coups d'etat* in 1938 and 1939, but did not follow through with them. He remained a part of the system through the invasions of Poland, western Europe, and the USSR, trying to defend the traditions of the German General Staff and Army by quiet, sometimes clandestine, measures of defiance. Although Hitler awarded him the Knight's Cross in October 1939, he remained at serious odds with Hitler's plans for the war on the Eastern Front; he ignored numerous directives from Hitler, effectively sabotaging them. Often, he seemed to express contrary opinions for their own sake, and to delay the implementation of decisions in that way. Although none of what he did was enough to save Germany or the rest of Europe from Hitler and his adherents, Halder's actions unquestionably ruined many of Hitler's plans.

Hitler fired Brauchitsch in December 1941 and personally assumed command of the German Army. Despite constant bickering, he kept Halder on until 24 September 1942, however, before retiring him. After the 20 July 1944 attempted assassination of Hitler, Halder was arrested and thrown into the Flossenburg concentration camp. Eventually, he was taken to Dachau, but despite the fact that he had maintained liaison with the much more actively resisting Beck, not even the fanatics of the Nazi court system could find enough evidence to justify executing Halder. On 27 April 1945, along with about 120 other prominent anti-Nazis (and, in some cases, their families), he was taken under *SS* escort to the Tyrolian village of Niederdorf where a German Army detachment confronted the *SS* guards and took charge of the entire group. Evidence exists that this may have saved their lives, as Himmler had ordered some, if not all, of the group to be exterminated on 29 April. Having been dismissed from the German Army the previous December — and therefore no longer a combatant — Halder was liberated by the US Army on 4 May 1945.

After the war, Halder played a pivotal role in the assembly of vast amounts of historical material about the *Wehrmacht* for the US Army. In 1961, the US Army recognized his exceptional contributions by awarded him its highest civilian service decoration. Franz Halder passed away on 2 April 1972 in Aschau in his native Bavaria.

Josef Harpe was born on 21 September 1887 in Buer, Westphalia. A cavalry officer and veteran of extensive combat in the Great War, he earned both classes of the Iron Cross by September 1915. After the war, he remained in the Army and rose steadily, but not spectacularly, through the ranks. From 1934 to mid-1939, he commanded *Panzer Regiment 3,* and assumed command of the *1st Panzer Brigade, 1st Panzer Division* in July of that year. In this capacity, he participated in the invasion of Poland, but was transferred to command the Panzer Training School at Wünsdorf in February 1940 and promoted to *Generalmajor.*

In October 1940, Harpe assumed command of the new *12th Panzer Division,* and led it into action as part of *Army Group Center*'s *3d Panzer Group* during Operation Barbarossa. As such, Harpe's division took part in the great encirclements of Soviet forces around Minsk and Smolensk; Harpe was awarded the Knight's Cross for his actions in the USSR in August 1941.

Harpe and his *12th Panzer* were transferred to *Army Group North* in November 1941, and took part in the assault on the Leningrad defenses. The division suffered heavy casualties, but Harpe was promoted to *Generalleutnant* and assigned to command *XLI Panzer Corps,* which took part in the defensive fighting around Kalinin against elements of Konev's **Kalinin Front.** For this, Harpe received the Oakleaves to the Knight's Cross. Later, *XLI Corps* was redesignated *"Panzer Corps Harpe"* and participated in Operation *BLAU* in roughly the same area around Kalinin. Harpe continued in command throughout the remainder of 1942 and most of 1943, as the tide turned against the German army on the Eastern Front. He was promoted to *General der Panzertruppen* in the summer of 1942.

Josef Harpe

Awarded the Swords to his Knight's Cross in the late summer of 1943, Harpe succeeded Model in command of the *9th Army* in Kluge's *Army Group Center* in November. During this time, Harpe skillfully directed his army's defensive and delay operations through the Pripet Marshes. Promoted to *Generaloberst* in April 1944, he was assigned to command *4th Panzer Army* in June. Struck shortly thereafter by the Soviets' massive Operation BAGRATION offensive, Harpe and his army withdrew into Poland.

In September 1944, Harpe was assigned to command *Army Group A,* which was attempting to defend a sector of over 300 kilometers' width with three seriously weakened armies against Konev's entire **1st Ukrainian Front** and part of Rokossovsky's **1st Belorussian Front.** Displeased with his performance in this hopeless situation, Hitler replaced him in January 1945; Harpe was assigned to the nebulous "Leader Reserve," without a job. He was succeeded by Schörner, a commander known for his ruthlessness and absolute obedience to Hitler.

In March 1945, Harpe was assigned to command *5th Panzer Army* during the final days before and during the battle of the Ruhr Pocket. He and his men were captured there by the Americans in April.

Harpe was never at all interested in political intrigue, and owed his rapid rise in rank to professional competence. Never a favorite of Hitler, his tactical acumen nevertheless made him indispensable in the brutal, high tempo fighting on the Eastern Front. He passed away on 14 March 1968 in Nuremberg.

Paul Hausser was born to a military family in Brandenburg an der Havel on 7 October 1880. He graduated on 18 March 1899 from the Gross-Lichterfelde cadet academy, the future home barracks of the *Leibstandarte Adolf Hitler* (*LAH*).

Hausser first demonstrated his exceptional military abilities as a young *Leutnant* with infantry units, and he was selected for General Staff training. Accepted for the prestigious German General Staff, Hausser was promoted to *Hauptmann* several months before the Great War began.

During the war, Hausser was promoted to *Major* and received numerous German and Austrian decorations while serving as a staff officer with various infantry units, and on the staff of Crown Prince Rupprecht of Bavaria.

Shortly after the war, Hausser commanded *Füsilier Regiment "Generalfeldmarschall Graf von Moltke,"* as well as border defense units in eastern Germany. Taken into the 100,000-man *Reichswehr*, he spent the ensuing years typically alternating between staff postings and field commands, gradually advancing in rank until his promotion to *Generalmajor* on 1 February 1931. On 31 January 1932, he retired with a *Generalleutnant*'s pension. A year later, Hausser joined the *Stahlhelm* ("Steel Helmet") veterans' association, and his leadership position in that brought him an *SA* (*Sturmabteilungen*, or Storm Troopers; the Nazi party "Brownshirts") commission when the *Stahlhelm* was merged with the *SA* during 1934. *SA-Standartenführer* Paul Hausser was out of his element, and soon accepted Heinrich Himmler's invitation to switch to the *SS* as an *SS-Standartenführer*, receiving that rank on 15 November 1934.

Paul Hausser

Hausser came to the *SS* specifically to oversee training in the newly-forming military units of the *Waffen-SS*. He founded the *SS-Officer Training School* at Braunschweig, and set the curriculum for that establishment and the sister school at Bad Tölz. His talents, his humor, and his concern for his men, along with his relatively advanced age, quickly brought him the nickname "Papa Hausser," one which he kept throughout his life.

Hausser excelled as a division commander, leading his *SS-Verfügung Division* soldiers in France during 1940, and in Yugoslavia and the Soviet Union the next year. As a long time professional army officer with wide experience, he had very good relations with his Army counterparts. He was awarded the Knight's Cross for his leadership during the Western European campaign and the summer 1941 advance to the Dnepr River.

Hausser was badly wounded by shrapnel on 14 October 1941, losing sight in his right eye. Following his recovery, he began to organize the headquarters for the first *SS* corps during May 1942. Initially known as the *SS-Panzer Corps*, it consisted of his previous command (renamed *Das Reich*) and the *SS-LAH* and *SS-Totenkopf Divisions*. These units trained and rebuilt during 1942.

The *SS-Panzer Corps* arrived in the Kharkov sector during January 1943, in the midst of the Stalingrad-Caucasus disaster. The corps, including the elite Army *Panzer-Grenadier Division Grossdeutschland*, was almost surrounded in Kharkov by the middle of February. Hitler ordered the defense of the city, but Hausser ignored the command and directed a breakout from near-encirclement on 15 February. In later years, Hausser shrugged off the potential consequences of his action, stating that he wasn't punished because of the obvious correctness of his decision.

The *SS-Panzer Corps* was joined by *SS-Totenkopf* for the successful counteroffensive that began in late February 1943 and which recaptured Kharkov the next month. In light of his official disobediance, Hausser could not be decorated for his decisive leadership during the campaign.

The *SS-Panzer Corps* fought effectively at Kursk during early July 1943, and again along the Mius River later that month. Hausser was recommended for the Oakleaves to his Knight's Cross by *4th Panzer Army* commander Hermann Hoth, with the award granted on 28 July 1943.

Hausser's corps was retitled *II SS-Panzer Corps* and by the time it returned to combat in March 1944, it controlled the *SS-Hohenstaufen* and *SS-Frundsberg Divisions*. Hausser directed his corps in the successful relief of the encircled *1st Panzer Army*, and then in further heavy fighting in Galicia.

The *II SS-Panzer Corps* was sent to Normandy during June 1944, and went into action on 28 June, counterattacking the British EPSOM offensive across the Odon River. The *7th Army* commander, Friedrich Dollmann, committed suicide that day, and Hausser was named to succeed him, becoming the first *Waffen-SS* officer to assume army-level command. Hausser personally led his men out of the Falaise encirclement until he was wounded by mortar fragments on 20 August 1944. He was driven out of the pocket in an armored personnel carrier of the *SS-Hitlerjugend Division*.

Hausser was awarded the Swords to his Knight's Cross days later on 26 August 1944, for his short tenure as *7th Army* commander. He spent the rest of the year convalescing, and then replaced Himmler as the commander of *Army Group Upper Rhine* on 23 January 1945. Five days later, the command was dissolved, and Hausser took over *Army Group G*, becoming the only *Waffen-SS* officer to hold army-group-level command. He was dismissed from the post on 3 April 1945, after arguing with Hitler, and finished the war in an unimportant staff position.

Hausser's army service and his later influence of a generation of *Waffen-SS* officers lent a degree of legitimacy to the early *Waffen-SS*, setting a professional standard without which the Army might not have allowed it to have modern weapons and equipment.

Hausser testified at Nuremberg on behalf of the *Waffen-SS* as a defense witness. He then wrote the first basic military history of his mens' campaigns, *Waffen-SS im Einsatz* [The Waffen-SS in action], published in 1953. He was recognized as "the Senior" by *Waffen-SS* veterans, and he continued to look out for the welfare of his men for the rest of his life. As increased documentary material became available, he expanded his book into *Soldaten wie andere Auch* [Soldiers also like the others], published during 1968, the year he turned 88. A man of remarkable vitality, he remained in control of his faculties until his death at age 92 on 21 December 1972.

Alfred Jodl was born 10 May 1890 in Würzburg, Bavaria. He was commissioned into the field artillery and saw extensive combat during WWI. Severely wounded in the leg, he remained in the Army after the war, and rose steadily throughout mainly staff, but also some line, assignments. A convinced anti-monarchist, Jodl was awed by Hitler from their first meeting, and he broke with the ancient German tradition of non-politicism to become an outspoken admirer of Hitler and equally outspoken critic of German officers who did not share his fondness for the *Führer*.

Jodl ultimately served as the Chief of the German High Command Operations staff in August 1939, and as such, was a principal strategic advisor to Hitler throughout the war. An excellent administrator and highly-efficient staff officer, Jodl was an aloof, sometimes cold manager whose dogged devotion to Hitler and complete lack of front experience during the Second World War did not endear him to even the highest ranking field commanders. His promotion to *Generaloberst* in early 1944 made him even less popular, as he was selected for this promotion in preference to many more senior, combat-experienced officers. To add final aggravation to the corps of German combat commanders, Admiral Dönitz awarded Jodl the Knight's Cross and the Oakleaves on the next to last day of the war, 7 May 1945.

Alfred Jodl

At the Nuremberg International Military Tribunal, Jodl was tried and sentenced to death for his part in planning the German invasions of most countries in Europe. He was hanged on 16 October 1946. Interestingly, in 1953, a Munich court found him not guilty of the main charges, thus eliminating penalties against his estate.

Wilhelm Keitel was born in the city and state of Brunswick, on 22 September 1882. He saw a lot of action in the Great War, and was seriously wounded. Remaining in the Army after the war, Keitel rose through the ranks, but was assigned strictly as a high-level staff officer from 1929 on. An ambitious, if unimaginative, officer, he married the War Minister's daughter in 1937, and was named by Hitler to serve as the *Wehrmacht* Chief of Staff the following year and remained there for the rest of the war. For his part in the planning and direction of the campaign in Poland, he received the Knight's Cross.

Although often hailed as a lackey, Keitel in fact did on occasion oppose his *Führer's* wishes: he recommended against the prosecution of Operation BARBAROSSA;

Wilhelm Keitel

he offered to resign on several occasions, and even seriously considered suicide more than once. However, whether his duty concept overruled his moral inclinations or he was simply weak, his opposition to Hitler was never enough to either get him sacked or to compel him to join the German Resistance. Indeed, along with *Generals* Guderian and Jodl, *Generalfeldmarschall* Keitel sat in judgment of fellow German officers in the "Honor Courts" which met in the wake of the 20 July 1944 attempt on Hitler's life; in the process, he dismissed hundreds of innocent parties, putting them at the mercy of the infamous and patently unjust "People's Courts."

Keitel was convicted by the International Military Tribunal at Nuremburg, and sentenced to death for planning and waging aggressive warfare, as well as for passing on Hitler's orders to murder Communist commissars and Jews in the USSR. After conviction, he admitted his culpability, ordered his attorney to not appeal, and, despite his request to be shot, was hanged on 16 October 1946.

Ewald von Kleist was born on 8 August 1881 in Braunfels an der Lahn in Hesse to an ancient military family whose progeny had served German monarchs since at least the last Middle Ages. A devout monarchist, Kleist was not enthusiastic about the National Socialist regime, and was an exceptional field commander.

Commissioned into a field artillery regiment in 1901, Kleist transferred to cavalry in 1909 and was assigned as a *Rittmeister* (Captain of Cavalry) in the *14th Hussar Regiment* at the outbreak of the Great

War. In late 1914, he assumed command of a squadron (a company-sized element) of the *1st Life Hussar Regiment*, but a year later, was assigned as a staff officer in the *85th Landwehr Division* on the Eastern Front.

After a course at the artillery school at Wahn, Kleist was assigned as chief of staff of the *Guard Cavalry Division*, and saw action on the Eastern and Western Fronts. In the summer of 1918, he reached his ultimate Great War assignment, serving as the chief of staff of the *225th Infantry Division* on the Western Front. He earned both classes of the Iron Cross during his wartime service.

Ewald von Kleist

Retained in the Army after the war, throughout the 1920s, Kleist served in a variety of staff positions and on the faculty of the cavalry school at Hannover. He was promoted to *Oberst* in 1929 and assumed command of the prestigious *"Graf Neun," Infantry Regiment 9*. A year later, he was awarded command of the *2d Cavalry Division*, and was promoted to *Generalmajor* later the same year. From this point, promotions came quickly. Kleist was promoted to *Generalleutnant* in 1933, and to *General* of Cavalry in 1936, at roughly the same time he assumed command of *Wehrkreis VIII* in Silesia.

Despite his rapid rise in the 1930s, Kleist was forcibly retired in 1938 due to Hitler's perception of his "uncooperative" attitude. However, like Rundstedt and many others, he was recalled to active duty in 1939 to command *XXII Corps* in the invasion of Poland. This was followed by service as commander of *Panzer Group Kleist* in the invasion of Western Europe; he and his men won fame for being the first across the Meuse at Sedan, for which Kleist was awarded the Knight's Cross. Although *Panzer Group Kleist* was also the first German unit to reach the English Channel, the drive across France was marked by Kleist's arguments with Guderian: Kleist argued on the side of convention and due caution, while Guderian insisted on risk and audacity. By the end of the campaign, however, Kleist's cavalry instincts helped him overcome his reticence to press the advantage with the new armored formations, and he became recognized as an expert in mobile combined arms operations.

Promoted to *Generaloberst* in July 1940, Kleist commanded *1st Panzer Group* in the invasion of the Balkans in April 1941. Still in command of the same organization, he and his men were assigned to *Army Group South* during Operation BARBAROSSA in June 1941. As such, they were largely responsible for encircling and destroying the Soviet **6th** and **12th Armies** near Uman by August; Kleist's panzer group also provided the southern prong of the great encirclement, conducted in cooperation with *Army Group Center,* of the **Southwestern Front** around Kiev. The Soviets lost the **5th**, **21st**, **26th**, and **37th Armies** in the process.

Kleist's panzer group, redesignated as "*1st Panzer Army*" in early October 1941, seized Rostov, but failed to hold it as the winter set in and the Soviets launched their winter offensive. Despite this, Kleist received the Oakleaves to the Knight's Cross for his achievements in early 1942. With the coming of summer, *1st Panzer Army* played the lead role in *Army Group South*'s part of Operation *BLAU,* and penetrated all the way to the Caucasus Mountains. Kleist was awarded command of *Army Group A,* deep in the Caucasus Mountains, on 22 November 1942.

A few weeks after he assumed command, the Soviet **North Caucasus** and **Trans-Caucasus Fronts** began their winter offensive. Coupled with the massive Soviet operations to the north against Army Groups B and *Don,* these succeeded in pushing Kleist's field army back over 300 kilometers. Despite this, Kleist was promoted to *Generalfeldmarschall* on 1 February 1943 . . . the day after Paulus surrendered at Stalingrad. Kleist remained in command of a shrunken *Army Group A,* which for most of 1943 and early 1944 controlled only the *17th Army,* and successfully defended the Crimea until the early spring. After the Crimea was cut off, but six weeks before the *17th Army* surrendered, Hitler relieved Kleist and awarded him the Swords to the Knight's Cross. Kleist remained uselessly assigned to the "Leader Reserve" for the remainder of the war.

In 1948, Kleist was found guilty by a court in Tito's Yugoslavia for war crimes committed in the 1941 Balkans campaign. He was sentenced to 15 years' imprisonment, but was handed over to the Soviets in 1949. They found him guilty of war crimes, too, and Kleist died in a Soviet prison camp in 1954.

Günther Hans Kluge was born in Posen on 30 October 1982 and commissioned in the field artillery in 1901. He saw extensive combat during the Great War, and also qualified as a pilot. Remaining in the Army after WWI, he rose to general officer rank, and commanded *Wehrkreis VI* (Westphalia) in the mid-1930s. After Hitler and his henchmen engineered the disgrace and dismissals of *Generals* von Blomberg and Fritsch in 1938, Kluge was one of 16 other generals also dismissed for being "uncooperative" with the effort to clear the way for pure sycophancy at the top of the German general officer corps.

Kluge was recalled to active duty in time for the invasion of Poland, in which he commanded *4th Army*. His army performed with distinction in the campaign, and he was awarded the Knight's Cross. He commanded the same formation during the invasion of western Europe less than a year later. The successful prosecution of *4th Army's* mission in the west earned Kluge his field marshal's baton in July 1940.

Kluge continued in command of *4th Army* during Operation BARBAROSSA, but had much more numerous and powerful assets at his disposal for this operation. During *Army Group Center's* spectacular successive encirclements of huge Soviet formations at Minsk, Smolensk, Viazma, and Briansk, Kluge quarreled increasingly with Guderian, whose *2d Panzer Group* was under *4th Army's* operational control.

In December, as the final thrust of BARBAROSSA toward Moscow slowed, Kluge was promoted to command of *Army Group Center*, replacing Bock. Kluge remained in command throughout the next year and a half, and was deco-

Günther Hans Kluge

rated with the Oakleaves to the Knight's Cross in January 1943. He again ran into conflict with Guderian when the latter was appointed

Inspector of Armored Troops in March of that year. As the bickering between the two rose to a crescendo over the planning for Operation ZITADELLE at Kursk (Guderian opposed it, Kluge favored it), the feud became so rancorous that Kluge actually proposed a duel. This did not come to pass, and ZITADELLE continued, with disastrous consequences for the Germans.

Kluge was seriously wounded in a car accident in October 1943, and was placed on convalescent leave to recover. He was awarded the Swords to the Knight's Cross shortly thereafter. He was still not completely healthy when he was assigned to replace Rundstedt as the Supreme Commander-West in July 1944. While attempting to shore up the increasingly-tenuous German containment of the Allied beachhead, Kluge committed suicide by taking a cyanide capsule. Although Hitler suspected that Kluge had been secretly trying to contact the Allies to initiate and armistice—a charge that history has not born out—Kluge received full military honors upon his death.

Georg von Küchler was born 30 May 1881 near the Hessian city of Hanau to a Junker family. Commissioned in the artillery in 1901, he commanded an artillery battery on the Western Front during the opening phases of the Great War, and took part in the fighting on the Somme and around Verdun. He became a staff officer of the *206th Infantry Division* in 1916. By war's end, he had established himself as a keen staff officer and combat leader.

Just after the war, Küchler joined a *Freikorps* and fought the Communists in Poland. After returning to Germany he was allowed to remain in the Army and was assigned to the staff at the Artillery School at Jüterbog.

Promoted to *Oberst* in 1931, Küchler was assigned as Deputy Commander of the *1st Infantry Division* in East Prussia in 1932. From this point, his rise became especially swift. He was promoted to *Generalmajor* in April 1934, and assumed command of the *1st Infantry Division* later that year. In December 1935, he was promoted to *Generalleutnant,* and to *General* of Artillery in April 1937; he commanded *I Corps*, headquartered in Königsberg, East Prussia. He took part in the occupation of Lithuanian Memelland in March 1939.

Küchler commanded the *3d Army* in the invasion of Poland in 1939, and was subsequently awarded the Knight's Cross for his performance in that campaign. While in command, he court-martialed those who had committed atrocities in his area of responsibility, greatly displeasing Himmler in the process.

In the invasion of western Europe in 1940, Küchler's *18th Army* played a critical role, sweeping through the Netherlands and linking up with airborne forces at key road junctions and bridges on the right flank of *Army Group B*. This enabled *18th Army* to occupy Antwerp and outflank Allied positions on the Scheldt. Although halted before Dunkirk by Hitler's order, Küchler's army eventually drove on into France, entering Paris and continuing south before the armistice.

Promoted to *Generaloberst* in July 1940, Küchler remained in command of *18th Army* in Operation BARBAROSSA. As

Georg von Küchler

part of the *Ritter* von Leeb's *Army Group North*, its mission was to advance along the northern (right) flank, clearing Soviet resistance from the Baltic coast and inland. In the process, elements of the *18th Army* encountered fierce Soviet resistance in the Baltic states, and on a few occasions used Soviet prisoners of war as human mine sweepers. Küchler also enforced Hitler's infamous "Commissar Order," by which German troops were to summarily execute Communist Party officials as they advanced.

In mid-January 1942, as *Army Group North* was suffering through the first winter of the siege of Leningrad, Küchler assumed command of *Army Group North* after the retirement of the *Ritter* von Leeb. Küchler remained in command throughout the next two years, fighting a see-saw battle to starve out the "cradle of Bolshevism." He was promoted to *Generalfeldmarschall* in June 1942, and was awarded the Oakleaves to the Knight's Cross in August 1943. However, when the Soviet Leningrad-Novgorod Offensive threatened to cut off *Army Group North*'s *18th Army* near Leningrad in January, Küchler disobeyed Hitler's order to stand fast and ordered a withdrawal. He was "temporarily" replaced the next day by Model, and formally sacked on the last day of the month. Küchler was then officially placed on the retired list.

Not long thereafter, Küchler was approached by some of the officers planning to assassinate Hitler. Although he expressed sympathy for their cause, he neither joined them nor turned in any of them to the *Gestapo*.

In 1948, Küchler was tried for the war crimes committed by some of his men in the Baltic States in 1941. He was found guilty and sentenced to 20 years' imprisonment, but was released in early 1955. Küchler died on 25 May 1968 and was interred in Darmstadt.

Wilhelm *Ritter* (Knight) von Leeb was born 5 September 1876 into an old Bavarian officer family. As a young artillery officer, he served in China (1901–02), and after three years of instruction in the Munich War Academy, was admitted to the General Staff of the Bavarian Army, a part of the German Imperial Army as it was then organized. He commanded a battery of the *Bavarian 10th Field Artillery Regiment* in Erlangen (1912–13), and was assigned to the Bavarian General Staff when the war broke out in the next year.

Leeb served as the first general staff officer (a combination of the US chief of staff and operations officer) for the *Bavarian 11th Infantry Division* during the Great War. As such, Leeb saw action on both the Western and Eastern fronts, and was awarded the Order of Max-Joseph, the possession of which conferred a non-hereditary Knight's status (hence the inclusion of the title "*Ritter*" in his name from this point forward.) In 1916, he was assigned to the staff of Crown Prince Rupprecht, and spent the remainder of the war there.

After the war, Leeb was retained in the Army, and served in a variety of command and staff positions, including chief of staff of *Wehrkreis II* (Pomerania and Mecklenburg) in 1920; in 1922, he was assumed the same position in *Wehrkreis VII*, in his native Bavaria. While assigned there, he contributed to the suppression of the Munich Beer Hall Putsch in 1923. It was not to be the first act that would displease Hitler.

Leeb returned to a combat unit in 1924, assuming command of a mountain artillery battalion of *Artillery Regiment 7*. He was promoted to *Generalmajor* in 1929 and assumed command of *Wehrkreis VII*. After hearing a speech by Hitler just a week before Hindenburg nominated him as Chancellor on 30 January 1933, Leeb remarked, "A businessman whose wares are good does not need to boost them in the loudest tones of a market crier."

Although he was put under surveillance by the *Gestapo*, Leeb was promoted to *General* of Artillery in 1934 and assumed command of *Army Group 2*. In his book, *Die Abwehr* [*The Defense*], published in

1937, Leeb argued that Germany could not win a swift victory against the Soviet Union if it became embroiled in a two-front war. Coupled with his opposition to the appointment of Reichenau as Commander-in-Chief of the German Armed Forces in 1935, this prompted Hitler to ask for his retirement in 1938.

Leeb was recalled to duty in 1939, and attempted to convince Rundstedt and Bock, among others, to resign rather than take part in the invasion of western Europe, which Leeb deemed "insane" in his own diary. He pointed out the criminality of the German plans to invade neutral countries, such as Belgium, the Netherlands, and Luxembourg, but to no avail. Rebuffed by both, he dutifully commanded *Army Group C,* and achieved two penetrations of the Maginot Line, the major one near Saarbrücken, and a minor one in the Low Vosges near Lembach. For his battlefield accomplishments, he was awarded the Knight's Cross and promoted to *Generalfeldmarschall* in July 1940.

Leeb commanded *Army Group North* during Operation BARBAROSSA, and was responsible for seizing Leningrad. His armies penetrated the city's outer defenses in September, but Hitler decided to besiege and starve, rather than conquer, the "cradle of Bolshevism." With no prospect of quick victory in sight by the vicious winter of 1941–42, Leeb recommended a general German withdrawal from the Soviet Union to allow regrouping and to spare German forces the effects of weather for which they were not prepared. Although many other German generals concurred, Hitler, of course, disagreed and had his way.

Leeb requested permission to retire "for health reasons" in January 1942, and Hitler instantly granted his permission. Leeb spent the rest of the war assigned to the "Leader Reserve," but performed no active duty. Tried at Nuremberg in 1948 for passing on illegal orders, he was sentenced to time served as a prisoner of war, and released.

Leeb was elevated to Grand Chancellor of the Order of Max-Joseph in 1954, and passed away on 29 April 1956 in Hohenschwangau near Füssen, in his native Bavaria. In 1976, the Federal German government published Leeb's diary and situation estimates from the war.

Carl Gustav Emil Mannerheim was born in Finland in 1867, the son of aristocratic parents with Swedish connections. A difficult student, he was sent to a military academy at age 14 to settle himself; however, he was expelled for disciplinary infractions.

He joined the Imperial Russian Army's cavalry in 1887 and had a varied and adventurous career. Rising through officer grades and having taken part in the Russo-Japanese War (1904–05), he received a battlefield promotion to colonel. By 1911, Mannerheim was a Russian Army Major General and commanded its Warsaw-based Emperor's **Uhlans-Guard** unit. Despite his rank and uniform, he and the Polish aristocracy got along well.

In World War I, Mannerheim earned the coveted Cross of St. George for his leadership against Austrian forces. By war's end, he had attained the rank of lieutenant general.

When the Bolsheviks came to power in Russia, Finland declared its independence and Mannerheim came home. His country was unsettled and a large number of Russian troops remained within its borders. The young country's government asked him to form a national army to restore order. During an ensuing three-month civil war in 1918, Finland secured its borders and eliminated the threat of Russian control. Mannerheim and the Finnish Army could take much credit for this success.

Also in 1918, Mannerheim spent time abroad, having come to odds with the Finnish Senate over its policy toward Imperial Germany. During that time, he informally and actively sought (and achieved) favorable attitudes toward Finland by France and Great Britain. Returning to his homeland in 1919, he was a signatory of Finland's constitution. He tried to influence a Finnish role in counterrevolutionary armed actions against the Bolsheviks but did not succeed. He then left public life and was active in such organizations as the Finnish Red Cross and a national league for child welfare.

War with the USSR broke out in 1939 when Mannerheim was head of the national Defense Council with the rank of field marshal. During the ensuiing "Winter War" (1939–40), his grotesquely outnumbered Finnish Army fought the Soviets and their recently-purged officer corps to a standstill that remains one of the great martial feats of modern times. Eventually, however, the overwhelming Soviet numerical superiority had its effect, and the Finns were forced to sign an armistice under unfavorable terms, losing territory and about 500,000 citizens in the process.

When the Finnish government collaborated with the Germans and took part in what Finns saw as the "Continuation War" (1941–44), Mannerheim led the Finnish forces that reclaimed the stolen territory and liberated the conquered populace. His forces outfought the Russians and regained some eastern territory previously lost to them.

From his leadership position, he led both military and political initiatives—most of which were to maintain a highly-sensitive balance between Finnish sovereignty and relations with Nazi Germany—whose forces were in Finland. As "Marshal of Finland," he also had to deal with divergent internal political factions and their goals.

All the while, Mannerheim had to keep Finland's national interests in the forefront. Key to it all was his high international prestige. His objective was to preserve Finland—and detach it from the war.

Appointed President of the Republic near the war's end, his skillful action resulted in Finland being the only Axis ally not occupied by foreign forces. By concluding a separate armistice with the USSR in September 1944, Mannerheim spared his land the hardships later experienced by much of Europe, and retained at least some of the territory and citizens otherwise lost to the Soviets in 1940. The most distasteful aspect of this was that the Soviets forced the Finns to attack their erstwhile allies of four years, the Germans, as they struggled to leave Finland under the impossible conditions dictated to them under the Finnish-Soviet armistice. To ensure Finnish compliance with these conditions of the armistice that were clearly designed to poison Finnish-German military relations, the Soviets occupied several Finnish border cities, essentially holding them hostage.

Marshal "Gustav" Mannerheim withdrew from public life when he resigned the presidency in 1946. In ill health thereafter until his death, he resided mainly in Switzerland, and passed away there, in Lausanne, on 27 January 1951.

Erich von Manstein was born Erich von Lewinski on 24 November 1887 in Berlin. (He later formally took the name of an adoptive uncle, von Manstein.) An imperial court page as a boy, he was commissioned into the *3d Foot Guards Regiment* and as adjutant of the *2d Foot Guards Regiment* saw action on the Western and Eastern fronts early in the war. After sustaining a serious wound on the Eastern Front, he was assigned to successive staff positions on the Eastern Front and in Serbia with *Army Group Gallwitz*, on the Western Front with *11th* and *1st Armies*, and, as operations officer, to the *4th Cavalry Division* in Kurland. His ultimate position during the Great War was as operations officer for the *213th (Assault) Reserve Division* on the Western Front. For his achievements during the war, he garnered numerous decorations, including both classes of the Iron Cross and the Royal Hohenzollern Knight's Cross with swords, a predecessor

Erich von Manstein

of the Third Reich's Knight's Cross of the Iron Cross.

Remaining in the Army after the war, Manstein served in a variety of infantry command and staff assignments, eventually rising to the rank of *Generalmajor* by the time of Hitler's humiliation of von Blomberg and Fritsch in 1938. Identified as a troublemaker, he was sent off to a division command in Silesia, but was brought back to the limelight as chief of staff to von Leeb in time for the seizure of the Sudetenland later that year.

Manstein rose meteorically during WWII. He served consecutively as chief of staff of *Army Group A* (commanded by Rundstedt) during the invasion of Poland, and conceived an alternative to the original plan for the invasion of western Europe. Calling for a drive not through Liége and Namur, as the rival plan dictated, but for an armored thrust through the Ardennes, his plan was rejected and he was further identified as something other than a team player. However, after the plan was compromised, Manstein's plan was adopted, and the Allies were caught preparing for exactly the wrong contingencies. Manstein, however, was only allowed to participate in the later phases of the campaign in the west, as even the spectacular success of his plan could not completely obliterate the stigma associated with advocating an idea different from many of his superiors. Nevertheless, he was awarded the Knight's Cross for his service in France.

During Operation BARBAROSSA, Manstein initially commanded *LXI Panzer Corps* of *Army Group North* under Leeb. After three months of intensive operations, he was awarded command of the *11th Army* under Rundstedt in *Army Group South* after the death of its former commander, *Generaloberst Ritter* von Schobert in a plane crash in the Crimea. After repelling the Soviet Army's winter offensive, Manstein's army was assigned to seize the Crimea. Although the siege of Sevastopol took longer than expected, the mission was complete by early July, and Manstein was promoted to *Generalfeldmarschall*.

Transferred to *Army Group North* with his army to assist in the siege of Leningrad in September 1942, Manstein's divisions destroyed Vlasov's **2d Shock Army** when it attacked later that month. In November, Manstein assumed command of *Army Group Don* and was given the mission of resuing Paulus's trapped *6th Army* at Stalingrad. Although the effort failed, *Army Group Don* managed to create and hold a corridor through which the *1st Panzer Army* escaped, although outnumbered seven to one by the Soviet forces opposing them. Manstein received the Oakleaves to the Knight's Cross for his achievements in this action.

Still in command of his now-redesignated *Army Group South,* Manstein orchestrated a miraculous feat that preserved German fortunes in the region. Employing forces withdrawn from the Caucasus and fresh forces from the West, on 20 February he struck the flanks of the exploiting **Southwestern Front**'s forces as they neared the Dnepr River. Within days, the entire Soviet force collapsed, and the Germans drove Soviet forces back to the Northern Donets River in disorder. In early March, Manstein's army group then struck the **Voronezh Front**'s forces and recaptured Kharkov and Belgorod on 16 and 18 March. In addition to thwarting the Soviets' ambitious offensive, Manstein's counterstroke produced utter consternation within the *Stavka*. To forestall further defeat, the Soviets transferred fresh forces into the Kursk and Belgorod regions, which, with deteriorating weather, forced the Germans to postpone further action.

Overruled by Hitler regarding what should constitute followup operations, Manstein was forced to participate in the doomed Operation ZITADELLE, in which the carefully reconstructed German armored forces on the Eastern Front were thrown away in an orgy of destruction. Although he remained in command for the better part of seven more months, doggedly defending against and delaying the Soviet offensives of the second half of 1943, Manstein was relieved by Hitler in April 1944. He received the Swords to the Knight's Cross at the same time, but remained unemployed in the "Leader Reserve" for the rest of the war.

Manstein was quite possibly the most brilliant and competent of all of Germany's higher-level field commanders. Regarding operational matters, he was quite capable of firmly and candidly expressing contrary opinions to Hitler, and he suffered the fate of practically all such officers. He was not, however, as forthright in his objections on other matters. Very strong evidence was produced at Nuremberg after the war that Manstein had been aware of the activities of the *SS-Einsatzgruppen* in his commands' areas, and had done nothing other than to direct that none of his officers were to be present during their murder sprees. For knowingly tolerating these activities, in 1950 he was sentenced to 18 years in prison, but was released in 1953 for poor health.

Manstein's famous memoirs, *Lost Victories*, published in 1955, remain a classic study of operations on the Eastern Front even today. He passed away 12 June 1973 in Irschenhausen, Bavaria.

Hasso von Manteuffel was born at Potsdam, Germany, in 1897 to a well-known Prussian aristocratic family of military and political influence. Forebears had been lauded for both Army and diplomatic successes in Prussia's nineteenth-century wars with France and Denmark. Typical of those familial characteristics, Manteuffel was noted not only for his combat efficiency and leadership, but also for his courteous treatment of subordinates.

Manteuffel graduated from the cadet school at Gross-Lichterfelde and in May 1916, was assigned as an officer in the *3d Brandenburg Hussar-Regiment*, seeing combat in France. He spent the rest of the war assigned to this regiment, although his company was attached to other divisions on the Western Front at various times throughout that two year period.

After the war, Manteuffel served in the von Oven *Freikorps* in and around Berlin, and he was retained in the *Reichswehr* after his service there. Among command and staff assignments, he served as a director of training in its Armor School, during which, he rose to *Major*.

On 1 April 1939, Manteuffel was promoted to *Oberstleutnant* and remained in the Armored Training School through the outset of the invasion of Poland. His WWII baptism of fire came as a battalion commander in a motorized infantry regiment of the *7th Panzer Division*; he assumed command of the other motorized infantry regiment of that division late summer in 1941. He was promoted to *Oberst* in October 1941 and in December earned the Knight's Cross for his outstanding leadership as regimental commander.

In the summer of 1942, when the 7th Panzer was transferred to France, Manteuffel was transferred to the German forces in North Africa. He assumed command of a provisional armored group through the spring of 1943. Taken ill, he was evacuated by ship just before Tunis was closed by Allied blockade. He was promoted to *Generalmajor* on 1 May.

In August 1943, Manteuffel assumed command of his old outfit, the *7th Panzer Division,* once again engaged on the Eastern Front, near Zhitomir. He was awarded the Oak-leaves for outstanding combat achievements during his tenure in command.

Manteuffel assumed command of the elite *Panzer-Grenadier Division Grossdeutschland* on 27 December 1943, and was promoted to *Generalleutnant* just over a month later His troops were credited with slowing and then stopping the Soviet advance into Romania, and Manteuffel was awarded the Swords to the Knight's Cross for his part in this achievement. In September 1944, Manteuffel assumed command of the *5th Panzer Army*

Hasso von Manteuffel

and, simultaneously, was promoted to the rank of *General* of Armored Troops. The *5th Panzer Army* was actively engaged in late 1944 on the Western Front and played the pivotal role in the Ardennes Offensive from December 1944 to January 1945. On 18 February 1945, he was awarded the Diamonds to the Knight's Cross. ultimately being one of only 11 Army officers to receive this award. After the Ardennes Offensive failed, Manteuffel was named commander, *3d Panzer Army* in the East. That force fought the Soviets along the Vistula River, somewhat slowing the Russian advance on Berlin. He surrendered his command to the Western Allies on 3 May 1945.

A prisoner of war after Germany surrendered, Allied reviewers vetted his wartime activities. Manteuffel was released from detention in 1947 and returned home.

Thereafter, he was active in post-War West German politics. That included his ardent support for a revitalized West German armed force and, as well, his election to the national parliament (1953–57) as a member of the Free Democratic Party. Due to controversy over his WWII position supporting an Armed Forces loyalty oath to Hitler, Manteuffel's post-War prominence in reestablishment of a Federal German military was deemed inappropriate. In 1959, Manteuffel was charged with, convicted of, and sentenced for his order to execute a German soldier who had deserted a unit in 1944. He was ordered remanded for 18 months, but was released after four.

He then withdrew from professional life and died in Reith (Tyrol), Austria, in 1978.

Walter Model was born 24 January 1891, near Berlin, his father a royal Prussian director of music. Commissioned in the infantry, Model saw a great deal of combat in the Great War, earning both classes of the Iron Cross, the Wounds Badge, and the Hohenzollern Knight's Cross with Swords (a predecessor of the Knight's Cross of the Iron Cross, which was a Third Reich-era award). He also earned a reputation as a flexible and innovative officer, as well as an effective battlefield leader.

A *Hauptmann* when the war ended, Model was promoted to *Major* in 1929, but promotions began coming quickly after that. In 1930, Model was assigned to the *Reichswehr*'s "technical warfare" section, which worked on plans for building forbidden mechanized and armored formations and doctrine for using them. Promoted to *Oberst* in October 1934, Model commanded the *2d Infantry Regiment* from 1934 to 1935. After completion of his command tour, he was back to work on armored weapons thereafter, serving as Chief of the 8th Section of the General Staff, which was responsible for technical matters such as the integration of new weapons and emerging tactical doctrine. While in this assignment, he gained Hitler's favorable attention for his straightforward, optimistic attitude.

At the end of his work on the General Staff, he was promoted to *Generalmajor* and assigned as chief of staff of *IV Corps*, the position he held during the invasion of Poland. During this period, he began to inspire the dislike of many of the older, more conservative generals who, while they begrudgingly worked for Hitler, they did not share Model's enthusiasm for National Socialism, nor his optimism about the future. Hiring a *Waffen-SS* officer to serve as his aide further alienated many of the Old Guard who were, after all, watching their numbers dwindle as Hitler humiliated some into retirement (Blomberg, Fritsch) while others either retired voluntarily (Beck, Rundstedt) or were ordered to retire (the *Ritter* von Leeb and the other "uncooperative officers").

Promoted to *Generalleutnant* in April 1940, Model served during the invasion of western Europe as chief of staff for *16th Army*, which attacked through the Ardennes on the left flank of Rundstedt's *Army Group A*. It wheeled left (east) and met elements of Leeb's *Army Group C* near Metz, after the latter had broken through the Maginot Line in the Saar. Although not as spectacular as the successes of other *Army Group A* field armies, *16th Army's* achievements in France nevertheless helped earn Model command of the *3d Panzer Division*. He participated in Operation BARBAROSSA in this position, and as part of Guderian's *2d Panzer Group*, played a key role in the massive encir-

Walter Model

clement of Soviet forces at Minsk and Smolensk. His accomplishments were recognized with the award of the Knight's Cross for his actions in the initial phase of BARBAROSSA.

In October 1941, Model was promoted to *General* of Panzer Troops and assumed command of *XLI Panzer Corps* of Hoth's *3d Panzer Group*, still assigned to *Army Group Center*. During his brief command of *XLI Panzer,* Model participated in the Viazma encirclement and the drive to envelop Moscow. He was awarded the Oakleaves to the Knight's Cross for his achievements in these operations.

As the Soviets counterattacked and began to drive *Army Group Center* elements back northwest of Moscow, Model was transferred to command *9th Army*, which at that time was endangered in a narrow salient from Viazma in the south to Rzhev in the north. In a fiery confrontation with Hitler shortly after assuming command, much to the amazement of all present, Model convinced Hitler to allow him to maneuver his corps as he, not the *Führer*, saw fit. A few days later, he became the youngest German *Generaloberst*. Throughout the next twelve months, Model and his *9th Army* held the Rzhev Salient, but when authorized to withdraw in early 1943, Model instituted a "scorched earth" policy which included the destruction of many Soviet towns and villages . . . and their inhabitants. Hitler awarded Model the Swords to the Knight's Cross for his successful conduct of operations in the Rzhev salient.

Model and the *9th Army* were next ordered to participate in Operation ZITADELLE, and Model was one of many senior German officers, including Guderian, to strongly recommend to Hitler that it be called off. After the failure of this last major German offensive in the USSR, Model's *9th Army* was pressed back by the Soviets' massive Operation RUMIANTSEV in August 1943. From there, the remainder of *Army Group Center* could only do their best to defend a series of successive lines before being forced back to the next by the Soviets, but Model often exhibited his flair for "saving the day" in a long series of difficult and intricate defensive maneuvers.

In late January 1944, Model replaced Küchler as commander of the hard-pressed *Army Group North*. A little over a month later, Model was promoted to *Generalfeldmarschall* and was quickly reassigned to command *Army Group South* upon the relief of Manstein. (It was redesignated *Army Group North Ukraine* shortly thereafter.) To add to his burden as he attempted to stave off the destruction of *4th Panzer Army* at the hands of Konev's **2d Ukrainian Front**, Model was also awarded command — simultaneously — of *Army Group Center*. Severely pressed by the attack of four Soviet fronts (**1st Baltic** and **1st**, **2d,** and **3d Belorussian**), there was little Model could do without Hitler's permission to withdraw elements of *Army Group Center* to establish a defensive line along the Dvina River. As a consequence, *4th* and *9th Armies* were encircled and largely destroyed, and Model had to reconstitute both while establishing a new line of defense all the way back in Poland, along the Vistula River.

Despite his mammoth losses, for his accomplishments, Model was awarded the Diamonds to the Knight's Cross, becoming only the seventeenth recipient of this prestigious award. (Only three Army field marshals received *"die Brillanten,"* the other two being Rommel and Schörner.)

In August 1944, Model was transferred to the Western Front and assigned to replace Kluge as Supreme Commander-West. After a brief assessment of the situation in the West, Model requested 30 more divisions and hundreds of thousands of replacements for units shattered in the Normandy fighting . . . and was replaced after less than three weeks by Rundstedt. Model was assigned to command *Army Group B* in the Low Countries, and was quite effective in defeating Operation MARKET-GARDEN.

After the failure of *Army Group B's* Ardennes Offensive in December/January 1945, much of *Army Group B* was encircled in the Ruhr Pocket and destroyed by the middle of April. Model committed suicide on 21 April 1945.

Few commanders, in any army during WWII, could match Model's record for repeated successes against the odds. Although said by some to be more adept at defensive operations than offensive ones, the fact is that by the time Model rose to higher rank, the few offensive missions in which he took part (Kursk, the Ardennes) were lost causes. Model possessed unquestionable physical courage; his insistence on being "up front" is documented by high decorations in both world wars. It was this insistence on developing and maintaining an intimate personal knowledge of the situation and, even more importantly, for his soldiers' capacities, that contributed to the exceptional success he enjoyed as a combat commander.

Friedrich Paulus was born on 23 September 1890 in the Hessian town of Breitenau. The son of the administrator of a reform school and the daughter of the school's headmaster, his lifelong dream of becoming a naval officer was destroyed when the German Navy rejected him for an inadequate social background. After briefly studying law at the University of Munich, Paulus was accepted for officer training in the Army and secured a commission in the *Baden 3d Infantry Regiment.* He saw extensive staff service on the Eastern and Western fronts during the Great War, serving with this regiment's *3d Battalion*, then with the Prussian *2d Jäger Regiment* for two years. In 1917, he was transferred to the staff of the German Alpine Corps.

Remaining in the Army after the war, the completely non-political Paulus rose steadily through a variety of mostly staff positions, but became a member of the panzer community with varous assignments. He served as chief of staff of *10th Army* during the invasion of Poland, and in the same capacity for *6th Army* during the invasion of western Europe. From there, he was catapulted into frequent contact with Hitler when he succeeded Halder as operations officer on the Army staff in Berlin.

Hitler appreciated the quiet, competent, efficient Paulus, and rewarded him with command of the *6th Army* in January 1942. During Operation BLAU in the late spring, *6th Army* was tasked to seize Stalingrad. Not only did it fail to secure its objective, but the entire army became encircled there by the end of the year. Nevertheless, Hitler awarded Paulus the Knight's Cross in August 1942. Ordered

Friedrich Paulus

by Hitler to hold out and not attempt a breakout to the west, the *6th Army's* situation deteriorated continuously throughout the winter of 1942–43. Despite all of Göring's pompous promises, the *Luftwaffe* utterly failed to deliver the supplies necessary for sustainment of the isolated German forces, and by late January, the end was near. Hitler awarded Paulus the Oakleaves to the Knight's Cross on 15 January and then, either cynically or wishfully—knowing that no German field marshal had ever surrendered—Hitler promoted Paulus to *Generalfeldmarschall* on 30 January (the tenth anniversary of the Nazis' ascendance to national power). The end came less than 24 hours later, as Paulus and his staff surrendered; all German resistance ended two days later. It was an enormous disaster: somewhere between 70,000 and 100,000 Axis soldiers died at Stalingrad, and more than 100,000 were taken prisoner. Only about 6,000 returned from captivity, long after the war. After this catastrophe, Germany was clearly going to lose the war.

Soviet captivity did not mean the war was over for Paulus, however. After getting no cooperation from Paulus for the first nineteen months of his captivity, the Soviets presented him with proof of Hitler's rampage in the wake of the 20 July assassination attempt. Horrified by the brutal executions of several of his friends, Paulus became the ranking member of the *Nationalkomitee Freies Deutschland (NFD),* or the "National Committee for a Free Germany," the group of German officers and enlisted men in Soviet captivity who agreed to help undermine the Nazi government (and received much better treatment that their more recalcitrant prisoner-peers in the process). Although nominally not a Communist organization (its colors were even the black-white-red of the German Empire), the *NFD's* political orientation was completely dominated by the minority of its members who were German Communists in exile, such as the future

Communist chief of the German Democratic Republic (GDR) and architect of the Berlin Wall, Walter Ulbricht.

As a member of the *NFD*, Paulus participated in the Soviet effort to demoralize German forces through propaganda delivered via radio and leaflet. Hitler ordered Paulus's wife to change her name, and arrested Paulus's son, Ernst, a German officer already seriously wounded at Kharkov in 1942, for the crime of being his father's offspring. (Paulus's other son, Friedrich, had already been killed in action at Anzio). Paulus's wife died in 1949, having not seen her husband since 1942.

At Nuremberg, Paulus testified as a Soviet witness for the prosecution. After release from Soviet captivity, Paulus briefly worked in the *Volkspolizei*, the East German shadow army founded in violation of the 1945 Potsdam accords. As a result of this and his *NFD* activities, to many Germans, Paulus's failings as a field commander are eclipsed by his late-war decision to help the Soviets undermine *Wehrmacht* morale, and his postwar decision to help the Stalinist regime in the GDR. No matter how well intended the apolitical field marshal may have been, his historical legacy is one of colossal battlefield disaster and, to many minds, moral, if not political, treachery. Paulus died in Dresden in 1957.

Walter von Reichenau was born to an army family (his father was a Prussian *Generalleutnant*) in Karlsruhe, Baden, on 8 October 1884. He was commissioned in the Prussian Army in 1903, initially serving in the *1st Guards Field Artillery Regiment*. By the outbreak of the Great War, von Reichenau had attended the *Kriegsakademie* and was a *Hauptmann* and General Staff officer, in which capacity he served on the Western Front for the duration of the war.

A professional soldier, von Reichenau remained in the army after the Great War, serving in routine, but varied, command and staff assignments. In 1932, while serving under Blomberg as Chief of Staff of *Wehrkreis I* in East Prussia, he was introduced to Hitler by an uncle who was an ardent Nazi. Reichenau was immensely attracted by Hitler's views and he arranged an introduction to Blomberg. After Hitler gained power in 1933, he selected Blomberg to be Minister of War, and Reichenau was appointed head of the *Reichswehr's* Ministerial Office, which coordinated affairs between the Party and the armed forces. In this capacity, Reichenau worked hard to establish the supremacy of the armed forces over the *SA*, and actively supported Hitler's "Night of the Long Knives" attack on the *SA* leadership.

Upon promotion to *Generalleutnant* in 1935, Reichenau command-ed *Wehrkreis VII* in Munich. Only a year later, he was promoted to *General* of Artillery, and in 1938, Hitler proposed to appoint him to the post of Commander in Chief of the Army. By this time, howev-

Walter von Reichenau

er, Reichenau was known throughout the army as an overly ambitious, politically-inspired officer and many of his contemporaries aligned themselves against him. Sever-al senior officers objected to the appointment so vocifer-ously—von Rundstedt, Hal-der, and Beck flatly refused to serve under him—that Werner von Fritsch received the appointment.

After serving as comman-der of *4th Army Group* in Leipzig, Reichenau command-ed the *10th Army* in the occu-pation of the Sudetenland and in the campaign in Poland, for which he was awarded the Knight's Cross. Promotion to *Generaloberst* in October 1939 brought a transfer to com-mand the *6th Army,* which he led on the Western Front. Despite his views, which he twice unsuccessfully attempted to convey to Hitler, that the invasion of Belgium was a criminal act, he performed his duties most ably. In recognition of his achievements in Poland and in the west, he was promoted to *Generalfeldmarschall* on 19 July 1940.

In the summer of 1941, the *6th Army* was transferred to the east and participated in operations around Kiev and Kharkov in the southern sector of the Eastern Front. Always fiercely athletic, Reichenau awed his troops (and startled his peers) by diving into the Vistula River and swimming across it during the advance. His most notable deed in his rather short service on the Eastern Front, how-ever, was the proclamation on 10 October 1941 of the infamous secret "Reichenau Order." Though parts of this order are often quot-ed out of context to falsely infer that Reichenau openly encouraged his troops to murder all Jews (his directive calling for ruthlessness was aimed specifically at guerillas and partisans), it was nonetheless clearly inspired by his Nazi values. Once again demonstrating his fealty to Hitler and his own strong beliefs in Nazi doctrine, Reichenau called upon his soldiers to view themselves as bearers of a "merciless national ideology." The soldier, he wrote, "must have full understanding for the necessity of a severe but just revenge on subhuman Jewry." He called for the "annihilation" of uprisings behind the German lines "which, as experience proves, have always been caused by Jews."

Soviet resistance, bolstered by commitment of huge reserves from Siberia and coupled with the devastating effects of the brutal winter of 1941 forced the German Army's offensive operations to a halt. Rundstedt, commander of *Army Group South* (and von Reichenau's superior) requested permission from Hitler to withdraw from the Rostov area to better defensive positions along the Mius River. When Hitler hotly denied the request, vRundstedt resigned in protest. Succeeding Rundstedt as commander of *Army Group South* on 3 December 1941, Reichenau ordered the withdrawal to the Mius River that Rundstedt had been refused.

There is some disagreement about the nature of the illness that caused Reichenau's untimely death. One story is that he suffered an incapacitating "apoplectic fit" on 15 January 1942, perhaps in response to continued interference by Hitler in his military decisions. Another account contends that he suffered a massive heart attack after jogging on 12 January. Whatever the true reason, it was decided to evacuate him by air to a military hospital in Leipzig for treatment. The airplane experienced mechanical troubles and crashed on takeoff from an airfield near his headquarters at Poltava, Russia, on 17 January 1942. It is unclear whether he died in the crash or immediately thereafter. *Generalfeldmarschall* Walter von Reichenau received a state funeral on 24 January 1942 and was buried in the heroes' cemetery, the *Invalidenfriedhof*, in Berlin.

Gerd von Rundstedt was born on 12 December 1875 in Aschersleben, Prussian Saxony, and was one of the German Army's most able and respected commanders. The scion of an old Army family, he fought in Belgium as the operations officer for the *22d Reserve Infantry Division*, and was later assigned to the staff of the Military Governor of Belgium. Rundstedt was next assigned as the chief of staff for the *86th Infantry Division* on the Eastern Front, then served successively as operations officer and, later, acting chief of staff, *XXV Reserve Corps* in the Carpathians; chief of staff, *LIII Corps* on the

Baltic coast; and finally as chief of staff of *XV Corps* on the Western Front.

After the war, Rundstedt was allowed to remain in uniform, and, through numerous troop commands and staff assignments including command of the *18th Infantry Regiment* at Paderborn and commander of the *2d Cavalry Division* at Breslau (1928–32), he rose to *General* of Infantry. He eventually commanded *Wehrkreis III* around the capital, Berlin. When martial law was declared under Hitler, Rundstedt attempted to resign his commission, but was dissuaded, and returned to his duties . . . which involved arresting Social Democrats and ejecting them from the government. In conjunction mainly with the *Ritter* von Leeb, he blocked Hitler's attempt to nominate the pro-Nazi Reichenau as Commander-in-Chief of the German Army in 1935. He later again demonstrated good soldierly intentions when he retired, at his own request, after Hitler's duplicity over the Munich Conference and the invasion of Czechoslovakia.

One year later, however, he answered the call to active duty, and commanded *Army Group South* during the invasion of Poland, for which he was awarded the Knight's Cross. After a brief stint as military commander in the occupation of Poland, he was assigned to command *Army Group A* in the invasion of western Europe. *Army Group A* played the pivotal part of rushing across Belgium and defeating the French Army there while forcing the British Expeditionary Force off the European continent; later, *Army Group A* raced south, around the Maginot Line, and used its ten mobile divisions to wreak havoc with this deep penetrations into the French lines.

Promoted to *Generalfeldmarschall* on 19 July 1940, after a tour as commander of German occupation forces in western Europe, Rundstedt was assigned to command *Army Group South* in BARBAROSSA. Probably due in part to his experience in the east in the Great War, and in part to his exceptional professional acuity, Rundstedt openly doubted that BARBAROSSA would result in the swift defeat of the Soviet Army. Nevertheless, he commanded *Army Group South* with aplomb, trapping and destroying the Soviet **6th** and **12th Armies** near Uman and deftly cooperating with Bock's *Army Group Center* to annihilate the Soviet **5th**, **21st**, **26th**, and **37th Armies** around Kiev.

As the winter approached, Rundstedt became more vociferous about his concerns that German forces were becoming overextended. His warnings fell on deaf ears, and in early November, the nearly 66-year-old field marshal suffered a heart attack from sheer exhaustion. He refused to relinquish command, however, and just a few weeks later personally and forcefully criticized Hitler's strategic conduct of the war on the Eastern Front to the *Führer's* face. Rundstedt was relieved of his command within a few days.

Rundstedt then assumed supreme command in the West in early 1942, and as such, was in charge of preparing defenses against an Allied invasion. When that invasion finally came in early June 1944, and German forces proved unable to quickly wipe out the burgeoning Allied beachheads, Rundstedt abruptly advised *OKW* to sue for peace. A few days later, Rundstedt was again relieved and placed on convalescent leave. He was awarded then the Oakleaves to the Knight's Cross shortly thereafter.

Gerd von Rundstedt

After the failure of the 20 July 1944 attempt on Hitler's life, in concert with *Generaloberst* Guderian and *Generalfeldmarschall* Keitel, Rundstedt presided over a military "honor court" which dismissed dozens of innocent officers from the Army. This action turned them over to the infamous "People's Courts," kangaroo affairs that were essentially lethal show trials.

Reinstated not long after *Generalfeldmarschall* Kluge, Rundstedt's replacement as Supreme Commander-West, committed suicide, Rundstedt was appalled by Hitler's plans for the Ardennes Offensive. Again, he realized that the plan was highly risky at best, and would likely result in squandering precious assets that could better be used for defending the crumbling Reich. He acceded to the plan, however, which, of course, failed and only hastened the end for Germany. Nevertheless, he was awarded the Swords to the Knight's Cross in February 1945. Hitler relieved him again on 10 March 1945, and this was the last time that the by-then 69-year-old field marshal commanded troops.

Rundstedt lived quietly after the war, unable to return to Soviet-occupied Saxony. He passed away in Hannover on 24 February 1953.

Ferdinand Schörner was born the son of a policeman in Munich on 12 May 1892. Following brief service as an enlisted man and NCO, he attended the Universities of Munich, Lausanne, and Grenoble in pursuit of qualifications for a teaching career. On the outbreak of war in August 1914, however, he returned to the army, and was never to become a school teacher. Quickly commissioned from the ranks, *Leutnant* Schörner served with great distinction in mountain infantry units during the Great War. He was awarded the *Pour le Merité*, Imperial Germany's highest decoration for battlefield valor, for actions near Caporetto, on the Italian Front. His unit was later transferred to the Western Front, where it participated in the brutal fighting around Verdun and Rheims. In 1918, Schörner suffered a serious head wound, which took him out of action for the rest of the war.

Discharged from the army after the Armistice, Schörner joined the *Ritter* von Epp's *Freikorps* and fought Communists in the Ruhr and in Upper Silesia. He returned to the army in 1919, and in 1922 became a General Staff officer. Schörner's outstanding war record, his first-rate professional qualities, and the open knowledge that he was an early adherent of Nazi philosophy served him well under Hitler.

Despite his potentially career enhancing qualification as a General Staff officer, Schörner actively campaigned to return to troop duty. After a three-year assignment as a staff officer in Berlin, the newly-promoted *Oberstleutnant* Schörner assumed command of *Mountain Infantry Regiment 98* on 1 March 1937. Schörner led his regiment into combat in southern Poland on 1 September 1939, where it engaged in the hard fighting to capture and hold Lvov.

Promoted to *Oberst* in January 1940, his successes in the Polish campaign (and possibly his unabashed affinity for National Socialism) led to an early promotion to *Generalmajor*, on 1 August of the same year, as well as command of the *6th Mountain Division,* which he led in the invasion of France. After the capitulation of France, Schörner's division fought with distinction and great success against Allied forces in Greece. His superb leadership in this campaign resulted in award of the Knight's Cross on 20 April 1941.

Soon after the successful conclusion of the campaign in Greece, the *6th Mountain Division* was transferred to the Arctic Front, where it held the Litsa sector throughout the winter of 1941–42. On 15 January 1942, Schörner was promoted to *Generalleutnant* and was placed in command of *Mountain Corps Norway*. In April 1942, Schörner's corps was instrumental in blunting a Soviet offensive aimed at cutting off Dietl's *Army of Lapland*; in these actions it is said that Schörner demonstrated conspicuous bravery by personally leading counterattacks. His toughness, however, was not always fully appreciated by his troops, who were not amused when Schörner played down the meteorological challenges of combat in the Arctic, thus belittling the misery of his own men.

On 1 June 1942, he was promoted to *General* of Mountain Troops and remained in command of his corps, now designated *XIX Mountain Corps*. Schörner's accomplishments in the north brought him to the attention of Hitler who began

Ferdinand Schörner

using him as a sort of troubleshooter. Hitler pulled Schörner from the Arctic Front on 23 October 1943 and transferred him to the Ukraine to command "Army Detachment-Nikopol," charged with the defense of that key city. Schörner was able to hold for some time in the face of fierce Soviet attacks, and was awarded the Oakleaves on 17 February 1944. Eventually, however, he had to withdraw his forces into Hungary to avoid their destruction at the hands of the swarming Soviet forces. Hitler so valued Schörner's services that he escaped the *Führer*'s wrath when he defied the standing order forbidding withdrawals. His determination to hold his positions in Hungary was demonstrated by the severe disciplinary measures he enacted in his unit's rear areas, including summary execution of deserters and stragglers. Such "drum-head" courts-martial were to become a hallmark of Schörner's command style, and only further endeared him to Hitler.

In March 1944, he was appointed to head the National Socialist Command Staff of the Army High Command *(OKH)*. Although in consonance with his personality and outlook as a confirmed zealot, this semi-military high staff position was also in conflict with Schörner's professional perspective, and he loathed the assignment. After two weeks in Berlin, Schörner was promoted to *Generaloberst*

on 31 March 1944 and was appointed to succeed Model as commander of *Army Group South.*

The impact of Schörner's promotion from *Oberstleutnant* to *Generaloberst* in the space of little more than four years was evident during this assignment. As he had no experience with the operational
level of war, he wisely left such matters to his staff, while he devoted the lion's share of his time to gaining first-hand knowledge of
conditions at the front. Typically, he also used these visits to zeal-
ously encourage his men to greater efforts. He was, however, not
averse to making the hard decisions dictated by the overwhelming
nature of the Soviet forces arrayed against him. Once again, he
defied Hitler's "no retreat" order, and pulled his newly-reformed
6th Army back from the Odessa sector, thereby sparing it from
destruction.

On 21 July 1944, the day after the most famous attempt on Hitler's
life, Schörner was assigned to command *Army Group North,* which
had been pushed back into Estonia and northern Latvia.. A month
later, on 28 August 1944, he was awarded the Swords for his leadership in this desperate situation. Schörner, however, had inherited a
major disaster-in-the-making and decided to apply his usual leadership techniques. One instance of terrorizing his own men is illustra-
tive: he once radioed an order to a subordinate to "report by 2100
hours which commanders he has shot or is having shot for cow-
ardice"* Despite these motivational measures, Schörner was forced
to abandon Estonia to protect the Latvian capital of Riga, with his
back to the Baltic. By 10 October 1944, the massive Soviet offensive
had forced the abandonment of Riga and Schörner's army group of
33 divisions had been pushed into the Kurland Peninsula, where it
was able to hold the Soviets at bay until the end of the war.

Schörner did not remain in the Kurland Pocket with his men,
however. Hitler awarded him the Diamonds ot the Knight's Cross
on 1 January 1945 and almost immediately (17 January) transferred
him to replace Harpe in command of *Army Group Center.* His new
command had been nearly destroyed by the Soviet Operation
Bagration and associated operations in the previous summer, and
continued to be pressed ever backwards toward the Reich. Schörner
notified Hitler that the forces he had available were not sufficient to
defend against the Soviet onslaught, and that he intended instead to
conduct a delaying operation to the Oder River, which he considered a strong defensive position, to buy time for German refugees to

*From *The Mammoth Book of the Third Reich at War,* edited by Michael Veranov (page
485), Carroll & Graf, NY, 1997.

flee across the river. As had become customary, he instituted his program of summary executions even for trivial offenses. Hitler promoted him to *Generalfeldmarschall* on 5 April 1945, the last such promotion in the German Army in the twentieth century. The final tribute accorded to Schörner came on 29 April 1945 when Hitler named him as his own successor as Commander in Chief of the *Wehrmacht*.

Despite his success in fleeing to Austria to surrender to American forces, Schörner was turned over to the Soviets and was tried and convicted of war crimes. After less than ten years, Schörner was released and returned to Munich in 1955. The Federal German government then tried him for murder in connection with the many summary executions carried out on his orders. His chief accuser was his own former chief of staff, Natzmer. The civil court found him guilty only of manslaughter, but sentenced him to four and a half years in prison and forfeiture of his pension.

Penniless when he got out of prison, Schörner found that his harsh discipline had not alienated all of his former soldiers. Veterans of the *6th Mountain Division* raised and gave to him funds sufficient nearly to match his vanished pension. He remained in Munich until his death on 6 July 1973, after which the Socialist Federal German Defense Minister, Georg Leber, denied the participation of *Bundeswehr* soldiers in uniform at his funeral in recognition of Schörner's record. Schörner is buried in a small cemetery in Mittenwald, home of the German mountain troops.

Felix Martin Julius Steiner was born on 23 May 1896 in East Prussia. His military service began shortly before the Great War with his enlistment in the German Army. He was quickly promoted to NCO, and was commissioned in January 1915, less than a year after entering the service. He was assigned to *Stosstrupp* ("strike troop") formations that broke the deadlock on the Eastern Front during the 1917 Riga campaign. He then participated in similar actions on the Western Front during the spring of 1918. He came away from the war convinced that such highly-trained, flexible units could be successful on a much greater scale in future warfare.

After service in a *Freikorps* in Lithuania, Steiner found a place in the *Reichswehr*, but retired as a *Hauptmann* at the end of 1933. He was frustrated by what he considered a lack of innovation, and sought a venue for his concept of an elite soldier-athlete. He first sought this through joining the *SA*, but on in April 1935, he switched to the *SS*. Here, with carefully screened volunteers under his leadership, he at last was able to demonstrate the validity of his ideas. The continued success of his training methods earned the approval of Paul Hausser, who spread them throughout the early units of the burgeoning *Waffen-SS*. Steiner also popularized the use of the camouflage smock, developed by his subordinate, Dr. Wim Brandt. Camouflage

Felix Steiner

clothing later spread to the rest of the *Waffen-SS* and eventually to armies around the world.

Steiner's regiment, *SS-Deutschland*, fought effectively in the invasions of Poland and Western Europe, and Steiner was one of the first *Waffen-SS* members to earn the Knight's Cross on 17 June 1940. He was promoted to *SS-Brigadeführer* on 9 November 1940, and on 1 December assumed command of the newly-formed *SS-Wiking Division*. Here he discovered a phenomenon that became a personal cause for the rest of his life.

SS-Wiking included the recently raised *SS-Nordland* and *SS-Westland* Regiments. The former included volunteers from Norway and Denmark, while the latter had men from Flanders and the Netherlands. While many more traditional German officers were skeptical of the value of foreign volunteers, Steiner embraced them enthusiastically.

The Finns, Swiss, Swedes, Danes, Norwegians, and Flemings entrusted to him came to admire Steiner for his firm, but caring leadership. He became known for shaking hands with every man in formations drawn up for inspection, and for emphasizing military efficiency over politics. Steiner was reprimanded by Himmler on several occasions for downplaying *SS* and Nazi ideology, and also for never abandoning his Christian faith, but he retained his commands because of his military abilities. His influence extended to the officer corps of *SS-Wiking*, so that the foreign volunteers were always respected and well treated.

During the Caucasus campaign, Steiner assumed temporary command of the army's *III Panzer Corps* (November 1942–January 1943).

This was an unusual step, but he had earned the respect and cooperation of his Army colleagues, including General Staff officer Joachim Ziegler. Steiner earned the Oakleaves to his Knight's Cross on 23 December 1942. He was marked for a permanent corps command, and this became official during May 1943, when he became the first commander of the *III (Germanic) SS-Panzer Corps,* which collected most of the available Western European volunteers.

The *III (Germanic) SS-Panzer Corps* fought very effectively during 1944 against heavy odds in the retreat from the Oranienbaum front to the Narva bridgehead, and finally on the Tannenberg defense line. Steiner received the Swords to his Knight's Cross in recognition of this on 10 August 1944. Steiner continued to lead his corps until late January 1945, when he preceded it to Pomerania to organize an offensive. The scattered units available were given the grandiose title *"11th SS-Panzer Army,"* though they were below conventional army strength.

Steiner resumed command of the *III (Germanic) SS-Panzer Corps* west of the Oder River during April 1945, and soon after defied Hitler's order to launch a hopeless relief attack on Berlin. The decision spared the lives of many of his men. Steiner intended to surrender all of the remaining Western European volunteers to the Western Allies, under the faintest of hopes that they might be used against the Communists in a post-war struggle.

In captivity, Steiner refused to testify against British volunteers who had joined the *Waffen-SS.* He later helped organize the *Hilfsgemeinschaft auf Gegenseitigkeit der Soldaten der ehemaligen Waffen-SS* (the HIAG, or Mutual Aid Society for Former Members of the *Waffen-SS*), and then devoted his time to writing studies of military history.

Steiner died in Munich on 17 May 1966.

Maximillian, *Reichsfreiherr* **von Weichs,** was born on 12 November 1881 in Dessau, Prussian Saxony. Weichs completed schooling and commenced military service, entering the *Bavarian Second Heavy Cavalry Regiment* in July 1900. Two years later, he was promoted to *Leutnant* and, prior to the commencement of the First World War, was promoted to *Rittmeister.* His first combat experience in the Great War was as a horse cavalryman, and he later served as a staff officer.

Retained in the army after the war, Weichs commanded the *18th Cavalry Regiment* (1928–30), and was assigned after that as chief of staff of the *1st Cavalry Division,* one of three mandated by the Versailles Treaty. Rising to *Oberst* in November 1930, in rapid fashion three years later he attained the rank of *Generalmajor* shortly after Adolf Hitler had been named German Chancellor.

In 1935, Weichs was promoted to *Generalleutnant* and assumed command of the *1st Panzer Division*. While in that assignment, he was promoted to *General* of Cavalry on 1 October 1936. In October 1937, he assumed command of *XIII Corps*, but was retired as one of the "uncooperative" generals Hitler purged in 1938. However, he was soon recalled to active duty, and resumed command of *XIII Corps* from then through the Polish Campaign.

After the opening campaign ended, Weichs assumed command of *2d Army* on 29 October 1939. In ensuing months, he commanded that force in the invasion of Western Europe, the invasion of the Balkans, and later still, Operation BARBAROSSA. He received the Knight's Cross for his performance in the West and, in July 1940, was promoted to *Generaloberst*.

Under *Army Group Center*, Weichs's army seized Brest-Litovsk, then participated in the reduction of several of the huge pockets of encircled troops that had been cut off by the *2d* and *3d Panzer Groups*. After weathering some health challenges in late 1941, Weichs was back in action by January to guide his army through the brutal Russian winter. In Operation *BLAU*, he commanded a provisional army group, named for him, which temporarily included *2d Army*, *4th Panzer Army*, and the *Hungarian 2d Army*.

The *Reichsfreiherr* von Weichs

Part way through the summer offensive, Weichs assumed command of *Army Group B*. His responsibilities were significant, as multiple German forces rapidly converged upon the Don and Volga River areas. As they advanced, Weichs's army grew to huge size, including not only *2d*, *6th*, and *4th Panzer Armies*, but also the *Hungarian 2d*, the *Italian 8th*, and the *Romanian 3d* and *4th Armies*. (The *4th*

Panzer, 6th, and *Romanian 3d* and *4th Armies* were transferred to *Army Group Don* in late November 1942.)

It was precisely the Hungarian and Italian field armies—poorly equipped and sometimes poorly led as they were—that were some of Stalin's prime targets in the Soviet winter offensive in early 1943. The better part of the **Voronezh** and **Southwestern Fronts** fell upon Weichs's Hungarians and Italians, and shattered them as they drove westward.

Army Group B was disbanded and its surviving forces absorbed into *Army Group South* following the winter debacle, but Weichs had already risen to *Generalfeldmarschall* in February. In August 1943, he was named Supreme Commander in the southeastern theater (*OB Südost*) and Commander of *Army Group F* as well. This made him responsible for military operations in Bulgaria, Yugoslavia, Albania, and Greece. He continued to command those elements until they were disestablished in early 1945, as Soviet forces ripped through the area and into Austria. Nevertheless, Weichs was further recognized in February 1945 with the addition of the Oakleaves to the Knight's Cross, upon the occasion of his relief of command and final retirement.

On 2 May 1945, American forces interned Weichs as a prisoner of war. Allied authorities demanded his trial as a war criminal. Shortly before one of a number of war crimes tribunals for German higher officers, he was exempted from prosecution due to poor health.

Weichs was a highly competent, versatile commander, a veritable workhorse in a wide variety of combat command assignments throughout the war. The *Reichsfreiherr* von Weichs died in 1954, at Rössberg bei Bonn.

Biographies
of Important Soviets

The top 25 Soviet commanders of WWII are summarized below. Two Soviet Marshals stand out above the others, Marshal Georgii K. Zhukov, the Deputy Supreme Commander during the war, and Marshal Alexander M. Vasilevsky, the Chief of the General Staff and *Stavka* representative. They are presented first. The remaining officers are listed alphabetically. Brief descriptions are presented for a number of other significant commanders at the end of the section.

Georgii K. Zhukov was born 1 December 1896, the son of a shoemaker in the village of Strelkovka, about 60 miles east of Moscow.

Highest rank achieved: Marshal of the Soviet Union, 1943

Four times awarded Hero of the Soviet Union (1939, 1944, 1945, 1956) and twice decorated with the Order of Victory

Standing at the pinnacle of Soviet military excellence during WWII is one man, Marshal G. K. Zhukov. Although Zhukov experienced a few notable operational failures (for example, Operation MARS in mid-1942), by and large, his record of service during the war as Deputy Supreme Commander, *Stavka* member, and coordinator of multi-front major campaigns, is one of a string of defensive masterpieces from late 1941 through 1942 and offensive victories thereafter. Together with Vasilevsky, Zhukov was primarily responsible for the strategic and operational planning and preparations behind many of the great Soviet campaigns of the Eastern Front. His name will always be associated with the strategic defensive stand at Moscow that burst the bubble of *blitzkrieg* as a war-winning doctrine; with the defense and counteroffensive at Stalingrad that so weakened the German Army in the east that it could no longer mount a strategic offensive; with the breaking of the siege of Leningrad; and with the defeat of Axis forces at Kursk, after which the Germans assumed a permanent defensive posture, no longer able to mount offensive operations above the higher tactical level. From 1944–45, Zhukov's masterful regrouping of forces between major campaigns enabled the Soviet Army to conduct a nearly continuous series of offensive campaigns, from the Baltic to the Black Sea, that maintained overwhelming pressure against Axis forces and consistently broke down their defenses through deep penetrations and operational-level encirclements. Naturally, in all of these stunning victories, Zhukov was supported by the masterful planning of the General Staff, the assistance of able, experienced front commanders, the ever-increasing output of Soviet military industry, and an advantage in correlation of forces that grew more decisive from month to month until the end of the war.

Zhukov began his long military career as a private and non-commissioned officer in the tsarist army, during which he earned two St. George's Crosses for bravery. Joining the Red Army in 1918, he commanded a cavalry platoon and troop during the Civil War. Between the wars, perhaps favored by his connection with Semyon Budyonny, he commanded cavalry units at all levels from regiment to corps and served as Red Army inspector of cavalry forces. He achieved initial fame as the commander of the **1st Army Group,** a combined Soviet and Mongol army in 1939 that defeated a strong Japanese force at the Battle of Khalkin Gol in a dispute over boundaries. Although criticized for the high losses suffered during the battle, Zhukov is credited with executing a form of mechanized warfare and deep battle that is considered to be a precursor to Soviet deep operations and encirclements during WWII.

Zhukov's success at Khalkin Gol pushed him ahead of many of his contemporaries. In 1940, he was appointed commander in chief of the Kiev Special Military District. At the end of that year, commanding "enemy" forces during special high-level wargames, he defeated Soviet forces executing war plans prepared by the General Staff, leading immediately to the reassignment of then-Chief of the General Staff Kiril Meretskov and Zhukov's appointment in his stead in January 1941 (simultaneously named a Deputy Commissar of Defense). By the time WWII began, Zhukov had clearly risen to the top of the ladder as an undisputed master of the military craft.

In the first months of the war, Zhukov was assigned as commander of the **Reserve, Leningrad,** and **Western Fronts,** each time

Georgii K. Zhukov

assuming command at a critical time and place in desperate defensive battles to halt the advance of Germany *Army Groups North* and *Center*. He was a primary planner and director of the December 1941 counteroffensive that relieved pressure on Moscow, as well as the general winter offensive that followed.

From 1942 on, he served almost continuously as a *Stavka* representative to various fronts and groups of fronts, charged with primary responsibility for planning and directing major campaigns. Occasionally, when the situation demanded it, he assumed personal command of specific fronts to ensure their completion of assigned missions and tasks, most notably of the **1st Ukrainian Front** from March through May 1944 (replaced by Konev) and the **1st Belorussian Front** from November 1944 through May 1945 (Vistula-Oder and Berlin offensive campaigns). Yet, even when assigned as front commander, Zhukov often visited other fronts as a *Stavka* representative to direct planning and oversee preparations for major campaigns. Zhukov personally received the surrender of German forces on 8 May 1945.

After the war, Zhukov initially commanded the **Soviet Group of Forces** in Germany and served as Commander in Chief of Ground Forces, but he was recalled after a year and charged with exaggerating his role in the war. Seen as a rival by Stalin and envied by others, he was removed from the limelight and forced to languish, humiliatingly, as a military district commander. He returned to prominence after Stalin's death, playing a key and personal role in the removal of Beria as Stalin's erstwhile successor. Zhukov was then as Minister of Defense and supported Khrushchev during a 1957 mini-palace coup attempt (by flying loyal troops to Moscow), although he eventually fell out of favor again and was retired.

Zhukov died 18 June 1974 and was buried with full honors in the Kremlin wall.

Alexander M. Vasilevsky was the son of a Russian Orthodox priest, born in 1895.

Highest rank achieved: Marshal of the Soviet Union, 1943

Twice awarded Hero of the Soviet Union and twice decorated with the Order of Victory

Not far below Zhukov, yet rising above all other Soviet commanders of the war, stands Marshal Alexander M. Vasilevsky. Combining his roles as Chief of the General Staff for 30 months in wartime, almost continuous service as a *Stavka* representative to many of the pivotal battles and campaigns of the war, and Commander-in-Chief of the Manchurian Campaign (August–September 1945), Vasilevsky exercised a level of influence on the course and outcome of the war that no other Soviet general officer can match, with the single exception of Zhukov. He is featured in Soviet military history as having made significant contributions to the evolution of Soviet military art with respect to: the preparation of reserve forces; the formation, equipping, and direction of large combined arms units; the planning and conduct of multi-front campaigns; and the employment of mounted and dismounted formations to create operational-level penetrations and encirclements.

Alexander M. Vasilevsky

Vasilevsky enlisted in the Tsarist Army in January 1915 and immediately completed a four-month course for junior officers. Over the next two years, he acquired significant combat experience, both defensive and offensive, including action in the Brusilov offensive of 1916. Joining the Red Army in 1919, he served as a battalion and assistant regimental commander during the Civil War, then served in command and staff positions following the war. He graduated from the General Staff Academy in 1937 and soon began long years of service within the General Staff.

Early in the war, as a general major, he was appointed as Chief of the Operations Department of the General Staff. In June 1942, he assumed duties as Chief of the General Staff, a post he was to hold for the next thirty months. He spent, however, only twelve months of that time period in Moscow, the rest of the time consumed with duties as a *Stavka* representative that compelled him to stay at the front. Vasilevsky was a primary author of both the Stalingrad Counteroffensive (November to December 1942) that broke the siege of Stalingrad and encircled *Army Group B,* and Operation RING (January–February 1943), the elimination of the German *6th Army* within the Stalingrad cauldron. He directed the coordinated action of the **Voronezh** and **Steppe Fronts** in the Battle of Kursk in 1943, followed by the same role in the clearing of the Donbas by the **Southern** and **Southwestern Fronts** later that year.

In January and February 1944, he directed the **3d** and **4th Ukrainian Fronts** in the Nikopol-Krivoi Rog operation; in April, the liberation of Crimea; and from June–August 1944, he oversaw the conduct of Operation BAGRATION, the Soviet Army's huge offensive campaign in Belorussia, executed by the **1st, 2d,** and **3d Belorussian,** and **1st Baltic Fronts** (commanded respectively by K. K. Rokossovsky, G. F. Zakharov, I. D. Chernyakovsky, and I. X. Bagramian). In February 1945, he was promoted to membership within the *Stavka* and assumed command of the **3d Belorussian Front** for the final campaign to defeat Germany. Marshal Vasilevsky culminated his wartime service as commander in chief of Soviet Forces in the Far East and planned and executed the Manchurian Offensive cited above.

Following the war, he resumed duties as Chief of the General Staff and was named a Deputy and 1st Deputy Minister of the Armed Forces. From 1949 to 1953, he held the top post in the Ministry. He retired in 1958 and was buried within the walls of the Kremlin after his death in 1977.

Alexei A. Antonov was born 15 September 1895 in Grodno, the son of an artillery officer.

Highest rank achieved: Army General, 1943

Awarded the Order of Victory

Antonov participated in WWI, joined the Red Army in 1919, and fought in the Civil War. A career staff officer, he graduated from the Frunze Academy in 1931, from the General Staff Academy in 1937, and then served on the General Staff in the years leading up to WWII. By June 1941, he had been promoted to general major.

Antonov spent the first year of the war in south Russia as the chief of staff of the **Southern, North Caucasus,** and **Transcaucasian Fronts,** then chief of staff of the **Black Sea Group of Forces.** In 1942, he was appointed 1st Deputy Chief of the General Staff to General A. M. Vasilevsky, simultaneously acting as Chief of the Operations Directorate responsible for operational-strategic planning. When Vasilevsky assumed command of the **3d Belorussian Front** in February 1945, Antonov was named Chief of the General Staff and became a member of the *Stavka.*

After the war, General Antonov reverted to 1st Deputy Chief of the General Staff under Vasilevsky once more and later served as Deputy Commander in Chief and Commander in Chief of the Trans-caucasus Military District. From 1955 to 1962, he occupied the position of Chief of Staff of the Combined Forces of the Warsaw Pact. He died in office on 18 June 1962 and is buried in the Kremlin wall.

Antonov is best remembered and honored in Soviet military history as the chief planner of many of the great battles on the Eastern Front and for accompanying Stalin, as his senior military advisor, to the great Allied councils at Yalta and Potsdam.

Ivan X. Bagramian was born 2 December 1897 in Elizavetpol, Azerbaijan, the son of an ethnically Armenian railroad worker.

Highest rank achieved: Marshal of the Soviet Union, 1955

Twice awarded Hero of the Soviet Union (1944, 1977)

Bagramian joined the Red Army in 1920 and participated in the establishment of Soviet authority in Georgia and Armenia. He completed the Frunze Academy in 1934 and the General Staff Academy in 1938. In 1940, he served as chief of the operations department of an army assigned to the Kiev Special Military District.

His initial wartime assignment was as Chief of Staff of the **Southwestern Front,** simultaneously holding the same position for the **Southwestern Direction** first under Marshall Budyonny, then Marshal Timoshenko, to mid-1942. In July 1942, Bagramian took command of the **16th Army** when Rokossovsky was promoted to front commander. Bagramian retained command of the army through 1943, during which the **16th** was renamed the **11th Guards Army.**

Fighting in the north in the last two years of the war, Bagramian was promoted to command the **1st Baltic Front** (November 1943), the **Zemland Group of Forces** (February 1945) and the **3d Belorussian Front** (April 1945). His service included participation in the

Kursk, Govodok, Belorussian, Polotsk, Riga, Memel, and East Prussian offensive operations and campaigns.

After the war, General Bagramian commanded the pri-Baltic Military District, served as Inspector General of the Ministry of Defense (1955), and Head of the General Staff Academy from 1956 to 1958. He then served for ten years as Chief of Rear Services of the Armed Forces, retiring in 1968. He died 21 September 1982 and was buried within the Kremlin wall.

Semyon M. Budyonny was born in Kozyurin, near Rostov, on 25 April 1883, the son of peasants.

Highest rank achieved: Marshal of the Soviet Union, 1935.

Three times awarded Hero of the Soviet Union, but all after WWII.

Marshal Budyonny achieved his fame during the Russian Civil War and played a relatively minor role compared to many others in WWII, although he held the rank of Marshal throughout the war. As a trusted crony of Stalin and member of the *Stavka* during WWII, however, he must be included within the larger group of significant Soviet wartime commanders.

Older by at least a decade than most of his fellow senior generals and marshals in WWII, Budyonny's military experience began with his participation in both the Russo-Japanese War and WWI. As a "Red Commander," Budyonny commanded cavalry units from regiment to corps, culminating his participation in the Russian Civil War as commander of the famous **1st Cavalry Army** (November 1919) in operations against the White General Denekin, from which also dates his close association with Stalin. Service in the **1st Cavalry Army** was to prove to be a significant boost to future promotion. The number of Soviet marshals and senior generals that had roots in this organization, in addition to Budyonny, included Zhukov, K. Ye. Voroshilov, S. K. Timoshenko, K. A. Meretskov, A. V. Khrulev, P. A. Rybalko, and others.

Budyonny completed the Frunze Academy in 1932 and was one of five famous Civil War veterans promoted to marshal in the mid-1930s . . . only two of which survived the purges—Budyonny and Voroshilov. In the 1930s, he served as inspector of cavalry of the Red Army as well as deputy commander in chief and commander in chief of a military district. By August 1940, Budyonny held the position of Deputy Commissar of Defense.

Budyonny began the war as a member of the *Stavka* and commander of the *Stavka* group of reserve armies. In July 1941, he served as commander in chief of the **Southwestern Direction,** but he was quickly replaced in that position by Timoshenko (September 1941) and given command of the **Reserve Front.** The following year, he was placed in charge of the short-lived **North Caucasus Strategic Direction** from April to May 1942, then shifted to command of the **North Caucasus Front.** Beginning in 1943, Budyonny was named commander in chief of Soviet cavalry troops and held no more operational commands.

After the war, Marshal Budyonny was appointed Deputy Minister of Agriculture (1947–53). A member of the Central Committee (1935–52), he retired from active service in 1954 and was laid to rest near the Lenin Mausoleum in 1973.

Ivan D. Chernyakovsky was born 29 June 1906, in Uman, in Ukraine. He was the son of a railroad worker.

Highest rank achieved: Army General, 1944

Twice awarded the Hero of the Soviet Union (1943, 1944)

Chernyakovsky was ten years younger than almost all of the senior officers that rose along with him to front command during World War II. He joined the Red Army in 1924 and completed the Mechanized and Motorized Military Academy in 1936. During the 1930s, Chernyakovsky commanded a tank battalion, a regiment, and a division.

By June 1941, Chernyakovsky had achieved the rank of colonel, initially serving as a tank division commander, but rising quickly to the command of **18th Tank Corps,** then command of **60th Army** from July 1942 through April 1944. He then commanded the **Western Front,** which was reformed as the **3d Belorussian Front,** from April 1944 to February 1945. As an army and front commander, General Chernyakovsky fought in the Battle of Kursk, forced the Desna and Dnieper rivers, and participated in operations at Kiev, Zhitomir-Berdichev, Rovno-Lutsk, Belorussia, Vilnius, Kaunass, Memel, and East Prussia. He was mortally wounded 18 February 1945 while on an inspection tour near Königsberg. He was buried with honors in Vilnius. General Chernyakovsky was perhaps the fastest rising star in the Soviet Army, highly regarded by both Marshal Zhukov and Marshal Vasilevsky, and undoubtedly would have continued to command at high levels but for his early death.

Vasily I. Chuikov was born 12 February 1900 in the village of Sere-bryanye, near Moscow.

Highest rank achieved: Marshal of the Soviet Union, 1955

Twice awarded Hero of the Soviet Union (1944, 1945)

Although never rising above the level of Army command, Vasily I. Chuikov is one of the best remembered names from the Eastern Front because of his heroic leadership of the **62d Army,** in tandem with General Mikhail S. Shumilov of the **64th Army,** of the gates of Stalingrad.

Chuikov joined the Red Army in 1918 and rose to command of a regiment during the Civil War at a very young age. An early gradu-ate of the Frunze Academy (1925), he had a non-standard interwar service that included duty as chief of a department within the staff of the **Special Far Eastern Army,** command of a brigade and corps, command of the **Bobruisk Group of Forces** and **4th Army,** which carried out operations to occu-py western Belorussia in con-nection with the Soviet-Ger-man partition of Poland. Chuikov commanded the **9th Army** during the Soviet-Finnish War, after which he was posted as a military advi-sor in China from December 1940 through March 1942. He held the rank of general lieu-tenant in June 1941.

Vasily I. Chuikov

Returning from China, Chuikov took command in May 1942 of the **1st Reserve Army,** which became the **64th Army** in July. Two months later, Chuikov assumed command of the **62d Army,** spending most of the autumn and early winter pinned against the banks of the Volga, along with the **64th Army** under Shumilov, in the stalwart defense of Stalingrad, before finally join-ing the **Don Front** in the elimination of the encircled German *6th*

Army in early 1943 in Operation RING. In April 1943, the **62d Army** reformed into the **8th Guards,** with General Chuikov still in command. Over the course of the next two years, Chuikov led his forces from the banks of the Don and Dnieper Rivers through Odessa and across Ukraine, across the Vistula, through Warsaw and Poznan, to the final battle of Berlin.

After the war, General Chuikov remained in Germany as Deputy, 1st Deputy, then Commander in Chief of the **Soviet Group of Forces.** In the 1950s, he served as Commander of the Kiev Military District, then was named Commander in Chief of **Ground Forces** in 1960. From 1964 to 1972, Marshal Chuikov headed the national civil defense organization within the Soviet Union. In honor of his role at the Battle of Stalingrad, upon his death in 1982, Chuikov was buried at the hillside site of the battle memorial on Mamayev Kurgan.

Yakov N. Federenko was born 22 November 1896 in Tsareborisovo, near Moscow, the son of a longshoreman.

Highest rank achieved: Marshal of Tank Troops, 1944

Federenko joined the Red Army in 1918 and served as a commissar of an army staff and as commander and commissar of an armored train. In the 1920s, he completed the Higher Artillery Command School (1924) and commanded a battalion and regiment of armored trains. As the Red Army moved to mechanization, Federenko became an early tank commander at regimental and brigade level. He graduated from the Frunze Academy in 1934.

By June 1941, he held the rank of general lieutenant of tank troops and had been Chief of the Automotive-Tank Department for a year. In December 1942, Federenko was named commander in chief of Tank and Mechanized Forces (simultaneously a Deputy Minister of Defense) with responsibilities for raising, equipping, and training tank formations for commitment to armies and fronts.

From time to time, the *Stavka* sent Federenko to the front as a *Stavka* representative to plan and coordinate the most effective employment of tank and mechanized forces in key operations. In that role, Federenko participated in the seminal battles of Moscow, Stalingrad, and Kursk and is credited with helping to instill the tactics and operational art of deep operations by mobile tank and mechanized forces.

Following the war, Federenko remained in position as commander in chief of Tank and Mechanized Forces until his death on 26 March 1947.

Philipp I. Golikov was born 16 July 1900 in Borisovo, east of the Urals.

Highest rank achieved: Marshal of the Soviet Union, 1961.

Golikov joined the Communist Party and Red Army in 1918 and participated in the Russian Civil War. A graduate of the Frunze Academy in 1933, he initially carried out party-political work, then commanded a variety of units in the 1930s, culminating in command of one of the early Soviet mechanized corps, a clear mark of favor, and the **6th Army.** By July 1940, he had risen to become a Deputy Chief of the General Staff.

Promoted to general lieutenant by June 1941, Golikov commanded the **10th Army** for a short time, then assumed command of the **4th Shock Army** from February through April 1942. Subsequently in 1942, he commanded a variety of large formations including the **Briansk Front** (April 1942), the **Voronezh Front** (July 1942), and **1st Guards Army,** and served as Deputy Commander of the **Southwestern** and **Stalingrad Fronts.** Golikov was then reappointed to command of the **Voronezh Front** from October 1942 through March 1943, during which he directed offensive operations in the region of the Upper Don.

From this point on in the war, Golikov appears to have filled no additional operational commands. Instead, he served as Deputy Commissar of Defense for Cadres with auxiliary responsibilities for repatriating Soviet citizens, a position which reflected his parallel involvement in party affairs.

For a number of years after the war, Golikov returned to duty with troop units, then became the Head of the Mechanized and Tank Military Academy (1956–58). From 1958 to 1962, he served as the Chief of the Main Political Administration of the Soviet Army as his last active post.

Golikov died 29 July 1980.

Leonid A. Govorov was born 22 February 1897 in Butyrki, near Kirov, the son of an office worker.

Highest rank achieved: Marshal of the Soviet Union, 1944.

Awarded Hero of the Soviet Union (1945) and the Order of Victory.

Govorov joined the Red Army in 1920 and fought in the Russian Civil War. He completed the Frunze Academy in 1933 and the General Staff Academy in 1938. During the Soviet-Finnish War, Govorov served as chief of staff of artillery of the **7th Army.**

At the start of WWII, Govorov was posted as Head of the Dzerzhinsky Artillery Academy in the rank of general major of artillery. During the first confused months of the war, he filled many different posts including Chief of Artillery Troops of the **Northwestern Direction** (July 1941), the same position in the **Reserve Front,** then deputy commander of troops in the Moscow line of defense from August through October 1941. He took command of the **5th Army** in October 1941 and later assumed long-term command of the **Leningrad Front** from 1942–44, during the long (900-day) siege of the city by

Leonid A. Govorov

Army Group North. In January 1943, in coordination with actions of the **Volkov Front** under General Meretskov, with Marshal Voroshilov as *Stavka* representative, Govorov managed to break the siege of Leningrad sufficiently to establish reliable lines of communication for supplies of food and ammunition. In October 1944, while commanding the **Leningrad Front,** he simultaneously coordinated offensive operations by the **2d** and **3d Baltic Fronts.** Govorov is credited by Soviet military historians with adding significantly to military art with respect to defensive operations.

In the post-war years, Govorov remained in Leningrad as commander in chief of the Leningrad Military District, before serving as commander in chief of Strategic Air Defenses (PVO Strany) and Deputy Minister of Defense 1948–52 and 1954–55. Govorov died in 1955 and was buried in the Kremlin wall.

Andrei V. Khrulev (1892–1962)

Highest rank achieved: Army General, 1943

Khrulev initially made his way in the Red Army, joining in 1918, as a military-political officer, most notably as the commissar of a cavalry division within the **1st Cavalry Army.** His formal military education, apparently, went no farther than the Military-Political Courses for Higher Political Staff in 1925. Between the wars, he served as commissar of a regiment and division, then as chief of the political department of a military district, chief of the central military finance department, and chief of the housing construction directorate of the Red Army. In October 1939, he was named chief of the Department of Supply, then Chief Quartermaster of the Army a year later.

In the first months of the war, General Lieutenant Khrulev was appointed a Deputy Minister of Defense and Chief of Rear Services. From 1942 through 1943, he also held the post of Commissar of Lines of Communications. In both roles, Khrulev was charged with the continuous material-technical sustainment of armies and fleets, an extraordinarily difficult task given the losses suffered by the USSR during the first year of the war and the expanse of territory over which supplies and materiel had to be organized and delivered.

He retained his post for several years after the war ended. From 1951 through 1958, Khrulev occupied a series of posts as a deputy defense minister in the military-industrial-transportation sectors of the Soviet economy. A widely-published author on matters of logistics, Khrulev retired in 1958 and was later buried upon his death in the Kremlin cemetery.

Ivan S. Konev was born in Ladino, near Kirov, on 28 December 1897.

Highest rank achieved: Marshal of the Soviet Union, 1944

Twice awarded Hero of the Soviet Union (1944, 1944) and the Order of Victory

A veteran of WWI and the Civil War, Konev joined the Red Army in 1918, performing duties as the commissar of an armored train unit, a brigade, and a division. In the early 1920s, he was posted as Chief of Staff of the People's Revolutionary Army of the short-lived Soviet puppet, Far Eastern Republic. After the Civil War, he initially served as a military commissar, then commanded units from regimental to army size, as well as the Transbaikal and North Caucasus Military Districts (1940–41). A graduate of the Frunze Academy in 1934, Konev achieved the rank of general lieutenant by June 1941.

At the start of the war, Konev was given command of the **19th Army,** then quickly promoted to command of **Western Front.** Seeking to strengthen the defense of the approaches to Moscow, the *Stavka* replaced Konev as front commander with Zhukov in October

1941, perhaps heating the rivalry that would seem to characterize the relationship of the two commanders for the rest of their lives.

After a stint as commander of the **Kalinin Front,** he resumed command of the **Western Front** from August 1942 through February 1943, then moved to command of the **North Caucasus Front** in March 1943. After four months, he assumed command of the **Steppe Front,** which, along with the **Central Front** under Rokossovsky and the **Voronezh Front** under Vatutin, defeated Axis forces in the great Battle of Kursk. Konev then commanded the **2d Ukrainian Front** from October 1943 to May 1944,

Ivan S. Konev

playing a central role in the Korsun-Shevchenkovskii and Uman-Botoshansky offensive operations. From May 1944 to May 1945, Konev headed the **1st Ukrainian Front** which he led across Poland to the streets of Berlin and Prague. In the battle for Berlin, Stalin manipulated Konev and Zhukov against each other, each in command of adjacent fronts, challenging them to see who would reach Berlin first. Ultimately, a boundary line was re-drawn between the two fronts, pushing Konev's forces to the south of Berlin and leaving the main approach within the sector of Zhukov's **1st Belorussian Front.** Unlike Zhukov and others, Konev appears not to have been used as a *Stavka* representative to coordinate the actions of multiple fronts.

After the war, Konev served as commander in chief of the **Central Group of Forces** and Supreme Commissar in Austria (1945–46), then four years as commander in chief of **Ground Forces** and Deputy Minister of the Armed Forces, his star rising as Zhukov's fell temporarily. From 1950 through 1955, he was relegated to the post of Inspector General and commander in chief of the pri-Carpathian Military District. Subsequently, he reappeared on the main stage and briefly resumed position as commander in chief of **Ground Forces** before spending 1956–60 as Commander in Chief of the Combined Armed Forces of the Warsaw Pact (while Zhukov held the post of Soviet Minister of Defense). From 1961 through 1962, Konev moved to Germany as commander in chief of the **Soviet Group of Forces** in that country. After his death on 21 May 1973, he was buried in the Kremlin wall.

Rodion Ya. Malinovsky was born 23 November 1898 in Odessa, the illegitimate son of a railroad worker and hospital cook.

Highest rank achieved: Marshal of the Soviet Union, 1944

Twice awarded Hero of the Soviet Union (1945, 1958) and the Order of Victory

Malinovsky was a veteran of both WWI and the Russian Civil War. Between the world wars, he served as a staff officer and as chief of staff of a cavalry regiment and cavalry corps. He graduated from the Frunze Academy in 1930 and participated in the Spanish Civil War from 1936 to 1939. In 1939, Malinovsky was on the faculty of the Frunze Academy, possibly as a result of his recent experiences in Spain.

By June 1941, he held the rank of general major and commanded the **48th Rifle Corps,** in which position he was one of the first to face invading Axis forces on the Prut River in the opening days of the war. He was promoted to command of the **6th Army** in August 1941, then commanded the **Southern Front** for the first seven months of 1942, taking part in the failed, poorly-prepared counteroffensive in the Kharhov region in May.

From October through November 1942, Malinovsky was Deputy commander in chief of the **Voronezh Front** before assuming command of the **2d Guards Army,** which distinguished itself in the counteroffensive at Stalingrad as one of the two formations committed late in the operation, the other being P. A. Rotmistrov's **7th Tank Corps,** to halt Manstein's desperate (and nearly successful) attempt to break through the Soviet encirclement and provide a means of escape for Paulus's **6th Army.**

In February 1943, Malinovsky assumed command of the **Southwestern Front** in an unbroken string of front commands that took him from southern Russian to Vienna. The **Southwestern Front** was renamed the **3d Ukrainian Front** in October 1943, remaining under Malinovsky's command.

Beginning in March 1944, Malinovsky commanded the **2d Ukrainian Front** and remained at its head until the end of the war in Europe, fighting in the southern theater of operations. Together, the **2d** and **3d Ukrainian Front** (under Tolbukhin) drove the Axis forces out of Soviet territory, liberated Romania, and occupied the Balkans. In the course of his service in WWII, Marshal Malinovsky participated in defensive and offensive operations at Barvenk-Lozovaia, (1st) Kharkov, Donbas (1942), Stalingrad, Donbas (1943), Right Bank Ukraine, Zaporozhe, Nikopol-Krivoi Rog, Bereznegovatoye-Snigirovka, Odessa, Iassy-Kishinev, Debrecen, Budapest, and Vienna.

In July 1945, Malinovsky assumed command of the **Trans-Baikal Front** during the Manchurian Campaign. Striking from the west, Malinovsky delivered the main blow that fractured the Japanese Kwantung Army, with the **6th Guards Tank Army** under General Kravechenko and a combined Soviet-Mongolian cavalry-mechanized group under Marshal Choibalsan striking hundreds of kilometers deep into the Japanese rear toward Mukden.

He remained in the Transbaikal after the war as commander in chief of the military district, then moved further east as commander in chief of the Far East Military District from 1947 to 1956. In March 1956, he returned to Moscow as Commander in Chief of Ground Forces, then was promoted to Minister of Defense, a post which he held for ten years, 1957–67.

Like so many of his fellow marshals and recipients of the Hero of the Soviet Union, he was buried in the Kremlin cemetery after he died on 31 March 1967.

Kiril A. Meretskov was born 7 June 1897, the son of a clerk in Nazaryevo, near Moscow.

Highest rank achieved: Marshal of the Soviet Union, 1944.

Awarded Hero of the Soviet Union (1940) and Order of Victory

Meretskov served on brigade- and division-level staffs during the Russian Civil War. After graduating from the Red Army Military Academy in 1921, he later served as chief of staff of a cavalry division and rifle corps, commander and commissar of a rifle division, and Chief of Staff of the **Separate Far Eastern Army.** He participated in the Spanish Civil War, then joined the General Staff as a deputy to Boris M. Shaposnikov. In the late 1930s, he commanded the Volga Military District. During the Soviet-Finnish War, he simultaneously commanded the **Leningrad Front** and the **7th Army,** after which he was named the Chief of the General Staff until replaced by Zhukov in January 1941.

Holding the rank of General of the Army in June 1941, Meretskov spent the entire war on the Eastern Front in command of armies and fronts, most notably the **Volkhov** and **Karelia Fronts,** in the northern area of operations. He played a key role with General Govorov, **Leningrad Front** commander, in the breaking of the blockade at Leningrad in early 1943 and the liberation of Karelia and polar regions. Operations in which Meretskov held high command position include Tikhvin, Lubansk, Siniavino, Svir-Petrozavodsk, and Petsamo-Kirkenes.

In early 1945, Meretskov was directed to take command of the **Maritime Group of Forces** and prepare it for strategic movement to the Far East. There, it was reformed into the **1st Far Eastern Front** and committed under Marshal Meretskov's command to offensive operations against Japanese forces in eastern Manchuria and northern Korea.

After WWII, Marshal Meretskov served as military district commander, Head of the Vystrel Course, and president of the Soviet Committee of War Veterans. He died on 30 December 1968 and is buried in the Kremlin wall.

Markian M. Popov was born 15 November 1902, the son of a clerk in the village of Ust-Mikhaylovich near Volgograd.

Highest rank achieved: Army General, 1953.

Awarded Hero of the Soviet Union, 1965

Popov joined the Red Army in 1920 and fought in the Civil War against White forces under General Wrangel in the Crimea. He graduated from the Frunze Academy in 1936. By January 1941, Popov occupied the post of commander of the Leningrad Military District. His fortunes and favor with Stalin and the *Stavka* appeared to fluctuate occasionally during WWII, like several other senior Soviet commanders, although he remained in almost continuous command of large formations.

Holding the rank of general lieutenant in June 1941, Popov initially commanded the **Northern** and **Leningrad Fronts** from June through September 1941, but was removed from the post of front commander and given command of the **61st** and **40th Armies** from November 1941 through October 1942. During the pivotal Battle of Stalingrad, Popov served as deputy commander of the **Stalingrad** and **Southwestern Fronts,** before assuming the command of **5th Shock Army** and **5th Tank Army,** both of which performed key roles during the Soviet counteroffensive, Operation URANUS. Forces under Popov's command (**24th Tank Corps**) penetrated the deepest into German-occupied held territory at this time, to a depth of 240 kilometers, before being forced to withdraw and assume the defense once again in 1943.

Based on these successes, Popov took command of the Steppe Military District from April to May 1943 to prepare it for commitment to future operations, then was again named to front command of the **Reserve** and **Briansk Fronts** from June to October 1943, during which his forces participated in offensive operations in connection with the Battle of Kursk. Subsequently, he commanded the **1st** and **2d Baltic Fronts** from October 1943 to April 1944, followed by lower positions as chief of staff of the **Leningrad** and **2d Baltic Fronts.** Overall, his wartime service included the defense of Leningrad, Moscow, and Stalingrad, the Battle of Kursk, and the liberation of Karelia and Baltic regions.

After the war, Popov commanded a military district and was appointed as 1st Deputy Commander in Chief of Ground Forces in 1956, retiring from service in 1962. He passed away 22 April 1969 and was buried in the Novodvichy Monastery.

Konstantin K. Rokossovsky was born to a Polish father (a railroad machinist) and Russian mother in Velikye Luki on 21 December 1896.

> Highest rank achieved: Marshal of the Soviet Union

> Twice awarded the Hero of the Soviet Union (1944, 1955) and the Order of Victory

Rokossovsky must be counted as one of the most important and capable Soviet commanders of WWII. Few other commanders participated in as many important battles and campaigns from the beginning of the war until the capture of Berlin.

Rokossovsky served as a non-commissioned officer in WWI and joined the Red Army in 1918, commanding a cavalry battalion and regiment. During the interwar period, he continued to command cavalry units from regimental size to corps. He completed Frunze Academy courses for higher staff officers in 1929. Briefly imprisoned for a time in connection with the purge of the Red Army; he was released in time to assume command of the **9th Mechanized Corps** in November 1940. By June 1941, he held the rank of general major.

When the Axis invaded, Rokossovsky's corps was one of the first to be committed in failed counterattacks to slow the German advance. He contested German offensive progress along the Moscow direction, participating in the fierce battle to hold Smolensk. Rokossovsky commanded the **16th Army** from August 1941 until the July of 1942, when he was given the first of many front commands, the **Briansk Front.** From September 1942 through February 1943, he commanded the **Don Front,** first defending against the advance of *Army Group B* to Stalingrad and then participating in the Stalingrad counteroffensive reduction of the encircled forces. The **Don Front** may have had the most difficult role during this operation in that it was charged — along with the **Southwestern Front** — with attacking to create the western arc of the encirclement, while simultaneously holding the inner circle and Volga line against enemy attempts to break out.

Konstantin K. Rokossovsky

In February 1943, Rokossovsky took command of the **Central Front** and participated in the planning and preparation for the great battle of Kursk. Strengthened by dense, mutually supporting, layered defensive lines, thickened with anti-tank obstacles, the **Central Front** absorbed the initial German offensive, then went over to the offensive to eliminate the encircled forces. In October 1943, Rokossovsky assumed command of the **Belorussian Front,** reformed later into the **1st Belorussian** in February 1944. From November 1944 to June 1945, he commanded the **2d Belorussian Front** and played a major role in the East Prussian and East Pomeranian offensive operations, culminating with a supporting role from the north in the final seizure of Berlin. In June 1945, he was given the high honor of commanding the victory parade in Moscow.

After the war, Rokossovsky held command of the **Northern Group of Forces** from 1945 through 1949, then was "named" Minister of Defense and Deputy Chairman of the Council of Ministers in Poland. He returned to the USSR in 1956 as a Deputy Minister of Defense and held the position of Inspector General from 1957 through 1962, with a brief stint as commander in chief of the Transcaucasus Military District in 1957. He retired from service in 1962 and passed away on 3 August 1968; his remains were buried in the Kremlin wall.

Boris M. Shaposhnikov was born 2 October 1882 in Zlatoust, in the southern Urals, the son of a distillery manager and a schoolmistress.

Highest rank achieved: Marshal of the Soviet Union, 1940

As the only senior officer from the tsarist army to remain in service in the Red Army into the WWII period, Marshal Shaposhnikov occupies a unique place in Soviet military history. Generally considered to be one of the fathers of the Soviet General Staff, many of the preeminent general staff officers of the war were trained and mentored by him. He is perhaps best know in the West for his writing and ruminations on the general staff as the "brain of the Army."

Shaposhnikov graduated from the tsarist General Staff Academy (1910) and served in positions of responsibility during WWI. Joining the Red Army in 1918, he was appointed assistant chief of the operations department of the Higher Military Council, then chief of the field staff of the Revolutionary Military Committee under Trotsky. He was appointed Chief of the General Staff (May 1937), a position which he held for most of the immediate pre-war years and the initial period of WWII. He was one of the chief planners for the defensive and offensive battles at Smolensk in 1941, as well as the Moscow counteroffensive and general winter offensive of 1941–42. His health eventually forced him into limited service, so, from 1943 until his death 26 March 1945, Shaposhnikov served as Head of the General Staff Academy. His remains were buried in the Kremlin wall.

Vasily D. Sokolovsky was born 21 July 1897, the son of peasants in Grodna, Poland.

Highest rank achieved: Marshal of the Soviet Union, 1946

Awarded Hero of the Soviet Union (1945)

Sokolovsky joined the Red Army in 1918 and served as a regimental and brigade commander and division chief of staff during

Vasily D. Sokolovsky

the Civil War. He completed the Red Army Military Academy in 1921 and higher-level Frunze Academy courses in 1928. Between the wars, Sokolovsky served as chief of staff of a division and a corps, commander of a division and "group of forces," and chief of staff of a military district. By June 1941, he had achieved the rank of general lieutenant and held the post of a Deputy Chief of the General Staff.

Sokolovsky simultaneously served as Chief of Staff of the **Western Front** (July 1941 through January 1942) and of the **Western Direction** under Marshal Timoshenko (July–September 1941). Apparently a short pause in assignment occurred before he again assumed the post of Chief of Staff of the **Western Front** (May 1942–February 1943). Sokolovsky was then promoted to commander of the **Western Front** (February 1943–April 1944), then again performed front chief of staff duties for the **1st Ukrainian Front** (April 1944–April 1945).

He spent April–May 1945 as Deputy Commander of the **1st Belorussian Front.** During the course of his wartime service, Sokolovsky helped plan and execute the Moscow Counteroffensive of 1941, the elimination of the Rzhev-Vyazemsk bridgehead, the Orlov and Smolensk offensive operations from July through August 1943, as well as Lvov-Sandomir, Vistula-Oder, and the final seizure of Berlin.

After the war, Marshal Sokolovsky served as Deputy and commander in chief of the Group of Soviet Forces in Germany (1946–49), 1st Deputy Minister of Armed Forces (1946–52), and spent a long stint as Chief of the General Staff (1952–60). He retired in 1960 and was laid to rest with honors in the Kremlin wall after his death on 10 May 1968.

Semyon K. Timoshenko was born on 18 February 1895, the son of ethnically Ukrainian peasants in Furmanka, Bessarabia.

Highest rank achieved: Marshal of the Soviet Union, 1940.

Twice awarded Hero of the Soviet Union (1940, 1965) and the Order of Victory

A veteran of both WWI and the Russian Civil War, Timoshenko joined the Red Army in 1918, serving as commander, in turn, of a cavalry regiment, brigade, and division in the struggle against White forces. He was not a graduate of either the Frunze or General Staff academies, but completed higher courses for "Red Commanders" in 1922 and 1927.

During the Soviet-Finnish War, Timoshenko served as Commander of the **Northwestern Front,** then replaced Marshal Voroshilov as Commissar of Defense from May 40 through July 1941, after which Stalin himself assumed that title. He was a permanent member of the *Stavka* throughout the war and a Deputy Commissar of Defense.

Semyon K. Timoshenko

In the summer of 1941, Marshal Timoshenko initially commanded the short-lived **Western Direction** (July–September 1941), then replaced Marshal Budyonny as commander in chief of the **Southwestern Direction** (September 1941) until its disbandment in June 1942. During these assignments, he simultaneously commanded the **Western Front** (July–September 1941) and the **Southwestern Front** (September–December 1941 and April–July 1942).

During the German strategic offensive in south Russia in 1942, Timoshenko temporarily commanded the **Stalingrad Front,** then moved to the Leningrad region to assume command of the **Northwestern Front** (October 1942–March 1943). Subsequently, Stalin employed the Marshal quite frequently through the end of the war as a *Stavka* representative to coordinate the action of multiple fronts. From March to June 1943, he synchronized operations of the

Leningrad and **Volkhov Fronts**; from June through November 1943, he was again in south Russia, coordinating the actions of the **North Caucasus Front** and **Black Sea Fleet**; from February through June 1944, he acted as *Stavka* representative to the **2d** and **3d Baltic Fronts**. Timoshenko completed his service during the war as *Stavka* representative to coordinate the operations of the **2d, 3d,** and **4th Ukrainian Fronts** as they drove Axis forces out of Eastern Europe.

Although Timoshenko participated in many of the great campaigns on the Eastern Front, he is perhaps best remembered for orchestrating the first successful Soviet counteroffensive against the initial German invasion at Rostov-on-Don in 1941; for the elimination of the German bridgehead at Demiansk in 1943; and for coordinating the very successful encirclement operation, Iassy-Kishinev (highly regarded in Soviet military history as an example of high operational art) in 1944, which led to the rapid liberation of Romania and the collapse of German *Army Group Southern Ukraine,* including the destruction of 22 enemy divisions.

After the war, Marshal Timoshenko continued in command of a series of military districts, most notably the Belorussian Military District from 1949 to 1960. He retired in 1960 and was buried with honors in the Kremlin wall following his death on 31 March 1970.

Fyodor I. Tolbukhin was born 16 June 1894, the son of a peasant artisan in Androniki, near Yaroslavl.

Highest rank achieved: Marshal of the Soviet Union, 1944

Awarded the Hero of the Soviet Union (1965, posthumously) and the Order of Victory

Tolbukhin participated in WWI, joined the Red Army in 1918, and served in a variety of positions during the Russian Civil War, including chief of staff of a division and Head of the Operations Directorate in the Red Army staff. During the interwar period, he served as a division and corps chief of staff and as a division commander. Completing the Frunze Academy in 1935, Tolbukhin was appointed as chief of staff of the Transcaucasus Military District in July 1938 and was promoted to general major by June 1941.

From 1941 to 1942, General Tolbukhin performed duties as chief of staff of the **Transcaucasus, Caucasus,** and **Crimean Fronts.** From May through June 1942, he was assigned as Deputy Commander in Chief of the Stalingrad Military District, before it converted to a front organization. In July 1942, Tolbukhin assumed command of the **57th Army** and led it during the defense and counteroffensive at

Stalingrad. In February 1943, he was appointed to be commander of the **68th Army,** then assigned a month later to command the **Southern Front.** From October 1943 to May 1944, he commanded the **4th Ukrainian Front** as Soviet forces inexorably drove Axis forces out of the southern theater of operations. He achieved greatest acclaim, however, as Commander of the **3d Ukrainian Front** from May 1944 to June 1945, leading it from southern Ukraine to Vienna.

Fyodor I. Tolbukhin

Tolbukhin finished the war as one of the Soviet Army's most experienced and respected commanders. He participated in a continuous string of important operations, including the battles of Stalingrad, Donbas, Melitopol, Nikopol-Krivoi Rog, Crimea, Bereznegovatoye-Snigirovka, Odessa, Iassy-Kishinev, Belgrade, Budapest, Lake Balaton, and Vienna.

Following the war's end, Tolbukhin commanded the **Southern Group of Forces** from July 1945 through January 1947, then assumed command of the Transcaucasus Military District. He died on 17 October 1949 and his remains were buried with honors in the Kremlin cemetery. The Bulgarian city of Dobrich was renamed Tolbukhin in his honor.

Nikolai F. Vatutin was born 16 December 1901, the son of peasants in the village of Chepukhino, near Belgorod.

Highest rank achieved: Army General, 1943.

Awarded Hero of the Soviet Union posthumously in 1965.

Nikolai N. Vatutin is considered to be one of the most outstanding Soviet commanders of WWII, a master of operational art of both defensive and offensive operations. He entered the Red Army in

Nikolai F. Vatutin

1920 and fought in the Russian Civil War. He graduated from the Frunze Academy in 1929 and from the General Staff Academy eight years later. He then served on the General Staff from 1937 to 1940, rising to the position of 1st Deputy. By June 1941, he had been promoted to general lieutenant.

Vatutin's initial wartime duties were as chief of staff of the **Northwestern Front,** after which he rejoined the General Staff as 1st Deputy to A. M. Vasilevsky. Antonov replaced him in that post, when Vatutin was briefly named commander of the **Voronezh Front** in October 1942, before assuming command of the **Southwestern Front** from October 1942 to March 1943. As the focus of conflict moved westward after the Battle of Stalingrad, so did Vatutin. He resumed command of the **Voronezh Front** from March to October 1943, followed by command of the **1st Ukrainian Front** from October 1943 to March 1944. As a front commander, he played key roles in the battles of Stalingrad, Kursk, the campaigns to clear the left and right banks of the Dnepr River, the Zhitomir-Berdichev operation, and the Korsun-Shevchenkovskii encirclement. Seriously wounded in February 1944, he died two months later on 15 April and was buried in Kiev. Had he survived, it is likely he would have ascended to the rank of Marshal before the end of the war.

In Soviet military history, Vatutin's name is most associated with Stalingrad, Kursk, Kiev, and the art of large encirclement operations requiring synchronized actions of a group of fronts.

Nikolai N. Voronov (1899–1968)

Highest rank achieved: Chief Marshal of Artillery, 1944

Awarded Hero of the Soviet Union, 1965

Voronov began service in the Red Army in 1918, fought in the Russian Civil War, and spent almost his entire career as an artillery commander, staff officer, and military academician.

A graduate of the Frunze Academy (1930), Voronov participated in the Spanish Civil War (1936–39) and the Soviet Finnish War of 1939–40. From 1937 to 1940, he held the post of Chief of Artillery of the Soviet Army and in 1940 and 1941, Deputy Chief of the Main Artillery Department. By the beginning of WWII, Voronov had reached the rank of general lieutenant, serving as Chief of Strategic Air Defense Forces (PVO Strany). In July 1941, he was again named as Chief of Artillery and appointed a Deputy Commissar of Defense. In March 1943, his position was upgraded to commander in chief of Soviet Artillery.

Nikolai N. Voronov

During the course of the war, in addition to his duties to raise, train, and equip Soviet artillery forces, Voronov often was dispatched as a *Stavka* representative to key combat zones, and in that role, participated in the planning and direction of large operations on many fronts, including "exceptional direction" with A. M. Vasilevsky, of the reduction of German forces caught within the Stalingrad encirclement. He is credited with working out the military art of the employment of artillery in offensive campaigns in order to achieve tactical and operational penetrations and in support of mechanized and tank formations committed to exploitation. Soviet military histories also praise him for the design and organization of the large artillery formations that came to characterize Soviet offensives and sieges in the long Soviet drive to Berlin.

After the war, Voronov retained his position as Chief of Artillery and later became president of the Academy of Artillery Sciences and Head of the Academy for Artillery Command.

He retired from active service in 1958.

Kliment Ye. Voroshilov was born 4 February 1881, the son of a railroad worker in the village of Verkhneye, near Dnepropetrovosk.

Highest rank achieved: Marshal of the Soviet Union, 1935

Twice awarded Hero of the Soviet Union, both after WWII (1956, 1968)

Kliment Voroshilov was one of the most enduring active military and political figures in the first 40 years of the existence of the Soviet Union — an adroit political survivor, who, although closely associated with Stalin, remained active in the party even after Stalin's death. A member of the Communist Party since 1903, he participated in both the October Revolution and the Russian Civil War, having joined the Red Army in 1918. Recognized as one the primary organizers of the Red Army, Voroshilov served as Commissar of Military and Naval Affairs and Chairman of the Revolutionary Military Council (1925–35) and as Minister of Defense (1934–40). Among the first five Army officers promoted to marshal in the mid-1930s, Voroshilov headed the Soviet delegation in the pre-war military negotiations with Great Britain and France to coordinate possible military action against Hitler.

Kliment Ye. Voroshilov

Although a member of the *Stavka* and Supreme High Command from 1941 through 1944, Marshal Voroshilov fell short of expectatons as an operational commander. During the first months of Operation BARBAROSSA, he commanded the **Northwestern Direction** (10 July–27 August 41), then assumed command of the **Leningrad Front** for only one week, supposedly requesting to be relieved. Voroshilov's poor performance as **Northwestern Direction** and **Leningrad Front** commander (and age) conspired to eliminate him from further consideration for command of large formations during the remainder of the war.

Like Budyonny, the higher demands and more sophisticated methods of warfare of WWII clearly exceeded his capabilities. Nevertheless, he remained a member of the *Stavka* and was occasionally employed after 1943 as a *Stavka* representative to fronts preparing for major operations. He also is identified as the commander-in-chief of the partisan movement.

In January 1943, Voroshilov coordinated the actions of the **Leningrad** and **Volkhov Fronts** (in concert with Zhukov) to relieve the siege of Leningrad. At the end of that year, he helped developed plans for the liberation of the Crimea. As a member of Stalin's inner circle, Voroshilov participated in the Moscow Conference of 1941 and the Teheran Conference of 1943.

After the war, Marshal Voroshilov acted as Chairman of the United Control Commission in Hungary (1945–47). A member of the Politboro for 35 years (1926–60), he was named Chairman of the Presidium of the Supreme Soviet from 1953–60. He passed away 2 December 1969 and was interred in the Kremlin wall.

Andrei I. Yeremenko was born 14 October 1892, the son of peasants who were from a village near what is today the city of Luhansk, Ukraine.

Highest rank achieved: Marshal of the Soviet Union, 1955.

Awarded Hero of the Soviet Union in 1944.

Yeremenko fought in the Tsarist Army during WWI, joined the Red Army in 1918, and then fought in the Russian Civil War as the chief of staff of a cavalry regiment and brigade. He completed the Higher Cavalry School in 1923 and the Frunze Academy in 1935. Yeremenko accumulated significant command experience during the inter-war years, successively commanding cavalry units from regimental to corps size. His development culminated with the command of one of the early Soviet mechanized corps and the **1st Red Banner Army.** By June 1941, had risen to general lieutenant.

General Yeremenko's initial wartime assignment was as Deputy commander in chief of the **Western Front** (July 1941), but he was quickly shifted to command of the **Briansk Front** from August to October of that year. Wounded during the Battle of Smolensk, Yeremenko led a staunch defense of the city which slowed the advance of the German *Army Group Center* toward Moscow and provided the Supreme High Command extra time to organize and deploy reserve forces to strengthen the defense of the approaches to Moscow.

From December 1941 through February 1942, Yeremenko was appointed to command of the newly formed **4th Shock Army.** Subsequently, he commanded the **Southeastern Front** (August 1942) before assuming command of the **Stalingrad Front** (late September–December 1942), retaining command when it was reformed as the **Southern Front** (January–February 1943).

Later, he moved north to take charge of the **Kalinin Front** (April–October 1943), and the **1st Baltic Front** (October–November 1943). In early 1944, Yeremenko returned to southern Russia in command of the **Separate Maritime (Morskaya) Army** during the liberation of the Crimea. After a few months, Yeremenko again moved north to command the **2d Baltic Front** (April 1944–February 1945). After March 1945, he served as commander in chief of the **4th Ukrainian Front.**

According to Marshal Vasilevsky's memoirs, Yeremenko's success as a defensive commander before Moscow and at Stalingrad earned Stalin's respect and the sobriquet "general of defense."

After the war, General Yeremenko commanded a series of military districts, including the Carpathian, Western Siberia, and North Caucasus. He retired in 1958 and was buried in the Kremlin wall upon his death on 19 November 1970.

Matvei V. Zakharov was born 17 August 1899, the son of peasants in the village of Voylovo, near Kalinin.

Highest rank achieved: Marshal of the Soviet Union, 1959.

Twice awarded the Hero of the Soviet Union (1945, 1971)

Matvei Zakharov got an early start to life in the Army, fighting in the Tsarist Army in WWI and being among the first to join the Red Army in 1918. His revolutionary credentials were bolstered by his participation in the storming of the Winter Palace in 1917. During the Civil War, he commanded an artillery battery and battalion and served as assistant chief of staff of a rifle brigade and division.

Like A. A. Antonov, Zakharov made his name in the Soviet Army as a superb senior staff officer. He graduated from Frunze in 1933, followed by the General Staff Academy in 1937. By 1940, Zakharov was assigned as Chief of Staff of the **12th Army,** then of the Odessa Military District.

Zakharov began the war in the rank of general major, posted as Chief of Staff of **9th Army,** but quickly assumed the same position on the command staff of the **Northwestern Direction** under

Voroshilov. From August through December 1941, he served as Deputy Chief of the Main Department of Rear Services of the Soviet Army.

He returned to front-line duty in January 1942 as chief of staff of a series of fronts, including: **Kalinin Front** (January 1942–April 1943), **Reserve and Steppe Front** (April–October 1943), and **2d Ukrainian Front** (1943–1945). In 1945, he participated in the Manchurian Offensive as Chief of Staff of the **Transbaikal Front** with responsibilities as chief planner and organizer of the front's deep operations from Xingan to Mukden.

In his various positions as a front chief of staff, General Zakharov played a key role in the planning, preparation, and conduct of many important operations and campaigns including: the defense of Moscow; large offensive campaigns at Belgorod-Kharkov, Kirovograd, Korsun-Shevchenkovskii, Uman-Botashanskii, Yassi-Kishinev; and the liberation of Budapest, Vienna, and Prague.

After the war, Zakharov served as Head of the General Staff Academy (1945–49 and 1963–64) and Deputy Chief of the General Staff (1949–52). Next, he was appointed commander in chief of the Leningrad Military District, then named commander in chief of the **Group of Soviet Forces** in Germany from 1957–60. He twice served as Chief of the General Staff and 1st Deputy Minister of Defense (1960–63 and 1964–71), spending nearly ten years in that critically important position. He died in 1972.

Other Important Senior Soviet General Officers

Khorlogiin Choibalsan (1895–1952)

Highest rank achieved: Marshal of the Mongolian People's Republic, 1936

Twice awarded Hero of the Mongolian People's Republic (1941, 1945)

Although a chief military and political actor in the Mongolian's People Republic, Choibalsan's fortunes and activities were closely connected to the Soviet Army. He served as commander in chief of Mongolian Army from 1924–28 and was named Prime Minister in 1939.

During the pre-war Battle of Khalgin-Gol, Choibalsan commanded the Mongolian contingent under Zhukov's overall direction. Then, in 1945, he commanded the combined Soviet-Mongolian cavalry mechanized group that formed the southern arm of the **Transbaikal Front.**

Alexander Ye. Golovanov was born on 2 July 1904.

Highest rank achieved: Chief Marshal of Aviation, 1944

A Red Army member since 1919 and veteran of the Russian Civil War, Golovanov completed pilot training in 1932 and participated in battles at Khalkin-Gol (1930) against the Japanese, and in the Soviet-Finnish War. During WWII, he initially commanded a long-range bomber regiment and division. From 1942 to 1944, he was in charge of all long-range Soviet aviation, then commanded the **18th Army** after December 1944, executing the bombardments of Königsberg, Danzig, and Berlin. After the war, he resumed command of Soviet long-range aviation. Golovanov died in 1975.

Ivan I. Maslennikov was born on 16 September 1900.

Highest rank achieved: Army General, 1944

Awarded Hero of the Soviet Union, 1945

A Red Army member beginning 1918, and 1935 graduate of the Frunze Academy, Maslennikov's service between the wars included postings within the NKVD and Soviet Internal Troops. During WWII, he commanded the **29th, 39th, 8th Guards,** and **42d Armies,** the **North Caucasus Front** (January–May 1943), served as deputy commander of a series of fronts (**Volkov, Southwestern,** and **3d Ukrainian**), and culminated his wartime duty as commander of the **3d Baltic Front** (April-October 1944). In 1945, he served as Deputy commander in chief to Vasilevsky of Soviet forces in the Far East.

In 1953, Maslennikov committed suicide after being arrested on suspicion of collaborating with Beria, who had been arrested three months earlier.

Alexander A. Novikov (1900–1976)

Highest rank achieved: Chief Marshal of Aviation, 1944.

Twice awarded Hero of the Soviet Union in 1944.

Novikov joined the Red Army in 1919, completed the Vystrel (1922) and Frunze Academies (1930), and served as Chief of Staff of Aviation for the **Northwestern Front** during the Soviet-Finnish War. By June 1941, he held the rank of general major of aviation.

During the first year of the war, General Novikov commanded the air forces of the **Northern** and **Leningrad Fronts,** then was named as Commander of the Air Forces of the Soviet Army, a position which he held through the rest of the war. Novikov also commanded the air forces that supported the Manchurian Campaign. He often acted as a *Stavka* representative to plan and coordinate the participation of Soviet air armies in multi-front operations and held parallel responsbilites to raise, equip, and train new aviation units for the war.

After the war, like his naval counterpart Admiral Kuznetsov, Marshal Novikov assumed positions of lower responsibility, then resumed command of all Soviet Air Forces (1954–55) after Stalin's death.

Issa A. Pliyev (1903–1979)

Highest rank achieved: Army General, 1962.

Twice awarded Hero of the Soviet Union (1944, 1945)

Pliyev joined the Red Army cavalry in 1922, completed the Frunze Academy in 1933, and the General Staff Academy in 1941. He spent much of his service during the inter-war period as a cavalry officer, commander, and staff officer in the Mongolian People's Republic, rising to the rank of colonel by June 1941.

During the war, he commanded the **50th Cavalry Division** (reconstituted and renamed **3d Guards** in late 1941). From December 1941 to 1944, he commanded various cavalry corps, including **3d Guards Cavalry Corps.** Pliyev culminated his wartime service commanding a combined cavalry-mechanized group that participated in many of the large encirclement operations of that timeframe, perhaps most notably the Korsun-Shevchenkovskii operation, known in German sources as the Cherkassy Pocket, where the fighting to break out of the trap was particularly vicious. Overall, he commanded cavalry units on the **Southern, Southwestern, Steppe, 3d Ukrainian, 1st Belorussian,** and **Transbaikal Fronts.**

Max A. Reiter (1886–1950)

Highest rank achieved: General Colonel, 1943

A member of the Red Army since 1919, Reiter completed the Frunze Academy in 1935. Initially during the war, as a general major, he served as chief of logistics for the **Central** and **Briansk Fronts.** In March 1942, he assumed command of the **20th Army,** then served as a front commander of the **Briansk** (September 1942) and **Reserve** (March 1943) **Fronts,** followed by the Steppe Military District (June 1943), and the **Voronezh Fronts** (as deputy commander). From late 1943 to the end of the war, he commanded military districts to the rear of the fighting fronts.

Pavel S. Rybalko (1892–1948)

Highest rank achieved: Marshal of Tank Forces, 1945

Twice awarded Hero the Soviet Union (1943, 1945)

Rybalko was one of the great Soviet tank commanders of WWII, often found in the forefront of deep penetration and exploitation operations. A 1934 Frunze Academy graduate, Rybalko served as a cavalry commander in both the Civil War and the inter-war period and served as a military attaché to Poland and China (1937–40). During the war, he initially served as deputy commander of the **5th Tank Army.** Beginning in July 42, he commanded a series of tank armies, including the **5th, 3d,** and **3d Guards.** After the war, he was appointed as Commander of Soviet Tank and Mechanized Forces.

Mikhail S. Shumilov (1895–1975)

Highest rank achieved: General Colonel, 1943

Hero of the Soviet Union, 1943

Shumilov served as a corps commander during the Soviet-Finnish War, then moved to Army-level command for most of WWII. Appointed as commander of the **64th Army** in August 1942, Shumilov achieved long-term fame as one of the two great defenders of Stalingrad, the other being V. I. Chuikov of the **62d Army.** Subsequently, Shumilov commanded the **7th Guards Army** (formerly **64th**) and led it in across the western USSR to Germany. He retired in 1958 and was buried on his death in 1975 alongside Chuikov on Mamayev-Kurgan in Volgograd (formerly Stalingrad).

Georgii F. Zahkarov was born 5 May 1897, the son of peasants in a village near Saratov.

Highest rank achieved: Army General, 1944

A veteran of the Russian Civil War, Zakharov joined the Red Army in 1919, and completed the Vystrel Academy in 1923, the

Frunze Academy in 1933, and the General Staff Academy in 1939. By June 1941, he had risen to the rank of general major.

Zakharov spent most of the war as a front chief of staff, Army commander, deputy front commander, and front commander, moving frequently between the different levels. At various intervals from 1943 to 1945, he commanded the **51st, 2d Guards,** and **4th Guards Army.** He had a brief stint in command of the **Briansk Front** in October–November 1941, but spent June–November 1944 in command of the **2d Belorussian Front** and participated in the Belorussian Campaign of the summer of 1944. Zakharov served out the war as deputy commander of the **4th Ukrainian Front.** He died 26 January 1957 in Moscow.

German and Their Allies' Units on the Eastern Front

Army Groups

uArmy Group A

1939	Formed in West
1940	Offensive opns in France; designated High Command, West
Apr 41	Relocated to East; for deception purposes redesignated Staff "Winter," then "Schliessen"
Jun 41	Converted to Army Group South; split into Army Group B (Stalingrad drive) and Army Group A (Caucasas area)
Jun 41–Apr 44	Opns in Caucasus, Crimea, southern Ukraine
Apr 44	Redesignated Army Group South Ukraine
Sep 44	Absorbed Army Group North Ukraine
Sep 44–Feb 45	Opns in southern Poland and Carpathians; conducted breakout from Baranow bridgehead; withdrew across southern Poland to Slovakia and Silesia
Feb 45	Redesignated Army Group Center

Commanders

Gen.Feldm. von Rundstedt, Sep 39
Gen.Feldm. List, May 42
Adolf Hitler, Oct 42 (part-time)
Gen.Feldm. von Kleist, Nov 42
Gen.Oberst Harpe, Jul 44
Gen.Feldm. Schörner, Jan–May 45

Army Group B

Oct 39	Controlled armies in the northern section of Western Front during the attack through Holland and Belgium; seized Paris and drove to Spanish border
Oct 40	Transferred to Prussia and Poland
Jun 41	Converted to Army Group Center
Jun 42	Reformed at the start of the German offensive to

control the seven armies advancing into the region between Stalingrad and Kursk

Spring 43 Replaced by Army Group South after the retreat beyond Rostov; designation transferred to HQ in northern Italy

Nov 43– Renamed Army Group C
Apr 45   in Italy; later reestablished in France and renamed Army Group B, Rommel's HQ; charged with defense of the Atlantic coast of France. Participated in defensive opns in France, controlling the Ardennes offensive. In early 1945, it was responsible under Army Group D for the sector from the Moselle River to north of Aachen

Apr 45   Destroyed in the Ruhr Pocket

Commanders
Gen.Feldm. von Bock, Sep 39
Gen.Feldm. *Freiherr* von Weichs, Jul 42
Gen.Feldm. Rommel, Jul 43
Gen.Feldm. von Kluge, Jul 44
Gen.Feldm. Model, Aug 44

Army Group C

Aug 39   Controlled Western Front units during the invasion of Poland and southern flank armies during the invasion of France

Apr 41   Transferred to the Eastern Front as "Staff East Prussia"

Jun 41   Redesignated Army Group North

Nov 43   Reformed as Kesselring's HQ to control all forces in Italy; also known as "High Command Southwest"

Commanders
Gen.Feldm. *Ritter* von Leeb, Aug 39
Gen.Feldm. Kesselring, Nov 43
Gen.Oberst von Vietinghoff, Mar 45

Army Group Center

Jun 41   Formed for BARBAROSSA to control the armies charged with capturing Moscow

Nov 41   Defensive opns

Jul 43   Controlled Operation *ZITADELLE* vic. Kursk

Jul 44   Nearly destroyed by the Soviet summer offensive in the withdrawal from the Vitebsk-Mogilev area

Late sum- Defensive opns in East
mer 44–   Prussia and Warsaw
Jan 45   areas

Jan 45   Redesignted Army Group North

Commanders
Gen.Feldm. von Kluge, Jun 41
Gen.Feldm. Busch, Oct 43
Gen.Feldm. Model, Jun 44
Gen.Oberst Reinhardt, Aug 44

Army Group Don

Nov 42   Formed from the 11th Army, charged with the defense of the southern front between Army Groups A and B. Originally intended to be a Romanian command under Antonescu. With the loss of Army Group B, it was redesignated Army Group South

Commander
Gen.Feldm. von Manstein, Nov 42– Feb 43

Army Group E

42–43   Formed in the Balkans by expansion of the 12th Army to control German and Bulgarian units in the Aegean area

Jan–　　Designated High Com
　Aug 43　mand Southeast
Sep 43　Subordinated to Army
　　　　Group F
Late 44　Withdrew from southern
　　　　Balkans; extended its con-
　　　　trol north to vic. between
　　　　Drava and Sava Rivers
Mar 45　Removed from subordina-
　　　　tion to Army Group F
Apr 45　Redesignated High Com-
　　　　mand Southeast
Commander
Gen.Oberst Lohr, Dec 42–May 45

Army Group F

Summer 43 Formed to control German
　　　　operational and occupa-
　　　　tional forces in the Bal-
　　　　kans; also carried the title
　　　　High Command Southeast
Late 44　During the withdrawal
　　　　from the Balkans, subordi-
　　　　nate units were transferred
　　　　to Army Group E (which
　　　　had been subordinated to
　　　　Army Group F, but was
　　　　considered disbanded)
Commander
Gen.Feldm. *Freiherr* von Weichs,
　Jul 43–Mar 45

Army Group Kurland

Jan–　　Formed as Army Group
　May 45　Kurland from Army
　　　　Group North after the
　　　　withdrawal from the
　　　　Leningrad-Lake Ilmen
　　　　areas to the Narva River-
　　　　Lake Peipus line. With-
　　　　drew to the Latvian coast
Commanders
Gen.Oberst von Vietinghoff, Jan 45
Gen.Oberst Dr. Rendulic, Mar 45
Gen.Oberst Hilpert, Apr 45

Army Group North

Sep 39　Formed in preparation of
　　　　the invasion of Poland,

but redesignated as Army
Group B
Jun 41　Reestablished in prepara-
　　　　tion for invasion of Russia
　　　　by redesignation of Army
　　　　Group C; controlled 16th
　　　　and 18th Armies
Jan 45　Redesignated Army
　　　　Group Kurland, where-
　　　　upon Army Group Center
　　　　was redesignated Army
　　　　Group North
Apr 45　Disbanded; staff used to
　　　　form 12th Army Staff
Commanders
Gen.Feldm. von Bock, 1939
Gen.Feldm. *Ritter* von Leeb,
　Jun 41
Gen.d.Art. von Küchler, Jan 42
Gen.Feldm. Model, Jan 44
Gen.Oberst Lindemann, Apr 44
Gen.Oberst Friessner, Jul 44
Gen.Feldm. Schörner, Jul 44
Gen.Oberst Dr. Rendulic, Jan 45
Gen.Oberst Weiss, Mar 45

Army Group North Ukraine

Mar 44　Formed by redesignation
　　　　of Army Group South;
　　　　charged with defense of
　　　　eastern Galicia and north-
　　　　ern Carpathians
Sep 44　Redesignated Army
　　　　Group A
Commanders
Gen.Feldm. Model, Apr 44
Gen.Oberst Harpe, Jun 44

Army Group South

Sep 39　Formed for invasion of
　　　　Poland
1940　Redesignated Army
　　　　Group A for invasion of
　　　　Western Europe
1941　Reformed for invasion of
　　　　Russia by redesignating
　　　　Army Group A; controlled
　　　　6th, 11th, 17th, and 1st
　　　　Panzer Armies

Jul 42	Formed Army Groups A and B	Gen.Feldm. von Bock, Jan 42
Feb 43	Reestablished by redesig- nating Army Group Don	Gen.Feldm. von Manstein, Nov 42
Mar 44	Redesignated as Army Group North Ukraine by converting Army Group South Ukraine; charged with defense of Hungary	Gen.Oberst Friessner, Sep 44 Gen.d.Inf. Wöhler, Dec 44
1945	Renamed Army Group Ostmark in the last weeks of the war	

Commanders

Gen.Feldm. von Rundstedt, 1939
Gen.Feldm. von Reichenau, Dec 41

Army Group South Ukraine

Mar 44	Converted from Army Group A; nearly destroyed in Romania by Sep 44; remnants absorbed by Army Group South

Commanders

Gen.Feldm. Schörner, Mar 44
Gen.Oberst Friessner, Aug 44

Armies

2d Army

39–40	Campaigns in Poland, the West and the Balkans
1941	Employed on the Eastern Front
Jul 41	Covered the southern flank of the central sector; with- drew through the Pripet Marshes during the Soviet Summer Offensive
Fall 44	On the Narev Line, north of Warsaw
Apr 45	Redesignated Army East Prussia

Commanders

Gen.Feldm. *Freiherr* von Weichs, Oct 39
Gen.Oberst von Salmuth, Jul 42
Gen.Oberst Weiss, Feb 43
Gen.d.Pz.Tr. von Saucken, Mar 45

3d Army

1939	Took part in the Polish campaign, then disbanded in Oct; most of the staff used to form the 16th Army

Commander

Gen. von Küchler, Sep 39

4th Army

39–40	Took part in campaigns in Poland and in the West
Jun 41	On the central sector of the Eastern Front
Jul 44	Withdrew from the upper Dnepr to the East Prussian frontier
Fall 44	Heavily engaged in defense of East Prussia
Apr 45	Destroyed in north Prussia

Commanders

GenFeldm. von Kluge, Sep 39
Gen.d.Geb. Kübler, Dec 41
Gen.Oberst Heinrici, Jan 42
Gen.d.Inf. Hossbach, Jul 44
Gen.d.Inf. Müller, Feb 45

6th Army

Oct 39–40	Campaign in the West
Jun 41	Southern sector of Eastern Front; engaged at Kiev, Kharkov, and Stalingrad
Jan 43	Destroyed at Stalingrad
Spring 43	Reformed in southern Russia

Mar 44	Suffered heavy losses in withdrawal from the lower Dnepr River bend
Aug 44	Encircled and virtually destroyed; withdrew from lower Dnester River sector as a combat group
Late 44–45	Rebuilt largely with Hungarian units; fought defensive battles in Romania and Hungary; responsible for defense of Budapest; withdrew to East Alps, south of Danube River

Commanders

Gen.Feldm. von Reichenau, Oct 39
Gen.Feldm. Paulus, Jan 42
Gen.Oberst Hollidt, Mar 43
Gen.d.Art. de Angelis, Apr 44
Gen.d.Art. Fretter-Pico, Jul 44
Gen.d.Pz.Tr. Balck, Dec 44

8th Army

1939	Took part in the campaign in Poland, then disbanded
Jul 43	Reformed and employed on the Eastern Front, southern sector
Feb 44	Heavy losses in encirclement of major forces at Korsun, west of lower Dnepr River
Mar 44	Withdrew to the eastern Carpathians and lower Dnester River sector
Aug 44	Withdrew through the Carpathian passes and Transylvania
Late 44	Hungarian sector, northern flank

Commanders

Gen.Oberst Blaskowitz, Sep 39
Gen.d.Inf. Wöhler, Aug 43
Gen.d.Geb. Kreysing, Dec 44

9th Army

| Spring 40 | Campaign in the West |
| Jun 41 | Eastern Front, central sector |

Jul 41	Withdrew from upper Dnepr River sector
Fall 44	Reponsible for the defense of Warsaw
Jan 45	Withdrew from Warsaw area and across central Poland along the Lodz-Posen-Berlin axis

Commanders

Gen.Oberst Strauss, May 40; Jun 40
Gen.Oberst Blaskowitz, May 40
Gen.Feldm. Model, Jan 42
Gen.Oberst von Vietinghoff, May 43
Gen.Feldm. Model, Aug 44
Gen.Oberst Harpe, Nov 43
Gen.d.Pz.Tr. von Vormann, Jun 44
Gen.d.Pz.Tr. *Freiherr* von Lüttwitz, Sep 44
Gen.d.Inf. Busse, Jan 45

11th Army

Late 40	Probable date of formation
Jun 41	Southern sector of the Eastern Front
1942	Successful assault on Sevastopol; moved to the northern sector and disbanded, staff used to form Army Group Don
Jan 45	Rebuilt as an SS unit under Army Group Vistula
Apr 45	Transferred to the West; surrendered

Commanders

Gen.Oberst *Ritter* von Schobert, Oct 40
Gen.Feldm. von Manstein, Sep 41
SS-Ogruf Steiner, Jan 45
Gen.d.Art. Lucht, Mar 45

12th Army

Oct 39	Formed
1940	Campaign in the West and in the Balkans, where it remained
Winter 42–43	Expanded to Army Group E
Apr 45	Rebuilt from the staff of the former Army Group

North and with newly-forming units; main mission was to break through to Berlin

Commanders

Gen.Feldm. List, Oct 39
Gen.d.Pz.Tr. Wenck, Apr 45

16th Army

Oct 39	Formed
1940	Campaign in the West
Jun 41	On the northern sector of the Eastern Front
Feb 44	Withdrew from vic. Lake Ilmen to Pskov
Summer 44	Heavily engaged in defensive battles during the withdrawal to Riga
Oct 44	Responsible for the Riga bridgehead; withdrew to the Latvian coast

Commanders

Gen.Feldm. Busch, Oct 39
Gen.d.Art. Hansen, Oct 43
Gen.d.Inf. Laux, Jun 44
Gen.Oberst Hilpert, Sep 44
Gen.d.Inf. von Krosigk, Mar 45
Gen.d.Geb. von Kirchensittenbach, Mar 45

17th Army

Dec 40	Formed
Jun 41	On the southern sector of the Eastern Front
Late 43	Withdrew to the Crimea
Apr 44	Evacuated from the Crimea
Sep 44	Defensive opns vic. Cracow

Commanders

Gen.d.Inf. von Stülpnagel, Dec 40
Gen.Oberst Hoth, Oct 41
Gen.Oberst Ruoff, Jun 42
Gen.Oberst Jaenecke, Jun 43
Gen.d.Inf. Almendinger, May 44
Gen.d.Inf. Schulz, Jul 44
Gen.d.Inf. Hasse, Apr 45

18th Army

Spring 39	Formed
1940	Campaign in the West
Jun 41	On the northern sector of the Eastern Front
Jan 44	Withdrew from the Leningrad area to the Narva River; on the Lake Peipus line
Fall 44	Withdrew from the Narva bridgehead through Estonia to the Latvian coast

Commanders

Gen.d.Art. von Küchler, Nov 39
Gen.Oberst Lindemann, Jan 42
Gen.d.Art. Loch, Mar 44
Gen.d.Inf. Boege, Sep 44

20th Army

Winter 41–42	Formed in northern Finland to control opns on the Murmansk sector; referred to as a Mountain Army and, until summer 1942, as the Army of Lapland
Fall 44	Withdrew from northern Finland to Norway
Late 44	Absorbed 21st Army; redesignated High Command, Norway
Spring 45	Reappeared in East Prussia in the last weeks of the war

Commanders

Gen.Oberst Dietl, Jan 42
Gen.Oberst Dr. Rendulic, Jun 44
Gen.d.Geb. Böhme, Jan 45

21st Army "Norway"

1939	Formed as XXI Infantry Corps, and took part in the campaign in Poland as such; as "Group XXI," it organized the conquest of Norway
Summer 41	Expanded to army; controlled occupation forces in Norway; responsible for

German opns in Finland
until the formation of the
20th Army

Late 44   Absorbed by 20th Army
               after the withdrawal
               through Finland to
               Norway

Commander

Gen.Oberst von Falkenhorst, Dec 40–
   Dec 44

1st Panzer Army

Summer 39 Formed as XXII Infantry
               Corps and took part in the
               Polish campaign; fought in
               the West as Group Kleist
               and in the Balkans as 1st
               Panzer Group

Summer 41 Fought in the East,
               assigned to Army Group
               South

Late 41   Redesignated 1st Panzer
               Army

Early 44   Moved from the lower
               Dnepr River bend to the
               northern Ukraine

Feb–   Withdrew through the
   Mar 44   Ukraine, then to southern
               Poland and Slovakia

Commanders

Gen.Feldm. von Kleist, Nov 40
Gen.Oberst von Mackensen, Nov 42
Gen.Oberst von Hube, Oct 43
Gen.Oberst Raus, Apr 44
Gen.Oberst Heinrici, Aug 44
Gen.d.Pz.Tr. Nehring, Mar 45

2d Panzer Army

May 39   Formed as XIX Motorized
               Corps and took part as
               such in the Polish cam-
               paign; fought in the West
               as Group Guderian

Summer 41 Fought in the East as 2d
               Panzer Group, assigned to
               Army Group Center

Late 41   Redesignated 2d Panzer
               Army on the central sector
               of the Eastern Front

Late 43   Transferred to the Balkans
               for counter-guerilla opns

Dec 44   Engaged vic. Brod (eastern
               Croatia), and subsequently
               against the Soviets in
               southern Hungary

Commanders

Gen.Oberst Guderian, Nov 40
Gen.Oberst Schmidt, Dec 41
Gen.Feldm. Model, Jul 43
Gen.Oberst Dr. Rendulic, Aug 43
Gen.d.Geb. Böhme, Jun 44
Gen.d.Art. de Angelis, Jul 44

3d Panzer Army

1937   Formed at Jena as XV
               Corps to control the three
               original motorized light
               divisions

39–40   Fought in Poland as XV
               Corps and in the West as
               Group Hoth

Summer 41 Fought in East as 3d Pan-
               zer Group, part of Army
               Group Center

Late 41   Redesignated 3d Panzer
               Army

Jul 44   Responsible for the
               defense of Vitebsk; with-
               drew during Soviet sum-
               mer offensive

Oct 44   Responsible for the
               defense of the northern
               frontier of East Prussia

Commanders

Gen.Oberst Hoth, Nov 40
Gen.Oberst Reinhardt, Nov 41
Gen.Oberst Raus, Aug 44
Gen.d.Pz.Tr. Hasso von Manteuffel,
   Mar 45

4th Panzer Army

1937   Formed in Berlin as XVI
               Corps to control the active
               panzer divisions

39–40   Fought in Poland and in
               the West

Summer 41 Offensive opns in the East
               as 4th Panzer Group,

	assigned to Army Group North
Late 41	Redesignated 4th Panzer Army, assigned to Army Group Center
Summer 42	Transferred to the southern sector of the Eastern Front and heavily engaged at Stalingrad
Fall 43	Heavily engaged in defensive and offensive opns west of Kiev
Early 44	Withdrew across northern Ukraine

Jul 44	Withdrew to defensive positions along the Vistula River
Jan 45	Withdrew from the Vistula across Poland to Upper Silesia

Commanders

Gen.Oberst Hoeppner, Feb 41
Gen.Oberst Ruoff, Jan 42
Gen.Oberst Hoth, Jun 42
Gen.Oberst Raus, Nov 43
Gen.Oberst Josef Harpe, May 44
Gen.d.Pz.Tr. Balck, Jun 44
Gen.d.Pz.Tr. Gräser, Oct 44

Corps

Cavalry Corps

I Corps

Summer 1944	Southern sector
Nov 44	East Prussia
Jan 45	Hungary
May 45	Austria

Infantry Corps

I Corps

1941	Northern sector, vic. Lake Ilmen
1945	Defensive opns in Latvia

II Corps

41–44	Northern sector
1944	Narva Bridgehead

V Corps

41–44	Southern sector; also Crimea area

VI Corps

Early 44	Southern sector
Aug 44	To East Prussia

VII Corps

Early 44	Southern sector
Jan 45	Central sector
Mar 45	Danzig Pocket

VIII Corps

41–43	Southern sector; destroyed at Stalingrad
43–45	Rebuilt; fought in central and southern sectors; defensive opns in Silesia

IX Corps

41–44	Southern and Central sectors

X Corps

41–45	Northern sector; ended at Kurland

XI Corps

41–43	Southern sector; destroyed at Stalingrad
Summer 43	Reformed in Southern sector
1944	Korsun Pocket/Dnepr
1945	Ended at Olmütz

XII Corps

1944	Central sector
Jul 44	Destroyed at Minsk
Apr 45	Reformed in Germany

XIII Corps

Early 44	Southern sector; destroyed in Soviet summer offensive

XVII Corps

1944	Southern sector
Dec 44	Moved west and ended in Silesia

XX Corps

41–44	Central sector; ended war in East Prussia

XXIII Corps

Early 44	Central sector
1945	Retrograde through Poland; ended at Danzig

XXVI Corps

41–43	North sector
Post-Aug 44	Central sector

XXVII Corps

41–late 44	Central sector; heavy losses at Minsk Jul 44
1945	Ended at Danzig

XXVIII Corps

1941	Northern sector; vic. Memel
1944	Samland at end

XXIX Corps

Early 44	Southern sector
Oct 44	Ended at Olmütz

XXXIV Corps

41–42	Central sector; disbanded Feb 42
1944	Balkans; retreat to Croatia at end

XXXV Corps

41–44	Central sector; destroyed at Bobruisk
Jul 44	Disbanded

XXXVI Corps

41–Dec 44	Arctic sector, vic. Kiestinki-Louhi

XLII Corps

Early 44	Southern sector; destroyed at Cherkassy
1945	Reformed; destroyed at Baranow, Poland

XLIII Corps

Early 44	Central sector; evacuated 45 through Baltics to East Prussia

XLIV Corps

Early 44	Southern sector; heavy losses at the lower Dniestr
Aug 44	Disbanded

L Corps

Early 44	Northern sector; in Latvia at end

LII Corps

Early 44	South sector; suffered heavy losses at Dniestr Mar 44; withdrawal; destroyed near Kishniev

LIII Corps

Early 44	Central sector; destroyed at Vitebsk offensive
1944	Reformed for last duty in the West

LIV Corps

Early 44	Northern sector

LV Corps

Early 44	Central sector; in East Prussia at end

LIX Corps

Early 44	Southern sector; commended Mar 44; end at Olmütz

LXVIII Corps

Late 44	Hungary sector opns

LXXII Corps

1944	Southern sector; Romania/Hungary

Mountain Corps

XVIII Corps

Fall 44	Northern sector; Samland; end in Danzig Pocket

XIX Corps

43–44	Arctic sector, vic. Murmansk

XXII Corps

Dec 44	Central sector; Hungary and withdrawal to Austria at end

XLIX Corps

Early–Dec 44	Southern sector; ended at Olmütz

LI Corps

41–43	Southern sector; destroyed at Stalingrad; rebuilt; ended war in Italy

Panzer Corps

III Corps

41–44	Southern sector
44–45	Hungary to Austria at end

IV Corps

1942	Southern sector; virtually destroyed at Stalingrad

1944	Heavy losses on lower Dnepr
1945	Retrograde to Austria via Hungary and Slovakia

XIV Corps

41–42	Southern sector; destroyed at Stalingrad
Summer 42	Reformed in Sicily

XXIV Corps

Early 44	Southern sector; Moved to Brünn at end

XXXIX Corps

41–44	Southern sector; Jul 44 suffered heavy losses at Minsk; retrograde through Baltics to West
1945	Returned to Eastern Front; ended in Silesia/Elbe areas

XL Corps

Early 44	Southern sector; retrograde through Poland

XLI Corps

Early 44	Central sector; destroyed at Bobruisk
Late 44	Reformed; final action in East Prussia (Heiligenbeil Pocket)

XLVI Corps

Early 44	Central sector
Jan 45	Heavy engagement in Silesia

XLVII Corps

Early 44	Southern sector
Jun 44	Transferred to West

XLVIII Corps

Early 44	Southern sector; transferred to Central sector
Sep 44	Retrograde through Poland

LVII Corps

Jun 41–Jun 42	Central sector
Jul 42	Southern sector
late 44	Hungary/Budapest area

Waffen-SS Corps

I SS-Panzer Corps
Leibstandarte Adolf Hitler

Oct–Nov 43	Corps staff formed in Italy
Jun–Sep 44	Assumed control of 1st and 12th SS-Panzer Divisions and conducted offensive, defensive, and retrograde opns in Normandy; conducted retrograde opns across northern France and Belgium
Dec 44–Jan 45	Offensive opns in the Ardennes; subsequent defensive opns in Belgium
Feb 45	Conducted the *SÜDWIND* offensive agaisnt the Gran bridgehead in Hungary
Mar 45	Participated in the *FRÜHLINGSERWACHEN* offensive south of Budapest
Mar–May 45	Retrograde opns through Hungary into Austria; surrendered to American forces vic. Steyr

Commanders

SS-Oberstgruf. und Panzergeneraloberst der W-SS Dietrich, Jul 43–Aug 44

SS-Brif. und Gen.Major d.W-SS und Oberst i.G. Kraemer, Aug 44

SS-Ogruf. und Gen.d.W-SS Keppler, Aug–Oct 44

SS-Gruf. und Gen.Lt.d.W-SS Priess, Oct 44–May 45

II SS-Panzer Corps

Sep 42	Began as Headquarters, SS-Panzer Corps, to control the first three *Waffen-SS* divisions
Feb–Mar 43	Defensive opns vic. Kharkov; subsequently conducted retrograde opns to the southwest before participating in offensive opns vic. Kharkov and Belgorod
Jul 43	After refitting, conducted offensive opns as part of the southern wing of the *ZITADELLE* offensive
Jul 43	Destroyed the bridgehead across the Mius River, and retitled as the II SS-Panzer Corps
Aug 43	Corps headquarters redeployed to northern Italy
Mar 44	Assumed control of the 9th and 10th SS-Panzer Divisions in France; redeployed to Galicia.
Apr–Jun 44	Participated in the relief of the encircled 1st Panzer Army, the attempted relief of Ternopol, Galicia, and then placed in reserve
Jun–Sep 44	Offensive, defensive, and retrograde opns in Normandy; subsequently conducted retrograde opns across northern France and Belgium
Dec 44–Jan 45	Offensive opns in the Ardennes; subsequent defensive opns in Belgium
Mar 45	Participated in the *FRÜHLINGSERWACHEN* offensive south of Budapest
Mar–May 45	Retrograde opns through Hungary into Austria; surrendered to American forces vic. Steyr

Commanders

SS-Ogruf. und Gen.d.W-SS Hausser, May 42–Jun 44

SS-Ogruf. und Gen.d.W-SS Bittrich, Jun 44–May 45

III (Germanic) SS-Panzer Corps

Apr–Aug 43	Corps organized and trained in Bavaria, taking control of the 11th SS-Volunteer-Panzer Grenadier Division and the 4th SS-Volunteer Panzer Grenadier Brigade, which became the 23d SS-Volunteer-Panzer Grenadier Division
Sep–Dec 43	Anti-partisan opns in Croatia as some subunits continued to organize at various training camps
Dec 43	Corps sub-units gradually redeployed to Oranienbaum front west of Leningrad
Jan–Feb 44	Retrograde opns vic. Leningrad area to the Luga River line, and then to the Narva River line
Feb–Jul 44	Defensive opns vic. Narva
Jul–Sep 44	Withdrawal to and defensive opns vic. the Tannenberg line
Sep–Oct 44	After evacuating Estonia, defensive opns vic. Riga to facilitate the redeployment of Army Group North into defensive positions in Kurland
Oct 44–Jan 45	Defensive opns vic. Kurland
Feb–Mar 45	Defensive opns in Pomerania; participated in the SONNENWENDE offensive, followed by defensive opns in the Altdamm bridgehead
Apr–May 45	After refitting west of the Oder River, pressed back toward Berlin. Elements destroyed vic. Berlin; the remainder of the corps surrendered to Allied forces along the Elbe River

Commanders

SS-Ogruf. und Gen.d.W-SS Steiner, May 43–Feb 44; Apr–Oct 44; and Apr–May 45

SS-Gruf. und Gen.Lt.d.W-SS Kleinheisterkamp, Feb–Apr 44

SS-Ogruf. und Gen.d.W-SS Keppler, Oct 44–Feb 45

Gen.Lt. Unrein, Feb–Apr 45

IV SS-Panzer Corps

Jun 44	Created by renaming the staff of the forming VII SS-Panzer Corps
Jul–Dec 44	Took control of the 3d and 5th SS-Panzer Divisions; heavy combat vic. Warsaw
Jan 45	After redeployment to Hungary, participated in the three unsuccessful KONRAD offensives to relieve encircled Budapest
Feb–May 45	Defensive fighting during the gradual withdrawal from Hungary into Austria. Surrendered to American forces west of Graz at the end of the war

Commanders

SS-Ogruf. und Gen.d.W-SS und Polizei Wünnenberg, Jun–Aug 43

SS-Gruf. und Gen.Lt.d.W-SS Kleinheisterkamp, Jun–Jul 44

Gruf. und Gen.Lt.d.W-SS Gille, Jul 44–May 45

V SS-Mountain Corps

Jul 43–Sep 44	Anti-partisan opns in Yugoslavia
Dec 44	Defensive opns in Serbia against Soviet and Bulgarian Army forces
Jan 45	Corps headquarters and support elements redeployed to the Oder River front to control Waffen-SS units east of Berlin

Feb– Apr 45	Defensive opns along the Oder, followed by brief refitting
Apr– May 45	Defensive opns vic. Berlin; retrograde opns to Halbe pocket, where most of the corps was destroyed or captured; individual survivors escaped west to surrender to American forces

Commanders

SS-Ogruf. und Gen.d.W-SS Phleps, Jul 43–Sep 44

SS-Ogruf. und Gen.d.W-SS und Polizei Krüger, Sep 44–Mar 45

SS-Ogruf. und Gen.d.W-SS und Polizei Jeckeln, Mar–May 45

VI Waffen-Army Corps of the SS

Oct 43	Created to control the two Latvian *Waffen-SS* divisions
Mar– Apr 44	Assumed control of the 15th and 19th Waffen-Grenadier Divisions in defensive opns along the Velikaya River.
Jul– Sep 44	Retrograde opns from western Russia through Latvia to vic. Riga
Oct 44– May 45	Defensive opns in Kurland. Survivors captured by Soviets or became anti-Soviet partisans

Commanders

SS-Gruf. und Gen.Lt.d.W-SS und Polizei Pfeffer-Wildenbruch, Sep 43–Jun 44

SS-Gruf. und Gen.Lt.d.W-SS von Treuenfeld, Jun–Jul 44

SS-Ogruf. und Gen.d.W-SS Krüger, Jul 44–May 45

IX Waffen-Mountain Corps of the SS

Jun 44	Created to control the Bosnian 13th and 23d Waffen-Mountain Divisions

Nov 44	Assumed control of the 8th SS-Cavalry and 22d SS-Volunteer Cavalry Divisions vic. Budapest
Dec 44– Feb 45	Defensive opns in encircled Budapest; destroyed attempting to break out

Commanders

SS-Gruf. und Gen.Lt.d.W-SS Sauberzweig, Jun–Nov 44

SS-Ogruf. und Gen.d.W-SS und Polizei Pfeffer-Wildenbruch, Nov 44–Feb 45

X SS-Army Corps

Feb 45	Created by retitling the headquarters of XIV SS-Army Corps. Controlled miscellaneous, mainly non-*Waffen-SS* units until dissolved the next month

Commanders

SS-Ogruf. und Gen.d.W-SS und Polizei von dem Bach, Feb 45

Gen.Lt. Kappe, Feb–Mar 45

XI SS-Panzer Corps

Aug 44	Created as the XI SS-Army Corps to control German Army infantry units in western Poland
Sep 44– Jan 45	Defensive opns in Poland and Slovakia
Feb– Apr 45	Retitled XI SS-Panzer Corps; conducted defensive opns vic. Oder River
Apr– May 45	Defensive opns east of Berlin; then led the partially successful breakout from the Halbe pocket; most corps elements destroyed; individual survivors escaped west to surrender to American forces

Commander

SS-Ogruf. und Gen.d.W-SS Kleinheisterkamp, Aug 44–May 45

XV (Cossack) SS-Cavalry Corps

Feb– May 45	Created by a largely paper transfer of the German Army Cossack Cavalry Corps to the *Waffen-SS*. Defensive opns against Soviet and Bulgarian forces in Croatia and Slovenia. Surrendered to British forces in Carinthia; later turned over to the Soviets

Commander

Gen.Lt. von Pannwitz, Feb–May 45

XVI SS-Army Corps

Jan– Mar 45	Created by retitling the "Leadership Staff-East Baltic Coast," and used to control miscellaneous units in Pomerania; dissolved after the corps' withdrawal from Pomerania

Commander

SS-Ogruf. und Gen.d.W-SS Demelhuber, Jan–Apr 45

XVII Waffen-Army Corps of the SS

Jan– May 45	Created to control the Hungarian 25th and 26th Waffen-Grenadier Divisions. Only small subunits of the corps saw combat, screening the withdrawal of the corps from its training camp in Silesia during early Feb 45. The corps staff surrendered to American forces in Austria

Commanders

Waffen-Gen.d.W-SS Zeidner, Jan–Mar 45

Waffen-Gen.d.W-SS Ranzenberger, Mar–May 45

Divisions

Panzer Divisions

Panzer and panzer-grenadier divisions by their nature covered much more ground than infantry divisions and thus generally fought in many more areas. It is beyond the scope of the summaries in this work to provide the same in-depth detail for these divisions as it has been possible to do for infantry divisions. Therefore, the general areas in which panzer and panzer-grenadier divisions fought are listed.

1st Panzer Division

1935	Activated and formed in Weimar
Sep 39	Offensive opns in Poland
May– Jun 40	Offensive opns in Western Europe
Jun 41– Dec 42	Offensive opns Eastern Front, northern sector
Jan–Feb 43	Redeployed to France
Spring 43	Redeployed to Greece
Aug 43	Offensive and defensive opns on Eastern Front, Southern Sector
Nov– Dec 43	Offensive and defensive opns vic. Kiev
Oct 44	Redeployed to Hungary
Oct 44– May 45	Defensive and retrograde opns in Hungary and Austria
May 45	Capitulated to American forces in Austria

Commanders

Gen.Lt. Rudolf Schmidt, Sep–Nov 39

Gen.Lt. Kirchner, Nov 39–Jul 41

Gen.Lt. Walter Krüger, Jul 41–Jan 44

Gen.Lt. Koll, Jan–Feb 44
Gen.Lt. Werner Marcks, Feb–Sep 44
Gen.Lt. Thunert, Sep 44–May 45

2d Panzer Division

1936	Activated and formed in Bavaria
1938	Transferred to Austria following *Anschluss*
Sep 39	Offensive opns in Poland
May–Jun 40	Offensive opns in Western Europe
Apr 41	Offensive opns in the Balkans
Sep 41–Jul 43	Offensive opns Eastern Front, central sector
Jul 43	Offensive opns vic. Kursk (Operation ZITADELLE)
Fall 43–Spring 44	Defensive and retrograde opns on Eastern Front, central sector
Spring 44	Redeployed to France for refitting
Jun–Sep 44	Offensive, defensive, and retrograde opns from Normandy across France to Belgium and Germany
Dec 44	Offensive opns in the Ardennes
Jan–May 45	Defensive and retrograde opns from the Ardennes across Germany to Czechoslovakia
May 45	Capitulation to American forces in Czechoslovakia

Commanders

Gen.Lt. Veiel, Sep 39–Feb 42
Gen.Major von Esebeck, Feb–Jun 42
Gen.Lt. von Lenski, Jun–Sep 42
Gen.Lt. Lübbe, Sep 42–Feb 44
Gen.Lt. Heinrich, *Freiherr* von Lüttwitz, Feb–May 44 and May–Aug 44
Gen.Lt. Westhoven, May 44
Gen.Major Schönfeld, Aug–Dec 44
Gen.Major von Lauchert, Dec 44–Mar 45
Gen.Major Munzel, Mar–Apr 45
Oberst Carl Stollbrock, Apr–May 45

3d Panzer Division

Oct 1935	Activated and formed at Wunsdorf
Sep 39	Offensive opns in Poland
May–Jun 40	Offensive opns in Western Europe
Jun 41–Mar 42	Offensive opns on Eastern Front, central sector
Mar–Dec 42	Offensive opns on Eastern Front, southern sector
Summer 43	Offensive and defensive opns vic. Kharkov
Fall 43–Jan 44	Defensive opns in the Dnepr Bend
Summer–Fall 44	Defensive opns along the Vistula River
Dec 44–Apr 45	Offensive and defensive opns in Hungary
Apr–May 45	Defensive opns in Austria; capitulation to American forces in Austria

Commanders

Gen.Lt. *Freiherr* Geyr von Schweppenburg, Sep–Oct 39
Gen.Lt. Horst Stumpff, Oct 39–Sep 40 and Oct–Nov 40
Gen.Lt. Friedrich Kühn, Sep–Oct 40
Gen.Lt. Walter Model, Nov 40–Oct 41
Gen.Lt. Breith, Oct 41–Oct 42
Gen.Lt. Westhoven. Oct 42–Oct 43
Gen.Lt. Bayerlein, Oct 43–Jan 44
Oberst Rudolf Lang, Jan–May 44
Gen.Lt. Wilhelm Philipps, May 44–Jan 45
Gen.Major Söth, Jan–Apr 45
Oberst Volkmar Schöne, Apr–May 45

4th Panzer Division

1938	Activated and formed in Bavaria
Sep 39–	Offensive opns in Poland
May–Jun 40	Offensive opns in Western Europe
Summer 41–Summer 43	Offensive, defensive, and retrograde opns on Eastern Front, central sector
Jul 43	Offensive opns vic. Kursk (Operation ZITADELLE)

Fall 43–Summer 44	Offensive, defensive, and retrograde opns on Eastern Front, central sector
Fall 44–May 45	Defensive and retrograde opns in Latvia, Poland, East Prussia
May 45	Destroyed vic. Danzig

Commanders

Gen.Lt. Georg-Hans Reinhardt, Sep 39–Feb 40

Gen.Lt. *Ritter* von Radlmeier, Feb–Jun 40

Gen.Lt. Stever, Jun–Jul 40

Gen.Lt. *Freiherr* von Boineburg-Lengsfeld, Jul–Sep 40

Gen.Lt. *Freiherr* von Langermann und Erlencamp, Sep 40–Dec 41 and Jan 42

Gen.Lt. von Saucken, Dec 41–Jan 42; May 43–Jan 44; and Feb–May 44

Gen.Lt. Heinrich Eberbach, Jan–Mar 42; Apr–Nov 42

Gen.Lt. Heidkämper, Mar–Apr 42

Gen.Lt. Erich Schneider, Nov 42–May 43

Gen.Lt. Junck, Jan–Feb 44

Gen.Lt. Betzel, May 44–Mar 45

Oberst Ernst Hoffmann, Mar–May 45

5th Panzer Division

1938	Activated and formed in Oppeln, Silesia.
Sep 39	Offensive opns in Poland
May–Jun 40	Offensive opns in Western Europe
Apr 41	Offensive opns in the Balkans
Jun–Dec 41	Offensive opns on Eastern Front, central sector
Summer 41–Summer 43	Offensive, defensive, and retrograde opns on Eastern Front, central sector
Jul 43	Offensive opns vic. Kursk (Operation ZITADELLE)
Fall 43–Summer 44	Opns west of the middle Defensive and retrograde opns on Eastern Front, central sector

Fall 44–Apr 45	Defensive and retrograde opns in Poland and East Prussia
Apr 45	Capitulated to Soviet forces vic. Pillau

Commanders

Gen.Lt. von Viettinghoff-Scheel, Sep–Oct 39

Gen.Lt. von Hartlieb-Walsporn, Oct 39–May 40

Gen.Lt. Lemelsen, May–Nov 40

Gen.Lt. Fehn, Nov 40–Aug 42

Gen.Lt. Eduard Metz, Aug 42–Feb 43

Gen.Major Nedtwig, Feb–Jun 43

Gen.Lt. Fäckenstedt, Jun–Sep 43

Gen.Lt. Karl Decker, Sep 43–Oct 44

Gen.Major Lippert, Oct 44–Feb 45

Gen.Major Hoffmann-Schönborn, Feb–Apr 45

Oberst d.Res. Hans Herzog, Apr–May 45

6th Panzer Division

1939	Converted from 1st Light Division at Wuppertal
Sep 39	Offensive opns in Poland
May–Jun 40	Offensive opns in Western Europe
Jun–Dec 41	Offensive opns on Eastern Front, northern sector
Summer 41–May 42	Offensive opns on Eastern Front, central sector
May 42	Transferred to France for refitting and rehabilitation
Oct 42–Summer 43	Offensive, defensive, and retrograde opns Eastern Front, southern sector
Jul 43	Offensive opns vic. Kursk (Operation ZITADELLE)
Fall 43–Summer 44	Defensive and retrograde opns vic. Karkhov, Kremenchug, Kirovograd, Cherkassy, and Yarmolinsky
Fall 44	Defensive and retrograde opns vic. Vilnius, Lithuania and East Prussia
Dec 44–May 45	Defensive and retrograde opns in Hungary and Austria

May 45   Capitulated to Soviet forces

Commanders

Gen.Lt. Werner Kempf, Oct 39–Jan 41

Gen.Lt. Franz Landgraf, Jan–Jun 41

Gen.Lt. Wilhelm *Ritter* von Thoma, Jun–Sep 41

Gen.Lt. Landgraf, Sep 41–Apr 42

Gen.Lt. Erhard Raus, Apr 42–Feb 43

Gen.Lt. von Hünersdorff, Feb–Jul 43

Gen.Major Crisolli, Jul–Aug 43

Gen.Lt. *Freiherr* von Waldenfels, Aug 43–Feb 44; Feb–Mar 44; Mar–Nov 44; and Jan–May 45

Gen.Lt. Werner Marcks, Feb 44

Gen.Lt. Walter Denkert, Mar 44

Oberst Friedrich-Wilhelm Jürgens, Nov 44–Jan 45

7th Panzer Division

Oct 39   Converted from 2d Light Division in Thuringia

Sep 39   Offensive opns in Poland

May–Jun 40   Offensive opns in Western Europe

Jun 41–May 42   Offensive and defensive opns Eastern Front, central sector

May 42   Transfer to France for refitting and rehabilitation

Feb 43–Summer 44   Offensive, defensive, and retrograde opns in the Ukraine vic. Belgorod, Kiev, and Zhitomir

Late summer 44–Jan 45   Defensive and retrograde opns through Lithuania and Poland

Jan–May 45   Defensive and retrograde opns in East Prussia, West Prussia, Pomerania, and Mecklenburg

May 45   Capitulated to British forces vic. Schwerin

Commanders

Gen.Lt. Georg Stumme, Oct 39–Feb 40

Gen.Major Rommel, Feb 40–Feb 41

Gen.Lt. *Freiherr* von Funck, Feb 41–Aug 43

Oberst Wolfgang Gläsemer, Aug 43 and Jan 44

Gen.Lt. Hasso von Manteuffel, Aug 43–Jan 44

Gen.Major Adalbert Schulz, Jan 44

Gen.Lt. Dr. Mauss, Jan–May 44; Sep–Oct 44; Nov 44–Jan 45; Jan–Mar 45

Gen.Major Schmidhuber, May–Sep 44

Gen.Major Mäder, Oct–Nov 44

Gen.Major Lemke, Jan 45

Oberst Christern, Mar 45–May 45

8th Panzer Division

Oct 39   Formed from 3d Light Division vic. Cottbus, Brandenburg

Sep 39   Offensive opns in Poland

May–Jun 40   Offensive opns in Western Europe

Apr 41   Offensive opns in the Balkans vic. Belgrade and Sarajevo

Jun–Dec 41   Offensive opns Eastern Front, northern sector

Mar 42–Aug 43   Offensive, defensive, and retrograde opns Eastern Front, central sector

Fall 43–Dec 44   Defensive and retrograde opns in Ukraine vic. Kiev, Zhitomir; and Galicia vic,. Ternopol, Brody, and Lvov

Dec 44–May 45   Defensive and retrograde opns in Hungary and Czechoslovakia

May 45   Capitulated to Soviet forces

Commanders

Gen.Lt. Kuntzen, Oct 39–Feb 41

Gen.Lt. Brandenburger, Feb–Apr 41; May–Dec 41; Mar–Aug 42; and Nov 42–Jan 43

Gen.Lt. Neumann-Silkow, Apr–May 41

Gen.Lt. Hühner, Dec 41–Mar 42

Gen.Lt. Schrötter, Aug–Nov 42

Gen.Lt. Fichtner, Jan–Sep 43

Gen.Major Frölich, Sep 43–Apr 44 and Jul 44–Jan 45

Gen.Major Friebe, Apr–Jul 44
Gen.Major Heinrich-Georg Hax, Jan–
    May 45

9th Panzer Division

1940	Formed from 4th Light Division in Austria
May–Jun 40	Offensive opns in Western Europe
Apr 41	Offensive opns in the Balkans
Summer 41	Offensive opns Eastern Front, southern sector
Fall 41–Summer 43	Offensive, defensive, and retrograde opns Eastern Front, central sector
Fall 43–Mar 44	Defensive and retrograde opns Eastern Front, southern sector
Spring 44	Transferred to France for refitting and rehabilitation
Jul–Sep 44	Offensive, defensive, and retrograde opns from Normandy across France to vic. Aachen
Fall 44	Defensive opns vic. Aachen
Dec 44–Apr 45	Offensive and defensive opns in the Ardennes
Apr 45	Destroyed in Ruhr Pocket; capitulation to American forces

Commanders

Gen.Lt. *Ritter* von Hubicki, Jan 40–
    Apr 42
Gen.Lt. Bässler, Apr–Jul 42
Gen.Major von Hülsen, Jul–
    Aug 42
Gen.Lt. Walter Scheller, Aug 42–Jul 43
Gen.Lt. Jolasse, Jul–Oct 43 and
    Nov 43–Aug 44
Gen.Major Dr. Johannes Schulz,
    Oct–Nov 43
Oberst Max Sperling, Aug–Sep 44
Gen.Major Gerhard Müller, Sep 44
Gen.Lt. *Freiherr* von Elverfeldt,
    Sep 44–Mar 45
Oberst Helmut Zollenkopf, Mar–
    Apr 45

10th Panzer Division

Apr 39	Formed vic. Prague
Sep 39	Offensive opns in Poland
May–Jun 40	Offensive opns in Western Europe
Jun 41–May 42	Offensive, defensive, and retrograde opns on Eastern Front, central sector
May–Nov 42	Refitting, rehabilitation and training in France
Dec 42–May 43	Offensive and defensive opns in Tunisia
May 43	Capitulation to American forces vic. Tunis

Commanders

Gen.Lt. Ferdinand Schaal, Sep 39–
    Aug 41
Gen.Lt. Wolfgang Fischer, Aug 41–
    Feb 43
Gen.Lt. *Freiherr* von Broich, Feb–
    May 43

11th Panzer Division

Aug 40	Formed in Silesia
Apr 41	Offensive opns in the Balkans
Jun–Oct 41	Offensive opns Eastern Front, southern sector
Oct 41–Jun 42	Offensive and defensive opns Eastern Front, central sector
Jun 42–Fall 43	Offensive, defensive, and retrograde opns in the Ukraine
Winter 44	Encircled vic. Korsun
Spring–Summer 44	Reconstitution and training in France
Aug 44	Defensive and retrograde opns in the Rhône Valley
Sep 44	Defensive and retrograde opns on the western slopes of the Vosges Mountains
Oct–Dec 44	Defensive opns in Lorraine
Dec 44–Jan 45	Offensive and defensive opns in the Ardennes
Jan–Mar 45	Defensive and retrograde opns in the Saar-Moselle triangle

Apr 45   Capitulated to American forces in Bavaria

Commanders

Gen.Lt. Crüwell, Aug 40–Aug 41

Gen.Lt. Angern, Aug 41

Gen.Lt. *Freiherr* von Esebeck, Aug–Oct 41

Gen.Lt. Scheller, Oct 41–May 42

Gen.Lt. Balck, May 42–Mar 43

Gen.Lt. von Choltitz, Mar–May 43

Gen.Lt. Mickl, May–Aug 43

Gen.Lt. von Wietersheim, Aug 43–Apr 45

Gen.Major *Freiherr* Treusch und Buttlar-Brandenfels, Apr–May 45

12th Panzer Division

Oct 40	Formed in Pomerania from 2d Motorized Infantry Division
Jun–Sep 41	Offensive opns on Eastern Front, central sector
Sep 41–Nov 42	Offensive and defensive opns Eastern Front, northern sector
Nov 42–Jun 43	Offensive and defensive opns Eastern Front, Central sector
Jul 43	Offensive opns vic. Kursk, (Operation ZITADELLE)
Aug 43–Feb 44	Defensive and retrograde opns Eastern Front, central sector
Feb–Sep 44	Defensive and retrograde opns Eastern Front, northern sector
Sep 44–May 45	Defensive opns in Kurland, capitulation to Soviet forces

Commanders

Gen.Lt. Harpe, Oct 40–Jan 42

Gen.Lt. Wessel, Jan 42–Mar 43

Gen.Lt. *Freiherr* von Bodenhausen, Mar 43–May 44 and Jul 44–Apr 45

Gen.Major Gerhard Müller, May–Jul 44

Oberst von Usedom, Apr–May 45

13th Panzer Division

Oct 40	Formed from the 13th Motorized Infantry Division
Winter 40–41	Deployed in Romania under cover as a training unit
Jun–Dec 41	Offensive opns on Eastern Front, southern sector
Early 42	Defensive opns on Eastern Front, southern sector
Spring–Summer 42	Offensive opns on Eastern Front, southern sector toward Caucusus Mountains
Late 42–early 43	Defensive and retrograde opns vic. Kuban
Summer 43	Defensive and retrograde opns, Eastern Front,
Summer 44	southern sector
Aug–Sep 44	Defensive and retrograde opns in Hungary
Sep–Oct 44	Reconstitution in Germany
Nov 44–Feb 45	Defensive and retrograde opns in Hungary
Mar 45	Redesignated as "Panzer Division *Feldherrnhalle* 2"
Mar–May 45	Defensive and retrograde opns in Hungary and Austria

Commanders

Gen.Lt. von Rotkirch und Panthen, Oct 40–Jun 41

Gen.Lt. Walther Düvert, Jun–Nov 41

Gen.Lt. Traugott Herr, Dec 41–Nov 42

Gen.Lt. von der Chevallerie, Nov–Dec 42 and May–Sep 43

Gen.Major Crisolli, Dec 42–May 43

Gen.Lt. Eduard Hauser, Sep–Dec 43

Gen.Lt. Mikosch, Dec 43–May 44

Oberst Friedrich von Hake, May 44

Gen.Lt. Tröger, May–Sep 44

Gen.Major Schmidhuber, Sep 44–Feb 45

Gen.Major Dr. Franz Bäke, Mar–May 45

14th Panzer Division

1940	Formed in Saxony from the 4th Motorized Infantry Division
Apr 41	Offensive opns in Yugoslavia
Jun–Dec 41	Offensive opns Eastern Front, southern sector
Jan–Apr 42	Defensive opns Eastern Front, southern sector
Spring–Fall 42	Offensive opns Eastern Front, southern sector
Winter 42–43	Defensive opns vic. Stalingrad; destroyed
Mar 43	Reconstituted in France
Oct 43	Defensive and retrograde opns Eastern Front, southern sector
Feb–Jul 44	Defensive opns in Bessarabia
Jul–Sep 44	Reconstituted in Moldavia
Sep 44–May 45	Defensive opns in Kurland; capitulated to Soviet forces

Commanders

Gen.Lt. Erik Hansen, Aug–Oct 40
Gen.Lt. von Prittwitz und Gaffron, Oct 40–Mar 41
Gen.Lt. Friedrich Kühn, Mar 41–Jul 42
Gen.Lt. Ferdinand Heim, Jul–Nov 42
Gen.Lt. *Freiherr* von Falkenstein, Nov 42
Gen.Lt. Bässler, Nov 42
Gen.Major Lattmann, Nov 42–Jan 43
Gen.Lt. Sieberg, Apr–Oct 43
Gen.Lt. Unrein, Oct 43–Sep 44 and Dec 44–Feb 45
Gen.Major Munzel, Sep–Dec 44
Oberst Friedrich-Wilhelm Jürgen, Feb–Mar 45
Oberst Karl Grässel, Apr 45

16th Panzer Division

Nov 40	Formed in Westphalia from elements of 16th Infantry Division
Jun–Dec 41	Offensive opns Eastern Front, southern sector
Jan–Spring 42	Defensive opns Eastern Front, southern sector
Spring–Sep 42	Offensive opns Eastern Front, southern sector
Nov 42–Jan 43	Defensive opns vic. Stalingrad; destroyed
Mar 43	Reconstitution in France
Jun 43	Transferred to Italy
Sep–Nov 43	Defensive opns vic. Solerno and Naples, Italy
Nov 43–Mar 45	Defensive and retrograde opns Eastern Front, central sector
Mar–May 45	Defensive and retrograde opns in Czechoslovakia
May 45	With the division deployed vic. Pilsen and Karlsbad, some elements capitulated to Soviet forces and some to American forces

Commanders

Gen.Lt. Hans-Valentin Hube Nov 40–Sep 42
Gen.Lt. Angern, Sep 42–Feb 43
Gen.Major Müller-Hillebrand, Mar–May 43
Gen.Major Sieckenius, May–Nov 43
Gen.Major Back, Nov 43–Aug 44
Gen.Lt. Dietrich von Müller, Aug 44–Apr 45
Oberst Kurt Treuhaupt, Apr–May 45

17th Panzer Division

Aug 40	Formed from 27th Infantry Division
Jun–Dec 41	Offensive opns Eastern Front, central sector
Jan–Apr 42	Defensive opns Eastern Front, central sector
Summer–Oct 42	Offensive opns Eastern Front, southern sector
Nov 42–Mar 44	Offensive, defensive, and retrograde opns Eastern Front, southern sector
Spring–Sep 44	Retrograde and defensive opns in the Ukraine

Sep 44–	Defensive opns in Romania
Oct 44–winter 45	Defensive opns along the Vistula River
Jan–May 45	Defensive and retrograde opns in Poland, Silesia, and Czechoslovakia
May 45	Some elements of the division capitulate to Soviet forces, others to American forces in Czechoslovakia

Commanders

Gen.Major Karl, *Ritter* von Weber, Nov 40–Jul 41
Gen.Lt. *Ritter* von Thoma, Jul–Sep 41
Gen.Lt. Hans-Jürgen von Arnim, Sep–Nov 41
Gen.Lt. Licht, Nov 41–Oct 42
Gen.Lt. von Senger und Etterlin, Oct 42–Jun 43
Gen.Lt. Walter Schilling, Jun–Jul 43
Gen.Lt. von der Meden, Jul 43–Sep 44
Gen.Major Demme, Sep–Dec 44
Oberst Albert Brux, Dec 44–Jan 45
Gen.Major Theodor Kretschmer, Feb–May 45

18th Panzer Division

Oct 40	Formed in Saxony from elements of the 4th and 14th Infantry Divisions
Jun–Dec 41	Offensive opns Eastern Front, central sector
Jan–Apr 42	Defensive opns Eastern Front, central sector
Summer–Fall 42	Offensive opns, Eastern Front, southern sector
Fall 42–Spring 43	Defensive and retrograde opns, Eastern Front, central sector
Summer 43	Offensive and defensive opns Eastern Front, southern sector
Jul 43	Offensive opns vic. Kursk (Operation ZITADELLE)
Fall 43	Defensive opns, Eastern Front, central sector; reorganized as the 18th Artillery Division

Commanders

Gen.Lt. Nehring, Oct 40–Jan 42
Gen.Lt. *Freiherr* von Thüngen, Jan–Jul 42; Aug–Sep 42; and Feb–Apr 43
Gen.Lt. Praun, Jul–Aug 42
Gen.Lt. Menny, Sep 42–Feb 43
Gen.Lt. von Schlieben, Apr–Sep 43

19th Panzer Division

Nov 40	Formed from 19th Infantry Division
Jun–Dec 41	Offensive opns Eastern Front, central sector
Jan–Apr 42	Defensive opns Eastern Front, central sector
Summer–Fall 43	Offensive opns Eastern Front, central sector
Winter 42-43	Defensive and retrograde opns Eastern Front, central sector
Spring–Summer 43	Offensive opns Eastern Front, southern sector
Jul 43	Offensive opns vic. Kursk (Operation ZITADELLE)
Fall 43–Spring 44	Defensive and retrograde opns Eastern Front, southern sector
Jun–Jul 44	Reconstituted vic. Breda, the Netherlands
Aug 44–Jan 45	Defensive opns along the Vistula River
Feb–May 45	Defensive and retrograde opns in Silesia and Czechoslovakia
May 45	Elements surrendered to Soviet forces in Czechoslovakia, others to US forces, then transferred to Soviets

Commanders

Gen.Lt. von Knobelsdorff, Nov 40–Jan 42
Gen.Lt. Gustav Schmidt, Jan 42–Aug 43
Gen.Lt. Källner, Aug 43–Mar 44 and May 44–Mar 45
Gen.Lt. Walter Denkert, Mar–May 44
Gen.Major Hans-Joachim Deckert, Mar–May 45

20th Panzer Division

Oct 40	Formed from elements of the 19th and 33d Infantry Divisions
Jun–Dec 41	Offensive opns Eastern Front, central sector
Jan–May 42	Defensive and retrograde opns Eastern Front, central sector
Summer 42	Anti-partisan, offensive, and defensive opns Eastern Front, central and southern sectors
Jul 43	Offensive opns vic. Kursk (Operation ZITADELLE)
Fall 43–Summer 44	Defensive and retrograde opns Eastern Front, central sector
Aug 44	Refitting, defensive, and retrograde opns in Romania
Fall 44	Reconstituted in East Prussia
Dec 44	Defensive and retrograde opns in Hungary
Jan 45	Defensive and retrograde opns in Poland
Feb–May 45	Defensive and retrograde opns in Silesia, Saxony, and Czechoslovakia
May 45	Capitulation to Soviet forces with minor elements surrendering to American forces

Commanders

Gen.Lt. Stumpff, Nov 40–Sep 41
Gen.Lt. Georg von Bismarck, Sep–Oct 41
Gen.Lt. *Ritter* von Thoma, Oct 41–Jul 42
Gen.Lt. Düvert, Jul–Oct 42
Gen.Lt. *Freiherr* von Lüttwitz, Oct 42–May 43
Gen.Lt. von Kessel, May 43–Jan 44; Feb–Nov 44
Gen.Lt. Werner Marcks, Jan–Feb 44
Gen.Major von Oppeln-Bronikowski, Nov 44–May 45

22d Panzer Division

Sep 41	Formed in France
Spring–Summer 42	Offensive and defensive opns in the Crimea
Summer 42	Offensive opns Eastern Front southern sector vic. Rostov and the Don River
Sep 42	Refitting west of Stalingrad
Oct–Nov 42	Offensive and defensive opns in the Don River bend
Jan 43	Remnants absorbed into 23d Panzer Division

Commanders

Gen.Lt. von Apell, Sep 41–Oct 42
Gen.Lt. von der Chevallerie, Oct–Nov 42
Gen.Lt. Rodt, Nov 42–Mar 43

23d Panzer Division

Sep 41	Formed in France
Spring–Fall 42	Offensive opns Eastern Front, southern sector vic. Caucusus Mountains
Winter 42 43	Defensive and retrograde opns vic. Stalingrad
Spring–Summer 43	Defensive and retrograde opns vic. Mius River
Fall 43	Defensive and retrograde opns in Dnepr River bend
Spring–Summer 44	Defensive and retrograde opns Eastern Front, southern sector
Sep 44	Defensive and retrograde opns in southern Poland along the Vistula River
Fall 44–Spring 45	Defensive and retrograde opns in Hungary
Apr 45	Defensive and retrograde opns in Austria
May 45	Capitulated to allied forces in Austria

Commanders

Gen.Lt. *Freiherr* von Boineburg-Lengsfeld, Sep–Nov 41; Nov 41–Jul 42; and Aug–Dec 42

Gen.Major, Werner-Ehrenfeucht, Nov 41 and Nov 43
Gen.Major Erwin Mack, Jul–Aug 42
Gen.Lt. von Vormann, Dec 42–Oct 43
Gen.Major Kräber, Oct–Nov 43 and Nov 43–Jun 44
Gen.Lt. Josef von Radowitz, Jun 44–May 45

24th Panzer Division

Nov 41	Formed from 1st Cavalry Division in East Prussia
Apr–May 42	Training in France
Summer–Fall 43	Offensive opns Eastern Front, southern sector
Winter 42–43	Defensive opns vic. Stalingrad; largely destroyed
Mar 43	Reconstituted in France
Aug–Sep 43	Participated in disarmament of Italian forces, northern Italy
Oct 43–Summer 44	Defensive and retrograde opns Eastern Front southern sector
Summer 44	Offensive and defensive opns in Romania
Fall 44–Jan 45	Defensive opns in Poland along the Vistula River; offensive and defensive opns in Hungary
Jan–Apr 45	Defensive and retrograde opns in East Prussia
Apr 45	Most of division capitulated to the Soviets in the Samland Pocket; the rest redeployed to Schleswig-Holstein and capitulated to British forces

Commanders
Gen.Lt. Kurt Feldt, Nov 41–Apr 42
Gen.Lt. *Ritter* von Hauenschild, Apr–Sep 42
Gen.Lt. von Lenski, Sep 42–Jan 43
Gen.Lt. *Freiherr* von Edelsheim, Mar 43–Aug 44
Gen.Major von Nostitz-Wallwitz, Aug 44–Mar 45

Major Rudolf von Knebel-Döberitz, Mar–May 45

25th Panzer Division

Feb 42	Formed in Norway
Jun 43	Brought to divisional strength
Aug–Oct 43	Training and security opns in Denmark and France
Oct 43–May 44	Defensive and retrograde opns Eastern Front, southern sector
Spring 44	Reconstution in Denmark and Germany
Sep 44–Feb 45	Defensive and retrograde opns in Poland
Spring 45	Defensive and retrograde opns in Silesia and Pomerania
Apr–May 45	Defensive and retrograde opns in Austria and Czechoslovakia
May 45	Capitulation to American forces in Austria; elements of the division transferred to Soviet custody

Commanders
Gen.Lt. Johann Haarde, Feb–Dec 42
Gen.Lt. Adolf von Schell, Jan–Nov 43
Gen.Lt. Georg Jauer, Nov 43
Gen.Lt. Hans Tröger, Nov 43–May 44
Gen.Major Oswin Grolig, Jun–Aug 44
Gen.Major Oskar Audörsch, Aug 44–May 45

27th Panzer Division

Oct 42	Division Formed on the Eastern Front, southern sector from elements of the 22d Panzer Division
Oct 42–Feb 43	Defensive and retrograde opns Eastern Front, southern sector vic. Voronezh
Feb 43	Disbanded

Commanders
Gen.Major Michalik, Oct 42–Nov 42
Gen.Lt. Hans Tröger, Nov 42–Feb 43

Motorized Infantry and Panzer-Grenadier Divisions

3d Motorized Infantry Division

1934–35	Formed in Frankfurt/Oder
Sep 39	Offensive opns in Poland
May–Jun 40	Offensive opns in Western Europe
Jun–Sep 41	Offensive opns Eastern Front, northern sector
Sep–Dec 41	Offensive opns Eastern Front, central sector west of Moscow
Jan–May 42	Defensive opns Eastern Front, central section
Summer–Fall 42	Offensive opns vic. Kursk and Voronezh
Fall 42	Offensive opns in the Don River Bend
Winter 42–43	Offensive and defensive opns vic. Stalingrad
Jan 43	Destroyed vic. Stalingrad

Commanders

Gen.Lt. Lichel, Sep 39–Oct 40
Gen.Lt. Bader, Oct 40–May 41
Gen.Lt. Jahn, May 41–Apr 42
Gen.Lt. Schlömer, Apr 42–Jan 43

10th Motorized Infantry (later PGD)

1934	Formed in Franconia
Sep 39	Offensive opns in Poland
May–Jun 40	Offensive opns in Western Europe
Jun–Dec 41	Offensive opns Eastern Front, central sector
Jan–May 42	Defensive and retrograde opns Eastern Front, central sector
Spring–Fall 42	Offensive opns Eastern Front, central sector
Winter 42–43	Defensive and retrograde opns Eastern Front, central sector
Summer 43	Reorganized as 10th Panzer-Grenaider Division
Fall 43	Transferred to southern sector; heavily engaged west of Kiev

Aug 44	Heavy losses during withdrawal The Dnestr; withdrew to reform
Nov 44–Jan 45	Relocated to central sector
Jan 45	Heavily engaged in Upper Silesia
May 45	Capitulated in Czechoslovakia

Commanders

Gen.Lt. Friedrich-Wilhelm Löper, Nov 40–Apr 42
Gen.Lt. August Schmidt, Apr 42–Oct 43; Dec 43–Sep 44
Gen.Lt. Mikosch, Oct–Dec 43
Gen.Major Herold, Sep–Nov 44
Oberst Vial, Nov 44–Jan 45
Gen.Major Kossmann, Jan–May 45

14th Motorized Infantry Division

Aug 40	Formed from 14th Infantry Division
Jun–Dec 41	Offensive opns Eastern Front, central sector; ending 35 km west of Moscow
Jan–May 42	Defensive and retrograde opns Eastern Front, central sector
Summer Fall 42	Offensive opns Eastern Front, central sector
Winter 42–43	Defensive and retrograde opns Eastern Front, central sector
Spring 43	Reorganized as conventional infantry division

Commanders

Gen.Lt. Dr. Rendulic, Jun–Nov 40
Gen.Lt. Friedrich Fürst, Nov 40–Jun 41
Gen.Lt. Wosch, Jun 41–Oct 42
Gen.Lt. Walther Krause, Oct 42–Jan 43
Gen.Lt. Holste, Jan–May 43
Gen.Lt. Flörke, May–Jun 43

16th Motorized Infantry (later Panzer-Grenadier) Division

Aug 40	Formed at Sennelager from elements of the 16th and 228th IDs

Apr 41	Offensive operations in the Balkans
Jun–Dec 41	Offensive operations on the Eastern Front, southern sector
Jan–May 42	Defensive and retrograde operations on the Eastern Front, southern sector
May 42	Refitting and rehabilitation, south of Kursk
Summer–Fall 42	Offensive operations on the Eastern Front, southern sector, toward the Caucasus Mtns.
Winter–Spring 43	Defensive and retrograde operations on the Eastern Front, southern sector
Jun 43	Reorganized as a panzer-grenadier division
Summer–Fall 43	Offensive, defensive, and retrograde operations on the Eastern Front, southern sector
Winter 43–44	Defensive and retrograde operations on the Eastern Front, southern sector
Spring 44	Retrograde operations from the Don River bend; extremely heavy casualties
Apr 44	Reconstituted in France as 116th Panzer Division

Commanders

Gen.Lt. von Chappius, Nov 40–Mar 41
Gen.Lt. Sigfrid Henrici, Mar–Oct 41; Nov 41–Nov 42
Gen.Lt. Streich, Oct–Nov 41
Gen.Lt. Gerhard *Graf* von Schwerin, Nov 42–May 43; Jun 43–Jan 44
Gen.Major Crisolli, May–Jun 43
Gen.Major Günther von Manteuffel, Jan–Mar 44
Gen.Major Stingl, Mar 44

18th Motorized Infantry (later Panzer-Grenadier) Division

Nov 40	Formed from 18th Infantry Division
Jun–Dec 41	Offensive operations Eastern Front, central sector

Jan–May 42	Defensive operations on the Eastern Front, northern sector
Summer–Fall 42	Offensive operations on the Eastern Front, northern sector
Winter 42–Spring 43	Defensive and retrograde operations on the Eastern Front, northern sector
Jun 43	Reorganized as a panzer-grenadier division
Summer–Fall 43	Offensive operations, on the Eastern Front, central sector
Winter 43–Spring 44	Defensive and retrograde operations, on the Eastern Front, central sector
Summer 44	Defensive operations vic. Minsk; practically destroyed. Remnants incorporated into Panzer Brigade 105
Dec 44	Reconstituted in East Prussia
Dec 44–Mar 45	Defensive and retrograde operations in East Prussia; destroyed in the Heiligen beil Pocket
Apr 45	Reconstituted in Eberswalde, Brandenburg
Apr–May 45	Defensive and retrograde operations vic. Berlin;

Commanders

Gen.Lt. Cranz, Nov 40–Mar 41
Gen.Lt. Herrlein, Mar–Dec 41
Gen.Lt. von Erdmannsdorff, Dec 41–Jun 43 and Jun–Aug 43
Gen.Lt. Zutavern, Aug 43–Apr 44 and May–Sep 44
Gen.Lt. Jahn, Apr–May 44
Gen.Lt. Dr. Bölsen, Sep 44–Jan 45
Gen.Major Josef Rauch, Jan–May 45

20th Motorized Infantry (later Panzer-Grenadier) Division

Fall 40	Formed from the 20th Infantry Division
Jun–Jul 41	Offensive opns Eastern Front, central sector

Jul–Dec 41	Offensive opns Eastern Front, northern sector
Jan–May 42	Defensive opns Eastern Front, northern sector
Summer–Fall 42	Offensive opns Eastern Front, northern sector
Winter 42–Spring 43	Defensive opns Eastern Front, northern sector
Jul 43	Reorganized as panzer-grenadier division
Jul–Sep 43	Offensive opns, Eastern Front, central sector
Fall 43–Spring 44	Defensive and retrograde opns, Eastern Front, southern sector
Apr–Jul 44	Refitting and rehabilitation
Summer–Fall 44	Defensive and retrograde opns along the Vistula River
Nov 44–Jan 45	In reserve, Army Group A
Jan–Apr 45	Defensive and retrograde opns, Poland, Silesia, Brandenburg
May 45	Defensive opns vic. Berlin; destroyed; minor elements broke out to capitulate to allied forces, but most of the division's members were captured by Soviet forces.

Commanders

Gen.Lt. von Wiktorin, Sep 39–Nov 40
Gen.Lt. Zorn, Nov 40–Jan 42
Gen.Lt. Jaschke, Jan 42–Jan 43
Gen.Lt. Jauer, Jan 43–Jan 45
Gen.Major Georg Scholze, Jan–May 45

25th Motorized Infantry (later Panzer-Grenadier) Division

Nov 40	Formed from 25th Infantry Division
Jun–Dec 41	Offensive opns, Eastern Front, southern sector
Jan–May 42	Defensive and retrograde opns, Eastern Front, central sector
Jun 42	Reorganized as a panzer-grenadier division

Summer–Fall 42	Offensive opns, Eastern Front, central sector
Winter 42–43	Defensive opns, Eastern Front, central sector
Spring–Fall 43	Offensive opns, Eastern Front, central sector
Winter 43–44	Defensive opns, Eastern Front, central sector
Spring–Summer 44	Defensive and retrograde opns, Eastern Front, central sector
Jul 44	Encircled and destroyed vic. Minsk
Aug 44	Remnants incorporated into Panzer Brigade 107
Nov 44	Division reconstituted, Panzer Brigade 107 incorporated
Dec 44	Defensive and retrograde opns vic. Bitche, Lorraine
Jan 45	Offensive opns in Alsace (Operation NORDWIND)
Jan–May 45	Defensive and retrograde opns in Brandenburg
May 45	Destroyed vic. Berlin; most of the division captured by Soviet forces, but some remnants capitulated to British forces west of Berlin

Commanders

Gen.Lt. Heinrich Clössner, Nov 40–Jan 42
Gen.Lt. Grasser, Feb 42–Nov 43
Gen.Lt. Dr. Benicke, Nov 43–Mar 44
Gen.Lt. Paul Schürmann, Mar–Jul 44; Oct–Dec 44
Gen.Major Arnold Burmeister, Dec 44–May 45

29th Motorized Infantry (later Panzer-Grenadier) Division

Fall 37	Formed from 29th Infantry Division
Sep 39	Offensive opns in Poland
May–Jun 40	Offensive opns in western Europe

Jun–Dec 41	Offensive opns Eastern Front, southern sector
Jan–May 42	Defensive opns Eastern Front, southern sector
May–Oct 42	Offensive opns Eastern Front, southern sector
Nov 42–Jan 43	Offensive and defensive opns vic. Stal
Jan 43	Destroyed at Stalingrad
Mar 43	Reconstituted in France
Jul 43–Apr 45	Offensive, defensive, and retrograde opns in Italy
Apr 45	Surrendered to British forces

Commanders

Gen.Lt. Lemelsen, Sep 39–May 40
Gen.Lt. Freiherr von Langermann und Erlencamp, May–Sep 40
Gen.Lt. von Boltenstern, Sep 40–Sep 41
Gen.Lt. Fremerey, Sep 41–Sep 42
Gen.Major Leyser, Sep 42–Jan 43

36th Motorized Infantry Division (later Infantry, later VGD)

Fall 40	Formed from 36th Infantry Division
Jun–Dec 41	Offensive opns, Eastern Front, northern sector
Jan–May 42	Defensive opns, northern sector
Summer–Fall 42	Offensive and defensive opns, central sector
Winter 42–43	Defensive and retrograde opns, central sector
May 43	Reorganized as a two-regiment infantry division

Commanders

Gen.Lt. Lindemann, 1939–Oct 40
Gen.Lt. Ottenbacher, Oct 40–Oct 41
Gen.Lt. Gollnick, Oct 41–Aug 43

60th Motorized Infantry Division

Aug 40	Formed from 60th Infantry Division
Apr 41	Offensive operations in the Balkans, Greece
Jun–Dec 41	Offensive operations Eastern Front, southern sector

Jan–May 42	Defensive and retrograde operations, southern sector
Summer–Fall 42	Offensive operations, southern sector
Nov 42–Jan 43	Defensive operations vic. Stalingrad; destroyed
Feb 43	Reconstituted in France
May 43	Reorganized as panzer-grenadier division
Jun 43	Awarded honorific *"Feldherrnhalle"*
Sep 43	Security operations vic. Franco-Italian border
Oct 43–Feb 44	Defensive and retrograde operations, Eastern Front, central sector
Feb–Jun 44	Defensive and retrograde operations, Eastern Front, northern sector
Jun–Oct 44	Defensive and retrograde operations, Eastern Front, central sector
Oct 44–Mar 45	Defensive and retrograde operations in Hungary
Mar–May 45	Defensive and retrograde operations in Austria and Czechoslovakia

Commanders

Gen.Lt. Friedrich-Georg Eberhardt, Aug 40–May 42
Gen.Lt. Kohlermann, May–Nov 42
Gen.Major von Arenstorff, Nov 42–Feb 43

Panzer-Grenadier Division Brandenburg

Sep 44	Formed in Baden
Oct–Nov 44	Reorganization in Yugoslavia
Jan 45	Defensive and retrograde opns along the Vistula River in Poland
Jan–Apr 45	Defensive and retrograde opns in Poland, Silesia, and Saxony
May 45	Destroyed.

Commanders

Gen.Lt. Kühlwein, Sep–Oct 44
Gen.Major Heuthaus, Oct 44–May 45

Motorized Infantry (later Panzer-Grenadier, later Panzer) Division "Grossdeutschland"

Apr 42	Formed from Motorized Infantry Regiment "Grossdeutschland"
Jun–Jul 42	Offensive opns Eastern Front, southern sector vic. Kursk and Voronezh.
Aug 42	Offensive opns toward the Caucasus vic. Manych
Sep–Dec 42	Offensive and defensive opns Eastern Front, central sector vic. Rzhev.
Jan 43	Defensive opns vic. Smolensk
Feb–Apr 43	Defensive opns vic. Kharkov
May 43	Refitted vic. Poltava
Jun 43	Redesignated as a PGD.
Jun–Aug 43	Defensive opns vic. Orel, Briansk, Sumy
Sep 43	Defensive and retrograde opns vic. Kremenchug
Oct–Dec 43	Defensive and retrograde opns vic. Krivoi Rog
Jan–Dec 43	Defensive and retrograde opns vic. Kirovograd
Apr–May 44	Defensive and retrograde opns vic. Yassy, Romania
Jun–Jul 44	Refitting and rehabilitation in Romania
Aug–Dec 44	Defensive and retrograde opns in Lithuania
Jan 45	Refitting and rehabilitation in East Prussia
Jan–May 45	Defensive and retrograde opns in East Prussia vic. Pillau and Samland; most of the division capitulated to the Soviets, but small elements were evacuated to Schleswig-Holstein and surrendered to British forces

Commanders

Gen.Lt. Hörnlein, Apr 42–Mar 43; Jun 43–Feb 44
Gen.Lt. Balck, Mar–Jun 43

Gen.Lt. Hasso von Manteuffel, Feb–Sep 44
Gen.Major Karl Lorenz, Sep 44–Feb 45
Gen.Major Mäder, Feb–May 45

Infantry Divisions

1st Infantry Division

34–35	Formed near Insterburg from 1st Regt., *Reichswehr*
Sep 39	Offensive opns in Poland
May–Jun 40	Offensive opns on Western Front
Jun–Dec 41	Offensive opns on Eastern Front, northern sector
Summer 43	Heavily engaged south of Lake Ladoga
Jan 44	Defensive opns Eastern Front, southern sector
Aug 44	Defensive opns Eastern Front, central sector
Oct 44	Defensive opns in East Prussia
Nov 44–Jan 45	Defensive opns vic. Schlossberg
Apr 45	Destroyed vic. Königsberg

Commanders

Gen.Lt. von Kortzfleisch, Sep 39–Mar 40
Gen.Lt. Kleffel, Mar 40–Jul 41, Sep 41–Jan 42
Gen.Lt. Dr. Altrichter, Jul–Sep 41
Gen.Lt. Grase, Jan 42–Jun 43
Gen.Lt. von Krosigk, Jul 43–May 44; Jun–Oct 44
Gen.Major Baurmeister, May–Jun 44
Gen.Lt. Schittnig, Oct 44–Feb 45
Gen.Lt. Henning von Thadden, Feb–May 45

4th Infantry Division—See 14th Panzer Division

5th Infantry Division

May 40	Offensive operations in Western Europe
Jun–Dec 41	Offensive opns Eastern Front, Viazma

Dec 41   Withdrawn to France and
            reorganized as a light
            infantry division

Commanders

Gen.d.Art. Fahrmbacher, Sep 39–
Oct 40

Gen.d.Inf. Allmendinger, Oct 40–
Dec 41

6th Infantry Division

34–35   Formed near Bielefeld
            from 18th Regt., *Reichswehr*

May–   Offensive opns on West-
Jun 40   ern Front

Jun–Dec 41 Offensive opns on Eastern
            Front, central sector

Summer 43   Offensive opns vic. Kursk
            (Operation ZITADELLE)

Winter   Defensive opns vic.
43–44   middle Dnepr sector

Jul 44   Destroyed near Bobruisk

Fall 44   Reformed as 6th VGD

Dec 44–   Defensive opns between
Mar 45   the Vistula River and
            Radom, Poland

Mar 45–   Reformed as 6th ID;
May 45   capitulated in Bohemia

Commanders

Gen.Lt. Arnold *Freiherr* von
Biegeleben, Sep 39–Oct 40

Gen.Lt. Auleb, Oct 40–Jan 42

Gen.Lt. Grossmann, Jan 42–Dec 43

Gen.Lt. von Neindorff, Dec 43–
Jan 44

Gen.Major Conrady, Jan 44

Gen.Major Klammt, Jan–May 44

Gen.Lt. Heyne, Jun 44

Gen.Lt. Brücker, Oct 44–May 45

7th Infantry Division

34–35   Formed in Munich from
            19th Regt., *Reichswehr*

Sep 39   Offensive opns in Poland

May–   Offensive opns on West-
Jun 40   ern Front

Jun–Dec 41 Offensive opns, Eastern
            Front central sector

Summer 43   Offensive opns vic. Kursk
            (Operation ZITADELLE)

Winter   Defensive opns vic.
43–44   middle Dnepr sector

Early 44   Defensive opns west of
            middle Dnepr sector

Dec 44   Defensive opns north of
            Warsaw

Mar 45   Withdrew to vic. Danzig;
            destroyed

Commanders

Gen.Lt. Ott, Sep 39

Gen.Lt. *Freiherr* von Gablenz, Sep 39–
Dec 41

Gen.Lt. Hans Jordan, Dec 41–Nov 42

Gen.Lt. von Rappard, Nov 42–Oct 43;
Feb–Aug 44; Aug 44–Feb 45

Gen.Major André, Oct–Nov 43

Gen.Major Gihr, Nov–Dec 43

Gen.Major Traut, Dec 43–Feb 44

Gen.Major Alois Weber, Aug 44

Gen.Major Noak, Feb–May 45

8th Infantry Division

Sep 39   Offensive opns in Poland

May–   Offensive opns in Western
Jun 40   Europe

Jun–Dec 41 Offensive opns Eastern
            Front, central sector vic.
            Suwalki, Grodno, Vitebsk,
            Smolensk, and Viazma.

Dec 41   Withdrawn to France and
            reorganized as a light
            infantry division

Commanders

Gen.d.Kav. Koch-Erpach, Sep 39–
Oct 40

Gen.d.Inf. Höhne, Oct 40–Dec 41

9th Infantry Division (later VGD)

Mar 35   Formed near Giessen

May–   Offensive opns on
Jun 40   Western Front

Jun–Dec 41 Offensive opns on
            Eastern Front, southern
            sector

Summer   Offensive opns in
42–43   Caucasus, withdrew vic.
            Kuban area

Fall 43   Defensive opns in lower
            Dnepr area

Fall 44	Retrograde opns through Romania; heavy losses
Oct 44	Remnants assembled at Wildflecken; reorganized as VGD
Late Oct 44– Mar 45	Redeployed to Western Front; destroyed vic. Trier

Commanders

Gen.Lt. von Apell, Sep 39–Aug 40
Gen.Lt. Vierow, Aug 40–Jan 41
Gen.Lt. *Freiherr* von Schleinitz, Jan 41– Aug 43
Gen.Lt. Friedrich Hofmann, Aug 43– May 44
Gen.Lt. Brücker, May–Jun 44
Gen.Major Gebb, Jun–Aug 44
Gen.Major Werner Kolb, Sep 44– May 45

10th Infantry Division—See 10th Motorized Infantry Division

11th Infantry Division

34–35	Formed near Allenstein, East Prussia, from 2d Regt., *Reichswehr*
Sep 39	Offensive opns in Poland
Jun– Dec 41	Offensive opns on Eastern Front, northern sector
Summer 43	Heavily engaged south of Lake Ladoga
Aug 44	Engaged at Narva
Sep–Oct 44	Withdrew to Kurland
Oct 44– May 45	Defensive opns in Kurland Capitulated to Soviets

Commanders

Gen.Lt. Max Bock, Sep–Oct 39
Gen.Lt. von Böckmann, Oct 39–Jan 42
Gen.Lt. Thomaschki, Jan 42–Sep 43
Gen.Lt. Burdach, Sep 43–Apr 44
Gen.Lt. Reymann, Apr–Nov 44
Gen.Lt. Feyerabend, Nov 44–May 45

12th Infantry Division (later VGD)

35–36	Formed in Schwerin, Mecklenburg during expansion of army
Sep 39	Offensive opns in Poland

May– Jun 40	Offensive opns on Western Front
Jun–Dec 41	Offensive opns on Eastern Front, northern sector
Early 43	Transferred to Eastern Front, central sector
Summer 44	Largely destroyed near Mogilev
Aug 44	Merged at Graudenz with partly formed 549th ID; redesignated as VGD
Sep 44– Apr 45	Transferred to Western Front; defensive opns vic. Aachen, Düren; offensive opns in Ardennes; destroyed in Ruhr Pocket

Commanders

Gen.Lt. von der Leyen, Sep 39–Mar 40
Gen.Lt. von Seydlitz-Kurzbach, Mar 40–Jan 42
Gen.Lt. Hernekamp, Jan–Mar 42
Gen.Major Gerhard Müller, Mar 42
Gen.Lt. Kurt-Jürgen *Freiherr* von Lützow, Mar–Jul 42; Jul 42–May 44
Gen.Major Wilhelm Lorenz, Jul 42
Gen.Lt. Jahn, May–Jun 44
Gen.Lt. Bamler, Jun 44
Gen.Lt. Gerhard Engel, Aug 44–Apr 45
Gen.Major Ernst König, Apr 45

14th Infantry Division

Jun 43	Formed from 14th Motorized Infantry Division
Aug 43	Offensive and defensive opns vic. Smolensk-Vitebsk
Jun 44	Defensive opns vic. Vitebsk; withdrawn to rest and refit
Aug 44	Defensive opns, central sector, north of Warsaw
Jan– May 45	Defensive and retrograde opns in East Prussia; part of division transported to Schleswig-Holstein and capitulated to British forces; rest of division destroyed in East Prussia, went into Soviet captivity

Commanders

Gen.Lt. Weyer, 1939–Jun 40

Gen.Lt. Dr. Rendulic, Jun–Nov 40

Gen.Lt. Friedrich Fürst, Nov 40–Jun 41

Gen.Lt. Wosch, Jun 41–Oct 42

Gen.Lt. Walther Krause, Oct 42–Jan 43

Gen.Lt. Holste, Jan–May 43

Gen.Lt. Flörke, May–Jun 43

15th Infantry Division

35–36	Formed in Kassel during expansion of army
Jun–Dec 41	Offensive opns on Eastern Front, central sector
Apr 42	Transferred to France
Mar 43	Offensive and defensive opns, Eastern Front, southern sector
Summer 43	Offensive opns vic. Dnepropetrovosk
Jan 44	Defensive opns, southern Ukraine
Aug 44	Heavy losses in encirclement vic. lower Dnestr River; reconstituted in eastern Hungary
Oct 44	Defensive opns in Hungary
Jan–Mar 45	Retreated to Tatras, Czechoslovakia; capitulated in Moravia

Commanders

Gen.Lt. Beschnitt, 1939

Gen.Lt. Hell, Oct 39–Jun 40, Aug 40–Jan 42

Gen.Lt. von Chappuis, Jun–Aug 40

Gen.Major Alfred Schreiber, Jan–Feb 42

Gen.Lt. Erich Buschenhagen, Jun 42–Nov 43

Gen.Major Sperl, Nov 43–Aug 44

Gen.Major Babel, Aug–Sep 44

Gen.Major Längenfelder, Oct 44–May 45

17th Infantry Division

34–35	Formed in Nuremberg from 21st Regt., *Reichswehr*
Sep 39	Offensive opns in Poland
May–Jun 40	Offensive opns on Western Front
Jun–Dec 41	Offensive opns Eastern Front, central sector
Summer 42	Transferred to France
Feb 43	Defensive opns, Eastern Front, southern sector
Summer 43	Offensive and defensive opns vic. Taganrog
Fall 43	Defensive opns, lower Dnepr River and southern Ukraine
Mar 44	Retrograde opns from lower Dnepr River bend
Summer 44	Withdrawn for reconstitution
Late 44	Defensive opns in southern Poland
Jan 45	Heavy losses east of Radom
Feb 45	Largely destroyed east of Breslau, Silesia
Apr 45	Rebuilt in Görlitz
May 45	Capitulated to Soviet forces in Silesia

Commanders

Gen.Lt. Loch, Sep 39–Oct 41

Gen.Lt. Güntzel, Oct–Dec 41

Gen.Lt. von Zangen, Dec 41–Apr 43

Gen.Lt. Richard Zimmer, Apr 43–Feb 44 and May–Sep 44

Gen.Lt. Brücker, Feb–Mar 44 and Apr–May 44

Gen.Major Haus, Mar–Apr 44

Gen.Major Sachsenheimer, Sep 44–Apr 45

21st Infantry Division

34–35	Formed near Mohrungen, East Prussia from 3d Regt., *Reichswehr*
Sep 39	Offensive opns in Poland
May–Jun 40	Offensive opns on Western Front
Jun–Dec 41	Offensive opns Eastern Front, northern sector through Lithuania, Latvia toward Novgorod, Chudovo and Volkhov

Jan 42–Jan 44	Offensive, defensive, and retrograde opns Eastern Front, northern sector
Feb 44	Retrograde opns vic. Leningrad
Fall 44	Defensive and retrograde opns Eastern Front, central sector
Jan 45	Defensive opns vic. Goldap, East Prussia
Mar 45	Retrograde opns to and defensive opns in Heiligenbeil Pocket

Commanders

Gen.Lt. von Both, Sep–Oct 39
Gen.Lt. Sponheimer, Oct 39–Jan 43
Gen.Lt. Matzky, Jan–Nov 43; Dec 43–Mar 44
Gen.Major Lamey, Nov–Dec 43
Gen.Lt. Sensfuss, Mar 44
Gen.Lt. Hermann Förtsch, Mar–Aug 44
Gen.Lt. Götz, Aug 44–Apr 45
Gen.Major Karl Kötz, Apr–May 45

22d Infantry Division ("Air Landing")

34–35	Formed in Oldenburg from 16th Regt., *Reichswehr*
May–Jun 40	Offensive opns in the Netherlands
Jun–Dec 41	Offensive opns Eastern Front, southern sector
Summer 42	Transferred to Greece, then Crete; reorganized as motorized division; evacuated from Crete; converted to field division; engaged in relief of divisions isolated in Montenegro
Fall 44	
Jan 45	Security and anti-partisan opns in Yugoslavia
Apr 45	Redesignated a VGD; remained on southeast front

Commanders

Gen.Lt. *Graf* von Sponeck, 1939–Oct 41
Gen.Lt. Ludwig Wolff, Oct 41–Aug 42
Gen.Lt. Friedrich-Wilhelm Müller, Aug 42–Feb 44
Gen.Major Kreipe, Feb 44–Mar 45

Gen.Lt. Friebe, Mar–Apr 45
Gen.Lt. Kühne, Apr–May 45

23d Infantry Division

34–35	Formed in Potsdam from 9th Regt., *Reichswehr*
Sep 39	Offensive opns in Poland
May–Jun 40	Offensive opns on Western Front
Jun–Dec 41	Offensive opns on Eastern Front
Spring 42	Converted to 26th Panzer Division in France
Fall 42	New 23d Infantry Division formed in Denmark
Winter 42–43	Defensive opns vic. Leningrad
Fall 44	Retrograde opns in Estonia; defended Saaremaa Island
Oct 44	Defensive opns on Latvian coast
Jan 45	Remnants rebuilt in Prussia
Mar 45	Defensive opns, Danzig Pocket; destroyed

Commanders

Gen.Lt. Graf von Brockdorff-Ahlefeldt, 39–Jun 40
Gen.Lt. Hellmich, Jun 40–Jan 42
Gen.Lt. Badinski, Jan–Jul 42
Gen.Major von Schellwitz, Nov 42–Aug 43
Gen.Lt. Horst von Mellenthin, Aug–Sep 43
Gen.Lt. Gurran, Sep 43–Feb 44
Gen.Lt. von Beaulieu, Feb–Aug 44
Gen.Lt. Schirmer, Aug 44–May 45

24th Infantry Division

35–36	Formed near Chemnitz
Sep 39	Offensive opns in Poland
May–Jun 40	Offensive opns on Western Front
Jun–Dec 41	Offensive opns, Eastern Front, southern sector
Winter 42–43	Defensive opns Eastern Front, northern sector

Feb–Jul 44	Defensive and Retrograde opns Eastern Front, northern sector
Oct 44	Withdrew to Latvian coast
Oct 44–May 45	Defensive opns along the Baltic coast in Latvia vic. Vietsaniki and Venteri

Commanders

Gen.d.Inf. Olbricht, 1939–Feb 40

Gen.Lt. von Obernitz, Feb–Jun 40

Gen.d.Inf. von Tettau, Jun 40–Feb 43

Gen.d.Geb. Versock, Feb 43–Feb 44, Jun–Sep 44

Gen.Lt. Hans *Freiherr* von Falkenstein, Feb–Jun 44

Gen.Major Harald Schultz, Sep 44–May 45

25th Infantry Division—See 25th Panzer Grenadier Division

26th Infantry Division (later VGD)

35–36	Formed near Cologne
May–Jun 40	Offensive opns on Western Front
Jun–Dec 41	Offensive opns Eastern Front, central sector vic. Lithuania, Polotsk (Belorussia), toward Rzhev
Jan 42–Summer 44	Offensive and defensive opns Eastern Front, central sector vic. Rzhev, Orel, Voronezh, Kursk, Mogilev, and Kovel; largely destroyed vic. Kovel
Summer 43	Offensive opns vic. Kursk (Operation ZITADELLE)
Jul 44	Defensive opns vic. Kovel
Sep 44	Destroyed in East Prussia; reconstituted vic. Posen as VGD
Nov 44	Defensive opns in Luxembourg
Dec 44	Offensive opns in Ardennes
Jan–May 45	Defensive opns on Western Front; surrendered to Allied forces

Commanders

Gen.Lt. Sigismund von Förster, Sep 39–Jan 41

Gen.Lt. Walter Weiss, Jan 41–Apr 42

Gen.Lt. Wiese, Apr 42–Aug 43

Gen.Lt. de Boer, Aug 43–Aug 44

Gen.Major Kokott, Aug–May 45

27th Infantry Division—See 17th Panzer Division

28th Infantry Division

Sep 39	Offensive opns in Poland
May–Jun 40	Offensive opns in Western Europe
Jun–Nov 41	Offensive opns Eastern Front, central sector vic. Smolensk, Viazma, and west of Moscow
Nov 41	Withdrawn to France and reorganized as light infantry division

Commanders

Gen.d.Inf. von Obstfelder, Sep 39–May 40

Gen.d.Art. Sinnhuber, May 40–Nov 41

30th Infantry Division

34–35	Formed in Lübeck from 6th Regt., *Reichswehr*
Sep 39	Offensive opns in Poland
May–Jun 40	Offensive opns in Belgium
Jun–Dec 41	Offensive opns Eastern Front, northern sector
Oct 44–May 45	Retrograde and defensive opns vic. Latvian coast; capitulated to Soviet forces

Commanders

Gen.Lt. von Briesen, 1939–Nov 40

Gen.Lt. von Tippelskirch, Jan 41–Jun 42

Gen.Lt. von Wickede, Jun 42–Oct 43

Gen.Lt. Hasse, Nov 43–Mar 44

Gen.Lt. von Basse, Mar–Aug 44

Gen.Major Barth, Aug 44–Jan 45

Gen.Lt. Henze, Jan 45–May 45

31st Infantry Division (later VGD)

34–35	Formed near Braunschweig from 12th and 17th Regts., *Reichswehr*
Sep 39	Offensive opns in Poland
May–Jun 40	Offensive opns on Western Front
Jun–Dec 41	Offensive opns Eastern Front, central sector
Summer 43	Offensive opns vic. Kursk (Operation ZITADELLE)
Fall 43	Defensive opns, middle Dnepr River sector
Jul 44	Defensive opns vic. Mogilev; nearly destroyed
Aug 44	Reformed as VGD
Sep 44	Defensive and retrograde opns Eastern Front, northern sector
Dec 44	Defensive opns on Latvian coast
Early 45	Withdrew to northern Germany (Army Group Center) and destroyed near Berlin

Commanders

Gen.Lt. Kämpfe, 1939 -May 41
Gen.Lt. Kalmukoff, May–Aug 41
Gen.Lt. Gerhard Berthold, Aug 41–Jan 42
Gen.d.Inf. Hossbach, Jan–Feb 42
Gen.Lt. Gerhard Berthold, Feb–Apr 42
Gen.Lt. Pflieger, Apr 42–Apr 43
Gen.Lt. Flörke, Apr–May 43
Gen.Lt. Hossbach, May–Aug 43
Gen.Lt. Ochsner, Aug 43–Jun 44
Gen.Major von Stolzmann, Oct 44–May 45

32d Infantry Division

34–35	Formed at Köslin from 4th Regt., *Reichswehr*
Sep 39	Offensive opns in Poland
May–Jun 40	Offensive opns on Western Front
Jun–Dec 41	Offensive opns Eastern Front, northern sector
Summer–Fall 41	Offensive opns north of Lake Ilmen, Valdai Hills
Jan 44	Defensive opns in Eastern Front, central sector
Feb 44	Defensive opns Eastern Front, northern sector
Late 44	Retrograde and defensive opns vic. Latvian coast
Jan–May 45	Redeployed to East Prussia vic. Platow, Linde, Grunau, Görsdorf
Mar 45	Defensive opns vic. Danzig

Commanders:

Gen.Lt. Böhme, Sep–Oct 39, Dec 39–Jun 40
Gen.Lt. *Freiherr* von Gablenz, Oct–Dec 39
Gen.Lt. Bohnstedt, Jun 40–Mar 42
Gen.Lt. Hernekamp, Mar–Jun 42
Gen.Lt. Wilhelm Wegener, Jun 42–Jun 43; Aug–Sep 43
Gen.Lt. Thielmann, Jun–Aug 43
Gen.Lt. Böckh-Behrens, Sep 43–Feb 44; Jun–Aug 44; Aug 44–May 45
Gen.Major Franz Schlieper, Feb–Jun 44
Gen.Major Georg Kossmala, Aug 44

33d Infantry Division—See 15th Panzer Division

34th Infantry Division

35–36	Activated vic. Heidelberg
May–Jun 40	Offensive opns on Western Front
Jun–Dec 41	Offensive opns Eastern Front, central sector
Aug 43	Offensive and defensive opns vic. Kharkov
Spring 44	Defensive and retrograde opns in northern Ukraine
Jul 44	Redeployed to northwestern Italy
Oct 44–Apr 45	Coastal defensive and defensive opns in northwest Italy; capitulated to American forces

Commanders

Gen.Lt. Behlendorff, 1939–May 40, Nov 40–Oct 41

Gen.Lt. Sanne, May–Nov 40
Gen.Lt. Fürst, Oct 41–Sep 42
Gen.Lt. Scherer, Sep–Nov 42
Gen.Lt. Hochbaum, Nov 42–May 44
Gen.Lt. Lieb, May 44–45
Oberst Ferdinand Hippel, 1945

35th Infantry Division

35–36	Activated at Karlsruhe
May–Jun 40	Offensive opns in Belgium
Jun–Dec 41	Offensive opns Eastern Front, central sector vic. Lithuania toward Smolensk, Kholm, Viazma, Moscow
Jan 42–Jun 44	Defensive, offensive, and retrograde opns Eastern Front, central sector between Moscow and Smolensk
Jul 44	Heavy losses vic. Bobruisk
Sep 44	Defensive opns vic. Modlin, Poland; retrograde and defensive opns vic. Danzig
Sep 44–May 45	Defensive and retrograde opns in Poland vic. Pultusk and East Prussia vic. Danzig; destroyed and capitulated to Soviets

Commanders
Gen.Lt. Hans Wolfgang Reinhard, 1939–Nov 40
Gen.Lt. Fischer von Weikersthal, Nov 40–Dec 41
Gen.Lt. *Freiherr* von Roman, Dec 41–Sep 42
Gen.Lt. Merker, Sep 42–Apr 43; Jun–Nov 43
Gen.Lt. Drescher, Apr–Jun 43
Gen.Lt. Richert, Nov 43–Apr 44; May–Aug 44
Gen.Major Gihr, Apr–May 44

36th Infantry Division (later VGD)

May 43	Reorganized as a two-regiment infantry division
Jul 43	Offensive opns vic. Kursk (Operation *ZITADELLE*)

Summer–Fall 43	Offensive, defensive, and retrograde opns, Eastern Front, central sector
Winter 43–44	Defensive and retrograde opns, Eastern Front, central sector
Jun 44	Destroyed in central sector vic. Bobruisk, remnants returned to Germany
Aug 44	Reformed at Baumholder as VGD
Sep 44	Defensive opns, Ardennes
Dec 44–Apr 45	Defensive opns in Saar; offensive opns in Lorraine and Alsace (Operation *NORDWIND*); surrendered to US forces in the Rhineland

Commanders
Gen.Lt. Lindemann, 1939–Oct 40
Gen.Lt. Ottenbacher, Oct 40–Oct 41
Gen.Lt. Gollnick, Oct 41–Aug 43
Gen.Lt. Stegmann, Aug 43; Sep 43–Jan 44
Gen.Major Fröhlich, Aug–Sep 43
Gen.Major Kadgien, Jan 44
Gen.Lt. von Neindorff, Jan 44
Gen.Major Conrady, Jan–Jul 44
Gen.Major Wellm, Oct 44–Mar 45
Gen.Major Kleikamp, Mar–May 45

39th Infantry Division

Summer 42	Activated in Netherlands
Mar 43	Defensive opns Eastern Front, southern sector
Dec 43	Defensive and retrograde opns vic. lower Dnepr River; disbanded and absorbed by 106th ID

Commanders
Gen.Lt. Höfl, Jul–Dec 42
Gen.Lt. Löweneck, Dec 42–May 43
Gen.Major, Hünten, May–Sep 43
Gen.Lt. Mahlmann, Sep–Nov 43

41st Infantry Division

Early 44	Formed in Greece as a fortress division
Sep–Nov 44	Rearguard opns, withdrew through Yugoslavia

Jan 45	Redesignated as 41st ID, defensive and retrograde opns in Croatia between Drava and Sava Rivers

Commanders

Gen.Lt. Krech, Nov 43–Apr 44
Gen.Lt. Dr. Benicke, Apr–Aug 44
Gen.Major Wolfgang Hauser, Aug 44–May 45

42d Infantry Division—See 42d *Jäger* Division

44th Infantry Division

1938	Formed in Vienna from 4th Regt., Austrian Army
Sep 39	Offensive opns in Poland
May–Jun 40	Offensive opns in France
Jun–Dec 41	Offensive opns Eastern Front, southern sector vic. Dubno, Kiev, Kharkov
Jan–May 42	Defensive and retrograde opns on Eastern Front, southern sector
May–Sep 42	Offensive opns on Eastern Front, southern sector vic. Millerovo, Don River bend
Sep 42–Jan 43	Offensive and defensive opns vic. Stalingrad; destroyed
Apr 43	Reformed in France as a two-regiment ID
Jun 43	Reconstituted as the "*Reichs-Grenadier-Division Hoch und Deutschmeister*"
Aug 43–Early 44	Redeployed to northern Italy, anti-partisan opns in Slovenia; defensive opns vic. Cassino, Italy
Late 44	Refitted in Venezia Giulia
Nov 44–Apr 45	Offensive, defensive and retrograde opns in Hungary vic. Komarom, Varpalota, Tapolca, and Austria vic. Radkersburg and Leibnitz; redeployed to vic. Seefeld

Late Apr–May 45	Defensive and retrograde opns in Austria vic. Seefeld, Gmünd
May 45	Capitulation vic. Hohenfurth and Rosenberg, Czechoslovakia; most of the division remained in American captivity, but a part was transferred to Soviet custody

Commanders

Gen.Lt. Schubert, Sep–Oct 39
Gen.Lt. Siebert, Oct 39–May 42
Gen.Lt. Deboi, May 42–Jan 43
Gen.Lt. Dr. Beyer, Mar 43–Jan 44
Gen.Lt. Dr. Franek, Jan–May 44
Gen.Lt. Ortner, May–Jun 44
Gen.Major Klatt, Jun 44
Gen.Lt. von Rost, Jun 44–Mar 45
Oberst Hoffmann, Mar–Apr 45
Gen.Major Langhäuser, Apr–May 45

45th Infantry Division (later VGD)

1938	Formed in Linz, Austria
Sep 39	Offensive opns in Poland
May–Jun 40	Offensive opns on Western Front
Jun–Dec 41	Offensive opns Eastern Front, central sector, including reduction of the Brest-Litovsk fortress, Pinsk, through the Pripet Marshes, to Gomel, Rylsk, Jelets
Jan–May 42	Defensive and retrograde opns vic. Eastern Front, central sector
Jul 43	Offensive opns vic. Eastern Front, central sector
Fall 43	Defensive opns Sozh River
Jul 44	Destroyed in Bobruisk area in Soviet Summer Offensive
Oct 44	Reorganized in Germany as VGD
Fall 44	Defensive opns, Eastern Front, central sector
Jan–May 45	Defensive opns south of Vistula River bend and

vic. Radom, Poland; sur-
rendered to Soviet forces

Commanders

Gen.Lt. Materna, 1939–Oct 40
Gen.Lt. Körner, Oct 40–Apr 41
Gen.Lt. Schlieper, Apr 41–Feb 42
Gen.Lt. Kühlwein, Feb 42–Apr 43
Gen.Lt. Hans, *Freiherr* von Falkenstein,
   Apr–Nov 43
Gen.Major Joachim Engel, Nov 43–
   Feb 44; Apr–Jun 44
Gen.Lt. Gihr, Feb–Apr 44
Gen.Major Richard Daniel, Oct 44–
   May 45

46th Infantry Division

1938	Formed in Karlsbad, Sudetenland
41–42	Offensive opns Eastern Front, southern sector; then in Crimea and Caucasus
Feb 43	Defensive opns vic. Donets River sector
Summer 43	Offensive opns vic. Belgorod
Fall 43	Offensive and defensive opns vic. Dnepropetrovosk
Mar 44	Defensive and retrograde opns vic. Krivoi Rog and Yassy, Romania
Sep 44	Defensive and retrograde opns vic. Transylvania
Late 44–Mar 45	Defensive and retrograde opns in Czechoslovakia
Mar 45	Offensive and defensive opns in Hungary
Apr–May 45	Defensive and retrograde opns in Czechoslovakia vic. Austerlitz, Adamsthal (Adamov), Deutsch Brod; destroyed; capitulated to Soviet forces

Commanders

Gen.Lt. von Hase, 1939–Jul 40
Gen.Lt. Kriebel, Jul 40–Sep 41
Gen.Lt. Himer, Sep 41–Mar 42
Gen.Lt. Haccius, Apr 42–Feb 43

Gen.Lt. Hauffe, Feb 43
Gen.Lt. von le Suire, Feb–May 43
Gen.Lt. Röpke, May 43–Jul 44
Oberst Curt Ewrigmann, Jul–Aug 44
Gen.Lt. Erich Reuter, Aug 44–May 45

50th Infantry Division

1939	Formed from border guard in Brandenburg
May–Jun 40	Offensive opns on Western Front
Apr 41	Offensive opns in Balkans
Jun–Dec 41	Offensive opns Eastern Front, southern sector; later in the Crimea and Caucasus
Winter 42–43	Defensive and retrograde opns vic. Kuban
Fall 43	Defensive and retrograde opns vic. lower Dnepr River
Early 44	Redeployed to the Crimea
Apr 44	Retrograde opns vic. Crimea; heavy losses
May 44	Reconstituted
Jul 44	Defensive opns Eastern Front, central sector
Late 44–Mar 45	Defensive and retrograde opns in Czechoslovakia
Mar 45	Offensive and defensive opns in Hungary
Apr–May 45	Defensive and retrograde opns in Czechoslovakia vic. Austerlitz, Adamsthal (Adamov), Deutsch Brod; destroyed; capitulated to Soviet forces

Commanders

Gen.Lt. Sorsche, 1939–Oct 40
Gen.Lt. Hollidt, Oct 40–Jan 42
Gen.Lt. August Schmidt, Jan–
   Mar 42
Gen.Lt. Friedrich Schmidt, Mar 42–
   Jun 43
Gen.Lt. Sixt, Jun 43–Apr 44
Gen.Lt. Paul Betz, Apr 44–May 44
Gen.Major Haus, May 44–Apr 45
Gen.Major Domansky, Apr–
   May 45

52d Infantry Division

Jun–Dec 41	Offensive opns on Eastern Front, central sector vic. Vilna, Minsk, Rogachev and Kaluga
Jan 42– Fall 43	Operations on Eastern Front, central sector: offensive opns vic. Tarussa and Yukhnov; anti-partisan opns vic. Roslavl; offensive and defensive opns vic. Sukhinichi; defensive opns vic. Maloye Beresnevo, near Smolensk; largely destroyed; remnants incorporated into 197th ID

Commanders

Gen.Lt. Hollidt, 1939
Gen.Lt. Hans-Jürgen von Arnim, Sep 39–Oct 40
Gen.Lt. Dr. Rendulic, Oct 40–Nov 42
Gen.Lt. Peschel, Nov 42–Nov 43

52d Security Division

1939	Formed vic. Kassel as 52d ID
Apr– Summer 1940	Operated partly in Norway and partly in the West
Jun 41	Offensive opns, central sector, Eastern Front
Fall 43	Heavy losses vic. Smolensk; withdrawn from combat
Nov 43	Remnants converted to field training division in Belorussia
May 44	Redesignated as a security division, for special employment
Summer 44	Destroyed in central sector, Eastern Front
Oct 44	Staff administered rear area security in Kurland
Apr 45	Staff redesignated as Libau Fortress Command

Commanders

Gen.Lt. Hollidt, Sep 39
Gen.Lt. Hans-Jürgen von Arnim, Sep 39–Oct 40

Gen.Lt. Dr. Rendulic, Oct 40–Nov 42
Gen.Lt. Peschel, Nov 42–Nov 43
Gen.Major Newiger, Dec 43–Apr 44

56th Infantry Division

Summer 39	Activated in Dresden
Sep 39	Offensive opns in Poland
May Jun 40	Offensive opns in Belgium
Jun– Dec 41	Offensive opns, southern sector, vic. Kovel and Korosten and to the Dnepr River
Jan– May 42	Defensive and security opns vic. Briansk, Orel
Summer– Fall 42	Offensive opns, Eastern Front, central sector
Summer 43	Offensive opns vic. Kursk (Operation ZITADELLE); heavy losses and incorporated into Corps Det D
Summer 44	Destroyed with Corps Det D
Fall 44	Reconstituted
Oct 44	Defensive and retrograde opns in East Prussia
Mar 45	Retrograde opns to Heiligenbeil Pocket, absorbed by the 197th ID

Commanders

Gen.Lt. Karl Kriebel, 1939–Jul 40
Gen.Lt. Paul von Hase, Aug–Nov 40
Gen.Lt. Karl von Oven, Nov 40– Jan 43
Gen.Lt. Otto Lüdecke, Jan–Sep 43
Gen.Major Bernhard Pampel umbenannt in Pamberg, Jun–Jul 44
Gen.Lt. Edmund Blaurock, Jul 44– Mar 45

57th Infantry Division

Summer 39	Formed at Bad Reichenhall
Sep 39	Offensive opns in Poland
May– Jun 40	Offensive opns on Western Front
Jun– Dec 41	Offensive opns Eastern Front, southern sector
Jan– May 42	Defensive opns, southern sector

Summer–Fall 42	Offensive opns, southern sector
Winter 42–43	Defensive and retrograde opns, southern sector
Summer 43	Offensive opns, southern sector
Fall 43–Early 44	Defensive and retrograde opns, southern sector
Feb 44	Defensive opns vic. Korsun; largely destroyed
Spring 44	Reconstituted
Jun 44	Defensive opns vic. Mogilev; destroyed
Jul 44	Disbanded

Commanders

Gen.Lt. Blümm, 1939–Sep 41; Apr–Oct 42

Gen.Lt. Dostler, Sep 41–Apr 42

Gen.Lt. Friedrich Siebert, Oct 42–Feb 43

Gen.Lt. Otto Fretter-Pico, Feb–Sep 43

Gen.Lt. Vinzenz Müller, Sep 43

Gen.Major Trowitz, Sep 43–Jul 44

58th Infantry Division

1939	Formed in Hamburg
Apr 40	Defensive opns, Saar Front
Jun–Dec 41	Offensive opns on Eastern Front, northern sector, through Latvia, Estonia, toward Leningrad
Jan 42–Jan 44	Defensive opns vic. Oranienbaum, Demjansk, Lake Ladoga, Mga, and Nevel
Jan 44–Feb 45	Defensive and retrograde opns vic. Estonia, Latvia, Lithuania
Feb–Mar 45	Defensive and retrograde opns in East Prussia; cut off in Samland Pocket; destroyed and capitulated to Soviet forces

Commanders

Gen.Lt. Iwan Heunert, 1939–Sep 41

Gen.Lt. Dr. Friedrich Altrichter, Sep–Apr 41

Gen.Lt. Karl von Graffen, Apr 41–May 43

Gen.Lt. Wilhelm Berlin, May–Jun 43

Gen.Lt. Siewert, Jun 43–Apr 45

60th Infantry Division—See 60th Motorized Infantry Division

61st Infantry Division (later VGD)

Summer 39	Formed in Königsberg
May–Jun 40	Offensive opns in Belgium
Jun–Dec 41	Offensive opns on Eastern Front, northern sector in Latvia, Estonia, the Baltic islands of Moon, ☐sel, and Dagö, toward Volkhov.
Jan 42–Jan 44	Offensive and defensive opns vic. Leningrad and Lake Ladoga
Jan 44–Jan 45	Defensive and retrograde opns in Estonia, Latvia
Jan–Apr 45	Defensive and retrograde opns in East Prussia, vic. Gumbinnen, Rominten, Zinten, Prussian Eylau, and the Heiligenbeil Pocket; destroyed and capitulated to Soviet forces

Commanders

Gen.Lt. Hänicke, 1939–Mar 42

Gen.Major Scheidies, Mar–Apr 42

Gen.Lt. Hühner, Apr 42–Feb 43

Gen.Lt. Krappe, Feb–Apr 43; May–Dec 43; Feb–Dec 44

Gen.Lt. Gottfried Weber, Apr–May 43

Gen.Major Joachim Albrecht von Blücher, Dec 43–Feb 44

Gen.Lt. Sperl, Dec 44–Apr 45

62d Infantry Division (later VGD)

1939	Formed in Glatz
Sep 39	Offensive opns in Poland
May–Jun 40	Offensive opns on Western Front
Jun–Dec 41	Offensive opns on Eastern Front, southern sector
Jan–May 42	Defensive opns on Eastern Front, southern sector
Jun–Sep 42	Offensive opns on Eastern Front, southern sector
Sep 42–Jan 43	Offensive, defensive, and retrograde opns vic. Stalingrad

Jan–Dec 43	Offensive, defensive, and retrograde opns Eastern Front, southern sector
Jan–Mar 44	Defensive and retrograde opns on Eastern Front, southern sector vic. Mius River, Ingul. Heavy losses; remainder of the division incorporated into "Corps Detachment F."
Jul 44	Reconstituted
Summer 44	Defensive and retrograde opns Romania; destroyed.
Sep 44	Reconstituted as 62d VGD
Nov 44–Apr 45	Defensive opns Western Front, Eifel area, Ardennes offensive vic. Monschau, retrograde opns to and encircled in Ruhr Pocket; capitulated to US forces

Commanders

Gen.Lt. Keiner, 1939–Sep 41
Gen.Lt. Rudolf Friedrich, Sep 41–Sep 42
Gen.Major von Reuss, Sep–Dec 42
Gen.Major Gruner, Dec 42–Jan 43
Gen.Lt. Huffmann, Jan–Nov 43
Gen.Lt. Graf von Hülsen, Nov 43–Mar 44
Gen.Major Tronnier, Mar–Aug 44

68th Infantry Division

Summer 39	Formed in Guben from reservists
May–Jun 40	Offensive opns on Western Front
Jun–Dec 41	Offensive opns Eastern Front, southern sector vic. Lvov, Vinnitsa, Cherkassy, Kharkov, Poltava
Jan–May 42	Defensive opns, Eastern Front, southern sector, vic. Dontes River sector, Slaviansk
Summer–Fall 42	Offensive opns, Eastern Front, southern sector
Winter 42–43	Defensive and retrograde opns Eastern Front, southern sector

Spring–Summer 43	Offensive operations vic. Eastern Front, southern sector
Fall 43	Defensive and retrograde opns Eastern Front, southern sector vic. Ukraine
Winter 43–44	Defensive and retrograde opns on Eastern Front, southern sector vic. Zhitomir, Berdichev
Spring–Summer 44	Defensive and retrograde opns vic. Galicia
Fall–Winter 44	Defensive and retrograde opns in Poland vic. Rakow, Dukla Pass, and Gorlice
Jan–May 45	Defensive and retrograde opns in Czechoslovakia vic. Krnov; capitulated to Soviet forces

Commanders

Gen.Lt. Georg Braun, 1939–Nov 41
Gen.Lt. Meissner, Nov 41–Jan 43
Gen.Lt. Hans Schmidt, Jan–Oct 43
Gen.Lt. Scheuerpflug, Oct 43–May 45

69th Infantry Division

Summer 39	Formed in Rheinland
Apr 40	Offensive opns and occupation of Norway
41–42	Grenadier Regiment 193 detached for duty in northern Finland
Spring 43	Offensive and defensive opns Eastern Front, northern sector
Fall 44	Defensive and retrograde opns Eastern Front, central sector
Jan 45	Defensive opns in East Prussia vic.Tilsit and Schillfelde
Mar 45	Remnants destroyed at Königsberg

Commanders

Gen.Lt. Tittel, 1939–Sep 41
Gen.Lt. Ortner, Sep 41–Feb 44
Gen.Lt. Rein, Feb 44–Jan 45

Oberst Grimme, Jan–Feb 45
Gen.Major Völker, Feb–Apr 45

71st Infantry Division

Summer 39	Formed at Hildesheim from reservists
May–Jun 40	Offensive opns on Western Front
Jun–Oct 41	Offensive opns Eastern Front, southern sector vic. Lvov, Brody, Zhitomir, Kiev
Oct 41–Jan 42	Refitting and rehabilitation in Belgium
Jan–Apr 42	Training activities in France
Apr–Sep 42	Offensive opns on Eastern Front, southern sector vic. Kharkov, Izyum, Mille-rovo, Chir, toward the Don River
Sep 42–Jan 43	Offensive and defensive opns vic. Stalingrad; destroyed
Mar 43	Reconstituted in Denmark.
Aug 43–Oct 44	Deployed to Italy; partici-pated in disarming the Italian Army upon their surrender; coastal defense, anti-partisan, and security duties in northeastern Italy; defensive opns vic. Cassino, Veletri, Monte Columbo
Nov 44–May 45	Offensive, defensive and retrograde opns in Hungary vic. Nagybajom, Kutas, Jako, and Kaposvar; defensive and retrograde opns in Austria vic. Lavamünd and St. Veit; destroyed

Commanders

Gen.Major Wolfgang Ziegler, Sep–Oct 39
Gen.Lt. Weisenberger, Oct 39–Feb 41
Gen.Lt. Herrlein, Feb–Mar 41
Gen.Lt. Alexander von Hartmann, Mar 41–Jan 43

Gen.Major Roske, Jan 43
Gen.Lt. Raapke, Mar 43–Jan 45
Gen.Major von Schuckmann, Jan–May 45

72d Infantry Division

1939	Formed from border troops vic. Trier
May–Jun 40	Offensive opns on Western Front
Apr 41	Offensive opns in the Balkans
Summer 41	Offensive opns Eastern Front, southern sector
Fall 42	Defensive and retrograde opns Eastern Front, central sector
Summer 43	Offensive opns vic. Kursk (Operation ZITADELLE)
Late 43	Defensive and retrograde opns Eastern Front, south-ern sector; Dnepr River bend; southern Ukraine
Feb 44	Encircled at Korsun, heavy losses
Spring 44	Reconstituted
Jul–Aug 44	Defensive opns vic. Vistula River
Jan 45	Defensive and retrograde opns in southern Poland, Baranow Bridgehead
Mar 45	Reconstituted
Mar–May 45	Defensive opns; destroyed in Czechoslovakia

Commanders

Gen.Lt. Mattenklott, 1939–Jul 40; Sep–Nov 40
Gen.Lt. Auleb, Jul–Sep 40
Gen.Lt. Müller-Gebhard, Nov 40–Jul 42; Nov 42–Feb 43; May–Nov 43
Gen.Major Souchay, Jul–Nov 42
Gen.Lt. Ralph, *Graf* von d'Oriola, Feb–May 43
Gen.Lt. Menny, Nov 43
Gen.Lt. Dr. Hohn, Nov 43–Mar 44; Jul 44–Apr 45
Gen.Major Arning, Jun–Jun 44
Gen.Lt. Harteneck, Jun–Jul 44
Gen.Lt. Beisswänger, Apr–May 45

73d Infantry Division

Summer 39	Formed in Würzburg
1939	Offensive opns in Poland
May– Jun 40	Offensive opns on the Western Front
Apr 41	Offensive opns in the Balkans vic. Romania and Bulgaria
Jun– Dec 41	Offensive opns on the Eastern Front, southern sector vic. Nikolayev, Perekop, the Crimea
Jan– May 42	Defensive opns in the Crimea
Spring– Fall 42	Offensive opns on the Eastern Front, southern sector vic. Taganrog, and toward the Caucasus Mountains
Winter 42–43	Defensive and retrograde opns vic. Kuban, the Taman Peninsula
Spring– Sum- mer 43	Defensive opns vic. Crimea, Taman Peninsula
Fall 43– Early 44	Defensive opns vic. Melitopol and Berislav (between Dnepr River and Sea of Azov)
Apr 44	Defensive opns vic. Sev- astopol, Crimea; largely destroyed
Summer 44	Reconstituted in Hungary
Sep 44– Jan 45	Defensive opns along the Vistula River vic. Modlin and Warsaw
Jan– Apr 45	Defensive and retrograde opns in East Prussia vic. Schwetz, Graudenz, Danzig; destroyed

Commanders
Gen.Lt. von Rabenau, Sep 39
Gen.Lt. Bieler, Sep 39–Oct 41
Gen.Lt. von Bünau, Nov 41–Feb 43
Gen.Major Nedtwig, Feb–Sep 43
Gen.Lt. Böhme, Sep 43–May 44
Gen.Lt. Dr. Franek, Jun–Jul 44
Gen.Major Hähling, Jul–Sep 44
Gen.Major Schlieper, Sep 44–Apr 45

75th Infantry Division

1939	Formed in Pomerania
May– Jun 40	Offensive opns on Western Front
Jun– Dec 41	Offensive opns, Eastern Front, southern sector
Fall 43	Defensive and retrograde opns vic. Kiev
Winter 43–44	Defensive and retrograde opns in northern Ukraine
Dec 44– Jan 45	Defensive and retrograde opns Eastern Front, central sector
Apr 45	Defensive opns in Moravia; destroyed

Commanders
Gen.Lt. Hammer, 1939–Sep 42
Gen.Lt. Diestel, Sep 42
Gen.Lt. Beukemann, Sep 42–Jul 44
Gen.Major Arning, Jul 44–Apr 45
Gen.Major Lothar Berger, Apr–May 45

76th Infantry Division

1939	Formed in Berlin from reservists
May– Jun 40	Offensive opns on Western Front
Jun–Dec 41	Offensive opns on Eastern Front, southern sector from Romania through Bessarabia, toward the Dnestr River, Mogilev, and the Dnepr River south of Kremenchug
Jan– May 42	Defensive opns on East- ern Front, southern sector
Spring– Fall 42	Offensive opns on East- ern Front, southern sector vic. Kobelyaki, Grabov- china, Artemovsk
Sep 42– Jan 43	Offensive and defensive opns vic. Stalingrad
Spring 43	Reconstituted in Brittany
Summer 43	Redeployed to northern Italy
Fall 43	Defensive and retrograde opns vic. Dnepr River bend, Eastern Front, southern sector

Mar 44	Retrograde opns from lower Dnepr River bend
Aug 44	Defensive opns vic. Debrecen
Oct 44–Jan 45	Defensive and retrograde opns in Hungary and Czechoslovakia

Commanders

Gen.Lt. de Angelis, 1939–Jan 42
Gen.Lt. Rodenburg, Jan 42–Jan 43
Gen.Lt. Abraham, Apr 43–Jul 44
Gen.Lt. Brücker, Jul 44
Gen.Lt. Abraham, Aug 44–Oct 44
Gen.Lt. von Rekowski, Oct 44–Feb 45
Oberst Dr. *Freiherr* von Bissing, Feb 45
Gen.Major Berner, Feb–May 45

78th Infantry Division (later a *Sturm*, Grenadier, and VGD)

Summer 39	Formed in Ulm
May–Jun 40	Offensive opns on Western Front
Jun–Dec 41	Offensive opns Eastern Front, central sector
Jan–May 42	Defensive opns vic. Moscow
Spring–Summer 42	Offensive and defensive opns on Eastern Front, central sector
Fall 42–Winter 42–43	Defensive opns vic. Rzhev
Dec 42	Redesignated as a Sturm Division
Summer 43	Offensive opns vic. Kursk (Operation ZITADELLE)
Fall 43	Offensive and defensive opns vic. Smolensk
Jul 44	Defensive opns vic. Minsk
Oct 44	Reformed at Konstanz as a Grenadier Division
Fall–Winter 44	Defensive and retrograde opns in southern Poland
Jan 45	Defensive and retrograde opns in Silesia; designated as a *Volkssturm* division; heavy losses vic. Jaslo
Feb 45	Reorganized as a VGD
May 45	Capitulated in Moravia

Commanders

Gen.Lt. Fritz Brand, Sep–Oct 39
Gen.Lt. Gallenkamp, Oct 39–Sep 41
Gen.Lt. Markgraf, Sep–Nov 41
Gen.Lt. Völckers, Nov 1941–Apr 43
Gen.Lt. Traut, Apr–Nov 43
Gen.Lt. von Larisch, Nov 43–Feb 44
Gen.Lt. Rasp, Jul–Sep 44
Gen.Major Alois Weber, Sep–Dec 44
Gen.Lt. von Hirschfeld, Dec 44–Jan 45
Gen.Major Nagel, Jan–Feb 45

79th Infantry Division (later VGD)

1939	Formed in Koblenz
May–Jun 40	Offensive opns on Western Front
Jun–Dec 41	Offensive opns Eastern Front, southern sector
Jan–May 42	Defensive and retrograde opns on Eastern Front, southern sector
Spring–Summer 43	Offensive opns on Eastern Front, southern sector vic. Olchavatka, Kupyansk
Sep 42–Jan 43	Offensive and defensive opns vic. Stalingrad; destroyed
Mar 43	Reconstituted vic. Stalino
Spring–Fall 43	Offensive and defensive opns vic. Kuban, Kerch (Crimea) and Melitopol
Fall 43–Spring 44	Defensive and retrograde opns on Eastern Front, southern sector, through Ukraine and eastern Romania; largely destroyed vic. Vutcani, Romania
Oct 44	Reconstituted in West Prussia from "Volks-Grenadier Division Katzbach"
Nov 44–May 45	Offensive and defensive opns on Western Front vic. Ardennes, Rhineland; capitulated to American forces

Commanders

Gen.Lt. Strecker, 1939–Jan 42
Gen.Lt. Richard von Schwerin, Jan 42–
 Jun 43
Gen.Major Kreipe, Jun–Oct 43
Gen.Lt. Weinknecht, Oct 43–Aug 44
Gen.Major Alois Weber, Oct 44–Feb 45
Oberst Reinherr, Feb–Mar 45
Oberst Kurt Hummel, Mar 45
Obstlt. von Hobe, Mar 45

81st Infantry Division

1939	Formed in Silesia
May–Jun 40	Offensive opns on Western Front
Feb–Jun 42	Division(-) conducted defensive opns vic. Demiansk and Lake Ilmen; one combat group (Infantry Regiment 189 and an artillery battalion) conducted defensive opns vic. Veliki Luki and was largely destroyed; a second combat group (Infantry Regiment 161 and an artillery battalion) conducted offensive and defensive opns between Novgorod and Chudovo and vic. Volkhov
Summer 42	Division was assembled, refitted, and rehabilitated
Fall 42–Jan 44	Defensive and retrograde opns vic. Leningrad and Nevel
Jan–Sep 44	Retrograde opns from vic. Nevel toward Latvian coast
Sep 44–May 45	Defensive opns vic. Kurland; capitulated to Soviet forces

Commanders

Gen.Lt. von Löper, 1939–Oct 40
Gen.Major Ribstein, Oct 40–Dec 41
Gen.Lt. Schopper, Dec 41–Mar 43,
 Mar–Jun 43
Gen.Lt. Gottfried Weber, Mar 43,
 Jun 43

Gen.Lt. Schopper, Jun 43–Apr 44
Gen.Lt. Lübbe, Apr–Jul 44
Gen.Major d.Res. Dr. Meiners, Jul 44
Gen.Lt. von Bentivegni, Jul 44–May 45

82d Infantry Division

1939	Formed in Kassel
Late 41	Occupation in the Netherlands
May 42	Offensive opns in Eastern Front, southern sector
Summer 43	Transferred to Eastern Front, central sector; offensive opns vic. Kursk (Operation ZITADELLE)
Fall 43–Winter 43–44	Redeployed to Eastern Front, southern sector; defensive and retrograde opns in Ukraine
Feb 44	Defensive and breakthrough opns vic. Korsun
Jul 44	Defensive and retrograde opns in southern Poland; withdrawn from action and disbanded

Commanders

Gen.Lt. Josef Lehmann, 1939–Apr 42
Gen.d.Inf. Hossbach, Apr–Jul 42
Gen.Lt. Bäntsch, Jul 42–Jan 43
Gen.Lt. Faulenbach, Jan–Mar 43
Gen.Lt. Heyne, Mar–Apr 43; May 43–
 May 44
Gen.Lt. Weinknecht, Apr–May 43

83d Infantry Division

1939	Formed in Hamburg
Sep 39	Offensive opns in Poland
May–Early 42	Offensive opns on Western Front; remained in France
Early–Fall 42	Defensive opns Eastern Front, northern sector
Winter 42–43	Defensive and retrograde opns vic. Veliki Luki; largely destroyed; rebuilt as two-regiment ID
Aug 43–Aug 44	Defensive and retrograde opns Eastern Front, northern sector

Sep– Oct 44	Retrograde opns to Latvian coast
Jan 45	Evaculated from Kurland by sea to East Prussia; one regiment defends Grau- denz until May 45
Mar– May 45	Remainder of division conducts retrograde and defensive opns in East Prussia; most of the divi- sion capitulates to Soviet forces with small elements capitulated to British forces in Schleswig- Holstein

Commanders

Gen.Lt. von der Chevallerie, 1939–
Dec 40
Gen.Lt. von Zülow, Dec 40–Feb 42
Gen.Lt. Sinzinger, Feb–Nov 42
Gen.Lt. Scherer, Nov 42–Mar 44
Gen.Lt. Heun, Mar–Jun 44
Gen.Lt. Götz, Jun–Aug 44
Gen.Lt. Heun, Aug 44–Mar 45
Gen.Major d. R. Wengler, Mar–Apr 45

86th Infantry Division

1939	Formed in Rhineland
May– Jun 40	Offensive opns on Western Front
Jun–Dec 41	Offensive opns Eastern Front, central sector
Jan 42– Spring 43	Offensive, defensive, and retrograde opns Eastern Front, central sector
Summer 43	Offensive opns vic. Kursk (Operation ZITADELLE)
Fall 43– Sum- mer 44	Defensive opns Eastern Front, central sector
Oct 44	Heavy losses; disbanded

Commanders

Gen.Lt. Witthöft, 1939–Jan 42
Gen.Lt. Weidling, Jan 42–Oct 43

87th Infantry Division

Fall 39	Formed in Saxony
May– Jun 40	Offensive opns on Western Front

Jun–Dec 41	Offensive opns Eastern Front, central sector
Jan 42– Sum- mer 43	Offensive, defensive, and retrograde opns Eastern Front, central sector
Fall 43	Defensive opns vic. Nevel; one regiment disbanded
Spring 44– May 45	Transferred to Eastern Front, northern sector; retrograde opns to Latvian coast; defensive opns vic. Kurland; capitulated to Soviet forces

Commanders

Gen.Lt. von Studnitz, 1939–Feb 42;
Mar–Aug 42
Gen.Lt. Lucht, Feb–Mar 42
Gen.Lt. Richter, Aug 42–Feb 43
Gen.Lt. Walter Hartmann, Feb–Nov 43
Gen.Lt. Mauritz *Freiherr* von Strach-
witz, Nov 43–Aug 44; Jan–May 45
Gen.Lt. Feyerabend, Aug–Sep 44
Gen.Major Helmuth Walter, Sep 44–
Jan 45

88th Infantry Division

Fall 39	Formed in Franconia
May– Jun 40	Offensive opns on Western Front
Aug 40– Early 42	Occupation of France
Jan– May 42	Deployed in southern sector as three separate combat groups conducting offensive and defensive opns in various locations
Jun 42	Divisional units assembled vic. Kursk
Summer– Fall 42	Offensive opns Eastern Front, southern sector vic. Voronezh and Belgorod
Fall 42– Winter 42–43	Defensive and retrograde opns Eastern Front, southern sector
Fall 43	Retrograde opns Ukraine
Winter 43–44	Defensive and breakout opns vic. Korsun; heavy casualties; withdrew to reform

Jun 44	Defensive opns in southern Poland
Jul 44	Heavily engaged vic. Lvov
Aug 44	Defensive opns in Vistula River bend
Dec 44–Jan 45	Remaining elements absorbed by Panzer Division *Grossdeutschland* and 17th Infantry Division

Commanders

Gen.Major Georg Lang, 1939–Feb 40
Gen.Lt. Gollwitzer, Feb 40–Mar 43
Gen.Lt. Heinrich Roth, Mar–Nov 43
Gen.Lt. von Rittberg, Nov 43–Jan 45
Gen.Major Anders, Jan 45

93d Infantry Division

Fall 39	Formed in Brandenburg
Nov 39	Located in upper Rhine area, later in Mosel area
Spring 40	Offensive opns on Western Front
40–41	Occupation of French coastal area
Jun–Dec 41	Offensive opns Eastern Front, northern sector vic. Estonia and Latvia toward Leningrad
Jan 42–Summer 43	Offensive and defensive opns vic. Oranienbaum, Volkhov, Veliki Luki, and Nevel
Summer 43	Transferred to Poland as two-regiment division, then returned to Eastern Front, northern sector
Early 44	Reformed as three-regiment division
Summer–Fall 44	Defensive and retrograde opns Eastern Front, northern sector to the Latvian coast
Winter 44–45	Defensive and retrograde opns in East Prussia
Mar 45	Destroyed vic. Samland and Hela Pockets; remnants incorporated into 58th Infantry Division

Commanders

Gen.Lt. Tiemann, 1939–May 43 and May–Sep 43
Gen.Lt. Gottfried Weber, May 43
Gen.Lt. Horst von Mellenthin, Sep–Oct 43
Gen.Lt. Löwrick, Oct 43–Jun 44
Gen.Lt. Erich Hofmann, Jun–Jul 44
Oberst Hermann, Jul–Sep 44
Gen.Major Domansky, Sep 44–Mar 45

94th Infantry Division

Sep 39	Formed in Saxony
May–Jun 40	Offensive opns on Western Front
Jun–Dec 41	Offensive opns Eastern Front, southern sector vic. Lvov, Ternopol, and Vinnitsa toward the Dnepr and beyond to Poltava
Jan–May 42	Defensive opns Eastern Front, southern sector
Summer–Fall 42	Offensive opns Eastern Front, southern sector to Voroshilovgrad
Sep 42–Jan 43	Offensive and defensive opns vic. Stalingrad; division destroyed
Mar 43	Reconstituted in Brittany
Apr 43–Apr 45	Offensive, defensive, and retrograde opns in Italy, heavy losses vic. Rome, remnants destroyed on Po River; capitulated to American forces vic. northern Italy

Commanders

Gen.Lt. Volkmann, 1939–Aug 40
Gen.Lt. Georg Pfeiffer, Aug 40–Jan 43, Mar 43–Jan 44
Gen.Lt. Steinmetz, Jan 44–Apr 45

95th Infantry Division (later VGD)

1939	Formed in Rhineland
1940	Western Front, Saar area
Jun–Dec 41	Offensive opns Eastern Front, central sector vic. Viazma and Briansk

Jan 42–
Jul 44 — Defensive and retrograde opns central sector

Jul 44 — Largely destroyed south of Vitebsk

Sep 44 — Reconstituted

Fall 44–
May 45 — Defensive and retrograde opns in Lithuania vic. the Memel River bridgehead and in East Prussia vic. Cranz, Pobethen, Galtgarben, and Pillau; capitulated to Soviet forces

Commanders

Gen.Lt. Hans-Heinrich Sixt von Arnim, 1939–May 42

Gen.Lt. Zickwolff, May–Sep 42

Gen.Lt. Karst, Sep–Oct 42

Gen.Lt. Aldrian, Oct 42

Gen.Lt. Röhricht, Oct 42–Sep 43

Gen.Major Gihr, Sep 43–Feb 44

Gen.Major Michaelis, Feb–Jun 44

Gen.Major Joachim-Friedrich Lang, Jun 44–Apr 45

96th Infantry Division

1939 — Formed vic. Braunschweig

May–
Jun 40 — Offensive opns on Western Front

Jun–Dec 41 — Offensive opns Eastern Front, northern sector vic. Lithuania, Latvia, and Estonia toward Novgorod

Jan 42–
Jan 44 — Defensive and retrograde opns vic. Novgorod and Mga; defensive opns in the Sinyavino Heights and along the Tigoda River

Jan–
Dec 44 — Redeployed to Eastern Front, southern sector; defensive and retrograde opns vic. Shepetovka and along the Bug and Dnestr Rivers; defensive and retrograde opns in Galicia vic. Sanok and Brody

Dec 44–
May 45 — Defensive and retrograde opns in Czechoslovakia vic. the Beskid Mountains;

offensive and defensive opns in Hungary; defensive and retrograde opns, Vienna vic. Linz; capitulated to American forces but part of the division was transferred to Soviet custody

Commanders

Gen.Lt. Vierow, 1939–Aug 40

Gen.Lt. Schede, Aug 40–Apr 42

Gen.Lt. *Freiherr* von Schleinitz, Apr–Oct 42

Gen.Lt. Nöldechen, Oct 42–Jul 43

Gen.Lt. Richard Wirtz, Jul 43–Sep 44 and Sep–Nov 44

Gen.Lt. Dürking, Sep 44

Gen.Major Harrendorf, Nov 44–May 45

98th Infantry Division (later VGD)

1939 — Formed in Franconia

May–
Jun 40 — Offensive opns on Western Front

Jun–
Nov 41 — Offensive opns Eastern Front, southern sector vic. Rovno, Zhitomir, Korosten toward the Dnepr

Nov 41–
Mar 43 — Offensive, defensive, and retrograde opns vic. west of Moscow, Kaluga, and Spas Demensk; anti-partisan opns vic. Roslavl

Mar 43–
Spring 44 — Defensive and retrograde opns vic. the Kuban and Crimea; destroyed vic. Stevastopol

Jun 44 — Reconstituted in Croatia

Sep 44–
May 45 — Coastal defense, defensive and retrograde opns in Italy vic. Rimini, the Senio Valley, the Futa Pass, Santerno, and the Po Valley; capitulated to American forces in the Cordevole Valley

Commanders

Gen.Lt. Schröck, 1939–Apr 40 and Jun 40–Dec 41

Gen.Lt. Stimmel, Apr–Jun 40
Gen.Lt. Gareis, Dec 41–Feb 44
Gen.Lt. Reinhardt, Feb 44–Apr 45
Gen.Major Schiel, Apr–May 45

102d Infantry Division

Oct 40	Formed in Pomerania from cadres of 8th and 28th IDs
Jun–Dec 41	Offensive opns, Eastern Front, central sector vic. Estonia, Nevel, Veliki Luki, and Rzhev
Jan–Jun 42	Defensive opns vic. Rzhev
Summer 42	Offensive opns Eastern Front, central sector (Operation SEYDLITZ)
Fall 42–Sum-- mer 43	Defensive opns vic. Osuga River
Jul 43	Offensive and defensive opns vic. Kursk (Operation ZITADELLE)
Summer 43–Dec 44	Defensive and retrograde opns Eastern Front, central sector vic. Gomel, Pripet Marshes, Pinsk, Brest-Litovsk, Ostrolenka, and Lomsha
Jan–May 45	Defensive and retrograde opns in East Prussia vic. Sensburg, Seeburg, Frauendorf, and Bonkenwalde; destroyed in Heiligenbeil Pocket, capitulated to Soviet forces

Commanders

Gen.Lt. Ansat, Dec 40–Feb 42
Gen.Lt. Albrecht Baier, Feb–Mar 42
Gen.Major von Räsfeld, Mar–May 42
Gen.Lt. Friessner, May 42–Jan 43
Gen.Lt. Hitzfeld, Jan–Nov 43
Gen.Lt. von Bercken, Nov 43–May 45

106th Infantry Division

Oct 40	Formed in Rheinland from cadres of 6th and 26th IDs
Jun–Dec 41	Offensive opns, Eastern Front, central sector vic. Lithuania, Vitebsk, and Smolensk toward Moscow
Jan–May 42	Defensive and retrograde opns Eastern Front, central sector vic. Volokolamsk and Gshatsk
May 42–Mar 43	Reconstitution in France
Apr–Jul 43	Offensive and defensive opns vic. Kharkov
Jul 43	Offensive opns vic. Kursk (Operation ZITADELLE)
Summer 43–Summer 44	Offensive, defensive, and retrograde opns, Ukraine and Romania; destroyed vic. Yassy, Romania
Mar–May 45	Reconstituted and defensive opns in Baden and Württemberg; capitulated to allied forces

Commanders

Gen.Major Ernst Dehner, Nov 40–May 42
Gen.Lt. Hitter, May–Nov 42
Gen.Lt. Kullmer, Nov 42–Jan 43
Gen.Lt. Werner Forst, Jan 43–Feb 44
Gen.Lt. von Rekowski, Feb–Aug 44
Oberst Rintenberg, Mar–May 45

110th Infantry Division

Oct 40	Formed in Oldenburg from cadres of 12th and 30th IDs
Jun–Dec 41	Offensive opns Eastern Front, central sector vic. Lithuania, Nevel, Veliki Luki, and the upper Dvina River toward Rzhev
Jan–May 42	Defensive opns Eastern Front, central sector
Summer–Fall 42	Offensive opns vic. Rzhev, Briansk
Winter 42–43–Summer 44	Defensive and retrograde opns Eastern Front, central sector vic. Lyudinovo, Garbovka, Rogachev, the Pripet Marshes, Mogilev, and Minsk; destroyed

Commanders

Gen.Lt. Ernst Seifert, Dec 40–Jan 42
Gen.Lt. Martin Gilbert, Feb 42–Jun 43
Gen.Lt. von Kurowski, Jun–Sep 43;
  Dec 43–May 44; May–Jul 44
Gen.Lt. Wüstenhagen, Sep–Dec 43
Gen.Major Gustav Gihr, May 44

111th Infantry Division

Oct 40	Formed vic. Braunschweig, incorporating one infantry regiment each from 3d and 36th IDs
Jun–Dec 41	Offensive opns Eastern Front, southern sector vic. Dubno and Zhitomir, and Poltava, and Artemovsk toward the Donets River
Jan–May 42	Defensive opns Eastern Front, southern sector
Summer–Fall 42	Offensive opns toward the Caucasus Mountains
Winter 42–43–Summer 43	Defensive and retrograde opns Eastern Front, southern sector vic. Mozdok, Rostov, Taganrog
Fall 43–May 44	Defensive and retrograde opns southern sector vic. Kuibishev, Melitopol, Nikopol, and the Crimea; capitulated to Soviet forces vic. Sevastopol

Commanders

Gen.Lt. Stapf, Nov 40–Jan 42
Gen.Lt. Recknagel, Jan 42–Aug 43;
  Aug–Nov 43
Gen.Major von Bülow, Aug 43
Gen.Major Gruner, Nov 43–May 44

112th Infantry Division

Oct 40	Formed in Bavaria, incorporating one infantry regiment each from 33d and 34th IDs
Jun–Dec 41	Offensive opns Eastern Front, central sector vic. Bialystok, Klintsy, Ivangorod, Tula, Orggarevo, and Yepifan

Jan 42–Jun 43	Defensive and retrograde opns Eastern Front, central sector
Summer 43	Offensive opns vic. Belgorod
Fall 43–May 44	Defensive and retrograde opns Eastern Front, southern sector; destroyed vic. Grigorovka, Moldavia

Commanders

Gen.Lt. Mieth, Dec 40–Nov 42
Gen.Major Newiger, Nov 42–Jun 43
Gen.Lt. Rolf Wuthmann, Jun–Sep 43
Gen.Lt. Theobald Lieb, Sep–Nov 43

113th Infantry Division

Oct 40	Formed in Franconia from cadres of 15th and 34th IDs
Jul–Nov 41	Offensive opns Eastern Front, southern sector vic. Zhitomir and Kiev
Nov 41	Redeployed to Germany
Dec 41	Anti-partisan opns (opposing Chetniks and Communist partisans) in Serbia
Jan–May 42	Defensive and offensive opns vic. Mius River, Kharkov, and Taranovka
Summer–Fall 42	Offensive operations Eastern Front, southern sector toward Stalingrad
Fall 42–Jan 43	Offensive and defensive opns vic. Stalingrad; destroyed
Mar 43	Reconstituted
Aug–Nov 43	Defensive and retrograde opns vic. Smolensk and Nevel; destroyed

Commanders

Gen.Lt. Güntzel, Dec 40–Jun 41
Gen.Lt. Zickwolff, Jun 41–May 42
Gen.Lt. Sixt von Arnim, May 42–Jan 43
Gen.Major Prüter, Mar–Nov 43

121st Infantry Division

Sep 40	Formed vic. Hamburg from cadres of 1st and 21st IDs

Jun–Dec 41	Offensive opns Eastern Front, northern sector through Lithuania toward Leningrad
Jan 42–Jun 44	Offensive, defensive, and retrograde opns Eastern Front, northern sector
Jun–Sep 44	Retrograde opns toward the Latvian coast
Sep 44–May 45	Defensive opns vic. Kurland; capitulated to Soviet forces

Commanders

Gen.Lt. Jahn, Oct 40–May 41
Gen.Lt. Lancelle, May–Jul 41
Gen.Lt. Wandel, Jul 41–Nov 42
Gen.Lt. Priess, Nov 42–Mar 44 and Jun–Jul 44
Gen.Major Pauer von Arlau, Mar–Jun 44
Gen.Lt. Bamler, Jun 44
Gen.Lt. Busse, Jul–Aug 44
Gen.Lt. Ranck, Aug 44–Apr 45
Gen.Major Ottomar Hansen, Apr–May 45

122d Infantry Division

Sep 40	Formed in Pomerania from cadres of 32d and 258th IDs
Jun–Dec 41	Offensive opns Eastern Front, northern sector
Fall 43	Transferred to Eastern Front, central sector, engaged at Nevel
Mar 44	Transferred to Eastern Front, northern sector
Jun 44	Transferred to Helsinki
Aug 44	Transferred to Estonia
Sep 44–May 45	Retrograde opns to Latvian coast; defensive opns in Kurland; capitulated to Soviet forces

Commanders

Gen.Lt. Macholz, Oct 40–Dec 41; Feb–Aug 42; Nov–Dec 42
Gen.Lt. Friedrich Bayer, Dec 41–Feb 42
Gen.Lt. Chill, Aug–Oct 42; Jun 43–Feb 44

Gen.Lt. Hundt, Oct–Nov 42
Gen.Major Westhoff, Dec 42–Jan 43
Gen.Major Adolf Trowitz, Jan–May 43
Gen.Lt. Thielmann, May–Jun 43
Gen.Major Johann-Albrecht von Blücher, Feb 44
Gen.Major Breusing, Feb–Aug 44
Gen.Lt. Fangohr, Aug 44–Jan 45
Gen.Major Schatz, Jan–May 45

123d Infantry Division

Sep 40	Formed in Braunschweig from cadres of 23d and 257th IDs
Jun–Dec 41	Offensive opns Eastern Front, northern sector through Lithuania and Kholm toward Demiansk
Jan–Sep 43	Defensive opns vic. Demiansk, Kholm, and Staraya Russa
Sep 43–Mar 44	Deployed to Ukraine; offensive and defensive opns vic. Zaporozhe; defensive and retrograde opns vic. Nikopol and Krivoi Rog toward the Dnestr; defensive opns vic. Yassy, Romania; destroyed

Commanders

Gen.Lt. Lichel, Oct 40–Aug 41
Gen.Lt. Erwin Rauch, Aug 41–Oct 43; Oct–Nov 43
Gen.Lt. Menny, Oct–Nov 43
Gen.Major Tronnier, Jan–Mar 44

125th Infantry Division

Sep 40	Formed in Württemberg from cadres of 5th and 260th IDs
Jun–Dec 41	Offensive opns Eastern Front, southern sector vic. Ternopol, Michaelovka, Uman, Kremenchug, and Stalino
Jan–May 42	Defensive opns vic. the Mius River sector

Summer– Fall 42	Offensive opns vic. Rostov and toward the Caucasus Mountains
Winter 42–43	Retrograde and defensive operations vic. Kuban
Spring– Fall 43	Defensive and retrograde opns vic. Kuban and in Ukraine
Fall 43– Mar 44	Defensive and retrograde opns from the lower Dnepr River through Krivoi Rog; destroyed
Mar 44	Heavy losses in withdrawal from lower Dnepr River bend; subsequently disbanded

Commanders

Gen.Lt. Schneckenburg, Oct 40–Dec 42

Gen.Lt. Helmut Friebe, Dec 42–Mar 44

126th Infantry Division

Sep 40	Formed in Rhineland
Jun–Dec 41	Offensive opns Eastern Front, northern sector vic. Lithuania Novgorod, and Staraya Russa toward Leningrad
Jan 42– Jan 44	Defensive and retrograde opns Eastern Front, northern sector vic. Demiansk, Lake Ladoga, Luga, and Lake Peipus
Jan–Sep 44	Retrograde and defensive opns from vic. Leningrad toward the Latvian coast
Sep 44– May 45	Defensive opns vic. Kurland; capitulated to Soviet forces

Commanders

Gen.Lt. Laux, Oct 40–Oct 42

Gen.Lt. Harry Hoppe, Oct 42–Apr 43; Jul–Nov 43

Gen.Lt. Friedrich Hofmann, Apr–Jul 43

Gen.Lt. Gotthard Fischer, Nov 43–Jan 45

Gen.Major Hähling, Jan–May 45

129th Infantry Division

Sep 40– Jun–Dec 41	Formed in Fulda Offensive opns Eastern Front, central sector vic. Vitebsk, Smolensk, and Kalinin
Jan 42– Fall 43	Defensive opns vic. Demiansk, Rzhev, Briansk, Propoisk, and Nevel
Winter 43–44– Summer 44	Retrograde opns through Belorussia to Poland
Fall 44– Spring 45	Defensive and retrograde opns in East Prussia vic. Allenstein, Guttstadt, and Heilsberg; capitulated to Soviet forces

Commanders

Gen.Lt. Rittau, Oct 40–Aug 42

Gen.Lt. Albert Praun, Aug 42–Sep 43

Gen.Major Fabiunke, Sep 43–Jan 44

Gen.Lt. von Larisch, Jan 44–Feb 45

Gen.Major Bernhard Ueberschär, Feb–May 45

131st Infantry Division

Sep 40	Formed from cadres of 9th and 251st IDs
Aug 41	Offensive opns in Eastern Front, central sector
Nov 41	Participated in Moscow offensive
Summer 43	Transferred to Eastern Front, southern sector
May 44	Defensive opns in Eastern Front, central sector, vic. Kovel
Jul 44	Heavy losses; absorbed remnants of 196th ID and 10th Brigade
Jan 45	Defensive opns in East Prussia
Feb 45	Destroyed in Heiligenbeil Pocket

Commanders

Gen.Inf. Meyer-Bürdorf, Oct 40–Jan 44

Gen.Lt. Friedrich Weber, Jan–Oct 44

Gen.Major d. Res. Werner Schulze, Oct 44–Feb 45

132d Infantry Division

Sep 40	Formed in Bavaria from cadres of 263d and 255th IDs
Jul 41	Offensive opns, Eastern Front, southern sector; heavy losses in the Crimea
Fall 42	Transferred to Eastern Front, northern sector
Apr 44	Transferred to the Eastern Front, central sector; subsequently returned to the northern sector
Sep 44–May 45	Withdrew to Latvian coast; defensive opns vic. Kurland; capitulated to Soviet forces

Commanders

Gen.Lt. Sintzenich, Oct 40–Jan 42
Gen.Lt. Lindemann, Jan 42–Aug 43
Gen.Lt. Herbert Wagner, Aug 43–Jan 45
Gen.Major Demme, Jan–May 45

134th Infantry Division

Sep 40	Formed in Franconia from cadres of 252d and 255th IDs
Jun 41–Spring 42	Offensive opns, Eastern Front central sector
Summer 43	Defensive opns vic. Briansk and Gomel
Jul 44	Heavy losses at beginning of Soviet summer offensive; remnants destroyed vic. Minsk

Commanders

Gen.Lt. von Cochenhausen, Oct 40–Dec 41
Gen.Lt. Schlemmer, Dec 41–Feb 44
Gen.Major Rudolf Bader, Feb–Jun 44
Gen.Lt. Ernst Philipp, Jun 44

137th Infantry Division

Sep 40	Formed from cadres from 44th and 262d IDs
Aug 41–Spring 43	Offensive opns in central sector, Eastern Front

Summer 43	Participated in Operation *ZITADELLE*
Fall 43	Disbanded after heavy losses

Commanders

Gen.Lt. Friedrich Bergmann, Oct 40–Dec 41
Oberst Heine, Dec 41
Oberst Muhl, Dec 41–Jan 42
Gen.Lt. Kamecke, Jan–Feb 42
Gen.Lt. Dr. Rüdiger, Feb 42
Gen.Lt. Kamecke, Feb 42–Oct 43
Gen.Lt. von Neindorff, Oct–Dec 43

161st Infantry Division

Nov 39	Formed in Allenstein and Goldap, East Prussia
Jun 40	Offensive opns on Western Front in Luxembourg, France; attacked Maginot Line
Jul 40	Transferred to the east, began training for invasion of Soviet Union
Jun 41	Offensive opns, Eastern Front vic. Grodino, Lida, Borisov, Orsch
Aug 41	Offensive opns, Eastern Front vic. Smolensk, Yartsevo, Nikitinka, Rzhev
Nov 41	Defensive opns, Kalinin
Dec 41	Withdrawal from Rzhev area; reformed as Group Recke; counterattacked in Volga River area
Jan 43	Group Recke disbanded; reorganized as 161st ID; defensive opns vic. Rzhev, Zubtsov
Mar 42	Group Recke reformed; defensive opns vic. Volga River, Rzhev
May 42	Grroup Recke disbanded; reorganized as 161st ID; defensive opns vic. near Rzhev
Sep 42	Withdrawal from Dorogobuzh area

Oct 42	Transferred to France; reorganized, coastal defense opns
Apr 43	Transferred to Eastern Front; offensive, defensive opns vic. Merefa, Kharkov
Sep 43	Withdrawal vic. Krasnograd for rehabilitation
Sep 43	Defensive opns vic. Kremenchug
Oct 43	Disengagement and withdrawal vic. Krasnograd, Dnepropetrovosk, Zaporozhe); reorganized as *Kampfgruppe* 161
Nov 43	Incorporated into "Corps Detachment A" near Krivoi Rog
Dec 43	Redesignated 161st ID near Krivoi Rog
Jul 44	Defensive opns vic. Grigoriopol, Moldavia
Aug 44	Encircled at Husi, Romania
Oct 44	Disbanded and absorbed by other units, vic. Dej, Romania

Commanders

Gen.Lt. Wilck, 1939–Sep 41
Gen.Lt. Recke, Sep 41–Aug 42
Gen.Major Schell, Aug 42
Gen.Lt. von Groddeck, Aug 42–Aug 43
Gen.Lt. Dreckmann, Aug 43–Jan 44; Jul–Aug 44

162d Infantry Division (later 162d Turkistan Infantry Division)

Dec 39	Formed Gross-Born Training area, Stettin, Pomerania
Jan 40	Transferred to Schivelbein for training
May 40	Transferred to the west (Darmstadt, Bingen, Trier)
May–Jun 40	Offensive opns in Luxembourg and France
Jul 40	Transferred to Poland
May 41	Border control near Ortelsburg, Poland; training

Jun 43	Offensive opns in Poland vic. Szczebra, Augow and USSR vic. Grodno, Ostryna, Baranovichi, Slutsk, Glussk, Bobruisk
Aug 41	Defensive and offensive opns vic. Smolensk, Rzhev, Kalinin, Klin)
Dec 41	Disengagement and breakup of the division vic. Staritsa; units absorbed by 86th, 129th, and 251st IDs
May 42	Division reformed at Stettin, Pomerania
May 43	Training in Germany and Poland; division made mainly of foreign soldiers, mostly former Soviet POWs from Turkestan, Georgia, and Azerbaijan
May 43	Redesignated 162d (Turk) ID at Neuhammer training area
Jan 44	Transferred to Ljubljana, Yugoslavia
Mar 44	Transferred to Italian Front (Trieste, Livorno)
Jun 44	Defensive opns near Orbetello and Valentano
Jun 44–Apr 45	Withdrawn from combat near Massa due to poor performance; engaged in security and anti-partisan opns until capitulation

Commanders

Gen.Lt. Hermann Franke, Dec 39–Jan 42
Gen.Major Prof. Dr. *Ritter* von Niedermayer, May 43–May 44
Gen.Lt. von Heygendorff, May 44–May 45

163d Infantry Division

Nov 39	Formed in Potsdam
Mar 40	Movement and embarkation for Norway
Apr 40–Jun 41	Participated in invasion of Norway

Jun 41	Transferred to Finland
Jun 41	Assembly, preparation for combat
Jul 41	Offensive opns in Finland, USSR vic. Tolvavarvi, Yaglyajärvi, Suojärvi, Lake Koti-Järvi
Sep 41	Offensive and security opns vic. Lake Ladoga, Lodelnoye
Jan 42	Defensive opns vic. Svir River, Sviritsa, Lodelnoye
May 42	Defensive opns vic. Uksu, Alakurtti
Jul 42	Defensive and offensive opns vic. Tumcha, Voyta River, Lake Tolvand
Jan–Jul 43	Defensive, offensive and security opns vic. Alakurtti, Vuorijärvi, Tumcha, Lake Tolvand, Lake Verman
Jan 44	Defensive opns, Lake Tolvand
Oct 44	Movement to Finland, defensive opns vic. Ivalo, Kaamanen; withdrawal across northern Finland to Norway
Nov 44– Dec 44	Security opns in Norway vic. Laksalv, Nordreisa, Bodo, Donna, Trondheim
Feb 45	Transferred to Eastern Front; defensive opns vic. Falkenberg, Stettin, Pomerania
Mar 45– Apr 45	Defensive opns and virtual destruction near Swinemünde; remnants absorbed by 3d Naval Div

Commanders

Gen.Lt. Engelbrecht, Oct 39–Jun 42
Gen.Major Dostler, Jun–Dec 42
Gen.Major Rübel, Dec 42–Mar 45

167th Infantry Division (VGD)

Nov 39	Formed as 167th ID at Heuberg training area, near Munich
May 40– May 41	Offensive opns on Western Front; occupation of France
May 41	Transferred to Germany
Jun 41	Transferred to Poland; offensive opns across Bug River; vic. Prushany, Slonim, Baranovichi, Nesvizh
Jul 41	Offensive opns in vic. Berezina River, Bobruisk, Rogachev, Briansk
Dec 41	Disengagement and defensive opns vic. Shchekino, Belev, Orel
Apr 42	Transferred to the Netherlands for rehabilitation
Apr 42	Coastal defense and training in Netherlands
Feb 43	Transferred to Poltava, Russia
Mar 43	Defensive opns vic. Akhtyrka, Belgorod, Kharkov
Aug 43	Withdrawal and reorganization as *Kampfgruppe* 167; defensive opns vic. Kremenchug, Chigrin, Cherkassy, Kanev
Oct 43	Offensive and defensive opns vic. Aleksandriya, Novaya Praga, Zybkovo, Adzhamka
Nov 43	Movement to and defensive opns near Krivoi Rog and Kirovograd
Jan 44	Redesignated as Division Group 167
Jan 44	Division disbanded; remnants absorbed by 376th ID
Oct 44	Reformed as 167th VGD at Döllersheim training
Nov 44	Transferred to Slovakia for defensive opns
Dec 44	Transferred to Western Front; offensive opns in Ardennes Offensive; defensive opns near Bitburg, Prüm

Mar 45 Destroyed in the Eifel

Commanders
Gen.Major Gilbert, Dec 39–Jan 40
Gen.Lt. Vogl, Jan–May 40
Gen.Major Schönhärl, May 40–Aug 41
Oberst Wenk, Aug 41
Gen.Major Schartow, Aug 41
Gen.Lt. Trierenberg, Aug 41–
    Nov 43
Gen.Major Hüttner, Nov 43–Feb 44
Gen.Lt. Höcker, Oct 44–Apr 45

168th Infantry Division

Dec 39	Formed in Breslau
Jan 41	Transferred to Döllersheim training area
Apr 40	Transferred to Austria
May 40	Transferred to Saar/Palatinate
Jun 40	Opns in France as a reserve unit
Jul 40	Transferred to Poland
Jun 41	Offensive opns in Poland vic. Hrubieszow, Poritsk, Brody, Dubno and USSR vic. Shepetovka, Zhitomir
Aug 41	Offensive opns vic. Kiev, Makarov, Kozelets
Sep 41	Offensive opns vic. Priluki, Sumy, Belgorod
Oct 41	Defensive opns vic. Donets River, Kharkov
Dec 41	Defensive opns vic. Kursk, Belgorod, Oboyan; redesignated Group Kraiss
Apr 42	Redesignated as 168th ID
Jul 42	Offensive opns vic. Voronezh, Svoboda
Jan 43	Disengagement opns vic. Novy Oskol, Chernyanka, Belgorod
Feb 43	Rehabilitation and defensive opns near Mirgorod
Apr 43	Transfer and defensive opns vic. Poltava, Kharkov, Belgorod
Sep 43	Reorganized as *Kampfgruppe 168*; disengagement vic. Poltava, Cherkassy

Nov 43	Reorganization near Rzhishchev, incorporating elements of 223d ID
Jan 44	Withdrawal and defensive engagements vic. Kazatin, Vinnitsa; encircled at Korsun, virtually destroyed
Aug 44	Disengagement and defensive opns near Rzeszow, Poland
Sep 44	Withdrawal and defensive opns near Presov, Slovakia
Dec 44	Withdrawal and defensive opns in Poland
Jan 45	Disengagement and defensive opns in Upper Silesia vic. Oppeln, Neisse; nearly destroyed at Baranow
Apr 45	Withdrawal and defensive opns near Otmuchow, Upper Silesia
Apr 45	Rebuilt in Silesia

Commanders
Gen.Major Boysen, Dec 39–Jan 40
Gen.Lt. Dr. Mundt, Jan 40–Jul 41
Gen.Lt. Dietrich Kraiss, Jul 41–Mar 43
Gen.Lt. von Beaulieu, Mar–Dec 43
Gen.Lt. Schmidt-Hammer, Dec 43–Sep 44; Dec 44–Jan 45; Apr 45
Gen.Major Anders, Sep–Dec 44
Gen.Major Dr. Rosskopf, Jan–Feb 45

169th Infantry Division

Nov 39	Formed in Kassel
Apr 40	Movement to Darmstadt
Apr 40–Feb 41	Offensive opns on Western Front Meuse and Moselle Rivers, Maginot Line, Margut, Montmedy, Verdun, Metz and occupation of France
Feb 41	Transferred to Saxony
May 41	Transferred to Stettin, Pomerania
Jun 41	Transferred to Finland
Jun 41	Movement and assembly in Finland vic. Kemijärvi
Jun 41	Offensive opns vic. Salla

Jul 41	Offensive opns vic. Alakurtti		Dniester Rivers; capture of Soroki, Yampol
Aug 41	Advanced to Voyta River, Verman; defensive opns	Jul 41	Offensive opns on Eastern Front vic. Klembovka,
Jan 42	Defensive opns and withdrawal from Verman Front		Balta, Berezovka; crossed Bug River at Troitskoye
Feb 42	Return to Verman Front area; defensive, offensive and reconnaissance opns	Aug 41	Offensive opns on Eastern Front vic. Novaya Odessa, Tarasovka, Berislav; crossing of Ingulets and Dnepr Rivers
Jan 43	Defense, reconnaissance and offensive opns, Verman Front	Oct 41	Movement to the Crimea; defensive and offensive opns vic. Armyansk, Feodosiya
Jul 43	Defensive opns, Verman front		
Oct 44	Withdrawal to Finland; defensive opns vic. Savukoski, Ivalo	Nov 41	Offensive opns vic. Kerch, Sudak, Feodosiya; coastal defense on Black Sea
Oct 44	Withdrawal to Norway	Dec 41	Offensive and defensive opns near Sevastopol
Jan 45	Movement to Mosjoen, Norway; security opns	Jan 42	Recapture of Feodosiya and Sudak (Operation SEEGANG)
Mar 45	Transferred to Oslo, Norway		
Mar– May 45	Transferred to Eastern Front; defensive opns vic. Frankfurt/Oder	Feb 42	Defensive engagements and counterattack, Kerch Peninsula
		Apr 42	Movement to and capture of Simferopol, Alupka, Sevastopol (Operation STÖRFANG)

Commanders

Gen.Lt. Müller-Gebhard, Nov–Dec 39
Gen.Lt. Kirchheim, Dec 39–Feb 41
Gen.Lt. Dittmar, Feb–Sep 41
Gen.d.Art. Tittel, Sep 41–Jun 43
Gen.Lt. Radziej, Jun 43–May 45

170th Infantry Division

Nov 39	Formed in Bremen	Aug 42	Transferred to Leningrad Front; defensive opns and counterattacks vic. Mga, Gatchina, Neva River, Kolpino, Krasny Bor
Apr 40	Occupation opns in Denmark		
May– Jun 40	Offensive opns, Netherlands, Belgium, France	Mar 43	Defensive opns vic. Kresnoye Selo, Krasny Bor, Pushkin, Verkhneye Koyrovo
Jun 40	Occupation and coastal defense opns in France		
Feb 41	Transferred to Hannover	Jul 43	Defensive and assault opns vic. Gatchina, Verkhneye Koyrovo
Apr 41	Transferred to Buzau, Romania; training of Romanian units	Jan 44	Withdrawal and defensive opns vic. Gatchina, Narva
May 41	Transferred to Moldavia in preparation for invasion of USSR	Feb 44	Incorporated 10th *Luftwaffe* Field Division in Narva
		Jun 44	Defensive opns vic. Vilna, Lithuania
Jun 41	Offensive opns on Eastern Front; crossing of Prut and	Jul 44	Defensive opns vic. Suwalki, Poland

Oct 44	Defensive opns vic. Treuburg, East Prussia
Feb 45	Defense of Heiligenbeil Pocket
Apr 45	Defensive opns, Frische Nehrung
Apr 45	Remnants of division in defensive opns
May 45	Surrender

Commanders

Gen.Lt. Wittke, Dec 39–Jan 42
Gen.Lt. Sander, Jan 42–Feb 43
Gen.Lt. Walther Krause, Feb 43–
Feb 44
Gen.Major Griesbach, Feb 44
Gen.Lt. Hass, Feb 44–May 45

181st Infantry Division

Dec 39	Formed at Lager Falling- bostel, Hannover
Apr 40	Transferred to Norway
Apr 40	Offensive opns in Norway vic. Trondheim, Molde, Kristiansund
Jun 40– Sep 43	Completion of combat opns, regrouping, coastal defense, training
Sep 43	Transfer to Stettin, Pomerania
Oct 43	Movement to Pristina, Yugoslavia
Oct 43	Movement to Albania; coastal defense and anti- partisan opns
Nov 44	Movement and anti-parti- san warfare (Scutari, Pod- gorics, Montenegro); heavy losses in withdraw- al from Montenegro
Dec 44	Withdrawal and anti-parti- san opns in Titovo Uzice, Serbia
Jan 45	Movement and anti-parti- san opns vic. Sarajevo
Apr 45	Withdrawal vic. Daruvar, northern Croatia

Commanders

Gen.Lt. Bielfeld, Dec 39–Jan 40
Gen.Lt. Woytasch, Jan 40–Mar 42
Gen.Lt. Friedrich Bayer, Mar 42

Gen.Lt. Hermann Fischer, Mar 42–
Oct 44
Gen.Lt. Bleyer, Oct 44–May 45

183d Infantry Division (later VGD)

Dec 39	Formed at Münsterlager training area
Jan 40	Movement, training in Swabia and Rhineland
May– Jul 40	Offensive opns in Luxembourg, Belgium, France; occupation of France
Jul 40	Movement to Moravia
Mar 41	Movement to Austria- Yugoslavia border; offensive opns on Eastern Front vic. Maribor, Drava River
Apr 41	Offensive and security opns vic. Zagreb, Rijeka, Dubice, Banja Luka, Sarajevo
Jun 41	Movement to Styria, Aus- tria via Brod, Yugoslavia; reorganization and training
Aug 41	Transfer to Poland
Aug 41	Offensive opns vic. Schezh, Nevel, Velizh, Demidov, Smolensk, Yelnya
Sep 41	Offensive and defensive opns vic. Dorogobuzh, Zhulino, Yukhnov, Bor- ovsk, Naro-Fominsk, Nara River
Feb 42	Movement, defensive opns vic. Protva, Vorya and Istra Rivers
Aug 42	Movement, defensive and offensive opns vic. Chelis- chchevo,Tomkino, Viazma
Feb 43	Withdrawal, defensive opns, assembly vic. Spas- Demensk, Dorogobuzh, Yelnya, Shuitsa River
Aug 43	Withdrawal and defensive opns vic. Dyatkovo, Kono- top, Nezhin

Nov 43	Remnants of 183d, 153d, 217th, and 339th IDs incorporated into Corps-Detachment C
Nov 43	Withdrawal and defensive opns vic. Malin, Korosten, Rovno, Brody
Jul 44	Encirclement at Olesko, Zolochev; redesignated 183d ID; Breakout from encirclement
Aug 44	Transfer to Oberglogau, Upper Silesia; disbanded
Sep 44	Division reformed as 183d VGD at Döllersheim and Göpfritz by absorbing 564 VGD
Sep 44	Transferred to Western Front; heavy losses in defensive opns in Germany vic. Geilenkirchen, Jülich
Mar 45	Defensive opns in the West; destroyed in Ruhr Pocket

Commanders
Gen.Lt. Dippold, Nov 39–Oct 41
Gen.Lt. Stempel, Oct 41–Jan 42
Gen.Lt. Dettling, Jan 42–Nov 43
Gen.Lt. Wolfgang Lange, Nov 43–May 45
Gen.Major Warrelmann, May 45

196th Infantry Division

Nov 39	Formed in Danzig
Apr 40–Jul 44	Movement to Gotenhafen embarkation and transfer to Norway; participated in disarming Norwegian armed forces; coastal defense opns
Jul 44	Transferred to Kaunas, Lithuania; reformed as two-regiment ID
Jul 44	Defensive opns vic. Marijampole, Altus, Kalvaria
Aug 44	Defensive opns vic. Goldap, East Prussia
Sep 44	Disbanded; elements incorporated into 131st ID

Commanders
Gen.Lt. Pellengahr, Dec 39–Mar 42
Gen.Lt. Dr. Franek, Mar 42–Dec 43
Gen.Lt. Möhring, Dec 43–Feb 44
Oberst Klinge, Feb 44–Jun 44
Gen.Major von Unger, Jun 44–Sep 44

197th Infantry Division

Nov 39	Formed in Posen
Mar 40	Reorganization and training
Jul 40	Transferred to the Netherlands; coastal defense and training
Feb 41	Transferred to Karlsruhe, then Mannheim/Ludwigshafen for training
Jun 41	Transferred to Poland
Jun 41	Offensive opns in Poland vic. Bransk, Bielsk, Podlaski, Slonim and USSR vic. Baranovichi, Minsk, Borisov, Tolochin, Orsha
Jul 41	Offensive opns vic. Gorki, Desna River, Viazma
Oct 41	Offensive and defensive opns vic. Viazma and Mozhaisk
Jan 42	Defensive opns vic. Gzhatsk
May 42	Defensive opns vic. Viazma
Jun 42	Offensive and defensive opns vic. Smolensk, Dorogobuzh
Jun 42	Defensive opns vic. Yartzevo, Prechistoye, Bely
Jul 42	Preparations for and execution of offensive opns: Operation SEYDLITZ
Dec 42	Encirclement of enemy forces at Preschistoye, Bely
Jan 43	Defensive and offensive opns vic. Lomonosovo, Dukhovshchina
Mar 43	Withdrawal vic. Bely
Apr 43	Withdrawal; preparation of fortified positions vic. Ostrya, Teterino, Dukhovshchina

Sep 43	Movement, defensive opns vic. Dubrovno
Nov 43	Absorbed elements of 52d ID vic. Orsha
Dec 43	Defensive opns vic. Orsha, Vitebsk
Jun 44	Encircled vic. Vitebsk
Jul 44	Remnants incorporated into Corps Detachment H

Commanders

Gen.Lt. Meyer-Rabingen, Dec 39–Apr 42
Gen.Lt. Boege, Apr 42–Nov 43
Gen.Lt. Wössner, Nov 43–Mar 44
Gen.Major Hahne, Mar–Jun 44

198th Infantry Division

Dec 39	Formed at Prague, Czechoslovakia
Mar 40	Transferred to Perleberg, Germany for training
Apr 40	Occupation duty in Denmark
May 40	Transferred to Saarbrücken
Jun 40	Invasion of France, offensive opns in Maginot Line; security and occupation opns
Mar 41	Transferred to Romania
Apr 41	Assembly and movement in Romania and Bulgaria
May 41	Withdrawal and assembly in Romania
Jun 41	Movement to Yassy, Romania; preparation for invasion of USSR
Jun–Jul 41	Offensive opns across Prut River vic. Sculeni; offensive opns in Bessarabia; drive to the Dnestr River; offensive opns vic. Beresovka and Balta
Jul–Aug 41	Offensive and defensive opns in the Dneprpetrovsk bridgehead
Sep-Oct 41	Offensive opns vic. Pavlograd, Makeyevka
Nov 41	Offensive and defensive opns vic. Mius River bridgehead at Yanovka
Jun 42	Offensive opns vic. Mius bridgehead at Ivanovka
Aug 42	Offensive/defensive opns in western Caucasus vic. Goryachi Klyuch, Psekups Valley, Tri Duba, Kochkanova Mountains, Khrebet Inyagav Mountains
Jan 43	Withdrawal and defensive opns vic. Krasnodar, Pashkovskaya
Feb 43	Withdrawal in the Crimea vic. Novorossiisk, Krymskaya
Mar 43	Defensive opns vic. Zaporozhe
May 43	Defensive opns vic. Lyubitskiy, Shebeinka
Aug 43	Defensive opns and withdrawal with heavy losses vic. Belgorod, Kharkov, Merefa, Valki, Poltava, Kremenchug
Oct 43	Withdrawal and defensive opns with heavy losses vic. Kremenchug, Belaya Tserkov, Boguslav, Zhaskov, Talnoye, Uman
Mar 44	Disengagement and movement of remnants of division
Apr 44	Reorganized as *Kampfgruppe* 198 in Moldavia
Apr 44	Assembly in Romania
Jun 44	Transferred to Prague, Czechoslovakia
Jun 44–Aug 44	Coastal defense opns in southern France; defensive opns against Allied landings in southern France
Aug–Sep 44	Withdrawal in Rhône Valley
Sep 44–Feb 45	Defensive opns in Vosges Mountains; Colmar Pocket
Mar–May 45	Defensive opns in Rhineland, southern Germany

Commanders

Gen.Lt. Windeck, Nov 39–Jan 40
Gen.Lt. Roettig, Jan 40–Apr 42
Gen.Major Buck, Apr–Sep 42

Oberst Paul Schultz, Sep 42
Gen.Major Müller, Sep 42–Jan 43
Oberst Feldmann, Jan–Feb 43
Gen.Lt. Hans Joachim Horn, Feb 43–
    Jun 44
Gen.Major Otto Richter, Jun–Aug 44
Gen.Major Schiel, Sep 44–Jan 45
Gen.Major Barde, Jan–Apr 45
Gen.Major Kolb, Apr 45
Gen.Major Staedtke, Apr 45

201st Security Division

Jun 41	Formed in Fulda as Security Brigade 201
Jun 41	Redesignated Replacement Brigade 201
Jul 41	Transferred to Radom, Poland for training
Sep 41	Transferred to Lancut, Poland for training
Jan 42	Transferred to Vitebsk, USSR; security and anti-partisan opns
Feb 42	Redesignated Security Brigade 201
Feb 42	Movement, security opns in vic. Gomel, Klintsy
Mar 42	Movement, security of rear areas vic. Lepel
Jun 42	Redesignated 201st Security Division; anti-partisan opns vic. Lepel, Vitebsk, Polotsk, Nevel
Jan 43	Participated in anti-partisan operation Operation *SCHNEEHASE* vic. Nevel, Polotsk
Feb 43	Participated in anti-partisan Operation *KUGELBLITZ* vic. Lake Sennitsa, Gerodok
Mar 43	Participated in anti-partisan Operation *DONNERKEIL* vic. Polotsk, Sirotino, Dretun, Trudy, Obol River
Jun 43	Training, regrouping, opns against partisans vic. Lepel, Vitebsk, Nevel, Polotsk
Nov 43	Defensive opns vic. Polotsk, Lepel
Jul 44	Disengagement through Lithuania
Aug 44	Defensive opns vic. Mazeikiai
Nov 44	Defensive opns vic. Kurland Pocket
May 45	Surrendered

Commanders
Gen.Major Schellmann, Jun 41–Apr 42
Gen.Lt. Demoll, Mar–May 42
Oberst Roenicke, May 42
Gen.Lt. Jacobi, May 42–Oct 44
Gen.Major Martin Berg, Oct 44
Gen.Major Eberth, Oct 44–May 45

203d Security Division

Jun 41	Formed in Berlin as Brigade 203
Dec 41	Redesignated Security Brigade 203
Jan 42	Transferred to Bobruisk, USSR for training and security duty
Jun 42	Redesignated Security Division 203; anti-partisan opns vic. Bobruisk, Rogachev, Klichev
Nov 42	Redesignated 203d Security Division; security duty in Bobruisk sector
Jul 43	Heavy losses in security duty, Bobruisk sector
Sep 43	Security opns vic. Bobruisk, Zhlobin, Gorval, Chernigov, Gome)
Nov 43	Security opns vic. Kalinkovichi, Mozyr, Bogushevak
Jan 44	Security opns vic.David-Gorodok, Luninets
Jul 44	Retreat, defensive opns vic. Luninetz, Brest-Litovsk, and Poland vic. Sokolow, Warsaw
Nov 44	Redesignated 203d ID; defensive opns and retreat vic. Jedwabne, Lomza

Mar 45   Surrender vic.
Gotenhafen

Commanders

Gen.Major Barton, Jun 41–Jan 43

Gen.Lt. Pilz, Jan 43–Aug 44

Gen.Lt. Max Horn, Aug–Nov 44

Gen.Lt. Wilhelm Thomas, Nov–Dec 44

Gen.Lt. Gädicke, Dec 44–Mar 45

205th Infantry Division

Aug 39	Formed from 14th *Land-wehr* Division in Freiburg
Nov 39	Border security opns, offensive opns in France, occupation of France, return to Freiburg, training in Germany, return to occupation and coastal defense opns in France
Jan 42	Transferred to Vitebsk, USSR
Feb 42	Defensive opns vic. Velish, Velikie Luki, Demidov
Jul 42	Offensive and anti-partisan opns vic. western Dvina River, Surazh
Jan 43	Movement, rehabilitation, relief of encircled forces vic. Nevel, Velikie Luki
Jan 43	Defensive opns vic. Novosokolniki
Apr 43	Defensive opns vic. Velikie Luki, Novosokolniki
Apr 43	One regiment disbanded
Dec 43	Defensive and offensive opns vic. Novosokolniki
Feb 44	Withdrawal, defensive opns vic. Polotsk
Jul 44	Withdrawal, defensive opns in Lithuania vic. Zarasel and Latvia vic. Jaunjelgava, Plavinas
Oct 44	Defensive opns vic. Riga, Tukums
Nov 44–May 45	Retrograde opns to Latvian coast; defensive opns vic. Kurland; capitulated to Soviet forces

Commanders

Gen.Lt. Ernst Richter, Aug 39–Mar 42

Gen.Lt. Paul Seyffardt, Mar 42–Nov 43

Gen.Major Ernst Michael, Nov–Dec 43

Gen.Lt. Horst von Mellenthin, Dec 43–Nov 44

Gen.Major Biehler, Nov 44

Gen.Major Giesse, Nov 44–May 45

206th Infantry Division

Aug 39	Formed in Potsdam
Aug 39	Training, assembly, movement through East Prussia; offensive opns in Poland vic. Nidzica, Ostrow, Mazowiecka, Bielsk, Podlaski
Sep 39	Withdrawal, security duty vic. Lomza, Ostroleka, Narev River
Jun 40	Offensive opns in Belgium and France
Aug 40	Transferred to Arys and Allenstein, East Prussia for training
Jun 41	Movement and training in Bishofstein, Insterburg, and Angersburg, East Prussia
Jun 41	Offensive opns in Poland and the USSR vic. Polotsk, Nevel, Velikie Luki
Aug 41	Offensive opns vic. Western Dvina River, Zapadnaya Dvina, Nelidovo, Olenino, Rzhev
Oct 41	Offensive and defensive opns, withdrawal vic. Staritsa and the Volga River
Dec 41	Defensive opns vic. Rzhev, Olenino, Molodoi Tud
Sep 42	Defensive opns, counterattack, disengagement vic. Olenino. Molodoi Tud, Urdom
Jan 43	Defensive and offensive opns vic. Urdom, Borodatovo

Mar 43	Disengagement movement through Olenino, Nikitin-ka, Vorobi
Mar 43	One regiment disbanded
Aug 43	Defensive opns vic. Demidov
Sep 43	Disengagement, defensive opns vic. Liozno, Vitebsk
Jun 44	Encircled at Vitebsk, virtually destroyed
Aug 44	Division disbanded

Commanders

Gen.Lt. Höfl, Sep 39–Jul 42
Gen.Lt. Hitter, Jul 42–Jul 43 and Jul 43–Jun 44
Gen.Major André, Jul–Sep 43

207th Infantry (later Security) Division

Aug 39	Formed in Stargard, Pomerania, as 207th ID
Oct 39	Training, security and occupation duty in Poland Leba River sector
Nov 39	Transferred to Germany for training
Jan 40	Training, preparation for invasion of the Netherlands
Apr–Jul 40	Offensive opns in the Netherlands; occupation duty in France
Jul 40	Transferred to Stettin, Pomerania
Mar 41	Redesignated 207th Security Division
Apr 41	Transferred to Köslin, East Prussia; training
Sep 41	Security opns in Estonia vic. Dorpat and USSR vic. Pskov, Lake Peipus
Jan 42	Security duty, coastal defense, anti-partisan opns in Estonia vic. Reval, Dorpat) and USSR vic. Lake Peipus, Pskov
Jul 43	Security duty, training, regrouping in Estonia and vic. Gdov, Pskov
Oct 43	Formation of Group von Below; defensive and

	offensive opns vic. Nevel, Dorpat, Ostrov
Nov 43	Disbandment of Group Below; security and anti-partisan opns vic. Dorpat
Feb 44	Anti-partisan, security, and defensive opns, coastal defense vic. Dorpat, Lake Peipus, Pskov
Aug 44	Reorganized as *Kampfgruppe* 207th Security Division vic. Dorpat
Sep 44	Remnants of *Kampfgruppe* retreat from Dorpat and Lake Peipus to Riga
Oct 44	Remnants of *Kampfgruppe* destroyed
Oct 44	207th Security Division reconstituted at Windau, Latvia
Oct 44	Division redesignated "for special duties," staff used to control foreign units at Sassmacken
Jan 45	Division disbanded after defensive engagements

Commanders

Gen.Lt. von Tiedemann, Sep 39–Jan 43
Gen.Lt. Erich Hofmann, Jan–Nov 43
Gen.Lt. Boglislav, *Graf* von Schwerin, Nov 43–Sep 44
Gen.Major Martin Berg, Sep–Dec 44

208th Infantry Division

Aug 39	Formed at Lübben
Sep 39	Offensive opns in Poland, vic. Grudziadz, Bromberg, Modlin, Kutno
Oct 39	Occupation duty in Poland
Nov 39–Jan 42	Transferred to Germany; invasion of the Netherlands and France; occupation and coastal defense
Jan 42	Transferred to USSR
Apr 42	Defensive opns vic. Zhizdra, Sukhinichi
Apr 42	Formation of Corps Scheele near Zhizdra

Mar 43	Disbandment of Corps Scheele; defensive and withdrawal opns vic. Zhizdra, Sudimir, Bolkhov, Belev
Jun 43	Defensive opns vic. Bolkhov and Oka River
Jul 43	Disengagement; reorganized as *Kampfgruppe* 208th ID; opns vic. Bolkhov, Karachev, Navlya, Konotop, Oster, Nezhin, Dymer
Nov 43	Defensive opns vic. Radomyshl, Zhitomir, Chernyakhov
Dec 43	Defensive opns; regrouping vic. Malin, Radomyshl
Jan 44	Disengagement opns vic. Kalinovka, Vinnitsa, Staro Konstantinov
Jan 44	Reconstituted as 208th ID vic. Medzhibozh
Mar 44	Withdrawal, heavy losses in Galicia vic. Proskurov, Chertkov, Stanislav, Sanok, Gorlice, Krosno, Jaslo, Tarnow, Nowy Sacy
Dec 44	Withdrawal and defensive opns in Hungary vic. omarom-Esztergom; Slovakia; and Silesia
Apr 45	In Liegnitz, Lower Silesia

Commanders

Gen.Lt. Moritz Andreas, 1939–Dec 41
Gen.d.Inf. von Scheele, Dec 41–Feb 43
Oberst von Schlieben, Feb–Apr 43
Gen.Major Zwade, Apr–Jun 43
Gen.Lt. Pieckenbrock, Jun 43–
    May 45

211th Infantry Division (later VGD)

Feb 39	Formed in Cologne by conversion of 211th *Landwehr* Division
Oct 39	Training in Germany and staging for invasion of Belgium and France
May 40– Jan 42	Offensive opns in Belgium and France;
	occupation and coastal defense opns in France
Jan 42	Transferred to Briansk, USSR
Jan 42	Assembly in USSR vic. Shchigry, Sudimir
Jan 42	Defensive opns vic. Zhizdra, Rechitsa, Chernychi, Lutovnya, Klintsy, Duminichi
Apr 42	Defensive and offensive opns vic. Zhizdra-Resseta Rivers sector
Jul 43	Disengagement and defensive opns vic. Granki, Lyubegoshchi, Shchigry
Aug 43	Defensive opns vic. Zhizdra, Dyatkovo, Lyudinovo, Kirov
Sep 43	Disengagement and defensive opns vic. Luzhnitsa, Slavgorod, Starry Bych, Mogachev
Nov 43	Renamed *Sperrgruppe* ("Blocking Group") Eckhardt vic. Polotsk
Nov– Dec 43	Defensive opns vic. Polotsk
Jan 44	Redesignated as 211th ID vic. Polotsk
Feb 44	Disengagement through USSR vic. Vitebsk, Bykhov, Bobruisk, Rogachev and Poland vic. Kamen, Kashirski
Jul 44	Retreat through Poland vic. Siedlce, Sokolow, Bielsk Podlaski, Pultusk, Makow Mazowiecki; heavy losses vic. Nevel
Nov 44	Withdrawn for reconstitution
Dec 44	Movement vic. Angerapp, East Prussia
Jan 45	Transfer to Czechoslovakia vic. Nitra, Nove Zamky; redesignated 211th VGD
Feb 45	Defensive opns vic. Estergom, Hungary

Mar 45   Last trace on maps vic.
              Estergom

Commanders

Gen.Lt. Renner, 1939–Feb 42

Gen.Major Richard Müller, Feb 42–
    Jul 43

Gen.Lt. Johann-Heinrich Eckhardt,
    Jul 43–May 45

212th Infantry Division (later VGD)

Feb 39   Formed in Rhineland I by
              redesignation of 212th
              Landwehr Division

Aug 39–   Training in Germany
Oct 41   for invasion of Belgium
              and France; offensive
              opns in Belgium and
              France; withdrawal to
              Germany; occupation and
              coastal in France

Oct 41   Transferred to USSR;
              offensive opns vic. Gatchi-
              na, Pushkin, Krasnoye
              Selo, Petrodvorets

Nov 41   Offensive and defensive
              opns; withdrawal vic.
              Oranienbaum, Krasnoye
              Selo

Feb 42   Defensive and offensive
              opns vic. Volkhov and
              Tigoda Rivers

Apr 42   Offensive and defensive
              opns vic. Oranienbaum
              and Krasnoye Selo

Jul 42   Defensive, training, and
              security opns vic. Nov-
              gorod, Volkhov River,
              Podberezye

Jan 43   Training, rehabilitation,
              defensive opns vic. Mga,
              Krasny Bor

Jun 43   Anti-partisan and offen-
              sive opns vic. Pogostye,
              Chernaya River, Maluksa
              Stantsiya, Lodva, and
              Voronovo

Dec 43   Defensive of Mga River
              sector

Jan 44   Disengagement; defensive
              opns vic. Tosno, Luga,

Strugi Krasnye, Pakov,
Ostrov

Jun 44   Withdrawal with heavy
              losses in USSR vic. Drissa,
              Glubkoye; and Lithuania
              vic. Svencionys, Ukmerge,
              Dotnuva, Raseinial

Sep 44   Withdrawal vic. Sieradz,
              Poland; redesignated
              212th VGD

Nov 44–   Transferred to Germany;
Apr 45   defensive opns on Western
              Front

Apr 45   Defensive opns vic.
              Dachau and Munich

Commanders

Gen.Major Walter Friedrichs, Sep 39

Gen.Lt. Endres, Sep 39–Oct 42

Gen.Lt. Reymann, Oct 42–Oct 43

Gen.Major Dr. Koske, Oct 43–May 44

Gen.Lt. Sensfuss, May 44–Mar 45

Oberst von Hobe, Apr 45

Gen.Major Max Ulich, Apr 45

Gen.Major *Freiherr* von Buddenbrock,
    Apr–May 45

213th Infantry (later Security) Division

Feb 39   Formed in Glogau, Silesia
              by redesignation of 213th
              Landwehr Division

Aug 39   Training vic. Glogau, Lieg-
              nitz and Breslau, Silesia

Sep 39   Offensive opns in Poland
              vic. Sycow, Ostrow,
              Kalisz, Leczyca, Podde-
              bice, Aleksandrow, Lodz-
              ki, Kutno, Modlin

Oct 39   Security opns and training
              in Poland

Apr 40   Transfer to Posen and
              Mosina for training and
              security opns

Jun–   Transferred to Germany;
Jul 40   security opns vic.
              Mulhouse, France

Jul 40   Transferred to Glogau,
              Silesia for training

Mar 41   Training vic. Szprotawa,
              Poland; dedesignated
              213th Security Division

May 41	Assembly, entraining, movement
Jul 41	Anti-partisan and security opns in USSR vic. Kovel, Lutsk, Sarny, Dubno, Rovno, Kostopol, Shepetovka, Novograd-Volynski, Berdichev, Zhitomir, Korosten, Kalinovka, Zhaskov, Skvira
Sep 41	Security and anti-partisan opns vic. Uman, Novo-Arkhangelsk, Smeln, Kirovograd, Belaya Tserkov, Krivoi Rog, Dnepropetrovosk
Oct 41	Security and anti-partisan opns vic. Aleksandriya, Cherkassy, Poltava, Kremenchug, Kobelyaki, Mirgorod, Gadyach
Jan 42	Security and anti-partisan opns vic. Kremenchug, Ysarichanka, Lubnykobelyaki, Romny, Piryatin, Pereyaslav-Khminitski, Kiev, Globino, Zolotonosha
Jun 42	Security and anti-partisan opns, regrouping vic. Kremenchug, Voroshilovgrad, Kupyansk, Valuiki, Belgorod, Kursk, Sumy, Akhtyrka, Izyum, Kharkov, Krasnograd, Lozovaia, Rubezhnoe
Jan 43	Security and anti-partisan opns, regrouping vic. Kharkov, Chuguev, Volchansk, Merefa, Borispol, Kiev, Oster, Dymer, Makarov, Vasilkov, Desna River, Dnepr River
Jul 43	Security and anti-partisan opns vic. Kiev, Yagotin, Romny, Krolevets, Glukhov, Borzna, Nezhin, Nosovka, Chernigov, Zhitomir, Vasilkov
Dec 43	Defensive opns; withdrawal vic. Fastov,

	Verbov, Zhitomir, Vilsk, Kolodiyevka
Jan 44	Disengagement with heavy losses vic. Korsun
Apr 44	Withdrawal through Ukraine vic. Sokal, Nemirov and Poland vic. Bilgoraj, Zamosc, Chelm
Aug 44	Defensive opns in Poland vic. Ostrowiec, Kielce

Commanders
Gen.Lt. de Coubiere, 1939–Aug 42
Gen.Lt. Göschen, Aug 42–Sep 44

214th Infantry Division

Feb 39	Formed in Hanau by redesignation of 214th *Landwehr* Division
Aug 39–Feb 44	Training in Germany; deployment to Norway for coastal defense and security opns
Feb 44	Defensive opns in Estonia
Mar 44	Redesignated Staff, 214th Security Unit in Mustvee
Apr 44	Reconstituted as 214th ID; defensive opns vic. Vladimir-Volynski, Ukraine
Jul 44	Defensive opns vic. Radom, Poland
Jan 45	Encircled at Lodz, Poland; virtually destroyed

Commanders
Gen.Lt. Groppe, 1939–Jan 40
Gen.Lt. Max Horn, Feb 40–Dec 43; Feb–Mar 44
Gen.Major Wahle, Dec 43–Feb 44
Gen.Lt. von Kirchbach, Mar 44–Jan 45

215th Infantry Division

Feb 39	Formed at Heilbronn by redesignation of 215th *Landwehr* Division
Aug 39–Nov 41	Training and border defense in Germany; offensive opns in invasion of France; occupation opns
Nov 41	Offensive and defensive opns in USSR vic.

	Chudovo, Budgoshch, Tikhvin, Oskuya River, Grusino, Novgorod
Jan 42	Defensive opns vic. Chudovo, Volkhovo-Stantsiya, Dymno, Volkhov River
Jul 42	Defensive opns vic. Tosno, Oranienbaum, Leningrad,
Sep 43	Defensive opns vic. Verkhnaya-Kipen and Mga
Oct 43	Defensive opns vic. Pushkin
Jan 44	Disengagement through Krasnoye Selo, Krasnogvardeisk, Luga, Seredka
Feb 44	Defensive opns vic. Pskov
Jun 44	Withdrawal and defensive opns in Poland (vic. Ostrow) and Lithuania (vic. Zarasai)
Sep 44	Defensive opns vic. Baldone, Latvia
Oct 44	Withdrawal vic. Saldus, Auce, Dobele vic. Kurland
Feb 45	Withdrawal; defensive opns vic. Danzig, West Prussia
Apr 45	Division remnants absorbed by "Inf. Div. T. Korner" vic. Gotenhafen

Commanders

Gen.Lt. Kniess, 1939–Nov 42
Gen.Lt. Frankewitz, Nov 42–Apr 45

216th Infantry Division

Feb 39	Formed at Hannover by redesignation of 216th *Landwehr* Division
Aug 39	Training; offensive opns in Netherlands, Belgium and France; occupation and coastal defense in France
Dec 41	Transferred to USSR; defensive opns vic. Smolensk, Viazma, Rzhev; formation of Group Gilsa; defensive opns and breakout from encirclement vic. Sukhinichi

Feb 42	Group Gilsa disbanded
Jun 42	Assembly and rehabilitation vic. Zhizdra; reformation of Group Gilsa; defensive and anti-partisan opns vic. Zhizdra, Yelnya, Briansk, Navlya, Altukhovo, Dmitrovsk-Orlovski)
Sep 42	Disbandment of Group Gilsa; offensive and defensive opns vic. Lyudinovo and Kirov
Nov 42	Offensive and defensive opns vic. Novo-Dugino, Sychevka, Milyatino, Viazma
Feb 43	In reserve, then defensive opns and withdrawal vic. Orel, Briansk, Altukhovo, Pochep, Starodub, Dobrush, Rechitsa
Nov 43	Offensive and defensive opns with heavy losses vic. Khoyniki, Yurevichi, Kalinkovichi, Belshiye, Avtyuki; redesignated 216th Division Group; remnants of division absorbed by 102d ID

Commanders

Gen.Lt. Hermann Böttcher, 1939–Sep 40
Gen.Lt. Himer, Sep 40–Apr 41
Gen.Major *Freiherr* von und zu Gilsa, Apr 41–Apr 43
Gen.Lt. Schack, May–Oct 43
Gen.Lt. von Neindorff, Oct 43
Gen.Major Gihr, Oct–Nov 43

217th Infantry Division

Feb 39	Formed in Allenstein, East Prussia by redesignation of 217th *Landwehr* Division
Sep 39	Offensive opns in Poland vic. Soldau, Mlawa, Pultusk, Serock, Zegrze security of demarcation line vic. Bug River

Nov 39	Security opns in Poland; redeployment for invasion of Low Countries
Apr–Jul 40	Offensive opns in the Netherlands, Belgium and France; occupation of France
Jul 40	Redeployment to the east vic. Tilsit, Memel
Jun 41	Offensive opns in Lithuania vic. Rietavas, Silute, Varnial, Kursenal, Joniskis and Latvia vic. Jelgava
Jul 41	Offensive opns in Latvia vic. Riga and Estonia vic. Parnu, Turi, Paide
Aug 41	Offensive opns in Estonia; coastal defense
Sep 41	Offensive opns, in USSR vic. Koporye, Oranienbaum
Mar 42	Defensive opns vic. Koporye
Apr 42	Defensive opns vic. Gomontova and Lyuban
Oct 42	Defensive opns vic. Kirishi
Sep 43	Transferred to southern sector vic. Nezhin; defensive opns vic. Nezhin and Pripet River
Oct 43	Redesignated *Kampfgruppe* 217 vic. Gornostaypol and Dymer
Nov 43	Remnants incorporated into Corps Detachment C

Commanders

Gen.Lt. Baltzer, 1939–Feb 42
Gen.Lt. Friedrich Bayer, Feb–Sep 42
Gen.d.Inf. Otto Lasch, Sep 42–Oct 43
Gen.Lt. Walter Poppe, Oct–Nov 43

218th Infantry Division

Feb 39	Formed in Berlin by redesignation of 218th *Landwehr* Division
Aug 39	Training; security duty, in East and West Prussia
Oct 39	Occupation opns in Poland

Apr–Jul 40	Transferred to Germany; offensive opns and occupation of France; withdrawal to Germany
Mar 41	Coastal defense and training in Denmark
Jan 42	Offensive opns in USSR vic. Demiansk, Velikie Luki, Ostrov, Pushkinskiye Gory, Loknya, Podberezye, Kholm
Feb 42–Dec 43	Offensive and defensive opns vic. Kholm; antipartisan opns
Feb 44	Defensive opns vic. Novorzhev, Opochka, Ostrov
Jul 44	Withdrawal into Latvia; reorganized as *Kampfgruppe* 218
Aug 44	Reconstitution as 218th Inf Div; defensive opns; reorganized as *Kampfgruppe* 218; withdrawal to Torva and Saare Island, Estonia
Dec 44	Defensive opns vic. Mazeikiai and Priekule; reconstitution as 218th Inf Div
Apr 45	Defensive opns vic. Saldus and Tukums

Commanders

Gen.Lt. *Freiherr* von Grote, 1939–Dec 41
Gen.Major *Freiherr* von Uckermann, Jan–Mar 42
Gen.Lt. Viktor Lang, Mar 42–Dec 44
Gen.Major von Collani, Dec 44–May 45
Gen.Lt. Ranck, May 45

221st Infantry (later Security) Division

Feb 39	Formed in Breslau as 221st Inf Div by redesignation of 221st *Landwehr* Division
Aug 39–Apr 40	Training; Polish campaign; occupation and security opns
Apr–Jul 40	Transferred to Germany; invasion of France

Jul 40	Training and rehabilitation vic. Breslau
Mar 41	Reorganization as 221st Security Division; security opns vic. Narev River, Ostrolenka, Lomza, Bial-ystok, Brest, Kobrin
Aug 41	Movement and anti-parti-san opns vic. Prushany, Baranovichi, Pinak, Slutsk, Bobruisk, Mozyr, Gomel, Briansk, Roslavl, Mogilev
Dec 41	Reorganized as 221st Inf Div; defensive and assault opns vic. Orel, Ust Leski, Trudki, Nizhnyaya, Zale-goshch, Trudy Taryayeva
Mar 42	Security and anti-partisan opns vic. Briansk, Smolen-sk, Pochinok, Velnya, Bal-tutino. Pavilnovo, Koro-bets, Ugra River
Jul– Nov 42	Anti-partisan opns vic. Gomel, Pochep, Klintsy, Unecha, Surazh, Mglin, Krichev, Korma, Novo-Zybkov, Chechersk
Jan 43	Anti-partisan and security opns
Sep 43	Anti-partisan opns vic. Novozybkov, Klintsy, Ubecha, Pogar, Starodub, Khotimak, Klimovichi, Stavgorod, Dovsk, Vetka, Semenovka, Mglin, Aku-lichi, Surazh, Kostyuko-vichi; defensive and disen-gagement opns vic. Gomel, Voronezh, Stary Oskol, Koryukovka
Oct 43	Anti-partisan and security opns vic. Minsk, Vileika, Molodechno, Oshmyany
Jul 44	Disengagement with heavy losses. Disbanded.

Commanders

Gen.Lt. Johann Pflugbeil, Sep 39–Jul 42
Gen.Lt. Hubert Lendle, Jul 42–Aug 43; Sep 43–Mar 44

Gen.Major Böttger, Aug–Sep 43
Gen.Lt. Bogislav, *Graf* von Schwerin, Mar–Jul 44

223d Infantry Division

Aug 39	Formed in Dresden by redesignating 223d *Landwehr* Division
Aug 39– Mar 40	Training; occupation and security opns in Poland
Mar 40	Preparation for invasion of Belgium and France
May– Jun 40	Offensive opns in Belgium and France
Jul 40– Oct 41	Occupation and coastal defense opns in France
Oct 41	Transferred to USSR; offensive and defensive opns vic. Pakov, Lyuban, Tosno, Mga, Chernaya, Voronova, Shapki, Khandrovo
Aug 42	Participation in first battle of Lake Ladoga; defensive opns vic. Mga, Voronovo, Kirsino, Nishkino, Lake Ladoga
Sep 42	Defensive opns vic. Pore-chye, Karbusel, Markovo, Siniavino, Maluksa, Lodva
Jan 43	Participated in second bat-tle of Lake Ladoga and defensive opns
May 43	Rehabilitation, security and anti-partisan opns vic. Dno, Porkhov, Nororzhev, Opochka, Idritsa, Pustoshka
Aug 43	Defensive Opns vic. Kharkov
Sep 43	Disengagement opns vic. Poltava, Kremenchug, Cherkassy, Dnepr River
Oct 43	Defensive and anti-parti-san opns vic. Cherkassy and Dnepr River sector; division virtually destroyed west of Kiev;

remnants incorporated into *Kampfgruppe* 168

Nov 43 Staff and other remnants transferred to France to be incorporated into 352d ID

Dec 43 Last elements of the division in the east incorporated into 168th Inf Div

Commanders

Gen.Lt. Körner, 1939–May 41
Gen.d.Inf. Lüters, May 41–Oct 42
Gen.Lt. Usinger, Oct 42–Sep 43
Oberst Schmidt-Hammer, Oct–Nov 43

225th Infantry Division

Feb 39 Formed in Hamburg by redesignation of 225th *Landwehr* Division

Aug 39– Training, preparation
Dec 41 for invasion of Low Countries; offensive opns in the Netherlands, Belgium and France; occupation and coastal defense opns in France

Dec 41 Transferred to USSR via Danzig

Jan 42 Defensive opns vic. Lisino-Korpus, Kastenskaya

Feb 42 Formation of Group von Rasse; offensive and defensive opns vic. Lyuban and Tigoda River

May 42 Disbandment of Group von Rasse; reestablishment of 225th ID; defensive and assault opns; coastal defense vic. Koporye, Gorki, Oranienbaum front

Dec 42 Defensive opns vic. Volosovo, Koty, Veymarn, Shimsk, Demiansk Pocket

Jan– Attached to 254th ID in
Feb 43 the Demiansk Pocket

Feb 43 Defensive opns vic. Staraya Russa, Lake Ilmen

May 43 Defensive and security opns vic. Tosno, Lyuban, Shapki

Aug 43 Defensive opns vic. Mga

Jan 44 Disengagement opns vic. Tosno, Gatchina, Volosovo; reorganization as *Kampfgruppe* 225

Feb– Incorporated remnants of
May 44 9th *Luftwaffe* Field Div. reformed as 225th ID; defensive opns in Estonia

Jul 44 Disengagement in Latvia

Oct 44– Retrograde opns to Lat-
May 45 vian coast; defensive opns vic. Kurland; capitulated to Soviet forces

Commanders

Gen.Lt. Schaumburg, 1939–Jul 40
Gen.Major Karl von Wachter, Jul 40–May 41
Gen.Lt. von Basse, May 41–Sep 42
Gen.Lt. Risse, Sep 42–May 45

227th Infantry Division

Feb 39 Formed in Düsseldorf by redesignation of 227th *Landwehr* Division

Mar 39 Training; offensive opns in the Netherlands and Belgium; coastal defense and occupation opns in France

Oct 41 Transferred to USSR; defensive and assault opns; coastal defense; regrouping vic. Mga, Gaytolovo, Siniavino, Likpa, Lake Ladoga

Aug 42 Offensive and defensive opns; coastal defense; participated in first battle of Lake Ladoga

Jan 43 Defensive opns; second battle of Lake Ladoga; rehabilitation vic. Kirsino, Chudovo

Feb 43 Defensive opns in participated in third battle of Lake Ladoga

Sep 43 Offensive and defensive opns vic. Mga, Gaytolovo, Siniavino

Dec 43	Withdrawal to Mga; defensive opns
Jan 44	Disengagement opns with heavy losses vic. Kineisepp, Narva
May 44	Movements to Latvia, defensive opns north of Lake Peipus
Jul 44	Withdrawal; defensive opns in Latvia
Jan 45	Transferred to Danzig
Feb 45	Withdrawal and defensive opns in Poland
Mar 45	Surrendered

Commanders

Gen.Major Zickwolff, 1939–May 40 and Jul 40–Apr 41
Gen.Lt. von Wachter, May–Jul 40
Gen.Lt. von Scotti, Apr 41–Jun 43
Gen.Lt. Berlin, Jun 43–May 44
Gen.Major Wengler, May 44–Mar 45

239th Infantry Division

Feb 39	Formed at Gleiwitz by redesignation of 239th *Landwehr* Division
Sep 39– May 40	Invasion of Poland; security and occupation opns
Jun– Jul 40	Offensive opns in France; occupation of France; return to Germany
Jul 40	Transferred to Gleiwitz for rehabilitation and training
Apr 41	Transferred to Romania; training of Romanian units
Jul 41	Offensive opns in USSR across Prut River and vic. Zguritsa, Yanpl, Balta, Dniester and Kolyma Rivers, Dnepr River, Psel River, Kremenchug
Sep 41	Offensive and defensive opns vic. Orshitsa, Vorskla River, Poltava, Krasnokutsk, Bogodukhov
Oct 41	Defensive opns vic. Bogodukhov; offensive opns vic. Kharkov

Nov 41	Defensive and security opns vic. Donets River sector; heavy losses vic. Bjelgorod
Feb 42	Disbanded vic. Bogodukhov

Commander

Gen.Lt. Neuling, Sep 39–Mar 42

246th Infantry Division (later VGD)

Feb 39	Formed at Darmstadt by redesignation of 246th *Landwehr* Division
May 40– Jan 42	Offensive opns in France; occupation of France
Jan 42	Defensive opns in USSR vic. Liezno, Smolensk
Jul 42	Offensive opns vic. Bely, Nelidovo, Pushkari
Nov 42	Offensive and defensive opns vic. Bely, Obsha River, Lomonosovo, Repino
Apr 43	Defensive opns vic. Troitskoye, Vorotyshino
Sep 43	Defensive opns vic. Rudnya, Liozno
Oct 43	Defensive opns vic. Shelokhovo and Zelenskoye Lakes, Vysochany, Pogostishche, Babinovichi
Jan 44	Defensive opns vic. Vysochany, Starobobylye; withdrawal; defensive opns vic. Vitebsk
Jun 44	Encirclement at Vitebsk; much of division captured
Sep 44	Division reformed as VGD in Milowitz, Czechoslovakia from remnants, elements of the newly-formed 565 VGD, and naval personnel
Sep 44	Transferred to Germany and the Western Front
May 45	Surrendered in Germany

Commanders

Gen.Lt. Denecke, Sep 39–Dec 41
Gen.Lt. Siry, Dec 41–May 43

Gen.Major von Alberti, May–Sep 43
Oberst Heinz Fiebig, Sep–Oct 43
Gen.Lt. Falley, Oct 43–Apr 44
Gen.Major Müller-Bülow, Apr–
Jun 44
Oberst Hirschfeld, Sep 44
Oberst Neumann, Oct 44
Oberst Gerhard Wilck, Oct–Nov 44
Gen.Major Körte, Nov 44–Jan 45
Oberst List, Jan 45
Gen.Major Dr. Walter Kühn, Jan–
May 45

250th Infantry Division

Aug 41	Formed at Grafenwöhr training area from Spanish volunteers; known as the "Blue Division"
Late Aug 41	Transferred through Poland to USSR
Oct 41	Offensive and defensive opns vic.Volkhov and Vishera Rivers, Novgorod, Podberezye
Sep 42– Oct 42	Offensive, defensive, opns vic. Pushkin, Pavlovsk, Krasny Bor
Oct 43	Assembly in Gatchina for departure to Spain
Nov 43	Reorganization of elements of the division as the sub-divisional "Spanish Legion" in Kingisepp; completion of transfer of remainder of the division to Spain

Commanders

Gen.Major Antonio Muñoz Grandes,
Jul 41–Dec 42
Gen.Lt. Emilio Esteban Infantes,
Dec 42–Oct 43

251st Infantry Division

Mar 39	Formed at Hanau by redesignation of 251st *Landwehr* Division
Aug 39	Training
May 40	Offensive opns in Belgium and France; occupation, coastal defense and security opns in France
Apr 41	Transferred to Poland; preparation for invasion of USSR
Jun 41– Oct 41	Offensive opns in Lithuania and USSR vic. Nevel, Velikie Luki, Andreapol, Seilzharovo, Babino, Torshok, Staritsa, Dmitriyeva
Dec 41	Disengagement opns vic. Kalinin, Pushkino, Oshurkovo, Zubtsov
Jan 42	Defensive and anti-partisan opns vic. Rzhev, Volga River sector, Bykovo, Bakhmutovo
Jul 42	Defensive opns vic. Muzhischevo
Jan 43	Defensive opns vic. Trushkovo, Chertolino, Sychevka
Mar 43	Offensive, defensive opns and disengagement vic. Smolensk, Pogar, Gramysch, Novogorod-Severshi, Sevsk
Sep 43	Reduced to a single regiment vic. Kholmy and Lyubrech; reorganized as *Kampfgruppe* 251
Oct 43	Withdrawal and defensive opns vic. Bragin
Nov– Dec 43	Disbandment of *Kampfgruppe 251* vic. Bragin; reorganized as Division Group 251; movement, defensive, disengagement and offensive opns vic. Kotlovitsa, Beresnevka, Khoiniki, Yurevichi, Kalinovichi
Dec 43	Withdrawal vic. Mozyr; incorporation of Division Group 251 into Corps Detachment E
Jul 44	Heavy losses in the central sector

Sep 44	Redesignated as 251st ID in Warka, Poland; defensive opns
Jan 45	Disengagement; retreat through Poland vic. Grojec, Sochaczew, Golub, Chelmno, and Pomerania
Mar 45	Reorganized as *Kampfgruppe* 251; and withdrawal and defensive opns vic. Gotenhafen; destroyed

Commanders

Gen.Lt Kratzert, 1939–Aug 41
Gen.Lt. Burdach, Aug 41–Mar 43
Gen.Lt. Felzmann, Mar–Nov 43
Gen.Lt. Heucke, Oct 44–Feb 45
Oberst Mangold, Mar 45

252d Infantry Division

Mar 39	Formed at Neisse by redesignation of 252d *Landwehr* Division
Sep 39	Transferred to Poland for anti-partisan, security and occupation opns
Oct 39–Jul 40	Transferred to Germany for training; offensive opns in France, and return to Germany
Jul 40	Transferred to Poland for occupation duty vic. Warsaw, Radom
Jun–Dec 41	Offensive opns in Poland across Bug River, and USSR vic. Slutsk, Bobruisk, Rogachev, Krichev, Roslavi, Desna River, Yelnya, Viazma,
Dec 41	Defensive opns vic. Mozhaisk, Ruza
Jan 42	Withdrawal and defensive opns vic. Gzhatsk
Mar 43	Disenagagement and defensive opns vic. Shimonovo, Podmoshchye, Volochek, Sharipino, Dorogobuzh, Yelnya
Nov 43	Offensive and defensive opns near Nevel;

	redesignation as *Kampfgruppe* 252; defensive opns vic. Gorodok
Dec 43	Release of command elements of the division for defensive opns in the Obel River sector; movement of *Kampfgruppe* 252 to vic. Vitebsk for defensive opns
Jan 44	Reorganization as 252d ID in Obel River sector vic. Vitebsk and Polotsk; defensive opns
Jun 44	Disengagement opns in Lithuania
Jul 44	Reorganization as *Kampfgruppe* 252; withdrawal and disbandment vic. Kedainiai and Dotnuva, Lithuania
Aug 44	Reorganization as 252d ID; defensive opns vic. Raseiniai; disengagement vic. Krustpils, Plavinas, Madona, Latvia
Sep 44	Withdrawal through Poland; defensive opns vic. Ciechanow, Nasielsk
Jan 45	Disengagement movement and retreat through East Prussia and Pomerania
Mar 45	Defensive opns vic. Danzig; redesignation as *Kampfgruppe* 252
Apr 45	Withdrawal to Bohnsack, West Prussia; defensive opns
May 45	Surrendered

Commanders

Gen.Lt. von Böhm-Bezing, 1939–Feb 42
Gen.Lt. Hans Schäfer, Feb 42–Jan 43
Gen.Lt. Melzer, Jan 43–Oct 44
Gen.Lt. Dreckmann, Oct 44–May 45
Oberst von Unold, Mar–May 45

253d Infantry Division

Mar 39	Formed in Düsseldorf by redesignation of 253d *Landwehr* Division

Aug 39– Apr 41	Movement in Germany in preparation for invasion of France; offensive operations Belgium and France; occupation, security opns and training in France
Apr 41	Transferred to Allenstein, East Prussia
Jun– Dec 41	Offensive opns in Lithuania vic. Vistytis, Kaunas, Zamoshye, Drissa, Polotsk and the USSR vic. Idritsa, Ushcha River, Nevel, Velikie Luki, Lakes Otolovo and Luchanskoye, Selizharova, Volga and Tikhvina Rivers
Dec 41	Disengagement vic. Volga River area and Molodoi Tud
Jan 42	Defensive opns vic. Olenino, Mostovaya, Kholmets, Khmelevka
Feb 42	Disengagement west of Olenino, Obsha and Belaya Rivers, Nikitinka
Mar 43	Defensive opns vic. Vop River sector, Vopets and Tsarevich Rivers
Aug– Dec 43	Withdrawal and defensive opns; reorganization as *Kampfgruppe* 252, then again as 253d ID near Briansk; disengagement vic. Gorodets, Pochep, Unecha, Klintsy, Peretin, Vetka, Zhlobin, Pykhan, Chechersk, Tursk, Zhlobin
Dec 43	Defensive opns vic. Shatilki, Parichi
Apr 44	Transfer to Poland; defensive opns vic. Kovel, Lyubomi, Olesk
Jul 44	Withdrawal vic. Krasnik, Poland; redesignation as *Kampfgruppe* 253
Aug 44	Defensive opns vic. Solec, Ostrowiec; reorganization as 253d ID

Sep 44	Defensive opns vic. Kielce, Gryhow, Dukla, Krepna
Oct– Nov 44	Redesignation as *Kampfgruppe* 252, then reorganization as 253d ID vic. Dukla
Dec 44	Transferred to Czechoslovakia; defensive opns vic. Nizna Polianka and Janske Lazne
Jan 45	Redesignation as Division Group 252; disengagement vic. Bardejov, Spisska Stara Ves, Bialka, Polhora; reorganized as 253d ID in Polhora
Feb 45	Defensive engagements in Poland vic. Skotschau [Skoczow], Zywiec and Czechoslovakia vic. Karvina, Darkov
Apr 45	Defensive opns vic. Mosty
May 45	Surrender

Commanders

Gen.Lt. Fritz Kühne, 1939–Mar 41
Gen.Lt. Schellert, Mar 41–Jan 43
Gen.Lt. Carl Becker, Jan 43–Jun 44;
    Jun 44–May 45
Gen.Lt. Junck, Jun 44
Gen.Major Schwatlogesterding,
    May 45

254th Infantry Division

Mar 39	Formed in Lingen, Oldenburg by redesignation of 254th *Landwehr* Division
Sep 39– Jun 40	Training; offensive opns in the Netherlands, Belgium and France; occupation, coastal defense and security opns in France
Apr 41	Transferred to Preussisch Stargard and Dirschau, West Prussia
Jun 41	Offensive opns in Lithuania vic. Taurage, Kelme, Seduva, Birzai, Pasvalys
Jul 41	Offensive opns in Latvia vic. Plavinas, Jaunjelgava

and Estonia vic. Aseri, Jogeva, Paide, Tapa, Kunde, Viljandi

Aug 41 Security opns vic. Sonda and Reval, Estonia

Sep 41 Defensive opns in Estonia vic. Narva-Joesuu and the USSR vic. Kingisepp, Krasnoye Selo, Mga, Glazhevo, Volkhov River, Kirishi, Chudovo, Lyuban

Apr 42 Defensive opns vic. Rubino, Apraksin Bor, Chervino, Finev Lug, Krivion, Rogavka, Spasskays Polist

Jan 43 Defensive opns vic. Demiansk; defensive opns vic. Olkhovets, Zdrinoga, Fedorovo

Feb 43 Disengagement vic. Pustoshka, Lyadiny, Soltsy

Mar 43 Defensive opns vic. Gatchina, Krasnoye Selo, Krasny Bor, Ishora River

Jul 43–Jan 44 Defensive opns vic. Mga

Jan 44 Transferred to fic. Vinnitsa; defensive opns vic. Lipovets, Ilintsy, Nemirov

Mar 44 Disengagement through Dzhurin, Bar, Olkhovets; redesignated as *Kampfgruppe* 254 vic. Borshchev, Chortkov

May 44 Reorganization as 254th ID; defensive opns vic. Monastyriska

Jul 44 Defensive opns vic. Podgaitsy, Vybranovka, Stry

Jul 44 Redesignation as *Kampfgruppe* 254; defensive opns vic. Sambor, Poland

Aug 44 Reorganization as 254th ID; defensive opns in Galicia vic. Sanok and Rymanow, and Dukla and Snina, Czechoslovakia

Oct 44 Defensive opns vic. Vysna, Radvan, Presov, Bidovce, Geinica, Levoca, Czechoslovakia

Jan 45 Withdrawal; defensive opns in Silesia

Mar–Apr 45 Withdrawal; defensive opns vic. Ziegenhals, Silesia

Commanders

Gen.Lt. Fritz Koch, 1939–Apr 40
Gen.Lt. Behschnitt, Apr 40–Mar 42
Gen.Lt. Köchling, Mar–Sep 42 and Nov 42–Aug 43
Gen.Major Reymann, Sep–Nov 42
Gen.Lt. Thielmann, Aug 43–Mar 44 and Apr–Dec 44
Gen.Major Richard Schmidt, Dec 44–May 45

255th Infantry Division

Mar 39 Formed in Löbau, Saxony by redesignation of 255th *Landwehr* Division

Sep 39 Transferred to Czechoslovakia for training

Dec 39–Mar 41 Training and offensive opns in the Netherlands, Belgium, France; occupation and coastal defense opns in France

Mar 41 Transferred to Silesia

Apr 41 Movement to Poland; preparation for invasion of USSR

Jun 41 Offensive opns vic. Wlodawa, Poland and Kobrin, Soviet-occupied Poland; Pruzhany, Slonim, Baranovichi, Bobruisk, USSR

Jul 41 Defensive and security opns vic.Rogachev, Zhlobin, Dnepr River

Aug 41 Offensive opns vic. Gadilovichi, Cherikov, Krichev, Mstislavl, Khislavichi, Smolensk,

Sep 41 Defensive opns vic. Yartsevo and Koprovshchina

Oct 41 Movement and security opns vic. Levino, Bely,

	Smolensk, Yartsevo, Dukhoshchina, Sychevka, Gzhatsk, Rzhev, Dorogobuzh		in the Netherlands, Belgium and France; coastal defense and occupation opns in France
Dec 41	Defensive and anti-partisan opns vic. Ruza, Volokolamsk, Mozhaisk	Mar 41	Transferred to Poland
Dec 41	Disengagement; defensive opns vic. Iznoski, Gzhatsk, Yukhnov, Temkino	Jun 41	Offensive and anti-partisan opns in USSR vic.Grodno, Mosty, Polotsk, Vitebsk, Vevel, Velikie Luki, Olenino, Staritsa, Rzhev, Zubtsov
Feb 42	Defensive and security opns, regrouping vic. Ugryumovskiye Vyselki, Valukhovo, Ivanovskoye, Berezki, Vorya and Ugra Rivers, Rocharovo	Dec 41	Disengagement and defensive opns vic. Burukovo, Zybino, Sychevka, Karmanovo
Feb 43	Transferred to southern sector; defensive and offensive opns vic. Konotop, Boromlya, Psel, Vorskia and Pena Rivers, Trostyanets, Rakitnoye	Apr 42	Defensive and assault opns vic. Rzhev
		Jan 42	Defensive opns vic. Volga-Locha River sector, Rzhev, Vladimirskoye, Nikitinka
Jul 43	Disengagement vic. Graivoron	Feb 42	Disengagement, defensive, and anti-partisan opns vic. Yesennaya, Pochinok, Krivets, Dukhovshchina, Rudnya, Liozno, Babinovichi, Vysochany, Dobromysl, Lyubavichi, Vitebsk
Aug 43	Breakout from encirclement; defensive opns; division merged with 332d ID vic. Golovchina, Akhtyrka, Lebedin, Oposhnya, Gadyach, Psel River		
Sep–Oct 43	Disbandment of the division vic. Gadyach; combat units assigned to 57th and 112th IDs; reorganization of division staff and remnants	Fall 43	Heavy losses vic. Smolensk
		Jun 44	Encirclement of division elements vic. Smolyany and Tolochin
		Jul 44	Breakout, movement and assembly vic. Borisov, Molodechno, USSR and Vilna, Kaunas, Virbalis, Lithuania

Commanders

Gen.Lt. Wetzel, 1939–Jan 42

Gen.Lt. Poppe, Jan 42–Oct 43

256th Infantry Division (later VGD)

Mar 39	Formed in Chemnitz, Saxony by redesignating the 256th *Landwehr* Division	Jul 44	Remnants of division incorporated into Corps Detachment H vic. Borisov
Sep 39	Transferred to Czechoslovakia	Sep 44	Redesignation of 568th VGD as 256th VGD in Königsbrück, Saxony
Nov 39–Mar 41	Transferred to Germamy; training; offensive opns	Sep 44	Transferred to the Western Front; defensive opns in the Netherlands, France and Germany

Jan 45	Offensive opns in Low Vosges (Operation *NORDWIND*)
Mar 45	Disbanded in Bruchsal, Germany

Commanders

Gen.Major Folttmann, 1939–Jan 40
Gen.Major Gerhard Kauffmann, Jan 40–Jan 42
Oberst Friedrich Weber, Jan–Feb 42
Gen.Lt. Dannhauser, Feb 42–Nov 43
Gen.Lt. Wüstenhagen, Nov 43–Jul 44
Gen.Major Gerhard Franz, Sep 44– Apr 45
Gen. Major Warnecke, Apr–May 45

257th Infantry Division (later VGD)

Mar 39	Formed in Potsdam by redesignation of 257th *Landwehr* Division
Aug 39– Jul 40	Transferred to Poland for occupation opns, then to Germany for training; offensive opns in Saar and against the Maginot Line; occupation opns in France
Jul 40	Transferred to Cracow area, Poland for occupation duty and training
Jun 41	Offensive opns in USSR vic. Radymno, San River, Mikolayev, Rogatin, Chortkov, Gorodok, Sobolevka, Dunayevtsy, Luchinets, Olshanka, Kirovograd
Aug 41	Offensive opns vic. Psel River, Kremenchug, Dnepr River, Gradizhsk, Zhovnin, Cherkassy, Mirgorod, Krasnograd, Dmitriyevka, Poltava
Nov 41	Defensive opns vic. Donets River, Barvenkovo, Bolgenkoye, Golaya Bolina, Slavyansk, Belbasovka
Jul 42– Apr 43	Transferred to France for occupation duty and coastal defense

Apr 43	Transferred to USSR; offensive and defensive opns vic. Lozovaia, Barvenkovo, Slavyansk, Bereka River, Petrovskaya, Petropolye, Semenovka, Zavodskoy, Donets River, Velikaya, Kamyshevakha
Sep 43	Disengagement vic. Mechebilovo, Lozovaia, Grigoryevka
Nov 43	Defensive opns vic. Chumaki, Tomahovka, Gurovka, Selenaya, Lozovatka
Mar 44	Disengagement and defensive opns vic. Dolinskaya, Yelanets, Tiraspol, Bendery
Mar– Aug 44	Heavy losses in withdrawal from Dnepr River bend and in encirclement vic. Kishinev
Aug 44	Withdrawal into Romania
Aug 44	Encirclement and destruction of combat units in Romania vic. Yassy, Husi and Prut River
Oct 44	Disbandment of division at Dubrecen, Hungary
Oct– Dec 44	Reorganization as 257th VGD at Wandern training area; transferred to Western Front; defensive opns in France and Germany
Jan 45	Offensive opns in Low Vosges Mountains (Operation *NORDWIND*)
Mar 45	Withdrawal and defensive opns vic. Bergzabern and Landau; capitulation

Commanders

Gen.Lt. Viebahn, 1939–Mar 41
Gen.Lt. Sachs, Mar 41–May 42
Gen.Lt. Püchler, May 42–Nov 43
Gen.Lt. *Freiherr* von Mauchenheim-von Bechtolsheim, Nov 43–Jul 44
Gen.Major Blümke, Jul–Aug 44
Gen.Major Seidel, Oct 44–May 45

258th Infantry Division

Mar 39	Formed at Stettin, Pomerania by redesignation of 258th *Landwehr* Division
Sep 39–Jul 40	Movement to Poland then Germany in preparation for invasion of France; offensive opns and occupation duty in France
Jul 40	Transferred to Poland for occupation opns and preparation for invasion of Russia
Jun 41	Offensive opns in USSR vic. Malkinia, Bielsk, Grodek, Nowa Wola, Podozierany, Volkovysk, Slonim, Berezino, Bykhov, Barkalabovo
Jul 41	Offensive and defensive opns vic. Sozh River, Cherikov, Krichev, Rodnya, Dolgaya, Mileykovo, Snopot River sector, Yukhnov
Oct 41	Offensive and anti-partisan opns vic. Medyn, Nara River, Smolinskove, Tashirovo, Borovsk, Naro-Fominsk
Dec 41	Defensive opns and disengagement vic. Desna, Nara, Shanva, Istya and Protva River positions, Medyn
Jan 42	Defensive and anti-partisan opns vic. Vorya and Rudnya River sector, Prechistove, Kholm, Trasya, Masalovka, Ryabiki, Tenloye
Jan 43	Defensive opns vic. Prechistoye, Shakhovo, Vorya River
Feb 43	Defensive opns vic. Yukhnov, Orel, Trosna
Jun 43	Offensive and defensive opns vic. Trosna, Malakhova, Sloboda
Aug 43	Reorganization as *Kampfgruppe* 258; defensive opns vic. Dmitrovsk-Orlovski, Briansk, Kirov
Aug 43	Redeployed to southern sector; defensive opns and disengagement vic. Stalino, Volonovakha, Pavlovka, Kremenchug, Zaporozhe, Voroshilovo, Nikopol
Jan 44	Reorganized as 258th ID at Novo Petrovka
Feb 44	Defensive opns vic. Malaya Lepetikha, Pokrovskoye
Feb 44	Routed during withdrawal vic. Apostolovo, Veselinovo, Novaya Odessa, Berezovka
Apr 44	Reorganization as *Kampfgruppe* 258; encirclement; breakout vic. Blagoyevo, Katarzhino, Betsilovo
Jun 44	Reorganized as 258th ID; defensive opns vic. Kishinev, Orgeyev, Hashkautsy
Aug 44	Disengagement through Poganeshty, Kalarash into Husi, Romania
Aug 44	Encirclement; attempted breakout vic. Husi, Barlad, Vutcani
Sep 44	Surrendered or destroyed vic. Barlad and Vutcani, Romania

Commanders

Gen.Lt. Wollmann, 1939–Aug 40
Gen.Lt. Waldemar Henrici, Aug 40–Oct 41
Gen.Major Pflaum, Oct 41–Jan 42
Gen.Lt. Höcker, Jan 42–Oct 43
Gen.Lt. Bleyer, Oct 43–Sep 44
Oberst Hielscher, Sep 44

260th Infantry Division

Mar 39	Formed in Stuttgart; moved to Sudetenland for formation and training

Aug 39– Jun 41	Redeployed to Germany; offensive, occupation, and coastal defense opns in France
Jun 41	Redeployed to Biala Podlaska, Poland, offensive opns in USSR vic. Brest, Ivatsevichi, Baranovichi, Parichi
Sep 41	Offensive and defensive opns vic. Gorval, Rechitsa, Gomel, Antonovka, Vibli, Yatsevo, Chernigov, Starodub, Kirov, Petrovskiy, Kremenki, Tarusa, Medyn, Yukhnov
May 42	Defensive and assault opns vic. Rossa and Ugra Rivers
Mar– Jul 43	Withdrawal, defensive and assault opns vic. Dubrovnya to Lazinki, Sluzna, Suglitsa
Aug 43	Disengagement vic. Spas-Demensk, Lyubun, Kokhany, Saveyevo, Lobkovichi, Krichev
Oct 43	Defensive opns vic. Dolgiy Mokh, Chausy, Volkovichi, Bykhov, Vyun, Chigrinka
Apr– Jun 44	Defensive and disengagement opns vic. Chigrinka, Bykhov, Mogilev, Lenino, Bobryn, Orsha, Kozlovichi, Kopys, Kopysitsa, Dnepr River; encirclement vic. Komsenichi and Belynichi
Jun 44	Breakout, retrograde, and defensive opns vic. Drut River, Glubokoye, Shepelevichi, Somry, Gibaylovichi, Mikheyevichi, Berezina River
Jul 44	Surrendered or destroyed along Berezina River, south of Minsk

Aug 44	Assembly of remnants; incorporation into Corps Detachment G

Commanders

Gen.Lt. Hans Schmidt, 1939–Dec 41

Gen.Lt. Hahm, Jan–Aug 42 and Oct 42–Nov 43

Gen.Lt. Dietrich von Choltitz, Aug–Oct 42

Gen.Major Schlüter, Nov 43–Apr 44

Gen.Major Klammt, Apr–Jul 44

262d Infantry Division

Mar 39	Formed in Vienna by redesignation of 262d *Landwehr* Division
Aug 39– Sep 40	Transferred to Germany; offensive opns and occupation duty in France
Sep 40	Transferred to Lower Silesia for training
Apr 41	Assembled in Poland
Jun 41	Offensive opns vic. Irava-Russkaya, Krystynopol, Radekhov, Kremenets, Zubhar, Zhitomir, Radomyshl
Aug 41	Offensive opns vic. Malin, Reznya, Makalevichi, Mircha, Dymer, Glebovka, Manuilsk, Dnepr and Desna Rivers, Chemer, Yagotin
Sep 41	Offensive and security opn vic. Nazhin, Borzna, Novgorod-Severski, Seredina-Buda, Dobrun, Terebushka, Komarichi, Dmitrovsk-Orlovski, Kromy
Dec 41	Defensive opns vic. Grunin Vorgol, Lamskoye, Novosil, Zalegoshch, Kazar-Gorka, Voroshilovo, Bogodukhovo
Apr 42	Defensive and offensive opns vic. Novosil, east of Orel, Neruch and Zusha Rivers sector

Jul 43	Disengagement and defensive opns south of Orel, Karachev, Briansk, Ugra River sector, Yelnya	Jul 42	Defensive and security opns vic. Glagolnya, Pochenok, Zhupanovo
Aug 43	Heavy losses in disengagement vic. Verbilovo, Vaskovo, Khislavichi, Chausy	Jan 43	Offensive and defensive opns vic. Krasnyy Poselok, Nevel, Kobylino
		May 43	Withdrawal; offensive opns vic. Krasnyy Poselok, Opukhliki, Lake Ushcho, Vaulino
Sep 43	Defensive opns vic. Slavgorod, Gomel, Sozh and Dnepr Rivers, Zhlobin, Bykhov, Mogilev	Aug 43	Offensive and defensive opns vic. Opukhliki, Nevel, Krasnyy Poselok, Bogdanovo
Oct 43	Consolidation of units as Division Group 262 vic. Chausy	Jan 44	Defensive opns and withdrawal vic. Novosokolniki, Pustoshka, Yukhovichi, Nishcha, Idritsa
Oct 43	Incorporation into 56th ID and then into Corps Detachment D vic. Gomel	Jul 44	Disengagement through and defensive opns in Latvia vic. Madona, Vestiena, Liezere
Nov 43	Division disbanded		

Commanders

Gen.Lt. Theissen, 1939–Sep 42
Gen.Lt. Karst, Sep 42–Jul 43
Gen.Lt. Wössner, Jul–Oct 43

263d Infantry Division

Mar 39	Formed in Mainz by redesignation of 263d *Landwehr* division
Aug 39– Apr 41	Training in Germany; offensive opns in Belgium and France; coastal defense; occupation opns in France
Apr 41	Training in Poland
Jun– Sep 41	Offensive opns in Poland vic. Zareby, Bielsk and the USSR Volkovysk, Slonim, Gorodishche, Minsk, Borisov, Gorki, Khislavichi, Orsha, Pochinok, Peresna, Dorogobuzh, Yukhov, Yermolino, Kamenka, Komarovo
Dec 41	Withdrawal vic. Dubrovka and Makoyaroslavets
Jan 42	Withdrawal, defensive opns vic. Adamovskoye, Myatlevo,Yukhov, Yelnya, Roslavl, Spas-Demensk

Sep 44	Withdrawal to defensive positions vic. Tekava, south of Riga
Oct 44	Disengagement vic. Pienava, Grivaisi, Mazdrogas
Nov 44– May 45	Retrograde opns to Latvian coast; defensive opns vic. Kurland; capitulated to Soviet forces

Commanders

Gen.Lt. Karl, 1939–Nov 40
Gen.Lt. Häckel, Nov 40–Apr 42
Gen.Lt. Traut, Apr 42–Apr 43
Gen.Lt. Werner Richter, Apr 43– May 44
Gen.Major Sieckenius, May–Jun 44; Apr 45
Gen.Lt. Hemmann, Jun 44–Apr 45
Gen.Lt. Risse, Apr–May 45

264th Infantry Division

Jul 43	Formed in Brussels, Belgium
Aug 43	Coastal defense in France
Oct 43– Jan 45	Transferred to Bihac, Yugoslavia; anti-partisan opns, coastal defense

	vic. Zadar, Sibenik, Split Drnis, Knin, Gracac, Srb, Nebljusi	Aug 43	Movement, defensive opns vic. Ugra River sector, Velnya
Jan 45	Transferred to Germany and disbanded	Aug 43	Disengagement and defensive opns vic. Kokhany, Shui, Koski, Shumyachi, Krichev, Cherikov, Slavgorod

Commanders

Gen.Lt. Nake, Jun 43–Apr 44
Gen.Lt. Lüdecke, Apr–May 44
Gen.Lt. Gareis, May–Sep 44
Gen.Major Paul Hermann, Sep–Oct 44
Gen.Major Windisch, Oct–Dec 44

267th Infantry Division

Aug 39	Formed in Hannover
Sep 39–May 41	Training; offensive opns in Belgium and France; occupation of France and coastal defense
May 41	Transferred to Poland; training
Jun–Dec 41	Offensive opns in Poland vic. Slawatycze and USSR vic. Kobrin, Slutsk, Parichi, Zhlobin, Checkersk, Krichev, Roslavl, Bogdanovo, Kostyri, Yermolino, Desna, Shuitsa, Snopot River, Gredyakino, Viazma, Prudnya, Mozhaisk, Tuchkovo, Moskva River, Zvenigorod, Kubinka
Dec 41	Disengagement; defensive opns vic. Mozhaisk, Dorokhovo, Ruza, Vereya, Yurlovo, Protva River
Jan 42	Withdrawal; defensive opns vic. Peredel, Terekhovo, Sorokino, Shanya and Istra Rivers, Nochalniki
Apr 42	Offensive and defensive opns vic. Viazma, Gzhatsk, Tenkino, Fomino, Fomino Pervoye, Milyatino
Mar 43	Withdrawal; defensive opns vic. Chiplyayevo, Belskaya, Kusemki, Ipot, Spas-Demensk

Nov 43	Disengagement and defensive opns vic. Usokhi, Nikonovichi, Bykhov
Jun 44	Disengagement vic. Bykhov, Glukhi, Gorodets, Pogost, Berezino
Jul 44	Delay opns vic. Berezino, Rudnya, Minsk
Jul 44	Heavy losses in breakout from Rudnya
Aug 44	Remnants of the division reach German lines vic. Vilna, Lithuania and the Augow Canal, Poland; division disbanded

Commanders

Gen.Lt. Fessmann, 1939–Jun 41
Gen.Lt. von Wachter, Jun–Nov 41 and Jan 42
Gen.Lt. Martinek, Nov 41–Jan 42
Gen.Lt. Friedrich Stephan, Jan–Feb 42
Gen.Major Karl Fischer, Feb–Mar 42
Gen.Lt. Stephan, Mar 42–Jun 43
Gen.Lt. Drescher, Jun 43–Aug 44

268th Infantry Division

Mar 39	Formed in Munich by redesignation of the 268th *Landwehr* Division
Aug 39–Aug 40	Training in Germany; offensive operations in France; occupation and security opns in France
Aug 40	Training in Poland
Jun 41	Offensive opns in USSR vic. Bialystok, Volkovysk, Tolochin, Beresina River, Borisov, Ursna, Vysokoye, yelino, Rossasna, Gusino
Jul 41	Defensive opns vic. Syrokorenye, Peresna,

	Baltutino, Leonidovo, Yelnya, Pochinok
Sep 41	Transferred south of Baltutino for rehabilitation
Sep 41	Offensive opns vic. Koski, Novyye Golovachi, Stryana and Desna Rivers, Bogdanovo, Sewlevo, Viazma
Oct 41	Offensive opns vic. Uspenskoye to Vyrubovo, southwest of Gzhatsk, Medyn
Nov 41	Defensive opns (Protva River, Vysokinichi, Vyazovnya, Makarovo, Voronino
Dec 41	Withdrawal, disengagement battles (Nedelnoye, Bashmakovka)
Jan 42	Reconnaissance, movement and defense (Ugra-Shanya River sector, Polotnyanyy)
Jan 42	Disengagement battles (Ugra River, Slyadnevo, Rozhdestvo, Dorokhi, Bogdanovo, Nefedovo)
Jan 42	Movement; offensive opns (Ladysnkino, Kunovka, Kolodkino, Ugra River)
Feb 42–Aug 43	Defensive and assault opns in Ugra River sector
Aug 43	Heavy losses in disengagement movements to Snopot River positions
Aug 43	Redesignated *Kampfgruppe* 268
Sep 43	Reorganized as 268th ID in Snopot River sector
Sep 43	Disengagement movements; defensive opns (Saveyevo, Yermolino, Shumyachi, Krichev, Cherikov, Pronya-Sozh River sector, Slavgorod)
Oct 43	Disengagement and defensive opns (Kliny, Rudnya, Gayshin)

Oct 43	Incorporation of remnants of division into 36th ID at Rudnya
Nov 43	Division staff used to activate 362d ID in Rimini, Italy
Nov 43	Division disbanded

Commanders

Gen.Lt. Straube, 1939–Jan 42
Gen.Lt. Greiner, Jan 42–Nov 43

269th Infantry Division

Mar 39	Formed at Delmenhorst, Oldenburg by redesignation of 269th *Landwehr* Division
Aug 39–Jul 40	Training in Germany; offensive opns in Belgium; reserve opns in France
Jul 40–Mar 41	Transferred to Denmark via Germany; coastal defense, occupation opns in Denmark
Mar 41	Training in Poland
Jun 41–Apr 42	Offensive opns in Lithuania vic. Taurage, Nemaksciai, Slapaberze; Latvia vic. Livani; and the USSR vic. Pytalovo, Lyutyye, Bolota, Porkhov, Nooselye, Zapolye, Strugi Krasnye, Serebryanka, Dobrovka, Smerdi, Korpovo, Luga, Mshinskaya, Siverskaye, Mikolskoye, Bolshoye Zamostye, Gatchina, Tosno, Shapki, Pogostye, Vinyagolovo, Mga, Maluksa, Berezovka, Starostino, Smerdynya, Lipki
Apr 42	Defensive opns vic. Tigoda River, Shala, Konduya, Tur
May 42	Defensive opns vic. Tur
Sep 42	Defensive opns vic. Kirishi
Oct 42	Transferred to Norway for coastal defense and occupation opns

Oct 44	Transferred to Colmar, France; defensive opns
Dec 44	Transferred to Poland
Jan–Apr 45	Defensive opns in Poland vic. Cracow, Trzebinia; Silesia vic. Breslau, Jauer, Jordansmühl, Gleinitz

Commanders

Gen.Lt. Hell, 1939–Aug 40
Gen.Lt. *Edler Herr und Freiherr* von Plotho, Aug 40–Apr 41
Gen.Lt. von Leyser, Apr 41–Sep 42
Gen.Major Badinski, Sep 42–Nov 43
Gen.Lt. Hans Wagner, Nov 43–May 45

271st Infantry Division (later VGD)

Dec 43	Formation in Franconia; included staff and other elements of former 137th ID
Jan 44	Completed formation in the Netherlands
Mar 44–Summer 1944	Transferred to France for coastal defense, then to Normandy, where it was destroyed;
Sep 44	Reconstituted as a VGD
Nov 44	Transferred to Czechoslovakia
Dec 44–May 45	Defensive opns in Hungary and Czechoslovakia

Commanders

Gen.Lt. Danhauser, Dec 43–Aug 44
Gen.Major Bieber, Sep 44–May 45

275th Infantry Division

Dec 43	Formation of division, included elements of 223d ID
Jan 43–Nov 44	Training in France; defensive opns in Normandy; heavy losses at Falaise; defensive opns and destruction vic. Aachen
Jan 45	Reformed vic. Flensburg
Jan–May 45	Defensive opns vic. Guben, Cotttbus, Lübben,

	Brandenburg; destroyed in the southern suburbs of Berlin

Commander

Gen.Lt. Hans Schmidt, Dec 43–Apr 45

281st Security Division (later Infantry Division)

Mar 41	Activated as Security Division 281 at Gross Born training area in Pomerania
May 41	Transferred to Poland for training
Jun 41	Transferred to Gordauen, East Prussia in preparation for invasion of Russia
Jun 41	Mopping up actions and security in Lithuania (Vilkaviskis, Kaunas, Jonava, Ukwerge, Utena, Zarasai)
Jul 41	Mopping up actions and security in Latvia (Daugavpils, Rezekne, Karsava)
Jul 41–Apr 42	Anti-partisan and security opns in Russia (Ostrov, Pskov, Novorznev, Podberezye, Knolw, Poddorye, Staraya Russa, Novgorod, Uno, Strugi Krasnye, Porknov, Sebeza, Idritsa, Kholm, Pustosnka, Novosokolniki, Loknya)
Apr 42	Redesignated 281st Security Division at Ostrov
Jan 43–Jan 44	Anti-partisan and security opns (Ostrov, Pusnkinskiye Gory, Opochka, Zarechye, Idritsa, Pustosnka, Pskov, Slavkovicai, Novorznev)
Jul 44	Movement, defensive, anti-partisan and security opns in Russia (Osveya) and Latvia (Kaunata, Rezekne, Luuza, Kiebini, Preili, Viesite)
Aug 44	Withdrawal; reorganization as *Kampfgruppe*

Security Division 281;
defensive and security
opns vic. Bauska

Sep 44 Withdrawal; defensive
opns vic. Jelgava, Klive,
Dzueksto

Nov 44 Reorganization as 281st
ID; defensive opns vic.
Dzueksto

Feb 45 Assembly vic. Saka and
Liepaja, Latvia; transfer to
Gotenhafen, Poland

Mar 45 Assembly, defensive opns
vic. Stargard, Pomerania

Mar 45 Movement, defensive opns
vic. Stettin, Pomerania

Apr 45 Probably surrendered or
destroyed vic. Stoeven

Commanders

Gen.Lt. Friedrich Bayer, Mar–Oct 41
Gen.Lt. Scherer, Oct 41–Jun 42
Gen.Lt. von Stockhausen, Jun–Dec 42
  and May 43–Jul 44
Gen.Major Scultetus, Dec 42–May 43
Gen.Lt. Ortner, Jul 44 and Sep 44–
  May 45
Gen.Major Windisch, Jul–Sep 44

282d Infantry Division (originally Division Gümbel and Division Karl)

Sep 39 Activated in Wehrkreis XII
as Division Number 182

Dec 39– Movement in Germany;
Apr 43 transfer to France (forma
tion of Division Gümbel),
coastal defense opns in
France (redesignation as
Division Karl, then as
182d ID); formation of
282d ID from 182d ID
and Division Schacky;
transfer to Poltava,
Russia

Apr 43 Movement, defensive opns
(Kharkov, Ternovaya,
Volchansk, Bolsnaya
Danilovka, Udy River)

Aug 43 Disengagement to Merefa;
defensive opns

Sep 43 Disengagement move-
ments (Novaya Vodolaga,
Krestishche, Krutaya
Balka, Kobelyanki, Vorskla
River, Keleberda,
Kremenchug); Crossed
Dnepr River at Keleberda
and Kremenchug; defen-
sive of bridgehead at
Kryukov and Pavlysn

Oct 43 Movement, defensive opns
vic. Uspenka

Nov 43 Disengagement move-
ments (Kolentayev,
Chigrin, Zhamenka,
Kirovograd)

Jan 44 Defensive opns vic. Bolshaya Viska

Feb 44 Movement, defensive opns
(Martynosa, Novo-Mir-
gorod, Lysaya Gora,
Pervomaisk)

Mar 44 Disengagement move-
ments, defensive opns
(Antonovka, Malovata,
Masnkautsy, Dniester
River, Kishinev)

Aug 44 Disengagement move-
ments (Ivancha, Kotoy-
skoye, Sarata-Galbena)

Aug 44 Partly encircled; movement toward Leovo

Aug 44 Encircled east of Husi,
Romania; probably surren-
dered or destroyed

Oct 44 Disbanded in Germany

Commanders

Gen.Major von Basse, May 40–May 41
Gen.Lt. Franz Karl, May 41–Apr 43
Gen.Major Wilhelm Kohler, Apr–
  Aug 43
Gen.Major Frenking, Aug 43–Aug 44

285th Security Division

Mar 41 Activated at Gross Born
training area, Pomerania

Mar–Jul 41 Training in East Prussia

Jul– Offensive opns in
Aug 41 Lithuania vic. Kybartai,

	Vilkaviskis, Kaunas, Utena, Zarasai; Latvia vic. Griva, Rezekne, Karsava; the USSR vic. Pytalovo, Ostrov, Pskov, Strugi Krasnye, Plyussa, Zaoplye, Lyady, Seredka, Pulna, Luga
Aug–Dec 41	Defensive opns vic. Luga River sector, Voloskovo, Vyritsa, Gatchina
Dec 41–Apr 42	Anti-partisan and security opns vic. Novoselye, Novgorod, Chudovo, Lyuban, Volknov River, Pskov, Strugi Krasnye, Luga, Volosnovo, Tolwachevo, Gatchina
Apr 42	Formation of *Kampfgruppe* Security Division 285; defensive and offensive opns vic. Yam-Tesovo, Rogavka, Volkhov River Pocket
Jul 42	Anti-partisan and security opns vic. Plyussa, Lyady, Glov, Luga, Tolwachevo, Krasnyye Gory, Novoselye, Voloshovo, Pushkin
Jul 42	Movement to Luga and disbandment of *Kampfgruppe* Security Division 285
Jan 43	Anti-partisan and security opns vic. Strugi Krasnye, Plyussa, Lyady, Luga, Novoselye, Volosnovo, Staraya Russa, Pskov, Gorodots, Ostrov, Krasnyye Gory
Feb 44	Movement; anti-partisan and security opns in Estonia vic. Reval and Salmistu
Feb 44	Redesignation as 285th Security Division
Apr–Aug 44	Movement, assignment as Coastal Defense West 285th Security Division;

	coastal defense and anti-partisan opns
Jun –Aug 44	Movement and defensive opns in Latvia vic. Skaume, Kaunata, Preili, Viesite, Bauska
Aug 44	Defensive opns vic. Pagari, Estonia
Sep 44	Coastal defense opns in the West; disbanded

Commanders

Gen.Lt. *Edler Herr und Freiherr* von Plotho, Apr 41–Sep 42

Gen.Lt. Auffenberg-Komarow, Sep 42–Aug 44

Gen.Lt. Ortner, Aug–Sep 44

286th Security (later Infantry) Division

Mar 41	Activated in Silesia as 286th Security Division
Mar 41	Transfer to Poland
Jun 41	Deployment in the USSR vic. Brest, Kobrin, Baranovichi
Jul 41	Anti-partisan and security opns vic. Volkovysk, Luninets, Liua, Minsk, Borisov, Krupki, Tolochin, Lepel, Orsna, Smolensk
Jul 41	Formation of Engagement Group for security of rail lines vic. Borisov, Ursna
Aug 41	Disbandment of Engagement Group
Sep 41–Dec 42	Anti-partisan and security opns vic. Vitebsk, Borisov, Osipovichi, Mogilev, Orsna, Liozno, Mstislavl, Pochinok, Krasnoye, Byknov, Slavgorod, Roslavl, Kirov, Spas-Demensk, Cherven, Cherikov, Orsha, Tolochin, Krupki
Dec 42	Formation of Division Richert; anti-partisan opns vic. Vitebsk, Nevel, Polotsk
Jan 43	Disbandment of Division Richert vic. Ursha

Jan–Jul 43   Anti-partisan and security opns vic. Borisov, Cherven, Byknov, Cherikov, Slavgorod, Krichev, Roslavl, Gorki, Bogusnevsk, Causy, Lepel, Belynichi, Shkiov, Orsna, Senno, Krupi, Toilochin, Krugloye

Dec 43   Redesignation as 286th Security Division

Jun 44   Defensive opns and attachment to Group Altrock vic. Krupki, Borisov

Jul 44   Transferred to Germany for rehabilitation

Aug 44   Defensive opns vic. Augow, Szczuczyn, Poland

Dec 44   Attached to 541st VGD; defensive opns vic. Przecnody

Dec 44   Formation of staff of 286th ID in Kuckemeese, East Prussia

Jan 45   Completion of formation of 286th ID, defensive opns vic. Karkeln, East Prussia

Jan 45   Defensive opns vic. Laibau

Feb–
May 45   Defensive opns in East Prussia; surrender

Commanders

Gen.Lt. Kurt Müller, Mar 41–Jun 42
Gen.Lt. Johann-Georg Richert, Jun 42–Nov 43
Gen.Lt. Oschmann, Nov 43–Aug 44
Gen.Lt. Friedrich-Georg Eberhardt, Aug–Dec 44
Gen.Lt. Wilhelm Thomas, Dec 44–Jan 45
Oberst Willi Schmidt, Jan 45
Gen.Major von Roden, Jan–May 45

290th Infantry Division

Feb 40   Activated at Münster

May 40–
Feb 41   Training in Germany and Belgium; offensive opns in Belgium and France; security, coastal defense and occupation opns in France

Feb 41   Transferred to Poland

Jun 41   Offensive opns in Lithuania vic. Paalsys, Taurage, Ariogala, Jonava, Ukmerge, Utens, Zarasai

Jul–
Aug 41   Offensive opns in Latvia vic. Daugavpils, Kraslava, and the USSR vic. Sebezh, Idritsa, Opochka, Pustoshka, Norozhev, Gorodovik, Slavitino

Aug 41–
Feb 43   Offensive and defensive opns vic. Ivanovskoye, Velikoye Selo, Pola and Lovat River sectors, Strelitsy, Nalyuchi, Demiansk Pocket

Feb 43   Anti-partisan and security opns, rehabilitation vic. Staraya Russa, Dedovichi, Gorodtsy, Dunyani, Novorzhev, Loknya

May 43   Transferred to Tusno area south of Leningrad; defensive opns vic. Shapki, ostye, Lyuban, Gaytolovo, Siniavino, Novo-Lisino

Oct 43   Transferred to Luga and Pskov

Nov 43   Offensive and defensive opns vic. Lovets, Ushcha River, Lakes Ushcho and Dolysskoye

Jan 44   Withdrawal east of Pustoshka and west of Novosokolniki

Jan–
Jul 44   Defensive opns vic. Marino, Loknyz, Soltsy, Albrekntovo, Yuknovichi, Borkovichi, Drissa, Druya

Jul 44   Reorganization as *Kampfgruppe* 290th ID; defensive opns in Latvia vic. Rubeniski, Subata, Jaunjelgava

Aug 44   Reorganization as 290th ID vic. Bauska

Sep 44   Reorganization as *Kampf-gruppe* 290th ID vic. Jelgava

Oct 44   Reorganization as 290th ID; defensive opns vic. Tukums, Dobele, Saldus, Priekule, Durbe (Kurland Pocket)

Mar 45   Reorganization as 290th ID at Skrunda

Apr–May 45   Defensive opns in Kurland Pocket; capitulation to Soviet forces

Commanders

Gen.Lt. Dennerlein, Feb–Jun 40
Gen.Lt. *Freiherr* von Wrede, Jun–Sep 40 and Oct 40–May 42
Gen.Lt. Auleb, Sep–Oct 40
Gen.Lt. Heinrichs, May 42–Feb 44
Gen.Major Henke, Feb–Jun 44 and Apr 45
Gen.Major Goltzsch, Jun–Aug 44
Gen.Major Baurmeister, Aug 44–Apr 45
Gen.Lt. Hemmann, Apr–May 45

291st Infantry Division

Feb 40   Activated in Königsberg, East Prussia

May–Jul 40   Movement in Germany, Holland, Belgium; offensive opns in France

Jul 40   Transferred to East Prussia in preparation for invasion of Russia

Jun–Dec 41   Offensive opns in Lithuania vic. Kretinga, Palanga, Skuodas; Latvia vic. Priekule, Liepaja, Saldus, Ventspils, Sabile, Taisi, Tukums; Estonia vic. Parnu, Haapsalu, Vandra, Turi, Palde, Kunda, Aseri, Sonda, Toila, Narva; and the USSR vic. Fedorovka, Kotly, Koporye, Krasnoye Selo, Petrodvorets,

Vyritsa, Lyuban, Lisino-Korpus, Mga

Dec 41–Nov 42   Offensive and defensive opns vic. Memino, Babino, Kirishi, Tur, Nechanye, Fedosino, Kamenka

Nov 42   Defensive and offensive opns vic. Chudovo, Babino, Nevel, Velikie Luki, Isocha, Ptakhino, Opukhliki, Novosokolniki, Kobylino, Pechishche, Dolshino, Borshchanka, Gushchino

Sep 43   Transfer to vic. Smolensk and Kiev

Sep 43   Defensive opns vic. Kiev and Lubyanka

Oct 43   Disengagement and defensive opns vic. Karpilovka, Malin, Volchkov, Korosten

Jan 44   Disengagement and defensive opns vic. Gorodnitsa, Berezdov, Shepetovka

Feb 44   Withdrawal, defensive opns vic. Borshchev, Buchach, Barysh, Chortkov

May 44   Withdrawal from Gorokhov; defensive opns south of Lutsk

Jul 44   Transferred to Germany for rehabilitation

Aug 44   Transferred to Poland; defensive opns vic. Sandomir, Opatow, Slupia Nowa

Jan 45   Withdrawal, defensive opns vic. Konskie, Skarzysko Kamienna

Jan 45   Encirclement vic. Belchatow, south of Lodz; division destroyed

Commanders

Gen.Lt. Herzog, Feb 40–Jun 42
Gen.Lt. Goeritz, Jun 42–Jan 44
Gen.Major Oskar Eckholt, Jan–Jul 44
Gen.Major Finger, Jul 44–Jan 45

292d Infantry Division

Feb 40	Activated at Stettin, Pomerania
May–Jul 40	Movement in Germany in preparation for invasion of low countries; offensive opns in Belgium and France; occupation opns in France
Jul 40	Transferred to Poland in preparation for invasion of Russia
Jun 41	Assembled along Bug River
Jun–Aug 41	Offensive opns in Poland vic. Bielsk, Podlaski, Bialowieza and the USSR vic. Slonim, Baranovichi, Gorodishehe, Berezino, Tolochin, Gorki, Khislavichi, Roslavl
Aug 41	Defensive and offensive opns, rehabilitation vic. Yelnya, Verbilovo, Bor, Vorovka
Oct 41	Offensive and defensive opns vic. Fedotkovo, Medyn, Borovsk, Naro-Fominsk
Dec 41	Offensive, withdrawal, and defensive opns vic. Troitskoye, Burtsevo, Naro-Fominsk
Jan 42	Disengagement vic. Vereya, Borovsk, Shanya River, Guseva, Pavlishchevo, Volyntsy, Protva River
Feb 42	Defensive opns vic. Chelishchevo, Dubna, Orlovo
Aug 42	Offensive and defense, opns vic. Ilovo, Mikheyevo, Upolozy
Feb 43	Defense and participation in Operation *BÜFFEL* vic. Upolozy, Isakovo, Besovo, Blokhino, Kudinovo, Sukhanova
Mar 43	Rehabilitation vic. Amsharovo and Roslavl
Apr 43	Defensive and anti-partisan opns vic. Briansk, Orel, Stish, Savsk, Trubchevsk, Suzenka
Jul 43	Offensive opns (Operation *ZITADELLE*) vic. Novyy Khutor, Ozerki, Sokolniki, Veselyy Berezhok, Ponyri; Disengagement opns vic. Ochka River sector, Pokhvalnoye, Shakovo, Shakhovtsy
Aug 43	Defensive and retrograde opns vic. Dobrik, Navlya, Klinskoye, Katiyakova, Starodub, Novozybkov
Oct 43	Defensive opns vic. Sozh River, Gomel
Nov 43	Movement, defensive opns vic. Malodusha, Valikiy Bor; Disengagement and defensive opns vic. Pervoye Maya, Barbarov, Rechitsa, Kalinkovichi, Bronnoye, Zhlobin, Rogachev, Bykhov
Jan 44	Withdrawal, defensive opns vic. Sukovichi, Klinsk, Kopatkevichi, Chelyushchevichi, Ptich River, Petrikov
Jun 44	Disengagement vic. Kopatkevichi, Rudnya, Subovka, Oressa River, Lyuban, Luninets, Pinsk, Bereza, Zabinka, Kobrin
Jul 44	Withdrawal through Poland; defensive opns vic. Kleszczele, Nielnik, Czyzewo, Ostrow, Gasewo
Jan 45	Reorganized as *Kampfgruppe* 292; defensive opns vic. Baranowo, Kadzidlo, Myszyniec, Rozogi
Jan 45	Withdrawal into East Prussia; defensive opns vic. Hensguth, Rothfliess, Heilsberg, Landsberg, Lichtenfeld

Feb 45	Defensive opns vic. Eisenberg, Heiligenbeil
Apr 45	Destroyed in East Prussia

Commanders

Gen.Lt. Dehmel, Feb 40–Sep 41
Gen.Lt. Seeger, Sep 41–Aug 42
Gen.Lt. Badinski, Aug–Sep 42
Gen.Lt. von Kluge, Sep 42–Oct 43
Gen.Lt. John, Oct 43–Jun 44
Gen.Major Gittner, Jul–Sep 44
Gen.Major Reichert, Sep 44–Apr 45

293d Infantry Division

Feb 40	Activated at Frankfurt/Oder
May 40–May 41	Training in Germany; offensive opns in Belgium and France; occupation and coastal defense opns in France
May 41	Transferred to Poland
Jun–Oct 41	Offensive opns in USSR vic. Kaments-Litovskiy, Brest, Kamianka, Pripet Marshes, Luninets, Pinsk, David-Gorodok, Petrikov, Ptich River, Denemka, Lesets, Donavovichi, Grodnya, Mezhin, Ipa River, Tsidov, Dnepr River, Desna River, Kovchin, Kiev, Priluki, Piryatin, Gorodishche, Zolotonosha, Lubny, Bakhmach, Glukhov, Seredina-Buda, Briansk, Sevsk
Oct 41	Defensive and offensive opns vic. Suzemka, Negino, Aleshkovichi, Usezha River, Trostnaya, Nerussa and Oka Rivers, Orel, Sobakino, Novosil
Nov 41	Offensive opns vic. Kulyashi, Yefremov, Alekseycvka, Semenek and Lyubovsha Rivers, Poganets, Volynskoye, Chemodanove
Dec 41–Sep 42	Defensive opns vic. Pankovo, Novomikhaylovskoye, Chulkovo, Zhelyabug, Glubki-Gorodilevo, Susha River sector, Ulyanovo
Jul 43	Heavy losses in Operation ZITADELLE vic. Kursk, Ulyanovo, Karachev, Orel
Aug 43	Disengagement opns vic. Poltava, Kharkov
Sep 43	Retreat vic. Dnepr River, Kremenchug
Oct 43	Retreat, heavy losses in Dnepr River bend; incorporation of elements of the division into 161st ID; formation of Corps Detachment A; Assembly, movement of staff and remnants to Novo-Arkhangelsk
Nov 43	Disbanded in Radom, Poland

Commanders

Gen.Major Russwurm, Feb–Jul 40
Gen.Lt. von Obernitz, Jun 40–Feb 42
Gen.Lt. Werner Forst, Feb 42–Jan 43
Gen.Lt. Arndt, Jan–Nov 43

294th Infantry Division

Feb 40	Activated in Leipzig
May 40–Mar 41	Training in Germany; offensive opns in Belgium and France; occupation duty in France
Mar 41	Transferred to Caracal, Romania
Jun 41	Transferred to Germany via Belgrade, Yugoslavia
Jul 41	Transferred to Poland, then to Zhitomir, Russia
Aug 41	Defensive opns vic. Radomyshl and Tripolye
Sep 41–Mar 42	Offensive opns vic. Dnepr River, Rzhishchev, Kiev, Pereyaslav-Khmelnitski, Mirgorod, Lubny, Kuzemin, Vorskla River, Akhtyrka, Bogodukhov,

Liptsy, Ternovaya, Stary Saltov, Donets River, Rubezhnoye

Mar 42   Withdrawal, defensive opns vic. Nepokrytoye, Peremoga, Ternovaya, Russikiye Tishki

Jun 42   Offensive opns vic. Prikolotnoye, Khatneye, Urazovo, Pervoye Mandrovo, Polatovka

Jul 42   Offensive and defensive opns vic. Don River, Novaya Kalitva, Nikolayevka, Semeyka

Sep–
Dec 42   Defensive and offensive opns vic. Saprino, Sergeyevka, Rossosh, Podgornoye, Bokovskaya, Krasnokutskaya, Chir River sector

Dec 42   Heavy losses in withdrawal and defensive opns vic. Verkhne-Svechnikov, Malakhov, Chapura, Morozovsk, , Kovylkin, Krasnodonetskaya, Bystraya River, Ust-Bystryy, Vinogradnyy

Feb 43   Withdrawal and defensive opns vic. Kuybyshevo, Dmitriyevka, Mius River sector

Jun 43   Defensive and offensive opns vic. Kuybyshevo, Dmitriyevka

Aug 43   Redesignated as *Kampfgruppe* 294

Sep 43   Disengagement vic. Lavino, Makeyevka, Dolya, Bolshaya Novoselka, Zaporozhe

Nov 43   Reorganized as full division; defensive opns, withdrawal vic. Kankrinovka, Verkhne Tarasovka, Krivol Rog, Lozovatka

Feb 44   Defensive opns, withdrawal vic. Krasnogrigo-

ryevka, Nikopol, Arkhangelskoye, Veselinovo

Mar 44   Redesignated as *Kampfgruppe* 294; withdrawal with heavy losses vic. Kashperovka, Novaya Odessa, Berezovka, lower Dnepr River bend

Apr 44   Defensive opns, withdrawal vic. Dnepr River, Bulboka, Chimisheny, Kishinev

Jun 44   Reorganized as full division; defensive opns vic. Delakau, Grigoriopol

Aug 44   Encircled and destroyed west of lower Dnepr River

Commanders

Gen.Lt. Gabcke, Feb 40–Mar 43

Gen.Lt. Johannes Block, Mar 42–
    Aug 43

Gen.Major Frenking, Aug–Dec 43

Gen.Major von Eichstädt, Dec 43–
    Aug 44

295th Infantry Division

Feb 40   Activation in Magdeburg

May 40–
Apr 41   Training in Germany; offensive opns in Belgium and France; occupation and coastal defense opns in France

Apr 41   Transferred to Poland

Jun 41   Offensive opns vic. Zlochow, Poland, and in the USSR vic. Rava-Russkaya, Ternopol, Seret and Zbruch Rivers

Jul 41   Offensive opns vic. Klininy, Karpovtsy, Bug River, Sieniava, Lipovets, Granov, Velikaya Sevastyanovka

Aug 41   Offensive opns vic. Verkhnyachka, Semiduby, Belaya Tserkov, Boguslav, Shpola, Onufriyevka, Deriyevka

Sep 41	Offensive opns vic. Kolesniki, Maltsy, Kobelyaki, Sukhinovka, Andreyevka, Pavlovka, Konstantinograd, Tishenkovka, Krasnograd
Oct 41	Petrovka, Krasnopavlovka, Akimovka, Bliznetsy, Barvenkovo
Nov 41–Sep 42	Defensive opns vic. Slavyansk, Mikiforovka, Donets River sector
Sep 42–Feb 43	Offensive opns; destroyed at Stalingrad
Mar 43	Reconstituted vic. Wernigerode, Saxony
May 43–May 45	Transferred to Norway; Occupation opns

Commanders

Gen.Major Geitner, Feb 40–Dec 41
Gen.Lt. Karl Gümbel, Dec 41–May 42
Gen.Lt. Wuthmann, May–Nov 42
Gen.Major Dr. Korfes, Nov 42–Jan 43
Gen.Lt. Dinter, Apr 43–Jul 44
Gen.Lt. Karl-Ludwig Rhein, Jul 44–Jan 45
Gen.Lt. Sigfrid Macholz, Jan–May 45

296th Infantry Division

Feb 40	Activation in Nuremberg
May 40–Jun 41	Offensive opns in Belgium and France; occupation opns in France
Jun–Jul 41	Offensive and defensive opns in Poland vic. Wierzbica, Jarczow, Werchrata; Ukraine vic. Rava Russkaya
Jul 41	Offensive opns in Ukraine vic.Velikiye Mosty, Brody, Busk, Zhitomir, Vatskov, Radomyshl, Malin, Maydanovka, Kodra
Aug 41	Defensive opns in Ukraine vic. Irpen River
Sep 41	Offensive opns vic. Kiev, Borzna, Nezhin
Oct 41	Offensive and defensive opns vic. Trubchevsk, Ostraya Luka, Altukhovo, Briansk
Nov 41	Offensive opns vic. Chern, Krapivna, Yasnaya Polyana
Dec 41	Withdrawal and defensive opns vic. Plava and Upa Rivers west of Tula, Belev
Apr 42	Defensive opns vic. Oka River, Bliznenskiye Dvory, Pozdnyakovo
Mar 43	Defensive opns vic. Zikeyevo, Oslinka, Akimovka, Zhizdra
Aug 43	Withdrawal and defensive opns in Ukraine, Belorussia vic. Sukreml, Mglin, Surazh, Sozh River sector
Dec 43	Defensive opns in Belorussia vic. Khalch, Luchin, Zhlobin
Feb 44	Defensive opns vic. Rogachev
Jun 44	Encirclement and breakout vic. Bobruisk
Aug 44	Disbanded in Munich

Commanders

Gen.Lt. Stemmermann, Feb 40–Jan 42
Gen.Lt. *Edler* von Wehregg, Jan–Apr 42
Gen.Major Ulrich Schütze, Apr–May 42
Gen.Lt. Faulenbach, May 42–Jan 43
Gen.Lt. Kullmer, Jan 43–Jun 44

297th Infantry Division

Jan 40	Activated in Vienna
Jan–May 40	Trained in Germany
May–Jun 40	Offensive opns in Belgium, France
Jun–Jul 40	Occupation of France
Jul 40–Jun 41	Training in Poland
Jun–Jul 41	Offensive opns vic. Krystynopol, Dobrotvor, Busk, Zolochev, Ternopol, Cherny Ostrov, Ulanov,

Priluka, Turbov, Tsybulev,
Zhabotin, Lomovatoye

Aug 41   Offensive and defensive
opns vic. Cherkassy,
Dnepr River sector

Sep 41   Offensive opns vic. Omel-
nik, Dolina, Kulikovo,
Voynovka

Oct 41   Offensive opns vic. Grya-
kova, Krestische, Novo-
Pokorovka, Chugavyev

Dec 41   Defensive opns along the
Donets River and vic.
Malinovka and
Korobochkino

Jun–   Offensive opns vic. Pech-
Oct 42   enegi, Martovaya, Topoli,
Belolutskaya, Markovka,
Koshary, Pervomayskoye,
Ust Gryaznovskiy,
Surovikino, Potemkin-
skaya, Abganerovo,
Tinguta, Beketovka

Nov 42   Encircled vic. Stalingrad

Jan 43   Destroyed

Mar–   Reconstituted vic.
Jun 43   Blaye-et-St. Luce, France

Jun 43   Deployed to Yugoslavia

Jul–Sep 43 Antipartisan opns vic.
Pristina, Novi Pasar

Sep 43– Anti-partisan opns and
Jan 44   training in Albania

Jan–   Coastal defense opns in
Apr 44   Albania; anti-partisan
opns in Yugoslavia

Sep–   Anti-partisan opns in
Nov 44   Yugoslavia

Apr 45   Surrendered in
Yugoslavia

Commanders
Gen.Lt. Pfeffer, Apr 40–Jan 43
Gen.Major von Drebber, Jan 43
Gen.Major Deutsch, Apr 43–Feb 44
Gen.Lt. Gullmann, Feb–Oct 44
Gen.Lt. Baier, Oct 44–Apr 45

298th Infantry Division

Feb 40   Activation in Breslau,
Silesia

May–   Offensive opns in
Jun 40   Belgium, France

Jul 40   Training in Poland and
Silesia

Jun–   Offensive opns vic.
Sep 41   Vladimir-Volynski, Lutsk
Torchin, Kostopol, Dniepr
River area, Novograd-
Volynski, Sushki, Federov-
ka, Tupaltsi, Chepovichi,
Vladovka, Makarov,
Dymer, Gornostaypol,
Oster, Kosolets, Borispol,
Yablonevo

Oct 41   Offensive opns vic. Orel
River, Verknyaya Orelka,
Aleksevskoye, Asayevka;
defensive opns vic. Donets
River sector

Nov 41   Defensive opns vic. Petro-
vskya, Mechebilovo,
Mikhaylovka, Lozovaya

Dec 41– Defensive opns vic.
May 42   Yuryevka and Ivanovka

Jun–   Offensive opns across the
Sep 42   Don River and toward the
Caucasus Mtns vic.
Slavyansk, Taganrog,
Novoshaktinsk; defensive
opns vic. Millerovo,
Kransnokutskaya

Dec 42   Defensive opns vic.
Boguchar, Chertkovo,
Malinovka

Mar 43   Disbanded vic. Kremenchug; remnants combined-
with those of the 385th
and 387th IDs into the new
387th ID in France

Commanders
Gen.Major Grässner, Feb 40–Jan 42
Gen.Lt. Szelinski, Jan–Dec 42
Gen.Major Michaelis, Dec 42–
Mar 43

299th Infantry Division

Feb 40   Activation at Kassel

May–   Offensive opns in Belgium
Jun 40   France

Sep 40– Jun 41	Training in Poland
Jun 41–	Offensive opns vic. Vladimir-Volynski, Lutsk, Dubno, Zbytyn Rovno
Jul 41	Offensive opns vic. Novo Aleksandrovka, Dvorishche, Sluch River, Novograd-Volynski
Jul 41	Defensive opns vic. Staraya Guta, Barashi, Mikhaylovka, Sergeyevka
Aug 41	Offensive opns vic. Yasnogorodka, Glevakha, Irpen River; Kiev
Sep 41	Security opns and rehabilitation vic. Romny, Ilek, Gotnya, Butovo, Sumy
Dec 41	Offensive and defensive opns vic. Droskovo, Sidorovka, Lazarevka, Rozhdestvenskoye, Muratovka, Topki, Ponyri
Jun 42	Offensive opns vic. Malo-Arkhangelsk, Gubkino, Morozovo, Ust' Leski, Pokrovka, Mokhovoye
Nov 42	Defensive opns vic. Glazunovka, Malo-Arkhangelsk, Markino, Fedorovka
Jan 43	Defensive opns. vic. Droskovo, Vnukovo, Korsun, Lipovets
Feb– Mar 43	Defensive opns vic. Mikhaylovka, Gorodishche, Bogodukhovo, Mokhovoye, Nikolayevka, Novopetrovka, Masalovka
Jul 43	Retrograde and defensive opns vic. Lavrovo, Gorodishche, Gorodets, Klintsy
Oct– Nov 43	Defensive and retrograde opns vic, Gomel and Zhlobin
Jan 44	Defensive opns vic. Bogushevsk, Moshkany
Jun 44– Jul 44	Destruction of division vic. Gumny and Chernyavka

Sep 44	Reconstitution in Germany; return to front in Poland vic. Ostrolenka
Jan 45	Defensive opns in East Prussia vic. Willenberg, Hohenstein, Wormditt
Mar 45	Reorganized as *Kampfgruppe* 299 in Danzig

Commanders

Gen.Lt. Moser, Feb 40–Nov 42
Gen.Lt. Viktor Koch, Nov 42
Gen.Lt. Bergen, Nov 42–May 43
Gen.Lt. *Graf* von Oriola, May 43– Jan 44 and Mar–Jun 44
Gen.Lt. Reichelt, Jan–Mar 44
Gen.Lt. Junck, Jun–Jul 44
Gen.Major Göbel, Sep 44–Feb 45
Oberst Überschär, Feb–Mar 45

302d Infantry Division

Nov 40	Activation at Friedland, Mecklenburg
Jan 41– Nov 42	Occupation and coastal defense opns in France
Aug 42	Defensive opns vic. Dieppe
Jan 43	Defensive opns vic. Rovenki, Shakhty, Kamensk-Shakhtinskiy
Feb 43	Defensive opns vic. Pleshakovo, Voroshilov, Millerovo, Krasnodon, Makedonovka, Kosakovka, Ivanovka, Krasny Kut, Bokovo-Platovo
Jul 43	Defensive opns vic. Krasny Luch, Krasnya Polyana
Sep 43	Defensive opns vic. Dnepr River, Nikopol, Arkhangelskoye, Ingulets River
Sep 44	Encircled west of the Dniper River
Oct 44	Remnants incorporated into 15th and 76th IDs

Commanders

Gen.Lt. Haase, Nov 40–Nov 42
Gen.Major Elfeldt, Nov 42–Nov 43
Gen.Lt. Rüdiger, Nov 43–Jan 44

Gen.Lt. von Bogen, Jan–Jul 44
Oberst Willi Fischer, Jul–Aug 44

304th Infantry Division

Nov 40	Activated at Leipzig
Mar 41– Nov 42	Training in Belgium and France; coastal defense in the Pas de Calais
Dec 42	Defensive opns vic. Gorlovka, Mezhevaya, Donets River, Kamensk-Shakhtinski
Dec 42	Offensive opns vic. Millerovo, Staraya Stanitsa
Jan 43	Defensive opns vic. Pavlovka, Dyachkino, Dubovoy, Semeykino, Kokino
Mar 43	Defensive opns vic. Petrovenki, Nikitovka, Illiriya
May 43	Offensive and defensive opns vic. Bashtevich, Bugayevka
Jul 43	Defensive opns vic. Adrianopol, Shterovka, Malaya Nikolayevka
Aug 43	Retrograde and defensive opns vic. Sabovka, Debaltsevo, Andreyevka, Makeyevka, Stalino, Priluki
Sep 43	Defensive and retrograde opns vic. Dnepr River, Chervonoarmeyskoye, Zaporzhe, Novo Augustinovka
Nov 43	Defensive and retrograde opns vic. Lukashev, Grigoryevka, Sofiyevka
Jan 44	Defensive opns vic. Krivoi Rog
Feb 44	Retrograde opns vic. Gornostayevka, Snigirevka
Mar 44	Defensive and retrograde opns vic. Kalinovka, Nikolayev-Ternovka, Sadovoye, Odessa
Apr– Jul 44	Retrograde opns vic. Olanesti, Romania, Dniester River, Tiraspol; transfer to Baranov bridgehead
Aug 44	Defensive opns in Poland vic. Stopnica, Szczucin, Zabno
Jan– Feb 45	Defensive and retrograde opns across Poland, into Silesia vic. Gleiwitz and Katowice
Mar– May 45	Defensive opns in eastern Germany and northern Czechoslovakia

Commanders

Gen.Lt. Krampf, Nov 40–Nov 42
Gen.Lt. Sieler, Nov 42–Apr 45
Gen.Major Robert Bader, Apr–May 45

305th Infantry Division

Dec 40	Activated in Ravensburg
Dec 40– Mar 42	Training and security opns in France
May 42	Offensive and defensive opns vic. Rovno, Poltava, Kovyagi, Lyubotin, Mikhaylovskoye
Jun 42	Offensive opns vic. Krasnaya Polyana, Yablonovo, Volchansk, Chernyanka, Tikhaya Sosna River, Olkhovatka
Jul 42	Defensive opns vic. Krinitsa and Boguchar Rivers; Don River sector
Jul 42	Offensive opns vic. approaches to Stalingrad (Raspopinskaya, Orekhovski)
Dec 42– Feb 43	Encirclement and capitulation vic. Stalingrad
Mar 43	Reconstituted in France vic. Le Mans
Aug 43– Apr 45	Opns in Italy

Commanders

Gen.Lt. Pflugradt, Dec 40–Apr 42
Gen.Major Oppenländer, Apr–Nov 42
Gen.Lt. Steinmetz, Nov 42–Jan 43
Gen.Lt. Hauck, Mar 43–Dec 44
Oberst Trompeter, Dec 44
Gen.Major von Schellwitz, Dec 44–Apr 45

306th Infantry Division

Nov 40	Activation in Münster
Nov 40–Nov 42	Occupation, security, and coastal defense opns in Belgium and France
Dec 42	Defensive opns vic. Morozovsk and Taganrog
Jan 43	Defensive opns vic. Krylov, Ust-Bystryanskaya, Krasnodonetskaya, Donets River
Feb 43	Defensive and retrograde opns vic. Belaya Kalitva, Trifonov, Nikolskoye, Rovenki, Antratsit, Krasny Luch, Dmitriyevka, Novo-Pavlovka, Mius River
Jul 43	Defensive opns vic. Snezhnoye, Pervomaisk, Mius River sector
Aug 43	Retrograde opns vic. Chistyakovo, Makeyevka, Stalino, Krasnogorovka, Marinka, Bolshaya Novoselka
Sep 43	Defensive opns vic. Zaporozhe
Oct 43	Retrograde and defensive opns vic. Akimovka, Novo-Nikolayevka
Dec 43	Retrograde and defensive opns vic. Iverskoye, Tomakovka, Sadovod
Feb 44	Withdrawal vic. Novo Vorontsovka, Nikolayev, Konstantinovka, Ryasnopol
Mar 44	Retrograde opns vic. Ryasnopol, Odessa, Belgorod-Dnestrovski, Dnepr Bend
Apr 44	Defensive opns in Moldavia vic. Kaushany
Aug 44	Retrograde and encirclement of remnants vic. Leovo and Buzau, Romania
Oct 44	Disbanded in Germany

Commanders

Gen.Lt. von Sommerfeld, Nov 40–Nov 42
Gen.Lt. Pfeiffer, Nov 42–Feb 43
Gen.Major Lieb, Feb–Mar 43
Gen.Lt. Karl-Erik Köhler, Mar 43–Jan 44 and Jan–Aug 44
Gen.Major Bär, Jan 44
Gen.Lt. Hundt, Aug–Oct 44

320th Infantry Division (later VGD)

Nov 40	Activation at Hamburg; training
Apr 41	Training in Belgium and France
Dec 42	Defensive opns vic. Kharkov, Belokurakino
Jan 43	Retrograde and defensive opns vic. Tarasovka, Svatovo, Kislovka
Feb 43	Retrograde and defensive opns vic. Oskol River (Izyum), Balakleya, Andreyevka, Zmiyev
Mar 43	Offensive and defensive opns vic. Krasnograd-Borki, Malaya, Lichovaka, Lyubotin, Zolochev, Botkino
Jul 43	Offensive opns vic. Kursk (Operation ZITADELLE)
Aug 43	Defensive opns vic. Belgorod and Kharkov
Sep 43	Retrograde opns vic. Novaya Vodolaga, Pavlovka, Kremenchug
Oct 43	Defensive opns vic. Dnepr River, Andrusovka, Tyasmin River
Dec 43	Defensive opns vic. Dnepr River, Novomirgorod
Mar 44	Retrograde opns vic. Novomirgorod, Cherkassy, Ivanovka
Apr 44	Defensive and retrograde opns vic. Dubossary, Kishinev, Lower Dnister River, Grigoriopol

Aug 44	Retrograde opns in Moldavia vic. Cainari and Gura-Galbena; encircled vic. Husi
Oct 44	Breakout vic. Barlad, Romania
Oct 44	Reorganization as VGD in Pomerania
Nov–Dec 44	Training in Poland
Jan 45	Defensive opns vic. Jordanow and Sywec, Poland
Mar 45	Defensive opns vic. Dolny Kubin, Liptovsky, Rajec, Slovakia
Apr 45	Destroyed in Slovakia

Commanders

Gen.Lt. Maderholz, Dec 40–Dec 42
Gen.Lt. Postel, Dec 42–May 43 and Aug 43–Jul 44
Gen.Lt. Röpke, May–Aug 43
Gen.Major Otto Schell, Jul–Sep 44
Oberst Rolf Scherenberg, Dec 44–Feb 45
Gen.Major von Kiliani, Feb–May 45

321st Infantry Division

Dec 40	Activated in Braunschweig
Mar 41–Dec 42	Training and coastal defense opns in France
Dec 42	Defensive opns vic. Kirov, Dubrova, Bolva River sector
Aug 43	Retrograde and defensive opns vic. Betlysa, and Rognedino
Oct 43	Elements of division absorbed by 110th and 211th IDs; others transferred to France and incorporated into newly-formed 352d ID

Commanders

Gen.Lt. Löweneck, Dec 40–Nov 42
Gen.Lt. Wilhelm Thomas, Nov 42–Aug 43
Gen.Lt. Sievers, Aug–Sep 43
Gen.Major Heinrich Zwade, Sep–Nov 43

323d Infantry Division

Nov 40	Activation in Nuremberg
Apr 41–Mar 42	Training, occupation, and coastal defense opns in Belgium and France
May–Jun 42	Anti-partisan opns vic. Rovno, Zhitomir, Kiev
Jun 42	Anti-partisan and offensive opns vic. Dnepr River, Nezhin, Glukhov, Legov, Kursk, Shchigry, Kastornoye, Zemlyansk
Jul–Sep 42	Offensive and defensive opns vic. the Don River and Voronezh; Voronezh Bridgehead
Early 43	Retrograde opns vic. Khokhol, Nizhnedevitsk, Gorshechnoye
Summer 43	Defensive opns in Ukraine
Dec 43	Remnants incorporated into 88th ID

Commanders

Gen.Lt. Mühlmann, Nov 40–Feb 42
Gen.Major Bergen, Feb–Nov 42
Gen.Lt. Viktor Koch, Nov–Dec 42
Gen.Major Nebauer, Dec 42–Feb 43
Oberst Koschella, Feb–Sep 43

327th Infantry Division

Nov 40	Activated in Vienna
Nov 40–Apr 41	Assembly and training, Austria and Czechoslovakia
Feb 43	Defensive opns vic. Sudzha, Lgov, Derevenki, Tolpino
Mar 43	Defensive opns vic. Rylsk, Seym River
Sep 43	Retrograde and defensive opns vic. Samarka, Piryatin, Yasnogorodka, Katyuzhanka
Oct 43	Retrograde and defensive opns vic. Novaya Greblya
Nov 43	Disbanded; remnants absorbed by 208th, 340th, and 357th IDs

Commanders

Gen.Major Rupprecht, Nov 40–
  Oct 42

Gen.Major Theodor Fischer, Oct 42

Gen.Lt. Rudolf Friedrich, Oct 42–
  Aug 43

Oberst Walter Lange, Aug–Sep 43

328th Infantry Division

Dec 41	Activated at Kassel
Jan 42	Training and deployment in East Prussia, Poland, Lithuania and Belorussia
Feb 42	Anti-partisan opns vic. Borisov, Orsha, Vitebsk
Mar 42	Offensive and defensive opns vic. Sychevka, Lad-noye, Varvarino; Inf Regt 547 and 1st Bn/Art Regt 328 detached to 83d ID
Jun 42	Offensive opns vic. Tartarinka, Kolminka, Korbutovka
Jul 42	Anti-partsian opns vic. Sychevka; defensive opns vic. Rzhev, Zubtsov
Oct 42–May 43	Training and coastal defense opns in France
May 43	Defensive opns vic. Karlovka, Kaminka, Andreyevka, Balakleya
Sep 43	Offensive and defensive opns vic. Golubovka, Mag-dalinovka, Chaplinka, Dnepr River
Oct 43	Defensive opns vic. Prole-tarka, Petrovka; parts of division absorbed by 306th ID
Nov 43	Remnants transferred to France; incorporated into 353d ID

Commanders

Gen.Lt. Albert Fett, Dec 41 and
  Jan–Apr 42

Gen.Lt. Wilhelm Behrens, Dec 41

Gen.Lt. Joachim von Tresckow,
  Apr 42–Nov 43

329th Infantry Division

Dec 41	Activated in Aachen; training in Pomerania and East Prussia
Feb 42	Defensive opns vic. Lichino, Ivanovskoye
Mar 42	Offensive and defensive opns vic. Lichino, Mavreno, Velikoye Selo, Ozhedovo
May 42	Offensive and defensive opns vic. Kudrovo, Ramushevo, Glukhaya Gorushka
Jul 42	Defensive opns vic. Gorodok, Sutoki, Beglovo, Loznitsy, Strelitsy
Oct 42	Offensive opns vic. Strelitsy, Demiansk
Nov 42	Defensive and security opns vic. Mamayevshchi-na, Lukino, Krasnaya Gorka, Lobanovo
Feb 43	Retrograde opns vic. Demiansk
Feb 43	Defensive opns vic. Glukhaya, Gorushka, Karkachevo, Lyakhnova
Mar 43	Offensive and defensive opns vic. Sosnovka, Zimnik
May 43	Defensive opns vic. Bakochino, Solonitsko, Staraya Russa
Jul 43	Defensive opns vic. Staraya Russa
Nov 43	Defensive opns vic. Pustoshka
Mar 44	Defensive opns vic. Slobodka, Pustoshka
Jul 44	Defensive and retrograd opns vic. Sebech and in Latvia vic. Odziena
Aug 44	Defensive opns vic. Auce, Latvia
Nov 44	Defensive opns vic. Kur-sisi and Ezermali, Latvia
Apr 45	Defensive opns Striki and Saldus, Latvia; destroyed

Commanders

Gen.Major Castorf, Dec 41–Mar 42
Oberst Bruno Hippler, Mar 42
Gen.Lt. Johannes Mayer, Mar 42–
  Aug 43 and Sep 43–Jul 44
Gen.Lt. Winter, Aug–Sep 43
Gen.Major Werner Schulze, Jul–Oct 44;
  Jan 45
Gen.Lt. Konrad Menkel, Oct 44–
  Jan 45

330th Infantry Division

Dec 41	Activated in Munich
Jan 42	Training in Poland
Jan 42	Transfer to Rudnya, USSR
Feb–Mar 42	Offensive and defensive opns vic. Demidov
Apr 42	Rehabilitation and training vic. Seltso
May 42	Offensive opns vic. Shaury, Shvedy
May 42	Defensive opns vic. Demidov, Kolyski
Jun–Jul 42	Anti-partisan and security opns vic. Demidov
Jul 42	Offensive opns vic. Chepli
Aug–Sep 42	Security opns vic. Demidov
Sep 42	Defensive opns vic. Lugi, Pechenki
Nov 42	Security opns vic. Demidov
Apr 43	Defensive and security opns vic. Tokovnoye
Aug 43	Defensive opns vic. Gorki
Sep 43	Defensive opns vic. "Panther Position"
Oct 43	Retrograde, defensive, and security opns vic. Shklov
Nov 43	Remnants of division absorbed by 342d ID

Commanders

Gen.Lt. Karl Graf, Dec 41–Jan 42
Gen.Lt. *Graf* von Rothkirch und Trach,
  Jan 42–Jun 43
Oberst Georg Zwade, Jun–Sep 43
Gen.Lt. Falley, Sep–Oct 43
Gen.Major Sauerbrey, Oct–Nov 43

331st Infantry Division

Dec 41	Activated in Chemnitz
Jan 42	Defensive opns vic. Milyatino
May 42	Defensive opns vic. Usokhi, Dubrovo, Bolva River
Dec 42	Offensive and defensive opns vic. Velikiye Luki
Jan 43	Defensive opns vic. Ploskovo
Feb 43	Defensive opns vic. Kiselevichi, Korolevo
Jul 43	Offensive and defensive opns vic. Korolevo
Nov 43–Jan 44	Defensive opns vic. Rovni, Lipshane
Mar 44	Transfer to Germany, vic. Cologne
Apr–Jul 44	Training in France
Jul–Aug 44	Defensive and retrograde opns in France and Belgium
Sep 44	Coastal defense opns in the Netherlands
Oct 44–Apr 45	Disbanded as a division, but staff and some units used for coastal defense opns in the Netherlands and northwestern Germany

Commanders

Gen.Lt. Hengen, Dec 41
Gen.Lt. Dr. Beyer, Dec 41–Feb 43
Gen.Lt. Rhein, Feb 43–Jan 44 and
  Apr–Aug 44
Gen.Major Furbach, Jan–Apr 44
Gen.Major Steinmüller, Aug–Oct 44
Gen.Lt. Diestel, Oct 44–Apr 45

332d Infantry Division

Nov 40	Activation in Güstrow
Apr 41–Feb 43	Training and coastal defense opns in France
Feb 43	Defensive opns vic. Romny, Alenino, Psel River
Mar 43	Offensive and defensive opns vic. Oleshnaya,

	Tarasovka, Pochayevo, Krasny Kutok, Chulanovo
Late Mar–Apr 43	Defensive and security opns vic. Borisovka, Novo-Berezovka, Khotmyzhek
Jul 43	Offensive opns vic. Kursk (Operation ZITADELLE)
Aug 43	Withdrawal, defensive opns along Psel River
Sep 43	Elements incorporated into 57th, 112th, and 255th IDs

Commanders

Gen.Major Recke, Nov 40–Aug 41
Gen.Lt. Kessel, Aug 41–Dec 42
Gen.Major Walter Meltzer, Dec 42–Jan 43
Gen.Lt. Schäfer, Jan–Jun 43
Gen.Major Trowitz, Jun–Aug 43

333d Infantry Division

Nov 40	Activation in Perleberg
Mar 41–Jan 43	Training, coastal defense and security opns in France
Feb 43	Offensive and defensive opns vic. Donets River, Slavyansk, Izyum
Sep 43	Retrograde and defensive opns vic. Stepanovka, Aleksandropol, Bogdanov-ka, Pavlograd, Odinkovka, Dnepropetrovsk, Zaporozhe, Grigoryevka
Oct 43	Disbanded

Commanders

Gen.Lt. Pilz, Nov 40–Dec 42
Gen.Major Grassmann, Dec 42–Mar 43
Gen.Major Tschudi, Mar–Jul 43
Gen.Major Crisolli, Jul 43
Gen.Lt. Menny, Jul–Oct 43

335th Infantry Division

Nov 40	Activation in Stuttgart
May 41–Dec 42	Occupation and coastal defense opns in France
Aug 42	Offensive opns vic. the Russian bridgehead in the Don sector

Feb 43	Defensive opns vic. Kryk-skaya, Sentyanovka, Donets River
Sep 43	Defensive and retrograde opns vic. Popasnaya, Gorlovka, Yakovlevka
Sep 43	Defensive opns vic. Zaporozhe bridgehead
Oct 43	Retrograde and defensive opns vic. Belenkoye, Dnepr River
Nov 43	Defensive opns vic. Nikopol bridgehead
Feb 44	Defensive opns vic. Gavrilovka, Dnepr River
Mar 44	Defensive and retrograde opns vic. Petrovskoye
May 44	Defensive opns in Moldavia vic. Kryulyany, Dubossary
Aug 44	Encircled vic. Minzhir, Moldavia; destroyed

Commanders

Gen.Lt. Dennerlein, Nov 40–Oct 42
Gen.Lt. Casper, Oct 42–Sep 43
Gen.Lt. Rasp, Sep 43–Jun 44
Oberst Brechtel, Jun–Aug 44

336th Infantry Division

Dec 40	Activated in Minden
Feb 41–May 42	Training in Belgium and France
Jun 42	Offensive opns in Donets and Oskol River sectors
Jul 42	Defensive opns in the Don River sector and at Arkhangelskoye, Botkino, Podgonoye and others
Aug 42	Offensive opns vic. Soviet bridgehead in the Don sector
Nov–Dec 42	Defensive opns vic. Chir River sector south of Stalingrad; opns vic. Alekshin-Bogda Nov–Sizov Line
Jan–Feb 43	Retrograde and defensive opns east of the Donets and Mius Rivers

Aug 43	Retrograde opns vic. Fedorovka, Melitopol, Spasskoye and the Krynka River
Sep–Oct 43	Retrograde and defensive opns southward toward the Crimea
Nov–Dec 43	Regrouping, defense and counterattacks in Crimea area (Armyansk, Budanovka, at the Sivash Sea)
Jan–May 44	Defensive and retrograde opns in the Crimea
May 44	Division captured vic. Sevastopol

Comdanders

Gen.Lt. Stever, Dec 40–Mar 42
Gen.Lt. Lucht, Mar 42–Jul 43
Gen.Major Kunze, Jul–Dec 43
Gen.Major Hagemann, Dec 43–May 44

337th Infantry Division (later VGD)

Nov 40	Activation in Kempten im Allgäu, Bavaria
Jan 41–Jul 42	Training in Germany, then occupation and security opns in France
Oct 42	Transfer to Eastern Front vic. Smolensk, Russia
Nov 42	Offensive and defensive opns vic. Vazuza River sector, Viazma, and Kasnya areas
Mar 43	Retrograde and defensive opns vic. Dniepr River sector, Sosedovo, Novo-Dugino, and Tarbeyevo
Aug–Sep 43	Offensive opns vic. Dorogobuzh; disengagements at Lyady, Dudino, and Gusino; defense of the Panther position vic. Lipovka
Oct 43	Regrouping, training, and assault opns vic. Lenino, Gorki, and the Pronya River
Jan–Jun 44	Defensive opns vic. Panther position; withdrawal along the Dniepr
Jul 44	Division battered to remnants; movement to Kolpino, Poland; reorganization at Augów, Poland
Sep 44	Return of remnants and staff to Munich
Sep 44	337th VGD built around remnants at Gross Born training area, Pomerania; after brief training, deployed to Poland and conducted defensive opns vic. Karzcew
Jan 45	Retrograde opns vic. Chelmno, Poland and Stargard, Pomerania
Mar 45	Disbanded vic. Danzig

Commanders

Gen.Lt. Spang, Nov 40–May 41
Gen.Major Pflieger, May 41–Mar 42
Gen.Lt. Erich Marcks, Mar–Sep 42
Gen.Lt. Schünemann, Oct 42–Dec 43
Gen.Lt. Scheller, Dec 43–Jul 44
Gen.Lt. Kinzel, Sep 44–Mar 45

339th Infantry Division

Dec 40	Activated at Jena, Thuringia
Feb 40–Jun 41	Movement and training; occupation opns in France
Aug 41	Transfer to Kaunas, Lithuania
Aug 41	Deployed to Borisov, USSR
Sep 41	Security opns vic. Gomel Russia; anti-partisan opns vic. Bobruisk, Tolochin, Pochep, and Kletnya
Jan–Feb 42	Security and anti-partisan opns vic. Briansk, Berezovka, and Lyudinovo
Jun–Jul 42	Anti-partisan opns vic. Bolva and Vetma Rivers; also vic. Lyudinovo, Zhukovka, Seltso, and Glukhovka
Oct–Dec 42	Offensive, defensive, and anti-partisan opns along the Bolva River

Jan–early Sep 43	Anti-partisan opns vic. Lyudinovo to south of Kirov
mid-Sep 43	Withdrawal and defense opns through the Vetma River sector to vic. Roslavl
Nov 43	Disbanded

Commanders

Gen.Lt. Hewelke, Dec 40–Jan 42
Gen.Lt. Pflugradt, Jan–Dec 42
Gen.Major Ronicke, Dec 42–Oct 43
Gen.Major Lange, Oct–Nov 43

340th Infantry Division (later VGD)

Nov 40	Activated in Schleswig
May 41– May 42	Occupation and coastal defense opns in France
May 42	Transfer to Volkovysk, Russia; anti-partisan and defensive opns vic. Gomel and Dniepr River
Jul– Dec 42	Defensive opns vic. Donskaya, northwest of Voronezh, Spasskoye, and Semlyansk
Jan– Feb 43	Defensive and retrograde opns vic. Orekhovo; encircled south of Kastornoye; breakout and retrograde opns from Kursk to Rylsk
Mar– Aug 43	Defensive, retrograde, and anti-partisan opns vic. Rylsk, Akimovka, Konotop, Rudovka, and Amon Krupets
Sep– Dec 43	Retrograde opns from the Dniepr River to vic. Zhitomir; anti-partisan opns
Jan– Aug 44	Defensive opns southwest of Zhitomir; retrograde opns to Baramel, Lobchevka, Lutsk
Apr 44	Defensive opns vic. Stojanow, Poland
Jul 44	Encircled and destroyed vic. Lvov
Sep 44	Reorganized as VGD vic. Thorn, West Prussia
Oct 44	Defensive opns vic. Jülich

Dec 44	Offensive opns in the Ardennes
Feb– Mar 45	Defensive opns in the *Westwall*; retrograde opns to vic. Sinzig
Mar– Apr 45	Encircled and destroyed in the Ruhr pocket

Commanders

Gen.Lt. Friedrich-Wilhelm Neumann, Nov 40–Mar 42
Gen.Lt. Viktor Koch, Mar–Nov 42
Gen.Lt. Butze, Nov 42–Feb 43
Obstlt. Dr. Herbst, Feb 43
Gen.Major Prinner, Feb–Oct 43
Gen.Major Ehrig, Oct 43–Jun 44
Gen.Major Beutler, Jun–Jul 44
Gen.Major Tolsdorff, Sep 44–Apr 45

342d Infantry Division

Nov 40	Activated in Koblenz
May– Sep 41	Training and occupation opns in France
Sep 41	Transfer to Yugoslavia; anti-partisan opns
Feb 42	Transfer to Eastern Front from Serbia
Mar 42– Jan 43	Defensive and anti-partisan opns vic.Bykovo, Peski, and Gorodok
Mar– Aug 43	Retrograde and defensive opns vic. Lyapino, Ivanovka, Viazma, Spas-Demensk, Gudino, Gorodok, and Gogolevka
Sep 43	Retrograde and defensive opns vic. the Panther position
Oct 43– Jan 44	Defensive opns, vic. Gorki
Mar 44– May 45	Defensive and retrograde opns vic. Kovel; Vistula River, Poland; Opatov; Pilica; Glogau, Silesia; Naumburg; Forst; Cattbus, Brandenburg; Straupitz; and Lübben
May 45	Division surrendered to American forces vic. Tangermünde

Commanders

Gen.Major Wanger, Nov 40–Jul 41

Gen.Lt. Hinghofer, Jul–Nov 41

Gen.Major Paul Hoffmann, Nov 41– May 42; Jul–Aug 42

Gen.Major *Baron* (not *Freiherr*) Digeon von Monteton, May–Jul 42

Gen.Major Baier, Aug 42–Sep 43

Oberst Nickel, Sep 43–May 45

344th Infantry Division

Sep 42	Activated in Stuttgart
Sep 42– Jul 44	Training and coastal, defense opns in France
Jul 44	Defensive opns in Normandy; division largely destroyed
Aug– Sep 44	Defensive and retrograde opns through France and Belgium to the Netherlands
Oct 44	Division dissolved vic. Lintfort, Germany
Jan 45	Reconstituted and transferred to Tarnow, Poland
Jan– Mar 45	Retrograde and defensive opns vic. Brzeszcze, Poland; and Mechnitz, Oberglogau, and Neustadt, Silesia
Apr 45	Division destroyed vic. Ziegenhals, Silesia

Commanders

Gen.Lt. Schwalbe, Sep 42–Sep 44

Gen.Major Goltzsch, Sep–Oct 44

Gen.Major Kossmala, Oct 44–Feb 45

Gen.Major Rolf Scherenberg, Feb– Mar 45

Gen.Major Jollasse, Mar–May 45

349th Infantry Division (later VGD)

Nov 43	Activated in France
Nov 43– Mar 44	Training and coastal defense opns vic. Calais
Mar 44	Transfer to Eastern Front vic. Lvov
Apr 44– Aug 44	Defensive and retrograde opns vic. Brody and Ternopol, Galicia
Jul 44	Encircled vic. Brody and Sasov; breakout opns
Aug 44	Retrograde opns vic. Tukla
Aug 44	Disbanded
Sep 44	Reorganized as VGD
Sep 44– Apr 45	Defensive and retrograde opns along the Ebenrode-Schlossberg rail line in East Prussia; Prussian Eylau; Pillau; Heyse Peninsula
Apr 45	Division surrendered to Soviet Forces

Commanders

Gen.Lt. Lasch, Nov 43–Aug 44

Gen.Major Koetz, Sep 44–Apr 45

355th Infantry Division

Feb– May 43	Formation and training in France
May 43	Coastal defense and security opns vic. Feodosiya, Crimea
Aug 43	Defensive opns vic. Poltava-Kharkov
Aug 43	Retrograde and defensive opns Taranovka and Borki
Sep 43	Defensive and retrograde opns vic. Ryabukhino, Krasnograd, Glinsko, and Peski
Oct 43	Defensive opns in the Dniepr bend; division destroyed

Commander

Gen.Lt. Kraiss, May 43–Nov 43

356th Infantry Division

Early 43	Formed in France to provide company-sized unit replacements
Oct 43	Coastal defense opns vic. Ventimiglia and Savona, Italy; division Fusilier Battalion and 1st Battalion Grenadier Regiment 871 conducted defensive operations vic. Nettuno

May 44	Defensive and retrograde opns vic. Montefiascone, Montepulciano, and Castelnuova
Jun–Dec 44	Defensive and retrograde opns vic. San Marino, Meldola, Forli, Cesena, Montene, Lugo, Bagnacavallo
Jan–May 45	Deployed to Hungary; defensive opns vic. Stuhlweissenburg (Székesfehérvár), Hungary; offensive and defensive opns vic. Moha and Mor; retrograde opns in Hungary vic. Gönyü, Raab, Kapuvar, and Ödenburg; defensive and retrograde opns southwest and west of Wiener-Neustadt, Austria; retrograde opns in Austria vic. Fischau, Unterpiesting, and Grünbach
May 45	Surrendered to American forces

Commanders

Gen.Lt. Von Neindorff, May 43
Gen.Lt. Faulenbach, May 43–Oct 44
Oberst Kleinhenz, Oct 44–Feb 45
Oberst von Saldern, Feb–May 45

357th Infantry Division

Oct–Nov 43	Formed vic. Radom, Poland from remnants of 327th ID
Mar–Oct 44	Defensive and retrograde opns in Galicia vic. Zloczow, Trostyanetz, Sambor, and Sanok; defensive opns in Slovakia vic. Dukla and Kapisova
Nov 44–Apr 45	Defensive and retrograde opns northeast of Presov, Slovakia and vic. Buda pest, Hungary; retrograde opns in Hungary vic. Aszod and Gödöllö, the

	Gran bridgehead, Levice, Cifare, Nitra, Senica, and Kuty; in Czechoslovakia vic. Lundenburg (Breclav), Znaim, and Budweis
May 45	Surrender to Soviet forces with some able to escape west to surrender to US forces

Commanders

Gen.Lt. Wolfgang von Kluge, Dec 43–Apr 44
Gen.Major Eberding, Apr–May 44
Gen.Major Holm, May–Sep 44
Gen.Lt. Rintelen, Sep 44–May 45

359th Infantry Division

Nov 43	Activated in Radom, Poland from remnants of the 293d Infantry Division
Mar 44	Defensive opns vic. Ternopol, Galicia
Apr–May 44	Gren Regt 949 and 3d Bn, Art. Regt. 359 defend and are destroyed in Ternopol; remainder of division; conducts defense and delay along the Stripa River and vic. Slobodka, Galicia
Jun–Jul 44	Defensive and retrograde opns vic. Strypa River; along the Bereshany-Ternopol Road and vic. Koslow and Slobodka
Jul 44	Retrograde opns vic. Czarna and Radomysl, Galicia
Sep 44–Apr 45	Defensive and retrograde opns vic. the Vistula River, Poland; Slomniki, Kalvaria, Bielitz, and Skotschau, Silesia
Apr 45	Surrender to Soviet forces in the Owl Mountains, Silesia

Commander

Gen.Lt. Karl Arndt, Nov 43–Apr 45

361st Infantry Division (later VGD)

Sep 43	Activation in Denmark
Feb–Mar 44	Training and security opns in Denmark
Mar–May 44	Defensive and security opns vic. Brody and Ternopol, Galicia
Jul 44	Defensive opns in Galicia vic. Zloczow, Olesko, and Sasov
Jul 44	Retrograde, defensive opns, encirclement, and breakout opns in Galicia vic. Koltow, Toporow, and Bialy Kamien, Galicia
Aug 44	Division disbanded vic. Mukachevo, Galicia
Sep 44	Reorganization as VGD vic. Cologne
Sep 44	Training and defensive opns in the Netherlands
Oct–Nov 44	Defensive opns in the Netherlands, the Saar Valley
Dec 44	Retrograde and defensive opns in the Low Vosges
Jan 44	Offensive opns in the Low Vosges (Operation NORDWIND)
Feb 45	Dissolved, some remnants absorbed by the 559th VGD

Commanders

Gen.Lt. *Freiherr* von Schleinitz, Nov 43–May 44
Gen.Major Gerhard Lindemann, May–Jul 44
Gen.Major Philippi, Sep 44–Feb 45

367th Infantry Division

Oct–Nov 43	Unit formed in Bavaria
Dec 43–Feb 44	Anti-partisan opns in Croatia
Feb 44–Jan 45	Defensive opns on southern sector of Eastern Front
Jan–Mar 45	Defensive opns and surrender vic. Königsberg, East Prussia

Commanders

Gen.Major Georg Zwade, Nov 43–May 44
Gen.Major Adolf Fischer, May–Aug 44
Gen.Lt. Hermann Hähnle, Aug 44–Mar 45

370th Infantry Division

Feb 42	Activation in northern France
Feb–Jun 42	Training in France
Jul 42	Offensive opns vic. Kaganovicha, Sverdlovsk, Proletarskaya
Oct 42	Defensive opns in the Tarek River bend, Nalchik, and Kardzhin (Northern Caucasus Mountains)
Jan–May 43	Retrograde and defensive opns vic. Kuban River
Sep 43	Retrograde opns from Kuban River bridgehead to Crimea
Oct 43–Jan 44	Defensive and retrograde opns vic. Akimovka and Melitopol, Ukraine; and Mogolev and Antonovka, Belorussia; and Kherson, Ukraine
Mar 44	Retrograde opns vic. Odessa
Apr 44	Defensive opns vic. Cornesti, Romania
Aug 44	Encircled along the Prut River, vic. Gorban, Romania; breakout opns
Oct 44	Division disbanded in Hungary

Commanders

Gen.Lt. Dr. Klepp, Apr–Sep 42
Gen.Lt. Fritz Becker, Sep–Dec 42; Jan–Aug 43; and Sep 43–Jun 44
Gen.Lt. von Bogen, Dec 42–Jan 43
Gen.Lt. Hermann Böhme, Aug–Sep 43
Gen.Lt. Graf von Hülsen, Jun–Sep 44

371st Infantry Division

Feb–Mar 42	Formation vic. Cologne

Mar–May 42	Training in Belgium
Jul 42	Offensive opns vic. Voroshilovgrad, the Donets and Don River zones
Aug 42	Offensive opns vic. the Kalmuk Steppe
Sep 42	Offensive and defensive opns vic. the Volga River bend south of Stalingrad
Jan 43	Destroyed south of Stalingrad
Apr–May 43	Reconstituted in France
Jun–Aug 43	Training and coastal defense opns in France
Oct 43	Coastal defense and security opns vic. Viareggio, Italy
Dec 43	Anti-partisan opns in the Balkans
Jan 44	Defensive opns vic. Zhitomir and Vinnitsa
Jan 44–Jan 45	Offensive and defensive opns vic. Kamentz Podolsk, Ukraine (encircled); breakout toward Zbrucz and along the Strypa River; defensive opns vic. Buczacz, Galicia; retrograde opns south of Lvov and west of Przymsl; defensive opns along the Vistula River
Feb–May 45	Defensive and retrograde opns vic. Kattowitz, Cosel, and Jägerndorf, Silesia
May 45	Surrendered to Soviet forces

Commanders

Gen.Lt. Stempel, Apr 42–Jan 43
Gen.d.Inf. Niehoff, Apr 43–Jun 44; Jul 44–Mar 45
Gen.Major Baurmeister, Jun–Jul 44
Gen.Major Scherenberg, Mar–May 45

376th Infantry Division

Apr 42	Activation and training in France
Jun 42–Jan 43	Offensive opns vic. Novy Oskol, Prudki, Alexeyevka, and Varvarovka to the Don River; offensive and defensive opns vic. Akimovskiy and Rokotino; retrograde and defensive opns vic. Stalingrad
Jan 43	Surrendered vic. Stalingrad
Feb–Oct 43	Reconstituted and trained in the Netherlands
Oct 43	Deployed to Eastern Front
Jan 44	Defensive opns vic. Kirovograd
Feb 44	Defensive opns vic. Novomirgorod and Corsun
Aug 44	Defensive opns vic. Dnestr River
Oct 44	Encircled and destroyed in Romania

Commanders

Gen.Lt. *Edler* von Daniels Apr 42–Jan 43
Gen.Lt. Szelinski, Apr–Dec 43
Gen.Lt. Otto Schwarz, Dec 43–Sep 44

377th Infantry Division

Feb–Apr 42	Activation and training in France
Jun 42	Offensive opns in the upper Don River region vic. Yeletz
Jul 42	Defensive opns vic. Beresovka
Aug 42–Aug 43	Defensive and retrograde opns vic. Olchovatka, the Oskol River, and the Seym River vic. Rylsk
Feb 43	Division destroyed vic. Rylsk

Commanders

Gen.Major Baessler, Feb–Dec 42
Gen.Lt. Lechner, Dec 42–Jan 43
Gen.Lt. Sinzinger, Jan–Feb 43

383d Infantry Division

Jan 42	Activation in Pritzwalk, Brandenburg
Apr 42	Anti-partisan opns vic. Slutsk, Bobruisk, Briansk, Orel, Roslavl
Jun–Jul 42	Offensive and defensive opns vic. Berezovka, Zibrovo, Prudki, and to southwest of the Kshen River
Feb 43	Retrograde and defensive opns vic. Yudinka, Novopolevo, Akhtyrka
Jun 43	Defense opns vic. Stepanovskiy and Posdeyevo
Jul 43	Offensive opns (Operation *ZITADELLE*) vic. Kamenka, and Fedorovka
Jul 43	Retrograde and defensive opns vic. the Hagen position over the Navlya and Desna Rivers south of Briansk
Sep–Oct 43	Defensive and retrograde opns vic. Titovka, Slizhi, and the Sozh River sector
Nov–Dec 43	Retrograde and defensive opns vic. Merkulovichi and Garmovichi
Jan–Feb 44	Defensive opns vic. the Rogachev bridgehead southwest of Shlobin
Jun–Jul 44	Surrounded and destroyed vic. the Olza River
Aug 44	Unit officially disbanded

Commanders

Gen.Lt. Haarde, Jan–Feb 42
Gen.Lt. von Fabrice, Feb–Sep 42
Gen.Lt. John, Sep 42–Jul 43
Gen.Lt. Hoffmeister, Jul 43–Dec 44

384th Infantry Division

Dec 41–Jan 42	Activation and training in Saxony
Apr–May 42	Assembly, defensive opns vic. Slavyanka, Petropolye, Chepel, Kramatorsk
Jun 42	Offensive and security opns vic. Andreyevka-Bugayevka and the Oskol River sector
Jun 42	Defensive opns vic. Kryuchki and Kolodets
Jul 42	Offensive and security opns in the Don River sector
Aug 42	Offensive opns through Kalmykov, Akatov, Kotluben, and Panshino
Dec 42	Withdrawn from vic. Stalingrad; defensive and retrograde opns through Chir River sector to Surovikino-Tormosin
Jan 43	Defensive opns vic. Chekhalov-Krimskiy
Feb 43	Heavy losses during defensive opns vic. Nizhny Chirskaya
Feb–Mar 43	Retrograde opns over the Donets to the Mius River
Apr 43	Reconstituted vic. St. Omer, France
Apr–Oct 43	Training in France
Oct–Nov 43	Defensive opns vic. Krivoi Rog-Kirovograd railway line; retrograde opns over the Ingul and Bug Rivers
Dec 43–Jan 44	Defensive opns vic. Kutsovka and Shevchenkovo
Jan–Aug 44	Defensive and retrograde opns vic. the Dnestr River; defensive opns in Moldavia vic. Tighina and Bulboka
Aug 44	Defensive and retrograde opns vic. Guragalbina, Moldavia; destroyed
Oct 44	Officially disbanded

Commanders

Gen.Major Kurt Hoffman, Jan–Feb 42
Gen.Lt. *Freiherr* von Gablenz, Feb 42–Jan 43
Gen.Major Dörr, Jan 43 and Feb 43

Gen.Lt. de Salengre-Drabbe, Feb 43–
Aug 44

385th Infantry Division

Dec 41	Activated in Münster
Dec 41– Mar 42	Training
Mar– Nov 42	Infantry Regiment 538 and 2d Battalion, Artillery Regiment 385 detached to Army Group North for opns vic. Leningrad; returned to division Nov 42
Mar 42	Division (-) conducts security and anti-partisan opns vic. Polotsk, Nevel, and Bobruisk
Apr 42	Defensive opns vic. Spaz Demensk
May 42	Defensive opns vic. Orel and Ivanovskoye
Jun 42	Defensive opns vic. Lebedki
Jun 42	Offensive opns vic. the Kshen River
Jul 42	Offensive opns vic. Ozerki and defensive opns in the Vereyka and Don River sectors
Dec 42	Defensive opns vic. Rossosh
Jan 43	Destroyed
Mar 43	Officially disbanded

Commanders
Gen.Major Eibl, Jan 42–Dec 42
Gen.Major von Schuckmann, Dec 42–
Feb 43

387th Infantry Division

Feb 42	Activation and train Döllersheim, Austria
Apr 42– Feb 43	Offensive and defensive opns vic. Kursk; offensive and defensive opns vic. Stary Oskol; defensive opns toward the Don River vic. Voronezh; offensive and defensive

opns vic. the Voronezh bridgehead; in reserve vic. the Don bend vic. Rossosh; defensive opsn along the Don vic. Michalovka and Kulakovka

Mar 43	Reconstituted vic. Kremenchug
Apr 43– Mar 44	Defensive opns vic. Kremenaya; retrograde opns vic. Constantinovka to the Dnepr; defensive opns vic. Dneprpetrovsk and Krivoi Rog; defensive opns in the Nikopol bridgehead and Marinskoye and Kamenka; retrograde opns vic. Apostolovo, Olgino, and Novo Pavlovka
Mar 44	Division destroyed and disbanded

Commanders
Gen.Lt. Jahr, Feb 42–Jan 43
Gen.Major von Schuckmann, Feb–
May 43; Jul–Oct 43; Dec 43–
Mar 44
Gen.Lt. Menny, May–Jul 43
Gen.Major von Eichstädt, Oct–Dec 43

389th Infantry Division

Jan–Apr 42	Activation in Bitche, Lorraine; training in Czechoslovakia
May– Jun 42	Offensive and defensive opns vic. Kharkov, Svobda; offensive opns between the Chir and Don Rivers vic. Kalach
Sep 42– Jan 43	Encircled and destroyed vic. Stalingrad
Feb– Aug 43	Reconstituted and trained in France
Oct 43	Offensive opns vic. Chigirin
Nov 43	Offensive opns vic. Kremenchug; retrograde and defensive opns vic. Chigirin and Telepino

Jan 44	Retrograde and defensive opns vic Kutsovka and Lebedin
Jan–Feb 44	Division encircled and destroyed vic. Cherkassy
Apr–May 44	Division reconstituted in western Hungary
May 44	Retrograde and defensive opns vic. Tofili
Jul 44	Retrograde opns through Belorussia into Latvia; continued retrograde and defensive opns in the Baltics
Sep 44	Baltic area retrograde through Liepaja
Feb 45	Transferred from Poland to Germany via ship; subsequently disbanded

Commanders

Gen.Lt. Jänecke, Feb–Nov 42
Gen.Major Magnus, Nov 42–Jan 43
Gen.Major Erwin Gerlach, Apr–Jun 43; Jul–Nov 43
Gen.Lt. Kruse, Jun–Jul 43
Gen.Major Paul Herbert Forster, Nov 43–Apr 44
Gen.Lt. Walther Hahm, Apr–Sep 44
Gen.Lt. Fritz Becker, Sep 44–Mar 45

403d Security Division

Oct 39	Activation in Strausberg, Berlin
Mar–Jun 41	Security activities in Silesia and Poland
Jun 41–May 43	Security activities in occupied western and central Russia; anti-partisan actions and reconnaisance; supply security, air raid protection, and defense against enemy penetrating actions
May 43	Transfer to Bergen, Lower Saxony; disbanded

Commanders

Gen.Lt. von Ditfurth, Mar 41–May 42
Gen.Lt. Russwurm, May 42–Apr 43

444th Security Division

Feb 40	Redesignation as divisional command in Alzey, Germany
May 40	Security opns in Germany
Jun 40	Security opns in Alsace and Lorraine
Jul–Apr 41	Security opns in France
Apr–May 41	Training in Poland
Jun 41–Aug 43	Defense, movement, anti-partisan, security, and related activities across central and southwestern USSR; assisted in building defense barriers in the Psel and Samara River areas.
May 44	Disbanded

Commanders

Gen.Major *Ritter* von Molo, Mar–Apr 41
Gen.Lt. Russwurm, Apr 41–Feb 42
Gen.Lt. Auleb, Feb–Mar 42
Gen.Lt. Mikulicz, Mar 42–Oct 43

454th Security Division

Mar 41	Organization as Security Division vic. Trebnitz, Silesia
May 41	Security opns in Galicia
Jun 41–May 42	Security duties across Ukraine; POW supervision; reconnaissance; anti-partisan opns defensive opns and construction projects
May 41–Apr 43	Security and anti-partisan opns in south and central Soviet Union
Jul 44	Destroyed

Commanders

Gen.Lt. Krantz, Mar–Sep 41
Gen.Lt. Wilck, Sep–Dec 41
Gen.Lt. Hellmuth Koch, Dec 41–Apr 44
Oberst Joachim Wagner, Apr–May 44
Gen.Major Nedtwig, May–Jul 44

541st Grenadier Division (later VGD)

Jul 44	Activated in Brandenburg
Oct 44	Redesignated as VGD
Sep–Nov 44	Defensive opns in Poland vic. Ostrow Mazowieckie and Nagoszevo; retrograde and defensive opns in the Narev bridgehead vic. Rozan
Dec 44	Defensive and retrograde opns vic. Grayevo and Bialystok, Poland
Jan–Feb 45	Retrograde opns through Poland to Bischofstein, East Prussia
Feb–Mar 45	Defensive and retrograde opns in East Prussia, vic. Bischdorf, Bartenstein, Landsberg, and Zinten
Mar 45	Dissolved

Commander

Gen.Major Hagemann, Jul 44–Mar 45

542d Grenadier Division (later Infantry Div and finally VGD)

Jul–Sep 44	Defensive and retrograde opns vic. Suwalki and Augustovo
Aug 44	Redesignation as infantry division
Sep 44–Apr 45	Defensive and retrograde opns in Poland, vic. Serock, Nasilsk, and Polntz; defenive and retro grade opns vic. Bromberg, East Prussia, and and Schwetz; defensive opns vic. Stargard, West Prus sia, and retrograde opns vic. Danzig; defensive and retrograde opns vic. Schiewenhorst, West Prussia
Apr 45	Division destroyed vic. Tiegenhof, West Prussia

Commander

Gen.Lt. Löwrick, Jul 44–Apr 45

544th Grenadier Division (later VGD)

Jul 44	Activated in Bavaria
Oct 44	Redesignated as VGD
Sep 44–Apr 45	Defensive opns in Poland, Czechoslovakia

Commander

Gen.Lt. Ehrig, Jul 44–May 45

545th Grenadier Division (later VGD)

Jul 44	Activated in the Saar/Palatinate
Oct 44	Redesignated as VGD
Sep 44–Apr 45	Defensive opns in Poland, Silesia

Commanders

Gen.Major Obenaus, Jul 44–Jan 45
Gen.Major Kohlsdorfer, Jan–Apr 45

547th Grenadier Division (later VGD)

Jul 44	Activated in Bavaria
Aug–Sep 44	Defensive and retrograde opns in Lithuania vic. Kalvaria; defensive opns in East Prussia vic. Rominten and Tollmingen and in Pomerania vic. Wartenstein
Oct 44	Redesignated as VGD
Nov–Feb 45	Redeployed to vic. Lomsha, Poland; defensive opns in Poland vic. Novo-grod and the Lipnicki Forest; retrograde opns in East Prussia vic. Sensburg, Bartenstein, Prussian Eylau, and Zinten; division destroyed vic. Mühlhausen, East Prussia
Mar 45	Division reconstituted minus Gr. Regt. 1093 vic. Schwedt/Oder
May 45	Capitulated to American forces vic. Schwerin

Commanders

Gen.Major d.Res. Dr. Meiners, Jul 44–Feb 45
Gen.Major Fronhöfer, Feb–May 45

548th Grenadier Division (later VGD)

Jul 44	Activated in Saxony
Oct 44	Redesignated as VGD
Nov 44– Apr 45	Defensive opns in Poland, East Prussia; destroyed in the Samland Pocket0

Commander

Gen.Major Sudau, Jul 44–Apr 45

549th Grenadier Division (later VGD)

Jul 44	Activated in Pomerania
Oct 44	Redesignated as VGD
Sep 44– Apr 45	Defensive opns in East Prussia and Pomerania
Apr 45	Division destroyed vic. Stettin, Pomerania

Commander

Gen.Major Jank, Jul 44–May 45

551st Grenadier Division (later VGD)

Jul 44	Formed in Thorn, West Prussia
Oct 44	Redesignated as VGD
Late summer 44	Assigned to Eastern Front, central sector
Jan 45	East Prussia

Commander

Gen.Lt. Verhein, Jul 44–May 45

558th Grenadier Division (later VGD)

Jul 44	Activated in Bavaria
Oct 44	Redesignated as VGD
Sep 44– Apr 45	Defensive opns in East Prussia and Pomerania
Apr 45	Capitulated to Soviet forces in East Prussia

Commanders

Gen.Lt. Kullmer, Aug–Oct 44

Gen.Lt. von Bercken, Oct 44–Apr 45

561st Grenadier Division (later VGD)

Aug 44	Activated in East Prussia
Sep– Oct 44	Defensive opns in East Prussia vic. Wierballen, Schlassbach, Haldenau, Göritten, and Ebenrode
Oct 44	Redesignated as VGD
Oct 44	Redeployed vic. Willuhnen, East Prussia

Nov 44– Mar 45	Defensive and retrograde opns vic. the Trappen Forest, Hohensalzburg, Schillen, and Kreuzingen; defensive ops vic. Königsberg
Mar 45	Destroyed vic. Königsberg

Commanders

Gen.Major Gorn, Jul 44–Mar 45

Oberst Becker, Mar 45

562d Grenadier Division (later VGD)

Aug 44	Activated
Oct 44	Redesignated as VGD
Fall 44	Defensive opns in Poland, East Prussia
Mar 45	Destroyed in East Prussia

Commanders

Gen.Major Johannes-Oskar Brauer, Jul 44–Jan 45

Gen.Major Hufenbach, Jan–Mar 45

563d Grenadier Division (later VGD)

Aug 44	Activated in Brandenburg
Late summer 44	Defensive opns on central sector of Eastern Front
Sep 44	Transferred to northern sector
Oct 44	Redesignated as VGD
Nov 44– May 45	Retrograde opns to Latvian coast; defensive opns vic. Kurland; capitulated to Soviet forces

Commanders

Gen.Major Brühl, Aug 44–Feb 45

Gen.Major Werner Neumann, Feb–May 45

707th Infantry Division

May 41	Activated in Munich; formation and training
Aug 41– Mar 42	Anti-partisan and security opns and training in Belorussia vic. Baranovichi, Minsk, and Gorodishche
Mar 42	Anti-partisan opns vic. Bobruisk
Apr 42– Feb 43	Anti-partisan and security opns in Belorussia vic.

Briansk, Lyudinovo, and
Dubrovka

Feb 43	Defensive opns vic. Pogodino
Mar 43	Defensive, anti-partisan, and security opns, vic. Komarichi and Lokot
May 43	Anti-partisan and security opns vic. Zhukovka and Bezhitsa
Jul 43	Defensive opns vic. Buki
Aug 43	Anti-partisan and security opns vic. Zhukovka and Rhzanitsa
Oct 43	Anti-partisan and security opns vic. Korma and Bobruisk
Nov–Dec 43	Defensive opns vic. Shatilki and Berezina River sector
Jan–Jun 44	Defensive opns vic. Shatilki, Luchin, Rogachev, and Brobruisk
Jul 44	Encircled and destroyed vic. Brobruisk
Aug 44	Disbanded

Commanders

Gen.Major *Freiherr* von Mauchenheim gennant von Bechtoldsheim, May 41–Feb 43

Gen.Lt. Hans *Freiherr* von Falkenstein, Feb–Apr 43

Gen.Lt. Russwurm, Apr–Jun 43

Gen.Lt. Busich, Jun–Dec 43; Jan–May 44

Gen.Major Conrady, Dec 43–Jan 44

Gen.Major Gihr, May–Jun 44

710th Infantry Division

May 41	Activated vic. Hamburg
Jun 41–Dec 44	Coastal defense, occupation, and security duties in Norway
Dec 44–Mar 45	Defensive opns in Italy
Apr–May 45	Defensive opns in Austria vic. St. Pölten, Neulengbach, and Herzogenburg

May 45	Capitulated to American forces vic. Steyr

Commanders

Gen.d.Inf. Petsch, May 41–Nov 44

Gen.Lt. Licht, Nov 44–Apr 45

Gen.Major Gorn, Apr–May 45

711th Infantry Division

Apr 41	Formed in Brunswick
Aug 41–Jun 44	Occupation and coastal defense duties in France
Jun–Aug 44	Defensive opns in Normandy
Sep–Oct 44	Retrograde opns from Normandy through Belgium to the Netherlands; reconstituted and reinforced in the Netherlands
Jan–May 45	Offensive and defensive opns in Hungary vic. Tokod, Gran, Estergom, Szob, and the Pilis Mountains; retrograde opns in Czechoslovakia vic. Nitra and Piestany
May 45	Capitulated to Soviet forces vic. Deutsch-Brod

Commanders

Gen.Major von Reinersdorff-Paczensky und Tenczin, May 41–Apr 42

Gen.Major Haverkamp, Apr–Jul 42

Gen.Lt. Friedrich-Wilhelm Deutsch, Jul 42–Mar 43

Gen.Lt. Josef Reichert, Mar 43–May 45

712th Infantry Division

May 41	Activated and trained in the Rhineland and Saar
Jun 41–May 42	Occupation and security opns and training in France
Jun 42–Aug 44	Coastal defense and occupation opns in Belgium
Sep 44–Jan 45	Defensive and retrograde opns in Belgium and the Netherlands
Jan 45	Defensive opns in East Prussia vic. Georgenberg,

and Silesia vic. Warthen-
hau and Königshütte

Feb–
Apr 45

Defensive opns in Silesia
vic. Sohrau; destroyed

Commanders

Gen.Major von Döhren, May 41–
Apr 42

Gen.Lt. Friedrich-Wilhelm Neumann,
Apr 42–Feb 45

Gen.Major von Siegroth, Feb–Apr 45

715th Infantry Division

May 41	Activation and training in Swabia
Jun 41–Jan 44	Coastal defense and occupation opns and training in France
Jan 44–Feb 45	Defensive opns in Italy
Mar 45	Defensive opns in with regimental combat groups in Poland vic. Rajcza; Silesia vic. Sohrau and Loslau; and Czechoslovakia vic. Bohumin
Apr–May 45	Capitulated to Soviet forces in Czechoslovakia

Commanders

Gen.Major Wening, May 41–Jul 42

Gen.Lt. Kurt Hoffmann, Jul 42–Jan 44

Gen.Lt. Hans-Georg Hildebrandt,
Jul 44

Gen.Major Hanns von Rohr, Jul–
Sep 44 and Sep 44–May 45

Gen.Major Hans-Joachim Ehlert,
Sep 44

Light Infantry Divisions

5th Light Infantry (later *Jäger*) Division—See 5th Infantry Division

Feb 42–late 43	Defensive and offensive opns Eastern Front, northern sector vic. Staraya Russa and Demiansk (redesignated as a *Jäger* division in Jul 42)

Winter 43–44	Redeployed to Eastern Front, central sector; defensive opns vic. Vitebsk
Spring–Dec 44	Defensive and retrograde opns in central sector vic. Brest-Litovsk, Kovel, Pripet Marshes, and across eastern Poland
Jan–May 45	Defensive and retrograde opns in West Prussia vic. Neuenburg and Reetz; defensive opns in Brandenburg vic. Wittenberge; capitulation to Soviets

Commanders

Gen.Lt. Allmendinger, Oct 41–Jan 43

Gen.Lt. Thumm, Jan 43–Mar 44 and
Jun–Nov 44

Gen.Major Gittner, Mar–Jun 44

Gen.Lt. Friedrich Sixt, Nov 44–Apr 45

Gen.Lt. Blaurock, Apr 45

8th Light Infantry (later *Jäger*) Division—See 8th Infantry Division

Spring 42–Spring 44	Defensive and offensive opns Eastern Front, northern sector vic. Staraya Russa, Demyansk, Novgorod, and Medved (redesignated as a *Jäger* Division in Jul 42)
Spring 44–Spring 45	Defensive, offensive, and retrograde opns in the Carpathian Mountains vic. Bistritza and Sirit, Romania; the Gran River sector in Hungary; Kremnica, Czechoslovakia; and Brünn, Austria; capitulated to Soviet forces.

Commanders

Gen.Lt. Gustav Höhne, Dec 41–Jul 42

Gen.Lt. Gerhard *Graf* von Schwerin,
Jul–Nov 42

Gen.Lt. Volckamer von Kirchensittenbach, Nov 42–Sep 44

Gen.Lt. Christian Philipp, Sep 44–
Apr 45

28th Light Infantry (later *Jäger*) Division

Feb–May 42	Offensive opns in the Crimea
Summer 42–Spring 44	Offensive, defensive opns Eastern Front, northern sector vic. Mga, Novgorod, and the Oranienbaum sector
Summer 44	Retrograde and defensive opns vic. Lvov, Minsk, Brest-Litovsk
Fall 44–Jan 45	Retrograde and defensive opns vic. Lomza and Ostrolenka, Poland, and Goldap and Angerapp, East Prussia
Jan–May 45	Retrograde and defensive opns in East Prussia vic. Heiligenbeil Pocket; capitulation to Soviet forces

Commanders
Gen.Lt. Sinnhuber, Oct 41–May 43
Gen.Lt. Friedrich Schulz, May–Nov 43
Gen.Major Lamey, Nov 43–Jan 44
Gen.Lt. Speth, Jan–Apr 44
Gen.Lt. Heistermann von Ziehlberg, Apr–Nov 44
Gen.Major Ernst König, Nov 44–Apr 45
Oberst Hans Tempelhoff, Apr–May 45

97th Light Infantry (later *Jäger*) Division

Dec 40	Formed in Bavaria
Jun–Dec 41	Offensive opns Eastern Front, southern sector vic. Lvov, Deriyevka, and Krasnograd
Jan–May 42	Defensive opns vic. Kramatorskaya, Artemovsk and Kharkov
Summer–Fall 42	Offensive opns into the Caucasus Mountains vic. Maikop and Krasnodar; redesignated a *Jäger* division in July 42
Winter 42–43	Retrograde opns to the Kuban bridgehead
Spring–Fall 43	Defensive opns vic. the Crimea
Winter 43–44	Defensive opns in the Nikopol bridgehead; retrograde opns Eastern Front, southern sector between the Ingulets and Bug Rivers; defensive opns along the Dnestr River
Spring 44–Winter 44–45	Defensive and retrograde opns in Poland and Czechoslovakia vic. the Beskid Mountains
Spring 45	Defensive and retrograde opns in Silesia vic. Kattowitz and Czechoslovakia; capitulated to Soviet forces

Commanders
Gen.Lt. Walter Weiss, Dec 40–Jan 41
Gen.Lt. Sigismund von Förster, Jan–Apr 41
Gen.Lt. Maximilian Fretter-Pico, Apr–Dec 41
Gen.Lt. Rupp, Jan–May 43
Gen.Major Otte, May–Jun 43
Gen.Lt. Ludwig Müller, Jun–Dec 43
Gen.Lt. Friedrich Rabe von Pappenheim, Dec 43–Apr 45
Gen.Major Robert Bader, Apr–May 45

99th Light Infantry Division (later 7th Mountain Division below)

Dec 40	Activated
Jun–Nov 41	Offensive opns Eastern Front, southern sector
Nov 41	Redeployed to Germany for refitting and reorganized as the 7th Mountain Division

Commander
Gen.Lt. von der Chevallerie, Dec 40–Oct 41

100th Light Infantry (later *Jäger*) Division

Dec 40	Formed vic. Döllersheim, Austria

Jun– Dec 41	Offensive opns Eastern Front, southern sector vic. Krasnoye, Kremnchug, Poltava, and Kharkov
Jan– May 42	Defensive and retrograde opns in Ukraine vic. Stepanovka, Bessabotovka, and Andreyevka
Summer– Fall 42	Offensive opns in the Don River bend; redesignated as a *Jäger* division in July 1942
Sep 42– Jan 43	Offensive and defensive opns vic. Stalingrad; destroyed
Mar 43	Reconstituted in Ukraine.
May 43– Apr 44	Anti-partisan opns in Croatia and Albania
Apr– Fall 44	Defensive and retrograde opns in Galicia and the Carpathian Mountains; defensive opns along the Czechoslovak-Hungarian frontier
Jan– May 45	Defensive and retrograde opns in Silesia and Czechoslovakia; capitulation to Soviet forces

Commanders

Gen.Lt. Sanne, Dec 40–Jan 43
Gen.Lt. Utz, Apr–Jan 43
Gen.Major Kreppel, Jan 43–May 45

101st Light Infantry (later *Jäger*) Division

Dec 40	Activated
Jun– Dec 41	Offensive opns Eastern Front, southern sector vic. Uman, Snamenka, Kremenchug, Poltava, and Kharkov
Jan– May 42	Defensive opns Martovaya, Gorlovka, and Izyum
Summer– Fall 42	Offensive opns toward the Don River and Caucasus Mountains redesignated as a *Jäger* Division in Jul 42

Winter 42–43	Retrograde and defensive opns vic. Maikop into the Kuban bridgehead
Spring– Summer 43	Defensive opns vic. the Crimea
Summer 43–Mar 44	Defensive and retrograde opns in northern Ukraine
Apr– Dec 44	Defensive and retrograde opns in Galicia and the Carpathian Mountains
Jan– May 45	Defensive and retrograde opns in Czechoslovakia and Austria; capitulated to American forces vic. Nesselbach

Commanders

Gen.Major Erich Marcks, Dec 40–Jun 41
Gen.Lt. von Haydringen, Jun 41–Apr 42
Gen.Lt. Diestel, Apr–Sep 42
Gen.Lt. Emil Vogel, Sep 42–Jul 44
Gen.Lt. Dr. Assmann, Jul 44–May 45

Skijäger Division

1st *Skijäger* Division

Jun 44	Formed on the Eastern Front, central sector from the 1st *Skijäger* Brigade
Jun– Oct 44	Defensive opns vic. the Pripet Marshes
Oct– Dec 44	Defensive and retrograde opns in Poland vic. Wojslawice and Annopol
Jan– May 45	Defensive and retrograde opns in the Carpathian Mountains and through Czechoslovakia; capitulated to Soviet forces

Commanders

Gen.Major Martin Berg, Jun 44–Oct 44
Gen.Lt. Hundt, Oct 44–Jan 45; and Feb–May 45
Gen.Major Steets, Jan 45–Feb 45

Mountain Divisions

1st Mountain Division

Apr 38	Formed vic. Garmisch-Partenkirchen
Sep 39	Offensive opns in Poland
May–Jun 40	Offensive opns in Western Europe
Apr 41	Offensive opns in the Balkans
Jun–Dec 41	Offensive opns Eastern Front, southern sector vic. Vinnitsa, Timoshevka, Stalino, and toward the Mius River
Jan–May 42	Defensive opns vic. Dimitrievka and Kharkov
Summer–Fall 42	Offensive opns into the Caucasus Mountains to Maikop and Mt. Elbrus
Winter 42–43	Defensive and retrograde opns to the Kuban bridgehead
Mar 43	Deployed to Greece.
Mar 43–Dec 44	Anti-partisan opns in the Balkans vic. northern Greece, Montenegro and Bosnia
Jan–May 45	Defensive and retrograde opns in Hungary and Austria; capitulation to American forces in Austria vic. Enns

Commanders

Gen.Major Kübler, Sep 39–Oct 40
Gen.Lt. Lanz, Oct 40–Jan 42
Gen.Lt. Martinek, Jan–Dec 42
Gen.Lt. Walter Stettner, *Ritter* von Grabenhofen, Dec 42–Oct 44
Gen.Lt. Josef Kübler, Oct 44–Mar 45
Gen.Lt. August Wittmann, Mar–May 45

2d Mountain Division

Apr 38	Formed vic. Innsbruck, Austria
Sep 39	Offensive opns in Poland.
Apr 40	Offensive opns in Norway
Jul–Dec 41	Offensive opns in the Arctic vic. Kirkenes, Norway toward Murmansk
Jan 42–Sep 44	Offensive and defensive opns west of Murmansk
Sep–Dec 44	Retrograde opns from west of Murmansk to Norway
Jan–Feb 45	Enroute from Denmark to the Saar
Feb–Mar 45	Defensive and retrograde opns in the Saar-Moselle Triangle
Mar–May 45	Defensive and retrograde opns in southern Germany; capitulation to American forces

Commanders

Gen.Lt. Feurstein, Sep 39–Mar 41
Gen.Major Schlemmer, Mar 41–Jan 42
Gen.Lt. Ritter von Hengl, Jan 42–Oct 43
Gen.Lt. Hans Degen, Oct 43–Feb 45
Gen.Lt. Utz, Feb–May 45

3d Mountain Division

Apr 38	Formed vic. Graz, Austria
Sep 39	Offensive opns in Poland
Apr 40	Offensive opns in Norway
Jul–Dec 41	Offensive opns in the Arctic vic. Kirkenes, Norway toward Murmansk
Dec–Apr 42	Training in Germany vic. Grafenwöhr
May–Aug 42	In reserve in Norway
Oct–Nov 42	Defensive opns Eastern Front, northern sector vic. Leningrad and Mga
Nov 42	Defensive and offensive opns Eastern Front, central sector vic. Veliki Luki
Dec 42	Deployed to southern sector
Dec 42–Mar 44	Offensive, defensive, and retrograde opns vic. Voroshilovgrad, Porkovo, Zaporozhe, Nikopol

Apr–Sep 44	Retrograde and defensive opns across southern Ukraine to the Carpathian Mountains
Oct 44	Defensive and retrograde opns in Hungary
Nov 44–Jan 45	Defensive and retrograde opns in Czechoslovakia
Feb–May 45	Defensive and retrograde opns in Czechoslovakia; capitulation to Soviet forces

Commanders

Gen.Lt. Dietl, Sep 39–Jun 40
Gen.Lt. Ringel, Jun–Oct 40
Gen.Lt. Kreysin, Oct 40–Aug 43
Gen.Major Picker, Aug 43; Sep 43
Gen.Lt. Rasp, Aug–Sep 43
Gen.Lt. August Wittmann, Sep 43–Jul 44
Gen.Lt. Klatt, Jul 44–May 45

4th Mountain Division

Oct 40	Formed vic. Heuberg
Apr 41	Offensive opns in the Balkans
Jun–Dec 41	Offensive opns Eastern Front, southern sector vic. Lvov, Vinnitsa, Berislav, Stalino to the Mius River
Jan–Jun 42	Defensive opns along the Mius River
Summer–Fall 42	Offensive opns vic. Rostov and Armavir to the Caucasus Mountains
Winter 42–43 –Sep 43	Defensive and retrograde opns vic. Novorossisk to the Kuban bridgehead
Oct 43	Defensive opns in the Crimea
Nov–Dec 43	Defensive and retrograde opns vic. Melitopol, Akimovka, and Kherson.
Jan–Feb 44	Defensive and retrograde opns vic. Uman, Vinnitsa
Mar 44	Defensive opns vic. Yassy, Romania
Apr–Aug 44	Defensive opns in Moldavia vic. Grigoriopol

Aug–Oct 44	Defensive and retrograde opns in the Carpathian Mountains
Nov–Dec 44	Defensive and retrograde opns in Hungary
Jan–May 45	Defensive and retrograde opns in Czechoslovakia; capitulation to Soviet forces

Commanders

Gen.Lt. Eglseer, Oct 40–Oct 42
Gen.Lt. Hermann Kress, Oct 42–Aug 43
Gen.Lt. Julius Braun, Aug 43–Jun 44
Gen.Lt. Jank, Jun–Jul 44
Gen.Lt. Breith, Jul 44–Feb 45; Apr–May 45
Gen.Major Robert Bader, Feb–451Apr 45

5th Mountain Division

Oct 40	Formed in Austria vic. Salzburg
Mar–Apr 41	Offensive opns in the Balkans
May 41	Offensive opns (airlanded) on Crete
Jun–Oct 41	Occupation and security opns on Crete
Nov 41–Mar 42	Redeployed to Germany for refitting, training
Apr 42–Nov 43	Offensive, and defensive opns Eastern Front, northern sector vic. Mga and Volkhov
Dec 43–Apr 45	Defensive and retrograde opns in Italy; capitulation to American forces

Commanders

Gen.Lt. Ringel, Nov 40–Feb 44
Gen.Lt. Max Schrank, Feb 44–Jan 45
Gen.Major Steets, Jan–May 45

6th Mountain Division

Jun 40	Formed vic. Heuberg, Austria
Jun 40	Limited offensive opns in France

Jun–Nov 40	Occupation opns in France vic. the Swiss border
Dec 40–Feb 41	Occupation and security opns in Poland
Mar–Apr 41	Offensive opns in the Balkans
May 41	*Gebirgsjäger* Regiment 141 conducts offensive opns on Crete
Sep 41–Sep 44	Offensive, defensive, and retrograde opns in the Arctic between Kirkenes, Norway and Murmansk
Sep–Dec 44	Retrograde and defensive opns in northern Finland and Norway
Jan–May 45	Occupation and security opns in Norway; capitulation to British forces

Commanders
Gen.Lt. Schörner, May 40–Jan 42
Gen.Lt. Philipp, Jan 42–Aug 44
Gen.Lt. Max Pemsel, Aug 44–Apr 45

7th Mountain Division

Nov 41	Formed from the 99th Light Infantry Division
Mar–Jul 42	Hoffmeister," elements of As "Combat Group the division conduct offensive operations on Eastern Front, northern sector vic. Lake Ilmen
July 42–Sep 44	Defensive opns in northern Karelia vic. Kiestinki and Uhtua
Sep–Dec 44	Retrograde opns through Finland to Norwegian frontier
Jan–May 45	Occupation and security opns in Norway; capitulated to British forces

Commanders
Gen.Lt. Rudolf Konrad, Nov–Dec 41
Gen.Major Wilhelm Weiss, Dec 41–Jan 42
Gen.Lt. Robert Martinek, Jan–May 42

Gen.Lt. August Krakau, May–Jul 42; Sep 42–May 45
Gen.Lt. Robert Martinek, Jul–Sep 42

Waffen-SS Divisions

1st SS-Panzer Division
Leibstandarte Adolf Hitler

Mar 33–Jun 40	Formation and gradual expansion to regimental strength. Offensive opns in Poland in Sep 39 and in the invasion of western Europe in May 40
Apr 41	After expansion to brigade strength, offensive opns in northern Greece
Jun–Nov 41	Offensive opns across Ukraine and southern Russia to vic. Rostov
Nov 41–Jul 42	Defensive opns along the Sambek River, and then briefly on the Sea of Azov, before redeploying to France to rebuild and expand to full divisional strength
Jan–Mar 43	Defensive opns vic. Kharkov, followed by offensive opns to recapture the city
Jul 43	Offensive opns on the southern wing of the *ZITADELLE* offensive
Oct 43–Apr 44	Security opns and rebuilding in Italy; defensive and retrograde opns west of Kiev, then south of Zhitomir and in opns to relieve the Cherkassy pocket; retrograde opns west with the encircled 1st Panzer Army
Jun–Sep 44	Offensive, defensive, and retrograde opns in Normandy; subsequently conducted retrograde opns

across northern France and Belgium

Dec 44– Jan 45 Offensive opns in the Ardennes; subsequent defensive opns in Belgium

Feb 45 Participated in the *SÜD-WIND* offensive against the Gran bridgehead in Hungary

Mar 45 Participated in the *FRÜH-LINGSERWACHEN* offensive south of Budapest

Mar– May 45 Retrograde opns through Hungary into Austria; surrendered to American forces vic. Steyr

Commanders

SS-Ogruf. und Gen.d.W-SS Dietrich, Mar 33–Jun 43

SS-Oberf. and SS-Brif. und Gen.Major d.W-SS Wisch, Jun 43–Aug 44

SS-Ostubaf. Steineck, temp., Aug 44

SS-Oberf. and SS-Brif. und Gen.Major d.W-SS Mohnke, Aug 44–Feb 45

SS-Brif. und Gen.Major d.W-SS Kumm, Feb–May 45

2d SS-Panzer Division *Das Reich*

Aug 34– Oct 39 Formation of separate battalions in Germany; which gradually became the regiments and supporting units for the division. Most participated in offensive opns in Poland during Sep 39

Oct 39– Jun 40 After uniting separate units into a division, offensive opns during invasion of western Europe, May 40

Apr 41 Occupation and security duties in Yugoslavia

Jun– Aug 41 Offensive opns toward Smolensk; defensive opns vic. Yelna

Sep 41 Offensive opns to reduce the Kiev pocket between Kiev and Kharkov

Oct– Dec 41 Offensive opns south of Smolensk toward Moscow

Feb– Jun 42 Defensive opns vic. Rzhev, followed by relief for rebuilding in France

Jan– Mar 43 Defensive opns vic. Kharkov followed by offensive opns to recapture the city

Jul 43 Offensive opns on the southern wing of the *ZITADELLE* offensive

Jul 43 Offensive opns vic. the Mius

Aug– Dec 43 Defensive opns west of Kharkov; retrograde opns west across the Dnepr River south of Kiev

Dec 43– Apr 44 A combat group remained in combat in Galicia as the main body of the division rebuilt in France. The combat group retreated west with the encircled 1st Panzer Army

Jun–Sep 44 Offensive, defensive, and retrograde opns in Normandy; subsequently conducted retrograde opns across northern France and Belgium

Dec 44– Jan 45 Offensive opns in the Ardennes; subsequent defensive opns in Belgium

Mar 45 Participated in the *FRÜH-LINGSERWACHEN* offensive south of Budapest

Mar– May 45 Retrograde opns through Hungary into Austria; defensive opns vic. Vienna; surrendered to American forces vic. St. Pölten, Austria at the end of the war. A detached element surrendered to American forces vic. Pilsen, Czechosolvakia at the same time

Commanders

SS-Ogruf. und Gen.d.W-SS Hausser,
Oct 39–Oct 41

SS-Brif. und Gen.Major d.W-SS
Bittrich, Oct–Dec 41

SS-Brif. und Gen.Major d.W-SS
Kleinheisterkamp, Jan–Apr 42

SS-Gruf. und Gen.Lt.d.W-SS Keppler,
Apr 42–Feb 43

SS-Oberf. Vahl, Feb–Mar 43

SS-Gruf. und Gen.Lt.d.W-SS Krüger,
Apr–Dec 43

SS-Brif. und Gen.Major d.W-SS
Lammerding, Dec 43–Jul 44 and
Nov 44–Jan 45

SS-Ostubaf. Tychsen, Jul 44

SS-Oberf. Baum, Jul–Oct 44

SS-Staf. Kreutz, Jan–Feb 45 and
Apr–May 45

SS-Gruf. und Gen.Lt.d.W-SS Osten-
dorff, Feb–Mar 45

SS-Staf. Rudolf Lehmann, Mar–Apr 45

3d SS-Panzer Division *Totenkopf*

Oct 39–Jun 40	Formation and training in Germany; then offensive opns during the invasion of western Europe, May 40
Jun 41–Feb 42	Offensive opns across the Baltic states and northern Russia, then defensive fighting vic. Staraya Russa
Feb–Oct 42	Defensive opns vic. Demyansk, with elements of the division gradually withdrawn to join newly-forming sub-units in France
Feb–Mar 43	Offensive opns to recapture Kharkov
Jul 43	Offensive opns on the southern wing of the *ZITADELLE* offensive
Jul 43	Offensive opns against the Mius bridgehead
Aug 43–Jun 44	Defensive opns west of Kharkov, followed by retrograde opns across the Dnepr and Dniester

	Rivers into Romania. Defensive and retrograde opns vic. Targul Frumos, followed by refitting in reserve
Jul–Dec 44	Defensive opns vic. Warsaw
Jan 45	Participation in the *KONRAD* offensives vic. Budapest
Feb–May 45	Retrograde opns through Hungary into Austria; surrendered to American forces. Most of the division turned over to the Soviets

Commanders

SS-Ogruf. und Gen.d.W-SS Eicke,
Nov 39–Jul 41 and Sep 41–Feb 43

SS-Brif. und Gen.Major d.W-SS Keppler, Jul–Sep 41

SS-Brif. und Gen.Major d.W-SS Simon,
Feb–Apr 43

SS-Brif. und Gen.Major d.W-SS and
SS-Gruf. und Gen.Lt.d.W-SS Priess,
Apr 43–Jun 44

SS-Ostubaf. Ullrich, Jun–Jul 44

SS-Brif. und Gen.Major d.W-SS Becker,
Jul 44–May 45

4th SS-Polizei Panzer-Grenadier Division

Oct 39–Jun 40	Formation and training in Germany; then security and limited objective attacks vic. Upper Rhine front during the invasion of western Europe
Jun 41–Feb 42	Offensive opns toward Leningrad; defensive opns vic. Leningrad
Feb–May 42	Defensive and offensive opns to contain and then reduce the Volkhov Pocket
Jun 42–Nov 43	Defensive combat vic. Leningrad
Nov 43–Apr 44	While most units redeployed to Greece, a combat group remained on the

Oranienbaum front which later conducted defensive opns southeast of Leningrad, then redeployed to join rest of division

Sep– Oct 44	Anti-partisan opns in Balkans, followed by defensive opns against Soviet forces in the Banat
Oct 44– Jan 45	Defensive opns east of Budapest; retrograde opns north into Slovakia
Feb 45	Offensive opns (Operation *SONNENWENDE*) in Pomerania
Feb– Apr 45	Defensive and retrograde opns toward Danzig
Apr– May 45	Defensive opns east of Berlin; retrograde opns toward the west. Surrendered to Allied forces in northern Germany

Commanders

SS-Gruf. und Gen.Lt.d.Polizei Pfeffer-Wildenbruch, Oct 39–Nov 40
SS-Gruf. und Gen.Lt.d.Schutzpolizei Mülverstedt, Nov 40–Aug 41
SS-Brif. und Gen.Major d.W-SS Krüger, Aug–Dec 41
SS-Gruf. und Gen.Lt.d.Polizei Wünnenberg, Dec 41–Jun 43
SS-Brif. und Gen.Major d.W-SS und Polizei Schmedes, Jun 43–Jun 44 and Aug–Nov 44
SS-Stanf. und Obstlt.d.Schutzpolizei Schümers, Jun–Jul 44 and Jul–Aug 44
SS-Brif. Vahl, Jul 44
SS-Staf. und Obstlt.d.Schutzpolizei Dörner, Aug 44
SS-Staf. Harzer, Nov 44–May 45

5th SS-Panzer Division *Wiking*

Dec 40– Jun 41	Formation and training in Swabia; transfer to Silesia
Jun– Dec 41	Offensive opns across Galicia and Ukraine; defensive opns along the Mius River
Jul– Dec 43	Offensive opns toward Rostov and across the Kuban River into the Caucasus Mtns
Dec 42– Mar 43	Defensive opns vic. the Kalmuk Steppe and on the Donets River; then offensive opns during the recapture of Kharkov
Jul–Oct 43	Defensive opns vic. Izyum; retrograde opns to the Dnepr River. Defensive opns along the Dnepr south of Kiev
Jan– Feb 44	Led the break out from the Cherkassy pocket
Mar– Apr 44	Offensive opns to relieve German forces encircled vic. Kovel
Jul–Dec 44	Defensive opns vic. Warsaw
Jan 45	Participation in the *KONRAD* offensives vic. Budapest
Jan– May 45	Retrograde opns west through Hungary into Austria; surrendered to American forces

Commanders

SS-Gruf. und Gen.Lt.d.W-SS Steiner, Dec 40–May 43
SS-Gruf. und Gen.Lt.d.W-SS Gille, May 43–Jul 44
SS-Stanf. Mühlenkamp, Jul–Oct 44
SS-Oberf. Ullrich, Oct 44–May 45

6th SS-Mountain Division *Nord*

Jul 41	As a motorized unit, offensive opns in Operation *SILBERFUCHS*, the liberation of Finnish Karelia and invasion of Soviet Karelia
Jul–Sep 41	Division's combat units attached to Finnish infantry formations for training and limited combat opns
Nov 41	Offensive opns between Kiestinki and Louhi

Jun 42	Reorganization as a *Waffen-SS* mountain division
Dec 41– Sep 44	Defensive opns against Soviet attacks between Kiestinki and Louhi; long-range patrols to sever the Murmansk railway
Sep– Nov 44	After Finnish/Soviet armistice, execution of Operation BIRKE, the withdrawal from Soviet Karelia and 1,600 km road march through Finland and part of Norway. As rear guard for XVIII Mountain Corps, combat against Finnish units during withdrawal
Jan 45	Offensive opns (Operation NORDWIND) in the Low Vosges Mountains
Feb– Mar 45	Defensive opns in the Low Vosges vic. Bitche
Mar– Apr 45	Defensive and retrograde opns in the Saar-Moselle triangle
Apr– May 45	Remnants surrender to American forces on the east bank of the Rhine

Commanders

SS-Brif. und Gen.Major d.W-SS Herrmann, Feb–May 41
SS-Brif. und Gen.Major d.W-SS Demelhuber, Jun 41–Apr 42
SS-Oberf. Scheider, Apr–Jun 42
SS-Gruf. und Gen.Lt.d.W-SS Kleinheisterkamp, Jun 42–Dec 43
SS-Gruf. und Gen.Lt.d.W-SS Debes, Dec 43–May 44
SS-Ogruf. und Gen.d.W-SS Krüger, May–Aug 44
SS-Gruf. und Gen.Lt.d.W-SS und Polizei Brenner, Sep 44–Apr 45
SS-Stanf. Schreiber, Apr–May 45

7th SS-Volunteer Mountain Division Prinz Eugen

Mar 43– Sep 44	Formation, training, and anti-partisan opns in occupied Yugoslavia
Sep– Nov 44	Defensive opns vs. Soviet and Bulgarian forces at Nish and Kraljevo
Dec 44– Feb 45	Offensive and defensive opns in western Serbia
Mar– Apr 45	Offensive and defensive opns in central Bosnia
Apr– May 45	Withdrawal into Croatia, surrendered to partisan forces west of Zagreb

Commanders

SS-Gruf. und Gen.Lt.d.W-SS and SS-Ogruf. und Gen.d.SS Phleps, Mar 42–Jul 43
SS-Brif. und Gen.Major d.W-SS *Reichsritter* (Imperial Knight) von Oberkamp, Jul–Nov 43 and Dec 43–Jan 44
SS-Stanf. Schmidhuber, Nov–Dec 43; Jan–Feb 44; and Jan–May 45
SS-Brif. und Gen.Major d.W-SS Kumm, Feb 44–Jan 45

8th SS-Cavalry Division Florian Geyer

Jun–Sep 42	Created in Poland around an existing brigade
Sep 42– Jan 43	Anti-partisan opns in the rear areas Army Group Center, while some combat groups fought in the front lines
Aug– Dec 43	After additional anti-partisan opns, defensive opns west of Kiev, followed by heavy fighting along the Dnepr River. When the bulk of the division withdrew to reorganize, combat groups remained on the front during early 44
Aug– Nov 44	Defensive opns in eastern Hungary; retrograde opns to vic. Budapest
Dec 44– Feb 45	Defensive opns vic. Budapest; encircled in the city alongside the 22d SS-Volunteer Cavalry Division and destroyed during breakout opns

Commanders

SS-Brif. und Gen.Major d.W-SS
  Bittrich, Jun–Nov 42
SS-Ostubaf. d.Res. Lombard, Nov 42–
  Jan 43
SS-Staf. und Obstlt. d.Schutzpolizei
  Freitag, Jan–Mar 43
SS-Staf. Zehender, Mar–May 43
SS-Brif. und Gen.Major d.W-SS
  Fegelein, May–Sep 43
Oberf. d.Res. Streckenbach, Sep 43–
  Apr 44
SS-Staf. and SS-Oberf. and SS-Brif. und
  Gen.Major d.W-SS Rumohr,
  Apr 44–Feb 45

9th SS-Panzer Division Hohenstaufen

Feb 43– Mar 44	Formation and training in France
Apr– Jun 44	Offensive opns to relieve encircled German units in Ternopol, Galicia.
Jun– Sep 44	Offensive, defensive, and retrograde opns in Normandy; retrograde opns across France and Belgium to the Netherlands
Sep 44	Offensive opns vic. Arnhem
Dec 44– Jan 45	Offensive opns in the Ardennes and subsequent defensive opns in Belgium
Mar– May 45	Offensive opns in Hungary (Operation *FRÜH-LINGSERWACHEN*); retrograde opns through Hungary to Austria. Surrendered to American forces vic. Steyr

Commanders

SS-Gruf. und Gen.Lt.d.W-SS Bittrich,
  Feb 43–Jun 44
SS-Staf. Müller, Jun–Jul 44
SS-Oberf. and SS-Brif. und Gen.Major
  d.W-SS Stadler, Jul 44 and Oct
  44–May 45
SS-Oberf. Bock, Jul–Oct 44

10th SS-Panzer Division Frundsberg

Feb 43– Mar 44	Formation and training in France
Apr– Jun 44	Offensive opns to relieve encircled 1st Panzer Army in Russia
Jun– Sep 44	Offensive, defensive, and retrograde opns in Normandy; retrograde opns across France and Belgium to the Netherlands
Sep 44	Offensive and defensive opns vic. Nijmegen
Nov 44– Jan 45	Defensive opns vic. Aachen
Jan 45	Offensive opns in Alsace during second phase of the *NORDWIND* offensive
Feb– Mar 45	Offensive opns (*SONNEN-WENDE* Offensive) in Pomerania, followed by defensive opns in the Altdamm bridgehead
Apr– May 45	Defensive opns vic. Dresden. Surrendered to Soviet forces

Commanders

SS-Brif. und Gen.Major d.W-SS Debes,
  Feb–Nov 43
SS-Gruf. und Gen.Lt.d.W-SS von
  Treuenfeld, Nov 43–Apr 44
SS-Oberf. and SS-Brif. und Gen.Major
  d.W-SS Harmel, Apr 44–Apr 45
SS-Ostubaf. d.Res. Roestel, Apr–
  May 45

11th SS-Volunteer Panzer-Grenadier Division *Nordland*

May– Aug 43	Formation and training in Bavaria
Aug– Dec 43	Training and anti-partisan opns in Croatia
Jan–Feb 44	Defensive and retrograde opns between Leningrad and the Luga and Narva Rivers
Feb–Jul 44	Defensive opns alongside the brigade that became the 23d SS-Volunteer

	Panzer-Grenadier Division vic. Narva
Jul–Sep 44	Retrograde opns between Narva and the Tannenberg Line
Sep 44– Jan 45	Retrograde opns to and defensive opns in the vic. of Riga; defensive opns in Kurland
Feb– Mar 45	Offensive opns (SONNEN-WENDE Offensive) in Pomerania, and then defensive opns in the Alt-damm bridgehead
Apr– May 45	Defensive opns east of Berlin; most of the division destroyed in the city. Survivors surrendered to Allied forces along the Elbe River

Commanders

SS-Gruf. und Gen.Lt.d.W-SS von
    Scholz, May 43–Jul 44
SS-Brif. und Gen.Major d.W-SS
    Ziegler, Jul 44–Apr 45
SS-Brif. und Gen.Major d.W-SS Dr.
    Krukenberg, Apr–May 45

12th SS-Panzer Division *Hitlerjugend*

Jul 43– May 44	Formation and training in Belgium and France
Jun– Sep 44	Offensive, defensive, and retrograde opns in Normandy; subsequently conducted retrograde opns across northern France and Belgium
Dec 44– Jan 45	Offensive opns in the Ardennes; subsequent defensive opns in Belgium
Feb 45	Participated in the SÜD-WIND offensive against the Gran bridgehead in Hungary
Mar 45	Participated in the FRÜH-LINGSERWACHEN offensive south of Budapest
Mar– May 45	Retrograde opns through Hungary into Austria;

	surrendered to American forces vic. Steyr

Commanders

SS-Brif. und Gen.Major d.W-SS Fritz
    Witt, Jul 43–Jun 44
SS-Oberf. and SS-Brif. und Gen.Major
    d.W-SS Kurt Meyer, Jun–Sep 44
SS-Stubaf. Hubert Meyer, Sep–
    Oct 44
SS-Brif. und Gen.Major d.W-SS und
    Oberst i.G. Fritz Kraemer, Oct–
    Nov 44
SS-Oberf. and SS-Brif. und Gen.Major
    d.W-SS Hugo Kraas, Nov 44–
    May 45

13th Waffen-Mountain Division of the SS Handschar, Croatian No. 1

Mar 43– Jan 44	Began formation in Bosnia, with most training taking place in France and Silesia
Feb– Aug 44	Anti-partisan opns in Bosnia
Sep 44	Division broke up as the Germans retreated from Bosnia, with most of the Bosnian personnel remain-ing to fight against Com-munist partisans and Chetniks (Serbian nationalists)
Oct 44– May 45	After being augmented with German personnel from miscellaneous units, the German cadre and remaining Bosnians con-ducted defensive opns vs. Soviets in Hungary; retrograde opns through Hungary to Austria; surrendered to British forces vic. Klagenfurt

Commanders

SS-Brif. und Gen.Major d.W-SS und
    Oberst i.G. Sauberzweig, Aug 43–
    Jun 44
SS-Oberf. and SS-Brif. und Gen.Major
    d.W-SS Hampel, Jun 44–May 45

14th Waffen-Grenadier Division of the SS, Ukrainian No. 1

Jul 43– Jul 44	Formation, training, and (with one combat group) anti-partisan opns in Ukraine
Jul 44	Defensive and break out opns in the Brody-Tarnov Pocket (in Galicia)
Oct 44– Feb 45	After rebuilding in Silesia, anti-partisan and security opns in Slovakia
Feb– Mar 45	Anti-partisan opns in Slovenia
Mar– May 45	Defensive opns vs. Soviet forces in Slovenia and Austria. On 27 Apr, reassigned to the Ukrainian Natioanal Army. Surrendered to British forces in Austria

Commanders

SS-Brif. und Gen.Major d.W-SS und Polizei Schimana, Jul–Oct 43

SS-Brif. und Gen.Major d.W-SS und Polizei Freitag, Oct 43–Apr 45

15th Waffen-Grenadier Division of the SS, Latvian No. 1

May 43	Began forming in Latvia, with manpower often reassigned to replace casualties in the brigade that later became the 19th Waffen-Grenadier Division
Nov 43– Jan 44	Divisional elements were gradually committed separately to defensive opns with German Army units west of Velikiye Luki
Feb 44	Defensive and retrograde opns south and west of Staraya Russa
Feb– Apr 44	Defensive opns along the Velikaya River
Jul– Aug 44	Defensive and retrograde opns western Russia and eastern Latvia; division evacuated by sea to

	Germany for reconstitution
Jan– Mar 45	Defensive and retrograde opns in West Prussia and Pomerania, to positions west of the mouth of the Oder River
Apr– May 45	One combat group conducted defensive opns vic. Berlin, but only one of its battalions became caught in the city, where it was destroyed. The remainder withdrew to the southwest and surrendered to American forces. The rest of the division surrendered to Canadian and American forces in northern Germany

Commanders

SS-Brif. und Gen.Major d.W-SS Hansen, Feb–May 43

SS-Brif. und Gen.Major d.W-SS *Graf* (Count) von Pückler-Burghauss, May 43–Feb 44

SS-Oberf. Heilmann, Feb–Jul 44

SS-Oberf. von Obwurzer, Jul 44–Jan 45

SS-Oberf. Ax, Jan–Feb 45

SS-Brif. und Gen.Major d.W-SS Burk, Feb–May 45

16th SS-Panzer-Grenadier Division *Reichsführer-SS*

Nov 43	Created in Slovenia by expanding an existing brigade
Jan– Apr 44	One combat group conducted defensive opns vic. Anzio, while the remainder of the division trained and participated in the occupation of Hungary
May 44– Jan 45	Defensive, retrograde, and anti-partisan opns in Italy
Feb– May 45	Conducted a supporting attack for Operation *FRÜHLINGSERWACHEN* in Hungary; subsequent

retrograde opns through Hungary to Austria. Surrendered to British forces vic. Klagenfurt

Commanders

SS-Gruf. und Gen.Lt.d.W-SS Simon, Oct 43–Nov 44

SS-Oberf. Baum, Nov 44–May 45

18th SS-Volunteer Panzer-Grenadier Division Horst Wessel

Jan 44	Created by expanding an existing brigade
Mar–Jun 44	Training and anti-partisan opns in Croatia; occupation duties in Hungary
Jul–Aug 44	One regimental combat group conducted defensive opns in Galicia while the division finished training
Sep–Oct 44	Anti-partisan and security duties in Slovakia insurrection
Nov 44–Jan 45	Defensive opns in Hungary
Feb–May 45	Defensive opns in Silesia and then in Czechoslovakia, with survivors surrendering to Czech partisans or Soviet forces

Commanders

SS-Oberf. Trabandt, Jan 44–Jan 45

SS-Stanf. Bochmann, Jan–Mar 45

SS-Staf. Petersen, Mar–May 45

19th Waffen-Grenadier Division of the SS, Latvian No. 2

Feb–Apr 44	Formed during heavy fighting along the Velikaya River by retitling an existing brigade, with new elements gradually added
Jul–Sep 44	Defensive and retrograde opns in western Russia and eastern Latvia
Oct 44–May 45	Defensive opns in Kurland; survivors surrendered to the Soviets or

became anti-Soviet partisans

Commanders

SS-Oberf. Schuldt, Feb–Mar 44

SS-Staf. Bock, Mar–Apr 44

SS-Brif. und Gen.Major d.W-SS and SS-Gruf. und Gen.Lt.d.W-SS und Polizei Streckenbach, Apr–May 45

20th Waffen-Grenadier Division of the SS, Estonian No. 1

Jan 44	Formed by retitling an existing brigade, with new elements gradually added. Defensive and retrograde opns west from the vic. of Staraya Russa
Feb–Jul 44	Defensive opns vic. the Narva River
Jul–Sep 44	Defensive opns along the Tannenberg Line west of Narva, and then evacuated to Germany for reconstitution in Silesia
Jan–Mar 45	Defensive and retrograde opns in Silesia, including breakout from the Oppeln pocket
Mar–May 45	Defensive and retrograde opns west through Saxony to the vic. of Prague; survivors surrendered to the Soviets or were killed by Czech partisans

Commanders

SS-Brif. und Gen.Major d.W-SS Augsburger, Jan 44–Mar 45

SS-Brif. und Gen.Major d.W-SS Maack, Mar–May 45

22d SS-Volunteer Cavalry Division Maria Theresia

May–Aug 44	Began to organize west of Budapest based around detached elements of the 8th SS-Cavalry Div. supplemented by ethnic German (*Volksdeutsche*) transfers from the Hungarian

Army, as well as ethnic German and ethnic Magyar conscripts

Aug–
Nov 44   Combat ready elements of the division conducted defensive and retrograde opns in eastern Hungary while the remainder aided the German occupation of Budapest

Nov 44–
Feb 45   Defensive and retrograde opns east of Budapest; the division was then encircled in the city alongside the 8th SS-Cavalry Division, and was destroyed during the breakout attempt in Feb

Commander
SS-Oberf. and SS-Brif. und Gen.Major d.W-SS Zehender, May 44–Feb 45

23d SS-Volunteer Panzer Grenadier Division Nederland, Dutch No. 1

Feb–
Mar 45   Created by retitling an existing brigade, which was conducting defensive opns in Pomerania

Apr–
May 45   After reorganization west of the Oder River, the division was split during defensive opns vic. Berlin. Part was forced west, and surrendered to Allied forces along the Elbe River. The remainder was destroyed in the Halbe pocket south of Berlin, with only a few survivors escaping to reach American captivity

Commander
SS-Brif. und Gen.Major d.W-SS Wagner, Feb–May 45

25th Waffen Grenadier Division of the SS Hunyadi, Hungarian No. 1

Nov 44   Began to organize in Hungary with Hungarian Army veterans, civilian

volunteers, and the latest group of Hungarian conscripts, before transferring to Silesia

Feb–
May 45   Two combat ready battalions defended the training camp in Silesia as the remainder of the division evacuated to Bavaria, before finishing the war in Austria

Commander
Waffen-Gruf.d.SS Grassy, Oct 44–May 45

26th Waffen Grenadier Division of the SS Hungaria, Hungarian No. 2

Nov–
Dec 44   Began to organize in Hungary with Hungarian Army veterans, civilian volunteers, and the latest group of Hungarian conscripts, before transferring to Silesia to join the 25th Waffen-Grenadier Division

Feb–
May 45   Two combat ready battalions defended the training camp in Silesia as the remainder of the division evacuated to Austria, where it ended of the war

Commanders
W-Oberf.d.SS von Pisky, Dec 44–Jan 45
SS-Brif. und Gen.Major d.W-SS Maack, Jan–Mar 45
W-Gruf.d.SS Grassy, Mar–May 45

27th SS-Volunteer Grenadier Division Langemarck, Flemish nr. 1

Sep 44–
Jan 45   Began to organize around an existing brigade, supplemented by workers in German industry and men from the collaborationist exile community

Jan–
Mar 45   Defensive and retrograde opns in Pomerania

Apr– May 45	After reorganization west of the Oder River, the divisional combat group conducted defensive and retrograde opns east of Berlin; surrendered to Allied forces in northern Germany

Commander

SS-Staf. Müller, Nov 44–May 45

28th SS-Volunteer Grenadier Division
Wallonien, Walloon nr. 1

Sep 44– Jan 45	Began to organize around an existing brigade, supplemented by workers in German industry and men from the collaborationist exile community
Jan– Mar 45	Defensive and retrograde opns in Pomerania
Apr– May 45	After reorganization west of the Oder River, the divisional combat group conducted defensive and retrograde opns east of Berlin; surrendered to Allied forces in northern Germany

Commanders

SS-Oberf. Burk, Sep–Dec 44
SS-Oberf. Heilmann, Dec 44–Jan 45
SS-Staf. Degrelle, Jan–May 45

31st SS-Volunteer Grenadier Division

Sep– Oct 44	Began to organize in the Batschka area around the German cadre of the former 23d Waffen-Mountain Division of the SS Kama and local ethnic-German manpower raised through draconian conscription
Nov 44	Defensive and retrograde opns vs. Soviet forces in Hungary on an emergency basis, before the completion of training
Jan– May 45	After replenishment, defensive and retrograde

	opns in Silesia; surrendered to the Soviets

Commander

SS-Brif. und Gen.Major d.W-SS Lombard, Oct 44–Apr 45

32d SS-Volunteer Grenadier Division
30. Januar

Feb 45	Began to organize piecemeal during heavy fighting vic. Frankfurt an d.Oder, as existing battalions and regiments were combined with the staffs and students of various training schools
Apr– May 45	Defensive and retrograde opns east of Berlin, destroyed in the Halbe Pocket, with a few survivors surrendering to American forces

Commanders

SS-Staf. Mühlenkamp, organized the division Jan–Feb 45
SS-Staf. Richter, Feb 45
SS-Oberf. Ax, Feb–Mar 45
SS-Ostubaf. Kempin, Mar–May 45

33d Waffen-Grenadier Division of the SS Charlemagne, French No. 1

Feb– May 45	Created by renaming an existing brigade; defensive and retrograde opns in Pomerania; reformed as a regiment; a small battalion of volunteers conducted defensive opns Berlin in late April; remainder of division surrendered to Allied forces in northern Germany, with a training element surrendering in southwest Germany

Commanders

W-Oberf. Puaud, Feb–Mar 45
SS-Brif. und Gen.Major d.W-SS Dr. Krukenberg, Mar–Apr 45
SS-Staf. Zimmermann, Apr–May 45

35th SS-Polizei Grenadier Division

Feb–
May 45

Created by renaming an existing brigade; defensive opns vic. Guben, then encircled in the Halbe Pocket and destroyed, with a few survivors surrendering to American forces

Commanders

SS-Oberf. und Oberst d.Schutzpolizei Wirth, Feb–Mar 45

SS-Staf. und Oberst i.G. Pipkorn, Mar–Apr 45

36th Waffen-Grenadier Division of the SS Dirlewanger

Feb–
May 45

Created by renaming an existing brigade; defensive opns vic. Guben; encircled in the Halbe Pocket and destroyed, with a few survivors surrendering to American forces

Commander

SS-Brif. und Gen.Major d.W-SS und Polizei Schmedes, Feb–May 45

37th SS-Volunteer Cavalry Division Lützow

Feb–
Mar 45

Organized in western Hungary

Mar–
May 45

Defensive and retrograde opns as two combat groups, one vic. Bratislava and the other vic. Gran. Most of the division surrendered to American forces

Commanders

SS-Staf. Fegelein, organized division Feb 45

SS-Ostubaf. Gesele, Mar–May 45

Luftwaffe Command Level Organization– Eastern Front, 1941–45

The *Luftwaffe* was organized into operational elements and support units. At senior command levels, the German Air Force was hierarchically stratified as follows:

High Command of the Air Force (Berlin) — *Oberkommando d.Luftwaffe (OKL)*
Regional Commands — *Luftgaue*
Air Fleets — *Luftflotten*
Subordinate Commanders
Tactical-Level Unit Commands

Command Responsibilities

Luftgaue (LG) were service commands with regional responsibilities. They are probably equivalent to modern-level entities whose administrative military responsibilities cross geographic or political boundaries. Combat and support elements under their control answered administratively to the LG commander. There were 14 numbered LGs and 10 others, designated by place names (for example, LG Moscow, LG Belgium/ Northern France, and so on.)

LGs pertinent to this report are: LGs 1, 2, and 8 and LGs Moscow, Kharkov, Kiev, Petersburg, and Rostov.

Luftflotten (LF) were the "Air Fleets." They were the highest sub-OKL units with operational missions. They may be likened to numbered fleets in the US Navy or numbered field armies. In the East, there were three numbered LFs: namely I, IV, and VI (Northern USSR,

Southern USSR, and Eastern Front, respectively), and LF "*Reich.*"

Luftwaffe Field Divisions (LWFD). These were ground divisions under the command of a general officer.

Luftgaue in the East

Luftgau I—Prussia and Poland
Gen.Lt. Lentzsch, Aug 38–Jan 39
Gen.Major Max Mohr, Feb–May 39
Gen. Musshoff, Jun 39–Feb 40
Gen.Lt. Wimmer, Feb–May 40
Gen.Lt. Süssmann, May 40–Jan 41
Gen.Lt. Putzier, Jan 41–Aug 43
Gen. Bieneck, Aug 43–Aug 44
Gen. Vierling, Aug 44–Feb 45

Luftgau II—Poland, General Government—See Luftgau VIII, below, as well

Luftgau VIII—Poland, General Government areas after Jan 43; 44: absorbed areas within Lower Silesia (From Luftgau III) and the *Warthegau* from Luftgau I; in Feb 45, absorbed the northern portion of Luftgau XVII (Protectorate of Bohemia-Moravia)
Commanders and Subordinates:
Gen. Bernhard Waber, May 39–
  Oct 41
Gen.d. Fleiger Sommé, Oct 41–
  Aug 44
Gen.d. Flieger Veit Fischer, Aug
  44–May 45
Subordinate Commanders:
Moscow—Gen. Veit Fischer, Nov 41–
  Feb 43
Gen.Major Siess, Feb 43–Apr 43
Kharkov—Gen. Bernhard Waber,
  Sep 42–Apr 43
Kiev—Gen. Bernhard Waber, Nov 41–
  Sep 42
Petersburg—Gen.Major Prockl,
  42–Apr 43
Rostov—Gen. Vierling, Oct 41–
  Apr 43

"Field" Luftgaue in the East (FLGK)

FLGK XXV–Dnepropetrovsk area
Gen. Vierling, Apr 43–Aug 44

FLGK XXVI–Baltic area
Gen.Major Prockl, Apr 43–Aug 43
Gen. Putzier, Aug 43–Aug 44

FLGK XXVII–Smolensk/Minsk areas
Gen. Veit Fischer, Apr 43–Aug 44

FLGK XXX–North Balkans
Gen. Bernhard Waber, Jul 43–Aug 44

Luftflotten (LF)

The Air Fleets responsible for operations in the East were established for the following geographic locales:

Luftflotte I
  39–42   Northeast Areas
  42–44   Baltic Areas
  1945   Lithuania
Luftflotte IV
  39–42   Austria-Poland
  42–44   Southern USSR
  1945   Hungary/Yugoslavia
Luftflotte VI
  39–45   Eastern Front

Commanders:

Luftflotte I
Gen.Feldm. Kesselring, Feb 39–Jan 40
Gen.Oberst Stumpff, Jan–May 40
Gen. Wimmer, May–Aug 40
Gen.Oberst Alfred Keller, Aug 40–
  Jun 43
Gen.Oberst Korten, Jun–Aug 43
Gen. Pflugbeil, Aug 43–Apr 45

Luftflotte IV
Gen.Oberst Löhr, Mar 39–Jul 42
Gen.Feldm. *Freiherr* von Richthofen,
  Jul 42–Sep 43

Gen.Oberst Dessloch, Sep 43–Aug 44
Gen.Lt. Holle, Aug–Sep 44
Gen.Oberst Dessloch, Sep 44–Apr 45

Luftflotte VI

Gen.Feldm. *Ritter* von Greim, May 43–
Apr 45
Gen.Oberst Dessloch, Apr–May 45

Luftflotte "Reich"

Gen.Oberst Stumpff, Feb 44–
May 45

Luftwaffe Ground Forces on the Eastern Front

Luftwaffe Field Divisions

1st *Luftwaffe* Field Division

Sep 42   Formed in Germany
Nov 42–   Defensive opns Eastern
Feb 44   Front, northern sector vic.
           Leningrad; disbanded

Commanders
Gen.Lt. Wilke, Sep 42–Jan 43 and Apr–
Nov 43
Gen.Major Zech, Jan–Apr 43
Gen.Major Petrauschke, Nov 43–
Feb 44

2d *Luftwaffe* Field Division

Sep 42   Formed in Germany
Nov 42–   Defensive and retrograde
Nov 43   opns Eastern Front, central
           sector vic. Vitebsk;
           disbanded

Commander
Oberst Petzold, Sep 42–Nov 43

3d *Luftwaffe* Field Division

Sep 42   Formed in Germany
Nov 42–   Defensive and retrograde
Jan 44   opns Eastern Front, central
           sector; disbanded

Commander
Gen.Lt. Pistorius, Sep 42–Jan 44

4th *Luftwaffe* Field Division

Sep 42   Formed in Germany
Nov 42–   Defensive and retrograde
Jul 44   opns Eastern Front, central
           sector; destroyed vic.
           Vitebsk

Commanders
Oberst Rainer Stahel, Sep–Nov 42
Gen.Major Hans-Georg Schreder,
Nov 42–Apr 43
Gen.Major Wilhelm Völk, Apr–Nov 43
and Nov–Dec 43
Gen.Major Sauerbrey, Nov 43
Gen.Major Geerkens, Dec 43–Jan 44
Gen.Lt. Pistorius, Jan–Jun 44

5th *Luftwaffe* Field Division

Oct 42   Formed in Germany
Dec 42–   Defensive and retrograde
Jun 44   opns Eastern Front,
           southern sector; destroyed
           vic. Odessa

Commanders
Gen.Major von Arnim, Oct–Mar 44
Gen. Lt. Botho *Graf* von Hülsen,
Mar–Jun 44

6th *Luftwaffe* Field Division

Sep 42   Formed in Germany
Jan 43–   Defensive and retrograde
Jun 44   opns Eastern Front, central
           sector; destroyed vic.
           Vitebsk

Commanders
Gen.Major Ernst Weber, Sep–Nov 42
Gen.Lt. von Heyking, Nov 42–
Nov 43
Gen.Major Peschel, Nov 43–Jun 44

7th *Luftwaffe* Field Division

Sep 42   Formed in Germany
Jan–   Defensive and retrograde
May 43   opns Eastern Front,
           southern sector; destroyed
           vic. Don River bend

Commander
Gen.Major *Freiherr* von Biedermann,
Sep 42–Jan 43 and Feb–Mar 43
Gen.Lt. Spang, Jan–Feb 43

8th *Luftwaffe* Field Division

Oct 42	Formed in Germany
Dec 42– May 43	Defensive opns Eastern Front, central sector; destroyed vic. Don River bend

Commanders
Oberst Heidemeyer, Oct 42–Jan 43
Gen.Lt. Spang, Jan–Feb 43
Oberst Hähling (*Heer*), Feb–Mar 43

9th *Luftwaffe* Field Division

Oct 42	Formed in Germany
Dec 42– Feb 44	Defensive and retrograde opns Eastern Front, northern sector; destroyed during withdrawal from vic. Leningrad

Commanders
Gen.Major Erdmann, Oct 42–Aug 43
Gen.Major Longin, Aug–Nov 43
Gen.Lt. Paul Winter, Nov 43
Gen.Major Ernst Michael, Nov 43– Jan 44

10th *Luftwaffe* Field Division

Sep 42	Formed in Germany
Dec 42– Feb 44	Defensive and retrograde opns Eastern Front, northern sector; destroyed during withdrawal from vic. Leningrad

Commander
Gen.Major Wadehn, Sep 42–Nov 43
Gen.Lt. von Wedel, Nov 43–Jan 44

12th *Luftwaffe* Field Division

Dec 42	Formed in Germany
Mar 43– Jan 44	Defensive and retrograde opns Eastern Front, northern sector, vic. Leningrad
Feb 44– Apr 45	Retrograde opns to Kurland; defensive opns vic. Kurland
Apr– May 45	Remnants evacuated to vic. Danzig; defensive opns vic. Danzig; capitulated to Soviet forces

Commanders
Gen.Lt. Kettner, Dec 42–Nov 43
Gen.Lt Gottfried Weber, Nov 43– Apr 45
Gen.Major Schlieper, Apr– May 45

13th *Luftwaffe* Field Division

Nov 42	Formed in Germany
Feb 43– Apr 44	Defensive and retrograde opns Eastern front, northern sector; destroyed during withdrawal from vic. Leningrad

Commanders
Gen.Lt. Olbricht, Nov 42–Dec 42
Gen.Major Korte, Dec 42–Oct 43
Gen.Lt. Reymann, Oct 43–Apr 44

15th *Luftwaffe* Field Division

Nov 42	Formed in Germany
Dec 42– Nov 43	Defensive and retrograde opns Eastern Front, southern sector; destroyed vic. Taganrog

Commanders
Gen.Lt. Mahnke, Nov 42–Jan 43
Oberst Cornrody, Jan–Feb 43
Gen.Lt. Spang, Feb–Nov 43

21st *Luftwaffe* Field Division

Dec 42	Formed in Germany
Jan 43– Jan 44	Defensive and retrograde opns Eastern Front, northern sector vic. Leningrad and vic. Staraya Russa
Jan 44– May 45	Retrograde opns to Latvian coast; defensive opns in Kurland; capitulation to Soviet forces

Commanders
Gen.Lt. Schimpf, Dec 42–Oct 43
Gen.Lt. Licht, Oct 43–Apr 44
Gen.Major Goltzsch, Apr– Aug 44
Gen.Lt. Henze, Aug 44–Jan 45
Gen.Major Barth, Jan–May 45

Hermann Göring Divisions

Hermann Göring Division (later Panzer Division Hermann Göring, later Parachute Panzer Division Hermann Göring)

Oct 42	Formed from Brigade Hermann Göring in France
Jan–May 43	Offensive and defensive opns in Tunisia; capitulated to Allied forces
May 43	Reformed in Sicily as Panzer Division Hermann Göring
Jul–Aug 43	Defensive and retrograde opns in Sicily
Sep 43–Jul 44	Defensive and retrograde opns in Italy; redesignated as Parachute Panzer Division Hermann Göring in May 44
Jul 44–Jan 45	Defensive opns along the Vistula River
Jan–May 45	Defensive and retrograde opns in Poland, East Prussia, Silesia, Saxony; capitulated to Soviet forces vic. Dresden

Commander
Gen.Major Contath, Oct 42–Apr 44
Gen.Major Wilhelm Schmalz, Apr–Sep 44
Gen.Major von Necker, Oct 44–Feb 45
Gen.Major Lemke, Feb 45–May 45

Parachute Panzer-Grenadier Division Hermann Göring

Sep 44	Formed in Poland vic. Radom
Oct 44–Jan 45	Defensive and retrograde opns in Poland and East Prussia
Jan–Mar 45	Defensive opns in the Heiligenbeil Pocket; evacuated by sea to Germany
Mar–May 45	Defensive and retrograde opns in Silesia and Saxony; capitulated to Soviet forces

Commanders
Gen.Major Erich Walther, Sep–Nov 44 and Mar–May 45
Oberst Söth, Nov 44–Jan 45
Oberst Seegers, Feb–Mar 45
Oberst Hufenbach, Mar 45

Parachute Division

2d Parachute Division

Feb 43	Formed in France
Jun–Nov 43	Defensive and occupation opns in Italy
Nov 43–May 44	Defensive and retrograde opns Eastern front, central sector vic. Zhitomir
May 44	Withdrawn to Germany
May–Sep 44	Deployed to France; defensive and retrograde opns in Normandy and Brittany; capitulated to American forces at Brest
Nov 44	Reformed in Germany
Nov 44–Apr 45	Defensive and retrograde opns in the Netherlands and Germany; capitulated to Allied forces

Finnish Army Divisions

Armored Division

Jun 42	Formed
42–43	Offensive and defensive opns in eastern Karelia
1944	Defensive opns in the Karelian Isthmus against Jun 44 Soviet offensive

Commander
Maj. Gen. Lagus, Jun 42–Dec 44

1st Division

Jun 41	In reserve for the Karelian Army vic. Lake Ryhä
42–43	Deployed vic. Maaselkä Isthmus area
43–44	Moved from Maaselkä Isthmus to Karelia north of Lake Ladoga

Commanders

Maj. Gen. Paalu, Jun 41–Nov 43
Maj. Gen. Fagernäs, Nov 43– Nov 44

2d Division

Jun 41	Offensive opns in the Karelian Isthmus
Aug 41	Offensive opns vic. Lake Ladoga
Oct 41	Offensive opns west of Lake Seg
Nov– Dec 41	Offensive opns to Povenets
Jan 42–44	Defensive opns in the Karelian Isthmus area, vic. Tyjä and Siiranmäki

Commanders

Maj. Gen. Blick, Jun 41–Jan 42
Maj. Gen. Hannuksela, Feb–May 42
Maj. Gen. Martola, May 42–Jul 44
Maj. Gen. Blick, Jul–Nov 44

3d Division

Jun 41	Offensive opns vic. Suomussalmi and Kuusamo
Jul 41	Offensive opns toward Kiestinki
Aug 41– May 44	Defensive opns vic. Uhtua
Jun 44	Offensive and defensive opns vic. Karelian Isthmus

Commanders

Maj. Gen. Fagernäs, Jun 41–Oct 43
Maj. Gen. Pajari, Oct 43–Oct 44

4th Division

Jun 41	Deployed vic. Viipuri
Aug 41	Offensive opns between Virolahti and Enso

Sep 41	Offensive opns towards Pryazha
1942	Offensive and defensive opns vic. the Maaselkä Isthmus
Jun 44	Defensive opns in the Karelian Isthmus vic. Lakes Suula, Vvot, and Kauk

Commanders

Col. Viljanen, Jun 41–Apr 42
Col. Takkula, Apr 42–Mar 43
Maj. Gen. Autti, Mar 43–Nov 44

5th Division

Jun 41	Offensive opns from Värtsilä to Korpiselkä
Jul 41	Offensive opns toward Lake Ladoga
42–43	Offensive and defensive opns vic. the Svir River
1944	Defensive opns vic. the Svir River, Eastern Karelia, and the Karelian Isthmus

Commanders

Col. Koskimies, Jun–Jul 41
Col. Lagus, Jul 41
Col. Karhu, Jul 41–May 42
Maj. Gen. Tapola, May 42–Sep 44

6th Division

Jun 41	Offensive opns vic. Suomussalmi and Kuusamo
Aug 41	Offensive opns vic. Lake Towand
1942	Offensive and defensive opns vic. Maaselkä
1943	Moved to the Karelian Isthmus area

Commanders

Col. Viikla, Jun–Dec 41
Maj. Gen. Wihma, Dec 41–Aug 44
Col. Puroma, Aug–Nov 44

7th Division

Jun 41	Offensive opns vic Lake Ryhä and Lake Värtsilä
42–43	Offensive and defensive opns vic. the Svir River

1943   Offensive and defensive opns in East Karelia and the Karelian Isthmus

Commanders

Maj. Gen. Svensson, Jun 41–Aug 43
Unknown, Aug 43–Jan 44
Maj. Gen. Isakson, Jan–Nov 44

8th Division

Jun 41   Offensive opns vic. Viipuri
Aug 41   Offensive opns between Virolahti and Enso
42–43   Offensive and defensive opns vic. Svir River
1944   Defensive opns vic. Svir River, East Karelia, and the Karelian Isthmus

Commanders

Maj. Gen. Winell, Jun 41–Jan 43
Maj. Gen. Palojärvi, Jan 43–Feb 44
Maj. Gen. Kääriäinen, Feb–Nov 44

10th Division

Jun 41   Offensive opns vic. Viipuri
Aug 41   Offensive opns between Virolahti and Enso
42–43   Offensive and defensive opns in the Karelian Isthmus
Jun 44   Defensive opns in the Karelian Isthmus

Commanders

Maj. Gen. Sihvo, Jun 41–Jun 44
Col. Savonjousi, Jun–Dec 44

11th Division

Jun 41   Offensive opns from Värtsilä to Korpiselkä
Jul 41   Offensive opns toward Lake Ladoga
42–43   Offensive and defensive opns along the Svir River
1944   Defensive opns along the Svir River and the Karelian Isthmus

Commander

Maj. Gen. Heiskanen, Jun 41–Nov 44

12th Division

Jun 41   Offensive opns vic. Viipuri
Aug 41   Offensive opns between Virolahti and Enso
Sep–Dec 41 Disbanded

Commander

Col. Wihma, Jun–Dec 41

14th Division

Jun 41   Deployed vic. Lieksa
Jul–Sep 41   Offensive opns to and occupation of Rukajärvi
42–43   Offensive and defensive opns vic. Rukajärvi

Commander

Maj. Gen. Raappana, Jun 41–Aug 44

15th Division

Jun 41   Deployed vic. Lake Ladoga
Jul 41   Offensive opns vic. Lake Ladoga
Oct 41   Offensive opns to the west of Lake Seg
Nov–Dec 41   Offensive opns towards Povenets
42–43   Offensive and defensive opns on Karelian Isthmus; defensive opns against the Soviet Jun 44 offensive

Commander

Maj. Gen. Hersalo, Jun 41–Nov 44

17th Division

Jun 41   Deployed vic. Hanko
Jul 41   Offensive opns west of Värtsilä toward Ruskeala-Harlo
Aug 41   Offensive opns towards Pryazha
42–43   Offensive and defensive opns along the Svir River
1944   Defensive opns along the Svir River and the Karelian Isthmus

Commanders

Col. Snellman, Jun 41–Apr 42
Maj. Gen. Sundman, Apr 42–Nov 44

18th Division

Jun 41	Offensive opns from Lake Ladoga to Lake Pyhä
Aug 41	Offensive opns vic. Lake Ladoga
Oct 41	Offensive opns vic. Lake Seg
Nov–Dec 41	Offensive opns towards Povenets
Mar 42	Offensive opns to take the island Suursaari
43–44	Offensive and defensive opns in the Karelian Isthmus

Commanders

Maj. Gen. Pajari, Jun 41–Oct 43
Maj. Gen. Paalu, Nov 43–Jun 44
Col. Snellman, Jun–Jul 44
Col. Oinonen, Jul–Dec 44

19th Division

Jun 41	Offensive opns vic. Lake Pyhä to Värtsilä
Jul 41	Offensive opns vic. Ruskaela-Harlu
Aug 41	Offensive opns vic. Pryazha
1942	Disbanded

Commander

Maj. Gen. Hannuksela, Jun 41–Feb 42

1st Coast Division

| Jul 44 | Formed |
| Jul–Sep 44 | Deployed in defense of the Bay of Viipuri |

Commanders

Col. Enkainen, Jul–Aug 44
Maj. Gen. Järvinen, Aug–Nov 44

Division J

Aug 41	Formed
Aug–Dec 41	Offensive opns vic. Kiestinki
Dec 41–Late 42	Defensive opns vic. Maaselkä Isthmus
Late 42	Disbanded

Commander

Maj. Gen. Väinö Palojärvi, Aug 41–Aug 42

The Royal Hungarian Army

Most of the following information was found in the extremely comprehensive treatment of the Royal Hungarian Army in WWII by Dr. Leo Niehorster, *The Royal Hungarian Army, 1920–1945* (Axis Europa, 1998).

The Mobile Corps

| Jul–Nov 41 | Conducted offensive opns Eastern Front southern sector through Galicia and Ukraine along the axis of advance vic. Korömezö-Horodenka-Smotryes-Stanislavchik-Bersad-Konstantinovka-Suvorovka-Krivoi Rog-Nikopol-Dnjepropetrovsk-Izyum |
| Dec 41 | Withdrawn to Hungary |

The following major maneuver units were assigned to the mobile corps during these operations.

1st Cavalry Brigade

Commanders

Brig. Gen. Noák, May 38–Mar 40
Brig. Gen. Veress, Mar 40–Oct 41
Brig. Gen. Király, Oct 41–Sep 42

1st Motorized Infantry Brigade

Commanders

Brig. Gen. Zay, Oct 38–Mar 40
Brig. Gen. Major, Mar 40–Nov 41
Brig. Gen. Ankai-Anesini, Nov 41–May 42
Brig. Gen. Sáska, May–Jun 42

2d Motorized Infantry Brigade

Commanders

Col. Horáth, Jan 39–Mar 40
Brig. Gen. Heszlényi, Mar–Oct 40
Brig. Gen. Vörös, Oct 40–Dec 41
Col. Bisza, Dec 41

Divisions

1st Hussar Division

Apr–Jun 44	Security opns vic. Pinsk Jun 44
Jun–Jul 44	Defensive opns vic. Miszanka
Aug–Sep 44	Defensive and retrograde opns in Poland
Oct 44	Withdrawn to Hungary
Nov 44	Defensive and retrograde opns vic. Budapest
Jan–Apr 45	Defensive and retrograde opns through northern Hungary into Czechoslovakia; capitulated to American forces

Commanders

Maj. Gen. Vattay, Oct 42–Jul 44
Maj. Gen. Ibrányi, Jul–Nov 44
Col. Schell, Nov 44–Apr 45

1st Armored Field Division

Jun–Sep 42	Offensive and defensive opns vic. Karotyak
Sep 42–Jan 43	In Second Hungarian Army reserve along the west bank of the Don River south of Voronezh, east of Belgorod and north of Rossosh vic. Kamlonka
Jan 43	Defensive opns in the Don River bend; reduced to remnants
Spring 43	Remnants withdrawn for reorganization

Commanders

Maj. Gen. Veress, Apr–Oct 42
Col. Sáska, Oct–Dec 42
Brig.Gen Horváth, Dec 42–Apr 43

1st Armored Division

Sep 44	Activated in Hungary
Sep 44	Offensive and defensive opns vic. Arad, Hungary
Oct 44	Defensive and retrograde opns vic. Totkomlos, Hungary
Nov–Dec 44	Defensive and retrograde opns in western Hungary
Dec 44–Feb 45	Defensive opns vic. Budapest; capitulated to Soviet forces

Commanders

Col. Koszorus, Sep 44
Col. Deák, Sep–Oct 44
Col. Tiszay, Oct 44
Brig. Gen. Schell, Oct–Nov 44
Col. Mike, Nov–Dec 44
Col. Vértessy, Dec 44–Feb 45

2d Armored Division

Mar 44	Activated in Hungary
Apr 44	Offensive opns in Galicia vic. Nadvorna
May–Aug 44	Defensive and retrograde opns to Hungarian frontier
Sep 44	Offensive and defensive opns against the Romanians and Soviets in Transylvania
Oct 44	Defensive and retrograde opns in Transylvania
Nov–Dec 45	Defensive and retrograde opns in western Hungary
Jan–May 45	Defensive and retrograde opns through western Hungary into Czechoslovakia; capitulated to American forces

Commanders

Col. Osztovics, Mar–Jun 44
Brig. Gen. Zsedényi, Jun 44–Apr 45

1st Light Division

Dec 42–Aug 43	Security and anti-partisan opns in Ukraine
Aug–Sep 43	Defensive and retrograde opns vic. Shostka; destroyed

| Sep– Oct 43 | Reconstituted |
| May 44 | Dissolved; units incorporated into 5th, 12th, and 23d Reserve Divisions |

Nov 43– Apr 44 — Security and defensive opns in Belorussia

Commanders

Brig. Gen. Ungár, Oct 42–Aug 43
Brig. Gen. Deseö, Aug 43–May 44

2d Light Division (formerly 102d Security Division)

| May– Jul 43 | Security and anti-partisan opns in Ukraine |
| Jul 43 | Withdrawn to Hungary; dissolved |

Commander

May–Jul 43 Brig. Gen. Dèpold

5th Light Division (formerly 105th Security Division; after Mar 44, 5th Reserve Division)

May–Oct 43	Security and anti-partisan opns in Ukraine
Oct 43– May 44	Security and defensive opns in Belorussia
May 44– May 45	Defensive and retrograde opns with German forces in Belorussia into Czechoslovakia; capitulated to Soviet forces

Commanders

Brig.Gen. Algya-Papp, May–Oct 43
Brig.Gen. Lászlo János Szábo, Oct 43– May 45

6th Light Division (later 6th Infantry Division)

Jun 42	Offensive opns Eastern Front, southern sector vic. Staraya Oskol
Jul–Aug 42	Offensive and defensive opns vic. the Uryv bridgehead on the Don River
Sep 42– Jan 43	Defensive opns along Don River bend vic. Oskino
Spring 43	Remnants withdrawn for reorganization

May 44	Reconstituted as 6th Infantry Division
Aug– Oct 44	Defensive and retrograde opns in the Carpathian Mountains
Dec 44	Disbanded

Commanders

Col. Gödry, Feb–Aug 42
Brig. Gen. László Szabó, Aug 42
Brig. Gen. Dr. Temesy, Aug–Nov 42
Brig. Gen. Ginszkey, Dec 42–Mar 44
Brig. Gen. Horváth, Mar–Jul 44
Brig. Gen. Karátsony, Jul–Dec 44

7th Light Division (later 7th Infantry Division)

Jun 42	Offensive opns Eastern Front, southern sector vic. Staraya Oskol
Jul–Sep 42	Offensive and defensive opns vic. the Uryv bridgehead on the Don River
Sep 42– Jan 43	Defensive opns along the Don River bend vic. Uryv; destroyed
Spring 43	Remnants withdrawn for reorganization
May 44	Reconstituted as 7th Infantry Division
Aug 44	Defensive opns in the Carpathian Mountains; Disbanded; remnants transferred to 24th Infantry Division

Commanders

Brig. Gen. Mezö, Mar–Oct 42
Brig. Gen. László Szabó, Oct 42–Jun 44
Brig. Gen. Kudriczy, Jun–Aug 44

8th Light Division (formerly 108th Security Division)

| May– Jun 43 | Security and anti-partisan opns in Ukraine |
| Jul 43 | Withdrawn to Hungary; absorbed by 9th Light Division |

Commanders

Brig.Gen. Csiby, Mar–Jun 43
Brig.Gen. Makay, Jul 43

9th Light Division (reorganized as 9th Reserve Division by Mar 44)

Jun–Jul 42	Offensive opns Eastern Front, southern sector vic. Staraya Oskol
Jul–Aug 42	Offensive and defensive opns vic. the Uryv bridgehead on the Don River
Sep 42–Jan 43	Defensive opns along the Don River bend vic. Ivanovka
Spring 43	Remnants withdrawn for reorganization
Mar 44	Reconstituted as 9th Reserve Division
Apr 44	Disbanded

Commanders

Brig. Gen. Ujlaky, May–Nov 42
Brig. Gen. Oszlányi, Nov 42–Aug 43
Brig.Gen. Németh, Aug 43–Apr 44

10th Light Division (later 10th Infantry Division)

Aug–2 Sep 4	Offensive and defensive opns Eastern Front, southern sector vic. Karotyak bridgehead on Don River
Sep 42–Jan 43	Defensive opns along the Don River bend south of Svoboda; destroyed
Spring 43	Remnants withdrawn for reorganization
Jul 44	Reformed as 10th Infantry Division
Aug–Oct 44	Defensive and retrograde opns in the Carpathian Mountains
Nov–Dec 44	Defensive and retrograde opns in western Hungary
Dec 44–Feb 45	Defensive opns vic. Budapest; capitulated to Soviet forces

Commanders

Col. Tanitó, May 42–Sep 42
General Molnár, Sep 42–Aug 43
Brig. Gen. Kudriczy, Aug 43–Jun 44
Brig. Gen. Oszlányi, Jun–Dec 44
Brig. Gen. Kisfaludy, Dec 44
Col. András, Dec 44–Feb 45

12th Light Division (After August 43, 12th Reserve Division; after Oct 44, 12th Infantry Division)

Aug–Sep 42	Offensive and defensive opns Eastern Front, southern sector vic. Karotyak bridgehead on the Don River
Sep 42–Jan 43	Defensive opns along the Don River bend south of Stutye; destroyed
Spring 43	Remnants withdrawn for reorganization
Aug 43	Reconstituted as 12th Reserve Division
Sep 43–Aug 44	Security and defensive opns in Belorussia
Aug 44	Withdrawn to Hungary
Sep–Dec 44	Defensive and retrograde opns in southern and western Hungary
Oct 44	Redesignated as 12th Infantry Division
Dec–Feb 45	Defensive opns vic. Budapest; capitulated to Soviet forces

Commanders

Brig. Gen. Illésházy, Aug 41–Aug 42
Col. Sáska, Aug–Sep 42
Brig. Gen. Solymossy, Oct 42–Aug 43
Brig. Gen. Bor, Aug 43–Apr 44
Brig. Gen. Pötze, May 44
Brig. Gen. Németh, May–Sep 44
Col. Tömöry, Sep–Oct 44
Brig. Gen. Mikófalvy, Oct–Dec 44
Brig. Gen. István Baumann, Dec 44–Feb 45

13th Light Division (later 13th Infantry Division)

Aug–Sep 42	Offensive and defensive opns Eastern Front, southern sector vic. Karotyak bridgehead on Don River
Sep 42–Jan 43	Defensive opns along the Don River bend vic. Karotyak; destroyed
Spring 43	Remnants withdrawn for reorganization

Jul 44	Reconstituted as 13th Infantry Division
Aug–Oct 44	Defensive opns in the Carpathian Mountains
Nov 44	Disbanded

Commanders

Brig. Gen. Grassy, Apr–Nov 42
Brig. Gen. Hollósy-Kuthy, Nov 42–Feb 43
No officer assigned as commander, Feb–May 43
Brig. Gen. Hankovszky, Aug–Oct 44
Brig. Gen. Sövényházi-Herdiczky, Oct–Dec 44

16th Infantry Division

Mar 44	Mobilized in Hungary
Apr–May 44	Offensive and defensive opns in Galicia
May–Aug 44	Defensive and retrograde opns to the Hungarian frontier
Aug–Oct 44	Defensive and retrograde opns in the Carpathian Mountains
Nov–Dec 44	Defensive and retrograde opns in northern Hungary
Jan–May 45	Defensive and retrograde opns in Czechoslovakia; capitulated to Soviet forces

Commanders

Brig. Gen. Lengyel, Mar–Aug 44
Brig. Gen. József Vasváry, Aug–Nov 44
Brig. Gen. Mészöly, Nov–Dec 44
Brig. Gen. Karátsony, Dec 44–Mar 45
Col. Keresztes, Mar–Apr 45
Col. Pápay, Apr–May 45

18th Reserve Division

Apr 43–Oct 43	Security and anti-partisan opns in Ukraine
Oct 43–Apr 44	Security and defensive opns in Ukraine vic. Rovno
Apr–Aug 44	Defensive opns in Galicia
Aug 44	Disbanded

Commanders

Brig. Gen. Ujlaky, Oct 42–Aug 43
Brig. Gen. Ibrányi, Aug 43–Jan 44
Brig. Gen. Jószef Vasváry, Jan–Aug 44

19th Light Division (later 19th Reserve Division)

Jul 42–Jan 43	Defensive opns along the Don River bend vic. Marky; destroyed
Spring 43	Remnants withdrawn for reorganization
Aug 43	25th Light Division redesignated as 19th Reserve Division
Aug 43–Mar 44	Security and anti-partisan opns in Ukraine and Galicia
Mar–Apr 44	Defensive opns in Galicia
May 44	In Hungarian First Army Reserve
Aug 44	Disbanded

Commanders

Col. Deák, May–Aug 42
Col. Szász, Aug–Sep 42
Brig. Gen. Astalossy, Oct 42–Jun 43
Col. Kálmán, Aug 43–May 44
Brig. Gen. Miskey, May–Aug 44

20th Light Division (later 20th Infantry Division)

Aug–Sep 42	Offensive and defensive opns Eastern Front, southern sector vic. Karotyak bridgehead on Don River
Sep 42–Jan 43	Defensive opns along the Don River bend vic. Mastyugino; destroyed
Spring 43	Remnants withdrawn for reorganization
Mar 44	Reconstituted as 20th Infantry Division
Aug–Oct 44	Defensive opns in the Carpathian Mountains
Nov 44–Mar 45	Defensive and retrograde opns in western Hungary
Apr–May 45	Defensive and retrograde opns in northern Croatia

and southern Austria; capitulated to British forces in Carinthia

Commanders

Brig. Gen. Kovács, Aug 41–Aug 42
Col. Nagy, Aug–Oct 42
Brig. Gen. Frigyes Vasváry, Oct 42–Mar 43
Col. Németh, May–Aug 43
Brig. Gen. Frigyes Vasváry, Aug 43–Oct 44
Brig. Gen Tömöry, Oct 44–Mar 45
Brig. Gen. Tilger, Mar–May 45

21st Light Division (formerly 121st Security Division)

May–Oct 43	Security and anti-partisan opns in Ukraine
Oct 43–Apr 44	Security opns in Galicia and Ukraine
May 44	Dissolved; units absorbed by 18th Reserve Division

Commanders

Brig. Gen. Tarnay, May–Jun 43
Col. Pusztakürthy, Jun–Aug 43
Brig. Gen. Ehrlich, Aug 43–?44
Brig. Gen. Miskey, 44?–Mar 44
No officer assigned as commander, Mar–May 44

23d Light Division (later 23d Reserve Division)

Jul 42–Jan 43	Defensive opns along the Don River bend vic. Sahuny; destroyed
Spring 43	Remnants withdrawn for reorganization
Oct 43	Redesignated 23d Reserve Division
Sep 43–Sep 44	Security and defensive opns in Belorussia
Sep 44	Withdrawn to Hungary
Oct–Dec 44	Defensive and retrograde opns in western Hungary
Jan–May 45	Defensive and retrograde opns in Czechoslovakia and Austria; capitulated to American forces

Commanders

Brig. Gen. Kiss, Mar–Oct 42
Brig. Gen. Vargyassy, Oct 42–Jun 43
Brig. Gen. Dépold, Jun–Jul 43
Brig. Gen. Magyar, Jul–Jan 44
Col. Sövenyházi-Herdiczky, Jan–May 44
Brig. Gen. Deseö, May–Oct 44
Brig. Gen. Osztovics, Oct 44
Brig. Gen. Fehér, Nov 44–Apr 45
Col. Miklóssy, Apr–May 45

24th Light Division (formerly 124th Security Division; after Jan 44, 24th Infantry Division)

May–Aug 43	Security and anti-partisan opns in Ukraine
Aug 43	Disbanded
Jan 44	Mobilized in Hungary as 24th Infantry Division
Apr–May 44	Offensive and defensive opns in Galicia
May–Aug 44	Defensive and retrograde opns to the Hungarian frontier
Aug–Oct 44	Defensive and retrograde opns in the Carpathian Mountains
Nov–Dec 44	Defensive and retrograde opns in northern Hungary
Jan–May 45	Defensive and retrograde opns in Czechoslovakia; capitulated to Soviet forces

Commanders

Brig. Gen. Pintér, Aug 43–Jun 44
Brig. Gen. Markóczy, Jun–Oct 44
Col. Karlóczy, Oct–Nov 44
Col. Keresztes, Nov 44–Mar 45
Col. Rumy, Mar–May 45

25th Light Division (After Aug 43, redesignated as 19th Light Division, which see)

May–Aug 43	Security and anti-partisan opns in Ukraine
Aug 43	Renumbered as 19th Reserve Division

Commander

Brig. Gen. Kálmán, Aug 42–Aug 43

25th Infantry Division

Mar 44	Activated in Hungary
Apr–May 44	Offensive and defensive opns in Galicia
May–Aug 44	Defensive and retrograde opns to Hungarian frontier
Sep–Oct 44	Offensive, defensive, and retrograde opns against the Romanians and Soviets in Transylvania
Nov 44	Defensive and retrograde opns vic. Szolnok, Hungary
Dec 44	Defensive and retrograde opns in western Hungary
Jan–Mar 45	Defensive and retrograde opns vic. Lakes Balaton and Valence
Apr–May 45	Defensive and retrograde opns along the Drave and Mur Rivers; capitulated to Yugoslav partisans in northern Croatia

Commanders

Brig. Gen. Ibrányi, Mar–Jul 44
Brig. Gen. Kozma, Jul 44
Brig. Gen. Benda, Jul–Sep 44
Brig. Gen. Hollósy-Kuthy, Sep–Oct 44
Maj. Gen. Ferenc Horváth, Oct–Dec 44
Col. Kalkó, Dec 44–May 45

27th Light Division (later 27th Infantry Division)

Mar 44	Activated in Hungary and placed in reserve in Transylvania
Mar 44	In reserve positions in Transylvania
Apr 44	Defensive opns in the Carpathian Mountains
Apr 44	Offensive opns in Galicia vic. Zabie
Aug 44	Defensive opns in the Carpathian Mountains east of the Tartar Pass vic. Zabie
Sep–Oct 44	Defensive and retrograde opns in Transylvania
Nov 44	Reinforced and redesignated 27th Infantry Division

Dec 44–May 45	Defensive and retrograde opns in western Hungary and Austria; capitulated to Soviet forces

Commanders

Col. Zákó, Oct 43–Oct 44
Brig. Gen. Gyözö Horváth, Oct 44–May 45

102d Security Division (After May 43, 2d Light Division)

Spring 42	Security and defensive opns vic. Kharkov
Summer 42–May 43	Security and anti-partisan opns in Ukraine

Commanders

Brig. Gen. Bogányi, Oct 41–May 42
Brig. Gen. Dépold, May 42–May 43

105th Security Division (After May 43, 5th Light Division)

Feb 42–May 43	Security and anti-partisan opns in Ukraine

Commanders

Brig. Gen. Kollosváry, Mar 41–Oct 42
Brig. Gen Algya-Papp, Oct 42–May 43

108th Security Division (After May 43, 8th Light Division)

Feb–May 42	Security and defensive opns in Ukraine
May 42–May 43	Security and anti–partisan opns in Ukraine
Jun 43	Withdrawn to Hungary; absorbed by 9th Light Division

Commanders

Brig. Gen. Stemmer, Jan–Feb 42
Brig. Gen. Abt, Feb–Nov 42
Brig. Gen. Makay, Sep 42–Mar 43
Brig. Gen. Csiby, Mar–Jun 43

121st Security Division (After May 43, 21st Light Division)

Feb 42–May 43	Security and anti–partisan opns in Ukraine

Commanders

Brig. Gen. Tarnay, Feb 42–May 43

124th Security Division (After May 43, 24th Light Division)

Feb 42–   Security and anti-partisan
May 43   opns in Ukraine

Commanders

Brig. Gen. Sziklay, Aug 41–Oct 42
Brig. Gen. Széchy, Oct 42–May 43

201st Security Division (After May 43, 201st Light Division)

Dec 42–   Security and anti-partisan
Oct 43   opns in Ukraine
Oct 43–   Security and defensive
Mar 44   opns in Ukraine vic.
            Vinnitza and Berdichev
Mar–   Defensive and retrograde
May 44   opns in Galicia
May 44   Dissolved; units absorbed
            by 18th and 23d Reserve
            Divisions

Commanders

Brig. Gen. Vukováry, Nov 42–
   Jul 43
Col. Miskey, Jul 43–Jan 44
Brig. Gen Kisfaludy, Jan–May 44

St. László Division

Oct 44   Formed in Hungary
Dec 44   Defensive and retrograde
            opns vic. Esztergom,
            Hungary
Jan–   Defensive and retrograde
Mar 45   opns in western Hungary
Apr–   Defensive and retrograde
May 45   opns in northern Croatia
            and southern Austria;
            capitulated to British
            forces in Carinthia

Commander

Brig. Gen. Szügyi, Oct 44–May 45

Italian Units

All Italian units operated in the southern sector of the Eastern Front during their service in 1941–43.

3d Amedeo Duca D'Aosta Celere (Cavalry) Division

Home station: Verona
Jul 41   Campolung Romania
Aug 41   Offensive opns between the
            Dniestr and Bug rivers vic.
            Oligopol
Sep 41   Offensive opns along west
            bank of the Dniepr River
            vic. Dnieprodsershinsk
Nov 41   Advanced across the Mius
            River to Rykovo
Dec 41   Offensive and defensive
            opns southeast of Rykovo
            vic. Krestovka
Jan–   Defensive opns east of
Feb 42   Dnepropetrovsk
Mar 42   Defensive opns vic.
            Konstantinovka

Jul 42   Offensive opns toward
            Ivanovka and Krasnyj
            Luch
Aug 42   Offensive opns south of
            Don River vic. Jagodni
Nov–   Italian Eighth Army
Dec 42   reserve vic. Nikolskoye
Jan–   Defensive opns along Don
Feb 43   River; destroyed

Commander

Division General Marazzani

2d Tridentina Division (Alpine)

Home station: Merano
Nov–   Defensive opns along the
Dec 42   western bank of the Don
            River vic. Babka
Jan–   Defensive and retrograde
Feb 43   opns along the Don River
            between Rossosh and
            Millerovo

Commander

Brig. Gen. Reverberi

3d Julia Division (Alpine)

Home station: Udine

Nov–Dec 42	Defensive opns along the west bank of the Don River vic. Pavlosk
Jan–Feb 43	Defensive and retrograde opns vic. Don River between Rossosh and Millerovo; remnants returned to Italy

Commander

Division General Ricagno

4th Cuneese Division (Alpine)

Home station: Cuneo

Nov–Dec 42	Defensive opns along the west bank of the Don River vic. Nikolaivka
Jan–Feb 43	Defensive and retrograde opns along the Don River between Rossosh and Millerovo; destroyed; remnants returned to Italy

2d Sforzesca Division (Semi-Motorized)

Home station: Novara

Jul 42	Offensive opns east of Rykovo toward Ivanovka and Krasnyj Luch
Aug–Dec 42	Defensive opns along th Don River
Jan–Feb 43	Defensive opns along the Don River between Rossosh and Millerovo; destroyed; remnants returned to Italy

Commander

Division General Pellegrini

9th Pasubio Division (Semi-Motorized)

Home station: Verona

Jul 41	Sucuavo Romania
Aug 41	Offensive opns vic. Jsvorj on Dniester River and Voznesensk on Bug River
Sep 41	Defensive opns along the Orel River vic. Voinovka
Nov 41	Offensive opns vic. Gorlovka on Mius River

Dec 41	Offensive opns vic. Gorlovka and Klinisk; defensive opns vic. Rykovo
Jan–Feb 42	Defensive opns east of Dnepropetrovsk
Mar 42	Defensive opns vic. Konstantinovka
Jul 42	Offensive opns toward Utkino, east of Rykovo and Krasnaya Polyana
Aug 42	Defensive opns along the Don River
Nov–Dec 42	Defensive opns along the Don River
Jan–Mar 43	Defensive and retrograde along the Don River between Rossosh and Millerovo; destroyed; remnants returned to Italy

Commander

Brig. Gen. Olmi

52d Torino Division (Semi-Motorized)

Home station: Civitavecchia

Jul 41	Deployed vic. Falticeni, Romania
Aug 41	Deployed vic. Sorej, west of the Dnester River
Sep 41	Deployed east of the Dnepr River vic. Kamenka and Dnepropetrovsk
Nov 41	Redeployed from Yassninova to Krink
Dec 41	Offensive opns from Rykovo toward Chazepetovko; defensive opns vic. Rykovo
Jan–Feb 42	Defensive opns vic. Dnepropetrovsk
Mar 42	Defensive opns vic. Konstantinovka
Jul 42	Offensive opns east of Rykovo vic. Mius River
Aug 42	Defensive opns along the west bank of the Don River south of Buguchar
Sep–Dec 42	Defensive opns along the Don River vic. Paseka

Jan–
Feb 43   Defensive opns along the
Don River between
Rossosh and Millerovo;
destroyed; remnants
returned to Italy

Commander
Division General Lerici

11st Trieste Division (Semi-Motorized)

Home station: Piacenza

Jun 41   Offensive opns Eastern
Front, southern sector

Aug–
Sep 41   Transferred to North
Africa

3d Ravenna Division (Infantry)

Home station: Alessandria

Aug–
Sep 42   Defensive opns along the
west bank of the Don River
vic. Boguchar

Oct–
Dec 42   Defensive opns along the
Don River vic. Orechovo

Jan–
Feb 43   Defensive opns vic.
Orechovo; destroyed;
remnants returned to Italy

Commander
Division General Du Pont

5th Cosseria Division (Infantry)

Home station: Imperia

Aug–
Sep 42   Defensive opns along
the Don River vic.
Nikolayevka

Oct–
Dec 42   Defensive opns along
the Don River vic.
Deresovka

Jan–
Feb 43   Defensive opns vic.
Deresovka; destroyed
remnants withdrawn to
Italy

156th Vicenza Division (Infantry)

Home station: Brescia

Sep 42–
Feb 43   Defensive opns along the
Don River between
Millerovo and Rossosh;
destroyed

Commander
Corps General Brolia

Romanian Units

1st Armored Division

Jun–Dec 41 Offensive opns Eastern
Front, southern sector in
Bessarabia

Nov–
Dec 42   Offensive and defensive
opns Eastern Front, southern sector vic. Sredne-
Zarinski, Petrovka, and
the Chir River

Jan–
Mar 43   Rendered combat ineffec-
tive and withdrawn to
Romania

Aug–
Sep 44   Crossed the Moldava
River, captured by the
Soviets; some elements
participated in offensive
opns against the Germans
vic. the Ghimes Pass

Sep–
Nov 44   Offensive opns against the
Germans in Transylvania;
disbanded by the Soviets

Commanders
Brig. Gen. Sion, Jan 41–Jan 42
General–Division Gheorghe, Jan 42–
Mar 43
General–Division Stoenescu, Mar 43–
Apr 44
Brig. Gen. Korne, May–Sep 44

1st Armored Training Division

Aug–
Oct 44   Fought against German
forces vic. Baneasa,
Otopeni, and Ploesti

Nov 44   Disbanded by the Soviets

Commander
Col. Benedict, Sep 44

1st Cavalry Brigade (after Mar 42, redesignated as a "Division")

Jun–Oct 41	Offensive opns vic. Odessa
Nov 41–May 42	Security opns vic. Odessa
Jun–Oct 42	Offensive opns in Ukraine toward Stalingrad
Nov–Dec 42	Defensive opns south of Stalingrad, initially vic. Kletskaya
Dec 42–Jan 43	Retrograde and defensive opns; destroyed vic. Stalingrad
Mar 43	Remnants, rear echelon, returned to Romania to refit
Aug 44	Defensive opns vic. Dnestr River
Sep 44	Offensive opns against Axis forces forces in the Carpathian Mountains

Commanders
Brig. Gen. Manafu, Jan 41–Mar 42
Brig. Gen. Georgescu, Mar 42–Jun 42
Brig. Gen. Bratescu, Jul 42–Feb 43
Brig. Gen. Munteanu, Mar 43–Jul 44
Col. Constantinescu, Jul–Oct 44
Col. Talpes, Oct–Nov 44
Brig. Gen. Popescu, Dec 44–Jan 45

5th Cavalry Brigade (after Mar 42, redesignated as a "Division")

Jun–Jul 41	Offensive opns vic. Brinzeni, Ataki, and Mogilev
Aug–Sep 41	Offensive opns vic. Berislav and the Nogai Steppe toward Akimovka
Aug–Sep 42	Offensive opns from Rostov to Kuban River vic. Slavyanskaya, toward Nassurovo and Novorossiisk
Oct–Dec 42	Defensive opns south of Stalingrad
Jan–Jul 43	Withdrawn to Romania to refit

Commanders
No data

6th Cavalry Brigade (after Mar 42, redesignated as a "Division")

Jun–Jul 41	Offensive opns north of Bivolari and vic. Ripiceni, Movila Rupta, and Serbeni
Jul–Aug 41	Offensive opns vic. Alexandrovka, Odaya; established defensive positions vic. Gavrilovka
Sep–Oct 41	Defensive opns vic. Gavrilovka; offensive opns vic. Izvestia and Adamovista
Nov 41–Mar 42	Security opns vic. Mariupol to the mouth of Dnepr River
Mar–Jul 42	Coastal defense along the Sea of Azov vic. Berdyansk and Radionovka
Aug–Sep 42	Offensive opns in Ukraine vic. Rostov and Temruk, across the Kuban, to Varenkovskaya
Sep–Oct 42	Offensive opns on the Taman Peninsula; the Veselovska Isthmus; and the Caucasus Mountains; defensive opns southeast of Solmskaya and south of Ilskaya
Nov–Dec 42	Defensive opns vic. Azovskaya; security opns south of the Kuban River
Jan–Feb 43	Defensive opns vic. Krasnodar
Feb–Jul 43	Withdrawn and moved to the Black Sea coast vic. Anapskaya; defensive opns in the Kuban
Aug–Nov 43	Withdrawn from the Kuban to the Crimea; defensive opns in the Crimea
Dec 43–Apr 44	Defensive opns in the Crimea
Apr–May 44	Retrograde opns along the Kerch, Sudak, Sevastopol axis; heavy casualties; withdrawn to Romania to refit

Jun–
Nov 44   Security opns vic.
          Bucharest; disbanded
Commanders
General Racovita, Jun–Jul 41
Col. Munteanu, Jul–Aug 41
Col. Codreanu, Aug 41–Feb 42
Col. Cantuniar, Feb–Oct 42
General Teodorini, Oct 42–Jul 44
General Eftimiu, Jul 44–Sep 44
Col. Talpes, Sep–Oct 44

7th Cavalry Brigade (after Mar 42, redesignated as a "Division")

Jul–Aug 41   Offensive opns in Bessara-
              bia and security opns on
              the lower Nistru River
              along the Black Sea
Sep–
Oct 41   Offensive opns vic.
              Odessa
Nov 41–   Returned to Romania for
Sep 42   refit
Oct–   In Romanian Third Army
Nov 42   reserve west and south of
              Stalingrad
Nov–   Defensive opns south of
Dec 42   Staro Pronin; retrograde
              opns to Malakhov in
              Ukraine; defensive opns
              along the Chir River;
              retrograde and defensive
              opns vic. Morozovsk
Jan–   Withdrawn to Romania;
Mar 43   remnants merged with the
              1st Cavalry Division
Commanders
Col. Savoiu, Jul 41
Col. Cantuniar, Jul–Aug 41
Col. Râmniceanu, Aug–Oct 41
Col. Munteanu, Oct 41–Mar 43

8th Cavalry Brigade (after Mar 42, redesignated as a "Division")

Jun–Jul 41   Offensive opns vic.
              Brinzeni, Ataki and
              Mogilev
Aug–   Offensive opns vic. Beri-
Sep 41   slav and over the Nogai
              Steppe to Akimovka
Oct 41–   Offensive opns in the
Jul 42   Crimea

Nov–   Defensive opns vic. Aksai
Dec 42   River, south of Stalingrad;
              heavy casualties
Jan 43   Withdrawn to Romania
              for refitting
Oct 44–   Offensive opns against
May 45   Axis forces in Hungary
              and Czechoslovakia
Commanders
Col. Danescu, Jun–Oct 41
Col. Teodorini, Oct 41–May 42
Col. Carp, May 42–Jan 43
Brig. Gen. Korne, Jan 43–Apr 44
Brig. Gen. Vasile Mainescu, Apr–Jul 44
Brig. Gen. Teodorini, Jul–Oct 44
Col. Craciunescu, Nov 44
Brig. Gen. Fortunescu, Nov 44–Mar 45
Brig. Gen. Eftimiu, Mar–May 45

9th Cavalry Division (after Mar 42, redesignated as a "Division")

Aug–   Initially in Army reserve;
Oct 41   offensive opns vic. Odessa
Nov 41–   Refitted in Romania
Jul 42
Aug–   Offensive opns across
Sep 42   Ukraine from Rostov to
              the Kuban along the
              Slavyanskaya-Taman axis,
              defensive opns in the Cau-
              casus Mountains east of
              Gelendzhik
Oct 42–   Withdrawn from the Cau-
Oct 43   casus Mountains; defen-
              sive opns vic. the Kuban
              Peninsula until evacuated
              to the Crimea
Nov 43–   Defensive opns in the
May 44   Crimea vic. Sevastopol;
              evacuated by sea to
              Romania
Aug–   Offensive opns against
Oct 44   German forces in Romania
              vic. Timisoaro
Nov 44–   Offensive opns against
Jan 45   Axis forces in Hungary
              vic. Pest
Feb–   Offensive opns against
May 45   Axis forces in
              Czechoslovakia

Commanders

Lieutenant Col. Enescu, Aug 44

Maj. Gen. Popescu, Sep 44

1st Guards Division

Jun–Jul 41	Offensive opns vic. Bogdanesti
Jul–Oct 41	Offensive opns vic. Grigiriopol; offensive opns vic. Odessa
Nov 41– Dec 42	Redeployed to Romania
Dec 42– Mar 44	Defensive opns vic. Doroudja along the Black Sea
Mar–Jul 44	Defensive opns vic. Târgu Frumos, Moldavia
Aug– Sep 44	Defensive and retrograde opns along the Siret River, withdrawn over the Moldava River and encircled; remnants withdrawn to Bucharest
Jan– Apr 45	Reconstituted, deployed to Czechoslovakia against German forces

Commanders

General Teodorescu, Jun–Sep 40

General Georgescu, Sep 40–Jan 41

General–Division Sova, Jan 41–Feb 43

General Popescu, Feb–Apr 43

General–Division Voiculescu, Apr–Dec 43

Col. Popescu, Dec 43–Jan 44

General Korne, Jan–Mar 44

General–Division Niculescu-Cociu, Mar–Jun 44

General Opris, Jun–Jul 44

Brig. Gen. Antonescu, Jul–Oct 44

Brig. Gen. Ion Dumitru, Nov 44–Mar 45

Brig. Gen. Marinescu, Mar–Apr 45

1st Infantry Division

Sep–Oct 41	Offensive opns vic. Odessa, Kuanka
Nov– Dec 41	Security opns vic. Krivoi Rog
Jan 41– Feb 42	Defensive opns in Ukraine vic. Samoilovka
Feb– May 42	Offensive and defensive opns vic. Alexandrovka
May– Jun 42	Offensive opns in Ukraine across the Donets River
Jul–Aug 42	Offensive opns vic. Vasilyevka and toward Stalingrad
Sep– Nov 42	Conducted defensive opns vic. Lakes Barmanzak and Sarpa
Nov– Dec 42	Defensive opns south of Stalingrad vic. Plodovitoye and Aksai; destroyed
Jan– Mar 43	Remnants withdrawn to Romania
Apr– Aug 44	Reconstituted; defensive opns in Moldavia; capitulated

Commanders

Brig. Gen. Bârzotescu, Jun 40–Mar 42

Brig. Gen. Mihaescu, Mar–Apr 42

General-Division Panaitiu, Apr–Aug 42

Brig. Gen. Mihaescu, Aug 42–Mar 43

Brig. Gen. Saidac, Mar 43–Aug 44

2d Infantry Division

Sep–Oct 41	Offensive opns vic. Odessa
May 42	Offensive opns vic. Kharkov
Nov– Dec 43	Defensive opns south of Stalingrad; encircled and destroyed
Jan– Aug 43	Remnants withdrawn to Romania for refitting
Aug 44	Defensive opns in Bessarabia
Sep 44– May 45	Offensive opns against Axis forces in Hungary and Czechoslovakia

Commanders

No data

3d Infantry Division

Jul–Aug 41	Deployed to Bessarabia
Aug– Sep 41	Offensive opns vic. Ploska, Poniatovka, and vic. between Ostradovka and Brinovka

Sep–Oct 41   Offensive opns vic. Odessa; withdrawn for reconstitution in Romania.

Apr–Jul 44   Defensive opns in Moldavia; withdrawn after heavy losses

Aug–Oct 44   Offensive opns against German forces south of Ploesti; redeployed to Transylvania

Nov–Dec 44   Offensive opns against Axis forces in Hungary

Jan–May 45   Offensive opns against Axis forces in Czechoslovakia

Commanders

General Steflea, Feb 41–Jan 42
General Arhip, Jan–Feb 42
General Boibeanu, Feb 42–Mar 43
General Calotescu, Mar 43–Oct 44
General Dumitriu, Oct–Nov 44
General Popescu, Nov 44–Apr 45
General Tãnãsescu, Apr–May 45

4th Infantry Division

Sep 41–Mar 42   Security opns and in reserve vic. Odessa

Apr–May 42   Offensive opns vic. Andreevka

Jun–Jul 42   Offensive opns vic. Cervoni Sachter, Pristin, Krasni Oskol, and Krasnogusarovka

Aug–Oct 42   Offensive opns south of Tebektenerovo, defensive opns south of Tundutovo on the Kalmuck Steppe

Nov–Dec 42   Defensive and retrograde opns from vic. Sadevoye to vic. Kotelnikovo; heavy losses

Jan–Apr 43   Withdrawn and returned to Romania for refitting

Apr–Aug 44   Defensive opns in Moldavia; withdrawn and partly disarmed by the Soviets

Oct–Nov 44   Offensive opns against Axis forces in Hungary; heavy losses; disbanded

Commanders

General Cialâk, Feb 41–Aug 42
General Alinescu, Aug–Nov 42
General Dumitriu, Nov–Apr 43
General Mihãescu, Apr 43–Jul 44
General Petrescu, Jul–Sep 44
General Chirnoagã, Oct 44
General Voicu, Oct 44
Lieutenant Col. Ionescu, Nov–Dec 44

5th Infantry Division

Jun–Jul 41   Offensive opns in Bessarabia

Aug–Nov 41   Offensive opns vic. Odessa; withdrawn to Romania

Dec 41–Aug 42   Refitting in Romania

Sep–Oct 42   Defensive opns in the Don River bend east of Belosin

Nov–Dec 42   Defensive opns in the Don River bend

Jan–Mar 43   Remnants withdrawn for refitting vic. Odessa

Mar–Jun 44   Defensive opns vic. Balta

Jun–Jul 44   Defensive opns north of Podu Iloaiei

Aug–Nov 44   Conducted opns against German forces vic. Ploesti; disbanded

Commanders

General Vlãdescu, May 41–Feb 42
General Mazarini, Feb–Nov 42
General Nicolau, Mar 43–Oct 44

6th Infantry Division

Aug–Oct 41   Offensive opns vic. Odessa

Nov 41–Aug 42   Refitting in Romania

Sep–Oct 42   Defensive opns south of the Don River vic. Raspopinskaya

Nov–Dec 42   Defensive opns vic. Raspopinskaya; encircled and destroyed

Jan–Mar 43   Remnants returned to Romania for refitting

Sep 44–May 45	Offensive opns against Axis forces in Hungary and Czechoslovakia

Commanders

No data

7th Infantry Division

Jun–Jul 41	Defensive opns vic. Bucovina
Jul–Aug 41	Offensive opns vic. Hotin, Grigoriopol, and Kolosova, toward Odessa
Sep–Oct 41	Offensive opns vic. Odessa
Nov 41–Sep 42	Withdrawn to Romania for refitting
Oct–Nov 42	Established defensive positions along the Don River
Nov–Dec 42	Defensive opns vic. Gromok; retrograde opns to the Chir River, encircled and destroyed
Jan–Mar 43	Remnants withdrawn to Romania
Apr 43–Mar 44	Refitting in Romania
Apr–Sep 44	Defensive opns in Moldavia; retrograde opns to north of Vaslui toward Ploesti
Sep–Nov 44	Deployed to Transylvania and disbanded

Commanders

General-Division Stavrat, Jun 40–Aug 42

Brig. Gen. Trestioreanu, Aug 42–Mar 43

Brig. Gen. Poenaru, Mar 43–Apr 44

Brig. Gen. Filip, Apr–Sep 44 and Oct–Dec 44

Brig. Gen. Popescu, Sep-Oct 44

8th Infantry Division

Jun–Oct 41	Offensive opns vic. Odessa with heavy losses; returned to Romania to refit
Jul–Aug 44	Defensive opns vic. Bacau

Sep–Oct 44	Elements absorbed by other units

Commanders

No data

9th Infantry Division

Sep–Oct 42	Defensive opns along the Don River bend vic. Blinov
Nov–Dec 42	Offensive and defensive opns vic. the Don River bend; elements surrounded and destroyed west of the Krushka River
Mar 43–Aug 44	Reconstituted in Romania
Aug 44–May 45	Offensive opns against Axis forces in Hungary and Czechoslovakia

Commanders

Brig. Gen. Schwab, Jan 41–Jan 42

General-Division Panaitiu, Jan–Apr 42

Brig. Gen. Manafu, Apr–Aug 42

Brig. Gen. Panaitiu, Aug 42–Mar 43

General-Division Ionescu, Mar 43–Dec 44

Col. Iucal, May–Dec 44

Brig. Gen. Stanculescu, Jan 44–Mar 45

Col. Iucal, Mar–Apr 45

Brig. Gen. Stanculescu, Apr 45–Dec 45

10th Infantry Division

Aug–Oct 41	Offensive opns vic. Odessa
Apr–Jul 42	Offensive opns in the Crimea
Aug–Sep 42	Offensive opns across the Kerch Strait; offensive opns vic. Nassurovo and Novorossisk
Oct 42–Oct 43	Defensive opns along the southern coast of the Kuban Peninsula
Oct 43	Evacuated to the Crimea
Nov 43–May 44	Defensive opns in the Crimea west of the Perekop Isthmus and vic. Sevastopol; evacuated by sea to Romania

| Jun–Oct 44 | Refitting in Romania |
| Nov 44–May 45 | Offensive opns against Axis forces in Hungary and Czechoslovakia |

Commanders

No data

11th Infantry Division

Jun–Jul 41	Offensive opns toward Chisinow
Aug–Oct 41	Offensive opns vic. Odessa
Nov 41–Aug 42	Refitting in Romania
Sep–Oct 42	Defensive opns south of the Don River vic. the Kriushka River
Nov–Dec 42	Defensive opns in the Don River bend, retrograde opns to the Chir River; encircled and destroyed
Jan–Mar 43	Remnants used to form other units
Apr 43–Feb 44	Reformed
Mar–Aug 44	Defensive opns vic. Tirgu Frumos, Iassy, Chisinow
Sep 44–May 45	Offensive opns against Axis forces in Hungary and Czechoslovakia

Commanders

No data

13th Infantry Division

Jun–Jul 41	Offensive opns vic. Iassy and Soroca
Aug–Oct 41	Offensive opns vic. Odessa
Nov 41–Jul 42	Redeployed to Romania for refitting
Aug–Oct 42	Deployed vic. the Don River bend; defensive opns west of Kletskaya
Nov–Dec 42	Defensive opns vic. the Don River bend; part of division encircled and captured; another part of division conducted retro-

grade opns to the Chir River; heavy losses

Dec 42–Mar 44	Withdrawn, refitted and deployed to Moldavia north of Tecuci
May–Jul 44	Defensive opns south of Targu Frumos to east of Piatra Neamt
Aug–Sep 44	Capitulated south of Brosteni; disbanded

Commanders

General Rozin, Jan–Aug 41

General Zaharescu, Aug 41–Apr 42

General Ionescu-Sinaia, Apr 42–Mar 43

General Dimitriu, Mar 43–Sep 44

14th Infantry Division

Jun–Oct 41	Offensive opns vic. Odessa
Nov 41–Aug 42	Refitting in Romania
Sep–Oct 42	Defensive opns south of the Don River vic. Blinov
Nov–Dec 42	Defensive opns vic. Blinov in the Don River bend; heavy losses; remnants withrew south of the Chir River
Jan–Mar 43	Remnants returned to Romania to refit

Commanders

No data

15th Infantry Division

Jun–Oct 41	Offensive opns vic. Odessa
Nov 41–Aug 42	Returned to Romania for refit
Sep–Oct 42	Defensive opns south of the Don River vic. Gromki
Nov–Dec 42	Defensive opns vic. Gromki in the Don River bend; encircled; broke out toward Bolshaya Don-schinka sustaining heavy losses; remnants withdrew to south of the Chir River

Jan– Mar 43	Remnants returned to Romania for refitting
Dec 43	Security opns vic. lower Dnepr River
Aug 44	Coastal defense opns along Bessarabian coast vic. lower Dnestr River
Sep– Oct 44	Elements absorbed by other units

Commander

General Sion, Nov 42(?)

18th Infantry (redesignated a "Mountain Division" in mid-1942)

Jun– Oct 41	Offensive opns vic. Odessa
Nov 41– Jul 42	Offensive opns in the Crimea vic. Sevastopol
Nov– Dec 42	Defensive opns vic. Tinguta, south of Stalin- grad; encircled and destroyed
Jan– Mar 43	Remnants returned to Romania to refit
Jun 44	Defensive opns vic. Tirgu Frumos
Aug 44	In reserve vic. Prut River, counterattacked vic. Podul Iloaiei
Sep 44– May 45	Offensive opns against Axis forces in Hungary and Czechoslovakia

Commanders

Brig. Gen. Teodorescu, Jun–Sep 41
Brig. Gen. Costescu, Sep 41–Jan 42
Brig. Gen. Bāldescu, Jan 42–
  Apr 44
Brig. Gen. Pascu, Apr–Oct 44
Col. Gheorghiade, Oct 44
General-Division Camenida, Oct 44–
  Jan 45 and Feb–Apr 45
Brig. Gen. Corbuleanu, Jan–
  Feb 45
Brig. Gen. Paraschivescu, Apr 45
General-Division Alexiu, Apr–
  May 45
General-Division Cosma, May 45

1st Mountain Brigade (after Mar 42, redesignated as a "Division")

Jun–Jul 41	Deployed west of Radauti
Jul–Aug 41	Offensive opns vic. Cer- nauti; Revna, and west of Mogilev
Aug– Sep 41	Offensive opns fic. Balta and Kryvoe Lake; crossed the Bug vic. Konstantinov ka, then advanced to Dnepr River vic. Berislav
Sep– Oct 41	Crossed the Dnepr River vic. Berislav; defensive opns on the Nogai Steppe north of the Sea of Azov
Oct– Nov 41	Defensive opns vic. Timosevka; offensive opns vic Czernigovka and advanced to the Salkvo Isthmus; established defensive positions
Nov 41– Jul 42	Offensive opns in the Crimea vic. Sevastopol and Balaklava
Jul– Aug 42	Security opns in the Iaila Mountains
Sep 42– Jun 43	Coastal defense opns between Jalta and Feo- dosia; deployed between Sudak and Alusta
Jul– Aug 43	Defensive opns vic. the Kuban Peninsula vic. Novorossisk
Sep 43– Apr 44	Withdrawn to the Crimea; defensive opns along the southern coast; security and anti-partisan opns
Apr– May 44	Withdrawn to Sevastopol; defensive opns; evacuated by sea to Romania
May– Aug 44	Refitted south of Brasov
Sep– Nov 44	Conducted opns in Transylvania against Hungarian forces; disbanded

Commanders

Brig. Gen. Lascar, Jan 41–Feb 42

Brig. Gen. Vasiliu-Rascanu, Feb 42–
Oct 43

Brig. Gen. Voiculescu, Oct 43–
May 44

Brig. Gen. Beldiceanu, May–
Oct 44

2d Mountain Brigade (after Mar 42, redesignated as a "Division")

Jun–Jul 41	Offensive opns in Bucovina vic. Tarnauca
Jul–Aug 41	Offensive opns vic. Odessa, blocked Soviet attacks vic. Svaniec
Aug–Sep 41	Offensive opns vic. Mogilev, Voznesensk, and the Bug River
Sep–Nov 41	Offensive opns across the Dniepr River; offensive and defensive opns vic. Nikopol and Novo Grigirievka
Dec 41–Jun 42	Returned to Romania for refitting
Jul–Aug 42	Deployed to the Kuban Peninsula south of Piatigorsk
Sep–Oct 42	Offensive opns across the Baksan River to vic. Nalchik in the Caucasus Mountains
Nov–Dec 42	Offensive and defensive opns west of Vladikavkaz in the Caucasus Mountains
Dec 42–Mar 43	Retrograde opns to Nalchik, then to the Kuban River; defensive opns in the Kuban until evacuated to the Crimea
Apr–Sep 43	Security opns in the Crimea
Sep 43–Mar 44	Defensive opns and anti-partisan opns in the Crimea
Apr–May 44	Defensive opns vic. Sevastopol; withdrawn
Jun–Aug 44	Refitting
Aug 44	Offensive opns against German forces vic. Deva

Commanders

General-Division Dumitrache, Oct 40–
Aug 44

Col. Bartolomeu, Aug–Sep 44

Brig. Gen. Iordachescu, Sep 44–
May 45

3d Mountain Brigade (after Mar 42, redesignated as a "Division")

Jan–Aug 42	Security opns west of the Dnepr River
Sep–Oct 42	Offensive opns from Rostov to the Caucasus Mountains north of Gelendzhik, offensive opns vic. Novorossiisk
Oct 42–Oct 43	Retrograde opns from the Caucasus Mountains; defensive opns in the Kuban Peninsula
Oct 43	Evacuated to the Crimea
Nov 43–May 44	Defensive opns in the Crimea vic. Sevastopol; severe losses; withdrawn by sea to Romania
Jun–Oct 44	Refitting in Romania; offensive opns against the Hungarians vic. Finata
Nov 44–May 45	Offensive opns against Axis forces in Hungary and Czechoslovakia

Commanders

General–Division Leonard, Aug 44–
Apr 45

General-Division Demetrescu, Apr–
Jun 45

4th Mountain Brigade (after Mar 42, redesignated as a "Division")

Jun–Jul 41	Offensive opns in Bucovina and across the Dnestr River

Apr–Jul 42	Offensive opns in the Crimea vic. Sevastopol
Aug 42–Jul 43	Security and anti-partisan opns vic. the Kerch Peninsula
Aug–Sep 43	Defensive opns on the Kuban Peninsula
Sep–Nov 43	Withdrawn to the Crimea; security opns vic. the Nogai Steppe
Aug 44	Defensive opns on the Dnestr River; heavy casualties

Sep 44	Remnants absorbed by other units

Commanders

No data

103d Mountain Division

Sep–Oct 44	Formed from various elements by the Soviets; offensive opns in northern Transylvania against the Germans; disbanded

Commander

General Cretulescu

Soviet Forces
on the Eastern Front

Directions

Directions were an operational-strategic, command and control echelon, comparable to German or US Army Groups, established by the Soviets to direct the operation of groups of fronts and fleets. Directions were employed primarily during the first year of the war in the strategic defense.

After 1942, the Soviet High Command occasionally formed temporary headquarters under Stavka representatives, most notably Marshals Zhukov, Vasilevsky, and Timoshenko, to coordinate the actions of multiple fronts in particularly complex or important situations.

The first directions were created on 10 July 1941, facing each of the major German strategic axes in Operation BARBAROSSA.

The Northwestern Direction, commanded by Marshal K. M. Voroshilov, coordinated defensive operations along the Leningrad axis from 10 July to 27 August 1941, after which it was disbanded.

The Western Direction defended the approaches from Smolensk to Moscow from 10 July to 10 September 1941 under Marshal Timoshenko. It was reestablished under then-General Zhukov from 1 February to 5 May 1942.

The Southwestern Direction remained in existence the longest, from 10 July 1941 to 21 June 1942. The initial CINC, Marshal Budyonny, proved unequal to the task and was replaced by Marshal Timoshenko in September 1941.

The *Stavka* established a fourth direction in 1945, the Far East Direction (30 July–20 December 1945), under Marshal Vasilevsky, as the operational-strategic high command for the Manchurian Offensive against the Japanese Kwantung Army.

Fronts

Fronts were large enough to conduct their own large, independent operations, but were more often combined into groups of two to four for the major campaigns of the Soviet-German war. Depending on the period of the war, Stavka maintained 10–15 front formations. By the third period of the war in Soviet reckoning (1944–45), a front typically contained 5–9 combined arms armies, 1–3 tank armies, 1–2 air armies, 2–5 separate tank or mechanized corps, 1–2 cavalry corps, plus large artillery formations and other supporting units. Troop strength rose as high as 800,000 (for example, in the Vistula-Oder, East Prussia, and Berlin operations).

Baltic Front
(Oct–Oct 43, then became 2d Baltic Front)

Ten days of offensive opns against Army Group North
Commander
Army Gen. M. M. Popov

1st Baltic Front
(Oct 43–Feb 45)

1943	Primary front in the Vitebsk-Polotsk and Gorodok opns
44–45	Primary front in the Polotsk, Shyaulyai, and Memel offensive opns; participated in the Vitebsk-Orsha, Riga (1944), and East Prussian opns (1945)

Commanders
Army Gen. A. I. Yeremenko, Oct–Nov 43
Army Gen. Bagramian, Nov 43–Feb 45

2d Baltic Front
(Oct 43–Apr 45)

1943	Vitebsk-Polotsk offensive
44–45	Participated in Leningrad-Novgorod and Riga opns (1944) and destroyed enemy groupings within the Kurland pocket (1945)

Commanders
Army Gen. M. M. Popov, Oct 43–Apr 44; Feb 45
Army Gen. A. I. Yeremenko, Apr 44–Feb 45
Marshal L. A. Govorov, Feb–Mar 45

3d Baltic Front
(Apr–Oct 44)

Primary front in the Pskov-Ostrov and Tartus opns; participated in the capture of Riga
Commander
Army Gen. I. I. Maslennikov

Belorussian Front

1st est. Oct 43–Feb 44, then became the 1st Belorussian Front
2d est. Apr 44, then again became 1st Belorussian Front (2d est.)

1943	Gomel-Rechitsa offensive operation
1944	Kalinkov-Mozyr offensive operation

Commander
Army Gen. K. K. Rokossovsky

1st Belorussian Front

1st est. formed from Belorussian Front: Feb–Apr 44
2d est. Apr 44–Jun 45, again formed from Belorussian Front

44–45	Primary front in the Rogachev-Zhlobin,

Legend: CC–cavalry corps; CD–cavalry division; MC–mechanized corps; MD–military district; MRD–motorized rifle division; RC–rifle corps; RD–rifle division; TA–tank army; TB–tank brigade; TC–tank corps; TD–tank division.

Bobruisk, Lublin-Brest and Warsaw-Poznan offensive opns; participated in Belorussian, Vistula-Oder, and Berlin campaigns

Commanders

Army Gen. K. K. Rokossovsky, Feb–Nov 44

Marshal G. K. Zhukov, Nov 44–Jun 45

2d Belorussian Front

1st est. Feb 44–Apr 44

2d est. Apr 44–Jun 45

44–45 Primary front in the Mogilev, Belostok, Osobets, Mlava-Elbing opns; participated in the Belorussian, East Pomeranian, East Prussian, and Berlin campaigns

Commanders

Gen. Col. P. A. Kurochkin, Feb–Apr 44

Gen. Col. I. E. Petrov, Apr–Jun 44

Army Gen. G. F. Zakharov, Jun–Nov 44

Marshal K. K. Rokossovsky, Nov 44–Jun 45

3d Belorussian Front

(Apr 44–Aug 45)

44–45 Primary front in the Kaunass, Gumbinnen, Insterberg-Königsberg, and Zemland opns; participated in the Belorussian, Memel, and East Prussian campaigns

Commanders

Army Gen. I. D. Chernyakovsky, Apr 44–Feb 45

Marshal A. M. Vasilevsky, Feb–Apr 45

Army Gen. I. X. Bagramian, Apr–Aug 45

Briansk Front

1st est. Aug–Nov 41

2d est. Dec 41–Mar 43, then became the Reserve Front

3d est. Mar–Oct 43, then became the Baltic Front

1941 Orel-Briansk defensive operation

1943 Briansk, Voronezh-Kastornoe, Orel offensive opns

Commanders

Gen. Lt. A. I. Eremenko, Aug–Oct 41

Gen. Major G. F. Zakharov, Oct–Nov 41

Gen. Col. Ya. T. Cherevichenko, Dec 41–Apr 42

Gen. Lt. F. I. Golikov, Apr–Jul 42

Gen. Lt. N. E. Chibisov, Jul 42

Gen. Lt. K. K. Rokossovsky, Jul–Sep 42

Gen. Col. M. A. Reiter, Sep 42–Mar 43; Mar–Jun 43

Gen. Col. M. M. Popov, Jun–Oct 43

Caucasus Front

(Dec 41–Jan 42, then became the Crimean Front)

1942 Kerch-Feodosia defensive operation

Commander

Gen. Lt. D. T. Kozlov

Central Front

1st est. Jul–Aug 41

2d est. Feb–Oct 43, then became the Belorussian Front

1941 Smolensk defensive battle

1943 Participated in the Battle of Kursk; primary front in the Chernigov-Pripyat offensive operation

Commanders

Gen. Col. F. I. Kuznetsov, Jul–Aug 41

Gen. Lt. M. G. Yefremov, Aug–Aug 41

Army Gen. K. K. Rokossovsky, Feb–Oct 43

Crimean Front

(Jan–May 42)

Front forces were defeated in the defense of Crimea and evacuated

Commander

Gen. Lt. D. T. Kozlov

Don Front
(Sep 42–Feb 43, formed from the first Stalingrad Front, then became the Central Front)

1942   Defensive battles vic. Stalingrad and the Stalingrad counteroffensive
1943   Operation RING, the elimination of the encircled German 6th Army

Commanders
Gen. Col. K. K. Rokossovsky

Far Eastern Front
(pre-war to Aug 45, then became the 2d Far Eastern Front)

Defensive posture throughout war; source of units and equipment

Commanders
Army Gen. P. Apanasenko, Jun–Apr 45
Army Gen. M.A. Purkayev, Apr–Aug 45

1st Far Eastern Front
(Aug 45–Sep 45)

Harbin-Girin offensive operation during the Manchurian Campaign

Commander
Marshal K. A. Meretskov

2d Far Eastern Front
(Aug 45–Sep 45)

Sungari offensive opns during the Manchurian Campaign

Commander
Army Gen. M. A. Purkayev

Kalinin Front
(Oct 41–Oct 43, then became the 1st Baltic Front)

41–42   Defense of Kalinin; counteroffensive in Kalinin region
42–43   Offensive and defensive opns vic. Sychevka-Viazma, Velikie Luki, Dukhovshchina, Nevel, Rzhev-Sychevka, Rzhev-Viazma, Smolensk opns

Commanders
Gen. Col. I. S. Konev, Oct 41–Aug 42
Gen. Col. M. A. Purkayev, Aug 42–Apr 43
Army Gen. A. I. Yeremenko, Apr–Oct 43

Karelian Front
(Sep 41–Nov 44)

41–44   Defensive posture
1944   Svir-Petrozavodsk and Petsamo-Kirkenes offensive opns

Commanders
Gen. Col. V. A. Frolov, Sep 41–Feb 44
Marshal K. A. Meretskov, Feb–Nov 44

Kursk Front
(Mar 43, then became the Orel Front, also a temporary front)

No operations, a temporary formation

Commander
Col. General M. A. Reiter

Leningrad Front
(Aug 41–May 45)

41–44   Battle and siege of Leningrad
44–45   Participated in Baltic offensive operation and blockade of Kurland

Commanders
Gen. Lt. M. M. Popov, Jun–Sep 41
Marshal K. E. Voroshilov, Sep 41
Army Gen. Zhukov, Sep–Oct 41
Gen. Major I. I. Fedyuninsky, Oct 41
Gen. Lt. M. S. Khozin, Oct 41–Jun 43
Marshal L. A. Govorov, Jun 43–May 45

Maritime Group of Forces
(Apr–May 45, then became the 1st Far Eastern Front)

No opns. Group of Forces deployed from Baltic region to the Far East

Commander
Marshal K. A. Meretskov

North Caucasus Front

1st est. May–Sep 42, then became the Caucasus Front

2d est. Jan–Nov 43

1942	Defensive opns on the lower Don and defense of approaches to Stalingrad; Armavir-Maikop and Novorossiisk opns
1943	Krasnodar, Novorossiisk-Taman, Kerch-Eltigen, North Caucasus, and Malaya Zemlya opns

Commander

Marshal S. M. Budyonny, May–Sep 42

Gen. Col. I. I. Maslennikov, Jan–May 43

Gen. Lt. I. E. Petrov, May–Nov 43

Northern Front

(24 Jun–26 Aug 41, then dissolved into Leningrad and Karelia Fronts)

Border battles in the north, in Karelia, and the Kola Peninsula

Commander

Gen. Lt. M. M. Popov

Northwestern Front

(Jun 41–Nov 43)

1941	Border battles in the Northwestern Direction and defense of Leningrad
42–43	Toropets-Kholm, Staraia-Russa, and Demiansk opns

Commanders

Gen. Col. F. I. Kuznetsov, Jun–Jul 41

Gen. Major Sobennikov, Jul–Aug 41

Gen. Col. P. A. Kurochkin, Aug 41–Oct 42; Jun–Nov 43

Marshal S. K. Timoshenko, Oct 42–Mar 43

Gen. Col. I. S. Konev, Mar–Jun 43

Reserve Front

1st est. Jul–Oct 41

2d est. Mar 43, then became the Kursk Front

3d est. 10 Apr–15 Apr 43, then became the Steppe Front

Established to receive and organize reserve armies deployed to the rear of the Western Front as Army Group Center advanced. Participated in the Yelnin and Moscow defensive opns. In Oct 41, combined with the Western Front. Second and third establishments were temporary formations

Commanders

Army Gen. Zhukov, Jul–Sep 41

Marshal S. M. Budyonny, Oct 41

Gen. Col. M. A. Reiter, Mar 43

Gen. Col. M. M. Popov, Apr 43

Southeastern Front

(Aug 42–Sep 42)

Formed out of Stalingrad Front, then became the Stalingrad Front (2d est.) Defense against Axis forces on the approaches to Stalingrad

Commander

Gen. Col. A. I. Yeremenko

Southern Front

1st est. Jun 41–Jul 42

2d est. (formed from Stalingrad Front): Jan–Oct 43

1941	Border battles in southern Ukraine; defended Odessa; conducted the defense and successful counteroffensive at Rostov-on-Don
1942	Participated in the Donbas, Barvenko-Lozovaia, Voronezh-Volgograd opns. Suffered a notable failure in 2d Battle of Kharkov, May 42

Commanders

Army Gen. I. V. Tyulenev, Jun–Aug 41

Gen. Lt. D. I. Ryabishev, Aug–Oct 41

Gen. Col. Ya. T. Cherevichenko, Oct–Dec 41

Gen. Lt. R. Ya. Malinovsky, Dec 41–Jul 42; Feb–Mar 43

Gen. Col. A. I. Yeremenko, Jan–Feb 43

Army Gen. F. I. Tolbukhin, Mar–Oct 43

Southwestern Front
(formed from the Kiev
Special Military District)

1st est. Jun 41–Jul 42, then became the
Stalingrad Front
2d est. Oct 42–Oct 43, then became the
3d Ukrainian Front

1941	Conducted defensive tank battles at Dubno, Lutsk, Rovno, defensive opns at Kiev and Elets
1942	Participated in the Uman, Donbas, Barvenko-Lozo-vaia, and Voronezh-Voroshilovgrad opns
42–43	Second establishment conducted the Middle Don operation (1942) and participated in 3d Battle of Kharkov, Ostrogozhsk-Rossosh, Donbas, and Zaporozhe opns

Commanders
General M. P. Kirponos, Jun–Sep 41
Marshal S. K. Timoshenko, Sep–
 Dec 41; Apr–Jul 42
General F. Ya. Kostenko, Dec 41–
 Apr 42
Army Gen. N. F. Vatutin, Oct 42–
 Mar 43
Army Gen. R. Ya. Malinovsky,
 Mar–Oct 43

Stalingrad Front
1st est. Jul 42–Sep 42
2d est. Sep–Dec 42, then became
Southern Front
Defensive opns on the approaches to
Stalingrad, divided into the Southeast-
ern and Stalingrad Fronts on 7 Aug,
transformed into the Don and South-
western Fronts on 28 Sep with the
Southeastern Front becoming the Stal-
ingrad Front; conducted the defense of
Stalingrad and the Operation URANUS
counteroffensive (Nov–Dec 42)
Commanders
Marshal S. K. Timoshenko, Jul–Jul 42
Gen. Lt. V. N. Gordov, Jul–Aug 42

Gen. Col. A. I. Yeremenko, Aug–
 Dec 42

Steppe Front
(Jul–Oct 43, then became
2d Ukrainian Front)
Participated in the Battle of Kursk,
then the Belgorod-Kharkov offensive
Commander
Army Gen. I. S. Konev

Transbaikal Front
(Sep 41–Sep 45)
Defeat of the Japanese Army in Man-
churia, seizure of Xingan and Mukden
Commanders
Gen. Col. M. P. Kovalev, Sep 41–Jul 45
Marshal P. Ya. Malinovsky, Jul–Sep 45

Transcaucasus Front
1st est. Aug–Dec 41, then became the
Caucasus Front
2d est. May 42–May 45

1941	No opns
1942	Conducted a series of defensive battles: Mozdok-Malgobek, Nalchik-Ordzhonikidze, Novorossiisk, and Tuapse
43–45	No significant opns

Commanders
Gen. Lt. D. T. Kozlov, **1st est.**
Army Gen. I. V. Tyulenev, 2d est.

1st Ukrainian Front
(Oct 43–Jun 45, created
from the Voronezh Front)

1943	Primary front in the Kiev offensive and defensive opns
43–45	Primary front in Zhitomir-Berdichev, Rovno-Lutsk, Proskurov-Chernovtsy, Lvov-Sandomir, Sando-mir-Silesia, Lower and Upper Silesia opns; participated in offensive opns on the Dnepr (Left and Right Bank Ukraine),

Korsun-Shevchenkovskii,
Vistula-Oder, Berlin, and
Prague

Commanders

Army Gen. N. F. Vatutin, Oct 43–
Mar 44

Marshal G. K. Zhukov, Mar–May 44

Marshal I. S. Konev, May 44–May 45

2d Ukrainian Front
(Oct 43–Jun 45, created
from the Steppe Front)

1943   Left and Right Bank
Ukraine opns

1944   Primary front in the Kirovograd, Uman-Botoshany,
Debrecen opns; participated in Korsun-Shevchen-
kovsy and Iassy-Kishinev

1945   Participated in opns in
Hungary and the seizure
of Budapest and Prague

Commanders

Marshal I. S. Konev, Oct 43–May 44

Marshal R. Ya. Malinovsky, May 44–
Jun 45

3d Ukrainian Front
(Oct 43–Jun 45, formed
from the Southwestern Front)

1943   Left and Right Bank Bereznegovatoye-Snigirovka,
Dnepropetrovosk, Ukraine

44-45   Nikopol-Krivoi Rog,
Odessa, Iassy-Kishinev,
Belgrade, Budapest, Lake
Balaton

Commanders

Army Gen. R. Ya. Malinovsky, Oct 43–
May 44

Army Gen. F. I. Tolbukhin, Apr–
Jun 45

4th Ukrainian Front
1st est. Oct 43–May 44, formed from
Southern Front
2d est. Aug 44–Jul 45

1943   Primary front in the Melitopol operation

1944   With Separate Maritime
Army liberated Crimea;
participated in opns in
East and West Carpathia

1945   Seizure of Prague

Commander

Army Gen. F. I. Tolbukhin, Oct 43–
May 44

Army Gen. I. E. Petrov, Aug 44–
Mar 45

Army Gen. A. I. Yeremenko, Mar–
Jul 45

Volkhov Front
1st est. Dec 41–Apr 42
2d est. Jun 42–Feb 44

1942   Participated in the Siniavino, Lubansk opns

1943   With Leningrad Front,
lifted blockade of
Leningrad

1944   Participated in the Nov-
gorod-Luga operation

Commander

Army Gen. K. A. Meretskov

Voronezh Front
(Jul 42–Oct 43, then became the
1st Ukrainian Front)

1942   Participated in the Voronezh-Voroshilovgrad opn

1943   Primary front in the Ostrogozhsk-Rossosh and
Kharkov opns of early 43;
participated in the Kursk
defense, then the Belgo-
rod-Kharkov offensive

Commanders

Gen. Lt. F. I. Golikov, Jul 42; Oct 42–
Mar 43

Army Gen. N. F. Vatutin, Jul–Oct 42;
Mar–Oct 43

Western Front
(Jun 41–Apr 44, then became the
3d Belorussian Front)

1941   Border battles in summer
of 1941, Smolensk defen-
sive battle, Moscow

1942   Rzhev-Sychevka operation
1943   Rzhev-Viazma, Orel,
        Smolensk, Spas-Demiansk

Commanders

Army Gen. D. G. Pavlov, Jun 41
    (relieved and executed)
Gen. Lt. A. I. Yeremenko, Jun–Jul 41
    and Jul 41
Marshal S. K. Timoshenko, Jul 41;
    Jul–Sep 41

Gen. Col. I. S. Konev, Sep–Oct 41 and
    Aug 42–Feb 43
Army Gen. G. K. Zhukov, Oct 41–
    Aug 42 (continued as Stavka
    representative)
Army Gen. V. D. Sokolovsky, Feb 43–
    Apr 44
Gen. Col. I. D. Chernyakovsky,
    Apr 44

Armies

Combined Arms Armies

Combined arms armies were the basic fighting formations of the USSR during the war. Their composition varied greatly depending on the period of the war and the tasks assigned to the army. Armies typically did not remain with a single front, but were often transferred from one to the other. Those armies that distinguished themselves in battle were awarded the honorific of *Guards.* Shock armies were formed in the first half of the war for the primary purpose of overcoming difficult defensive dispositions in order to create a tactical penetration of sufficient breadth and depth to permit the commitment of mobile formations for deeper exploitation.

1st Guards Army

Aug 42   Formed on the base of the
         2d Reserve Army, compris-
         ing five Guards RDs; par-
         ticipated in the Battle of
         Stalingrad as part of the
         Stalingrad and Don Fronts
Oct 42   Disbanded; formations and
         units distributed to 24th
         Army and the command
         staff formed the Southwest-
         ern Front headquarters
Dec 42   Second establishment,
         formed from 63d Army,

including the 1st and 6th Guards RCs, 1st Guards MC, and three RDs. The reformed army participated briefly in the Battle of Stalingrad as part of the Southwestern Front, then converted to the 3d Guards Army

Dec 42   The Army was established a third time, again as part of the Southwestern Front. Command-staff provided from the 4th Reserve Army Forces: 4th and 6th Guards RCs and 18th TC

42–45   As part of the Voronezh, Southwestern, and 4th Ukrainian Fronts, the army took part in a series of offensives including: the Donbas (in early 43), Izyum-Barvenkovo, Left Bank Ukraine, Zhitomir-Berdichev, Proskurov-Chernovits, Lvov-Sandomir, East and West Carpathia, and Prague

Commanders

Seven commanders. Notable: Gen. Col. (future Marshal, Commander in Chief Ground Forces, and Minister of Defense) A. A. Grechko (44–45)

1st Red Banner Army

Jul 38	Formed in the Red Banner Far Eastern Front as the 1st Maritime Army, renamed as the 1st Separate Red Banner Army. Received its final designation as 1st Red Banner Army in Jul 40. Performed readiness and defensive functions during the course of the war in the west
Aug 45	Comprised of six RDs, three TBs, and three tank regiments, the army took part in the Harbin-Girin offensive against Japanese Kwantung Army in Manchuria as part of the 1st Far Eastern Front

Commanders
Three commanders

1st Shock Army

Nov 41	Formed in Stavka reserve from remnants of the 19th Army. Initial composition: eight separate rifle brigades and other units. Participated in the Battle of Moscow as part of the Western Front
42–44	Assigned to a variety of northern fronts, the army took part in the Demiansk, Leningrad-Novgorod, Pskov-Ostrov, Tartu, and Riga offensive opns
1945	Participated in the blockade of the Kurland peninsula

Commanders
Six commanders

2d Guards Army

Oct 42	Formed as part of the Stavka reserve; included the 1st, 13th Guards RC, and 2d Guards MC

42–43	Part of the Don and Stalingrad Fronts. Fought in the Battle of Stalingrad. Defense of the Mius River. As part of the Southern Front, participated in Donbas and Melitopol opns, then deployed to Perekop
Apr–May 44	Liberation of the Crimea
May–Jun 44	Redeployed to the north and joined the 1st Baltic Front; composition now included the 11th and 13th Guards and 54th RCs. Took part in the Shyaulyai and Memel offensive operations, then joined the 3d Belorussian Front
1945	Participated in the East Prussian offensive

Commanders
Four commanders. Notable: Marshal Rodion Ya. Malinovsky, Nov 42–Feb 43; and Army Gen. G. F. Zakharov, 43–44

2d Red Banner Army

Jul 38	Formed as 2d Army within the Red Banner Far East Front, renamed the 2d Red Banner Separate Army
Jul 40	Renamed as 2d Red Banner Army
41–45	Security opns in border areas; Stavka reserve as part of the 2d Far Eastern Front, participated in the Sungari offensive operation

Commander
Gen. Lt. M. F. Terekhin

2d Shock Army

Dec 41	Formed from the 26th Army in the Volkhov Front; composition included the 327th RD and 8 separate rifle brigades

1942	Took part in Lubansk and Siniavino battles
Jan 43	Participated in offensive opns to break the blockade at Leningrad. New composition included 12 RDs and 8 separate rifle, tank, and mobile brigades
Feb–Sep 43	Rotated between the Leningrad and Volkhov Fronts in defensive opns
Nov 43–Jan 44	Opns at the Oranienbaum bridgehead
1944	Offensive opns at Krasnosel, Ropshin, Narva, Tallinn, then placed in Stavka reserve in Sep 44
Oct 44	Joined 2d Belorussian Front through the end of the war; participated in Mlava-Elbing, East Pomeranian, Berlin offensives

Commanders

Four commanders. Notable: Army Gen. I. I. Fedyuninsky, 44–45

3d Army

1939	Formed in the Belorussian Special MD from the Vitebsk army operational group of forces. Participated in the occupation of western Belorussia in connection with the partition of Poland
Jun 41	Composition included the 4th RC and 11th MC. Fought defensive battles in 1941 at Grodno, Lida, and Novogrudok; enveloped, broke out, reformed in the Stavka reserve and re-equipped
Aug 41	As part of the Central, then Briansk Fronts, took part in the defense of Smolensk and Moscow
42–43	Defended vic. Orel

Jul 43–Feb 44	Transferred between a series of fronts, took part in offensive opns at Orel, Briansk, Gomel-Rechitsa, and Rogachev-Zhlobin
Summer 1944	Participated in the Belorussian Campaign.
1945	East Prussian and Berlin offensive opns

Commanders

Seven commanders

3d Guards Army

Dec 42	Formed in the Southwestern Front from the 14th RC, four RDs, 1st Guards MC, three separate brigades, and and three tank regiments
43–44	Assigned, in sequence, to the Southwestern, 3d, 4th, and 1st Ukrainian Fronts. Took part in Middle Don and Voroshilovgrad offensive opns, battles on northern Donets River, Donbas and Zaporozhe offensives. Later fought at Nikopol bridgehead, Nikopol-Krivoi Rog, Proskurov-Chernovits, and Lvov-Sandomir offensive opns
1945	Took part in offensive opns in Sandomir-Silesia, Lower Silesia, Berlin, and Prague

Commanders

Four commanders. Notable: Gen. Lt. (future front commander) V. N. Gordov

3d Shock Army

Dec 41	Formed from the 60th Army and placed initially in Stavka reserve. Consisted of three RDs and six separate brigades

| 42–43 | Assigned to a series of fronts. Participated in Toropets-Kholm, Velikie Luki, Nevel, and Rezhitsa-Dvina opns |
| 44–45 | Offensive opns at Madon and Riga. Participated in the Kurland blockade, Warsaw-Poznan, East Pomeranian and Berlin opns |

Commanders

Six commanders. Notable: Army Gen. M. A. Purkayev

4th Army

Aug 39	Formed in the Belorussian Special Military District from the Bobruisk army group. Took part in the partition of Poland
Jun 41	Assigned to the Western Front, comprising the 28th RC and 14th MC. Defended in the Brest Direction and the left bank of the Sozh River, vic. Propoisk (Slavgorod)
Jul 41	Disbanded. Command-staff formed the base of the Central Front headquarters
Sep 41	Reformed with three RDs and the 27th CD. Deployed to the right bank of the Volkhov River from Kirish to Gruzin; participated in the defensive battle and counterattack at Tikhvin
Dec 41–Nov 43	As part of the Voronezh then Leningrad Fronts, defended the Volkhov River line and the bridgehead on the left bank. Disbanded

Commanders

Five commanders. Notable: Marshal K. A. Meretskov

4th Guards Army

Feb 43	Converted from 24th Army, with the 20th and 21st Guards RCs and 3d Guards TC assigned
Aug 43	Participated in Voronezh Front offensive to Belgorod-Kharkov and the battle for the Dnepr River line; advancing in the Krivoi-Rog Direction, the army helped expand bridgeheads as part of the 2d Ukrainian Front
1944	Opns at Kirovograd, Korsun-Shevchenkovsky, Uman-Botoshany, and Iassy-Kishinev, then assigned to Stavka reserve
Nov 44–45	Participated in the Budapest, Balaton, and Vienna opns as part of the 3d Ukrainian Front

Commanders

Seven commanders. Notable: Army Gen. G. F. Zakharov, 44–45

4th Shock Army

Dec 41	Formed in the Northwestern Front from remnants of the 27th Army; initial composition: five RDs, one separate brigade
1942	Defended the eastern shore of the White Sea; took part in the Toropets-Kholm offensive operation by Kalinin Front
1943	Continued defensive opns on the approaches to Demidov
44–45	As part of the Kalinin, 1st, and 2d Baltic Fronts, took part in offensive opns at Nevel, Gorodok, Polotsk, Rezhitsa-Dvina, Riga, and Memel; participated in the Kurland blockade

Commanders

Six commanders. Notable: Army Gen. A. I. Yeremenko

5th Army

1939	Formed in the Kiev Special Military District
Jun 41	Assigned to the Southwestern Front. Composition: Two RDs, 9th and 12th MCs; participated in border battles, retreated in Kiev Direction and took part in defense of Kiev
Sep 41	Command-staff disbanded and units dispersed
Oct 41	Reformed in the Mozhaisk military region. New composition included two RDs and three TBs. Took part in the Battle of Moscow as part of the Western Front
1943	Participated in Rzhev-Viazma and Smolensk offensives
1944	As part of 3d Belorussian Front, particpated in the Belorussian Campaign
1945	East Prussian offensive opns, then redeployed to the 1st Far Eastern Front. Strengthened to four RCs and participated in the Harbin-Girin offensive

Commanders

Five commanders. Notable: Marshal L. A. Govorov, 41–42

5th Guards Army

Apr 43	Formerly the 66th Guards Army; initially assigned to the Voronezh, then Steppe and 2d Ukrainian Fronts
Jul–Aug 43	Critical participant in the great tank battle of Prokhorovka, Battle of Kursk; subsequently, forced the Dnepr River

44–45	Assigned to the 1st Ukrainian Front, participated in the Kirovograd, Uman-Botoshany, Lvov-Sandomir, Sandomir-Silesia, Lower and Upper Silesia, Berlin, and Prague offensives

Commander

Gen. Col. A. S. Zhadov

5th Shock Army

Dec 42	Formed within the Stavka reserve on the base of the 10th Reserve Army, comprising three RDs, the 4th MC, and 7th TC. As part of the Stalingrad and Southwestern Fronts, had the major task in the counteroffensive of destroying enemy forces in the Tormosin grouping
1943	Participated in the Rostov and Mius River line opns; offensive opns in the Donbas and Melitopol
1944	Right Bank Ukraine and Iassy-Kishinev opns; assigned to the 1st Belorussian Front in Oct 44
1945	Warsaw-Poznan and Berlin offensives

Commanders

Three commanders. Notable: Army Gen. M. M. Popov, Dec 1942 (initial breakthrough at Stalingrad)

6th Army

Four separate establishments

Aug 39	Initially created in the Kiev Special MD. Participated in the occupation of western Ukraine in conjunction with the Soviet-German partition of Poland
Jun 41	Composition: 6th and 37th RCs, 4th and 15th MCs, 5th CC. Deployed on the

Lvov axis, within the Southwestern Front. Fought border battles to the southwest of Lvov; fell back and helped defend Kiev, then disbanded in Aug 41

Aug 41   Immediately reformed in the Southern Front on the base of 48th RC and other units. Defended west bank of the Dnepr River northwest of Dnepropetrovosk

Sep 41–   Transferred to the South-
May42   western Front and participated in defensive operations in the Donbas, the Barvenkovo-Lozovaia operation, and the 2d Battle of Kharkov, then disbanded

Jul 42   Established the third time from the 6th Reserve Army, comprising eight RDs. Assigned, in sequence, to the Voronezh, Southwestern, and 3d Ukrainian Fronts; defensive opns: Voronezh-Voroshilovgrad and the Middle Don

1943   Participated in opns in the Donbas

1944   Participated in Nikopol-Krivoi Rog, Bereznogova-toye-Snigorovka, and Odessa offensive opns

Jun 44   Forces and command staff redistributed to other forces

Dec 44   Reformed with formations and units from the 3d Guards and 13th Armies

1945   Took part in Sandomir-Silesia, Lower-Silesia, and Bresla offensive opns

Commanders

Eight commanders. Notable: Marshal R. Ya. Malinovsky, 1941

6th Guards Army

Apr 43   Converted from the 21st Army; included multiple RDs that were combined into 22d and 23d Guards RCs

Jul–Aug 43 Participated in Kursk battle with Voronezh Front

Oct 43   Assigned to the Baltic, then 2d Baltic Front; defended northwest of Nevel

1944   Offensive opns at Nevel, Vitebsk-Orshan, Polotsk, Shyaulyai, Riga, and Memel

1945   Participated in the Kurland blockade

Commander

Gen. Col. I. M. Chistyakov

7th Army

1940   Formed in the Leningrad MD and defended Soviet borders vic. Lake Ladoga; a primary participant in the Soviet-Finnish War (winter 39–40), commanded at that time by Army Gen. K. A. Meretskov

Jun 41   With four RDs assigned, the army conducted defensive opns in Karelia

Sep 41   Converted to the 7th Separate Army and moved to Stavka reserve

Oct 41-   Defended the Sbir River line between Onega and Ladoga

Jun–   Participated in the Sbir-
Aug 44   Petrozavod offensive
Jan 45   Disbanded

Commanders

Three commanders. Notable: Marshal K. A. Meretskov, Sep–Nov 41

7th Guards Army

Apr 43   Created and renamed from the 64th Army, one of the hero armies of

Stalingrad. Comprised six Guards divisions, later combined into the 24th and 25th Guards RCs

Jul–Aug 43 Battle of Kursk, as part of Voronezh and Steppe Fronts, then fought for the control of Dnepr River line

44–45   Assigned to the 2d Ukrainian Front, the army participated in opns at Kirovograd, Uman-Botoshany, Iassy-Kishenev, Debrecen, Budapest, Bratislava-Brno, and Prague

Commander

Gen. Col. M. S. Shumilov

8th Army

Oct 39   Formed on the base of the Novgorod army operational group of forces in the Leningrad MD

Aug 40   Part of the Baltic Special MD which became the Northwestern Front on 22 Jun 41

Jun 41   Initial composition: 10th, 11th RCs; 12th MC, 9th Anti-Tank Brigade. Participated in border battles

Aug 41   Defensive opns, Leningrad Front

Sep–   Defensive opns, Oranien-
Nov 41   baum bridgehead

Jun 42   Siniavino offensive operation, part of Volkhov Front

Jan 43   Blockade breaking opns vic. Leningrad, then kept defensive posture

44–45   As part of the Leningrad Front, participated in offensive opns at Narva, Tallinn, and Moonzund archipelago, then defended the Estonian coastline

Commanders

Eight commanders

8th Guards Army

One of the most famous Soviet armies of WWII

Apr 43   Formerly the 62d Army; included the 28th, 29th, then 4th Guards RCs

1943   Participated in defensive opns as part of Southwestern Front (northern Donets River), followed by offensive opns: Izyum-Barvenkovo, Donbas, and battles for the Dnepr River line.

1944   Offensive opns: Nikopol-Krivoi Rog, Bereznegovatoye-Snigirovka, Odessa. From Apr to Jun 44, the Army was part of the Stavka reserve, then joined the 1st Belorussian Front and participated in the Belorussian offensive

1945   Warsaw-Poznan and Berlin offensive opns

Commander

Gen. Lt. V. I. Chuikov

9th Army

Jun 41   Formed in the Odessa MD on the base of the 9th Separate Army, comprising three RCs, the 2d CC, and the 2d and 18th MCs

1941   As part of the Southern Front, fought border battles along the Dnestr, southern Bug, and Dnepr rivers. Defensive opns in the Donbas and at Rostov. Participated in the Rostov and Barvenkovo-Lozovaia (Jan 42) counterattacks

42–43   Defended Caucasus region

Nov 43   Disbanded

Commanders

Eight commanders. Notable: Gen. Major (future Marshal, CINC Ground Forces, and Minister of Defense) A. A. Grechko

9th Guards Army

Jan 45	Formed on the base of 7th Army command-staff and a large Guards airborne unit; augmented by 37th, 38th, and 39th Guards RD in Hungary in Feb 45
Mar 45	As part of the 2d Ukrainian Front, conducted offensive opns, culminating in seizure of Prague

Commander

Gen. Lt. V. V. Glagolev

10th Army

1939	Formed in the Belorussian Special MD. Participated in the occupation of western Belorussia in connection with the Soviet-German partition of Poland
Jun 41	Assigned to the Western Front with 1st and 5th RCs, 6th and 13th MC, 6th CC, and the 155th RD; defended the Belostok Direction; participated in front counterattack vic. Grodno; encircled and largely destroyed
Oct 41	Reformed in the Southern Front, but process halted due to severe battle conditions
Nov 41	Third establishment in the Volga region, with nine (seven new) RDs assigned. Initially part of Stavka reserve, then assigned to the Western Front for the Battle of Moscow
1942	Defensive opns in the central region
1943	Smolensk offensive opn
Apr 44	Disbanded; command-staff formed the base for the 2d Belorussian Front headquarters; units distributed to 49th Army

Commanders

Four commanders. Notable: Gen. Lt. (future Marshal) F. I. Golikov, 41–42

10th Guards Army

Apr 43	Created from the 30th Army; composed of the 7th, 15th, and 19th Guards RCs
43–44	Assigned to the Western, then 2d Baltic Fronts, the army took part in a series of offensives including: Smolensk, Leningrad-Novgorod, Staraya Russa-Novogorod, Rezhitsa-Dvina, Madon, and Riga
From Oct 44	Part of the blockade force in Kurland

Commanders

Four commanders

11th Army

1939	Formed in the Belorussian Special MD. Occupied western Belorussia in connection with the Soviet-German partition of Poland
Jun 41	Assigned to the Northwestern Front with 16th, 29th RCs, 3d MC, and three RDs. Initially defended against Army Group North west and southwest of Kaunas and Vilnius
Jul 41	Command-staff participated in counterattacks at Soltsi and Staraya Russa.
42–43	Defended in the Demiansk region
Jul 43	Reformed with the 53d RC and five RDs, assigned to the Western, then Briansk Fronts
Oct 43	Participated in the Orel, Briansk, and Gomel-Richitsa offensives
Dec 43	Disbanded

Commanders
Four commanders. Notable: Army
Gen. I. I. Fedyuninsky, 1943

11th Guards Army

Apr 43	Formerly the 16th Army. Composition at this time: 8th and 16th RCs and one RD; initially assigned to the Western Front, then Briansk and Baltic Fronts
May 44–45	Participated in the Orel, Briansk, Gorodok, Belorussian, Gumbinnen, and East Prussian offensives, the later opns as part of the 3d Belorussian Front

Commanders
Three commanders. Notable: General
Marshal I. Kh. Bagramian, 1943

12th Army

1939	Formed in the Kiev Special Military District. Took part in the occupation of western Ukraine in connection with the Soviet-German partition of Poland
Jun 41	Assigned to the Southwestern and Southern Fronts; comprised the 13th and 17th RCs and 16th MC. Defensive border battles vic. Stanislava and the Uman Direction. Encircled and destroyed by Jul 41
Aug 41	Reformed in the Southern Front on the base of 17th RC, two RCs, and the 11th TD. Defended the left bank of the Dnepr vic. Zaporozhe
Sep–Dec 41	Defensive opns in the Donbas
From Jan 42	Barvenkovo-Lozovoya offensive, then pushed back to defensive positions in the Donbas and North Caucasus

Sep 42	Disbanded; command staff relocated to the Tuapse region and troops distributed to the 18th Army
Apr 43	Reformed in the Southwestern Front on the base of 5th Tank Army, comprising five RDs. Initially the front reserve, then participated in Donbas and Zaporozhe offensive opns
Nov 43	Disbanded

Commanders
Seven commanders. Notable: Gen. Lt.
(future Marshal, CINC Ground Forces,
and Minister of Defense) A. A.
Grechko, 1942

13th Army

Jun 41	Army command-staff was initially formed separately in the Western Special MD, then combined with a variety of formations and units when the war broke out, including one RC and one RD. The Army fought defensive battles vic. Minsk. Subsequently, assigned to a series of fronts, it defended at Smolensk and in the Orel-Briansk, Elets, and Voronezh-Voroshilovgrad opns
1943	Participated in the Battle of Kursk and the fight for the Dnepr River line
1944	Offensive opns included Right Bank Ukraine and approaches to Poland.
1945	Offensive opns in Poland, Berlin, and Prague

Commanders
Six commanders

14th Army

Oct 39	Formed in the Leningrad MD and took part in the Soviet-Finnish War

Jun 41	Composition: 42d RC, two RDs, 1st TD, and a mixed air division. Conducted defensive opns in the Murmansk, Kandalaksha, and Ukhtin Directions. Halted the German advance in the sector by July
To 1944	Assigned to the Karelian Front, conducted defensive opns in place
Late 44	Participated in Petsamo-Kirkenes offensive operation to recover Pechenga (Petsamo) and northern regions of Norway and restore Soviet borders
1945	Defended the northern borders

Commanders

Three commanders

15th Army

| Jul 40 | Formed as part of the Far Eastern Front including the 20th Rifle Corps and an assortment of other units. Remained in this front during the war in the west |
| Aug 45 | Composed of four RDs and three tank brigades, the army took part in the Sungari offensive by the 2d Far Eastern Front |

Commanders

Three commanders

16th Army

| Jun 40 | Formed in the Transbaikal MD |
| Jun 41 | Initially assigned to Stavka reserve, then rapidly deployed to the central region and assigned to the Western Front; composition: 32d RC and 5th MC; fought in defensive battles at Smolensk and Moscow through 1941 |

42–43	Defensive opns in the Zhizdra Direction; converted to the 11th Guards Army in Apr 43
Jul 43	16th Army reformed in the Far Eastern Front to defend Sakhalin Island and other missions
Aug 45	Led offensive opns in southern Sakhalin and then participated in the Kuril Islands operation

Commanders

Five commanders. Notables: Marshal K. K. Rokossovsky, 41–42; and Marshal I. Kh. Bargramyan, 42–43

17th Army

Jul 40	Formed in the Transbaikal MD and remainded in the Transbaikal during the war
41–45	Assumed a general defensive posture, including territory of Mongolia
Aug 45	With three RDs and two tank battalions, the relatively small army took part in the Khingan-Mukden offensive

Commanders

Three commanders

18th Army

| Jun 41 | Command-staff provided from the Kharkov MD and units from the Kiev Special MD. Initially composed of 17th CC, 16th MC, and two air divisions. Assigned in sequence to the Southern, North Caucasus, Transcaucasus, 1st, and 4th Ukrainian Fronts |
| 41–42 | Conducted defensive opns in western Ukraine, Donbas, Rostov. Conducted offensive opns in the battle for the Caucasus |

43–45	Participated in the Kerch-Eltigen amphibious and Malaya Zemlya opns; offensive opns in western Ukraine, then advances into Hungary, Poland, and Czechoslovakia

Commanders
Nine commanders. Notable: Gen. Major (future Marshal, CINC Ground Forces, and Minister of Defense) A. A. Grechko

19th Army

Jun 41	Formed in the North Caucasus MD; composition: 25th, 34th RCs, 26th MC, and 38th RD
Jul 41	Defensive opns in the Vitebsk Direction, Western Front; participated in the defense of Smolensk and Viazma; encircled, but broke out
Nov 41	Reformed into 1st Shock Army
Apr 42	19th Army resurrected on the Karelian front with two RDs, a naval infantry brigade and a light brigade
42–44	Defended the Kandalaksh Direction, then assumed the offensive in 1944 and restored Soviet-Finnish border
Nov 44	Placed in Stavka reserve, then assigned to 2d Belorussian Front
1945	East Pomeranian offensive opns

Commanders
Three commanders

20th Army

Jun–Oct 41	Formed within the Orel MD, consisting of the 61st and 64th RCs, 7th MC, and 15th RD; committed as

	part of Western Front to defensive battles in Belorussia, Smolensk, and Viazma; encircled and destroyed
Nov 41	Reformed for defense of Moscow; composition: 331st and 350th RDs, plus 3 separate brigades; Western Front
42–43	Opns at the Rzhev-Sychevka bridgehead; participated in the Rzhev-Viazma offensive operation
1944	Moved to Stavka reserve, then reassigned to the Kalinin and Leningrad Fronts
Apr 44	Disbanded into different formations, 3d Baltic Front

Commanders
Eleven commanders. Notable: Gen. Col. M. A. Reiter, 1942

21st Army

Jun 41	Formed in the Volga MD. Composition: 63d, 66th RCs, and the 25th MC.
1941	Defensive and counteroffensive opns in the Western Direction as part of the Central, Western, and Briansk Fronts. Took part in defense of Kiev as part of the Southwestern Front; encircled, but escaped and was re-equipped
May 42	Participated in second Battle of Kharkov
Jul 42	Defensive opns as part of the Stalingrad, then Don Fronts; took part in the Battle of Stalingrad
Apr 43	*Honored and renamed as 6th Guards Army*
Jul 43	21st Army reformed on the base of 3d Reserve Army, comprising 61st RC and 5 RDs; Western Front;

participated in Smolensk offensive operation

Oct 43   Disbanded with troops assigned to the 33d Army and the command-staff moving into reserve

1945   Participated in Vyborg, Sandomir-Silesia, Upper Silesia, and Prague offensive opns

Commanders

Eleven commanders. Notable: Army Gen. V. N. Gordov, 41–42

22d Army

Jun 41   Formed in the Urals MD from 51st and 62d RC. Initially part of Western Front, then transferred to Kalinin Front

1941   Defended series of lines from Idrits to Vitebsk and Smolensk; defended Kalinin and southwest of Rzhev

43–44   Took part in the Rzhev-Viazma offensive, then, as part of Northwest, Baltic, and 2d Baltic Fronts; participated in opns at Kholm, Velikie Luki, Leningrad-Novgorod, Staraia-Russa-Novorshev, and Rezhitsa-Dvina

From   Took part in the blockade
  Oct 44   of German forces in Kurland

Commanders

Five commanders

23d Army

May 41   Formed in the Leningrad MD from the 19th and 50th RCs, and the 10th MC

Jun–Jul 41   As part of the Northern Front, defended Soviet borders with Finland northeast of Vyborg

41–44   Defended in Karelia as part of Leningrad Front

Jun 44   Participated in the Vyborg offensive operation, then remained in area to secure Karelian border

Commanders

Four commanders

24th Army

Jun 41   Formed in the Siberian MD from the 52d and 53d RCs; initially assigned to Stavka reserve, then to the Reserve Front

Jul–Oct 41   Participated in the defense of Smolensk and Viazma; encircled and destroyed; remnants distributed to other units

Dec 41   Reformed in the Moscow MD as part of the reserve of the Moscow zone of defense

May 42   Became the 1st Reserve Army

Commanders

Two commanders

25th Army

Jun 41   Formed in the Far East MD, from 39th RC and six RDs

41–45   Conducted border security opns as part of the Far Eastern Front

Aug 45   Participated in the Harbin-Girin offensive operation in Manchuria, then deployed to Beijing to support Chinese Communist movement

Commanders

Three commanders

26th Army

Jul 40   Formed in the Kiev Special MD from the 8th RC and 6th MC

1941   Conducted defensive opns in the Western Direction.

	Encircled and destroyed during defense of Kiev
Oct 41	Reestablished in the Moscow MD on the base of 1st Guards RC, 1st Guards RD, 41st CD, and 5th Airborne Corps; conducted defensive opns in the Orel-Tula Direction; essentially destroyed; remnants distributed to the 50th Army of the Briansk Front and the command-staff was disbanded
Nov 41	Established the third time in the Volga MD from three RDs and two CDs. Assigned to the Volkhov Front
Dec 41	Reformed into the 2d Shock Army
Mar–Apr 42	Fourth establishment within Karelian Front, comprising six RDs and two naval infantry brigades
Apr 42–Sep44	Defensive opns in Karelia, then advanced to occupy the border with Finland
Nov 44	Placed in Stavka reserve
From Jan 45	Took part in the Budapest, Lake Balaton, and Vienna offensive opns as part of the 3d Ukrainian Front

Commanders

Five commanders

27th Army

May 41	Formed in the Baltic Special MD, comprised of the 22d and 24th RCs and the 16th and 67th RDs; assigned to the Northwestern Front for defensive opns in the Baltic region
Jun–Oct 41	Fought on the Dvina River and at Kholm and Demiansk; helped stop the

	advance of Army Group North at White Sea
Dec 41	Reformed into the 4th Shock Army
May 42	Second establishment in the Northwestern Front, comprising five RDs; conducted defensive opns
Apr 43	Stavka reserve
From Jul 43	Assigned to the Steppe then Voronezh Front; participated in the Belgorod-Kharkov offensive and Bukrina bridgehead
Oct 43	Participated in the Kiev offensive as part of 1st Ukrainian Front
44–45	Zhitomir-Berdichev, Korsun-Shevchenkovsky, Uman-Botoshany, Iassy-Kishinev, Debrecen, and Vienna offensive opns as part of 2d and 3d Ukrainian Fronts

Commanders

Three commanders

28th Army

Jun 41	Formed in the Archangel MD from 30th and 33d RDs
Jul–Sep 41	Assigned to the Western Front; encircled and destroyed in the defense of Smolensk
Nov 41	Reformed in the Moscow MD from five new RDs
1942	As part of Southwest Front, destroyed second time in the 2d Battle of Kharkov (May). Command-staff distributed to the 4th Tank Army, troops to the 21st Army
Sep 42	Re-established third time within the Stalingrad Front from existing forces; fought in the Battle of Stalingrad

43–45	Continuous opns in multiple fronts. Took part in series of offensive opns: Rostov, the Donbas, Melitopol, Nikopol-Krivoi Rog, Bereznegovatoye-Snigirovka, Belorussian campaign, East Prussia, Berlin, and Prague

Commanders

Seven commanders. Notable: Army Gen. I. V. Tyulenev, Nov 41–Mar 42

29th Army

Jul 41	Formed in the Moscow MD from five new RDs; assigned to the Reserve then Western Front; defended at Staraia-Russa, Demiansk, Ostashkov, Silezhorov, Smolensk, vic. Toropets and Rzhev
1942	As part of the Kalinin Front, took part in the defensive battle at Kalinin, then offensive opns Rzhev-Viazma (1st) and Rzhev-Sychevka, then defended along the Volga
Feb 43	Disbanded, with remaining troops assigned to the 5th and 20th Armies and the command-staff to 1st Guards Tank Army

Commanders

Three commanders. Notable: Army Gen. I. I. Maslennikov, Jul–Dec 41

30th Army

Jul 41	Formed as part of the Stavka reserve, comprising four RDs and a tank brigade. Assigned to the Reserve Front, it participated in defensive opns
41–43	As a part of the Western Front, the army participated in the Battles of Smolensk and Moscow; as

	part of the Kalinin Front, took part in the Rzhev-Sychevka and Rzhev-Viazma offensive opns
Apr 43	Converted into the 10th Guards Army

Commanders

Three commanders. Notable: Gen. Lt. (future Army Gen.) D. D. Lelyushenko, Nov 41–Nov 42. One of the Soviet Army's most experienced field commanders, General Lelyushenko commanded five different armies during the war.

31st Army

Jul 41	Formed in Moscow MD and placed in the Stavka reserve. Initial composition: 244th, 246th, 247th, and 249th RDs and other units. As a part of the Reserve Front, the army fortified the defense line vic. Ostashkov, Yeltsy, and Tishina. Defended enemy advance towards Rzhev
Oct 41–42	The army was disbanded, with formations distributed to the 29th Army and the command-staff joining the Kalinin Front. Subsequently, the command-staff combined with three RDs to reform the 31st Army, defending to the north and northwest of Kalinin
Jun 42	As part of the Western Front, the army participated in fighting vic. Moscow, then took part in the Rzhev-Sychevka, Rzhev-Viazma (1943) and Smolensk offensive opns. Later as a part of the 3d Belorussian Front it participated in the Belorussian, Gumbinnen, and East

Prussia offensive opns, concluding wartime service as a part of the 1st Ukrainian Front in the seizure of Prague

Commanders

Eight commanders

32d Army

Jul 41	Formed in Moscow Military District in Stavka reserve. Initial composition included five territorial divisions. Conducted defensive opns in the Reserve Front and on the Mozhaisk defensive line
Oct 41	Assigned to the Western Front, the 32d defended vic. Viazma, was encircled, and broke out. Army was then disbanded, with forces applied to the 16th and 19th Armies
Mar 42–44	Reformed in the Karelian Front comprising five RDs and four naval infantry and light brigades. Conducted defensive opns through the first half of 1944
Jun 44–45	Participated in the Sbir-Petrozavod offensive operation, then placed in Stavka reserve in Nov 44
Aug 45	Disbanded

Commanders

Five commanders. Notable: Gen. Major (future Army Gen.) I. I. Fedyuninsky, Aug–Sep 41.

33d Army

Jul 41	Formed in Moscow Military District, initially composed of four territorial divisions. Conducted defensive opns as part of the Mozhaisk Defense Line and the Reserve Front

Oct 41	Participated in defense of Moscow as part of the Western Front
1942	Took part in offensive and defensive opns vic. Viazma
43–45	As a part of the Western, 2d, 3d, and 1st Belorussian Fronts, participated in Rzhev-Viazma, Smolensk, Belorussian, Warsaw-Poznan and Berlin offensive opns

Commanders

Nine Commanders. Notables: Army Gen. (future Marshal) K. A. Meretskov, May–Jun 42; Army Gen. V. N. Gordov, Oct 42–Mar 44; Army Gen. I. E. Petrov, Mar–Apr 44

34th Army

Jul 41–43	Formed in Moscow MD, comprising three new RDs and two cavalry divisions. Assigned to the Northwestern Front, the army participated in counterattacks vic. Staraya Russa in Aug 41 and in opns vic. the Demiansk bridgehead for the next two years and the Staraya Russa offensive of Aug 43
Nov 43	Disbanded, with forces distributed to 1st Shock Army and the command-staff to the 4th Army

Commanders

Seven commanders.

35th Army

Jul 41	Formed as a part of the Far Eastern Front on the base of 18th Rifle Corps. Initial composition: three RDs and other units. Maintained defensive posture and readiness in the Primorye (coastal) region

Aug 45   Assigned to the 1st Far
          Eastern Front. Included
          three RDs. Took part in
          the Harbin-Girin offensive

Commanders

Two commanders

36th Army

Jul 41   Formed in Transbaikal
          MD on the base of 12th
          Rifle Corps, comprising
          four RDs. Maintained a
          defensive posture and
          readiness in the region
Aug 45   Reinforced significantly
          and comprising the 2d and
          86th Rifle Corps, plus two
          RDs, the army participated
          in Khingan-Mukden offen-
          sive operation

Commanders

Two commanders

37th Army

Aug 41   Formed as a part of the
          Southwestern Front from
          local forces and units of
          the Stavka reserve, com-
          prising six RDs. Fortified
          the defense line vic. Svy-
          atilnoye, west of Kiev and
          the left bank of Dnepr
          river until Zherebyatin. In
          defense of Kiev, the army
          was encircled, escaped,
          and then was disbanded in
          Sep 41. Participated in
          Kiev defensive opns
Nov 41   Reformed on the Southern
          Front with five RDs. Ini-
          tially defended approach-
          es to Rostov. Took part in
          the successful Rostov
          counteroffensive
42–43   Took part in Barvenkovo-
          Lozovaia offensive opera-
          tion south of Kharkov (Jan
          42) and opns in the Don-
          bas. Assigned to the

Caucasus and North Cau-
casus Fronts, took part in
the battle for the Caucasus

Jul 43   The army was temporarily
          disbanded. Units joined
          the 9th and 56th Armies;
          command staff assigned to
          Stavka reserve
Sep 43   Reformed and strength-
          ened with the 57th and
          82d RC, 53d RD and other
          units
1944   As a part of Steppe, 1st
          and 2d Ukrainian Fronts,
          the army participated in
          the battle for the Dnepr
          River line, helped liberate
          the Right Bank Ukraine,
          took part in Iassy-Kishinev
          offensive opns and the
          liberation of Bulgaria

Commanders

Six commanders

38th Army

Jul 41–42 Formed in the Southwest-
           ern Front, initally compris-
           ing two RDs. Fortified the
           defense line on the Dnepr
           River vic. Cherkassy. De-
           fended Kiev. Took part in
           Donbas operation, Jul 42
Jul 42   Disbanded. Units were
           distributed to the 21st
           Army and the command-
           staff was used to form 1st
           Tank Army headquarters
Aug 42   Army was reformed in the
           Briansk Front from the
           local operational group of
           forces and the 4th Reserve
           Army. Initial composition:
           five RDs and several sepa-
           rate brigades. Through
           1942, took part in defen-
           sive and offensive opns
           vic. Voronezh
1943   Assigned to the Voronezh
           Front, the army took part

in Voronezh-Kastornoesk and the third battle of Kharkov, followed by the Battle of Kursk. The army helped liberate the Left Bank Ukraine and participated in the crossing of Dnepr River

44–45   As a part of the 1st and then the 4th Ukrainian Fronts, it participated in Kiev, Zhitomir-Berdichev, Proskurov, Chernovits, Lvov-Sandomir, East and West Carpathians, Morava-Ostravka and Prague offensive opns

Commanders

Eight commanders.

39th Army

Nov 41   Formed in Archangelsk MD within Stavka reserve. Initial composition: 357th, 361st, 369th, 371st, 373d, 377th, and 381st RDs, plus the 76th and 94th cavalry divisions. Assigned to the Kalinin Front, the army took part in the defense of Moscow

Feb–Jul 42 Largely encircled, then wholly encircled, the Army defended under difficult conditions, eventually breaking out. Disbanded

Aug 42   New 39th Army formed as a part of Kalinin Front on the base of 58th Army (2d est.). New composition included four RDs

Aug 42–   Participated in defensive
Mar 43   and offensive opns directed towards Rzhev. Later the same year it took part in Rzhev-Viazma and Dukhovshchin-Demidov offensive opns

43–45   Subsequently assigned in sequence to the Baltic, Western, and 3d Belorussian Fronts. Participated in a series of offensive opns in the Direction of Vitebsk, followed by the Belorussian, Memel, and East-Prussian opns

Jun–   Moved to Mongolian
Aug 45   People's Republic and became a part of Transbaikal Front, with which it took part in Khingan-Mukden offensive

Commanders

Five commanders. Notable: Army Gen. I. I. Maslennikov, Dec 41–Jun 42.

40th Army

Aug 41   Formed on the Southwestern Front from an unusual combination: 2d Airborne Corps, the 135th and 239th RDs, and the 10th TD. Participated in opns vic. Desna River to the north and northwest of Konotop. Through Dec 41, defended approaches to the Desna and Tim Rivers

1942   As part of the Bryanks and Voronezh Fronts, participated in offensive opns directed towards Kursk and Belgorod and the Voronezh-Voroshilovgrad defensive operation of Jun-Jul 42

1943   Took part in the Ostrogozhsk-Rossosh offensive and third battle of Kharkov. Participated in battles for the Dnepr River line and Right Bank Ukraine as part of 1st Ukrainian Front

1944   Assigned to the 2d Ukrainian Front, participated in

Uman-Botoshany, Iassy-
Kishinev, Budapest,
Bratislava-Brno, and the
seizure of Prague

Commanders

Five commanders. Notable: Army
Gen. M. M. Popov, Jul–Oct 42.

41st Army

May 42	Formed on the Kalinin Front. Initial composition: five RDs. Initially conducted defensive opns to the west and southwest of the city of Bely
Mar 43	Participated in the Rzhev-Viazma offensive
Apr 43	Disbanded, with forces distributed to several armies and the command-staff provided to the Reserve Front

Commanders

Two commanders

42d Army

Aug 41–44	Formed on the Leningrad Front, comprising two Guards territorial divisions and the 6th naval infantry brigade, and other smaller units. Defended Leningrad, then assumed defensive positions along the line Ligovo, Kamen, and south of Pulkovo
1944	Participated in Leningrad-Novgorod and Pskov-Ostrov opns, the latter while assigned to the 3d Baltic Front
Aug 44–45	Reformed as part of the 2d Baltic Front with a new set of forces based on the 110th and 124th RCs. Participated in the Riga offensive and then helped hold the blockade of enemy forces in Kurland

Commanders

Seven commanders

43d Army

Jul 41	Formed on the base of the 33d Rifle Corps as a part of the Reserve Front. Initial composition: 38th, 53d, 145th, 149th, 211th, 222d, 279th, 203d Rifle Divisions, 104th and 109th Tank Divisions as well as other units
1941	Took part in the Smolensk battle, assigned to the Western Front in Oct 41, then defended Moscow
Oct 42–43	Continued defensive opns, assigned to the Kalinin and 1st Baltic Front to the southeast of Demidov. Subsequently, took part in the Smolensk offensive operation
44–45	Participated in the Belorussian and Baltic offensive opns (assigned to the 3d, then 2d Belorussian Fronts) and then helped seal the Kurland blockade

Commanders

Six commanders

44th Army

Jul 41	Formed in Caucasus Military District on the base of the 40th Rifle Corps, with two mountain RDs and the 17th Caucasus RD. Created to cover the borders of the USSR with Iran, the 44th Army participated in opns for control of the Caucasus region
41–42	Took part in the Kerch-Feodosiya amphibious operation, after which it fought on the Crimean

	peninsula as part of the Crimean Front
1942	Transferred between the Transcaucasus and Caucasus Fronts, the with a new set of five RDs, the Army participated in the battle for the Caucasus
1943	Assigned to the Southern Front (Feb 43) and then to the 4th Ukrainian Front (Oct 43), the army took part in offensive opns at Rostov, in the Donbas, and Melitopol
Nov 43	Disbanded

Commanders

Eight commanders. Notable: Army Gen. I. E. Petrov, Aug–Oct 42.

45th Army

Jul 41	Formed in Caucasus Military District on the base of the 23d Rifle Corps. Initial composition: 138th Mountain and 31st and 136th RDs, and the 1st Mountain Cavalry Division
Dec 41-	Defended USSR borders with Turkey
1945	Disbanded after the end of the war

Commanders

Four commanders.

46th Army

Jul 41	Formed in Caucasus MD on the base of 3d Rifle Corps. Initial composition: 9th and 47th Mountain and 4th Rifle Divisions
41–42	As a part of the Caucasus Front, the army defended the border of the USSR with Turkey, the Black Sea, and designated passes
1943	Participated in the battle for control of the Caucasus region

Sep 43	Assigned to the Steppe, then the 2d Ukrainian Front (Oct 43), participated in offensive opns in the Donbas and for control of the Dnepr River line
44–45	Assigned to 3d, then 2d Ukrainian Fronts, participated in a series of offensives, including: Right Bank Ukraine, Iassy-Kishinev, liberation of Romania and Bulgaria, Debrecen, Budapest, Vienna and Prague

Commanders

Ten commanders.

47th Army

Jul 41	Formed in the Transcaucasus MD on the base of the 28th Mechanized Corps for border defense with Iran. Initial composition: 63d and 76th Mountain RDs, 236th RD, and the 6th and 54th Tank Divisions
Jan 42	Transferred to the Crimean Front and participated in offensive and defensive opns on the Kerch peninsula
May 42	Evacuated to the Taman peninsula in defense of Novorossiisk, after which it was transferred between a variety of fronts and groupings
42–43	Took part in the battle for Caucasus, then participated in the Belogorod-Kharkov offensive under the Voronezh Front.
44–45	Opns to clear enemy forces from the Left Bank Ukraine. Assigned to the 1st Belorussian Front, the army took part in opns at

Lublin, Brest, Warsaw-
Poznan, East Pomerania,
and Berlin

Commanders
Fourteen commanders

48th Army

Aug 41	Formed on the Northwestern Front from the Novgorod operational army group. Initial composition: three RDs, the 21st TD, and one territorial division. Defended approaches to Novgorod, then was disbanded in Sep 41, with remaining forces assigned to the 54th Army
Apr 42	Reformed in the Briansk Front on the base of 28th Mechanized Corps with initial composition of two Guards and three rifle divisions, three separate rifle brigades and an independent tank brigade
Apr 42– Mar 43	Assigned to the Briansk, then Central Front, then contested with enemy forces in the direction of Malo-Archangel and Elets
Summer 43–May 1945	As a part of the Central, 1st, 2d, and 3d Belarussian Fronts, the army took part in the Battle of Kursk, followed by the Chernigov-Pripiat, Gomel, Rechitsa, Belorussian, and East-Prussian offensive opns

Commanders
Three commanders

49th Army

Aug 41	Formed in the Moscow MD with one mountain and three regular rifle divisions, plus a territorial

division. Assigned initially
to the Reserve Front, then
to the Western Front (Oct
41), for the defense of
Moscow

1943	Participated in Rzhev-Viazma and Smolensk offensive opns
44–45	As part of the 2d Belarussian Front, took part in the Belorussian East-Prussian, East-Pomeranian, and Berlin offensive opns. The army met the end of the war on the Elba River vic. Ludwigslust where it met the troops of the 2d English Army

Commanders
Two commanders

50th Army

Aug 41	Formed in the Briansk Front from the 2d Rifle Corps. Initial composition: 217th, 258th, 260th, 269th, 278th, 279th, 280th, 290th RDs, and the 55th Cavalry Division
41–42	Participated in the defense of Moscow and subsequent battles
Mar 43	Participated in Rzhev-Viazma offensive operation
Apr 43	16th Army was incorporated into the 50th Army
late 43	Participated in Orel, Smolensk and Briansk offensive opns, followed by Gomel-Rechitsa in Oct 43
1944	Assigned to 2d Belarussian Front, took part in the Belorussian Campaign
1945	East Prussian operation as part of the 3d Belarussian Front

Commanders
Four commanders

51st Army

Aug 41	Formed on the Crimean peninsula as the 51st Separate Army. Initial composition: 9th Rifle Corps, two RDs, three CDs, and four Crimean territorial divisions. Unsuccessful defense of Crimea forced its evacuation to the Taman peninsula in Nov 41, where the army was incorporated into the Transcaucasus Front
41–42	Participated in Kerch-Feodosia amphibious opn
May 42	Evacuated into the Kuban and incorporated into the North Caucasus Front
Jun 42	Relocated to Don River, incorporated into the Stalingrad, Southeastern, and again Stalingrad Front during the Battle of Stalingrad
43–44	Assigned in sequence to the Southern and 2d Ukrainian Fronts, the army took part in offensive opns at Rostov, the Donbas, Melitopol, and the recovery of Crimea
44–45	Relocated to the 1st Baltic Front, participated in opns on the territories of Latvia and Lithuania and accepted the surrender of enemy forces in Kurland

Commanders
Nine commanders

52d Army

Aug 41	Formed in the Northwestern Front from 25th RC and placed in Stavka reserve. Initial composition included seven RDs
41–42	Participated in Tihvin defensive and offensive opns. Took part in the Lyuban operation as part of the Volkhov Front
43–44	Placed in Stavka reserve in May, then assigned to the Voronezh Front for opns to control the Dnepr River line. Transferred in turn to the Steppe Front, then the 2d Ukrainian, the army took part in Korsun-Shevchenkovsky, Uman-Botoshany, and Iassy-Kishinev offensives
Dec 44–45	Transferred to the 1st Ukrainian Front, the army took part in the Sandomir-Silesia, Lower Silesia, Berlin, and Prague opns

Commanders
Three commanders

53d Army

Aug 41	Formed initially in Central Asia to defend southeastern borders
Dec 41	Disbanded
Apr 42	Reestablished in the Northwestern Front from 34th Army. Initial composition: eight RDs (including 22d Guards)
1943	Took part in the Demiansk offensive operation, after which the Army was transferred to the Steppe Front and reorganized with seven different divisions in preparation for the Battle of Kursk. Followed Kursk with participation in the battle for the Dnepr River line
44–45	Assigned to the 2d Ukrainian Front and participated in the Kirovograd, Korsun-Shevchenkovosky, Umansk-Botoshansk, Iassy-Kishinev, Debrecen,

Budapest, Bratislava-Brno
and Prague offensive opns

Summer   Redeployed to the Trans-
1945   baikal Front and took part
          in the Khingan-Mukden
          offensive

Commanders
Six commanders

54th Army

Aug 41–44 Formed in Moscow Mili-
           tary District from the 44th
           Rifle Corps. Initial compo-
           sition: 285th, 286th, 310th,
           314th RDs, 27th Cavalry
           Division, and the 122d
           Tank Brigade. Initially
           deployed from Stavka
           reserve to defend Volkhov
           River line. Remained in
           region as part of Lenin-
           grad Front for three-year
           long Leningrad campaign
1944   Incorporated into the 3d
           Baltic Front and participat-
           ed in the Pskov-Ostrov
           and Riga offensive opns
Oct 44   Disbanded; forces distrib-
           uted to other armies

Commanders
Five commanders

55th Army

Aug 41   Formed in the Leningrad
           Front. Initial composition:
           Four RDs, three territorial
           divisions. Initially defend-
           ed the southern approach-
           es into Leningrad
Oct 41–   Participated in selected
Feb 43   offensive opns with
           the aim of improving its
           operational dispositions
           while spoiling those of the
           enemy
Dec 43   Combined with the 67th
           Army

Commanders
Two commanders

56th Army

Oct 41   Formed in the North Cau-
           casus Military District as a
           separate Army. Initial
           composition: 31st, 317th,
           343d, 347th, 353d RDs;
           302d Mountain Rifle Divi-
           sion; 62d, 64th, 68th, 70th
           Cavalry Divisions; 6th
           Tank Brigade; and other
           units
Nov 41–42 Incorporated into the
           Southern Front. Took part
           in defensive and offensive
           opns at Rostov, later par-
           ticipated different opns in
           the Taganrog region
Jul 42–43 Transferred to the North
           Caucasus Front for partici-
           pation in defensive opns
           in Krasnodar and the
           Tuapse region, followed
           by offensive opns at
           Krasnodar, Novorossiisk-
           Taman, and the Kerch-Elti-
           gen amphibious operation
Nov 43   Reformed into the Sepa-
           rate Maritime Army

Commanders
Six commanders. Notable: Gen. Lt.
(future Marshal and Minister of
Defense) A. A. Grechko, Jan–
Oct 43

57th Army

Oct 41   Formed in the North Cau-
           casus MD in the Stalingrad
           region, assigned to the
           Stavka reserve. Initial
           composition: four newly-
           formed RDs and two
           newly-formed CDs
1942   Incorporated into the
           Southern Front and com-
           mitted to the Barvenkovo-
           Lozovaia operation. Later
           participated in the 2d Bat-
           tle of Kharkov (May 42),
           after which the army was

transferred to the South-
western (May), Stalingrad
(Jul), Southeastern (Aug),
and Don Fronts for participation in the Battle of
Stalingrad.

Feb 43   Disbanded, with the com-
         mand staff assigned to
         68th Army

Apr 43   Formed for the second
         time in the Southwestern
         Front on the base of the 3d
         Tank Army, comprising
         three Guards RDs, four
         other RDs, the 1st Fighter
         (air) Division, and two
         separate tank brigades.
         Initially, defended along
         the northern Donets River,
         then participated in the
         Battle of Kursk. Trans-
         ferred to the Steppe/2d
         Ukrainian Front, the army
         participated in Left Bank
         Ukraine offensive opns

1944   Assigned to the 3d Ukrain-
         ian Front, the army took
         part in: Bereznegovatoye-
         Snegirovka, Odessa, Iassy-
         Kishinev, the liberation of
         Bulgaria, Belgrade,
         Budapest, Balaton, and
         Vienna opns

Commanders
Seven commanders. Notable: Marshal
F. I. Tolbukhin, Jul 42–Jan 43

58th Army

Nov 41   Formed in Siberian MD
         from six newly formed
         divisions—the 362d, 364th,
         368th, 370th, 380th, 384th
         RDs—and the 77th CD.
         Deployed to Archangel
         MD

May 42   Converted into 3d Tank
         Army

Jun–   Formed for the second
  Aug 42 time in the Kalinin Front,

then converted to the 39th
Army. Formed for the
third time in the Transcau-
casus Front, comprising
three new RDs, the
Mahachkala Division of
NKVD, and the 3d Rifle
Brigade

42–43   Participated in the battle
         of the Caucasus. Defended
         the Azov sea coastline

Oct 43   Disbanded. Command
         staff provided to the Volga
         MD

Commanders
Two commanders

59th Army

Nov 41   Formed in Siberian MD,
         composed of six newly
         formed RDs and two new
         cavalry divisions

41–44   Participated in the Battle
         of Leningrad as part of the
         Volkhov and Leningrad
         Fronts. Defended the
         islands and the coast of
         Vyborg bay, the Soviet
         border in Karelia

Dec 44   Incorporated into Stavka
         reserve, then redeployed
         to Poland and assigned to
         the 1st Ukrainian Front,
         with seven different RDs.
         Participated in the San-
         domir-Silesia, Lower and
         Upper Silesia and Prague
         offensive opns

Commanders
Two commanders

60th Army

Nov 41   Formed in Moscow MD,
         placed in Stavka reserve.
         Initial composition: 334th,
         336th, 348th, 352d, 358th,
         360th RDs and the 11th
         Cavalry Division. Fortified
         the left bank of the Volga

river bank from Unza to Kosmodemiansk, then converted to the 3d Shock Army in late Dec 41

Jul 42   Formed for the second time from the 3d Reserve Army. Initial composition: 107th, 121st, 161st, 167th, 195th, 232d, 237th, 303d RDs. Incorporated into the Voronezh Front and defended along the Don River to the north of the city of Voronezh

43–45   Participated in the Voronezh-Kastornoe offensive and the 3d Battle of Kharkov. Assigned to the Central, then 1st Ukrainian (Oct 43) Fronts, the army took part in the battle of Kursk, the liberation of Left Bank Ukraine, Kiev offensive and defensive opns, Zhitomir-Berdichev, Rovno-Lutsk, Proskurov-Chernovits, Lvov-Sandomir, Sandomir-Silesia, Lower and Upper Silesia, Morava-Ostravka, and Prague offensive opns, the latter opns while assigned to 4th Ukrainian Front (Apr 45)

Commanders

Three commanders. Notable: Army Gen. I. D. Chernyakovsky, Jul 42–Apr 44

61st Army

Nov 41–42 Formed in the Volga MD in Stavka reserve. Initial composition: 342d, 346th, 350th, 356th, 385th, 387th, 391st RDs; 83d, and 91st CDs. Initially committed to the Battle of Moscow as part of the Briansk Front; participated in the winter

counteroffensive in the Orel and Volkhov Directions

Spring 42– Participated in defensive
mid 43   and offensive opns to the south of Beyov. Participated in the Orel offensive after Kursk

43–44   Subsequently, the army was assigned in sequence to the Central, Belorussian, 1st and 2d Belorussian, 3d and 1st Baltic, and again the 1st Belorussian Fronts. Took part in Chernigov-Pripiat, Gomel-Rechitsa, Kalinkov-Mozyr, Belorussian and Riga offensive opns

1945   Participated in the blockade of German forces in the Kurland peninsula, as well as the Warsaw-Poznan, East-Pomeranian and Berlin offensive opns

Commanders

Three commanders. Notable: Army Gen. M. M. Popov, Nov 41–Jul 42

62d Army

Jul 42   Formed from 7th Reserve Army. Initial composition of the army: 33d Guards, 147th, 181st, 184th, 192d, 196th Rifle Divisions, 121st Tank Brigade and other support units. Initially transferred from the Stalingrad Front to the Southeastern to the Don Front, the army won lasting fame under the command of Gen. Lt. V. I. Chuikov, for holding the center of the city at the Battle of Stalingrad

Spring 43 After helping to eliminate enemy forces trapped

within Stalingrad, the army advanced to defend the left bank of the Oskol River

Apr 43   *Honored and renamed as 8th Guards Army*

Commanders

Three commanders. Notable: Gen. Lt. (future Marshal) V. I. Chuikov, Sep 42–May 45

63d Army

Jun 42   Formed from the 5th Reserve Army with an unusual initial composition: 14th Guards and four other RDs. Committed to the Battle of Stalingrad

Nov 42   Converted into the 1st Guards' Army

Mar 43–44   Formed for the second time from 2d Reserve Army. Initial composition of the army: six RDs and supporting units. Assigned in sequence to the Briansk, Central, and Belorussian Fronts; initially conducted defensive opns along the Zusha and Neruch Rivers and the region southeast of Mtsensk. Participated in the Orel, Briansk, Gomel-Rechitsa opns

Feb 44   Disbanded

Commanders

Three commanders

64th Army

Jul 42   Formed from 1st Reserve Army, with an unusual composition of six RDs, two naval infantry brigades, two tank brigades, and cadet regiments from three military schools in the southern theater. Like its sister 62d Army, the

64th won fame at Stalingrad as the second rock upon which the German 6th Army foundered in its attempt to take the city

42–43   Contributed to the final reduction of encircled German forces at Stalingrad, then advanced westward and established defensive positions on the northern Donets River, Voronezh Front

Apr 43   *Honored and renamed as 7th Guards' Army*

Commanders

Two commanders. Notable: Gen. Lt. M. S. Shumilov, Aug 42–Apr 43

65th Army

Oct 42   Formed in the Don Front on the base of the 4th Tank Army. Initial composition: two Guards and four other RDs, plus a separate tank brigade. Participated in the Battle of Stalingrad, then transferred to the Central Front

43–44   Took part in the Battle of Kursk, Chernigov-Pripiat, Gomel-Rechitsa, and Kalinkov-Mozyr offensive opns

44–45   Transferred in Nov 44 to the 2d Belorussian Front, participated in the Belorussian Campaign, Mlava-Elba, East Prussian, East Pomeranian, and Berlin offensive opns

Commander

One commander

66th Army

Aug 42   Formed from 8th Reserve Army, comprising six RDs and four separate tank brigades. Participated in the Battle of Stalingrad as part of the Stalingrad and Don Fronts

Apr 43   *Incorporated into the Reserve Front, then honored and renamed as 5th Guards Army*

Commanders

Four commanders. Notable: Marshal R. Ya. Malinovsky, Aug–Oct 42

67th Army

Oct 42   Formed in the Leningrad Front from Neva operational group. Initial composition: 45th Guards and three other RDs. During the Battle of Leningrad, defended part of the right bank of Neva River and the ice road across Lake Ladoga

Jan 43   Participated in the lifting of the blockade of Leningrad

Dec 43   Combined with 55th Army, with the 55th command staff replacing that of the 67th

1944   Participated in Leningrad-Novgorod offensive operation, then transferred to the 3d Baltic Front, under which it took part in the Pskov-Ostrov, Tartu, and Riga opns. Subsequently, reincorporated into the Leningrad Front to defend Riga bay coastline

Commanders

Five commanders

68th Army

Feb 43   Formed in the Northwestern Front with the 57th Army command staff, initially comprising one RD, five Guards airborne

divisions, three separate brigades, and a ski brigade

1943   Participated in Demiansk offensive operation, then the army advanced between the Lovat and Redya rivers, assuming defensive positions along the latter

Jul 43   After a short stint in Stavka reserve, the army was transferred to the Western Front and participated in the Smolensk offensive

Nov 43   Disbanded

Commanders

Two commanders. Notable: Marshal F. I. Tolbukhin, Feb–Mar 43

69th Army

Feb 43   Formed in the Voronezh Front from 18th Separate Rifle Corps and including three rifle divisions, the 1st Fighter (air) Division, a separate rifle and tank brigade. Immediately took part in the offensive and defensive actions of the 3d Battle of Kharkov

Jul 43   Transferred to the Steppe Front, participated in the Battle of Kursk and for the Dnepr River line, then placed in Stavka reserve from Sep 43–Aug 44

Apr 44   Assigned to the 1st Belorussian Front, after which the army took part in Lublin-Brest, Warsaw-Poznan and Berlin offensive opns

Commanders

Three commanders

70th Army

Oct 42–   Formed from the Internal
Feb 43   Troops and Frontier

Guards of NKVD. Assigned to the Central Front with six RDs. Participated in the Battle of Kursk, then placed in Stavka reserve

Apr 44   Transferred to the 2d, then 1st, Belorussian Front, the army took part in the Poless and Lublin-Brest offensive opns

1945   Participated in the East-Prussian, East-Pomeranian, and Berlin offensive opns

Commanders

Seven commanders

Maritime Army (southern theater)

Jul 41   Formed in the Southern Front on the base of the Maritime Group of Forces, comprising three RDs, 1 corps artillery regiment, and a fighter air regiment

1941   Took part in the defense of Odessa and Sevastopol

Jul 42   Evacuated from Crimea to the Caucasus and disbanded

Nov 43   Reformed from the North Caucasus Front staff and units of the 56th Army as the Separate Maritime Army. The army was composed of two guards RDs, a mountain rifle corps, one RD

Early 44   Opns to expand the Kerch lodgment and opns to clear enemy forces from Crimea

44–45   Defense of Crimea

Commanders

Three commanders. Notable: Army Gen. I. E. Petrov, 43–44

Tank Armies

It took a year of wartime experience for the Soviet High Command to fully understand the significant role of massed tank formations in modern warfare. After June 1942, they began to form tank armies comprised of tank and mechanized corps, supported by rifle formations and dedicated air divisions. Initially, these large armored formations were sometimes used to help create tactical penetrations, then were committed to operational depths. That practice often limited the depth and duration of their advance. As time went on, infantry formations were strengthened sufficiently so that tank and mechanized corps and tank armies could be held out from battle until tactical penetrations were completed, thereby enabling the armored formations to be committed in depth to full strength. Overall, six tank armies were created, all eventually being awarded Guards status. They participated in all the major Soviet encirclement opns from 1943 until the end of the war.

1st Tank Army

Jul 42   Formed in the Stalingrad Front from the former 38th Army. Initial composition: 13th, 28th Tank Corps, 131st, 399th Rifle Divisions, 158th Tank Brigade. Participated in a counterstrike on the Don River to the north of Kalach

Aug 42   Disbanded; forces were incorporated into the Southeastern Front

Feb 43   Reformed again as 1st Guards' Tank Army

Commander

Gen. Major K. S. Moskalenko

1st Guards Tank Army

Feb 43   Formed in the Northwestern Front from the 1st Tank Army; command

staff was provided by the
29th Army; composition:
6th TC, 3d MC, 112th TB,
three light brigades, and
four separate tank regiments

1943   As part of the Voronezh
        Front, took part in the
        Battle of Kursk, then
        reverted to Stavka reserve

Nov 43– Assigned to the 1st
Nov 44   Ukrainian Front, the army
         took part in Zhitomir-
         Berdichev, Proskurov-
         Chernovits, and the Lvov-
         Sandomir offensive opns

1945   Participated in the War-
        saw-Poznan, East Pomeran-
        ian, and and Berlin opns
        (1st Belorussian Front)

Commander

Gen. Col. M. Ya. Katukov

2d Tank Army/2d Guards Tank Army

Jan-Feb 43 Formed from the 3d
            Reserve Army as 2d Tank
            Army. Composition: 11th,
            16th TC; 60th, 112th, 194th
            RDs, plus separate brigades

Feb–Sep 43 As part of the Central
            Front, conducted offensive
            opns in the Briansk Direc-
            tion; participated in the
            Kursk battle and Cher-
            nigov-Pripyat operation

Sep 43–   Stavka reserve
Jan 44

1944   As part of 1st Ukrainian
        Front, advanced in the Vin-
        nitsa Direction; took part in
        Korsun-Shevchenkovsky,
        then (2d Urkainian Front)
        in Uman-Botoshany, and
        Lublin-Brest opns

Nov 44   *Honored and renamed as 2d
          Guards Tank Army*

1945   Warsaw-Poznan, East
        Pomeranian, and Berlin
        offensives

Commanders

Four commanders. Notable: Gen. Col.
S. I. Bogdanov, 43–44, 45

3d Guards Tank Army

May 43   Formed in Stavka Reserve,
         assuming some forces from
         3d Tank Army, including
         the 12th and 15th TCs; aug-
         mented later by the 2d MC

1943   Took part in Orel offensive,
        then placed in Stavka
        reserve; subsequently
        assigned to the Voronezh
        and 1st Ukrainian Fronts
        and participated in the lib-
        eration of Left Bank
        Ukraine and forcing of the
        Dnepr River vic. Velikii
        Bukrina; Kiev offensive
        and defensive opns

1944   Offensive opns: Proskurov-
        Chernovits and Lvov-San-
        domir

1945   Took part in the Sandomir-
        Silesia, Lower Silesia,
        Berlin, and Prague offen-
        sive opns

Commander

Gen. Col. (future Marshal) P. S.
Rybalko

3d Tank Army

May 42   Formed in the Moscow MD
         on the base of the 55th
         Army; initial composition:
         12th and 15th TCs (later the
         6th and 7th Guards TC),
         one MRD, and two RDs.
         Strengthened later with the
         3d TC (Aug 42)

Aug 42   As part of the Western
         Front, participated in effec-
         tive counterstrike against
         the 2d German Tank Army
         south of Kozelsk

1943   Took part in Ostrogozhsk-
        Rossosh, 3d Battle of
        Kharkov (Feb–Mar, first

offensive, then defensive posture)

Apr 43   Reformed into the 57th Army

Commanders

Two commanders. Notable: Gen. Lt. (future Marshal) P. S. Rybalko, 42–43

4th Guards Tank Army

Feb 43   Initially organized as the second est. of 4th Tank Army, but severe battle-field conditions prevented its formation

Jul 43   Restarted organization in the Moscow MD, placed in Stavka reserve; composed of the 11th and 30th Urals Volunteer TCs and 6th Guards MC. Took part in the Orel offensive as part of the Briansk Front

Sep 43   Reverted to Stavka reserve

Feb 44–45 Assigned to 1st Ukrainian Front until the end of the war; battles in Proskurov-Chernovits, Lvov-Sando-mir, Sandomir-Silesia, Lower and Upper Silesia, Berlin, and Prague

Mar 45   Received the Guards honorific

Commanders

Two commanders

4th Tank Army

Jul 42–   Formed in the Stalingrad
Oct 42   Front from the 22d and 23d TCs, one RD, one TB, and the 8th Separate Fighter Air Brigade. Before completing its organiza-tion and equipping, it par-ticipated in a counterat-tack against an enemy grouping attempting to cross the Don at Kalach, halting the German advance. The success of

this counterattack helped prevent Army Group B from taking Stalingrad in stride. The army then conducted defensive retro-grade opns to Stalingrad. 4th Tank Army was then converted to 65th Army

Commander

Gen. Major V. D. Kryuchenkin

5th Guards Tank Army

Feb–   One of the most well-
Mar 43   known Soviet formations during the war, the 5th TA was formed from the 3d Guards and 29th TCs, the 5th Guards MC, and the 994th Light Bomber Regi-ment, an organization which supported the army's employment for deep opns

Jul 43   Key formation in the Sovi-et victory at Prokhorovka in the Battle of Kursk (Voronezh Front)

Oct 43   Assigned to the 2d Ukrain-ian Front, took part in the Belgorod-Kharkov opera-tion and the expansion of bridgeheads across the Dnepr

1944   Continued offensive opns: Kirovograd, Korsun-Shevchenkovsky, Uman-Botoshany, and the Belorussian Campaign (now assigned to the 2d Belorussian Front); as part of 1st Baltic Front, took part in the Memel offensive

1945   Offensive opns in East Prussia as part of the 2d and 3d Belorussian Fronts

Commanders

Four commanders. Notable: Marshal P. A. Rotmistrov, 43–44

5th Tank Army

Jun 42   Formed in the Moscow MD as part of Stavka reserve; composition: 2d, 11th TCs, one RD, and one TB

Jul 42   Assigned to the Briansk Front and strengthened by addition of the 7th TC, the army conducted defensive opns in the Voronezh Direction

Sep 42   After heavy losses, reformed with three TCs and one RD

late 42   Participated in the Battle of Stalingrad.

early 43   Attacked in the Donbas Direction. Advanced to the Mius River and assumed the defense

Apr 43   Disbanded with command staff and part of the forces forming the base for 12th Army

Commanders

Five commanders. Notable: Army Gen. M. M. Popov, Dec 42–Jan 43.

6th Tank Army/ 6th Guards Tank Army

Jan 44   The last of six tank armies formed, comprising the 5th Guards TC and 5th Guards MC. Initially assigned to the 1st Ukrainian Front, then 2d Ukrainian, ending in the 3d Ukrainian Front in 1945. Received the Guards honorific in Sep 44

1944   Took part in Korsun-Shevchenkovsky, Uman-Botoshany, Iassy-Kishinev, Debrecen, and Budapest opns

1945   Vienna opn, followed by the Bratislava-Brno and Prague offensive opns

Summer 1945   Deployed to Mongolia in the Transbaikal Front and led the deep penetration of Manchuria from the west in the Khingan-Mukden offensive; sustained from air by the 12th Air Army

Commander

Gen. Col. A. G. Kravchenko

Air Armies

1st Air Army

May 42   Formed from air forces of the Western Front; initial composition: five fighters, one bomber, one night bomber, one mixed, and five ground-attack divisions

1942   Supported offensive opns of the Western Front in the Yukhnov, Gzhat, and Rzhev sectors; took part in Rzev-Sychevka and Rzhev-Viazma offensives

Mar 43   French Fighter Division "Normandy" was included into the Army, later renamed into the "Normandy-Neman" Air Force group

43–45   Participated in Orel, Smolensk, Belorussian, Memel, Gumbinennen, and East Prussian offensive opns

Commanders

Four commanders

2d Air Army

May 42   Formed from air forces of the Briansk Front, comprising three fighter, one night bomber, one close bomber, and three ground-attack divisions

42–45   Supported defensive battles in the Voronezh Direction, then took part in the
Stalingrad counteroffen-
sive. With other air armies,
took part in the battle for
air supremacy. Supported
the Battle of Kursk, for the
Dnepr River line, Zhito-
mir-Berdichev, Korsun-
Shevchenkovsky, Rovno-
Lutsk, Proskurov-Cher-
novtsy, Lvov-Sandomir,
Sandomir-Silesia, Lower
and Upper Silesia, Berlin,
and Prague offensive
opns. Overall, conducted
more than 300,000
sorties

Commanders
Two commanders

3d Air Army

May 42   Formed from the air forces
of the Kalinin Front and
included three fighter, two
ground-attack, and one
bomber division. Initially
defended near the city of
Bely, then took part in
Rzhev-Sychevka and
Velikie Luki opns
1943   Participated in Northwestern Front opns at the
Demiansk bridgehead,
then supported ground
forces at Smolensk, Nevel,
and Gorodok
1944   Participated in the Belorussian Campaign and
Baltic opns
1945   Supported the East Prussian operation and the
blockade of Kurland; overall, the air army flew over
200,000 sorties during the
war

Commanders
Two commanders

4th Air Army

May 42   Formed from the air forces
of the Southern Front:
three fighter, one bomber,
one night bomber, and one
ground-attack division.
Assigned to a series of
fronts in the southern
theater. Conducted defen-
sive opns in the Donbas,
along the Don, and in the
battle for the Caucasus.
Supported Kerch-Eltigen
amphibious operation and
the battle for air supremacy in the Kuban (spring
1943)
Spring 44   Supported the Maritime
Army in the liberation of
Crimea
Summer   Assigned to the 2d Belo-
44–May   russian Front. Participated
1945   in the Belorussian, East
Prussian, East Pomeran-
ian, and Berlin opns. Overall, flew approximately
300,000 sorties

Commanders
Two commanders

5th Air Army

Jun 42   Formed from air forces in
the North Caucasus Front,
consisting of three fighter,
one ground-attack, and
one bomber division
42–43   Supported the Battle for
the Caucasus, including
both ground and Black Sea
forces. Fought the air campaign in the Kuban (spring
1943). Transferred to the
Steppe then 2d Ukrainian
Front and participated in
the Belgorod-Kharkov
operation and the battle
for the Dnepr River line
44–45   Took part in the
Kirovograd, Korsun-

Shevchenkovsky, Uman-Botoshany, Iassy-Kishinev, Debrecen, Budapest, Vienna, and Prague opns

Commander

Gen. Col. S. M. Goryunov

6th Air Army

Jun 42	Formed from air forces of the Northwestern Front; included two fighter, one bomber, one night bomber, and one ground-attack division. Assigned initially to the Northwestern Front through Feb 44, then to 2d and 1st Belorussian Fronts
1943	Supported the Demiansk and Nevel offensive opns, then placed in Stavka reserve in Nov 43
1944	Subordinated the 16th Army; participated in Belorussian campaign and opns in eastern Poland
Sep 44	Again placed in Stavka reserve. The command staff formed the initial headquarters of the Polish Air Force. The army flew approximately 120,000 sorties during the war

Commanders

Two commanders

7th Air Army

Nov 42	Formed from the air forces of the Karelian Front, comprising two fighter, one ground-attack, and one bomber division
42–43	Supported forces of the Karelian Front and Northern Fleet; protected convoy flow from the US and UK into Murmansk

1944	Took part in the Sbir-Petrozavod and Petsamo-Iassy offensive opns
Dec 44	Placed in Stavka reserve

Commander

Gen. Col. I. M. Sokolev

8th Air Army

1942	Formed in June in the Southwestern Front, comprising five fighter, three bomber, and two ground-attack divisions; initially supported front opns in the Poltava, Kupyan, and Valyuisk-Rossosh Directions. Subsequently, supported both the defensive and offensive periods of the Battle of Stalingrad. Struggle for regional air supremacy
43–44	Supported ground forces in the destruction of the Kotelnikov enemy formations. Took part in opns in the Rostov Direction, on the Mius River, in the liberation of the Donbas, Left Bank Ukraine, Melitopol, and the recovery of Crimea. Supporting the 1st and 4th Ukrainian Fronts, the air army participated in the Lvov-Sandomir and Carpathian opns
1945	Participated in opns in Czechoslovakia, culminating in the capitulation of German forces in Prague

Commanders

Two commanders

9th Air Army

Aug 42	Formed on the Far Eastern Front from three fighter, two bomber, and two ground-attack divisions

Apr 45	Included within the Maritime Group of Forces
Aug 45	Augmented by the 19th Bomber Corps, the army supported 1st Far Eastern Front offensive operation, Harbin-Girin; conducted airborne assaults at multiple airfields; overall, 4,400 sorties were flown in support of the offensive

Commanders

Three commanders

10th Air Army

Aug 42	Established in the Far Eastern Front with one fighter, three bomber, and one ground-attack division
Jul 45	Augmented with the 18th Air Corps (Mixed)
Aug 45	As part of the 2d Far Eastern Front, supported the Sungari offensive operation in the Tsitsihar Direction; supported follow-on opns in southern Sakhalin and the Kiril Islands. A total of 3,300 sorties were flown

Commanders

Three commanders

11th Air Army

Aug 42	Formed in the Far Eastern Front from the 2d Red Banner Army with three divisions: one fighter, one bomber, and one mixed
1944	Redesignated as the 18th Air Corps (mixed) and included in the 10th Air Army in Jul 45

Commander

Gen. Major V. I. Bibikov

12th Air Army

Aug 42	Formed from air forces units in the Transbaikal

	Front, including two bomber, two fighter, and one ground attack division
41–45	Defended Far East borders and prepared fighter pilots and cadres for air armies in the west
Aug 45	Comprising 13 air divisions of various kinds, supported the Khingan-Mukden offensive with bombing, ground support, and supplies, particularly to the 6th TA. Conducted four deep airborne opns. Overall, conducted 5,000 sorties and delivered 4,000 tons of supplies

Commanders

Two commanders

13th Air Army

Nov 42	Formed from air forces of the Leningrad Front, including one fighter, one bomber, and one ground-attack division
43–45	Supported forces of the Leningrad and other fronts in the the lifting of the Leningrad blockade (Jan 43), Leningrad-Novgorod, Vyborg, Narva, Tallinn, and the Moonzund opns. Flew approximately 120,000 sorties during this period

Commander

Gen. Col. of Aviation S. D. Rybalchenko

14th Air Army

Jun 42	Formed from the air forces of the Volkhov Front, including one bomber and one ground-attack division
Jan 43	Supported the lifting of the blockade of Leningrad by the Volkhov and

Leningrad Fronts. Participated in the Novgorod-
Luga operation

Feb 44   The command staff was
assigned to Stavka reserve,
with air units distributed
to other air armies

Apr 44   Reformed and assigned to
the 3d Baltic Front. Took
part in the Pskov-Ostro-
gozhsk, Tartu, and Riga
offensives

Nov 44   Command staff again subordinated to the Stavka
reserve and units distributed to other air armies

Commander
Gen. Lt. I. P. Zhuravlev

15th Air Army

Jul 42   Formed from air forces of
the Briansk Front, com-
prising one fighter, one
bomber, one ground attack
division, and three sepa-
rate regiments

1942   Defensive opns vic.
Voronezh

43–45   Voronezh-Kastornoe, Orel,
and Briansk offensives
Transferred to 2d Baltic
Front in Oct 43; took part
in the Vitebsk-Polotsk,
Staraya Russa-Novorzhev,
Rezhitsa-Dvina, and Riga
opns. Supported blockade
of enemy forces in Kur-
land in 1945. Overall, the
army flew approximately
160,000 sorties

Commanders
Two commanders

16th Air Army

Aug 42   Formed from units of 8th
Air Army; placed in Stav-
ka reserve. Initially
composed of two fighter
and two ground-attack

divisions. Fought in the
southern theater in a series
of fronts

1942   Battle of Stalingrad

1943   Battles of Kursk and the
Left Bank Ukraine

1944   Belorussian campaign

1945   Offensive opns across
Poland and the seizure of
Berlin; overall, it flew
approximately 780,000 sorties during the war

Commanders
Two commanders

17th Air Army

Nov 42   Formed from air forces of
the Southwestern Front,
including a mixed air
corps, two fighter, one
ground-attack, one
bomber, and one night
bomber division. Immedi-
ately took part in the Battle of Stalingrad

43–45   Participated in Ostrogozhsk-Rossosh, Left and Right
Bank Ukraine, the libera-
tion of Romania, Bulgaria,
Yugoslavia, Hungary, and
Austria. Over 200,00 sor-
ties flown

Commanders
Two commanders

18th Air Army

Dec 44   The last air army formed
during the war, with a
unique purpose and utili-
ty. The 18th was formed
from long-range aviation
units from the Stavka
reserve, including five
long-range bomber corps
and four separate bomber
divisions, for a total of 22
divisions. The army com-
mand staff remained in
Moscow, with a forward

command post at Bresla. The command was formed in order to centralize heavy, long-range bombing strikes throughout the depths of enemy dispositions in the final six months of the war

1945   Deep bombing opns in support of Vistula-Oder, East-Prussian, and Berlin offensives. Over 19,000 sorties were flown during this time period

Commander

Marshal of Aviation A. Ye. Golovanov

Corps

Infantry

Rifle Corps (RC)

Note: Number of commanders shown is for all establishments.

1st Separate RC. Apr 42–Sep 42. Disbanded.
  Two commanders
1st RC
  1st est. Apr 40–Sep 41. Disbanded.
  2d est. Sep 43–May 45.
  Three commanders
1st Light RC. Feb–Mar 44. Converted to the 125th Light Mountain RC
2d RC
  1st est. Jul 40–Aug 41. Disbanded.
  2d est. May 42–Sep 45.
  Two commanders
2d Light RC. Feb–Mar 44. Converted to 127th Light Mountain RC
3d RC. Apr 40–Jul 41. Disbanded
3d Mountain RC. Jul 42–May 45.
  Eight commanders
4th RC
  1st est. Feb 40–Sep 41. Disbanded.
  2d est. Apr 42–May 45.
  Three commanders
5th RC
  1st est. Feb 39–Jul 41. Disbanded.
  2d est. Jun 42–May 45.
  Three commanders
6th RC
  1st est. Jan 40–Sep 41. Disbanded.
  2d est. Nov 42–Apr 43. Became 19th Guards RC.

  3d est. Jun 43–May 45.
  Five commanders
7th RC
  1st est. Feb 38–Aug 41. Disbanded.
  2d est. Sep 42–Apr 43. Became 35th Guards RC.
  3d est. Jun 43–May 45.
  Six commanders
8th RC
  1st est. Aug 42–Aug 41. Disbanded.
  2d est. Sep 42–May 45.
  Three commanders
9th RC
  1st est. Jun 41–May 42.
  2d est. Oct 42–May 45
10th RC
  1st est. Feb 40–Sep 41. Disbanded.
  2d est. Oct 42–Dec 42. Disbanded.
  3d est. Feb 43–May 45.
  Five commanders
11th RC
  1st est. Apr 38–Nov 41. Disbanded.
  2d est. Oct 42–May 45.
  Six commanders
12th RC
  1st est. Jan–Jul 41. Disbanded.
  2d est. Dec 42–May 45.
  Two commanders
13th RC
  1st est. Feb 38–Aug 41. Disbanded.
  2d est. Dec 42–May 45.
  Two commanders
14th RC
  1st est. Jan–Aug 41. Disbanded.
  2d est. Nov 42–Apr 43. Converted to 27th Guards RC.

3d est. Aug 43–May 45.
Ten commanders
15th RC
    1st est. Feb 40–Aug 41.
    Disbanded.
    2d est. Nov 42–Apr 43. Converted
    to 28th Guards RC
16th RC
    1st est. Jan–Aug 41. Disbanded.
    2d est. Dec 42–May 45.
    Nine commanders
17th RC
    1st est. Mar–Aug 41. Disbanded.
    2d est. Dec 42–Aug 45.
    Two commanders
18th RC
    1st est. Mar–Jul 41. Disbanded.
    2d est. Dec 42–Feb 43. Disbanded.
    3d est. Feb–Apr 43. Converted to
    34th Guards RC.
    4th est. Jun 43–May 45
19th RC
    1st est. Jun 40–Sep 41. Disbanded.
    2d est. Feb–Apr 43. Converted to
    29th Guards RC.
    3d est. Jun 43–May 45.
    Four commanders
20th RC
    1st est. Jul 40–Aug 41.
    2d est. Feb 43–May 45.
    Five commanders
21st RC
    1st est. Mar–Jun 41.
    2d est. Mar 43–May 45.
    Five commanders
22d RC
    1st est. Jun–Sep 41. Disbanded.
    2d est. Mar 43–May 45.
    Four commanders
23d RC
    1st est. Dec 40–Aug 41. Disbanded.
    2d est. Mar 43–May 45.
    Three commanders
24th RC
    1st est. Jun–Sep 41.
    2d est. Feb 43–May 45.
    Three commanders
25th RC
    1st est. Jun–Jul 41.

2d est. Feb 43–May 45.
Six commanders
26th RC. Nov 40–Sep 45.
    Five commanders
27th RC
    1st est. Aug 39–Sep 41. Disbanded.
    2d est. Feb–Apr 43. Converted to
    18th Guards RC.
    3d est. Jun 43–May 45.
    Four commanders
28th RC
    1st est. Mar 40–Sep 41. Disbanded.
    2d est. Feb 43–May 45.
    Three commanders
29th RC
    1st est. Jun–Sep 41. Disbanded.
    2d est. Mar–Apr 43.
    3d est. Jun 43–May 45.
    Five commanders
30th RC
    1st est. Aug 39–Aug 41. Disbanded.
    2d est. Mar–Apr 43. Converted to
    26th Guards RC.
    3d est. Jun 43–May 45.
    Three commanders
31st RC
    1st est. Nov 40–Sep 41. Disbanded.
    2d est. May 43–May 45.
    Four commanders
32d RC
    1st est. Nov 39–Aug 41. Disbanded.
    2d est. May 43–May 45.
    Two commanders
34th RC
    1st est. Jun 40–Aug 41.
    Disbanded.
    2d est. May 43–May 45.
    Three commanders
35th RC
    1st est. Jul 40–Aug 41.
    Disbanded.
    2d est. May 43. Converted to 44th
    RC.
    3d est. Jun 43–May 45.
    Five commanders
36th RC
    1st est. Jun–Sep 41. Disbanded.
    2d est. May 43–May 45.
    Six commanders

37th RC
1st est. Mar–Sep 41. Disbanded.
2d est. May 43–May 45.
Six commanders
38th RC. May 43–May 45.
One commander
39th RC. Aug 41–Sep 45.
Five commanders
40th RC
1st est. Mar–Jul 41. Disbanded.
2d est. Jun 43–May 45.
Two commanders
41st RC
1st est. Mar–Jul 41. Disbanded.
2d est. Jun 43–May 45.
Two commanders
42d RC
1st est. Mar–Aug 41. Disbanded.
2d est. Jun 43–May 45.
Two commanders
43d RC. May 43–May 45.
One commander
44th RC
1st est. Mar–Sep 41. Disbanded.
2d est. May 43–May 45.
Two commanders
45th RC
1st est. Mar–Aug 41. Disbanded.
2d est. Jun 43–Sep 45.
Five commanders.
46th RC. Jun 43–May 45.
One commander
47th RC
1st est. Jun 40–Aug 41. Disbanded.
2d est. Jun 43–May 45.
Six commanders
48th RC
1st est. Mar–Aug 41. Disbanded.
2d est. Jun 43–Sep 45.
Four commanders
50th RC
1st est. Jan–Aug 41. Disbanded.
2d est. Jun 43–May 45.
Five commanders
51st RC
1st est. Mar–Nov 41. Disbanded.
2d est. Jun 43–May 45.
Five commanders
52d RC
1st est. Aug 39–Aug 41. Disbanded.

2d est. Jun 43–May 45.
Four commanders.
53d RC
1st est. Aug 39–Aug 41. Disbanded.
2d est. Jul 43–May 45.
Two commanders
54th RC. Jun 43–May 45.
Two commanders
55th RC
1st est. Mar–Sep 41. Disbanded.
2d est. Jun 43–May 45.
Four commanders
56th RC. Jul 43–Sep 45.
Two commanders
57th RC. Aug 43–Sep 45.
Three commanders
58th RC. Aug 39–May 45.
Three commanders
59th RC. Jun 40–Aug 45.
Three commanders
60th RC. Sep 43–May 45.
Three commanders
61st RC
1st est. Jan 40–Nov 41. Disbanded.
2d est. Aug 43–May 45.
Three commanders
62d RC
1st est. Aug 39–Sep 41. Disbanded.
2d est. Jul 43–May 45.
Four commanders
63d RC
1st est. Nov 40–Aug 41. Disbanded.
2d est. Aug 43–May 45.
Seven commanders
64th RC
1st est. Aug–Sep 41. Disbanded.
2d est. Jul 43–May 45.
Three commanders
65th RC
1st est. Mar–Aug 41. Disbanded.
2d est. Aug 43–Sep 45.
Five commanders
66th RC
1st est. Jun–Sep 41. Disbanded.
2d est. Jul 43–May 45.
Three commanders
67th RC
1st est. Mar–Oct 41. Disbanded.
2d est. Jun 43–May 45.
Three commanders

68th RC. Jul 43–May 45.
One commander
69th RC
   1st est. Mar–Sep 41. Disbanded.
   2d est. Aug 43–May 45.
   Three commanders
70th RC. Aug 43–May 45.
One commander
71st RC. Aug 43–May 45.
Three commanders
72d RC. Aug 43–Sep 45.
Three commanders
73d RC. Jul 43–May 45.
Two commanders
74th RC. Sep 43–May 45.
Three commanders
75th RC. Sep 43–May 45.
Five commanders
76th RC. Dec 43–May 45.
Two commanders
77th RC. Aug 43–Sep 45.
Three commanders
78th RC. Sep 43–May 45.
Two commanders
79th RC. Oct 43–May 45.
Two commanders
80th RC. Sep 43–May 45.
Three commanders
81st RC. Aug 43–May 45.
Eight commanders
82d RC. Jul 43–May 45.
One commander
83d RC. Jul 43–May 45.
Two commanders
84th RC. Jul 43–May 45.
Three commanders
85th RC. Sep 43–Sep 45.
Two commanders
86th RC. Aug 43–Sep 45.
Four commanders
87th RC. Aug 43–May 45.
Two commanders
88th RC. Jul 43–Sep 45.
Two commanders
89th RC. Sep 43–May 45.
Three commanders
90th RC. Aug 43–May 45.
Four commanders
91st RC. Aug 43–May 45.
One commander

92d RC. Aug 43–May 45.
Three commanders
93d RC. Sep 43–May 45.
Four commanders
94th RC. Aug 43–Sep 45.
One commander
95th RC. Oct 43–Sep 45.
Four commanders
96th RC. Aug 43–May 45.
Three commanders
97th RC. Nov 43–May 45.
Four commanders
98th RC. Nov 43–May 45.
Two commanders
99th RC. Dec 43–Dec 44.
Converted to 40th Guards RC.
100th RC. Nov 43–May 45.
Three commanders
101st RC. Dec 43–May 45.
Two commanders
102d RC. Jan 44–May 45.
Two commanders
103d RC. Jan 44–May 45.
Two commanders
104th RC. Dec 43–May 45.
Two commanders
105th RC. Dec 43–May 45.
One commander
106th RC. Nov 43–May 45.
Five commanders
107th RC. Oct 43–May 45.
One commander
108th RC. Jan 44–May 45.
Two commanders
109th RC. Nov 43–May 45.
Two commanders
110th RC. Nov 43–May 45.
Three commanders
111th RC. Nov 43–May 45.
One commander
112th RC. Nov 43–May 45.
Two commanders
113th RC. Dec 43–Sep 45.
Three commanders
114th RC. Jan 44–May 45.
Two commanders
115th RC. Nov 43–May 45.
One commander
116th RC. Dec 43–Jun 45.
Three commanders

117th RC. Dec 43–May 4.
One commander
118th RC. Dec 43–May 45.
Three commanders
119th RC. Dec 43–May 45.
Three commanders
120th RC. Jan 44–May 45.
Three commanders
121st RC. Dec 43–May 45.
One commander
122d RC. Dec 43–May 45.
Three commanders
123d RC. Jan 44–May 45.
Four commanders
124th RC. Jan 44–May 45.
Four commanders
125th RC. Jan 44–May 45.
Four commanders
126th Light Mountain RC. Mar 44–
Sep 45. One commander
127th Light Mountain RC. Mar 44–
May 45. Three commanders
128th RC. Apr 44–May 45.
Two commanders
129th RC. Apr 44–May 45.
Three commanders
130th RC. Jun 44–May 45.
One commander
131st RC. Aug 44–May 45.
Five commanders
132d RC. Aug 44–May 45.
Two commanders
133d RC. Sep 44–May 45.
Two commanders
134th RC. Sep 44–May 45.
Three commanders
135th RC. Nov 44–May 45.
One commander

Guards Rifle Corps (Gds RC)

1st Gds RC. Sep 41–May 45.
Four commanders
2d Gds RC. Dec 41–May 45.
Six commanders
3d Gds RC
  1st est. Jan 42–Aug 42.
  Command staff transferred to 10th
  Gds RC.
  2d est. Apr 43–May 45.
  Seven commanders

4th Gds RC. Jan 42–May 45.
Six commanders
5th Gds RC. Feb 42–Sep 45.
Seven commanders
6th Gds RC. Mar 42–May 45.
Seven commanders
7th Gds RC. Apr 42–May 45.
Nine commanders
8th Gds RC. Apr 42–May 45.
Six commanders
9th Gds RC. May 42–May 45.
Six commanders
10th Gds RC. Aug 42–May 45.
Four commanders
11th Gds RC. Aug 42–May 45.
Eight commanders
12th Gds RC. Dec 42–May 45.
Five commanders
13th Gds RC. Nov 42–May 45.
Three commanders
14th Gds RC. Dec 42–May 45.
One commander
15th Gds RC. Apr 43–May 45.
Four commanders
16th Gds RC. Apr 43–May 45.
Five commanders
17th Gds RC. Apr 43–May 45.
Three commanders
18th Gds RC. Apr 43–Sep 45.
Three commanders
19th Gds RC. Apr 43–May 45.
Five commanders
20th Gds RC. Apr 43–May 45.
Two commanders
21st Gds RC. Apr 43–May 45.
Two commanders
22d Gds RC. Apr 43–May 45.
Three commanders
23d Gds RC. Apr 43–May 45.
Three commanders
24th Gds RC. Apr 43–May 45.
Three commanders
25th Gds RC. Apr 43–May 45.
Two commanders
26th Gds RC. Apr 43–May 45.
One commander
27th Gds RC. Apr 43–May 45.
Three commanders
28th Gds RC. Apr 43–May 45.
Five commanders

29th Gds RC. Apr 43–May 45.
Seven commanders
30th Gds RC. Apr 43–May 45.
Two commanders
31st Gds RC. Apr 43–May 45.
Three commanders
32d Gds RC. Apr 43–May 45.
One commander
33d Gds RC. Apr 43–May 45.
Three commanders
34th Gds RC. Apr 43–May 45.
Five commanders
35th Gds RC. Apr 43–May 45.
Three commanders
36th Gds RC. Jun 43–May 45.
Four commanders
37th Gds RC. Jan 44–May 45.
One commander
38th Gds RC. Aug 44–May 45.
Two commanders
39th Gds RC. Aug 44–May 45.
One commander
40th Gds RC. Dec 44–May 45.
Two commanders

Rifle Corps Awarded with Place-Name Honorifics

9th Guards Rifle Corps (Brest)

Jun 42	Formed in the Kaluga region on the base of the 12th Gds RD as the 9th Gds RC. Spent entire war as part of the 61st Army
42–43	Participated in the Orel offensive after Kursk, Chernigov-Pripyat, and Gomel-Rechitsa opns
1944	Kalinkov-Mozyr, Belorussian, and Riga offensives
1945	Took part in the Kurland blockade; Warsaw-Poznan, East Pomeranian, and Berlin offensives
Aug 44	*Awarded the Brest place-name honorific*

Commanders
Gen. Major N. I. Kiryuhin, 1942
Col. F. E. Pochema, 1942
Gen. Major A. A. Boreiko, 42–44

Gen. Major M. A. Popov, 1944
Gen. Lt. G. A. Halyuzin, 44–45
Gen. Lt. A. D. Shemenkov, 1945
Other Names
Brest Rifle Corps

28th Guards Rifle Corps/ 15th Rifle Corps (2d est.) (Lublin)

Nov 42	Formed in the Voronezh region as 15th RD (2d est.). Initially part of 6th Army; assigned to the famous 8th Guards Army after April 1943, with rifle divisions
1943	Middle Don opns, 3d Battle of Kharkov, Izyum-Barvenkovo, liberation of the Donbas, and Dnepr River line opns
Apr 43	*Honored and renamed 28th Guards Rifle Corps*
44–45	Participated in all 8th Guards Army opns
Aug 44	*Awarded the Lublin place-name honorific*

Commanders
Gen. Major P. F. Privalov, 1942
Gen. Major A. S. Gryaznov, 1943
Gen. Major S. S. Guriev, 1943
Gen. Major D. P. Monahov, 1944
Gen. Lt. S. I. Morozov, 1944
Gen. Lt. A. I. Rizov, 44–45
Other Names
Lublin Rifle Corps

18th Guards Rifle Corps (Stanislav-Budapest)

Apr 43	Formed in Moscow region as the 18th Guards Rifle Corps. Assigned to a variety of armies, including the 13th, 60th, 1st Gds, 38th, 18th, 46th, and 53d
43–44	Participated in the Battle of Kursk, Left-Bank Ukraine, Kiev offensive and defensive opns, Zhito-mir-Berdichev, Rovno-Lutsk, Proskurov-

Chernovtsy, Lvov-Sando-
mir, and East Carpathian
opns

Aug 44   *Awarded the Stanislav place-*
          name honorific

1945   Budapest, Vienna, Bratisla-
          va-Brno, Prague, and
          Khingan-Mukden opns

Apr 45   *Awarded the Budapest place-*
          name honorific

Commanders
Gen. Lt. I. M. Afonin, 1943–Jan 45 and
   Apr–Sep 45
Gen. Major L. B. Sosedov, Jan–Apr 45
Other Names
Stanislav-Budapest Rifle Corps

Calvalry

Cavalry Corps (CC)

1st CC. Jan–Mar 42. Disbanded.
One commander
2d CC
   1st est. Mar–Nov 41. Converted to
   1st Guards CC.
   2d est. Dec 41–Jun 42. Disbanded.
   Five commanders
3d CC. Nov 41. Converted to 2d
Guards CC.
4th CC. Jan 41–May 43.
Two commanders
5th CC
   1st est. Mar 41–Dec 41. Converted
   to 3d Guards CC.
   2d est. Jan–Jul 42. Disbanded
6th CC
   1st est. Mar 40–Jul 41.
   2d est. Jan–May 42.
   Four commanders
7th CC. Dec 41–Jan 43. Converted to
6th Guards CC. Three commanders
8th CC. Jan–Feb 43. Four commanders
9th CC. Feb–Apr 42. Disbanded.
Two commanders
10th CC. Jan–Feb 42. Disbanded.
One commander
13th CC. Jan–Jul 42. Disbanded.
Two commanders

14th CC. Jan–Apr 42. Disbanded.
Two commanders
15th CC. Jan 42–May 45. Five
commanders
16th CC. Jan–Mar 42. Disposition not
clear. One commander
17th CC. Jun–Aug 42. Converted to
4th Guards CC. Two
commanders
18th CC. Aug 42–Aug 43. Disbanded.
Three commanders
19th CC. Feb–Jul 43. Disbanded.
One commander

Guards Cavalry Corps (Gds CC)

1st Gds CC. Nov 41–May 45.
Two commanders
2d Gds CC. Nov 41–May 45.
Three commanders
3d Gds CC. Dec 41–May 45.
Three commanders
4th Gds CC. Aug 42–May 45.
Four commanders
5th Gds CC. Nov 42–May 45.
Two commanders
6th Gds CC. Jan 43–May 45.
Two commanders
7th Gds CC. Feb 43–May 45.
Four commanders

Cavalry Corps Awarded with Place-Names Honorifics

4th Guards Kuban Cossack Cavalry Corps

Jan–   Formed in Krasnodar
Apr 42   region as 17th Kuban
         Cosack Cavalry Corps
42–45   Fought in the North Cau-
         casus, Caucasus, Southern,
         4th and 3d Ukrainian, 1st
         Belorussian and 2d
         Ukrainian Fronts. Partici-
         pated in the battle for the
         Caucasus, in the Donbas,
         Melitopol, Bereznegova-
         toye-Snigirovka, Odessa,
         Belorussian, Debrecen,

Budapest, Bratislava-Brno and Prague offensive opns

Aug 42   *Honored and renamed 4th Kuban Cossack Cavalry Division*

Commanders
Gen. Major M. F. Maleyev, 1942
Gen. Lt. N. Y. Kirichenko, 42–43
Gen. Lt. I. A. Pliyev, 43–44
Gen. Major V. S. Golovsky, 44–45
Gen. Lt. F. V. Kamkov, 1945

Other Names
Kuban Cossack Cavalry Corps,
17th Kuban Cossack Cavalry Corps

5th Guards Don Cossack Cavalry Corps

Nov 42   Formed as 5th Guards Cavalry Corps. Included the 11th and 12th Guards Don Cossack Cavalry Divisions, 63d Cavalry Division, and others

42–45   Fought as part of the Caucasus, North Caucasus, Southern, 4th , 2d and 3d Ukrainian Fronts. Helped liberate North Caucasus and Ukraine. Participated in Iassy-Kishinev, Debrecen, Budapest, and Vienna offensive opns

Apr 45   *Awarded with the name Budapest*

Commanders
Gen. Lt. A. G. Selivanov, 42–44
Gen. Lt. S. I. Gorshkov, 44–45

Other Names
Budapest Cavalry Corps, 5th Guards Cavalry Corps

7th Guards Cavalry Corps

Jan–Jun 42   Formed in Orel and Tula regions as 8th Cavalry Corps

1942   Fought on different fronts as a part of several armies. Defended Voronezh and Stalingrad

43–44   Helped liberate Left Bank Ukraine and Eastern Belorussia. Participated in Lublin-Brest operation

Feb 43   *Honored and renamed 7th Guards Cavalry Corps*

1945   Warsaw-Poznan, East-Pomeranian and Berlin offensive opns

Apr 45   *Awarded with the name Brandenburg*

Commanders
Gen. Lt. P. P. Korzun, 1942
Col. I. F. Lunev, 1942
Gen. Major M. D. Borisov, 42–43
Gen. Major Y. S. Sharaburko, 1943
Gen. Major M. F. Maleyev, 1943
Gen. Lt. M. P. Konstantinov, 43–45

Other Names
Brandenburg Cavalry Corps,
8th Cavalry Corps

Armor

Mechanized and Tank Corps (MC)

1st MC
1st est. Jan–Aug 41. Disbanded.
2d est. Aug 42–May 45.
Two commanders

2d MC
1st est. Jan 40–Aug 41. Disbanded. One commander.
2d est. Sep 42–Jul 43. Converted to 7th Guards MC.
Two commanders

3d MC
1st est. Jan–Aug 41. Disbanded.
2d est. Sep 42–Oct 43. Converted to 8th Guards MC.
Two commanders

4th MC
1st est. Jan–Aug 41. Disbanded.
2d est. Sep–Dec 42. Converted to 3d Guards MC.
Three commanders

5th MC
1st est. Mar–Aug 41. Disbanded.
2d est. Nov 42–Sep 44. Converted

to 9th Guards MC.
Two commanders

6th MC
  1st est. Jun 40–Jun 41. Disbanded.
  2d est. Sep 42–Jan 43. Converted to
  5th Guards MC.
  Two commanders

7th MC
  1st est. Jun 40–Aug 41. Disbanded.
  2d est. Aug 43–Sep 45.
  Three commanders

8th MC
  1st est. Jun 40–Aug 41. Disbanded.
  2d est. Aug 43–May 45.
  Three commanders

9th MC
  1st est. Nov 40–Aug 41. Disbanded.
  2d est. Aug 43–May 45.
  Four commanders

10th MC
  1st est. Mar–Jul 41. Disbanded.
  2d est. Dec 44–May 45.
  Three commanders

11th MC. Mar–Aug 41. Disbanded.
  One commander

12th MC. Mar–Aug 41. Disbanded.
  Three commanders

13th MC. Feb–Jul 41. Disbanded.
  One commander

14th MC. Mar–Jul 41. Disbanded.
  One commander

15th MC. Mar–Jun 41. Disbanded.
  One commander

16th MC. Mar–Jul 41. Disbanded.
  One commander

17th MC. Mar–Aug 41. Disbanded.
  One commander

18th MC. Mar–Aug 41. Disbanded.
  One commander

19th MC. Mar–Aug 41. Disbanded.
  One commander

20th MC. Mar–Jul 41. Disbanded.
  One commander

21st MC. Mar–Aug 41. Disbanded.
  One commander

22d MC. Mar–Sep 41. Disbanded.
  Three commanders

23d MC. Mar–Jul 41. Disbanded.
  One commander

24th MC. Mar–Jul 41. Disbanded.
  One commander

25th MC. Mar–Aug 41. Disbanded.
  One commander

26th MC. Mar–Jul 41. Disbanded.
  One commander

27th MC. Mar–Aug 41. Disbanded.
  One commander

28th MC. Mar–Aug 41. Disbanded.
  One commander

29th MC. Mar–May 41. Disbanded.
  One commander

30th MC. Mar–Jun 41. Disbanded.
  One commander

Guards Mechanized Corps (Gds MC)

1st Gds MC. Jun 42–May 45.
  One commander

2d Gds MC. Oct 42–May 45.
  One commander

3d Gds MC. Dec 42–May 45.
  Three commander

4th Gds MC. Jan 43–May 45.
  Two commanders

5th Gds MC. Jan 43–May 45.
  Three commanders

6th Gds MC. Jun 43–May 45.
  Four commanders

7th Gds MC. Jun 43–May 45.
  One commander

8th Gds MC. Jul 43–May 45.
  Two commanders

9th Gds MC. Sep 44–Jun 45.
  One commander

Tank Corps (TC)

1st TC. Mar 42–May 45. Two
  commanders

2d TC. Apr 42–Sep 43. Converted to
  8th Guards TC. Six commanders

3d TC. Mar 42–Nov 44. Converted to
  9th Guards TC. Six commanders

4th TC. Mar 42–Feb 43. Converted to
  5th Guards TC. Two commanders

5th TC. Apr 42–May 45.
  Four commanders

6th TC. Apr 42–Oct 43. Converted to 11th Guards TC. One commander

7th TC. Apr–Dec 42. Converted to 3d Guards TC. One commander. Gen. Major P. A. Rotmistrov

8th TC. Apr–Sep 42. Converted to 3d MC. Two commanders

9th TC. May 42–May 45. Seven commanders

10th TC. Apr 42–May 45. Five commanders

11th TC. May 42–May 45. Six commanders

12th TC. May 42–Jul 43. Converted to 6th Guards TC. Four commanders

13th TC. May 42–Jan 43. Converted to 4th Guards MC. Two commanders

14th TC. May–Sep 42. Converted to 6th MC (2d est.). One commander

15th TC. May 42–Jul 43. Converted to 7th Guards TC. Three commanders

16th TC. Jun 42–Nov 44. Converted to 12th Guards TC. Six commanders

17th TC. Jun 42–Jan 43. Converted to 4th Guards TC. Four commanders

18th TC. Jun 42–May 45. Nine commanders

19th TC. Dec 42–May 45. Three commanders

20th TC. Dec 42–May 45. Four commanders

21st TC. Apr–Jun 42. Disbanded. One commander

22d TC. Apr–Aug 42. Converted to 5th MC (2d est.)

23d TC. Apr 42–May 45. Six commanders

24th TC. Apr–Dec 42. Converted to 2d Guards TC

25th TC. Jul 42–May 45. Four commanders

26th TC. Jul–Dec 42. Converted to 1st Guards TC. One commander

27th TC. Jun–Sep 42. Converted to 1st MC. One commander

28th TC. Jul–Sep 42. Converted to 4th MC (2d est.). One commander

29th TC. Feb 43–May 45. Four commanders

30th TC. Feb–Oct 43. Converted to 10th Guards TC

31st TC. May 43–May 45. Four commanders

Guards Tank Corps (Gds TC)

1st Gds TC. Dec 42–May 45. Three commanders

2d Gds TC. Dec 42–May 45. Two commanders

3d Gds TC. Dec 42–May 45. Three commanders

4th Gds TC. Jan 43–May 45. One commander

5th Gds TC. Feb 43–Sep 45. Three commanders

6th Gds TC. Jul 42–May 45. Five commanders

7th Gds TC. Jul 43–May 45. Six commanders

8th Gds TC. Sep 43–May 45. One commander

9th Gds TC. Nov 44–May 45. One commander

10th Gds TC. Oct 43–May 45. Four commanders

11th Gds TC. Oct 43–May 45. Two commanders

12th Gds TC. Nov 44–May 45. Two commanders

Mechanized and Tank Corps Awarded Place-Name Honorifics

1st Guards Mechanized Corps (Vienna)

Nov 42	Formed in Tambov region as 1st Guards Mech Corps. Assigned to Southwestern and 3d Ukrainian Fronts
1942	Participated in the Battle of Stalingrad
1943	Offensive opns at Zaporozhe
44–45	Offensive opns at Prague, Lake Balaton, and Vienna
May 45	*Awarded the Vienna place-name honorific*

Commander
Gen. Lt. I. N. Russiyanov
Other Names
Vienna Mechanized Corps

2d Guards Mechanized Corps (Nikolayev-Budapest)

Nov 42	Formed in Tambov region as 2d Guards Mech Corps. Assigned in sequence to the Stalingrad, Southern, 4th, 3d, and 2d Ukrainian Fronts
42–43	Participated in the battles of Stalingrad, Rostov, the liberation of the Donbas, and Melitopol
1944	Took part in the Nikopol-Krivoi Rog, Bereznegovatoye-Snigirovka, and Odessa offensive opns
Apr 44	Awarded the Nikolayev place-name honorific
1945	Offensive opns at Budapest, Bratislava-Brno, Prague, and Vienna
Apr 45	*Awarded the Budapest place-name honorific*

Commander
Gen. Lt. K. V. Sviridov
Other Names
Nikolayev-Budapest Mechanized Corps

4th Guards Mechanized Corps (Stalingrad)

May 42	Formed in Stalingrad MD as 13th Tank Corps
Nov 42	Converted to a mechanized corps structure. Was assigned to many different armies and fronts
1942	Took part in Voronezh-Voroshilovgrad defensive operation and the Battle of Stalingrad
43–44	Rostov, Donbas, Melitopol, Nikopol-Krivoi Rog, Berezenegovatoye-

Snigirovka, Odessa, Iassy-Kishinev, liberation of Bulgaria, and Belgrade offensives

Jan 43	*Honored and renamed as 4th Guards Mechanized Corps. Awarded the Stalingrad place-name honorific*
1945	Capture of Budapest

Commanders
Gen. Major P. E. Shurov, 1942
Gen. Lt. T. I. Tanaschishin, 42–44
Gen. Lt. V. I. Zhdanov, 44–45
Other Names
Stalingrad Mechanized Corps, 13th Tank Corps

6th Guards Red Banner Mechanized Corps (Lvov)

1932	Formed in the Perm region as the 82d Self-Propelled Gun Division
1939	Participated in the Battle of Khalkhin Gol against the Japanese
1941	Name and structure changed to 82d Motorized Rifle Division. Initially assigned to the 5th Army, in which it participated in the Battle of Moscow
Mar 42	*Honored and renamed as the 3d Guards MRD*
42–43	As part of the Western Front, took part in defensive battles
Jun 43	Merged with the 49th Mechanized Brigade to be reformed into the 6th Guards Red Banner Mechanized Corps. Assigned to the 4th/4th Guards Tank Army
43–45	Participated in the Orel, Proskurov-Chernovits, Lvov-Sandomir, Sandomir-Silesia, Lower Silesia, Upper Silesia, Berlin, and Prague offensive opns

Aug 44   *Awarded the Lvov place-name honorific*

Commanders
Gen. Lt. A. I. Akimov, 43–44
Col. V. F. Orlov, 44–45
Col. V. I. Koretsky, 1945
Col. S. F. Pushkaryev, 1945
Other Names
Lvov Mechanized Corps

8th Guards Mechanized Corps (Carpathia-Berlin)

Oct 42   Formed in Kalinin as the 3d Mech Corps. Initially assigned to the 22d Army, Kalinin Front; from Feb 43 to end of war, assigned to the 1st/1st Guards Tank Army
1943   Took part in the Battle of Kursk
Oct 43   *Honored and renamed as 8th Guards Mech Corps*
1944   Participated in the battles of Zhitomir-Berdichev, Korsun-Shevchenkovsky, Proskurov-Chernovits, and Lvov-Sandomir
Apr 44   *Awarded the Carpathian place-name honorific*
1945   Warsaw-Poznan, East Pomeranian, and Berlin offensives
Jun 45   *Awarded Berlin as a place-name honorific*

Commanders
Gen. Lt. M. E. Katukov, 42–43
Gen. Lt. S. M. Krivoshein, 43–44
Gen. Major I. F. Dremov, 44–45
Other Names
Carpathian-Berlin Mechanized Corps, 3d Mechanized Corps

9th Mechanized Corps (2d est.) (Kiev-Zhitomir)

Sep 43   Formed in Tula as the 9th Mechanized Corps. Assigned continuously to the 3d Guards Tank Army

43–45   Took part in Left and Right Bank Ukraine, Lvov-Sandomir, San-domir-Silesia, Lower Silesia, Berlin, and Prague offensive opns
Jan 44   *Awarded the Zhitomir place-name honorific*
Mar 44   *Awarded Kiev as a place-name honorific*

Commanders
Gen. Major K. A. Malygin, 43–44
Gen. Lt. I. P. Sykhov, 44–45
Other Names:
Kiev-Zhitomir Mechanized Corps

1st Guards Tank Corps (Don)

Jul 42   Formed in the Moscow region as the 26th Tank Corps. Assigned in sequence to the Briansk, Southwestern, Don, Belorussian, 1st and 2d Belorussian Fronts
42–43   Took part in Battle of Stalingrad, 3d Battle of Kharkov, and Orel offensive
Dec 42   *Honored and renamed the 1st Guards Tank Corps*
Jan 43   *Awarded the Don place-name honorific*
44–45   Participated in operatons to liberate Belorussia and Poland; advanced to Berlin

Commanders
Gen. Lt. A. G. Gorodin, 42–43
Gen. Major A. V. Kukushkin, 1943
Gen. Lt. M. F. Panov, 43–45
Other Names
Don Tank Corps, 26th Tank Corps

2d Guards Tank Corps (Tatsinsk)

Apr 42   Formed in the Voroshilov-grad region as the 24th Tank Corps. Sequentially, part of the Southern, Briansk, Southwestern, West-ern, and 3d Belorussian

Fronts. Achieved fame in the Battle of Stalingrad

42–43   Initially participated in defensive battles in the Voronezh Direction and in the great bend of the Don River. Took part in the Stalingrad counteroffensive, opns in the Middle Don, 3d Battle of Kharkov, the Battle of Kursk, and the Smolensk offensive

Dec 42   *Honored and renamed as 2d Guards Tank Corps*

Jan 43   *Awarded Tatsinsk as a place-name honorific to commemorate its deep penetrations during the Stalingrad counteroffensive*

44–45   Distinguished itself in the Belorussian Campaign, during which its 4th Guards Tank Brigade was the first unit to enter Minsk. Subsequently took part in the Gumbinnen and Insterburg-Königsberg offensive opns

Commanders
Gen. Lt. V. M. Badanov, 42–43
Gen. Lt. A. S. Burdeiny, 43–45
Other Names
Tatskinsk Tank Corps, 24th Tank Corps

5th Guards Tank Corps (Stalingrad-Kiev)

Apr 42   Formed in Voronezh as the 4th Tank Corps. Assigned to a series of armies and fronts until Jan 45 when it joined the 6th/6th Guards Tank Army

42–43   Participated in the Voronezh-Voroshilovgrad defensive operation and the Battle of Stalingrad

43–44   Voronezh-Kastornoe, 3d Battle of Kharkov, Kursk, liberation of Left Bank Ukraine offensive opns; offensive and defensive opns at Kiev; battles of Zhitomir-Berdichev, Korsun-Shevchenkovsky, Uman-Botoshany, Iassy-Kishinev, Debrecen, and Budapest

Jan 43   *Awarded the Stalingrad place-name honorific*

Feb 43   *Honored and renamed as 5th Guards Tank Corps*

Nov 43   *Awarded Kiev as a place-name honorific*

1945   Opns at Vienna, Bratislava-Brno, and Prague. Transferred to Far East; participated in Khingan-Mukden operation with 6th Guards Tank Army as part of Transbaikal Front

Commanders
Gen. Lt. V. A. Mishulin, 1942
Gen. Lt. A. G. Kravchenko, 42–44
Gen. Lt. V. M. Alekseyev, 1944
Gen. Lt. M. I. Savelyev, 44–45
Other Names
Stalingrad-Kiev Tank Corps, 4th Tank Corps

6th Guards Tank Corps (Kiev-Berlin)

May 42   Formed in the Moscow region as the 12th Tank Corps. Assigned to the 3d/3d Guards Tank Army

1942   Participated in the counterstrike against enemy forces south of Kozel

1943   Took part in the Ostrogorzhsk-Rossosh offensive, 3d Battle of Kharkov, Orel, and Left Bank Ukraine offensive opns, including liberation of Kiev (43–44)

Jul 43	*Honored and renamed as 6th Guards Tank Corps*
Nov 43	*Awarded the Kiev place-name honorific*
1944	Right Bank Ukraine and Lvov-Sandomir offensives.
1945	Sandomir-Silesia, Lower Silesia, Berlin, and Prague offensive opns
Jun 45	*Awarded Berlin as a place-name honorific*

Commanders

Gen. Major S. I. Bogdanov, 1942
Col. M. I. Chesnokov, 1942
Gen. Major V. A. Mitrofanov, 42–43, 1945
Gen. Major M. I. Zinkovich, 1943
Gen. Major I. P. Sukhov, 1943
Gen. Lt. A. P. Panfilov, 43–44
Gen. Major V. V. Novikov, 44~45

Other Names

Kiev-Berlin Tank Corps, 12th Tank Corps

7th Guards Tank Corps (Kiev-Berlin)

May 42	Formed in the Moscow region as 15th Tank Corps. As a part of the 3d/3d Guards Tank Army, *this corps participated in the same opns and was awarded the same place-name honorifics*
Jul 43	*Honored and renamed as 7th Guards Tank Corps*
Nov 43	*Awarded the Kiev place-name honorific*
Jun 45	*Awarded Berlin as a place-name honorific*

Commanders

Gen. Major V. A. Koptsov, 42–43
Lt. Col. A. B. Lozovsky, 1943
Gen. Major F. N. Rudkin, 1943
Gen. Major K. F. Suleykov, 1943
Gen. Major S. A. Ivanov, 43–44, 44–45
Gen. Major V. A. Mitrofanov, 1944
Gen. Major V. V. Novikov, 1945

Other Names

Kiev-Berlin Tank Corps (2), 15th Tank Corps

9th Guards Tank Corps (Uman)

Oct 42	Formed in the Tula region as the 3d Tank Corps. Assigned to the Western, Southwestern, 1st and 2d Ukrainian Fronts. After Apr 1943, was part of the 2d/2d Guards Tank Army
1942	Initially participated in battles in Volkhov region, then in the defeat of the enemy advance in the Sukhinichev Direction
1943	Opns in the Donbas, the Battle of Kursk, and Chernigov-Pripiat
44–45	Took part in the Korsun-Shevchenkovsky, Uman-Botoshany, Lublin-Brest, Warsaw-Pozanan, East Pomeranian, and Berlin offensives
Mar 44	*Awarded the Uman place-name honorific*
Nov 44	*Honored and renamed as the 9th Guards Tank Corps*

Commanders

Gen. Major D. K. Mostovenko, 1942
Gen. Major M. D. Sinenko, 42–43
Gen. Major N. M. Telyakov, 1944, 1945
Gen. Major A. A. Shamshin, 1944
Gen. Lt. V. A. Mishulin, 1944
Gen. Major N. D. Vedeneyev, 44–45

Other Names

Uman Tank Corps, 3d Tank Corps

10th Guards Tank Corps (Ural Volunteers) (Ural-Lvov)

Apr 43	Formed in the Urals MD as the 30th Tank Corps (Ural) Volunteers. Guards Tank Army

43–45	Took part in the Orel, Briansk, Proskurov-Chernovits, Lvov-Sandomir, Lower Silesia, Upper Silesia, Berlin, and Prague offensive opns
Oct 43	*Honored and renamed as the 10th Guards Tank Corps (Ural Volunteers).*
Aug 44	*Awarded the Lvov place-name honorific*

Commanders
Col. V. I. Sokolov, 1943
Gen. Lt. G. S. Rodin, 43–44
Gen. Lt. Ye. Ye. Belov, 1944, 1945
Col. N. D. Chuprov, 44–45
Other Names
Ural-Lvov Volunteer Tank Corps,
30th Tank Corps (Ural Volunteer)

11th Guards Tank Corps (Carpathia-Berlin)

Apr 42	Formed in the Moscow region as the 6th Tank Corps. Initially assigned to the Western Front. From Feb 43 through the end of the war, the corps was assigned to the 1st/1st Guards Tank Army
1942	Participated in the Rzhev-Sychevka offensive.
1943	Took part in the Battle of Kursk
1944	Zhitomir-Berdichev, Korsun-Shevchenkovsky, Proskurov-Chernovits, and Lvov-Sandomir opns.
1945	Took part in Warsaw-Poznan, East Pomeranian, and Berlin offensive opns
Oct 43	*Honored and renamed as 11th Guards Tank Corps*
Apr 44	*Awarded the Carpathia place-name honorific*
Jun 45	*Awarded Berlin as a place-name honorific*

Commanders
Gen. Lt. A. L. Getman, 42–45
Col. A. Kh. Babadzhanyan, 44–45
Other Names
Carpathia-Berlin Tank Corps,
6th Tank Corps

Divisions

Rifle Divisions

On the eve of the war with Germany, the USSR had more than 200 rifle and mountain rifle divisions, 13 cavalry divisions, and 20 mechanized or motorized rifle divisions in existence in some form, in varying stages of readiness and personnel fill. By the end of 1941, the Soviets had expanded the number of rifle divisions to more than 400, moving toward a total of approximately 430 during the course of the war. Of those 430 divisions, 216 were reformed at least one time, with 52, approximately one-eighth of the total, requiring establishment from three to four times due to losses in battle; 117 rifle divisions earned Guards distinction.

Other Soviet division structures included: 38 artillery divisions (six earning Guards distinction); seven Guards mortar divisions; 78 anti-aircraft divisions (six earning Guards distinction); 19 national air defense divisions; and 41 territorial home guard divisions (28 of which were converted to regular rifle divisions and included in the total above). The force structure further included totals of:

140 rifle corps, of which 40 earned Guards distinction.

30 mechanized corps, of which 9 earned Guards

31 tank corps, of which 12 earned Guards

17 cavalry corps, of which 7 were awarded Guards

Guards Rifle Divisions (Gds RD)

1st Gds RD. First establishments, Sep 41–Oct 42, then reformed into 1st Guards Mechanized Corps; Jan 43–May 45. Six commanders

2d Gds RD. Sep 41–May 45. Six commanders

3d Gds RD. Sep 41–May 45. Six commanders

4th Gds RD. Sep 41–May 45. Eight commanders

5th Gds RD. Sep 41–May 45. Seven commanders

6th Gds RD. Sep 41–May 45. Five commanders

7th Gds RD. Sep 41–May 45. Five commanders

8th Gds RD. Nov 41–May 45. Ten commanders

9th Gds RD. Nov 41–May 45. Nine commanders

10th Gds RD. Dec 41–May 45. Five commanders

11th Gds RD. Jan 42–May 45. Six commanders

12th Gds RD. Jan 42–May 45. Three commanders

13th Gds RD. Jan 42–May 45. Seven commanders

14th Gds RD. Jan 42–May 45. Eight commanders

15th Gds RD. Feb 42–May 45. Five commanders

16th Gds RD. Feb 42–May 45. Eight commanders

17th Gds RD. Mar 42–Sep 45. Six commanders

18th Gds RD. Mar 42–May 45. Ten commanders

19th Gds RD. Mar 42–Sep 45. Twelve commanders

20th Gds RD. Mar 42–May 45. Five commanders

21st Gds RD. Mar 42–May 45. Six commanders

22d Gds RD.
1st est. Mar 43–Nov 42. Reformed into 2d Guards Mechanized Corps.
2d est. Apr 43–May 45. Four commanders

23d Gds RD. Mar 42–May 45. Five commanders

24th Gds RD. Mar 42–May 45. Eight commanders

25th Gds RD. Apr 42–May 45. Seven commanders

26th Gds RD. Apr 42–May 45. Two commanders

27th Gds RD. May 42–May 45. Two commanders

28th Gds RD. May 42–May 45. Four commanders

29th Gds RD. May 42–May 45. Four commanders

30th Gds RD. May 42–May 45. Three commanders

31st Gds RD. May 42–May 45. Four commanders

32d Gds RD. May 42–May 45. Five commanders

33d Gds RD. May 42–May 45. Ten commanders

34th Gds RD. Aug 42–May 45. Eight commanders

35th Gds RD. Aug 42–May 45. Five commanders

36th Gds RD. Aug 42–May 45. Two commanders

37th Gds RD. Jun 42–May 45. Seven commanders

38th Gds RD. Aug 42–May 45. Five commanders

39th Gds RD. Aug 42–May 45. Six commanders

40th Gds RD. Aug 42–May 45. Eight commanders

41st Gds RD. Aug 42–May 45. Three commanders

42d Gds RD. Sep 42–May 45. Three commanders

43d Gds RD. Oct 42–May 45. Four commanders

44th Gds RD. Oct 42–May 45. Four commanders

45th Gds RD. Oct 42–May 45.
Three commanders
46th Gds RD. Oct 42–May 45.
Four commanders
47th Gds RD. Oct 42–May 45.
Five commanders
48th Gds RD. Oct 42–May 45.
Three commanders
49th Gds RD. Oct 42–May 45.
Six commanders
50th Gds RD. Nov 42–May 45.
Four commanders
51st Gds RD. Nov 42–May 45.
Five commanders
52d Gds RD. Nov 42–May 45.
Four commanders
53d Gds RD. Dec 42–May 45.
Three commanders
54th Gds RD. Dec 42–May 45.
One commander
55th Gds RD. Dec 42–May 45.
Four commanders
56th Gds RD. Jun 43–May 45.
Three commanders
57th Gds RD. Dec 42–May 45.
Thee commanders
58th Gds RD. Dec 42–May 45.
Seven commanders
59th Gds RD. Jan 43–May 45.
Two commanders
60th Gds RD. Jan 43–May 45.
Two commanders
61st Gds RD. Jan 43–May 45.
Three commanders
62d Gds RD. Jan 43–May 45.
Three commanders
63d Gds RD. Jan 43–May 45.
Three commanders
64th Gds RD. Jan 43–May 45.
Four commanders
65th Gds RD. May 43–May 45.
Three commanders
66th Gds RD. Jan 43–May 45.
Two commanders
67th Gds RD. Jan 43–May 45.
Five commanders
68th Gds RD. Feb 43–May 45.
Three commanders
69th Gds RD. Feb 43–May 45.
One commander

70th Gds RD. Feb 43–May 45.
Five commanders
71st Gds RD. Mar 43–May 45.
Five commanders
72d Gds RD. Mar 43–May 45.
Three commanders
73d Gds RD. Mar 43–May 45.
Four commanders
74th Gds RD. Mar 43–May 45.
Five commanders
75th Gds RD. Mar 43–May 45.
One commander
76th Gds RD. Mar 43–May 45.
One commander
77th Gds RD. Mar 43–May 45.
Three commanders
78th Gds RD. Mar 43–May 45.
Three commanders
79th Gds RD. Mar 43–May 45.
Five commanders
80th Gds RD. Mar 43–May 45.
Four commanders
81st Gds RD. Mar 43–May 45.
Four commanders
82d Gds RD. Mar 43–May 45.
Four commanders
83d Gds RD. Mar 43–May 45.
Three commanders
84th Gds RD. Apr 43–May 45.
Two commanders
85th Gds RD. Apr 43–May 45.
Three commanders
86th Gds RD. Apr 43–May 45.
Two commanders
87th Gds RD. Apr 43–May 45.
One commander
88th Gds RD. Apr 43–May 45.
Six commanders
89th Gds RD. Apr 43–May 45.
Four commanders
90th Gds RD. Apr 43–May 45.
Two commanders
91st Gds RD. Apr 43–May 45.
Five commanders
92d Gds RD. Apr 43–May 45.
Three commanders
93d Gds RD. Apr 43–May 45.
Four commanders
94th Gds RD. Apr 43–May 45.
Three commanders

95th Gds RD. May 43–May 45.
Four commanders
96th Gds RD. May 43–May 45.
Two commanders
97th Gds RD. May 43–May 45.
Six commanders
98th Gds RD. Dec 43–May 45.
Two commanders
99th Gds RD. Jun 44–May 45.
Two commanders
100th Gds RD. Jun 44–May 45.
Two commanders
101st Gds RD. Jun 44–May 45.
Two commanders
102d Gds RD. Dec 44–May 45.
One commander
103d Gds RD. Dec 44–May 45.
One commander
104th Gds RD. Feb–May 45.
One commander
105th Gds RD. Feb–May 45.
One commander
106th Gds RD. Feb–May 45.
One commander
107th Gds RD. Dec 44–May 45.
One commander
108th Gds RD. Jul 43–May 45.
Two commander
109th Gds RD. Jul 43–May 45.
One commander
110th Gds RD. Aug 43–May 45.
Six commanders
114th Gds RD. Dec 44–May 45.
One commander
117th Gds RD. Oct 43–May 45.
Three commanders
119th Gds RD. Sep 43–May 45.
Three commanders
120th Gds RD. Sep 43–May 45.
Four commanders
128th Gds RD. Oct 43–May 45.
Three commanders

Motorized Rifle (MRD) and Mechanized Divisions (MD)

As the list below indicates, most of the Soviet motorized rifle and mechanized divisions were created in the year prior to the outbreak of the war with Germany. Most of these divisions were destroyed, with near complete loss of rolling stock, during the first months of the war and then converted to standard rifle divisions. Where unit disposition is shown below as unclear, it is likely that the unit was completely destroyed. By and large, commanders of these units employed them improperly and the organization was deemed subsequently to be unsuitable. Consequently, when the USSR began again to reform mechanized and armored formations in 1942, they organized mechanized and tank corps composed of brigades, and tank armies composed of corps. Apparently only two MRDs, the 36th and the 57th, survived in that organizational form through the end of the war.

1st MRD. Mar–Aug 41. Converted into 1st Tank Division. Commander Gen. Major Ya. G. Kreizer
7th MD. Jul 40–Sep 41. Converted into 7th RD. Commander Col. A. V. Gerasimov
15th MD. Apr–Aug 41. Converted into 15th RD. Commander Col. N. N. Belov
29th MD. Jul 40–Jul 41. Disposition unclear. Commander Col. I. P. Bikzhanov
36th MRD. Jan 41–Sep 45.
Five commanders
57th MRD. Jul 40–Sep 45.
Five commanders
69th MD. Mar–Jul 41. Converted to 107th Tank Division. Commander Col. P. N. Domrachev
81st MD. Jul 40–Jul 41. Converted to 81st RD. Three commanders
82d MRD. Mar 41–Mar 42. Converted to 3d Gds MRD.
Three commanders
84th MD. Jul 40–Jul 41. Converted to 84th RD. Commander Col. P. I. Fomenko
101st MRD. Sep–Oct 41. Disposition unclear. Commander Col. G. M. Mikhailov

103d MD. Mar–Aug 41. Converted to 103d RD. Two commanders

107th MRD. Jul 41–Jan 42. Converted to 2d Gds MRD. Two commanders

109th MD. Jun 39–Jul 41. Converted to 304th RD. Commander Col. N. P. Krasnoretsky

112th MRD. Jun–Sep 41. Converted into 112th RD. Commander Col. I. A. Kopyak

131st MD. Jun 40–Sep 41. Converted into 131st RD. Two commanders

163d MD. Jun 40–Jul 41. Converted into 163d RD. Commander Gen. Major I. M. Kuznetsov

185th MD. Mar–Aug 41. Converted into 185th RD. Two commanders

198th MD. Mar–Sep 41. Converted into 198th RD. Commander Gen. Major V. V. Kryukov

202d MD. Mar–Sep 41. Converted into 202d RD. Three commanders

204th MD. Mar–Sep 41. Disposition unclear. Commander Col. A. M. Pirov

205th MD. Mar–Jun 41. Disposition unclear. Commander Col. F. F. Kudyurov

208th MD. Mar–Sep 41. Disposition unclear. Commander Col. V. I. Nichiporovich

209th MD. Mar–Sep 41. Disposition unclear. Commander Col. A. I. Muravev

210th MD. Mar–Jul 41. Converted into 4th Cavalry Division. Commander Brigade Commander F. A. Parkhomenko

212th MD. Mar–Jul 41. Converted to 212th RD. Commander Gen. Major S. V. Baranov

213th MD. Mar–Sep 41. Disposition unclear. Commander Col. V. M. Osminsky

215th MD. Mar–Sep 41. Disposition unclear. Commander Col. P. A. Barabanov

216th MD. Mar–Sep 41. Disposition unclear. Commander Col. A. S. Sarkisyan

218th MD. Jun–Sep 41. Converted into 218th RD. Two commanders

219th MD. Mar–Sep 41. Converted into 219th RD. Commander Gen. Major P. P. Korzun

220th MD. Mar–Jul 41. Converted into 220th RD. Commander Gen. Major N. G. Khoruzhenko

221st MD. Mar–Aug 41. Disposition unclear. Commander Col. G. M. Roptenberg

240th MD. Mar–Aug 41. Converted to 240th RD. Commander Col. I. V. Gorbenko

Guards Motorized Rifle Divisions (Gds MRD)

1st Gds MRD. Sep 41–Jan 43. Reformed into 1st Guards RD. Nine commanders

2d Gds MRD. Jan 42–Oct 42. Reformed into 49th Guards RD. Commander Gen. Major P. G. Chanchibadze

3d Gds MRD. Mar 42–Jun 43. Reformed into 8th Guards Mechanized Corps. Commander Col. A. I. Akimov

Rifle Divisions Honored with Place-Name Honorifics

1st Guards Moscow Rifle Division (Moscow-Minsk)

Dec 1926	Formed in Moscow as the 1st Moscow Proletarian Division
Jan 40	Reformed into 1st Moscow Motorized Rifle Division. Assigned to the 20th, 16th, 40th, 33d, 43d, 3d Tank, 5th, and 10th Armies, then, from May 43, to the 11th Guards Army
1941	Defensive battles near Sumi and Moscow
Sep 41	*Honored and renamed as 1st Guards Moscow MRD*

1942	Rzhev-Sychevka offensive operation
1943	Orel, Briansk, and Gorodok offensives
Jan 43	Reformed as the 1st Guards Moscow RD
1944	Belorussian campaign
1945	Gumbinnen and East Prussian offensives
Jul 44	*Awarded the Minsk place-name honorific*

Commanders

Gen. Major Ya. G. Kreizer, Aug. 41
Col. A. I. Lizyukov, 1941
Gen. Major T. Ya. Novikov, 41–42
Gen. Major V. A. Revyakin, 1942
Gen. Major N. A. Kropotin, 42–44
Gen. Major P. F. Tolstikov, 44–45

Other Names

Proletarian Moscow-Minsk Rifle Division, 1st Moscow Motorized Rifle Division, 1st Guards Moscow-Minsk Motorized Rifle Division

2d Guards Rifle Division/
127th Rifle Division (Taman)

Sep 40	Formed as the 127th RD. Served in a series of armies and fronts; after May 44 as part of the 2d Guards Army
1941	Took part in the Battle of Smolensk; defensive opns near the cities of Glukhov, Kursk, and Tim
Sep 41	*Honored and renamed 2d Guards RD*
42–43	Defensive and offensive opns in the battle for the Caucasus region. Distinguished itself in the Kerch-Eltigen amphibious operation
Oct 43	*Awarded the Taman place-name honorific*
44–45	Took part in the recovery of Crimea, Shyaulyai, Memel, and East Prussian offensive opns

Commanders

Gen. Major T. G. Korneyev, 1941
Gen. Major A. Z. Akimenko, 41–42
Col. K. P. Neverov, 1942
Gen. Major F. V. Zakharov, 42–43
Gen. Major A. P. Turchinsky, 43–44
Gen. Major N. S. Samokhalov, 44–45

Other Names

Taman Rifle Division

5th Guards Rifle Division/
107th Rifle Division (Gorodok)

Aug 39	Formed in Alma-Aty (Kazakhstan) as the 107th RD. From 41–43, assigned to the 24th, 49th, 33d, and 16th Armies. After Jul 43, remained assigned to the 11th Guards Army
41–42	Defensive opns vic. Yelynya and Moscow.
Sep 41	*Honored and renamed as 5th Guards RD*
1943	Participated in the Orel, Briansk, Gorodok offensives
Dec 43	*Awarded the Gorodok place-name honorific*
44–45	Gumbinnen and East Prussian offensive opns

Commanders

Gen. Major P. V. Mironov, 41–42
Lt. Col. P. V. Maltsev, 1942
Gen. Major M. E. Yerokhin, 1942
Gen. Major A. K. Pavlov, 42–43
Gen. Major N. L. Soldatov, 43–44
Col. N. I. Kravtsov, 1944
Col. N. L. Volkov, 44–45
Gen. Major G. B. Peters, 1945

Other Names

Gorodok Rifle Division

6th Guards Rifle Division/
120th Rifle Division (Rovno)

Jul 40	Formed in the Orel region as the 120th RD. Assigned in sequence to the 24th,

26th, 3d, 48th, 13th, 70th, and 60th Armies

1941   Opns at Elnia and the defense of Moscow

Sep 41 *Honored and renamed 6th Guards RD*

1943   Battle of Kursk, Left Bank Ukraine, Kiev offensive and defensive opns, and Zhitomir-Berdichev

1944   Rovno-Lutsk and Lvov-Sandomir offensives

Feb 44 *Awarded the Rovno place-name honorific*

1945   Upper and Lower Silesia, Berlin, and Prague offensive opns

Commanders
Gen. Major K. I. Petrov, 41–42
Gen. Major F. M. Cherokmanov, 42–43
Gen. Major D. P. Onuprienko, 43–44
Col. M. A. Malatyan, 1944
Col. G.V. Ivanov, 44–45
Other Names
Rovno Rifle Division

8th Guards Rifle Division/
316th Rifle Division (Riga)

Aug 41 Formed in Alma-Aty as the 316th RD. Assigned in sequence to the 52d and 16th Armies, 2d Guards RC on the Northwest and Kalinin Fronts, 3d Shock, 22d, and, after Apr 44, the 10th Guards Armies

Nov 41 *Honored and renamed as the 8th Guards RD (Panfilov)*

41–43   Defensive opns near Malaya Vishera, the Moscow region, and Demiansk

1944   Offensive opns: Novo-gorod-Kaluga, Rezhitsa-Dvina, Madon, and Riga

Aug 44 *Awarded the Riga place-name honorific*

Commanders
Gen. Major I. V. Panfilov, 1941
Gen. Major V. A. Revyakin, 41–42

Gen. Major I. M. Chistyakov, 1942
Col. I. I. Serebryakov, 1942
Gen. Major S. S. Chernyugov, 42–44
Col. D. A. Dulov, 1944
Gen. Major E. Zh. Sedulin, 1944
Gen. Major A. D. Kuleshov, 1944
Col. G. I. Panishev, 1944
Col. G. I. Lomov, 44–45
Other Names
Riga Rifle Division

9th Caucasus Mountain Rifle Division (Krasnodar Plastun)

May 1918   Formed as the Kursk Infantry Division

1936   Renamed the 9th Caucasus Mountain RD. Assigned in sequence to the 46th, 37th, 56th, Separate Maritime, 69th, 18th, 5th Guards, and 60th Armies

41–43   Fought in the southern theater; in defensive and offensive opns in battle for the Caucasus

Sep 43 *Honored and renamed as the 9th Krasnodar-Plastun Red Banner Rifle Division*

44–45   Offensive opns at Lvov-Sandomir, Poland, and Czechoslovakia

Commanders
Col. V. T. Maslov, 1941
Col. V. S. Dzabakhidze, 41–42
Col. M. V. Yvstigneyev, 42–43
Col. A. E. Shapovalov, 1943
Col. S. M. Cherny, 1943
Gen. Major P. I. Metalnikov, 43–45
Other Names
Krasnodar-Plastun Rifle Division

10th Guards Rifle Division/
52d Rifle Division (Pechenga)

1935   Formed in Moscow MD as the 52d RD

1939   Took part in the occupation of western Belorussia as part of the Soviet-German partition of Poland

41–43	Split service between the 19th and 14th Armies in defensive opns in the Murmansk region
Dec 42	*Honored and renamed as the 10th Guards RD*
44–45	Took part in Petsamo-Iassy, East Pomeranian, and Berlin offensive opns
Oct 44	*Awarded the Pechenga place-name honorific*

Commanders

Gen. Major N. N. Nikishin, 1941
Col. G. A. Veshchezersky, 1941
Col. M. K. Pashkovsky, 41–42
Gen. Major D. E. Krasilnkov, 1942
Col. Kh. A. Khudalov, 42–43; 44–45
Col. F. A. Grebenkin, Nov 43–
    Mar 44

13th Guards' Rifle Division/
87th Rifle Division (Poltava)

Nov 41	Formed in the Kursk region as the 87th RD on the base of units of the 3d Airborne Corps. Served in sequence in the 40th, 38th, 28th, and 62d Armies; after Jul 43, in the 5th Guards Army
42–43	Participated in defensive opns in the Voronezh, Kharkov, Valuisk, and Rossosh Directions, on the Don River line, and in the Battle of Stalingrad. Took part in the Battle of Kursk and liberation of Left Bank Ukraine
Jan 42	*Honored and renamed 13th Guards Rifle Division*
Sep 43	*Awarded the Poltava place-name honorific. Two sister divisions were also awarded "Poltava" as an honorific: 95th Guards and 97th Guards RDs (see below) for similar combat performance in the 5th Guards Army*

1944	Kirovograd, Uman-Botoshany, Lvov-Sandomir offensives
1945	Upper and Lower Silesia, Berlin, and Prague opns

Commanders

Gen. Major A. I. Rodimtsev, 41–43
Gen. Major G. V. Baklanov, 43–44
Col. V. N. Komarov, 44–45

Other Names

Poltava Rifle Division

14th Guards Rifle Division/
96th Rifle Division (Vinnitsa)

Dec 1923	Formed in Vinnitsa as the 96th Vinnitsa RD
1939	Took part in the occupation of western Ukraine in connection with the Soviet-German partition of Poland. Assigned to various armies on Southern, Southwestern, Steppe, 2d and 3d Ukrainian Fronts. After Feb 44, assigned to the 5th Guards Army
41–43	Defensive opns in Pervomaisk, Nikolayev, Rostov-on-Don, Barvenkovo-Lozovaia, the Battle of Stalingrad, Kursk, and the liberation of the Ukraine
Jan 42	*Honored and renamed as the 14th Guards RD; retained its previous place-name, Vinnitsa*
44–45	Offensive opns in Ukraine, Poland, Berlin, and Prague

Commanders

Gen. Major I. M. Shepetov, 41–42
Gen. Major A. S. Gryaznov, 1943
Col. V. V. Rusakov, 1943
Col. G. P. Slatov, 43–44
Gen. Major V. V. Skriganov,
    44–45
Col. A. Ya. Goryachev, 1945
Col. S. A. Losik-Savitsky, 1945
Col. P. I. Sikorsky, 1945

Other Names

Vinnitsa Rifle Division

15th Guards Rifle Division/
136th Rifle Division (Kharkov-Prague)

Sep 39	Formed in Gorky as the 136th RD
39–40	Participated in the Soviet-Finnish War. Assigned in sequence to the 18th, 9th, 28th, 57th, 51st, and 64th/7th Guards Armies. After Jun 44, assigned to the 5th Guards Army
1941	Defended in battles near Melitopol, in the Donbas, and at Rostov
42–43	Battles of Stalingrad, Kursk, Left Bank Ukraine
Feb 42	*Honored and renamed as 15th Guards RD*
Aug 43	*Awarded the Kharkov place-name honorific*
44–45	Lvov-Sandomir, Sandomir-Silesia, Upper and Lower Silesia, Berlin, and Prague offensive opns
Jun 45	*Awarded the Prague place-name honorific*

Commanders
Gen. Major A. I. Andreev, 1941
Gen. Major E. I. Vasilenko, 41–42, 42–44
Col. N. P. Raevsky, 1942
Lt. Col. P. D. Kondratiyev, 1942
Lt. Col. A. E. Ovsienko, 1942
Gen. Major P. M. Chirkov, 44–45
Other Names
Kharkov-Prague Rifle Division

15th Rifle Division (Sivash-Stettin)

Jun 1918	Formed in Inza, Ulyanov region, as the Inza Revolutionary Division, later as the 15th Inza RD, then *awarded the Sivash place-name in 1921*
1939	Renamed 15th Mechanized Division. During the war, assigned to 9th, 18th, 6th, 12th, 37th, 13th, 70th, 61st, and 65th Armies
1941	Defended in the area of Moldavia, Uman, and the Donbas. Reformed as the 15th RD in Aug 41
42–43	Took part in Voronezh-Voroshilovgrad defensive, then in the Voronezh-Kastornoe, Kursk, Chernigov-Pripiat, and Gomel-Rechitsa offensive opns
44–45	Kalinkov-Mozyr, Belorussian, Mlava-Elbing, East Pomeranian, and Berlin opns
Jun 45	*Awarded the Stettin place-name honorific*

Commanders
Gen. Major N. N. Belov, 1941
Gen. Major A. N. Slyshkin, 41–43
Col. V. N. Dzhandzhgava, 1943
Col. V. I. Bulgakov, 1943
Gen. Major K. Ye. Grebennik, 43–45
Col. A. P. Varyukhin, 1945
Other Names
15th Inza RD, 15th Mechanized Division, Sivash-Stettin Rifle Division

19th Guards Rifle Division/
366th Rifle Division (Rudnen-Khingan)

Nov 1941	Formed in Tomsk region as the 366th RD. Assigned in sequence to the 2d Shock, 52d, 3d Shock Armies; after Aug 43, assigned to the 39th Army
42–43	Took part in the Lubansk, Siniavino, Velikie Luki, and Smolensk opns
Mar 42	*Honored and renamed the 19th Guards RD*
Sep 43	*Awarded the Rudnen place-name honorific*
1944	Participated in the Belorussian, Memel, Gumbinnen, East Prussian, and Khingan-Mukden (Manchuria) offensive opns
Sep 45	*Awarded the Khingan place-name*

Commanders

Col. S. I. Bulanov, 41–42

Gen. Major D. M. Barinov, 1942

Col. I. D. Vasiliyev, 42–43

Gen. Major I. P. Repin, 1943

Gen. Major B. S. Maslov, 43–44

Col. S. I. Tsukarev, 1944

Gen. Major P. N. Bibikov, 44–45

19th Rifle Division (Voronezh-Shumlin)

Jul 1922	Formed in Tambov as the 19th Rifle Division
1923	*Awarded the Tambov place-name; renamed the 19th Voronezh RD*
39–41	During the war, served in the 24th, 43d, 5th, 20th, 3d Guards Tank, 57th, 37th, 7th Guards, and 46th Armies. Defensive and offensive opns near Elnia and the Battle of Moscow
42–43	Defended vic. Gzatsk and Kharkov; took part in the Belgord-Kharkov offensive and the liberation of Ukraine
1944	Opns in Romania, Bulgaria, Yugoslavia, Hungary, Czechoslovakia
Sep 44	*Awarded the Shumlin place-name honorific*

Commanders

Gen. Major Ya. G. Kotelnikov, 1941

Col. A. I. Utvenko, 1941

Gen. Major N. S. Dronov, 41–42

Col. G. A. Gogolitsin, 42–43

Gen. Major P. E. Lazarev, 43–44

Col. S. V. Salychev, 44–45

Other Names

Voronezh-Shumlin Rifle Division, 19th Voronezh Rifle Division

20th Guards Rifle Division/ 174th Rifle Division (Krivoi Rog)

Aug 40	Formed in the Urals MD as the 174th RD. Served in the 22d, 29th, 30th, 31st, 6th, 1st Guards, 46th, 37th, and after Nov 44, the 57th Armies
41–42	Defensive opns near Polotsk, Velikie Luki, Andreapol, and Moscow. Took part in Rzhev-Sychevka offensive
Mar 42	*Honored and renamed as 20th Guards RD*
1943	Defended on the Northern Donets River; Izyum-Barvenkovo offensive operation and Left Bank Ukraine
44–45	Iassy-Kishinev offensive, followed by further opns Romania, Bulgaria, at Budapest, Vienna, and Lake Balaton
Feb 44	*Awarded the Krivoi Rog place-name honorific*

Commanders

Gen. Major A. I. Zygin, 1941

Col. P. F. Ilinykh, 1941

Col. P. P. Miroshnichenko, 1941

Col. S. Ya. Senchilov, 41–42

Col. A. A. Kutsenko, 1942

Gen. Major I. F. Dudarev, 1942

Gen. Major P. J. Tikhonov, 42–44

Gen. Major N. M. Dreier, 44–45

Lt. Col. G. S. Ivanishchev, 1945

Other Names

Krivoi Rog Rifle Division

24th Rifle Division (2d est.) (Samara-Ulyanov-Berdichev)

Jul 1918	Formed in Ulyanov region as the 1st Free Simbirsk Infantry Division. Renamed 24th RD in Nov 18. *Awarded the Samara place-name honorific and "Iron" distinction, resulting in renaming: 24th Samara Ulyanov "Iron" Rifle Division in 1924*
1939	Took part in the Soviet-Finnish War. Initially

assigned to the 13th Army then to several armies in the Western, Stalingrad, Don, and Southwestern Fronts After Apr 44, part of the 18th Army (1st and 4th Ukrainian Fronts)

1941   Defended in Belorussia and the approaches to Moscow

42–43   Battle of Stalingrad, offensive opns in the Donbas, Left Bank Ukraine, and Zhitomir-Berdichev opns

44–45   Proskurov-Chernovits, Lvov-Sandomir, East and West Carpathian, Morava-Ostravka, and Prague offensive opns

Jan 44 *Awarded the Berdichev place-name honorific*

Commanders

Gen. Major K. N. Galitsky, 1941
Gen. Major F. A. Prokhorov, 42–45

Other Names

24th Samara-Ulyanov "Iron" Rifle Division, Samara-Ulyanov-Berdichev Rifle Division

25th Guards Red Banner Rifle Division (Sinelnikov-Budapest)

Apr 42 Formed in the Kalinin region on the base of the 2d Guards Red Banner Brigade as the 25th Guards Red Banner RD. Assigned in sequence to the 6th Tank, 40th, 3d Tank, 8th Guards, 53d, and, after Nov 44, to the 7th Guards Army

1942   Defended on the Don River line

1943   Took part in Ostrogozhsk-Rossosh, Voronezh-Kastornoe offensives, and in the offensive and defensive battles for Kharkov

Sep 43 *Awarded the Sinelnikov place-name honorific*

44–45   Korsun-Shevchenkovsky, Uman-Botoshany, Iassy-Kishenev, Budapest, Bratislava-Brno, and Prague offensive opns

Apr 45 *Awarded the place-name Budapest*

Commanders

Col. Ya. P. Bezverhov, 1942
Gen. Major P. M. Shafarenko, 42–43
Col. A. G. Dashkevich, 1943
Col. K. V. Bilyutin, 1943
Gen. Major G. A. Krivilapov, 43–44
Col. N. P. Korkin, 1944
Col. A. M. Peremanov, 44–45

Other Names

Sinelnikov-Budapest Rifle Division

26th Guards Rifle Division/ 93d Rifle Division (Gorodok)

1936   Formed in the Transbaikal MD as the 93d RD and given the sobriquet "East Siberian." Assigned to the 43d, 33d, 20th, and 16th armies; after May 43, assigned to 11th Guards Army

41–43   Participated in the defensive and offensive battles around Moscow, then in the Orel, Briansk, and Gorodok offensive opns

Apr 42 *Honored and renamed as 26th Guards RD*

Dec 43 *Awarded the Gorodok place-name honorific*

44–45   Belorussian, Gumbinnen, and East Prussian offensive opns

Commanders

Gen. Major K. M. Erastov, 41–42
Gen. Major N. N. Korzenevsky, 42–44
Gen. Major G. I. Chernov, 44–45

Other Names

East Siberian-Gorodok Rifle Division

27th Guards Rifle Division (Omsk-Novobug)

1941	Initially organized as the 75th Naval Infantry Brigade at the end of 1941. Assigned in sequence to the 4th Tank, 1st Guards, 24th, 66th, 65th, and 62d/8th Guards Armies
42–43	Participated in Demiansk operation, Kalinin Front; Stalingrad, Izyum-Barvenkovo, the Donbas, and Zaporozhe
May 42	*Honored and reformed into 27th Guards RD and given the name Omsk from Russian Civil War association*
44–45	Took part in Nikopol-Krivoi Rog, Bereznegova-toye-Snigirovka, Odessa, Lublin-Brest, Warsaw-Poznan, and Berlin offensives
Mar 44	*Awarded the Novobug place-name honorific*

Commanders
Col. K. N. Vindushev, 1942
Gen. Major V. S. Glebov, 42–45
Other Names
Omsk-Novobug Rifle Division

31st Guards Rifle Division/ 328th Rifle Division (Irkutsk-Vitebsk)

Sep 41	Formed in the Yaroslavl region as the 328th RD. Assigned to the 10th, 16th, and 11th Guards Armies
1941	Defensive opns vic. Moscow
1942	Took part in the general winter offensive vic. Zhizdra and Kirov
May 42	*Honored and renamed as the 31st Guards RD*
1943	Participated in the Orel, Belorussian, Gumbinnen, and East Prussian offensive opns

Jul 44	*Awarded the Vitebsk place-name honorific*

Commanders
Col. P. A. Yeremin, 41–42
Col. P. M. Gudz, 1942
Gen. Major A. F. Naumov, 42–43
Gen. Major I. K. Shcherbina, 43–44
Gen. Major I. D. Burmakov, 44–45

35th Guards Rifle Division (Lozovaia)

Aug 42	Organized in the Moscow region on the base of the 8th Airborne Corps. Assigned to the 57th, 62d, 1st Guards, 6th, and 8th Guards Armies, with the majority of service, after Oct 43, in the 8th Guards
42–43	Participated in the Battle of Stalingrad, then conducted offensive opns in the Donbas, defensive opns at the 3d Battle of Kharkov, and Left Bank Ukraine
Sep 43	*Awarded the Lozovaia place-name honorific*
44–45	Continued opns in Right Bank Ukraine, followed by Lublin-Brest, Warsaw-Poznan, and Berlin offensives

Commanders
Gen. Major V. A. Glazkov, 1942
Col. V. P. Dubyansky, 1942
Col. F. A. Ostashenko, 1942
Gen. Major I. Ya. Kulagin, 42–44
Col. N. P. Grigoryev, 44–45
Col. G. B. Smolin, 1945

36th Guards Rifle Division (Upper Dnepr)

Aug 42	Organized in the Ivanovo region on the base of the 9th Airborne Corps. Assigned to 57th, 64th, 7th Guards, and 26th Armies
42–43	Took part in battles of Stalingrad, Kursk, and the liberation of the Ukraine

Oct 43   *Awarded the Upper
Dnepr place-name
honorific*
44–45   Participated in Iassy-
Kishinev, Debrecen,
Budapest, Balaton, and
Vienna offensive opns
Commanders
Gen. Major M. I. Denisenko, 42–44
Gen. Major G. P. Lilenkov, 44–45
Other Names
Upper Dnepr Rifle Division

37th Guards Rifle Division (Rechitsa)

Aug 42   Formed in the Moscow
region as the 37th Guards
RD. Assigned to the 4th
Tank, 62d, 65th, and 2d
Shock Armies
42–43   Participated in the Battle
of Stalingrad, offensive
opns in the Sevsk Direc-
tion, Orel, Chernigov-Prip-
iat, and Gomel-Rechitsa
battles
Nov 43   *Awarded the Rechitsa place-
name honorific*
44–45   Kalinkov-Mozyr, Belaruss-
ian, Mlava-Elbing, East
Pomeranian, and Berlin
offensive opns
Commanders
Gen. Major V. G. Zholudev, 42–43
Col. T. N. Vishnevsky, 1943
Gen. Major Ye. G. Ushakov, 43–44
Col. I. K. Brushko, Nov 1943
Gen. Major I. I. Sankovsky, Nov 1943
Gen. Major V. L. Morozov, 1944
Gen. Major S. U. Rakhimov, 1945
Gen. Major K. Ye. Grebennikov, 1945
Other Names
Rechitsa Rifle Division

39th Guards Rifle Division (Barvenkovo)

Aug 42   Organized in the Moscow
region on the base of the
5th Airborne Corps.
Assigned for almost the

entire war to the 62d/8th
Guards Army
42–44   Took part in the Battle of
Stalingrad, Left and Right
Bank Ukraine, Lublin-
Brest opns
Sep 43   *Awarded the Barvenkovo
place-name honorific*
1945   Warsaw-Poznan and
Berlin opns
Commanders
Gen. Major S. S. Guryev, 42–43
Gen. Major V. A. Leshchinin, 1943
Col. S. M. Kaminin, 43–44
Lt. Col. V. M. Shtrigol, 1944
Col. Ye. T. Marenko, 44–45
Other Names
Barvenkovo Rifle Division

40th Guards Rifle Division (Yenakiev-Danube)

Aug 42   Formed in the Moscow
region on the base of the
6th Airborne Corps.
Assigned in sequence to
the 1st Guards, 21st, 4th
Tank, 65th, 5th Tank, 5th
Shock, 46th, 4th Guards,
and again 46th Armies
42–44   Took part in the Battle of
Stalingrad, Left and Right
Bank Ukraine, Rostov
offensive, and opns in
Romania
Sep 43   *Awarded the Yenakiev place-
name honorific*
1945   Opns in Bulgaria, Yugosla-
via, Hungary, and Austria
Jan 45   *Awarded the Danube place-
name honorific*
Commanders
Gen. Major A. I. Pastrevich, 42–43
Gen. Major I. I. Shvigin, 1943
Col. D. V. Kazak, 1943
Col. K. A. Sergeyev, 1943
Gen. Major G. F. Panchenko, 43–44
Col. L. S. Bransburg, 44–45
Other Names
Yenakiev-Danube Rifle Division

42d Guards Red Banner Rifle Division (Priluga)

Jul 42	Formed in the Western Front on the base of the 1st Guards Red Banner Rifle Brigade. Assigned to the 5th, 20th, 31st, 5th Guards, 40th, and 53d Armies. Primarily served in the 40th Army (Dec 43–Mar 45)
42–43	Took part in the Rzhev-Sychevka and Rzhev Viazma offensive opns, the Battle of Kursk, Left Bank Ukraine, and offensive and defensive opns at Kiev
Sep 43	*Awarded the Priluga place-name honorific*
44–45	Uman-Botoshany, Iassy-Kishinev, Debrecen, Budapest, Bratislava-Brno, and Prague offensives

Commanders
Gen. Major F. A. Bobrov, 42–44
Gen. Major S. P. Timoshkov, 1944
Col. F. F. Bochkov, 44–45
Other Names
Priluga Rifle Division

44th Guards Rifle Division/ 5th Rifle Division (Baranovich)

Sep 1918	Formed as the 2d Penzen Infantry Division
Oct 1918	Renamed the 5th Rifle Division
1939	Took part in the occupation of western Belorussia in connection with the Soviet-German partition of Poland. Assigned in sequence to the 11th, 27th, 1st Guards, and 65th Armies during the war
41–42	Defensive opns as part of the Northwestern Front, then participated in the defense of Moscow and the Battle of Stalingrad
Oct 42	*Honored and renamed as the 44th Guards RD*
43–45	Offensive and defensive opns in the Donbas; Left Bank Ukraine, Gomel-Rechitsa, Belorussian Campaign, Mlava-Elbing, East Pomeranian, and Berlin offensive opns
Jul 44	*Awarded the Baranovich place-name honorific*

Commanders
Col. F. P. Ozerov, 1941
Col. A. I. Svetlyakov, 1941
Lieutenant-Col. P. S. Telkov, 1941
Gen. Major V. R. Vashkevich, 1941
Col. P. S. Yeroshenko, 41–42
Gen. Major D. A. Kupriyanov, 1941, 1943
Col. N. A. Krymsky, 1942
Col. N. V. Korkishko, 1943, 1944
Col. P. G. Petrov, 1944
Gen. Major V. A. Borisov, 44–45
Other Names
Baranovich Rifle Division

45th Guards Rifle Division/ 70th Rifle Division (Krasnosel)

1934	Formed in the Kuibyshev region as the 70th RD
39–40	Participated in the Soviet-Finnish War as part of 7th Army. Assigned during the course of the war to the 11th, 48th, 55th, 67th, 42d, 2d Shock, 21st, 8th, and 6th Guards Armies
1941	Participated in defensive opns vic. Leningrad
1942	Siniavino offensive operation
Oct 42	*Honored and renamed as 45th Guards RD*
1943	Lifting of the blockade at Leningrad; continued defensive opns
1944	Leningrad-Novgorod, Vyborg, and Tallinn offensives

Jan 44   *Awarded the Krasnosel place-
          name honorific*
1945   Part of the blocking force
          in the Kurland Peninsula

Commanders
Gen. Major A. Ye. Fedyunin, 1941
Col. V. P. Yakutovich, 1941
Col. Ye. Ye. Tsukanov, 1942
Gen. Major A. A. Krasnov, 42–43
Gen. Major S. M. Putilov, 43–44
Gen. Major I. I. Trusov, 44–45

Other Names
Krasnosel Rifle Division

50th Guards Rifle Division/
124th Rifle Division (Donets)

Dec 41   Formed in the Southwest
          Front in the Voronezh
          region as the 124th RD.
          Assigned in sequence to
          the 21st, 38th, 5th Tank, 3d
          Guards, 51st, 5th Shock,
          and 28th Army
42–43   Defensive opns on the
          Northern Donets River to
          the north of Belgorod; par-
          ticipated in the 2d Battle of
          Kharkov (May 42); defend-
          ed in the Ostrogozhsk
          Direction and the Battle of
          Stalingrad; Left Bank
          Ukraine opns
Nov 42   *Honored and renamed as
          50th Guards RD*
Sep 43   *Awarded the Donets place-
          name honorific*
44–45   Offensive opns: Belorussia,
          eastern Poland, Gumbin-
          nen, East Prussia, Berlin,
          and Prague

Commanders
Col. A. K. Berestov, 41–42
Gen. Major A. I. Belov, 42–43
Col. K. A. Sergeyev, 1943
Gen. Major A. S. Vladychansky,
    43–45
Col. G. L. Rybalko, 1944

Other Names
Donets Rifle Division

52d Guards Rifle Division/
63d Rifle Division (Riga-Berlin)

Dec 41   Formed in Voronezh as an
          NKVD mechanized
          division
Jan 42   Named the 8th MRD of
          NKVD. Assigned in
          sequence to the 21st, 3d
          Shock, and 1st Shock
          Armies
42–43   Took part in the Battle of
          Stalingrad, followed by
          the Battle of Kursk and
          Left Bank Ukraine offen-
          sive opns
Jul 42   Renamed the 63th RD
Apr 43   *Honored and renamed as the
          52d Guards RD*
44–45   Leningrad-Novgorod,
          Pskov-Ostrova, Riga,
          Warsaw-Poznan, East
          Pomeranian, and Berlin
          offensives
Oct 44   *Awarded the Riga place-
          name honorific*
Jun 45   *Awarded the Berlin place-
          name honorific*

Commanders
Col. F. M. Mazirin, 1941
Col. S. M. Rogachevsky, 1942
Gen. Major K. I. Goryunov, 1942
Gen. Major N. D. Kozin, 42–43, 44–45
Gen. Major I. M. Nekrasov, 1943
Col. B. K. Kolchigin, 1943
Col. N. V. Simonov, 43–44

Other Names
Riga-Berlin RD, 8th Motorized Rifle
Division of the NKVD

52d Rifle Division (2d est.)
(Shumlin-Vienna)

Feb 42   Formed in the Moscow
          region as the 52d RD (2d
          est.). Assigned to many
          different armies in the
          Kalinin, Steppe, Western,
          Southwestern, 2d and 3d
          Ukrainian, and Trans-
          baikal Fronts

1942	Participated in the Rzhev-Sychevka offensive opn
1943	Offensive opns in the Donbas, followed by defense of the Northern Donets River line, the Battle of Kursk, and liberation of Left Bank Ukraine
44–45	Right Bank Ukraine, Iassy-Kishinev, liberation of Romania, Bulgaria, Yugoslavia, Budapest, Bratislava-Brno and Prague offensive opns. Transferred to the Far East and participated in the Khingan-Mukden offensive
Sep 44	*Awarded the Shumlin place-name honorific*
May 45	*Awarded Vienna as a place-name*

Commanders
Lt. Col. K. K. Dzhukha, 1942
Col. V. S. Andreyev, 1942
Col. L. I. Vagin, 42–43
Lt. Col. K. P. Kozachuk, 1943
Lt. Col. P. D. Fadeyev, 1943
Col. A. Ya. Maksimov, 43–44
Gen. Major L. M. Milyaev, 44–45
Other Names
Shumlin-Vienna Rifle Division

54th Guards Rifle Division/ 119th Rifle Division (Makseyev)

Jul 42	Formed in the Kalinin region on the base of the 51st Rifle Brigade as 119th RD. Assigned to the 5th Tank, 51st, 5th Shock, and 28th Armies
42–43	Took part in the Battle of Stalingrad, offensive action in the Donbas, defensive opns at Voroshilovgrad, then the Melitopol and Krivoi Rog offensive opns
Dec 42	*Honored and renamed as 54th Guards RD*

Sep 43	*Awarded the Makseyev place-name honorific*
44–45	Took part in Bereznegova-toye-Snigirovka, Odessa, Belorussian, East Prussian, Berlin, and Prague offensives

Commanders
Col. I. J. Kulagin, 1942
Gen. Major M. M. Danilov, 42–45
Other Names
Makseyev Rifle Division

55th Guards Rifle Division/30th Irkutsk Rifle Division (Irkutsk-Pinsk)

Jul 1918	Initially formed as the Western RD, renamed 4th Urals RD, and again renamed 30th RD (Nov 1918)
1938	Awarded the Irkutsk place-name honorific
1940	Participated in the occupation of Bessarabia. During the war, assigned to the 9th, 56th, 37th, 58th, 18th, Armies; after May 44, to the 28th Army
41–42	Defensive opns in the southern theater 1942
Dec 42	*Honored and renamed as 55th Guards RD*
1943	Took part in the battle in the North Caucasus, Taman, and Kerch-Eltigen amphibious operation
1944	Participated in the Belorussian campaign, opns in the eastern part of Poland, East Prussian, Berlin, and Prague offensive operation
Jul 44	*Awarded the Pinsk place-name honorific*

Commanders
Gen. Major S. G. Galaktionov, 1941
Gen. Major M. D. Goncharov, 1941
Col. S. K. Potekhin, 41–42
Gen. Major B. N. Arshintsev, 42–43

Col. C. I. Semenov, 1943, 1944
Col. P. A. Murashev, 1944
Gen. Major A. P. Turchinsky, 44–45
Other Names
Irkutsk-Pinsk Rifle Division

58th Guards Rifle Division/ 1st Rifle Division (Krasnograd-Prague)

Jun 42	Formed in Kuibyshev area as the 1st RD. During the course of the war was assigned to the 63d, 3d Guards, 1st Guards (3d est.), 6th, and 3d Tank Armies
1942	Took part in the Battle of Stalingrad
Dec 42	*Honored and renamed as 58th Guards RD*
1943	Left and Right Bank Ukraine offensive opns
Sep 43	*Awarded the Krasnograd place-name honorific*
44–45	Lvov-Sandomir, Sandomir-Silesia, Lower and Upper Silesia, Berlin, and Prague offensive opns
Jun 45	*Awarded the Prague place-name honorific*

Commanders
Gen. Major A. I. Semenov, Nov 42–43
Gen. Major D. S. Zerebin, 1943
Col. G. S. Sorokin, 1943
Col. P. I. Kasatkin, 1943
Gen. Major V. V. Rusakov 43–44, 44–45
Col. V. I. Kazurin, 1944
Other Names
Krasnograd-Prague Rifle Division

59th Guards Rifle Division/ 197th Rifle Division (2d est.) (Kramator)

Mar 42	Formed in the Krasnodar region as the 197th RD (2d est.). Assigned to the 63d (later 1st Guards, then 3d Guards), 6th, and 46th Armies
42–43	Participated in battles at Stalingrad, Voroshilovgrad, the Donbas, Zaporozhe, and Nikopol-Krivoi Rog
Jan 43	*Honored and renamed as 59th Guards RD*
Sep 43	*Awarded the Kramator place-name honorific*
44–45	Offensive opns at Odessa, Iassy-Kishinev, Romania, Bulgaria, Debrecen, Budapest, and Vienna

Commanders
Gen. Major M. I. Zaporozhchenko, 42–43
Gen. Major G. P. Karamyshev, 43–45
Other Names
Kramator Rifle Division

62d Guards Rifle Division/127th Rifle Division (Zvenigorod-Buadapest)

Mar 42	Formed in the Volga MD as 127th RD. Assigned to different armies in the Stalingrad, Voronezh, Southwestern, Steppe, and 2d Ukrainian Fronts
42–43	Took part in Stalingrad and Ostrogozhsk-Rossosh battles; defensive and offensive opns at the 3d Battle of Kharkov; liberation of the Ukraine
Jan 43	*Honored and renamed as 62d Guards RD*
44–45	Iassy-Kishinev, Budapest, and Vienna offensive opns
Feb 44	*Awarded the Zvenigorod place-name honorific*
Apr 45	*Awarded Budapest as a place-name*

Commanders
Col. K. A. Sergeyev, 1942
Gen. Major G. M. Zaitsev, 42–43
Col. N. N. Moshlyak, 43–45
Gen. Major G. F. Panchenko, 1945
Other Names
Zvenigorod-Budapest Rifle Division

70th Guards Rifle Division/ 138th Rifle Division (Glukhov)

Sep 39   Formed in Kalinin region as the 138th RD. Also named the 138th Mountain Rifle Division from Apr 41 to Mar 42. Assigned in sequence to the 51st, 44th, 64th, 62d, 13th, 70th, 60th, and 38th Armies

39–40   Took part in the Soviet-Finnish War

41–43   Initially guarded the border with Turkey. Later, took part in defensive opns in Crimea, Taman, and the North Caucasus. Participated in battles of Stalingrad and Kursk, and liberation of the Ukraine

Feb 43   *Honored and renamed as the 70th Guards RD*

Aug 43   *Awarded the Glukov place-name honorific*

44–45   Offensive opns in Poland and Czechoslovakia

Commanders

Gen. Major Ya. A. Ishchenko, 1941
Col. P. M. Yagunov, 1941
Col. M. Ya. Pimenov, 1942
Gen. Major I. I. Lyudnikov, 42–43
Gen. Major I. A. Gusev, 43–44, 1945
Col. T. A. Andrienko, 1944
Gen. Major D. Ya. Grigoryev, 1945
Col. L. I. Gredinarenko, 1945

71st Guards Rifle Division/23d Kharkov Rifle Division (Kharkov-Vitebsk)

Oct 1918   Originally formed as the 1st Ust-Medvedits RD, renamed the 23d RD in Nov 18

1922   Awarded the Kharkov place-name honorific

1939   Assigned to the 11th, 27th, 3d Shock, 34th, 53d, 1st Guards, 21st, 4th Tank, 65th, again the 21st, and 43d Armies

41–42   Defensive opns west of Kaunass in the Kholm Direction. Took part in the Demiansk operation (Jan–Mar 42) and the Battle of Stalingrad

1943   Battle of Kursk and opns to clear Left Bank Ukraine

Mar 43   Honored and renamed the 71st Guards RD

44–45   Belorussian campaign; Shyaulyai, Riga, Memel offensive opns, then formed part of the blocking force on the Kurland Peninsula

Jul 44   *Awarded the Vitebsk place-name honorific*

Commanders

Gen. Major V. F. Pavlov, 1941
Gen. Major S. G. Goryachev, 1941
Col. A. M. Goryainov, 1941
Gen. Major P. P. Vakhrameyev, 41–42; 1943
Gen. Major I. P. Sivakov, Dec 1942, 43–44
Col. N. I. Babahin, 1944
Col. A. I. Ivanchenko, 1944
Gen. Major D. S. Kuropatenko, 1944
Col. N. N. Lozhkin, 44–45
Lt. Col. G. A. Inozemtsev, 1945

75th Guards Rifle Division/ 95th Rifle Division (Bakhmach)

Sep 42   Formed in the Tula region as the 95th Rifle Division. Assigned during the war to the 62d, 13th, 70th, 60th, 65th, and 61st Armies

42–43   Battles of Stalingrad and Kursk, Left Bank Ukraine, offensive opns at Kiev

Mar 43   *Honored and renamed as the 75th Guards RD*

Sep 43   *Awarded the Bakhmach honorific*

44–45   Belorussian campaign, opns in Latvia, Lithuania,

Estonia, Poland, and
Berlin

Commander
Gen. Major V. A. Gorishny, 43–45
Other Names
Bakhmach Rifle Division

77th Guards Rifle Division
173d Rifle Division (Chernigov)

Aug 40 — Formed in Moscow as the 21st Territorial (Home Guards) Division (Kiev district). Served in various armies in the Reserve, Western, Stalingrad, Don, Briansk, Central, Belorussian Fronts, and, after Apr 44, in the 69th Army, 1st Belorussian Front

1941 — Reformed into the 173d RD (2d est.). Participated in the Battle of Moscow

42–43 — Opns at Stalingrad, the Orel offensive, Left Bank Ukraine, and Gomel-Rechitsa

Mar 43 — *Honored and renamed as the 77th Guards RD*

Sep 43 — *Awarded the Chernigov place-name honorific*

44–45 — Kalinkov-Mozyr, Lublin-Brest, Warsaw-Poznan, and Berlin offensive opns

Commanders
Col. A. V. Bogdanov, 41–42
Col. P. J. Tikhanov, 1942
Lt. Col. V. A. Katyushin, 1942
Col. V. D. Khokhlov, 1942
Col. I. P. Khorikov, Nov–Dec 43
Gen. Major V. S. Askalepov, 42–45
Other Names
21st Territorial (Home Guards) Division (Moscow, Kiev District)

79th Guards Rifle Division/
443d Rifle Division (Zaporozhe)

Dec 41 — Formed in Tomsk as the 443d RD. Assigned initially to the Briansk Front,

then to the 62d/8th Guards Army for the rest of the war

42–43 — Initially conducted defensive opns in the Voronezh Direction, then took part in Battle of Stalingrad and opns to liberate Ukraine

Jan 42 — Reformed as the 284th RD

Mar 43 — *Honored and renamed as the 79th Guards RD*

Oct 43 — *Awarded the Zaporozhe place-name honorific*

1944 — Lublin-Brest offensive

1945 — Warsaw-Poznan and Berlin offensives

Commanders
Brigade Commander S. A. Ostroumov. 41–42
Gen. Major N. F. Batyuk, 42–43
Gen. Major L. I. Vagin, 43–45
Col. I. V. Semchenkov, 1945
Col. S. I. Gerasimenko, 1945
Gen. Major D. I. Stankevsky, 1945

84th Guards Rifle Division/
110th Rifle Division (Karachev)

Jul 41 — Originally formed as the 4th Territorial (Home Guards) Division, Moscow, Kuibyshev district

Sep 41 — Reformed into the 110th RD. Assigned as part of the 24th, 49th, 21st, 33d, and 11th Guards Armies, the latter from May 43-May 45

41–42 — Participated in defensive and offensive opns vic. Moscow

1943 — Participated in the Rzhev-Viazma and Orel offensives

Apr 43 — *Honored and renamed as the 84th Guards RD*

Aug 43 — *Awarded the Karachev place-name honorific*

44–45 — Took part in the Belorussian, Gumbinnen, and

East Prussian offensive
opns

Commanders

Gen. Major A. N. Sidelnikov, 1941
Col. A. D. Borisov, 1941
Col. S. T. Gladishev, 1941
Col. N. A. Bezzubov, 41–42
Col. A. N. Yurin, 1942
Col. P. A. Zaitsev, 1942
Gen. Major G. B. Peters, 42–44
Gen. Major I. K. Shcherbina, 44–45

Other Names

4th Territorial (Home Guards)
Division of Moscow

89th Guards Rifle Division/
160th Rifle Division (Belgorod-Kharkov)

Aug 40	Formed in the Gorky region as the 160th RD. Assigned to 13th, 40th, 6th, 3d Tank, 69th, 6th Guards, 37th, 53d, and 5th Shock Armies
41–43	Defensive opns in the western and southwestern Directions. Took part in the Battle of Kursk and Left Bank Ukraine offensive opns
Apr 43	*Honored and renamed 89th Guards RD*
Aug 43	*Awarded the Belgorod and Kharkov place-name honorifics*
44–45	Right Bank Ukraine, Iassy-Kishinev, Warsaw-Poznan, and Berlin offensives

Commanders

Gen. Major I. M. Skugarev, 1941
Col. M. B. Anashkin, 41–42
Gen. Major M. P. Seryugin, 42–45

Other Names

Belgorod-Kharkov Rifle Division

91st Guards Rifle Division/257th Rifle
Division (2d est.) (Dukhov-Khingan)

Dec 41	Formed in the Kalinin region as the 257th RD (2d est.). Assigned to the 3d

Shock and, after Jul 43, the
39th Army

1942	Defended in the Toropets-Kholm Direction, then on the Velikie Luki River
43–44	Took part in Velikie Luki, Smolensk, Belorussian, and Memel offensive opns
Apr 43	*Honored and renamed as 91st Guards RD*
Sep 43	*Awarded the Dukhov place-name honorific*
1945	East Prussian and Khingan-Mukden opns
Sep 45	*Awarded the Khingan place-name honorific*

Commanders

Gen. Major K. A. Zheleznikov, 41–42
Gen. Major A. A. Dyakonov, 42–43
Gen. Major M. I. Ozimin, 42–43
Col. V. L. Beilin, 1943
Lt. Col. P.G. Karamushko, 1943
Col. A. B. Rodionov, 43–44
Col. I. M. Starikov, 1944
Gen. Major V. I. Kozhanov, 44–45

Other Names

Dukhov-Khingan Rifle Division

93d Guards Red Banner Rifle Division
(Kharkov)

Apr 43	Formed in the Voronezh Front from the 92d and 13th Guards Red Banner separate rifle brigades. Assigned to 69th, 5th Guards, 7th Guards, 27th, again 7th Guards, and 53d Army
43–44	Took part in the Battle of Kursk, Left and Right Bank Ukraine, Iassy-Kishinev, and Debrecen opns
Aug 43	*Awarded the Kharkov place-name honorific*
1945	Offensive opns at Budapest, Bratislava-Brno, and Prague

Commanders

Gen. Major V. V. Tikhomirov, 43–44

Col. Ya. N. Vronsky, 1944

Gen. Major N. G. Zolotukhin, 1944

Col. P. M. Marol, 44–45

Other Names

Kharkov Rifle Division

95th Guards Rifle Division/
226th Rifle Division (Poltava)

Aug 41	Formed in the Zaporozhe region as 226th RD. Initially assigned to the 6th Army of the Southern Front, then a variety of armies; after Oct 42, assigned to the 66th/5th Guards Army
41–42	Defensive opns on Dnepr River northeast of Dnepropetrovsk, at Poltava, and Kharkov. Participated in the Battle of Stalingrad
1943	Battle of Kursk and liberation of Left Bank Ukraine
May 43	Honored and renamed as 95th Guards RD
Sep 43	*Awarded the Poltava place-name honorific*
44–45	Kirovograd, Uman-Botoshany, Lvov-Sandomir, Sandomir-Silesia, Upper and Lower Silesia, Berlin, and Prague offensive opns

Commanders

Col. V. A Chugunov, 1941

Col. A. S. Sergienko, 1941

Gen. Major A. V. Gorbatov, 41–42

Gen. Major M. A. Usenko, 1942

Gen. Major N. S. Nikitchenko, 1942, 1943

Gen. Major A. I. Oleinikov, 43–45

Other Names

Poltava Rifle Division

96th Guards Rifle Division/
258th Rifle Division (Ilovai)

Oct 41	Formed initially in Novosibirsk as the 43d

Separate Rifle Brigade. Assigned to the 49th, 1st Guards, 24th, 65th, 5th Tank, 5th Shock, and 28th Armies

1941	Battle of Moscow
42–43	Took part in the Stalingrad, Rostov, Donbas, Melitopol, and Nikopol-Krivoi Rog opns
Apr 42	Reformed into the 258th RD
May 43	*Honored and renamed as 96th Guards RD*
Sep 43	*Awarded the Ilovai place-name honorific*
1944	Bereznogovatoye-Snigirovka, Odessa, Belorussian offensives. Opns in eastern Poland
1945	East Prussian, Berlin, and Prague opns

Commanders

Col. Tsitaishvili, 1942

Col. P. S. Khaustovich, 1942

Col. S. S. Levin, 1942; 43–44

Col. I. Ya. Fursin, 42–43

Gen. Major S. N. Kuznetsov, 44–45

Other Names

Ilovai Rifle Division, 43d Separate Rifle Brigade

97th Guards Rifle Division/
343th Rifle Division (Poltava)

Sep 41	Formed in Stavropol as the 343d RD. Assigned during the war to the 56th, 6th, 9th, 21st, and 24th Armies; after Oct 42, assigned to the 66th/5th Guards Army
41–42	Participated in defensive opns at Rostov, then in the Rostov and Barvenko-Lozovaia offensive opns 2d Battle of Kharkov and defensive opns near Stalingrad
1943	Battle of Kursk and liberation of Left Bank Ukraine

May 43	*Honored and renamed as 97th Guards RD*
Sep 43	*Awarded the Poltava place-name honorific, along with its sister divisions, the 13th and 95th Guards RDs*
44–45	Kirovograd, Uman-Boto-shany, Lvov-Sandomir, Sandomir-Silesia, Upper and Lower Silesia, Berlin, and Prague offensive opns

Commanders
Col. P. P. Chuvashev, 41–42
Gen. Major M. A. Usenko, 42–43
Gen. Major I. I. Antsiferov, 43–44
Lt. Col. M. I. Lashkov, 1944
Col. Ye. M. Golub, 1944
Col. A. P. Garan, 44–45
Other Names
Poltava Rifle Division

101st Guards Rifle Division/ 14th Rifle Division (Pechenga)

1922	Formed in Moscow as the 14th RD
39–41	Participated in the Soviet-Finnish War
41–43	Defensive opns in the Murmansk area, assigned to the 19th, 14th, and, later, the 2d Shock Army
44–45	Participated in Petsamo-Iassy, East Pomeranian, and Berlin opns
Oct 44	*Honored and renamed as 101st Guards RD and awarded Pechenga as a place-name honorific. [One of two RDs so honored, the other being 10th Guards RD.]*

Commanders
Gen. Major A. A. Zhurba, 1941
Gen. Major N. N. Nikishin, 1941
Col. T. V. Tommola, 41–42
Col. Kh. A. Khudalov, 1942
Gen. Major F. F. Korotkov, 42–44
Col. F. A. Grebenkin, 44–45
Gen. Major E. G. Ushakov, 1945

Other Names
Pechenga Rifle Division

102d Guards Rifle Division/65th Rifle Division (Novgorod-Pomerania)

Jul 39	Formed in Tyumen as the 65th Rifle Division. Assigned to the 4th, 52d, 59th, 67th, 7th, 14th, and 19th Armies
1941	Defensive opns at Tikhvin
1942	Lubansk offensive operation
44–45	Participated in Leningrad-Novgorod, Sbir-Petroza-vod, Petsamo-Iassy, and East Pomeranian offensives
Jan 44	*Awarded the Novgorod place-name honorific*
Dec 44	*Honored and renamed the 102d Guards RD*
Apr 45	*Awarded the Pomerania place-name*

Commanders
Col. P. K. Koshevoi, 40–42
Col. V. J. Nikolayevsky, 42–43
Gen. Major G. Ye. Kalinovsky, 43–44
Col. S. I. Khramtsov, 44–45
Other Names
Novgorod-Pomerania Rifle Division

110th Guards Red Banner Rifle Division (Aleksander-Khingan)

Aug 43	Formed in Voronezh from the 5th Guards and 7th Guards Red Banner rifle brigades. Assigned to the 37th, 5th Guards, and 53d Armies
1943	Took part in the battle for the Dnepr River line
44–45	Right Bank Ukraine, opns in Romania, Hungary, and Czechoslovakia. Trans-ferred to the Transbaikal Front for the Khingan-Mukden offensive opns
Dec 43	*Awarded the Aleksander place-name honorific*

Sep 45   *Awarded Khingan as a place-name honorific*

Commanders

Gen. Major M. I. Ogorodov, 1943, 1944, 1945

Col. D. F. Sobolev, 1944

Col. I. A. Rotkevich, 1944

Col. I. A. Pigin, 1944

Col. A. I. Malchevsky, 1945

Gen. Major G. A. Krivolapov, 1945

Other Names

Aleksander-Khingan Rifle Division

120th Guards Rifle Division/ 308th Rifle Division (Rogachev)

May 42   Formed in Siberian MD as the 308th RD. Assigned to 24th, 62d, and after May 43, to the 3d Army

42–43   Took part in the battles of Stalingrad, Orel, Briansk, and Gomel-Rechitsa

Sep 43   *Honored and renamed as the 120th Guards RD*

Feb 44   *Awarded the Rogachev place-name honorific*

1944   Rogachev-Zhlobin and Belorussian offensive opns

1945   East Prussian and Berlin offensives

Commanders

Gen. Major L. N. Gurtiev, 42–43

Gen. Major N. K. Maslennikov, 1943

Gen. Major Ya. Ya. Fogel, 43–44

Gen. Major P. S. Telkov, 1944, 1945

Gen. Major N. A. Nikitin, 1944

121st Guards Rifle Division/ 342d Rifle Division (Gomel)

Nov 41   Formed in Saratov region as the 342d RD. Assigned during the war to the 61st, 3d, and 13th Armies

41–42   Offensive and defensive opns in the Western Direction

1943   Took part in the Orel, Briansk, and Gomel-Rechitsa offensive opns

Sep 43   *Honored and renamed as the 121st RD*

Nov 43   *Awarded the Gomel place-name honorific*

1944   Right Bank Ukraine, opns in Poland, Berlin, and Prague

Commanders

Col. A. I. Popov, 41–42

Col. G. I. Kanachadze, 42–43

Col. N. K. Maslennikov, 1943

Gen. Major L. D. Chervony, 43–45

Other Names

Gomel Rifle Division

140th Siberian Rifle Division (Novgorod-North)

Nov 42   Formed in Novosibirsk as the Siberian RD of the NKVD. Assigned to the 70th, 65th, 13th, 60th, and 38th Armies

1943   Took part in the battles of Kursk, Chernigov-Pripiat, Gomel-Rechitsa, and Zhitomir-Berdichev

Feb 43   Renamed 140th Siberian RD

Sep 43   *Awarded the Novgorod-North place-name honorific*

1944   Rovno-Lutsk, Proskurov-Chernovits, Lvov-Sandomir, and Carpathia-Duklin offensive opns

1945   West Carpathian, Morava-Ostravka, and Prague offensives

Commanders

Gen. Major M. A. Yenshin, 42–43

Col. Z. S. Shekhtman, 1943

Gen. Major A. J. Kiselev, 43–45

Col. M. M. Vlasov, 1945

Other Names

Siberian Rifle Division of the NKVD, Novgorod-North Rifle Division

144th Rifle Division (Vilnya)

Oct 39   Formed in the Ivanovo region as the 144th RD

1939	Participated in the Soviet-Finnish War
1940	Assigned to the 20th, 5th, 33d, and 5th Armies
1941	Took part in the Battle of Smolensk and defense of Moscow
42–43	Defensive and offensive opns vic. Smolensk and eastern Belorussia
44–45	Belorussian, Gumbinnen, East Prussian, and Harbin-Girin (1st Far Eastern Front) offensive opns
Jul 44	*Awarded the Vilensk place-name honorific*

Commanders

Gen. Major M. A. Pronin, 41–42
Col. I. N. Pleshakov, 1942
Col. F. D. Yablokov, 42–43
Col. A. A. Kaplun, 43–44
Gen. Major A. A. Donets, 44–45
Col. G. F. Perepich, 1945
Col. N. T. Zorin, 1945

Other Names

Vilnya Rifle Division

163d Rifle Division (Romnen-Kiev)

Sep 39	Formed in the Tula region as the 163d Mechanized Division. Took part in the Soviet Finnish War. During the war, assigned in sequence to the 27th, 11th, 34th, 27th, and 40th Armies
41–42	Defensive opns near Rezekne, Ostrov, Porkhov, Soltsi, Staraya Russa, and Demiansk
Sep 41	Reformed as the 163d Rifle Division
1943	Belgorod-Kharkov, Left Bank Ukraine, Kiev, and Zhitomir-Berdichev opns
Sep 43	*Awarded the Romnen place-name honorific*

Nov 43	*Awarded Kiev as a place-name honorific*
1944	Korsun-Shevchenkovsky, Uman-Botoshany, Iassy-Kishinev, and Debrecen opns
1945	Budapest, Balaton, and Vienna opns

Commanders

Col. G. P. Kotov, 41–42
Col. M. S. Nazarov, 1942
Col. K. A. Vasiliev, 42–43
Gen. Major F. V. Karlov, 43–45

Other Names

163 Mechanized Division, Romnen-Kiev Rifle Division

167th Rifle Division (2d est.)/ 438th Rifle Division (Sumi-Kiev)

Dec 41	Began forming in the Urals MD as the 438th RD. Renamed the formation in Jan 42 as the 167th RD, 2d est. Assigned to the 38th, 69th, again 38th, 40th, 27th, 6th Tank, and 1st Guards Armies
1942	Defensive opns to the west of Zadon
43–44	Voronezh-Kastornoe, Kharkov, Belgorod-Kharkov, and Left Bank Ukraine, Kiev offensive and defensive opns, Zhitomir-Berdichev, Korsun-Shevchenkovsky, Proskurov-Chernovits, Lvov-Sandomir, and East Carpathian opns
Sep 43	*Awarded the Sumi place-name honorific*
Nov 43	*Awarded Kiev as a place-name*
1945	Morava-Ostravka and Prague offensive opns

Commanders

Gen. Major I. I. Melnikov, 42–44
Col. I. D. Dryakhlov, 44–45
Col. I. S. Grechkosy, 1945

287th Rifle Division (Novgorod-Volyna)

Dec 41	Formed in Lipetsk region as 287th RD. Assigned to the 3d, 63, 13th, and 3d Guards Armies
1943	Took part in the Orel, Briansk, and Gomel-Rechitsa offensives
1944	Rovno-Lutsk, Proskurov-Chernovits, and Lvov-Sandomir offensives
Jan 44	*Awarded the Novogorod-Volyna place-honorific*
1945	Sandomir-Silesia, Lower Silesia, Berlin, and Prague offensive opns

Commanders

Col. I. P. Yeremin, 41–42
Col. M. V. Grachev, 1942
Gen. Major I. N. Pankratov, 42–45
Gen. Major I. N. Rizhkov, 1945

Cavalry

Cavalry and Mountain Cavalry Divisions (CD)

At the start of the war, the Soviet Army included nine cavalry and four mountain cavalry divisions. Nine of the divisions were organized into cavalry corps, one in a rifle corps, with three retained as separate cavalry divisions. Cavalry division organization formally called for 9,240 personnel and 64 light tanks, organized into four cavalry regiments and a tank regiment, with horse artillery and air defense subunits. Actually, the divisions numbered about 6,000. In the first months of the war, the personnel strength was reduced further to approximately 3,000 by direction of Stavka. By the end of 1941, 82 CDs had been formed, but that number was later reduced—largely as a result of the increasing number of mobile armored formations—to 26 CDs by the end of 1943. Organized into cavalry corps or cavalry-mechanized groups, cavalry divisions were used to exploit penetrations, pursue retreating forces, and conduct combat operations in the enemy rear. Seventeen cavalry divisions were awarded Guards distinctions; eight of those divisions were given place-name honorifics.

1st Odessa CD. Jul–Aug 41. Converted to 2d CD. Commander: Col. A. D. Alekseyev

2d CD. Aug–Nov 41. Combined into 2d RD. Two commanders

3d CD. Sep 39–Dec 41. Converted to 3d Guards CD. Commander: Gen. Major M. F. Maleyev

4th CD. Jul 41–Dec 42. Combined into 7th Cavalry Corps. Two commanders

5th CD. Mar–Nov 41. Converted to 1st Gds CD. Commander: Gen. Major V. K. Baranov

6th CD. Mar–Sep 41. Disposition unclear. Commander: Gen. Major M. P. Konstantinov

7th CD. Apr 42–Apr 43. Disbanded. Two commanders

8th CD. Jan 39–May 45. Two commanders.

9th CD. Jan–Nov 41. Converted to 2d Guards CD. Two commanders

10th CD. Jan–Apr 42. Combined into 12th and 13th CD. Commander: Col. I. P. Kalyuzhny

11th CD. Sep 41–Jan 43. Converted to 8th Guards CD. Commander: Col. M. I. Surzhikov

12th CD. Jan–Aug 42. Converted to 9th Guards CD. Three commanders

13th CD. Jan–Aug 42. Converted to 10th Guards CD. Two commanders

14th CD. Jun 38–Dec 41. Converted to 6th Guards CD. Two commanders

15th CD. Dec 41–Aug 42. Converted to 11th Guards CD. Commander: Col. S. I. Gorshkov

17th Mountain CD. Dec 39–Jul 42. Disbanded. Three commanders

18th CD. Mar 41–Jul 42. Disbanded. Commander: Gen. Major M. S. Ivanov

20th Mountain CD. Jan 41–Sep 43. Converted to 17th Guards CD. Four commanders

21st Mountain CD. Jun 41–Feb 43. Converted to 14th Guards CD. Three commanders

23d CD. Aug 41–May 45. Five commanders

24th CD. Feb 41–Jun 43. Combined into 2d Guards Cavalry Corps. Three commanders

25th CD. Jun 41–Jun 42. Disbanded. Two commanders

26th CD. Jun 41–Jun 42. Disposition unclear. Two commanders

27th CD. Jul 41–Mar 42. Disbanded. Two commanders

28th CD. Jul 41–May 42. Disposition unclear. Commander: Col. L. N. Sakovich

29th CD. Jul 41–Mar 42. Disbanded. Commander: Col. Ye. P. Serashev

30th Separate CD. Jul 41–May 45. Four commanders

31st CD. Jul 41–Jan 42. Converted to 7th Guards CD. Two commanders

32d CD. Oct 40–May 45. Seven commanders

34th CD. Jul 41–Jul 42. Combined into 30th CD. Two commanders. Notable: Col. A. A. Grechko, future Marshal and Minister of Defense

35th CD. Jun 41–Mar 42. Disbanded. Commander: Col. S. F. Sklyarev

36th CD. Apr–Jul 41. Disposition unclear. Commander: Col. Ye. S. Zybin

37th CD. Jul 41–Jun 42. Disbanded. Commander: Col. G. M. Roptenberg

38th CD. Jul 41–Jul 42. Disbanded. Three commanders

39th Separate Mountain CD. Jul 41–May 45. Three commanders

40th CD. Jul 41–Apr 42. Disbanded. Two commanders

41st CD. Jul 41–Jan 42. Disbanded. Two commanders

42d CD. Jul 41–Apr 42. Disbanded. Commander: Col. V. V. Glagolev

43d CD. Jun 41–Feb 42. Disbanded. Two commanders

44th CD. Jul 41–Apr 42. Combined into 17th CD. Commander: Col. P. F. Kuklin

45th CD. Jul 41–May 42. Disbanded. Commander: Col. N. M. Dreper

46th CD. Jul 41–Jul 42. Disbanded. Two commanders

47th CD. Jul–Dec 41. Combined into 32d CD. Commander: Gen. Major A. N. Sidelnkov

48th CD. Jul–Dec 41. Disbanded. Commander: Gen. Major D. Z. Aberkin

49th CD. Jul 41–Jul 42. Disbanded. Two commanders

50th CD. Jul–Nov 41. Commander: Army Gen. I. A. Pliyev, later commander of cavalry–mechanized groups

51st CD. Jul 41–Jul 43. Disbanded. Commander: Col. I. G. Pronin

52d CD. Jul 41–Mar 42. Disbanded. Commander: Col. N. P. Yakunin

53d CD. Jul–Nov 41. Converted to 4th Guards CD. Commander Brigade Commander: K. S. Melnik

54th CD. Jul 41–Jun 42. Disbanded. Two commanders

55th CD. Three commanders.
1st est. Jul 42. Combined into 73d CD.
2d est. Jul 42–Mar 43. Converted to 15th Guards CD

56th CD. Jul 41–Mar 42. Disbanded. Two commanders

57th CD. Aug 41–Feb 42. Combined into 1st Guards CD. Commander: Col. I. I. Murov

58th CD. Feb–Jun 43. Disposition unclear. Commander: Col. A. D. Alekseyev

59th CD. Feb 43–Sep 45. Three commanders

60th CD. Aug 41– Jul 42. Disposition unclear. Two commanders

61st CD. Sep 41–May 43. Disbanded. Four commanders

62d CD. Sep 41–Jul 42. Disbanded. Three commanders

63d CD. Aug 41–May 45. Two commanders

64th CD. Aug 41–May 42. Combined into 70th and 78th CDs. Two commanders

66th CD. Aug 41–Apr 42. Combined into 62d CD. Commander: Col. V. I. Grigorivich

67th CD. Mar–Jul 43. Disposition unclear. Commander: Col. V. V. Bardadin

68th CD. Sep 41–Mar 42. Disbanded. Two commanders

70th CD. Aug 41–Mar 42. Disbanded. Commander: Col. N. N. Yurchik

72d CD. Oct 41–Jun 42. Converted to a separate motorized rifle brigade. Commander: Gen. Major V. I. Kniga

73d CD. Oct 41–Jul 42. Converted to 55th CD, 2d establishment. Two commanders

74th CD. Aug 41–Apr 42. Disbanded. Two commanders

75th CD. Sep 41–Mar 42. Converted to 2d Guards CD. Two commanders

76th CD. Sep 41–May 42. Disbanded. Two commanders

77th CD. Sep 41–May 42. Disbanded. Commander: Col. I. V. Tutarinov

78th CD. Sep 41–May 42. Disbanded. Commander: Col. A. P. Gusev

79th CD. Nov 41–Apr 42. Disbanded. Commander: Col. V. S. Golovskoi

80th CD. Aug 41–Aug 42. Disbanded. Five commanders

81st CD. Sep 41–May 43. Disbanded. Three commanders

82d CD. Oct 41–Aug 42. Combined into 24th CD. Three commanders

83d CD. Sep 41–Jan 43. Converted to 13th Guards CD. Four commanders

84th CD. Feb 43–May 45. Three commanders

87th CD. Sep 41–Jul 42. Combined into 327th RD. Two commanders

91st CD. Jun 41–Mar 42. Disbanded. Three commanders

94th CD. Aug 41–Apr 42. Disbanded. Commander: Col. V. G. Baumshtern

97th CD. Dec 41–Mar 43. Disbanded. Five commanders

98th CD. Nov 41–Apr 42. Disbanded. Two commanders

99th CD. Dec 41–Jul 42. Disbanded. Commander: Col. D. N. Pavlov

100th CD. Nov–Jul 42. Disbanded. Three commanders

101st CD. Dec 41–Jul 42. Disbanded. Commander: Major D. S. Volkov

102d CD. Dec 41–Jun 42. Disbanded. Two commanders

103d CD. Dec 41–Mar 42. Disbanded. Commander: Col. M. V. Lavrentyev

104th CD. Nov 41–Jul 42. Disbanded. Commander: Col. G. I. Sheppak

105th CD. Nov 41–Jul 42. Disbanded. Two commanders

106th CD. Dec 41–Mar 42. Disbanded. Commander: Major B. N. Pankov

107th CD. Dec 41–Aug 42. Disbanded. Two commanders

108th CD. Dec 41–Mar 42. Disbanded. Commander: Col. V. I. Askalepov

109th CD. Dec 41–May 42. Disbanded. Commander: Col. I. I. Stetsenko

110th CD. May 42–Jan 43. Disbanded. Commander: Col. V. A. Khomutnikov

111th CD. Mar–Apr 42. Disbanded. Commander Col. G. A. Belousov

112th CD. Apr 42–Feb 43. Converted to 16th Guards CD. Commander: Gen. Major M. M. Shaimuratov

113th CD. Nov 41–Mar 42. Disbanded. Commander: Col. V. P. Karuna

114th CD. Jan–Mar 42. Converted to the 255th Separate Cavalry Regiment. Commander: Col. Kh. D. Mamsurov

115th CD. Feb–Oct 42. Disbanded.
Commander: Col. A. F. Skorokhod
Rostov Territorial CD. Oct–Dec 41.
Converted to 116th CD. Commander: Col. P. V. Strepukhov
116th Don Cossack CD. Jan 42–Aug
42. Converted to 12th Guards CD.
Two commanders

Guards Cavalry Divisions

1st Guards CD. Nov 41–May 45.
Seven commanders
2d Guards CD. Nov 41–May 45. Four
commanders
3d Guards CD. Nov 41–May 45. Three
commanders. Notable: Gen. Major
I. A. Pliyev, future Army Gen. and
commander of cavalry-mechanized
groups
4th Guards CD. Nov 41–May 45.
Six commanders
5th Guards CD. Dec 41–May 45.
Two commanders
6th Guards CD. Dec 41–May 45.
Two commanders
7th Guards CD. Jan 42–May 45.
Three commanders
8th Guards CD. Jan 43–May 45.
Four commanders
9th Guards CD. Aug 42–May 45.
Four commanders
10th Guards CD. Aug 42–May 45.
Seven commanders
11th Guards CD. Aug 42–May 45.
Four commanders
12th Guards CD. Aug 42–May 45.
Two commanders
13th Guards CD. Jan 43–May 44.
Five commanders
14th Guards CD. Feb 43–May 45.
Three commanders
15th Guards CD. Feb 43–May 45. Two
commanders
16th Guards CD. Feb 43–May 45. Two
commanders
17th Guards CD. Sep 43–May 45.
Commander: Gen. Major P. T.
Kursakov

Cavalry Divisions Awarded with Place-Names Honorifics

1st Guards Cavalry Division

Nov 1919	Formed as Caucasus Division of 9th Army
1920	Renamed 2d Stavropol Cavalry Division of Blinov
1924	Renamed 5th Stavropol Cavalry Division of Blinov
Jun 41	Part of the 2d Caucasus Corps
Nov 41	*Honored and renamed 1st Guards Cavalry Division*
Nov 41–45	Part of the 1st Guards Caucasus Corps. Fought as part of the Southern, Southwestern, Western, Voronezh and 1st Ukrainian Fronts
1941	Participated in defensive opns on the territory of Moldavia and vic. Moscow
1943	Opns to liberate Ukraine
1944	Lvov-Sandomir and Carpathian-Duklin offensives
1945	Sandomir-Silesia, Lower Silesia, Berlin and Prague offensive opns

Commanders
Gen. Major V. K. Baranov, 41–42
Col. A. I. Prilepsky, 1942
Gen. Major Y. I. Ovar, 42–43
Col. I. S. Borshchev, 43–44
Col. S. V. Aristov, 1944
Col. P. S. Vashurin, 44–45
Col. F. A. Blinov, 1945
Other Names
Stavropol Cavalry Division (of Blinov)

2d Guards Cavalry Division

Jul 1920	Formed in Samara region as 9th Cavalry Division
Jan 1921	Renamed 9th Crimea Cavalry Division of USSR SOVNARKOM (Soviet of People's Commissariats)

Jun–
  Nov 41   Part of the 2d Cavalry
            Corps; later part of the 1st
            Guards Cavalry Corps
May–   As a part of Southern,
  Jun 42   Southwestern, Western,
            Voronezh and 1st Ukrain-
            ian Fronts, it participated
            in initial defensive opns
            on the river Prut, on the
            territory of Moldavia and
            South Ukraine, vic.
            Moscow, Donbas, and
            Kharkov
43–45   Participated in the clearing
            of Left Bank and Right
            Bank Ukraine, Lvov-San-
            domir, Sandomir-Silesia,
            Lower Silesia, and Berlin
            offensive opns
Nov 41   *Honored and renamed 2d*
            Guard Cavalry Division

Commanders
Gen. Major A. F. Bychkovsky, 1941
Gen. Major N. S. Oslikovsky, 41–42
Col. V. D. Vasilyev, 1942
Col. V. G. Sinitsky, 42–43
Gen. Major Kh. D. Mamsurov, 43–45
Other Names
Crimea Cavalry Division, 9th Crimea
Cavalry Division SOVNARKOM

3d Bessarabia Cavalry Division of G.I. Kotovsky

Nov 1922   Formed as 4th Cavalry
            Division
Jan 1923   Renamed 3d Cavalry
            Division
39–40   Participated in occupa-
            tion/pacification of
            western Ukraine, northern
            Bukovina and Bessarabia
            during Soviet-German
            partition of Poland
41–42   Participated in defensive
            opns in Ukraine; Battle of
            Stalingrad
Dec 41   Honored and renamed 5th
            Guards Cavalry Division
43–45   Participated in Rostov,
            Smolensk, Belorussia,

            Mlava-Elbing, East-
            Pomeranian and Berlin
            offensive opns
Feb 45   *Awarded with the name of*
            Tannenberg

Commanders
Gen. Major M. F. Maleyev, 41–42
Gen. Major N. S. Chepurkin, 42–45
Other Names
Bessarabia-Tannenberg Cavalry Divi-
sion, 5th Guards Cavalry Division, 3d
Cavalry Division

6th Guards Cavalry Division

1920   Formed as 14th Cavalry
            Division
1930   Renamed 14th Cavalry
            Communist International
            Youth Division (COMIN-
            TERN) of Comrade Park-
            homenko. [Began the war
            under this name]
1941   Part of the 5th Cavalry
            Corps
Dec 41–45 Part of the 3d Guards Cav-
            alry Corps
Dec 41   *Honored and renamed 6th*
            Guards Cavalry Division
41–45   Assigned in sequence to
            the Southwestern, South-
            ern, Western, 3d and 2d
            Belorussian Fronts
41–42   Participated in battles vic.
            Dubno, Berdichev, Tara-
            scha, and in the Battle of
            Stalingrad
1943   Offensive opns in Rostov,
            Smolensk, and eastern
            Belorussia
1944   Participated in the
            Belorussian offensive
Jul 44   *Awarded with the name of*
            Grodno
1945   Took part in Mlava-Elbing,
            East Pomeranian, and
            Berlin offensive opns

Commanders
Gen. Major V. D. Kryuchenkin, 1941
Col. A. I. Belogorsky, 41–42
Gen. Major P. P. Brikel, 43–45

Other Names

Grodno Cavalry Division, 14th Cavalry Division COMINTERN

7th Guards Cavalry Division

Jul 41	Formed in Voronezh region as 31st Cavalry Division
41–45	Fought as part of the Southwestern, Western, Voronezh and 1st Ukrainian Fronts
1941	Participated in the battles vic. Moscow
Jan 42	Honored and renamed 7th Guards Cavalry Division
Mar 42– May 45	Part of 1st Guard Cavalry Corps
42–44	Opns in the Donbas, Kharkov region. Helped liberate Left and Right Bank Ukraine, Poland, Czechoslovakia
Nov 43	*Awarded with Zhitomir place-name honorific*
1945	Participated in Berlin and Prague offensive opns

Commanders

Lt. Col. M. D. Borisov, 1941, 1942
Col. Y. N. Pivnev, 1941
Lt. Col. B. V. Mansurov, 1942

Other Names

Zhitomir Cavalry Division, 31st Cavalry Division

9th Guards Kuban Cossack Cavalry Division

Jan 42	Formed in Krasnodar region as 12th Kuban Cossack Cavalry Division
41–42	Part of 17th Kuban Cossack Cavalry Corps
Aug 42–45	Participated in various military opns as a part of 4th Guards Kuban Cossack Cavalry Corps (see entry)
Aug 42	*Honored and renamed 9th Guards Kuban Cossack Cavalry Division*

Jul 44	*Awarded with the name of Baranovich*

Commanders

Col. A. F. Skhorohod, 42
Lt. Col. M. L. Porkhovnikov, 42
Col. I. V. Tutarinov, 42–44
Col. D. S. Demchuk, 1944
Col. V. G. Gagua, 44–45
Col. A. P. Smirnov, 1945

Other Names

Kuban-Baranovich Cossack Cavalry Division, 12th Kuban Cossack Cavalry Division

10th Guards Kuban Cossack Cavalry Division

Feb 42	Formed in Krasnodar region as the 13th Kuban Cossack Cavalry Division
41–42	Part of the 17th Kuban Cossack Cavalry Corps
Aug 42–45	Part of 4th Guards Kuban Kossack Cavalry Corps
42–45	Participated in military opns as a part of 4th Guards Kuban Cossack Cavalry Corps (see entry)
Aug 42	*Honored and renamed 10th Guards Kuban Cossack Cavalry Division*
Jul 44	*Awarded with the name of Slutsk*

Commanders

Col. N. F. Tsepliayev, 1942
Gen. Major B. S. Millerov, 42–43
Col. N. G. Gadalin, 43–44
Col. S. A. Shevchuk, 1944
Col. M. S. Poprikailo, 1944
Col. G. I. Reva, 1944
Col. V. V. Nikiforov, 44–45
Gen. Major S. T. Shmuilo, 1945

Other Names

Kuban-Slutsk Cossack Cavalry Division, 13th Kuban Cossack Cavalry Division

16th Guards Cavalry Division

Nov 41	Formed in South-Ural Military District as 112th Cavalry Division

41–43	Part of 8th Cavalry Corps
Feb 43	Part of the 7th Guard Cavalry Corps
41–45	Participated in various military opns as a part of the 8th Cavalry Corps and later of the 7th Guards Cavalry Corps (see corps entries)

| Feb 43 | *Honored and renamed 16th Guards Cavalry Division* |
| Sep 43 | *Awarded with the name of Chernigov* |

Commanders
Gen. Major M. M. Shaimuratov, 42–43
Gen. Major G. A. Belov, 43–45
Other Names
Chernigov Cavalry Division,
112th Cavalry Division

Air Forces

At the beginning of the war, Soviet air forces were assigned into three broad categories: high command air forces, frontal (military district) air forces, and air forces apportioned to combined arms armies (army aviation). Organization of air forces for combat opns experienced many fluctuations during the first year of the war, but began to be more regularized with the formation of air armies beginning in May 1942. The air division formed the basic tactical fighting unit of the air force. Soviet air divisions were organized into five main forms: basic air divisions with which the USSR started the war; mixed air divisions; bomber divisions; long-range aviation; ground attack divisions; and fighter divisions. Overall, the number of air divisions in the Soviet wartime force structure seems extraordinarily large—upwards of 300—until one realizes that many of these divisions were reformed or converted and renumbered during the course of the war. A total of 59 divisions were designated as Guards divisions during the course of the war.

Basic Air Divisions

On the eve of the war, Soviet Air Forces included 10 basic air divisions. During the course of the war, a total of 37 such divisions were formed, only three of which survived intact through the course of the war with this designation. Twenty of the divisions were destroyed or disbanded, and fourteen others converted to alternative structures, largely during 1941–42. From 1942 until the end of the war, this form of division essentially disappeared from the Soviet inventory. No Guards air divisions of this type were designated during the war.

Mixed Air Divisions

Seven mixed air divisions existed before the war, with 44 generated during its course. Thirteen were destroyed and disbanded, with the rest converted, largely during 1941–42, into other forms of divisions. In several instances, mixed divisions constituted the base for the formation of air armies in 1942. No division of this type survived through the end of the war and only one, the 1st Guards Mixed Air Division, commanded by Colonel F. S. Pushkarev, was awarded the Guards distinction from September 1943 to November 1944 before it, too, was converted to the 16th Guards Fighter Division.

Bomber Divisions

A total of 66 bomber divisions were included in the Soviet air force structure during the war, with only seven in being prior to its start. Of the 66, 27 were destroyed, disbanded, or converted in some fashion. Most bomber divisions were formed in 1942, although the generation process continued through the war years. Seven bomber divisions were especially designated for night bombing. Eighteen bomber divisions earned Guards distinction.

Long-Range Aviation Divisions

A total of 22 long-range aviation divisions were created during the war; no divisions of this type appear to have been included within the force structure prior to the beginning of the war (although the pre-war bomber divisions cited above were designated as long-range). Moreover, it appears that all long-range aviation divisions eventually were converted to bomber divisions. Nine long-range aviation divisions earned Guards distinction, but they, too, were converted to bomber units.

Ground-Attack Divisions

No ground-attack divisions existed in the inventory prior to the beginning of the war; 48 were formed during the course of the war, largely from 1942 to 1944. Apparently only two of these 48 were destroyed or disbanded. Eighteen divisions earned the Guards distinction.

Fighter Divisions

Fighter divisions formed the largest category of air forces within the Soviet structure, with a total of 109 being formed, of which 11 existed on the eve of the war. Eleven fighter divisions were destroyed or disbanded during the war, 15 were converted in some fashion, and 18 earned Guards distinction.

Guards Air Divisions

1st Gds Bomber Division. Mar 43– May 45. Commander: Col. F. I. Dobysh

2d Gds Bomber Division. Dec 44–May 45. Two commanders

2d Gds Night Bomber Division. Mar 43–Sep 44. Converted to 15th Gds Ground Attack Division. Commander: Gen. Major P. O. Kuznetsov

3d Gds Bomber Division. Sep 43–May 45. Commander: Col. S. P. Andreyev

4th Gds Bomber Division. Sep 43–May 45. Commander: Gen. Major F. P. Kotlyar

5th Gds Bomber Division. Sep 43–May 45. Commander: Gen. Major V. A. Sandalov

6th Gds Bomber Division. Oct 43–May 45. Commander: Gen. Major G. A. Chuchev

7th Gds Bomber Division. Dec 44–Apr 45. Commander: Gen. Major F. S. Shirokin

8th Gds Bomber Division. Feb 44–May 45. Commander: Col. G. V. Gribakin

9th Gds Bomber Division. Aug 44–May 45. Commander: Col. K. I. Rasskazov

11th Gds Bomber Division. Dec 44–May 45. Commander: Gen. Major I. F. Balashov

13th Gds Bomber Division. Dec 44–May 45. Commander: Gen. Major I. K. Brovko

14th Gds Bomber Division. Dec 44–May 45. Two commanders

15th Gds Bomber Division. Dec 44–May 45. Commander: Gen. Major S. A. Ulyankovsky

16th Gds Bomber Division. Dec 44–May 45. Commander: Gen. Major S. I. Chemodanov

18th Gds Bomber Division. Dec 44–May 45. Commander: Gen. Major V. G. Tikhonov

21st Gds Bomber Division. Aug–Sep 45. Commander: Gen. Major I. M. Gorsky

22d Gds Bomber Division. Dec 44–May 45. Commander: Gen. Major B. V. Blinov

1st Gds Long-Range Aviation Air Division. Mar 43–Dec 44. Converted to 11th Gds Bomber Division. Three commanders

2d Gds Long-Range Aviation Air Division. Mar 43–Dec 44. Converted to 2d Gds Bomber Division. Commander: Gen. Major A. I. Shcherbakov

3d Gds Long-Range Aviation Air Division. Mar 43–Dec 44. Converted to 13th Gds Bomber Division. Commander: Gen. Major I. K. Brovko

4th Gds Long-Range Aviation Air Division. Mar 43–Dec 44. Converted to 14th Gds Bomber Division. Commander: Col. I. I. Kozhemyakin

5th Gds Long-Range Aviation Air Division. Jun 43–Dec 44. Converted to 15th Gds Bomber Division. Three commanders

6th Gds Long-Range Aviation Air Division. May 43–Dec 44. Converted to 16th Gds Bomber Division. Commander: Gen. Major S. I. Chemodanov

7th Gds Long-Range Aviation Air Division. May 43–Dec 44. Converted to 7th Gds Bomber Division. Gen. Major F. S. Shirokin

8th Gds Long-Range Aviation Air Division. May 43–Dec 44. Converted to 18th Gds Bomber Division. Commander: Gen. Major V. G. Tikhonov

9th Gds Long-Range Aviation Air Division. Sep 43–Dec 44. Converted to 22d Gds Bomber Division. Two commanders

1st Gds Ground Attack Division. Mar 43–May 45. Two commanders

2d Gds Ground Attack Division. Mar 43–May 45. Commander: Gen. Major G. I. Komarov

3d Gds Ground Attack Division. Mar 43–May 45. Three commanders

4th Gds Ground Attack Division. May 43–May 45. Three commanders

5th Gds Ground Attack Division. May 43–May 45. Commander: Gen. Major L. V. Kolomeitsev

6th Gds Ground Attack Division. Sep 43–May 45. Commander: Gen. Major P. I. Mironenko

7th Gds Ground Attack Division. Sep 43–May 45. Two commanders

9th Gds Ground Attack Division. Feb 44–May 45. Two commanders

10th Gds Ground Attack Division. Feb 44–May 45. Commander: Gen. Major A. N. Vitruk

11th Gds Ground Attack Division. Aug 44–May 45. Two commanders

12th Gds Ground Attack Division. Oct 44–May 45. Commander: Col. L. A. Chizhikov

15th Gds Ground Attack Division. Sep 44–May 45. Commander: Gen. Major P. O. Kuznetsov

1st Gds Fighter Division. Feb 43–May 45. Three commanders

2d Gds Fighter Division. Mar 43–May 45. Commander: Gen. Major I. G. Puntus

3d Gds Fighter Division. Mar 43–May 45. Three commanders

4th Gds Fighter Division. Mar 43–May 45. Gen. Major V. A. Kitayev

5th Gds Fighter Division. Mar 43–May 45. Two commanders

6th Gds Fighter Division. Mar 43–May 45. Two commanders

7th Gds Fighter Division. May 43–May 45. Two commanders

8th Gds Fighter Division. May 43–Mar 45. Four commanders

9th Gds Fighter Division. Jun 43–May 45. Two commanders

10th Gds Fighter Division. Sep 43–May 45. Three commanders

11th Gds Fighter Division. Aug 43–May 45. Commander: Gen. Major A. P. Osadchy

13th Gds Fighter Division. Feb 44–May 45. Commander: Gen. Major K. G. Baranchuk

13th Gds Fighter Division. Jul 44–May 45. Commander: Col. I. A. Taranenko

14th Gds Fighter Division. Jul 44–May 45. Commander: Col. A. P. Yudakov

15th Gds Fighter Division. Aug 44–May 45. Gen. Major I. A. Lakayev

16th Gds Fighter Division. Nov 44–May 45. Two commanders

22d Gds Fighter Division. Oct 44–May 45. Col. L. I. Goreglyad

23d Gds Fighter Division. Oct 44–May 45. Two commanders

Airborne

Soviet Airborne Forces

The Soviet Armed Forces experimented with airborne forces during the interwar period and began to form airborne corps in April 1941. Those corps were intended to be organized with three airborne brigades, a tank battalion, an artillery battalion, and support troops. The advent of the war, however, prevented the completion of this process and largely limited development to the brigade level. Moreover, the desperate conditions of the first period of the war compelled the Soviets to use their airborne forces primarily as regular infantry. Only a few small tactical airborne drops were conducted in the vicinity of Kiev, Odessa, and the Kerch peninsula at this time.

Beginning in 1942, conditions permitted somewhat broader use of airborne forces. However, only two significant opns were conducted, the first being the Viazma airborne operation of February–March 1942, involving the 4th Airborne Corps, and the Dnepr/Kiev airborne operation of September 1943, again involving a temporary corps formation. All three of the fronts in the Far East Direction employed tactical airborne operations to seize key airfields and decisive points during the Manchurian Campaign.

Airborne corps were converted to airborne (and guards rifle) divisions in late 1942, with those divisions employed almost exclusively as regular infantry (rifle) formations. In October 1944, the majority of airborne forces were combined into the Separate Airborne Army, a short-lived formation that was converted/combined with the 9th Guards Army in January 1945. Overall, the history of Soviet airborne forces during the war, like that of the western belligerents, is primarily a history of airborne units employed as regular infantry.

Airborne Corps

1st Airborne Corps. Jun 41–Aug 42. Disbanded. Two commanders

2d Airborne Corps. Jun–Sep 41. Disbanded. One commander

3d Airborne Corps. Jun 41–Feb 42. Disposition not clear. Partly converted to the 87th RD in Nov 41. Two commanders

4th Airborne Corps. Jun 41–Dec 42. Two commanders

5th Airborne Corps. Jun 41–Aug 42. Converted to the 39th Gds RD. Two commanders

6th Airborne Corps. Aug–Dec 42. Converted in part to the 40th Gds RD. One commander

7th Airborne Corps. Dec 41–Aug 42. One commander

8th Airborne Corps. Aug–Dec 42. Converted in part to 35th Gds RD. One commander

9th Airborne Corps. Dec 41–Aug 42. Converted to 36th Gds RD. Two commanders

10th Airborne Corps. Dec 41–Aug 42. One commander

Although the disposition of the 4th–10th Airborne Corps is not indicated above, they were almost certainly converted to numbered guards airborne divisions when deactivated, as suggested in the introductory text.

Guards Airborne Divisions (AD)

All Soviet airborne divisions were awarded Guards honorific designation.

1st Guards AD. Dec 42–May 45. Four commanders

2d Guards AD. Dec 42–May 45. Three commanders

3d Guards AD. Dec 42–May 45. One commander

4th Guards AD. Dec 42–May 45. Four commanders

5th Guards AD. Dec 42–May 45. Five commanders

6th Guards AD. Dec 42–May 45. Three commanders

7th Guards AD. Dec 42–May 45. Three commanders

8th Guards AD. Dec 42–Dec 44. Converted to 107th Guards RD. Three commanders

9th Guards AD. Dec 42–May 45. One commander

10th Guards AD. Dec 42–May 45. Three commanders

11th Guards AD. Dec 43–Feb 45. Converted to 104th Guards RD. Two commanders

12th Guards AD. Dec 43–Feb 45. Converted to 105th Guards RD. One commander

13th Guards AD. Dec 43. Converted immediately to 98th Guards RD. One commander

14th Guards AD. Dec 43–Jun 44. Converted to 99th Guards RD. One commander

15th Guards AD. Dec 43–Jan 44. Converted to 100th Guards RD. One commander

16th Guards AD. Dec 43–Feb 45. Converted to 106th Guards RD. Two commanders

Guards Airborne Divisions Earning Place-Name Honorifics

The five airborne divisions summarized below distinguished themselves in battle to the degree that they were awarded place names as honorifics. Their battle histories, undoubtedly, are representative of all the airborne divisions.

1st Guards Airborne Division

Apr 41	Initially established as the 4th Airborne Corps in the Western Special MD
Dec 42	Designated the 1st Guards Airborne Division. Employed primarily as a rifle division during the course of the war. Fought, in sequence, as part of the 64th, 34th, 37th, and 53d armies, primarily in the southern theater
43–45	Notable opns include: Staraya Russa, Korsun-Shevchenkovsky, Uman-Botoshany, Iassy-Kishinev, Debrecen, Budapest,

Bratislava-Brno, Prague, and the Khingan-Mukden offensive in the Manchurian Campaign

Feb 44 *Awarded the name of Zvenigorod*

Sep 44 *Awarded the name of Budapest*

Commanders

Gen. Major A. F. Kazankin, 42–43
Col. B. I. Kashcheyev, 43–44
Col. Ya. S. Mikheyenko, 1944
Gen. Major D. F. Sobolev, 44–45

Other Names

Zvenigorod-Bucharest Airborne Division

3d Guards Airborne Division

Dec 42 Formed in the Moscow region on the base of the 8th Airborne Corps. Employed during the course of the war as a rifle division, assigned in sequence to the 1st Shock, 13th, 60th, and 27th Armies

1943 Participated in the Demiansk, Kursk, Chernigov-Pripiat, and Kiev opns

1944 Participated in Zhitomir-Berdichev, Uman-Botoshany, Iassy-Kishinev, and Debrecen opns

1945 Budapest, Balaton, and Vienna opns

Mar 45 *Awarded the name of Uman*

Commander

Gen. Major I. N. Konev

Other Names

Uman Airborne Division

4th Guards Airborne Division

Dec 42 Formed in the Moscow region as the 4th Guards Airborne Div. Employed during the course of the war as a rifle division assigned to the 1st Shock, 53d, 13th, 60th, 13th, 40th,

27th, and 7th Guards Armies

1943 Notable opns included offensive opns at Demiansk, Kursk, Chernigov-Pripiat, and Kiev

Nov 43 *Awarded the name Ovruch*

1944 Zhitomir-Berdichev, Korsun-Shevchenkovsky, Uman-Botoshany, Iassy-Kishinev, Debrecen, and Budapest

1945 Brataslava-Brno and Prague opns

Commander

Gen. Major P. A. Aleksandrov, 42–43
Gen. Major A. D. Rumyantsev, 43–44
Col. A. P. Kostrykin, 1944
Gen. Major N. V. Yeremin, 44–45

Other Names

Ovruchskaya Airborne Division

6th Guards Airborne Division

Dec 42 Formed in Moscow region from the 6th Airborne Corps; renamed 6th Guards Airborne Division. During the entire war, employed as a rifle division, assigned to the 1st Shock, 5th Guards, 5th Guards Tank, and 7th Guards Armies

43–45 Notable opns: Staraia-Russa, Kursk, the battle for Dnepr River line, Kirovograd, Korsun-Shevchenkovsky, Uman-Botoshany, Iassy-Kishinev, Debrecen, Budapest, Bratislava-Brno, and Prague

Sep 43 *Awarded the name of Kremenchug*

Dec 43 *Awarded the name of Znamen*

Commanders

Gen. Major A. I. Kirzimov, 42–43
Gen. Major M. N. Smirnov, 43–45

Other Names

Kremenchug-Znamen Airborne Division

9th Guards Airborne Division

Dec 42	Formed in the Moscow region and fought as a rifle division during the course of the war
41–43	As part of 1st Shock Army participated in the Moscow counteroffensive, then battles to the south of Staraia-Russa. Participated in the Battle of Kursk and the Left Bank Ukraine. Assigned to the 5th Guards Army from 43–45
Sep 43	*Awarded the name Poltava*
1944	Offensive opns at Kirovograd, Uman-Botoshany, and Lvov-Sandomir
1945	Participated in the Sandosmir-Silesia, Lower and Upper Silesia, Berlin, and Prague opns

Commander

Col. K. N. Vindushev, 42–43

Gen. Major A. M. Sazonov, 43–44

Gen. Major I. P. Pichugin, 1944

Col. F. A. Afanasev, 1944

Col. P. I. Shumeyev, 44–45

Col. Ye. M. Golub, 1945

Other Names

Poltava Airborne Division

Organization of
Military Units
on the Eastern Front

Tactical Unit Symbols

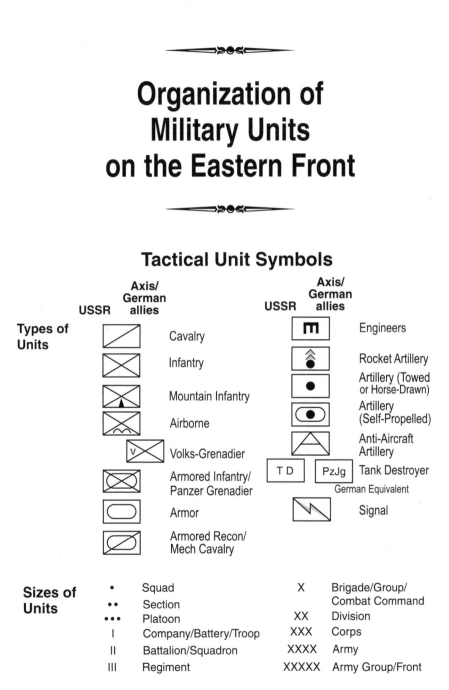

	USSR	Axis/German allies	
Types of Units			Cavalry
			Infantry
			Mountain Infantry
			Airborne
			Volks-Grenadier
			Armored Infantry/Panzer Grenadier
			Armor
			Armored Recon/Mech Cavalry

	USSR	Axis/German allies	
			Engineers
			Rocket Artillery
			Artillery (Towed or Horse-Drawn)
			Artillery (Self-Propelled)
			Anti-Aircraft Artillery
	T D	PzJg	Tank Destroyer
		German Equivalent	
			Signal

Sizes of Units

•	Squad	X	Brigade/Group/Combat Command
••	Section		
•••	Platoon	XX	Division
I	Company/Battery/Troop	XXX	Corps
II	Battalion/Squadron	XXXX	Army
III	Regiment	XXXXX	Army Group/Front

German Panzer Division, Late War

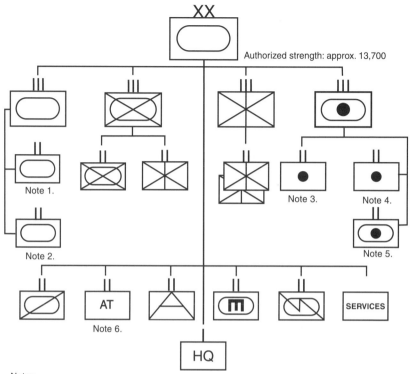

Authorized strength: approx. 13,700

Note 1.
Note 2.
Note 3.
Note 4.
Note 5.
Note 6.

AT

SERVICES

HQ

Notes
1. Consisted of 51 Panthers.
2. Consisted of 52 Panzer IVs.
3. Consisted of three 4-gun batteries of towed 105mm howitzers.
4. Consisted of three 4-gun batteries of towed 150mm howitzers.
5. Consisted of two 4-gun batteries of SP 105mm howitzers and one 4-gun battery of 150mm howitzers.
6. Consisted of two 14-gun batteries of 75mm assault guns or tank destroyers (with three more assault guns in the battalion HQ) and one 12-gun battery of towed 75mm AT guns.

German Panzer IV/G (NA)

Waffen-SS Panzer Division

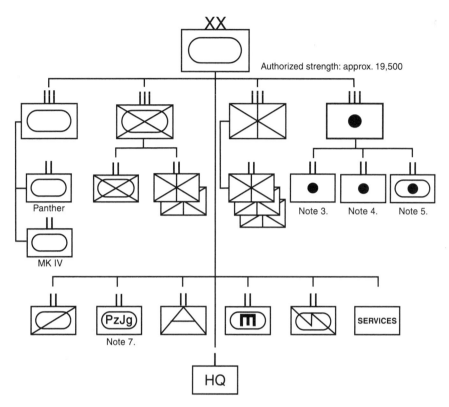

Authorized strength: approx. 19,500

Panther

MK IV

Note 3.   Note 4.   Note 5.

Note 7.

SERVICES

HQ

Notes

1. The quantity of tanks authorized in an SS Panzer regiment varied according to changing tables of organization and equipment during the war. In the last year of the war, a battalion was was authorized four companies, each of 17 tanks, with an additional 8 tanks in each battalion headquarters company for a total of 76 tanks per battalion. Another 8 in the regimental headquarters company brought the total to 160 tanks authorized for the regiment.
2. At the same time, the tank companies of the *SS-LAH* and *SS-Hitlerjugend* were authorized an additional platoon of five tanks each, bringing their totals to 96 tanks per battalion, and 200 tanks in the regiment.
3. Consisted of three 4-gun batteries of towed 105mm howitzers.
4. Consisted of two 4-gun batteries of towed 150mm howitzers and one of towed 105mm field guns.
5. Consisted of two batteries of SP 105mm howitzers and one battery of SP 150mm howitzers.
6. Late in the war, *SS-LAH* and *SS-Hitlerjugend* were each authorized a battalion of *Nebelwerfers* as well.
7. The *Panzerjäger* (antitank) battalion consisted of two companies of fourteen 75mm assault guns or tank destroyers each and a twelve-gun battery of towed antitank guns.

German Mountain Division

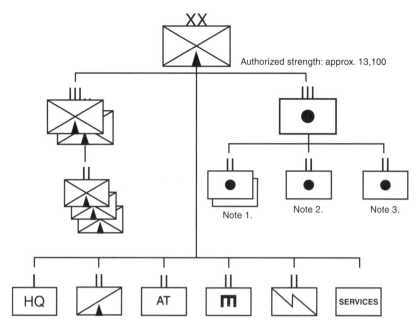

Authorized strength: approx. 13,100

Note 1.

Note 2.

Note 3.

HQ   AT   m   SERVICES

Notes
1. Each battalion consists of three 4-gun batteries of 75mm mountain guns, Model 1936, transported by mules.
2. Consists of three 4-gun batteries of horse-drawn 105mm howitzers.
3. Consists of three 4-gun batteries of towed 150mm howitzers.
4. The number of batteries in each battalion sometimes varied with each mountain division; also, some mountain artillery regiments possessed a battery of 105mm field guns.

Field Marshal von Rundstedt (standing, center) and others observe a ski training exercise (NA).

Waffen-SS Mountain Division

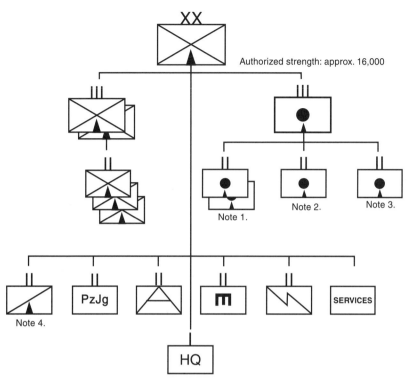

Authorized strength: approx. 16,000

Note 1.

Note 2.

Note 3.

PzJg

Note 4.

SERVICES

HQ

Notes
1. Each battalion consists of three 4-gun, mule-packed 75mm mountain howitzer batteries.
2. Consists of three 4-gun batteries of towed 105mm howitzers.
3. Consists of two four-gun batteries of towed 150mm howitzers and one 4-gun battery of towed 105mm field guns.
4. The reconnaissance battalion consisted of three infantry companies and one heavy weapons company.
5. *SS-Nord* also possessed SS-Motorized Infantry Battalion 6 (later SS-Panzer-Grenadier Battalion 506), a battalion of motorized infantry, left over from *SS-Nord's* days as a motorized division. Also, from September 1943 - September 1944. SS-Ski Battalion "Norge" was attached.
6. *SS-Prinz Eugen* differed in the following especially significant ways:
   a. Two mountain infantry regiments of four battalions each.
   b. The 75mm and 105mm battalions possessed only two batteries each.
   c. The division possessed two companies of horse cavalry.
7. *SS-Handschar* differed in the following especially significant ways:
   a. Two mountain infantry regiments of four battalions each.
   b. The 75mm and 105mm battalions possessed only two batteries each.
8. SS-Skanderbeg differed in the following especially significant ways:
   a. Three 75mm battalions, each of three four-gun batteries, and one truck-drawn battalion of 150mm howitzers.
   b. No anti-aircraft battalion.
9. *SS-Kama* never achieved full divisional status, and possessed two mountain infantry regiments of two battalions each, with some division support troops.
10. *SS-Karstjäger* differed in the following especially significant ways:
    a. The 105mm battalion of the artillery regiment was equipped with mule-drawn 105mm mountain howitzers.
    b. No anti-aircraft battalion.

German Panzer-Grenadier Division

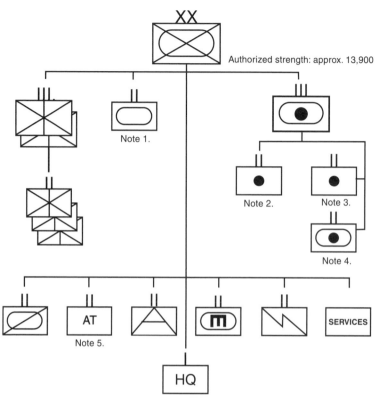

Authorized strength: approx. 13,900

Note 1.

Note 2.   Note 3.

Note 4.

Note 5.   AT   SERVICES

HQ

Notes
1. Consists of 48 75mm assault guns, tank destroyers, or tanks.
2. Consists of three 4-gun batteries of towed 105mm howitzers.
3. Consists of three 4-gun batteries of towed 150mm howitzers.
4. Consists of two 4-gun batteries of SP 105mm howitzers and one 4-gun battery of 150mm howitzers; some divisions had towed 150mm howitzers and 105mm field guns instead.
5. Consists of two 14-gun batteries of 75mm assault guns or tank destroyers (with three more assault guns in the battalion HQ) and one 12-gun battery of towed 75mm AT guns.

German Sdkfz. 251 half-tracked personnel carriers equipped the reconnaissance battalions of Army and *Waffen-SS* Panzer-Grenadier Divisions (NA)

Waffen-SS
Panzer-Grenadier Division

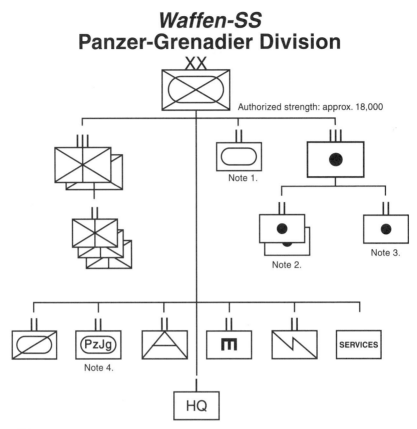

Authorized strength: approx. 18,000

Note 1.

Note 2.

Note 3.

Note 4.

SERVICES

HQ

Notes

1. The Panzer battalion was authorized 70-76 armored fighting vehicles, and was usually assigned assault guns.
2. Each battalion consisted of three 4-gun batteries of towed 105mm howitzers.
3. Consisted of two 6-gun batteries of towed 150mm howitzers and one 4-gun battery of 105mm field guns.
4. The *Panzerjäger* (anti-tank) battalion consisted of 45 75mm assault guns or tank destroyers.

German *Sturmgeschütz* III with natural camouflage for the Russian steppe. Assault guns such as these commonly equipped the *Panzerjäger* battalions of Panzer-Grenadier Divisions. (NA)

German Infantry Division, Early War

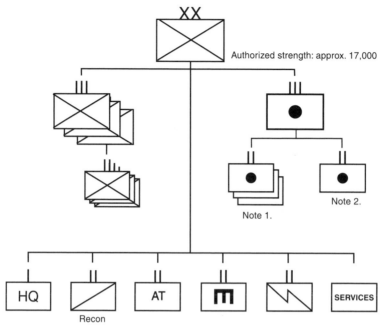

Authorized strength: approx. 17,000

Note 1.

Note 2.

HQ

Recon

AT

SERVICES

Notes
1. Each battalion consists of three 4-gun batteries of 105mm horse-drawn howitzers.
2. Consists of three 4-gun batteries of horse-drawn 150mm howitzers; later in the war, some had 105mm field guns substituted for one of the 150mm howitzer batteries.

German infantryman prepares to hurl a stick grenade, early war (NA)

Waffen-SS
Grenadier (Infantry) Division

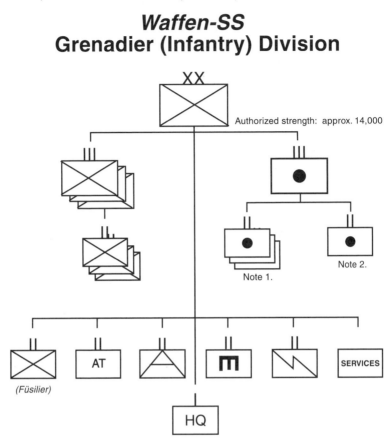

Authorized strength: approx. 14,000

Note 1.

Note 2.

(Füsilier)

AT

SERVICES

HQ

Notes
1. Consisted of three battalions of horse-drawn 105mm howitzers, each with three 4-gun batteries.
2. Consisted of three batteries, each with four horse-drawn 150mm howitzers.

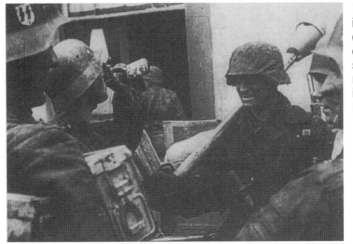

Waffen-SS infantrymen during a lull in combat; the soldier at center-right is shouldering a *Panzerfaust.* (NA)

German Infantry Division
1944 Type

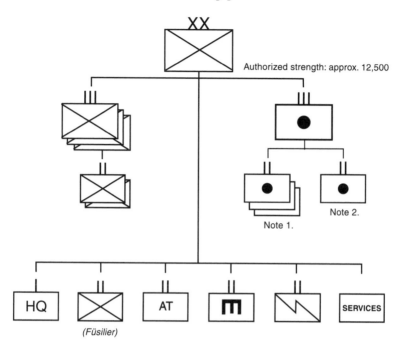

Authorized strength: approx. 12,500

Note 1.

Note 2.

HQ

(Füsilier)

AT

SERVICES

Notes
1. Each battalion consists of three 4-gun batteries of horse-drawn 105mm howitzers.
2. Consists of three 4-gun batteries of horse-drawn 150mm howitzers.

German
Volks-Grenadier Division

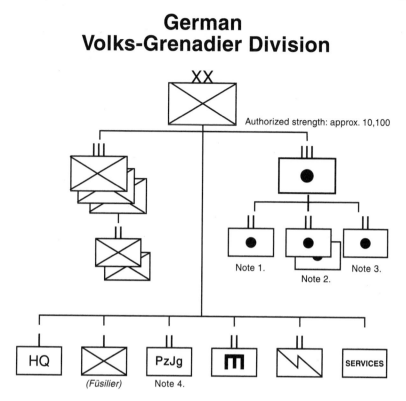

Authorized strength: approx. 10,100

Note 1.

Note 2.

Note 3.

HQ

(Füsilier)

PzJg

Note 4.

SERVICES

Notes
1. Consists of three 6-gun 75mm batteries.
2. Each battalion consists of three 4-gun 105mm howitzer batteries.
3. Consists of three 4-gun 150mm howitzer batteries.
4. Consists of a battery of nine 75mm towed AT guns; a battery of nine 37mm automatic AA guns; and one 14-gun company of 75mm assault guns or tank destroyers.

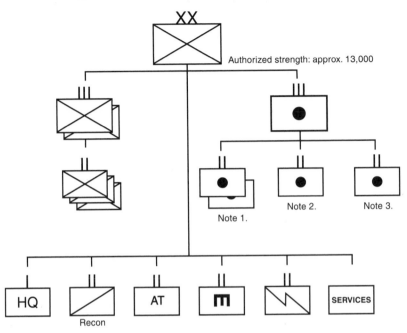

Authorized strength: approx. 13,000

Note 1.   Note 2.   Note 3.

HQ   Recon   AT   m   SERVICES

Notes
1. Each battalion consists of two 4-gun, horse-drawn 105mm howitzer batteries.
2. Consists of three 4-gun, horse-drawn 105mm howitzer batteries.
3. Consists of two 4-gun, motorized 150mm howitzer batteries.

German Infantry Division
Two-Regiment Type

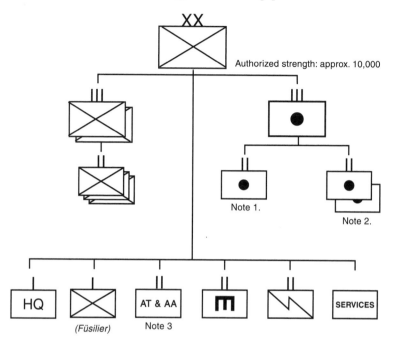

Authorized strength: approx. 10,000

Note 1.

Note 2.

HQ

(Füsilier)

AT & AA
Note 3

SERVICES

Notes
1. Consists of three 4-gun batteries of 88mm guns.
2. Each battalion consists of three 4-gun batteries of horse-drawn 105mm howitzers.
3. Consists of one 12-gun anti-aircraft battery equipped with 20mm automatic cannon and one 12-gun towed 75mm anti-tank gun battery.

Waffen-SS
Cavalry Division*

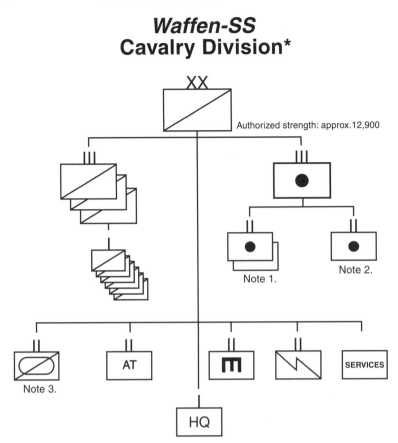

Authorized strength: approx.12,900

Note 1.

Note 2.

Note 3.

AT

SERVICES

HQ

Notes
1. Each battalion onsisted of three 4-gun batteries of horse-drawn 105mm howitzers.
2. Consists of two 4-gun batteries of horse-drawn 150mm howitzers and one 4-gun battery of 105mm field guns.
3. Later in the war, the armored reconnaissance battalion was redesignated as a *Füsilier* battalion, and became a dismounted organization.

Waffen-SS cavalry units were used as dragoons (mounted infantry).

German *Luftwaffe* Parachute Division

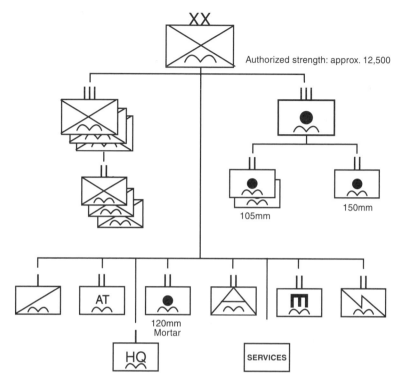

Authorized strength: approx. 12,500

105mm

150mm

AT

120mm
Mortar

HQ

SERVICES

Luftwaffe paratroopers with 81mm mortar (NA)

German
Luftwaffe Field Division, late 1943*

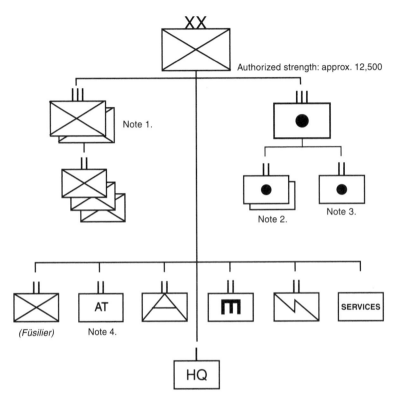

Notes:
Much of the following information was furnished or confirmed by Jason von Zerneck, author of a forthcoming book about Luftwaffe Field Divisions being published by Axis Europa Books of New York.
1. In Luftwaffe Field Divisions 1–10, from the time of organization in 1942 until mid- or late 1943, there were no infantry regimental headquarters, and only four infantry battalions, which were controlled directly by division headquarters.
2. Each battalion consists of three 4-gun batteries of light howitzers; this ordnance was usually of French or captured Soviet origins, but sometimes was German Pak 97/38 employed as field artillery.
3. Consists of three 4-gun batteries of medium howitzers; this ordnance was usually of French or captured Soviet origins.
4. Equipped with towed and, sometimes, horse-drawn 50mm and 75mm anti-tank guns; an assault gun battery with six to ten guns was also included.

*Until late 1943, Luftwaffe field divisions were often organized in unique, one-of-a-kind ways. By 1944, it was planned that all would become organized as "1944 Infantry Divisions." (See page 400)

Finnish Infantry Division, 1944

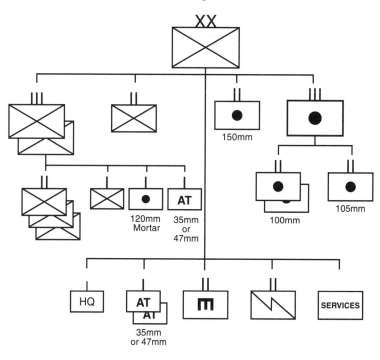

Finnish Infantry Brigade, 1944

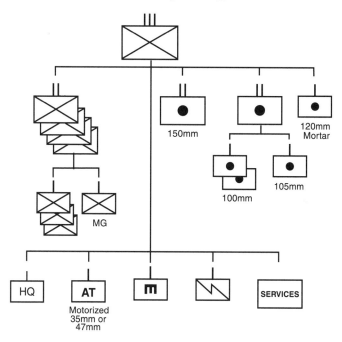

Finnish Armored Division, 1944

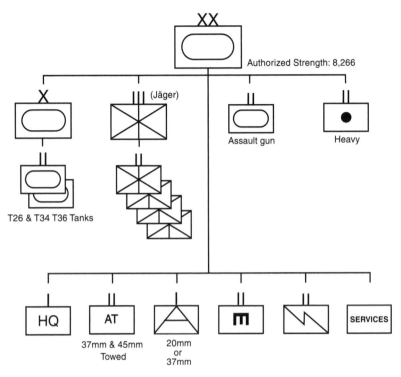

Authorized Strength: 8,266

(Jäger)

Assault gun

Heavy

T26 & T34 T36 Tanks

HQ

AT
37mm & 45mm
Towed

20mm
or
37mm

SERVICES

Hungarian Mobile Corps, 1941

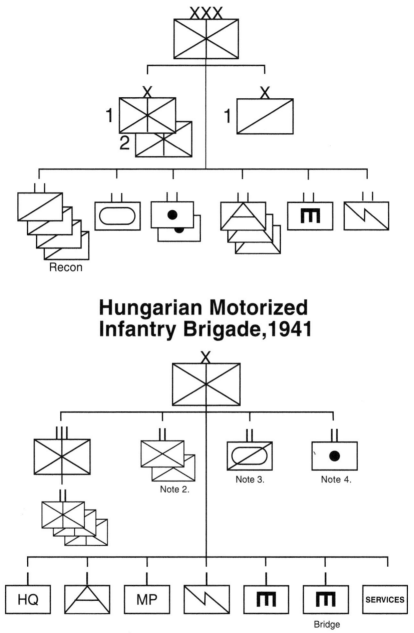

Recon

Hungarian Motorized Infantry Brigade,1941

Note 2.

Note 3.

Note 4.

HQ   MP

Bridge

SERVICES

Notes
1. All units in the brigade had motorized transportation except the infantry units of the bicycle infantry battalions.
2. The bicycle infantry battalion possessed a platoon of CV tankettes and a battery of towed 105mm howitzers.
3. Equpped with 20 Toldi tanks and 20 CV tankettes.
4. Consists of four 4-gun batteries of towed 105mm howitzers.

Hungarian Cavalry Brigade, 1941

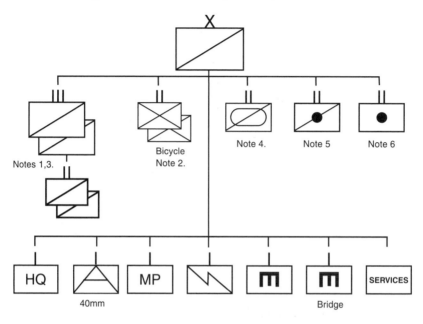

Notes
1. The cavalry regiments consisted of horse mounted squadrons with motoriized support units.
2. The bicycle battalions were organized with infantry companies mounted on bicycles and motorized support units.
3. The cavalry regiments and the infantry battalions each had 5 CV tankettes.
4. The armored reconnaissance battalion possessed 20 Toldi tanks and 20 CV tankettes.
5. Consists of two 4-gun batteries equipped with 76.5mm field guns.
6. Consists of two 4-gun batteries equipped with 100mm/105mm howitzers.

Hungarian Security Division, 1942–43

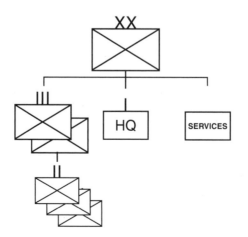

Hungarian Light Division,1942–43

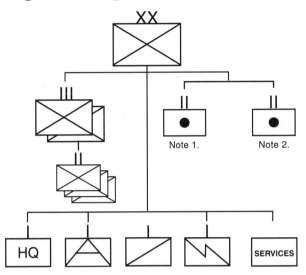

Notes
1. Consists of one 4-gun battery of 76.5mm field guns and one 4-gun battery of 100mm/105mm howitzers.
2. Consists of two batteries, each with 100mm/105mm howitzers, and two batteries with 149mm howitzers.

Hungarian Reserve Division,1944

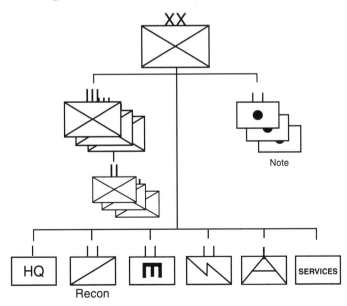

Note: Consists of two 4-gun batteries of 100mm/105mm howitzers, and one 4-gun battery of 149mm howitzers.

Hungarian Infantry Division, 1944

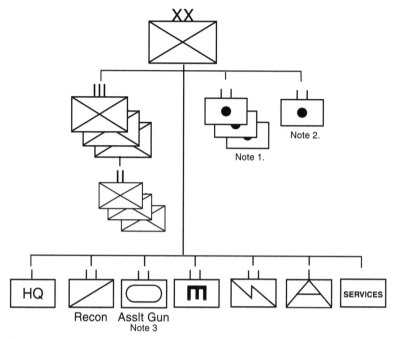

Notes
1. Consists of two 4-gun batteries of 100mm/105mm howitzers and one 4-gun battery of 149mm howitzers.
2. Consists of two 4-gun batteries of 149mm howitzers.
3. Consists of two 10-gun batteries equipped with 75mm assault guns, and one 10-gun battery equipped with 105mm assault guns.

Hungarian Hussar Division,1944

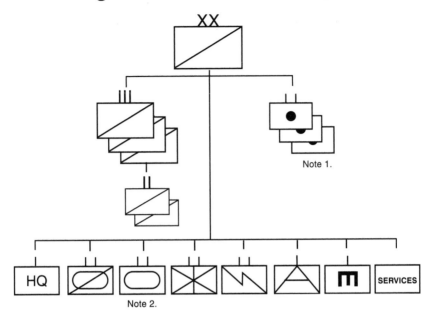

Note 1.

HQ

Note 2.

SERVICES

Notes
1. Each of the field artillery battalions was organized differently. One had three 4-gun batteries of
   75mm field guns; one had three 4-gun batteries of 75mm mountain guns, and one had three
   4-gun batteries of 100mm/105mm howitzers.
2. The tank battalion consisted of one "heavy" tank company equipped with 17 tanks mounting
   75mm main guns, and three "medium" tank companies, each equipped with 27 tanks mounting
   40mm main guns.

Hungarian St. László Division,1944

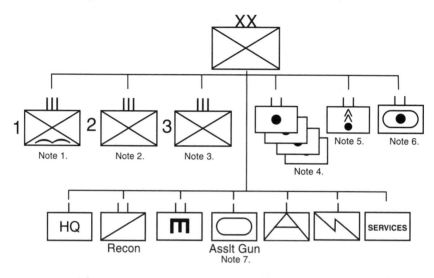

Notes
1. The 1st Parachute Regiment consisted of one parachute infantry battalion; one heavy weapons battalion, and one parachute training battalion.
2. The 2d Regiment consisted of the Royal Guard infantry battalion and a Royal *Gendarmerie* battalion.
3. The 3d Regiment consisted of two battalions of former Hungarian Air Force ground personnel.
4. Each of these field artillery battalions consisted of two 4-gun batteries equipped with 100mm/105mm howitzers, and one 4-gun battery equipped with 149mm howitzers.
5. Consisted of three batteries, each with four rocket launchers.
6. Consisted of three 10-piece batteries equipped with self-propelled "assault howitzers."
7. Consisted of 10 assault guns.

Italian *Celere* Division, 1940

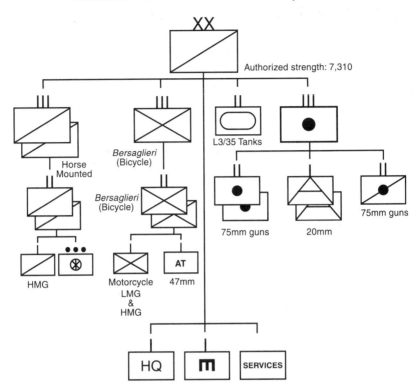

Authorized strength: 7,310

L3/35 Tanks

Horse
Mounted

Bersaglieri
(Bicycle)

75mm guns

Bersaglieri
(Bicycle)

75mm guns   20mm

HMG

Motorcycle   47mm
LMG
&
HMG

AT

HQ   m   SERVICES

Generale di
Corpo d'Armata
Italo Gariboldi
(NA)

Italian Alpini Division
(as organized on the Eastern Front)

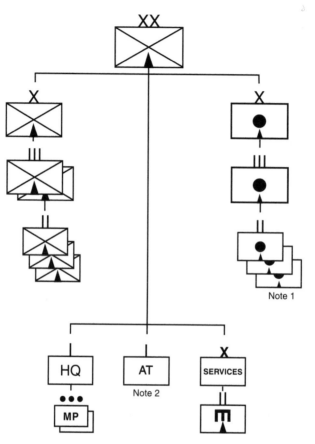

Note 1

Note 2

Notes
1. Each battalion consisted of three 4-gun batteries of mule-packed 75mm mountain howitzers.
2. Equipped with eight 75mm anti-tank guns.

Italian
Semi-Motorized Infantry Division
1940

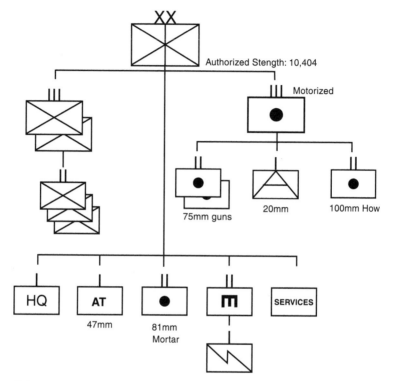

Authorized Stength: 10,404

Motorized

75mm guns

20mm   100mm How

HQ   AT   SERVICES

47mm   81mm Mortar

Notes
1. All elements in the division have motor transport except the infantry regiments.
2. The Artillery Regiment consisted of 2 battalions of 12 - 75mm guns, 1 battalion of 100mm howitzers, and 1 battalion of 8x 20mm AA guns.

Italian
Infantry Division

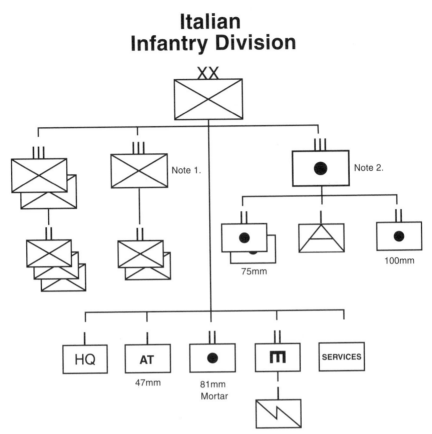

Note 1.

Note 2.

75mm

100mm

HQ

AT

47mm

81mm
Mortar

SERVICES

Notes
1. The third "regiment" of Italian infantry divisions was a "legion" of Italian Fascist militia.
2. Each battalion consisted of three four-gun 75mm batteries.
3. Consisted of three four-gun 100mm howitzer batteries.

Italian 47mm anti-tank gun and crew in Russia (NA)

Romanian 1st Armored Division, 1941–43*

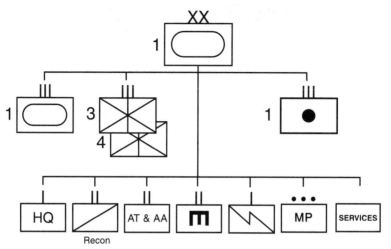

*Technically, this division had two tank regiments, but one was detached and served separately for the entirety of its combat service.

Romanian Cavalry Brigade, 1941
(5th, 6th, and 8th Cavalry Brigades)

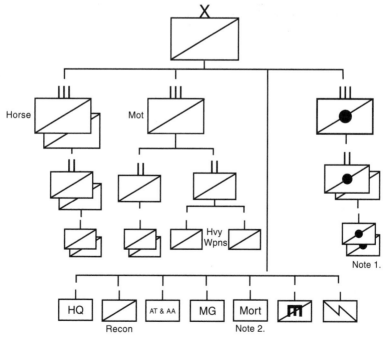

Notes
1. Each battery equipped with four 75mm howitzers.
2. Equipped with twelve 81.4mm mortars.

Romanian
Cavalry Brigade, 1941
(1st, 7th, and 9th Cavalry Brigades)

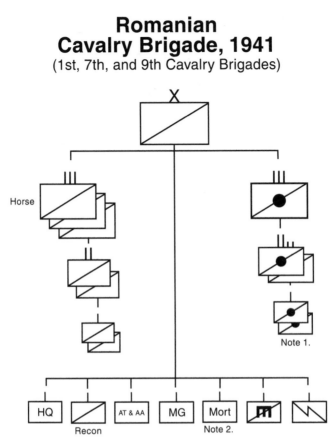

Notes
1. Each battery equipped with four 75mm howitzers.
2. Equipped with twelve 81.4mm mortars.

Romanian
Cavalry Division, 1942*

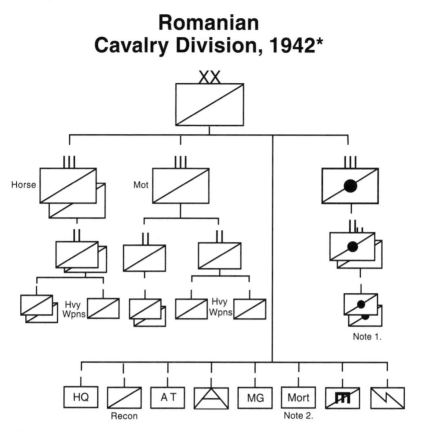

Notes
1. Each battery equipped with six 75mm howitzers.
2. Equipped with six 120mm mortars.

*In March 1942, all cavalry brigades were redesignated as "divisions," and their structure altered to this.

Romanian
Mountain Brigade/Division, 1941–43*

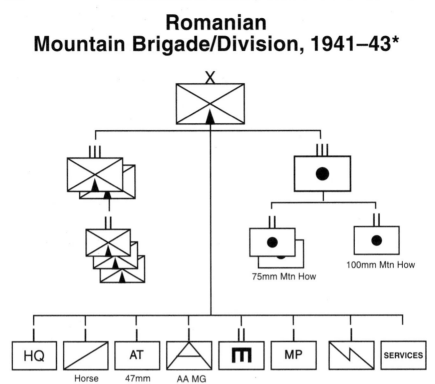

*In March 1942, all mountain brigades were redesignated as "divisions."

Romanian
Infantry Division, 1941

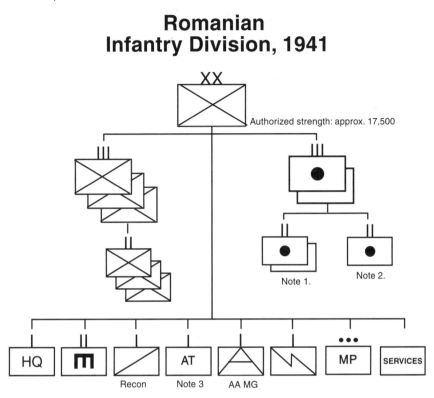

Authorized strength: approx. 17,500

Note 1.

Note 2.

HQ

Recon

AT

Note 3

AA MG

MP

SERVICES

Notes
1. Consisted of three 4-gun batteries of 75mm field guns.
2. Consisted of two 4-gun batteries of 100mm howitzers.
3. Equipped with six French 47mm anti-tank guns.

Romanian
Infantry Division, 1942*

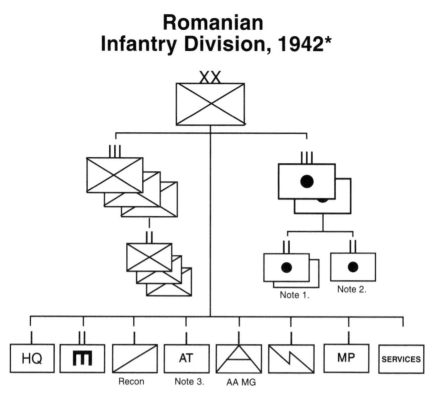

Notes
1. Consisted of three 4-gun batteries of 75mm field guns.
2. Consisted of two 4-gun batteries of 100mm howitzers.
3. Equipped with six German Pak 98/37 anti-tank guns.

*The most reliable sources, such as Dragos Pusca and Victor Nitu, *et al.*, indicate that in 1942, the infantry regiments actually possessed only two infantry battalions each. As Nitu, *et al.*, point out on their excellent website, *The Romanian Army in World War II* (http://www.wwii.home.ro/), although this reduced the strength of Romanian infantry divisions to about 13,500, other organizational developments actually mitigated in favor of increased combat power. Each infantry platoon gained an extra squad, and each regiment gained a recon company, a combat engineer company, and a battery of 120mm mortars, thus significantly increasing firepower, even while actual numbers of infantry soldiers dwindled. The authorized organization, which still included three infantry battalions per regiment, is clearly outlined on Pusca's website, *The Dutch Helmet* (www.armata.home.ro/).

Romanian
Infantry Division, 1943*

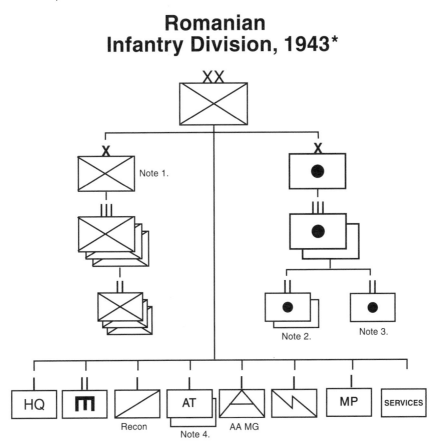

Notes
1. The infantry regiments lost the separate heavy weapons companies formerly integral to each
   (i.e the 120mm mortar battery, AT company, and combat engineer company); now there was only
   one such company of each, directly subordinated to the brigade HQ.
2. Consisted of three 4-gun batteries of 75mm field guns.
3. Consisted of two 4-gun batteries of 100mm howitzers.
4. Each battery equipped with six German Pak 98/37 or Pak 40 anti-tank guns.

*As with the 1942 organization, although each infantry regiment was authorized three battalions,
most operated in the field with only two.

Soviet Cavalry Corps, July 1943

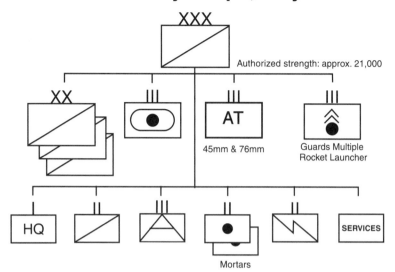

Authorized strength: approx. 21,000

45mm & 76mm

Guards Multiple
Rocket Launcher

HQ

Mortars

SERVICES

Note: Soviet cavalry corps evolved during the war from a strength of 19,430 personnel
in June 1941 to approximately 21,000 personnel in July 1943.

Soviet cavalry attack (NA)

Soviet Cavalry Division, July 1943

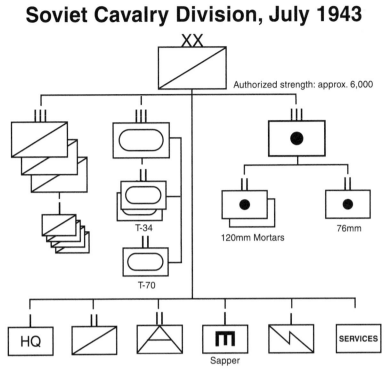

Authorized strength: approx. 6,000

T-34

T-70

120mm Mortars

76mm

HQ   Sapper   SERVICES

Note: Soviet cavalry divisions evolved during the war from a strength of 9,240 personnel in June 1941 to 6,000 personnel in July 1943.

Soviet Tank Corps January 1943

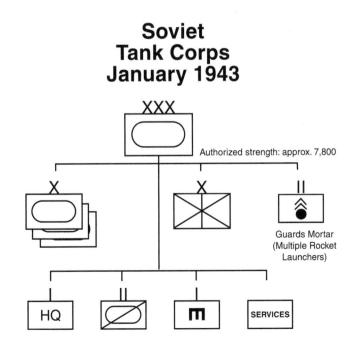

Authorized strength: approx. 7,800

Guards Mortar
(Multiple Rocket
Launchers)

HQ   SERVICES

Soviet
Tank Corps
January 1944

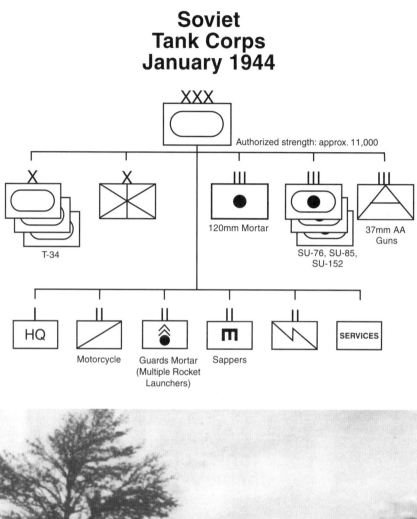

Authorized strength: approx. 11,000

120mm Mortar

37mm AA
Guns

T-34

SU-76, SU-85,
SU-152

HQ

Motorcycle

Guards Mortar
(Multiple Rocket
Launchers)

Sappers

SERVICES

Soviet infantry attack in conjunction with a T-34 (NA)

Soviet
Tank Brigade
November 1943

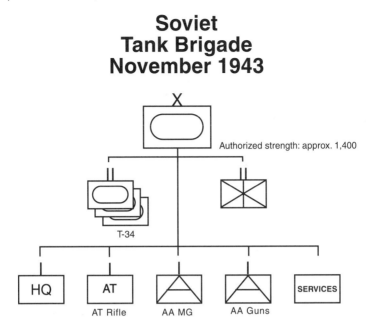

Authorized strength: approx. 1,400

T-34

HQ

AT

AT Rifle

AA MG

AA Guns

SERVICES

T34s and Soviet infantry attacking (MHI)

Soviet Mechanized Corps
January 1944

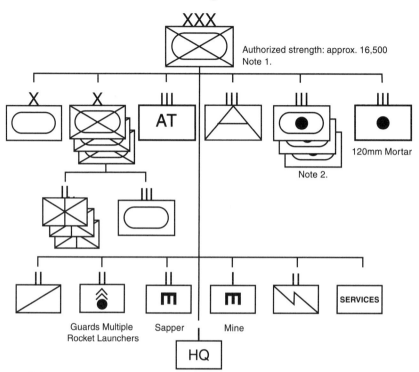

Authorized strength: approx. 16,500
Note 1.

AT

120mm Mortar

Note 2.

Guards Multiple
Rocket Launchers

Sapper

Mine

SERVICES

HQ

Notes
1. Soviet mechanized corps evolved over the course of the war; in September 1942, 13,559 personnel and 175 tanks & SP guns; January 1943, 15,018 personnel and 229 tanks & SPs guns; and January 1944, 16,442 personnel and 246 tanks & SP guns.
2. SP artillery battalions could be equipped with SU-76, SU-85, SU-122, SU-152, JSU-122 or JSU-152.

T-34 (right) and JSU-152 attack through a city (MHI)

Soviet
Motorized Rifle Brigade
November 1943

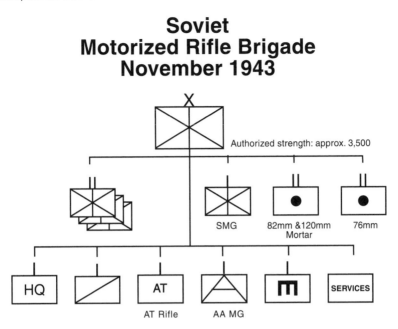

Note: Soviet motorized rifle brigades' strength changes; April 1942, 3,151;
November 1942, 3,161; January 1943, 3,537; and Novemeber 1943, 3,500.

Soviet Rifle Corps

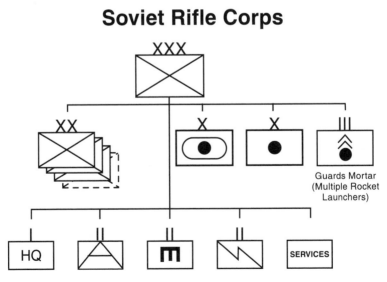

Notes
1. This is the 1944 Rifle Corps structure with 3 or 4 Rifle divisions.
2. The Rifle Corps structure from 1941 to 1943 generally had fewer artillery assets
   and no anti-aircraft battalion

Soviet
Guards Rifle
and Rifle Divisions

Authorized strengths:
Guards Rifle Division: approx. 10,700
Rifle Division: approx. 9,400

Note 1.

Note 2.

HQ

Recon

AT

SERVICES

Notes
1. Each battalion equipped with ten 76mm guns.
2. Equipped with twelve 122mm howitzers.
3. Rifle divsion strength changed from 1941 to 1943 from 14,483 to 9,380.
4. The primary difference between the organization of a Guards rifle division (GRD) and a rifle division (RD) was in the artillery regiment. The GRD had a 36 guns versus the RD 32 guns.
5. NKVD divisions which fought until 1943 were organized similiarly to rifle divisions.

Soviet infantry attacking through a city. (MHI)

Soviet Mountain Rifle Division

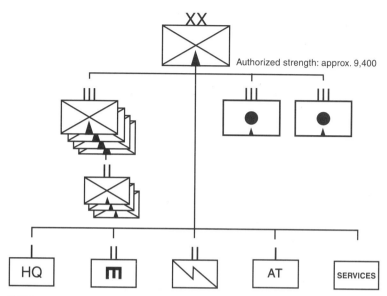

Authorized strength: approx. 9,400

Notes

1. Soviet mountain divisions possessed four mountain rifle regiments, and, at least early in the war, two artillery regiments.
2. The artillery regiments were equipped with 122mm pack howitzers, 76mm mountain guns, and 107mm mountain mortars.

Soviet infantry in winter camouflage attack aboard T-34 tanks (NA)

Soviet
Destroyer Division

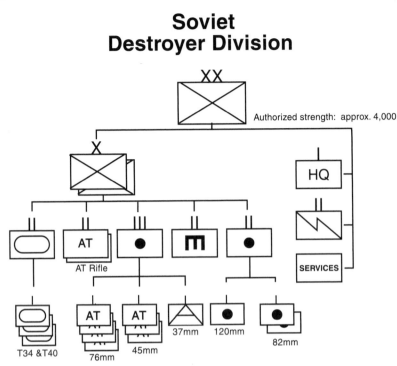

Note: Destroyer divisions' primary mission was to conduct antitank defense operations.

Soviet Ski Brigade

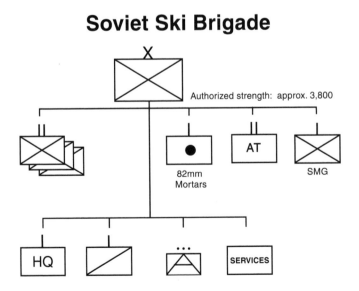

Soviet Airborne Brigade, 1943

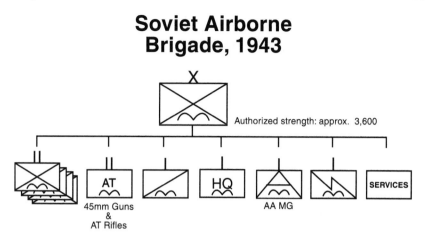

Authorized strength: approx. 3,600

45mm Guns
&
AT Rifles

AA MG

SERVICES

Note: Soviet Army Airborne forces changed over the course of the war.
By 1944 the Soviets had 12 Guards Airborne Divisions organized into three
Airborne Corps that eventually formed the Separate Airborne Army, which
became the 9th Guards Army in January 1945.

Soviet Naval Infantry Brigade

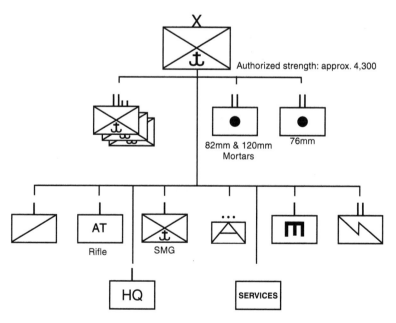

Authorized strength: approx. 4,300

82mm & 120mm
Mortars

76mm

Rifle

SMG

HQ

SERVICES

Soviet
Artillery Penetration Corps
April 1943

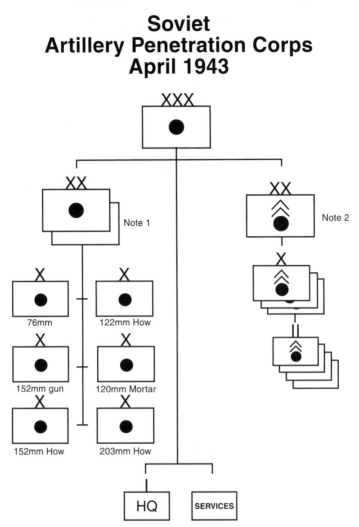

Notes
1. Each artillery penetration division was equipped with 356 guns and mortars;
   72 76mm guns, 84 122mm howitzers, 32 152mm howitzers, 36 152mm guns,
   24 203mm howitzers, and 108 120mm mortars.
2. The Guards Mortar Division (Multiple Rocket Launchers), January 1943 version,
   consisted of 864 launchers capable of delivering 3,456 rockets in a volley.

Soviet Artillery Division

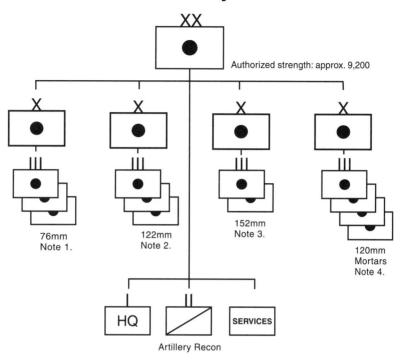

Authorized strength: approx. 9,200

76mm
Note 1.

122mm
Note 2.

152mm
Note 3.

120mm
Mortars
Note 4.

HQ

Artillery Recon

SERVICES

Notes
1. Each regiment is equipped with 24 76mm guns.
2. Each regiment is equipped with 20 122mm howitzers.
3. Each regiment is equipped with 18 152mm gun-howitzers.
4. Each regiment is equipped with 20 120mm mortars.

Weapons
of the Eastern Front

SMALL ARMS, RIFLES, MACHINE GUNS, & ANTI-TANK RIFLES

WEAPON	CALIBER (MM)	WEIGHT (LBS)	MAGAZINE (RDS)	CYCLIC RATE (RDS/MIN)	RANGE (M) (EFF./MAX.)
PISTOLS					
Tokarov TT-33	7.62x25	2.1	8	SA	50/—
Nagant 1895	7.62x38	1.9	7	Revolver	50/—
P08 "Luger"	**9x19**	**2**	**8**	**Toggle**	**50/—**
Walther P-38	**9x19**	**2.3**	**8**	**SA**	**50/—**
SUBMACHINE GUNS					
PPSh-41	7.62x25	8	71 or 35	900	200/—
PPS-43	7.62x25	8	35	700	200/—
MP28	**9x19**	**8.8**	**20/32/50**	**500**	**100/—**
MP38	**9x19**	**9**	**32**	**500**	**100/—**
MP40	**9x19**	**9**	**32**	**500**	**100/—**
MP41	**9x19**	**8.1**	**32**	**600**	**100/—**
Suomi	**9x19**	**11.3**	**25/50/70**	**850**	**100/—**
RIFLES AND CARBINES					
Mauser 98 Carbine	**7.92x57**	**9**	**5**	**Bolt**	**600/2,000**
Mosin-Nagant 91/30 rifle	7.62x54	9	5	Bolt	600/2,200
MP43 Assault Rifle	**7.92x33**	**11**	**30**	**600**	**400/—**
MP44 Assault Rifle	**7.92x33**	**11**	**30**	**600**	**400/—**
SKS 45	7.62x39	8.5	10	SA	450/—
G41 rifle	**7.92x57**	**10.9**	**10**	**SA**	**600/—**
G42	**7.92x57**	**9**	**10**	**SA**	**600/—**
G43 rifle	**7.92x57**	**10**	**10**	**SA**	**600/—**
SVT-40 rifle	7.62x54	9.5	10	SA	630/—
ANTI-TANK RIFLES					
Degtarev PTRD M1941	14.5	38.1	1		—/1,500
Simonov PTRS M1941	14.5	44.8	5		—/1,500

German weapons–boldface; Russian weapons–regular face

SMALL ARMS (CONTINUED)

WEAPON	CALIBER (MM)	WEIGHT (LBS)	MAGAZINE (RDS)	CYCLIC RATE (RDS/MIN)	RANGE (M) (EFF./MAX.)
MACHINE GUNS					
MG34 LMG	**7.92x57**	**26.5**	**Belt**	**900**	**800/3,500**
MG42 LMG	**7.92x57**	**23.8**	**Belt**	**1,400**	**800/3,500**
Degtarev DP LMG	7.62x54	19.6	47	600	800/1,640
Maxim M1910	7.62x54	145.5	250	580	—/1,500
AA M1931 AA MG	7.62x54	101.4	500	600	—/2,700
DT Tank MG	7.62x54	22.6	63	600	—/1,500
Goruniov M SG-1943	7.62x54	89	250	600–700	—/2,000
RPD M1944 MG	7.62x54	16.3	100	650–750	—/1,000
Degtarev DPM M1944	7.62x54	20.4	47	600	800/1,500
MG34 w/tripod (HMG)*	**7.92x57**	**68.5**	**Belt**	**900**	**2,500/3,500**
MG42 w/tripod (HMG)*	**7.92x57**	**65.8**	**Belt**	**1,400**	**2,500/3,500**
Czech ZB 30	**7.92x57**	**20**	**20**	**600**	**800/—**
Hotchkiss	**8x50R**	**52**	**Belt**	**600**	**1,100/—**
Maxim 08	**7.92x57**	**53**	**Belt**	**450**	**1,100/—**
DShK AA MG	12.7	374.8	Belt	575	2,000/6,000

*Including telescope and tables for overhead firing

German weapons–boldface; Russian weapons–regular face

SA=Semi-automatic; Bolt=bolt action; Toggle=toggle action; xx/xx/xx=optional magazine capacities

German MG34 configured as heavy machine gun with tripod and telescope. (NA)

Top: Soviet platoon
advances with PPSh-
41s (NA)

Above: Soviet M1910
Maxim machine gun
(NA)

Right: Soviet machine
gun team advancing.
Nagant carbine M91/30
and Model 1910 (Maxim
1910) machine gun
(MHI)

The crew in the left foreground is armed with a Soviet PTRS AT rifle Model 1941 (MHI)

Like so much of Western "knowledge" of the Eastern Front, the identifications in the photo show what Allied intelligence thought it knew about German small arms. Actual identifications are:
Top: G-41(W) semi-automatic rifle; Mauser KAR 98
Center: MG42; MG34
Bottom: MP 38 machine pistol; and MP 43 or 44 machine pistol (NA)

ROCKET LAUNCHERS

WEAPON	PROJECTILE WEIGHT (LBS)	RANGE (YDS)
82mm M-8 Model 1939	1.4	5468
105mm Nebelwerfer 35	**16**	**3300**
105mm Nebelwerfer 40	**19.1**	**6780**
132mm M-13 Model 1939	10.8	9263
132mm M-13 DD	10.8	12905
132mm M-20 Model 1942	40.5	5523
150mm Nebelwerfer 41	**75.3**	**7330**
150mm Panzerwerfer 42	**75.3**	**7330**
210mm Nebelwerfer 42	**248**	**8600**
280mm M-28	132	2133
280/320mm Schweres Wurfgerät 40	**184.5**	**2100**
280/320mm Schweres Wurfgerät 41	**184.5**	**2100**
280/320mm Schweres Wurfrahmen 40	**184.5**	**2100**
280/320mm Nebelwerfer 41	**184.5**	**2100**
300mm M-30 Model 1942	63.6	3062
300mm M-31 Model 1942/1944	63.6	4730
300mm M-31 uk Model 1944	63.6	4375
300mm BM-31-12 Model 1944	63.6	4375
300mm Nebelwerfer 42	**277**	**5000**

German weapons–boldface; Russian weapons–regular face

Soviet rockets firing (NA)

Top and above: Soviet rocket launchers (MHI)

Left: German 150mm Nebelwerfer (NA)

ARTILLERY & MORTARS

WEAPON	SYSTEM WEIGHT (LBS)	SHELL WEIGHT (LBS)	RANGE (YDS)
MORTAR			
50mm light mortar Model 1936	**31**	**2.2**	**570**
81mm heavy mortar Model 1934	**124**	**7.7**	**2625**
107mm mountain mortar Model 1938	374	17.6	5468
120mm mortar PM-120 Model 1938	605	35.2	6234
120mm Heavy Mortar Model 1942	**616**	**35**	**6600**
160mm mortar MT-13 Model 1943	2486	90.2	5523
280mm mortar BR-5 Model 1939	40480	541.2	11385
HOWITZER			
105mm mountain howitzer Model 1940	**3660**	**32.6**	**13810**
105mm light field howitzer Model 1918	**4320**	**32.7**	**13480**
122mm howitzer M-30 Model 1938	5500	47.7	12905
150mm heavy field howitzer Model 1918	**12096**	**95.7**	**14630**
152mm gun-howitzer ML-20 Model 1937	15684	95.7	18843
152mm howitzer M-10 Model 1938	9130	88	13550
152mm howitzer D-1 Model 1943	8030	88	13561
203mm howitzer B-4 Model 1931	38940	220	19707
210mm Mörser (heavy howitzer) 18	**36740**	**249–268**	**18300**
305mm howitzer BR-18 Model 1939	100540	726	18132

German weapons–boldface; Russian weapons–regular face

German 50mm mortar (NA)

ARTILLERY & MORTARS (CONTINUED)

WEAPON	SYSTEM WEIGHT (LBS)	SHELL WEIGHT (LBS)	RANGE (YDS)
GUN			
75mm light infantry gun Model 1918	**880**	**13.2**	**3900**
75mm light infantry gun Model 1937	**1124**	**12.1**	**5630**
75mm mountain gun Model 1936	**1650**	**9.8–12.8**	**10100**
76mm regimental gun Model 1927	1980	13.6	9295.71
76mm mountain gun Model 1938	1727	13.6	11046
76mm regimental gun Model 1936	3520	13.6	14983
76mm divisional gun USV Model 1939	3256	13.6	14534
105mm heavy field gun Model 1918	**11424**	**31.3–34.6**	**20850**
122mm gun A-19 Model 1931/1937	15664	55	21600
150mm heavy infantry gun Model 1933	**3360**	**84–197**	**5140**
150mm field gun Model 1918	**28440**	**94.6–95.7**	**27040**
152mm gun BR-2 Model 1935	40040	107.4	27417
170mm field gun	**38080**	**138–148**	**32370**

German weapons–boldface; Russian weapons–regular face

German 81mm mortar and crew (NA)

Above: Soviet 82mm
mortar and crew
(NA)

Right: Soviet 120mm
regimental mortar
(NA)

Above: German 75mm mountain howitzer (NA)

Below: German 105mm field gun (NA)

German 150mm howitzer (NA)

Top: German
170mm field gun
(NA)

Above: Soviet
76mm gun in
action (NA)

Left: Soviet towed
76mm gun (NA)

Soviet 122mm howitzer battery (MHI)

Soviet 152mm artillery battery (MHI)

ANTI-TANK

WEAPON	AMMO TYPE	EFFECTIVE RANGE	ARMOR PIERCING CAPABILITY
28mm/20mm s. Pz. B 41	**APCNR**	**1050m/sec**	**40mm/30°/500m**
37mm Pak 36	**AP**	**745 m/sec**	**29mm/30°/500m**
	AP40	**1030 m/sec**	**40mm/30°/500m**
42mm/28mm le. Pak 41	**APCNR**	**1270 m/sec**	**72mm/30°/500m**
			53mm/30°/1000m
45mm Model 1937	AP	820 m/sec	60mm/30°/500m
			38mm/30°/1000m
50mm Pak 38	**AP39**	**823 m/sec**	**61mm/30°/500m**
			50mm/30°/1000m
	AP40	**1180 m/sec**	**86mm/30°/500m**
			55mm/30°/1000m
57mm Model 1943	APCR	1270 m/sec	140mm/30°/500m
75mm Pak 40	**AP**	**792m/sec**	**106mm/30°/500m**
			94mm/30°/1000m
			83mm/30°/1500m
	AP40	**930m/sec**	**115mm/30°/500m**
			96mm/30°/1000m
			80mm/30°/1500m
75mm Pak 41	**APCNR**	**1125m/sec**	**171mm/30°/500m**
			145mm/30°/1000m
			122mm/30°/1500m
			102mm/30°/2000m
75mm Pak 97/38	**AP**	**450m/sec**	**100mm/30°/500m**
76mm Model 1942	AP	740m/sec	98mm/30°/500m
			88mm/30°/1000m
			71mm/30°/2000m
88mm Pak 43, 43/41	**AP40/43**	**1000m/sec**	**226mm/30°/500m**
			192mm/30°/1000m
			162mm/30°/1500m
			136mm/30°/2000m
			114mm/30°/2500m

Armor Piercing (AP). A solid steel round that used its own kinetic energy to pierce armor. The number associated with the term "AP" indicates the year of the round's introduction to combat.

Armor Piercing Composite Rigid (APCR). Made with a tungsten carbide core, a dense, extremely hard substance which enhances penetration capability. For better aerodynamic stability and accuracy, as well as to offset the brittleness of the core, APCR rounds had an aluminum alloy ballistic cap.

Armor Piercing Composite Non-Rigid (APCNR). Like APCR above, but with a softer metal jacket that could be compressed by a squeeze bore weapon (such as the German s. Pz. B 41, which fired a 28mm projectile fired through a bore that was only 20mm at the muzzle). This produced a sort of venturi effect that resulted in exceptionally high muzzle velocities, and, therefore, increased impact energy at closer ranges.

German weapons–boldface; Russian weapons–regular face

Top: German 50mm Pak 38 (NA)

Center: German 75mm Pak 97/38 (NA)

Bottom: German 37mm Pak 36 (NA)

Above: Soviet 45mm anti-tank gun in action (MHI)

Below: Soviet 76mm anti-tank gun (MHI)

ANTI-AIRCRAFT

WEAPON	WEIGHT (LBS)	MUZZLE VELOCITY (M/SEC)	RANGE (VERTICAL) (METERS)	ELEVATION (MIN/MAX) (DEGREES)	RATE OF FIRE (RDS/MIN)
20mm Flak 30	**1,021**	**900**	**2,200**	**-12/+90**	**120–280**
20mm Flak 38	**893**	**900**	**2,200**	**-20/+90**	**220–450**
20mm Flakvierling 38	**3,327**	**900**	**2,200**	**-10/+100**	**720–1800**
25mm Model 1940	2,332	910	2,000	-20/+85	250
37mm Flak 18, 36, 37	**3,858**	**820**	**2,000**	**-5/+85**	**80**
37mm Flak 43	**423**	**820**	**4,200**	**-6/+90**	**150–250**
37mm Model 1939	4,620	880	3,000	-5/+85	180
50mm Flak 41	**6,834**	**840**	**9,400**	**-10/+90**	**130**
76mm Model 1931	8,250	813	9,500	-3/+82	20
76mm Model 1938	9,460	813	9,500	-3/+82	20
85mm Model 1939	9,460	700	10,500	-3/+82	20
85mm Model 1944	11,000	700	10,500	-3/+82	20
88mm Flak 18, 36, 37	**8,179**	**830**	**10,600**	**-3/+85**	**15–20**
88mm Flak 41	**17,284**	**1,000**	**14,700**	**-3/+90**	**20**
105mm Flak 38, 39	**22,575**	**880**	**12,800**	**-3/+85**	**10–15**
128mm Flak 40	**57,320**	**880**	**14,800**	**0/+87**	**12–14**

German weapons–boldface; Russian weapons–regular face

German self-propelled quad 20mm Flak (NA)

Left: German self-propelled 37mm Flak (NA)

Below: German 88mm dual-purpose anti-aircraft and anti-tank gun, with SdKfz 8 prime mover (NA)

Bottom: Soviet SU 37 self-propelled anti-aircraft gun (NA)

TANK DESTROYERS

WEAPON	WEIGHT (TONS)	CREW	MAIN GUN/ RDS ON BOARD	MGS/ RDS ON BOARD	ARMOR FRONT/ BODY (INCHES)	SPEED (MI/HR)	COMBAT RADIUS (MI)
47mm AT Gun on Pz I Chassis	8.4	3	47mm L/43 86	None	.5@68° .5@68°	25	87
Marder II	11.9	3	76mm L/51 30	1 x 7.92mm 1,500	.38 .6	26	155
Marder III	11.6	4	75mm L/46 41	None	.3-2	29	124
Panzerjäger 38(t) Hetzer ("Harrier")	17.6	4	75mm L/48 41	1 x 7.92mm 600	2.4@60° .8@45°	24	111
Jagdpanzer IV	26.9	5	75mm L/48 or 75mm L/70	1 x 7.92mm	3.2@45° 1.6@30°	25	124
SU-85 1943	32.5	4	85mm 48	None	1.8@30-40° 1.8@70-90°	34	173
SU-100 1944	31.6	4	100mm 34	None	1.8@35-40° 1.8@70-90°	30	99 155
Nashorn ("Rhinocerous")	26.5	5	88mm L/71 40	1 x 7.92mm 300	2.0@30° 1.2@74°	25	133
Tiger (P) Ferdinand	71.7	6	88mm L/71 50	1 x 7.92mm* 600	7.8@55°-70° 2.3-3.1@60-90°	12	93
Jagdpanzer V "*Jagdpanther*" (Hunting Panther)	51.3	5	88mm L/71 60	1 x 7.92mm 3,000	3.2@55° 2.0@35°	29	124
Jagdpanzer VI "Jagdtiger"	79	6	128mm L/55 38	1 x 7.92mm 3,000	3.9-9.9@40-90° 3.2@65-90°	22	106

German weapons–boldface; Russian weapons–regular face

*In late production or rebuilt vehicles only.

German *Marder* III (NA)

Above: German
Ferdinand (NA)

Left: German
47mm AT gun on
Panzer I chassis
(NA)

Below left: German
Marder III with
Soviet 76.2mm
(NA)

SELF-PROPELLED ARTILLERY

WEAPON	WEIGHT (TONS)	CREW	MAIN GUN/ RDS ON BOARD	MGS/ RDS ON BOARD	ARMOR TURRET/ BODY (INCHES)	SPEED (MI/HR)	COMBAT RADIUS (MI)
SU-76M 1943	10.5	4	76mm 60		1.38@32°	28	180/ 199
Wespe	12.1	5	105mm How 32	1 x 7.92mm	.7 .6	25	87
Hummel	25.4	5	150mm How 20	1 x 7.92mm	2 1.2	25	133
Geschütz-Wagen Lorraine	9.4	4	150mm	None	.4 .4	22	84

German weapons–boldface; Russian weapons–regular face

Above: Soviet infantry advance with support from SU76s (MHI)

Right: German Lorraine self-propelled 150mm howitzer (NA)

Above: German *Wespe*
self-propelled 105mm
howitzer (NA)

Left: German *Hummel*,
self-propelled 150mm
howitzer (NA)

ASSAULT GUNS

WEAPON	WEIGHT (TONS)	CREW	MAIN GUN/ RDS ON BOARD	MGS/ RDS ON BOARD	ARMOR FRONT/ SIDE (INCHES)	SPEED (MI/HR)	COMBAT RADIUS (MI)
Sturmgeschütz III/D	**24.3**	**4**	**75mm L/24** **44**	**None**	**2.0@69-80°** **1.2@79-90°**	**24**	**96**
Sturmgeschütz 40 (Sturmgeschütz III/G)	**26.3**	**4**	**75mm L/48** **54**	**None**	**3.2@69-80°** **1.2@79-90°**	**24**	**96**
Sturmgeschütz IV	**26.7**	**4**	**75mm L/48** **54**	**None**	**3.2@76-80°** **1.2@79-90°**	**25**	**124**
Sturmhaubitze 42	**26.4**	**4**	**105mm L/28** **36**	**None**	**3.2@76-80°** **1.2@79-90°**	**25**	**96**
SU 122	34	5	122mm How	None	1.8@30-40° 1.8@50-90°	34	93
JSU 122	46	5	122mm Gun 30	12.7mm AA 450	3.0@12-60° 1.77@75-90°	23	150
Sturmpanzer IV **Brummbär**	**30.4**	**5**	**150mm/L12** **38**		**3.9@50-78°** **2.0@75-90°**	**25**	**124**
JSU 152	46	5	152mm How 20	12.7mm AA 1,000	3.6@60° 3.6@90°	23	132
Sturmmörser **Tiger**	**65.7**	**5**	**380mm Rocket** **13**		**3.9-5.9@45-65°** **3.2@60-90°**	**25**	**106**

German weapons–boldface; Russian weapons–regular face

Above: Soviet JSU 122 (NA)

Right: German *Sturmgeschütz* III/D (NA)

Above: German *Sturmgeschütz* III/G (NA)

Below: Soviet SU122 (MHI)

TANKS

WEAPON	WEIGHT (TONS)	CREW	MAIN GUN/ RDS ON BOARD	MGS/ RDS ON BOARD	ARMOR FRONT/ SIDE (IN)	SPEED (MI/HR)	COMBAT RADIUS (MI)
T-60 Model 1941	6.4	2	20mm/ 780	1 x 7.62mm 945	.59-.75@20-65° .59@65-90°	28	280
L3/35 Italy	7.5	2 256	20mm 1,560	1 x 8mm .25	1.9	25	125
T-70 Model 1942	10.2	2	45mm/ 94	1 x 7.62mm 945	1.4@30-60° .6-1.4@65-90°	28	155
Skoda 38t	10.4	4	37mm L/47.8 72	2 x 7.92mm 2,400	.6-1@90° .4-1@90°	26	155
Toldi I Hungary	9.57	3	20mm 52	1 x 8mm 2,400	.5 .5	30	136
Toldi III Hungary	10.3	3	40mm no data	1 x 8mm no data	.75-1.4 .8-1.0	30	136
Turan I Hungary	20	5	40mm	1 x 8mm	2.0-2.3 1.0-1.6	29	93
Turan II Hungary	20.25	5	75mm	1 x 8mm	2.0-2.3 1.0-1.6	27	102
Panzer III/L	25.4	5	50mm L/60 78	2 x 7.92mm 4,960	2.0-2.4@65-81° 1.2@65-90°	28	90
Panzer IV/F2	25.3	5	75mm L/43 87	2 x 7.92mm 3,159	2.0@76-80° 1.2@64-90°	25	124
Panzer IV/G	25.9		75mm L/48 87	2 x 7.92mm 3,150	3.2 @ 76-80° 1.2@64-90°	24	124
Panzer IV/H	27.6	5	75mm L/48 87	2 x 7.92mm 3,159	3.2@76-80° 1.2@64-90°	25	124
T-34 M1940	28.5	4	76mm 77	2 x 7.62mm 2,900-4,800	1.8@30° 1.8@50-90°	34	186
T-34 M1943	34	4	76mm 100	2 x 7.62mm 2,400	1.8-2.7@30-60° 1.8-2.0@50-90°	34	186
T-34-85	35	4	85mm 60	2 x 7.62mm 1,890	1.8-3.5@30-90° 1.8-2.9@50-70°	34	186
T-44	34.75	4	85mm 58	2 x 7.62mm 1,890	3.5@30-90° 2.9-3.5@70-90°	32	124
Panzer V/G "Panther"	50.2	5	75mm L/70 79	2 x 7.92mm 4,500	2.3-4.3@35-79° 1.6-2.0@60-90°	29	124
KV-1E 1940	52.5	5	76.2mm 114	3 x 7.62mm 3,000	1.6-4.3@25-70° 2.9-4.3@75-90°	22	155
KV-2	57.2	6	152mm How 36	3 x 7.62mm 3,100	1.6-2.9@25-90° 2.9@90°	16	155
KV-85 1943	50.5	4	85mm 70	3 x 7.62mm 3,300	1.6-3.9@25-60° 2.3-3.9@75-90°	26	155

Tanks (continued)

Weapon	Weight (tons)	Crew	Main Gun/ Rds on Board	MGs/ Rds on Board	Armor Front/ Side (in)	Speed (mi/hr)	Combat Radius (mi)
JS II 1944	50.5	4	122mm 28	2 x 7.62mm 2,331 1 x 12.7mm AA 945	3.5-4.7@30-60° 3.5@72-90°	23	149
JS-III 1945	51.5	4	122mm 28	2 x 7.62mm 1,000 1 x 12.7mm AA 945	4.7-6.3@18-47° 3.5-8.6@30-90°	25	118
Panzer VI/E "Tiger I"	**62.8**	**5**	**88mm L/56 92**	**2 x 7.92mm 3,920**	**3.9@66-82° 3.2@90°**	**23**	**73**
Panzer VI "King Tiger"	**76.9**	**5**	**88mm L/71 84**	**2 x 7.92mm 4,800**	**3.9-7.0@40-81° 3.2@65-90°**	**26**	**106**
Lend Lease[1]							
MKIII Valentine	17.6	3	40mm 79	1 x 7.92mm 3,150	2.3-2.5@21-90° 2.3@90°	15	90
MK II Matilda	29.7	4	40mm L/52 67	1 x .303" 4,000	2.9-3.2@23-90° 2.5-2.9@60-90°	15	90
MK IV Churchill	43.1	5	57mm L/52 84	2 x 7.92mm 9,350	1.5-4.0@25-90° 1.5-3.46	17	161
M-3 General Lee (Two main guns)	32	7	75mm L/31 41 37mm L/50 179	4 x .30"[2] 8,000	1.5-2.0@37-90° 1.5-2.0@90°	25	120
M-3 Stuart	14.3	4	37mm L/53 103	5 x .30"[3] 8,300	.63-1.7@21-80° 1.0@90°	36	125
M4A2 Sherman	35	5	75mm L/40[4] 97	2 x .30" 1 x .50" AA 6,750/300	2.0-4.0-@34-90° 1.5-2.0@85-90°	25	100

1. Lend-Lease provided the Soviet Army with 1,683 light tanks, 5,488 medium tanks from the U.S., and 5,218 British tanks. The quantity of Lend-Lease tanks equalled 16 percent of the total Soviet wartime production for tanks.

2. Two .30" MG in the bow; one mounted coaxially in turret; one in commander's cupola

3. One .30" MG in right and left sponsons; one in bow; one coaxially mounted in turret; one AA

4. Later versions mounted the 3" (76mm) L/53 main gun; ammo stowage was 71 rounds

German weapons–boldface; Russian weapons–regular face

Above: German Panther (NA)

Below: Soviet KV-1 heavy tank (NA)

Left: German Tiger I (NA)

Below: German Panzer III/L (NA)

Bottom: Soviet JS II heavy tank (NA)

FIGHTER AIRCRAFT

MODEL	MAXIMUM SPEED (MI/HR)	RANGE(MI)	CEILING(FT)	BOMB LOAD (TONS)	ARMAMENT MG/GUNS
I-15	226	450	32,100	None	4 x 7.62mm
I-15bis	228	388	26,250	.11	4 x 7.62mm
I-16	273	388	29,500	None	4 x 7.62
Bf 109C-1	**292**	**388**	**32,800**		**4 x 7.92mm**
I-16 Type 24	303	372	29,500	None	2 x 7 .62mm/ 2 x 20mm
LaGG-3	341	345	30,500	None	2 x 7.62mm 1 x 12.7mm 1 x 20mm
Bf 110C-4	**348**	**696**	**32,800**	**2.2**	**5 x 7.92mm 2 x 20mm**
Bf 109E-3	**351**	**410**	**32,800**		**2 x 7.92mm 2 x 20mm**
Yak-1	360	434	32,808	.22	2 x 7.62mm 1 x 20mm
Yak-9D	374	876	34,800		2 x 12.7mm 1 x 37mm
Yak-7b	381	509	32,800	.22	1 x 12.7mm 1 x 20mm
Bf 109G-10	**385**	**434**	**39,400**		**2 x 13mm 1 x 30mm**
FW190A-3	**395**	**497**	**37,400**	**.55**	**2 x 7.92mm 4 x 20mm***
MiG-3	398	621	39,370		2 x 7.62mm 1 x 12.7mm
La-5FN	403	475	31,200	.11	2 x 20mm
Yak-3	407	559	35,400		1 x 20mm 2 x 12.7mm
La-7	423	394	32,500	.1	3 x 20mm
FW190D-9	**426**	**519**	**39,400**	**.55**	**2 x 13mm 2 x 20mm**
Bf 109K	**450**	**356**	**41,000**		**2 x 15mm 1 x 30mm**
Ta 152	**472**	**1,240**	**48,560**		**1 x 30mm 4 x 20mm**
Me 262A-1	**541**	**652**	**37,566**		**4 x 30mm**

*Two of the 20mm were sometimes removed.

German weapons–boldface; Russian weapons–regular face

BOMBERS/CLOSE SUPPORT AIRCRAFT

Model	Maximum Speed (mi/hr)	Range(mi)	Ceiling(ft)	Bomb Load (tons)	Armament MG/Guns
Dornier 17E-1	220	988	16,700	.83	2 x 7.92mm
Dornier 17Z-2	255	720	26,900	1.1	6 x 7.92mm
He 111B-2	230	1,032	23,000	1.65	3 x 7.92mm
He 111H-16	252	1,280	27,900	3.6	5 x 7.92mm 1 x 20mm 1 x 13mm
DB-3F	264	1,680	32,800	2.75	3 x 7.62mm 2 x 20mm
Pe-2	335	683	28,900	1.1	4 x 7.62mm
Pe-8(TB-7)	273	2,920	22,965	4.4	2 x 7.62mm 2 x 12.7mm 2 x 20mm
SB-2	276	608	31,400	.66	4 x 7.62mm
Ju 88A-4	292	1,696	26,900	2.2	6 x 7.92mm
Su-2	302	684	27,600	.66	5 x 7.62mm
Tu-2	340	1,550	36,200	1.65	3 x 12.7mm 2 x 20mm
Close Support					
Ju-87 B-1	238	621	26,400	2.2	3 x 7.92mm
Ju-87 G-1	195	621	26,400	None	1 x 7.92mm 2 x 37mm
HS-129	254	546	29,700	.39	2 x 7.92mm 2 x 20mm 1 x
Il-2M3	255	475	21,000	2,200 or 8 rockets	2 x 7.62mm 1 x 12.7mm 2 x 23mm
Il-10	315	621	24,600	.44 or 8 rockets	2 x 7.62mm 1 x 20mm 2 x 23mm

German weapons–boldface; Russian weapons–regular face

LEND LEASE AIRCRAFT*

MODEL	SPEED (MI/HR)	MAX. RANGE (MI)	CEILING (FT)	BOMB LOAD (TONS)	ARMAMENT
FIGHTERS					
P-39D	335	600–1100	32,100	.25	1 x 37mm, 4 x .30 cal, 4 x .50 cal
P-40N	378	340–1490	38,000	.25	6 x .50 cal
P-47D	423	1030–1800	42,000	1.25	8 x .50 cal
P-63A	410	450–2000	43,000	.25	1 x 37mm, 4 x .50 cal
BOMBERS					
A-20G	341	1090	25,600	2.0	5 x.30 cal, 4 x 20mm
B-25J	272	1350	24,200	2.0	13 x .50 cal

Under Lend Lease, the United States furnished the following quantities of aircraft to the USSR: P-39 = 4,719, P-40 = 2,097, P-47 = 195, P-63 = 2,400, A-20 = 2,908, and B-25 = 862

German weapons–boldface; Russian weapons–regular face

——————⫸●⫷——————

Forgotten Battles

——————⫸●⫷——————

by David M. Glantz

Detecting and analyzing those military operations on the Eastern Front which have not been written about is a difficult and painstaking process for a number of reasons. First, general accounts of the war written by Soviet historians often have simply overlooked these operations; treated the actions as insignificant; or dismissed them, rightly or wrongly, as feints, demonstrations, or deceptions. Second, since many of these operations failed, they left no major "footprint" in terms of major territorial advance or impact on their opponent that can easily attract the historians attention. Finally, since the Germans routinely perceived massive Soviet forces arrayed against them, recorded almost constant Soviet counteraction, and had difficulty distinguishing precisely what forces were operating against them (because of the rapidity of their advance earlier in the war and their decaying intelligence capabilities late in the war), German historians have focused primarily on those major operations which their Soviet counterparts identify and describe. Thus, the gaps identified here are routinely subsumed and obscured by the context of larger operations, such as the BARBAROSSA advance; the battles of Moscow, Stalingrad, and Kursk; and the immense Soviet operations later in the war (for example, the advance to the Dnepr, the Right Bank of the Ukraine operation, and the Belorussian operation). Finally, these gaps tend to occur in the waning stages of a major Soviet offensive, when striking overall Soviet offensive successes and German confusion obscure renewed Soviet activity and ultimate Soviet offensive aims.

Based on *Forgotten Battles of the German-Soviet War (1941–1945)*, © 1998 by David M. Glantz. Self-published. Used by permission.

471

If historians did not write about these operations or if they were summarily dismissed as unimportant, how, then, can the historian identify these gaps in the coverage of the wartime operations? Further, how can these operations be identified and their intent be revealed? From the experience of this historian, there are two ways to do so. First, Soviet historiography has been marked by periods of candor, during which the authorities permitted more thorough coverage of the war. The most obvious of such periods was 1958 to the mid-1960s, when memoir literature, unit histories, and operational accounts were generally more thorough, more candid, and more detailed. It was during this period that some of the greatest Soviet wartime military failures received remarkable public airing, including the Kharkov disaster of May 1942 (covered by Bagramian and Moskalenko) and the Donbas and Kharkov defeats of February–March 1943 (covered by Morozov and Kazakov). While many of the gaps recorded here did not receive requisite attention, some were mentioned in the better memoirs and unit histories, such as Sandalov's and Katukov's memoirs and Solomatin's history of the **1st Mechanized Corps**. While one can reconstruct the shadowy outlines of these ignored operations from these Soviet works, full reconstruction is not possible. Recent releases of Soviet archival materials — in particular, the war experience volumes of the General Staff and works produced by the Voroshilov General Staff and Frunze Academies — sadly reveal that these works too often also ignore these historical gaps.

Thus, the failings and weaknesses of official and unofficial Soviet military historiography force the historian to turn elsewhere to identify the gaps and reconstruct the complete history of wartime operations. The second and most important alternative source of information of these forgotten operations is the vast repository of German archival materials on the war, supplemented by German unit histories. German archival materials on Eastern Front operations have been markedly underexploited. Those now-famous Germans military leaders who introduced the Soviet-German War to Western readers (such as Guderian, Mellenthin, and Manstein) usually wrote from memory and from their personal notes without benefit of archival materials. Thus, their accounts are far from complete regarding Soviet actions and intent; and they present Soviet forces in an utterly faceless fashion. They sketchily identify the gaps noted here, but these gaps are again subsumed by the context of larger operations. Subsequent general histories by Western historians have used these memoirs as points of departure and also miss the gaps, focusing only on that which has been already been identified as significant.

The failure of these German memoirs and secondary accounts to elucidate the war fully forces the researcher to turn to other sources, namely German unit histories—written more recently from archival materials—and primary archival materials themselves. The brevity, narrow focus, and spotty geographical coverage of the former make it difficult to base one's conclusions solely on these sources. Once the archives themselves identify a gap, however, the unit history is of value as context. It is the archives themselves that most fully reveal the lost pages of wartime operations. This author has employed a time-consuming, but fruitful, method for discovering ignored and neglected military operations. The most vivid and candid reflection of what took place on the field of battle appears on the daily operational and intelligence maps of German army groups, armies, corps, and divisions. These "pictures" of combat record the nature and intensity of combat in any front sector through changing front lines, and they visually and graphically record the intensity and scope of fighting in any region by the physical configuration of the front and the intelligence picture of concentrated and identified enemy forces. Supplemented by accompanying written operational and intelligence reports, large operations become readily identifiable and subject to at least rudimentary analysis.

The military operations covered in this chapter have been identified through this laborious process of studying German daily operational and intelligence maps. Once such operations are identified, German unit histories and earlier fragmentary Soviet accounts confirm, elucidate, and elaborate upon the existence, nature, and probable intent of these obscure, but often significant, operations. Admittedly, this research procedure is by no means infallible. The sources relied upon here can reliably detect major operations; accurately measure the nature, intensity, and scope of the operations; and identify the contending participants. They cannot, however, determine precisely the ultimate intent of the operation. Thus, definitive accounts of these and other neglected operations can be written only after the Soviet military archives are fully open and accessible to Western and Russian scholars alike.

Finally, the operations mentioned in this chapter are by no means the only neglected operations. These are examples only, based on an initial and rather perfunctory review of German archival materials.

They do, however, represent what we do not know about the war, and they represent what must be done if, in the future, the history of the war is to be revealed in full.

A Sample of Neglected Operations

Soviet Counterattacks and Counterstrokes During Operation BARBAROSSA (July–September 1941)

Historians and general readers alike have been fascinated with the sudden, deep, and relentless advance of German forces during Operation BARBAROSSA. Spearheaded by four powerful German panzer groups, the German advance from the Soviet Union's western borders to the approaches of Leningrad, Moscow, and Rostov has been portrayed as a series of successive offensive lunges culminating in the final November 1941 thrust on Moscow itself. While historians have identified the various stages of the advance and have argued about the sequencing, timing, and objectives of each stage, they have tended to accord it a seamless nature, whose various phases exist, but do not warrant excessive study in their own right. These primarily Western historians argue that German confusion over their ultimate objectives, the vast scale of Russian terrain, the terrors of a Russian winter, and weak German logistics ultimately produced German failure. They recount in some detail the complex Border Battles; the Minsk encirclement; the battles around Smolensk; the German September southward turn and subsequent Kiev encirclement; the German October victories around Viazma and Briansk; and the final failed drive on Moscow. Often they openly lament German confusion and the failure to secure Moscow.

Soviet sources cover the period in greater detail, properly underscoring the importance of these combat phases in the ultimate outcome of battle on the approaches to Moscow. Soviet historians highlight the confused ferocity of the Border Battles; the importance of the Battle of Smolensk; and the Herculean efforts of the *Stavka* to assemble, amass, and commit to combat those strategic reserves which, at the gates of Leningrad, Moscow, and Rostov, ultimately thwart the German BARBAROSSA offensive. In the context of their accounts, however, Soviet historians have mentioned, but not elaborated upon to a sufficient degree, the intense Soviet efforts to counter the German advance before it reached unprecedented depths.

Specifically, they have not covered in adequate detail the apparently concerted series of counterstrokes and counterattacks that periodically punctuated (and in the process, perhaps, wore down) the German advance.

In short, there are a series of Soviet counteractions, which occurred in clusters during July, August, and September 1941, which deserve further study and elaboration. At a minimum, these include the following:

July 1941

– **Western Front** operations toward Lepel (6–11 July)

– **Northwestern Front** operations at Stoltsy (14–18 July)

– **Western Front** Counterstrokes (planned or carried) out along the Dnepr (13–17 July), to include:

> – **22d Army** (at Gorodok)
>
> – **19th Army** (at Vitebsk)
>
> – **20th Army** (around Orsha)
>
> – **13th Army** (around Staryi Bykov)
>
> – **21st Army** (toward Bobruisk)
>
> – **4th** and **16th Army** remnants (to Gorki)

– **Southwestern Front** operations toward Dubno (1–2 July)

– **Southwestern Front** operations toward Novgorod-Volynski (10–14 July)

August 1941

– **Northwestern Front**'s Staraia-Russa offensive (12–13 August)

– **Western Front**'s Smolensk offensive (11 August–9 September)

– Continuation of the Bobruisk operation (to 7 August)

– **Southwestern Front**'s offensive around Korosten (5–8 August)

September 1941

– **Western Front**'s Elnia offensive (30 August–8 September)

– **Briansk Front**'s Roslavl-Novozybkov offensive (30 August–12 September)

Soviet historians have written in varying detail on each of these operations, but much of that detail is at the lower operational and tactical levels. For example, excellent accounts exist on the exploits of **63d** and **67th Rifle Corps** near Rogachev, and accounts of the Bobruisk operation are fairly clear, as are the experiences of **5th** and **7th Mechanized Corps** at Lepel.[3] One wonders if the factual detail here is in response to the detailed, if somewhat sensational, German accounts of the Bobruisk offensive as related in Guderian's memoirs and other German-based sources, under the rubric of the "Timoshenko counteroffensive." The same feature is apparent from operations in the north along the Leningrad axis. In his memoirs, Manstein mentions heated actions around Stoltsy and Staraia-Russa. Subsequently, Soviet sources mention the action, only in less detail than their German counterparts. Likewise, German popular accounts focus on the heavy combat around Smolensk, and Soviet accounts have responded with considerable detail, in particular, about the fate of **Group Kachalov,** which Guderian's panzer corps destroyed.[4] Unfortunately, Soviet accounts are less revealing about the operations and fate of the other Soviet operational groups which struggled around Smolensk.

Eremenko's memoirs do provide considerable detail about the Roslavl-Novozybkov operation, but again in apparent response to materials in Guderian's memoirs. There is, however, a dearth of other sources on this operation and on the Elnia operation further north. Finally, the excellent recent work by A. V. Vladimirsky, *Na kievskom nauravlenii* [On the Kiev axis], finally casts light on the intense efforts of the **Southwestern Front** to halt the German drive on the approaches to Kiev.[5] It remains, however, the only detailed source to do so.

Thus, there are many historical gaps to fill related to action during these critical phases of Operation BARBAROSSA. More detail is required on each of the operations mentioned above. Even more important, the strategic intent, nature, and import of these operations must be revealed. In their recent work entitled *Nezavershchaemie operatsii pervom periode voiny* [Uncompleted operations of the first period of war], the authors carefully describe the offensive mind-set of Red Army commanders, inherited from the prewar years which governed much of their 1941 planning and operations. They imply that the failed offensives of that period were largely prompted by this mind-set, but that requisite strategic appreciation and operational and tactical skills were lacking to carry out that tradition.[6] Further, in their 1976 article on restoration of the strategic front, B. Panov and N. Naumov wrote that, in late June and July 1941, the *Stavka* faced the complex and daunting task of "restoring the strategic defensive front from Polotsk to Polese," and that the mission of forces designated to do so was "to prevent an enemy penetration to Moscow, while destroying him with powerful counterstrokes by ground forces and aviation."[7] Therefore, the preeminent question is: to what extent were these counteractions interrelated and driven by *Stavka* orders? And if that guidance existed, to what extent did these counteractions contribute to subsequent Soviet failures or the ultimate defeat of BARBAROSSA?

Offensive Operations During the Soviet Winter Offensive (December 1941–April 1942)

Much has been written from both the German and Soviet perspectives about the Soviet strategic defense at Moscow and the two-phased Soviet strategic offensive which followed. German works, however, focus on the events in the immediate environs of Moscow, and Soviet sources expand the focus to embrace the front from Staraia-Russa to Elets. Events on the flanks and in less-known sectors have been largely ignored by German and Soviet historians alike (with the exception of action around Demiansk and Rostov). Two major and one minor example will suffice to demonstrate this neglect.

The Soviet Winter Campaign, like its component Moscow offensives, was an immense and complicated endeavor. While the principal Soviet operations drove the Germans back from the immediate approaches to Moscow, they did not achieve their ultimate aim of destroying *Army Group Center*. They did not, in part, because of failures on the flanks, which either produced no operational results and, hence, had no strategic impact, or which dissipated the striking power of the Soviet Army on the main (Moscow) axis. For these reasons, the ignored flank operations are important.

Among those operation which require further clarification are the following:

– **Volkhov** and **Leningrad Fronts'** Liuban offensive (7 January–30 April 1942)

– **Briansk Front's** Orel-Bolkhov offensive (7 January–18 February 1942)

- **Briansk Front**'s Kursk-Oboian offensive (January–February 1942)

- **Northwestern Front**'s Demiansk offensive (6 March–9 April 1942)

The first of these operations, which initially sought to end the German siege of Leningrad and, ultimately, involved the encirclement and destruction of Soviet **2d Shock Army,** has received great notoriety in the West because of the fate of the man sent by Stalin to save the army, General A. A. Vlasov. For the same reason, and because of Vlasov's subsequent perceived treason to the Soviet cause, Soviet historians routinely first ignored the operation and then referred to it without reference to Vlasov. While recent accounts now discuss the operation in full, largely for political motives, a full military assessment of the operation remains to be done.[8]

The twin **Briansk Front** offensives languish in obscurity, just as do the details of other Soviet operations. During the waning stages of the Moscow counteroffensive (such as **50th Army** attempts to reach and rescue Soviet forces encircled in *Army Group Center*'s rear from February–April 1942). Mention is made of the operations in separate chapters of memoirs (such as M. I. Kazakov) and unit histories, but the many Soviet encyclopedias on the war ignore the operations, and no other open-source detailed accounts exist to substantiate the ample German archival materials attesting to the operations' existence. Given the potential role these operations had in the stretching of German *Army Group Center* resources in a time of great peril, they deserve more attention than they have received.

The Demiansk example exists as a case study in the failures of Soviet Eastern Front historiography. German sources, in vivid detail (including operational and tactical reports, intercepts of Soviet radio transmissions, and hundreds of POW debriefings), describe a daring Soviet ground operation, supported by air, designed to reduce and destroy the Demiansk encirclement (*II Corps*). Three Soviet airborne brigades, supported by several ski battalions, penetrated into the German encirclement, while Soviet frontal forces attacked the encirclement from without.[9]

While the course of the operation has been reconstructed in detail from these German sources, virtually no Soviet work has even mentioned the operation or commented on the selfless performance of the over 7,000 airborne troopers who perished during its conduct. No doubt other such examples await the investigation of future historians.

Soviet Offensive and Counteroffensive Operations Within the Context of German Operation *BLAU* (June–July 1942)

Both German and Soviet sources have laid out in considerable detail the context and nature of operations during the spring and summer of 1942. Vasilevsky and Kazakov have detailed Soviet planning for the conduct of local offensive operations within the context of a Soviet strategic defense; Bagramian and Moskalenko have written extensively about the failure of the May 1942 Soviet Kharkov offensive; others have provided details on the Soviet tragedy at Kerch, and Kazakov has related in some detail operations on the approaches to Voronezh.[10] Accounts from both sides then relate in considerable detail the German offensive and subsequent advance into the Stalingrad and Caucasus region. Where open-source Soviet accounts are weak, recently-released war experience volumes fill in the gaps (in particular, on **5th Tank Army's** July counterstroke and subsequent fighting around Voronezh).[11] In other associated areas, major gaps exist. These include the following:

– **Briansk Front** counteroffensive operations (June–July 1942)

– **Western Front** offensive operations (July–August 1942), including:

    – The Bolkov offensive (**61st Army**, 5–12 June 1942)

    – The Zhizdra offensive (**16th Army**, 6–14 July 1942)

    – The Zhizdra offensive (**61st, 16th,** and **3d Tank Army,** August 1942)

– **Southern Front** defensive battles in the Voroshilograd operation (6–24 July 1942)

While operations by the **Briansk Front** require greater explanation in open accounts, **Western Front** operations remain utterly obscure except for occasional mention in some German unit histories and extensive German archival coverage. The various offensives, obviously designed to distract German attention and strength from the Stalingrad axis, involved sizable forces, especially the August offensive which was the first offensive operation by newly-created **3d Tank Army.**

Operations by the Soviet **Southern Front** have been described in outline but not in detail, and, again, we must look to the German archives to find detailed materials on the actions and fate of Soviet **9th, 12th, 24th, 37th,** and **38th Armies,** which were all at least partially encircled, but the bulk of whose forces escaped captivity to the ultimate detriment of the Germans. Why and how this occurred remains unclear. To a lesser extent, detailed accounts are also lacking on the battles of **62d, 64th,** and **1st** and **4th Tank Armies** on the immediate approaches to Stalingrad. Given the potentially critical influence of these operations on the course and outcome of the German Stalingrad offensive, historians and readers should possess more than a purely German interpretation.

Soviet Offensive Operations in Fall 1942

All readers and historians know about the course and outcome of the Soviet Stalingrad counteroffensive, codenamed Operation "URANUS." Most know about the subsequent planning for and conducting of Operations "SATURN" and "LITTLE SATURN" against German and Italian forces along the middle Don River. Few, however, know about the remaining "celestial" operation, codenamed "MARS." MARS remains an enigma, noticed by the most astute of Western and German observers, but ignored by all but a handful of Soviet sources. Contemporary to operation URANUS, unlike its successful counterpart, MARS has been dismissed and forgotten.

Operation "MARS": The Rzhev-Sychevka Operation (24 November–December 1942)

The four most prominent Soviet sources which refer to the operation demonstrate the historiographical dilemma and represent how many of these forgotten operations appear in Soviet works. Zhukov notes the existence of Operation MARS in his memoirs, and he apparently played a major role in its planning and conduct, along with the two participating front commanders, I. S. Konev, and M. A. Purkaev. Konev's memoirs ignore the operation (and others he participated in, by beginning in January 1943). Zhukov reports the parameters of the plan, which called for the destruction of German forces in the Rzhev salient. Then, after returning to his description of the Stalingrad victory, he briefly mentions the failure at Rzhev and dismisses the operation as simply a diversion, although it began on 24 November (five days after the commencement of the Stalingrad operation and one day after the encirclement of German *6th Army*) and continued through mid-December.[12]

The second major source, that of M. D. Solomatin, commander of the **1st Mechanized Corps,** mentions the necessity of tying down German reserves within the context of the Stalingrad battle and provides a superb and detailed description of the role of his corps in Operation MARS. His account mentions the actions of his corps and cooperating **41st Army** formations and mentions the fact that other **Kalinin** and **Western Front** forces were designated to participate in the offensive, whose aims, he described, were to "destroy the German-Fascist Olenino-Rzhev Group" in cooperation with **Western Front** forces.[13]

Katukov's memoirs mention the operation, but provide little detail. Katukov commanded **3d Mechanized Corps** subordinate to **22d Army.** He states briefly, "**3d Mechanized Corps** received an order to go over to the attack with cooperating rifle units. The Rzhev-Sychevka offensive operation of **Kalinin** and **Western Front** forces began on 25 November." After commenting in general on the course of operations, the heavy fighting, and the adverse weather conditions, Katukov laconically noted, "on 20 December, the Rzhev-Sychevka operation was completed."[14] A. Kh. Babdzhanian, who commanded the **3d Mechanized Brigade** of Katukov's corps, mentioned the operation only briefly in his memoirs by quoting a conversation with his army commander, V. A. Iushkevich, who said, "We will conduct a rather serious offensive together with **Western Front** forces—we must liquidate the enemy Rzhev grouping."[15] A final source, a history of Soviet cavalry forces, mentions joint operations by cavalry forces (**20th Cavalry Division** of **2d Guards Cavalry Corps**) and Soviet **6th Tank Corps** in penetration operations south of Rzhev, during which the cavalry division reached the German rear, where it operated for a month before being rescued by elements of Katukov's mechanized corps (also mentioned by Katukov).[16]

These sources, taken alone, indicate that a modest operation occurred, perhaps diversionary in nature, and that at least three armies (**22d, 41st,** and one **Western Front** army), supported by up to four mobile corps (**1st** and **2d Mechanized, 2d Guards Cavalry,** and **6th Tank Corps**), took part in the operation. These forces were of significant—but not overwhelming—size.

German archival intelligence and operational reports, however, cast the operation in a vastly different light. Records of the *9th Army* affirm that the **Kalinin Front's 22d** and **41st Armies,** supported by **1st** and **3d Mechanized Corps,** participated in the operation. According to these records, however, so also did the front's **39th Army,** and subordinate to **41st Army** was the elite **Stalin 6th Rifle Corps.** Moreover, three of **Western Front's** armies (**20th, 30th,** and **31st**) also took part, supported at various times by **6th, 7th,** and **8th**

Tank Corps, and **2d Guards Cavalry Corps.** At the same time, immediately to the west, **3d Shock Army** struck at German forces at Velikie Luki and achieved success (which Soviet historians have reported on in detail). Further, **2d Mechanized Corps** was available to support either **41st Army** operations against Belyi or **3d Shock Army** (which it ultimately supported). Detailed German order of battle reports indicate that the Soviet mobile forces were at or well above establishment armored strength, and that offensive preparations had been thorough.[17]

At Stalingrad, the Soviets committed six armies (**21st, 24th, 51st, 57th, 65th,** and **5th Tank**), containing or supported by nine mobile corps (**1st, 4th, 16th, 26th,** and **13th Tank; 4th Mechanized,** and **8th, 3d Guards,** and **4th Cavalry Corps**), against the *6th* and part of the *4th Panzer Army* and Romanian *3d* and *4th Armies,* while **62d** and **64th Armies** defended in the city. In the Rzhev-Sychevka operation, Zhukov committed six armies (**20th, 22d, 30th, 31st, 39th,** and **41st**), supported by up to seven mobile corps (**1st, 2d,** and **3d Mechanized, 5th, 6th,** and **8th Tank,** and **2d Guards Cavalry Corps**), against two thirds of *9th Army,* while **3d Shock Army** struck simultaneously at *9th Army* elements at Velikie Luki, and three more Soviet armies (**29th, 43d,** and **4th Shock**) protected the flanks. While armies are admittedly of varying size, Soviet strength and favorable correlation of forces at Rzhev probably approximated that of Stalingrad.

On 24 November, **22d** and **41st Armies,** spearheaded by **1st** and **3d Mechanized Corps,** attacked and penetrated German defenses north and south of Belyi, and within days, were driving salients deep into the German rear area. Deteriorating weather conditions and heavy German resistance finally halted the attacks and contained Katukov's and Solomatin's mechanized corps. Meanwhile to the east, Konev's armies pounded German defenses along the Osuga River to no avail. Heavy Soviet combined tank and infantry assaults struck German defenses repeatedly, but were repelled with heavy losses after only minimal Soviet gains. Elsewhere, to the north **39th Army** forces also struck German defenses northeast of Rzhev, slowly driving the defenders back, and, just west of Rzhev, **31st Army** forces struggled forward to cut the rail line from Rzhev to Olenino. The heavy fighting continued into December as German mobile reserves encircled and destroyed the bulk of Solomatin's mechanized corps along with supporting **6th Rifle Corps;** drove back Katukov's mechanized corps; and contained **31st** and **39th Armies** assaults north of the Rzhev-Olenino rail line. In mid-December, Zhukov and Konev launched one more attempt to break through and rescue Solomatin's force, but the attempt also ended in bloody failure. Total Soviet losses in the operation are unknown, but those recorded in German reports were high (an estimated 15,000 dead in Konev's sector alone, and 1,655 tanks destroyed from 24 November to 14 December) and included four general officers.[18]

Two factors differentiated operation URANUS from operation MARS. First, at Stalingrad Soviet armies chose Romanian sectors in which to conduct their initial penetration operations, and they penetrated Romanian defenses rather easily. At Rzhev, however, experienced German divisions (like the *102d*) were dug into well-prepared defenses. Unlike the case at Stalingrad, the Germans also had the *5th Panzer Division* deployed in defenses opposite Konev's main assault. Second, at Stalingrad, the Germans had burned up their armor in city fighting and had only two panzer divisions in reserve (*22d* and *1st Romanian*). At Rzhev, however, German *9th Army* had four mobile divisions in their immediate operational reserve (*1st* and *9th Panzer, Grossdeutschland* and the *14th Panzer-Grenadier*) and three other panzer divisions (*9th, 19th,* and *20th*) within striking distance in a matter of days. This spelled doom for the Soviet offensive.

One other marked characteristic differentiates Operation URANUS from Operation MARS. The former was fully recorded by historians; the latter was not!

Offensive Operations During the Winter and Spring 1943

Soviet historical coverage of the Winter Campaign (November 1942–March 1943) has generally mirrored or responded to that of the Germans. Obviously, both sides were transfixed by operations around Stalingrad from 19 November through 2 February, including the encirclement and destruction of German *6th Army,* German failed attempts to relieve their beleaguered garrison, the ultimate destruction of the encircled force, and Soviet expansion of the operation westward toward and into the Donbas. Both sides have provided adequate detail of the flow of operations through early February, when the tide of battle suddenly turned against the advancing Soviets. German accounts of action in February and March focus almost exclusively on Manstein's effective counterstroke in the Donbas, which cut off the spearheads of advancing Soviet forces; drove **Southwestern Front** forces back to the Northern Donets River; and, subsequently, collapsed advancing **Voronezh Front** forces and drove them northward through Kharkov and Belgorod to create, by mid-March, that particular bent segment of the Eastern Front popularly known as the Kursk bulge.

The Germans understandably wax poetic about Manstein's achievements in February and March 1943 and ponder what might have been achieved had the German advance continued. Soviet historians have written extensively about the Kharkov offensive and defense operations, but less about the details of the Donbas operation. The information is there, but one must work hard to dig it out of numerous scattered sources.[19] More surprising is the fact that the potentially most important Soviet offensive of late winter 1943 has been almost totally obscured — that is, the major offensive by **Central Front** on the Kursk-Briansk axis, an offensive which, if successful, could have destroyed German *Army Group Center,* reached the Dnepr River, and chopped the German Eastern Front in half.

Central and Western Fronts' Orel-Briansk-Smolensk Offensive (February–March 1943)

Close examination of Soviet memoir literature, in particular works by Vasilevsky, Rokossovsky, Bagramian, Chistiakov, and Moskalenko, and unit histories, such as **2d Tank, 13th Armies,** and **1st Guards Motorized Rifle Division,** permit the researcher to reconstruct the outlines of the February–March offensive.[20] German archival materials, particularly from the records of *2d* and *2d Panzer Armies,* confirm the Soviet data and add details on the complex operations.[21] What emerges is a significant, ambitious, and audacious offensive whose course, potential, and ultimate outcome increase the significance of Manstein's counterstroke.

In outline, in early February 1943, the *Stavka* planned an offensive to exploit **Briansk** and **Voronezh Front** successes along the Voronezh-Kursk axis and accompany the **Southwestern Front's** advance through the Donbas to the Dnepr and Sea of Azov. To do so, it planned to use the bulk of its "Stalingrad" armies, free after the 2 February surrender of German *6th Army,* and other strategic reserves to attack along the Kursk-Briansk axis toward the Dnepr River and Smolensk in concert with the **Western** and **Kalinin Front.** Rokossovsky's **Don Front,** renamed **Central Front,** would spearhead the mid-February offensive with **2d Tank Army** and **70th Army** from *Stavka* reserve and with **21st** and **65th Armies** redeployed by rail from the Stalingrad region. The multi-front offensive was to begin on 12 February, when forward armies of the **Western**

Front (16th) and **Briansk Front (13th** and **48th)** were to encircle German forces in the Orel salient.

Then, between 17 and 25 February, the two fronts, joined by **Central Front,** were to clear the Briansk region of German troops and secure bridgeheads over the Desna River. During the final phase of the operation, between 25 February and mid-March, the **Kalinin** and **Western Fronts** would join combat to seize Smolensk and, in concert with their sister fronts, destroy *Army Group Center* in the Rzhev-Viazma salient. The entire offensive was timed to coincide with anticipated successful operations by the **Voronezh** and **Southwestern Fronts** so that by mid-March, the strategic offensive would have propelled Soviet forces to the line of the Dnepr River from Smolensk to the Black Sea.

From the beginning, the offensive experienced serious difficulties. First, movement problems forced delay in the beginning of Rokossovsky's offensive to 25 February, by which time **Southwestern Front's** advance in the Donbas had already been thrown back by Manstein's counterstroke. Bagramian's **Western Front** assault in the Zhizdra sector also failed, although he repeatedly attempted to renew the attack. Nevertheless, Rokossovsky attacked on 25 February with **2d Tank Army, 65th Army,** and a **Cavalry-Rifle Group** formed around the nucleus of **2d Guards Cavalry Corps.** Other redeploying armies were to join the assault as they arrived.

Rokossovsky's offensive achieved spectacular initial success. By 7 March, Rodin's **2d Tank Army** had secured Sevsk and, with the **Cavalry-Rifle Group,** approached Trubchevsk and Novgorod-Severskii. Batov's **65th Army,** now joined by Tarasov's **70th Army,** made slow progress against German forces defending south of Orel, while **38th** and **60th Armies** on Rokossovsky's left flank attempted to turn *2d Army's* left flank in the Lgov region. Four factors, however, combined to deny Rokossovsky success. First, the redeployment of the "Stalingrad" armies by rail and road through Livny to the front went slowly, delaying the arrival of **21st Army,** which was essential for the attack on Orel to succeed. Second, bad weather and the ensuing thaw hindered this redeployment as well as the advance by Rokossovsky's force. Third, by early March, Manstein's counterstroke had also crushed **Voronezh Front** forces south of Kharkov and threatened both that city and Belgorod, on Rokossovsky's left flank. Finally, German abandonment of the Rzhev salient and the victories in the south permitted German *2d Panzer* and *2d Armies* to shift forces south and north against the flanks of Rokossovsky's attacking forces. As a result, on 7 March, Rokossovsky received

Stavka permission to regroup his forces to his right flank to begin a less ambitious operation against the Orel salient.

Subsequently, German resistance stiffened on the Fatezh-Orel axis, halting Rokossovsky's offensive, and redeployed German forces struck his overexposed forces in the Novgorod Severskii-Lgov sector. The final blow to his offensive plans occurred on 11 March when Chistiakov's **21st Army,** which had just arrived to join Rokossovsky's Orel offensive, was diverted to Oboian to deal with Manstein's continued advance toward Belgorod. Although desultory fighting continued along the Orel axis until 23 March, Rokossovsky's forces abandoned Sevsk and occupied new defenses along what would become the northern and central face of the Kursk bulge.

Thus, the ambitious strategic effort failed, and the *Stavk,* once again would have to postpone an advance to the line of the Dnepr River. The Soviet failure would have a major impact on how Soviet forces would operate at Kursk later in 1943. It also accorded strategic significance to Manstein's Donbas and Kharkov counterstrokes. Most important, from the standpoint of this work, is the apparent neglect of this operation by Soviet historians, which is extraordinary, given its potential importance. No single account exists, and even recent works ignore its conduct. For example, Krivosheev's new work on Soviet wartime losses provides no personnel loss figures for the operation (or for Operation MARS), nor does it recognize the very existence of the Central Front in February–March 1943.[22]

Offensive Operations into Belorussia in Fall 1943 and Winter 1944

German and Soviet historians cover in detail the dramatic series of Soviet offensives which followed the Kursk defense in July 1943 and the subsequent Soviet advance to the Dnepr River from August through October 1943. Volumes have been written on Operations "SUVOROV," "RUMIANTSEV," and "KUTUZOV" at Orel, Belgorod-Kharkov, and Smolensk. Equal attention has been devoted to the various phases of the Chernigov-Poltava operation, operations designed to breech the Dnepr River line (the Chernigov-Pripiat, Kiev, Gomel-Rechitsa, Krivoi Rog, and Nikopol operations), and operations on the flanks, such as the Nevel and Melitopol operations. The Germans, quite naturally, focus on Soviet failures, such as the unsuccessful multiple attempts to crush their Nikopol bridgehead. Thereafter, Soviet accounts focus on their successful and spectacular advance into the Ukraine, commencing with the Zhitornir-Berdichev operation in December 1943 and culminating with their encirclement of the German *1st Panzer Army* during the Proskurov-Chernovits operation and the arrival of Soviet forces along the borders of Romania and southern Poland in April. 1944. Lost in this coverage are important and repeated Soviet attempts to conquer Belorussia in late fall 1943 and early winter 1944.

The Belorussian Strategic Offensive (November 1943–February 1944)

The general outlines of this offensive can be pieced together from a wide variety of scattered Soviet sources. Portions of the initial operations to liberate Belorussia are covered in detail under the rubric of the continuation of the Nevel operation by **1st Baltic Front** and the Gomel-Rechitsa operation of the **Belorussian Front.** The overall *Stavka* plan, probably formulated in early November, called for **1st Baltic Front** to strike from its salient west of Nevel southward to Polotsk and west of Vitebsk to destroy the German Vitebsk Group in concert with **Western Front** attacks on the Orsha and Bogushevsk axes. Simultaneously, **Belorussian Front** forces would advance from their Dnepr bridgeheads near Loev along the Rechitsa-Bobruisk axis toward Minsk, supported on the right by **Western Front** forces attacking through Rogachev. One source set out the intent of the *Stavka* plan by quoting from a 1 October *Stavka* order: "While delivering the main blow in the general direction of Zhlobin, Bobruisk, and Minsk, destroy the enemy Zhlobin-Bobruisk group and secure the capital of Belorussia, Minsk. Detach a separate group of forces to attack along the northern bank of the Pripiat River in the direction of Kalinkovichi and Zhitkovichi."[23] In his memoirs, K. N. Galitsky, commander of **1st Baltic Front's 11th Guards Army**, also spells out initial *Stavka* intent to "isolate the Vitebsk-Gorodok enemy grouping," according to another source apparently in concert with an airborne operation into Belorussia.[24]

Obviously, the airborne operation was canceled, and the intended strategic offensive failed for a number of reasons, including bad weather and intense German resistance. Soviet historians have written about the series of operations west of Nevel, the Gorodok operations of November and December 1943, the Gomel-Rechitsa operation of November, and the Rogachev-Zhlobin operation of February 1944. They have been utterly silent, however, concerning subsequent operations by **1st Baltic** and **Belorussian Fronts** during the period and until recently, have ignored entirely operations by **Western Front**. Soviet military encyclopedic literature ignores the operations, and the recent Krivosheev volume fails to mention losses in these additional operations and the overall losses of participating fronts during the lengthy period. The only exception to this neglect is the recent important revelations by M. A. Gareev concerning the multiple failed operations by **Western Front** during this period.[25]

German unit histories, memoirs, and archival materials, however, amply attest to the scope, intensity, and duration of Soviet offensive efforts against German forces in Belorussia during this entire period.[26] Unless additional Soviet materials become available, the history of these operations will, of necessity, once again have to be based on German sources alone.

Soviet Attempts to Exploit Offensive Success in Spring 1944

One of the most difficult tasks of a military historian is to determine the ultimate scope and aims of a strategic operation, even if that strategic offensive is successful. According to its general pattern of behavior, the *Stavka* understandably tended to expand its strategic objectives while operations were underway. This occurred during the Winter Campaign of 1941–42, the Winter Campaign of 1942–43, and the Summer–Fall Campaign of 1943. In general, this expansion of offensive aims could be justified on the basis that one could not determine whether or when German collapse would occur, and, unless one pressed the attack, opportunities would be lost. Of course, relative risk had to be assessed, lest the attacking force fall victim to the kind of trap that Manstein sprang on Soviet forces in the Donbas.

The success of Soviet strategic offensives in 1944 and 1945 makes it more difficult to assess whether military operations at the end of the offensive were simply attempts to exploit success or were designed to posture forces more advantageously for subsequent offensive action (or to deceive the enemy regarding future offensive intentions). Two such operations pose serious questions for historians. The first involves a failed offensive late in the Winter–Spring Campaign of 1944, which the Germans label as major and which Soviet historians generally ignore; and the second (covered later) involves an apparent major attempt by Soviet forces at the end of the Summer–Fall Campaign of 1944 to penetrate deep into East Prussia.

The first of these operations is called the Battle of Targul-Frumos (2–4 May 1944), during which, according to German sources, German forces defeated a major Soviet offensive and inflicted heavy losses on the attacking Soviet forces. Subsequently, the battle has been used as a prime case study in officer tactical education (along with the Chir battles of December 1942 and the Nikopol battles of 1943–44).

The Battle of Targul-Frumos (2–4 May 1944)

According to German sources, foremost of which are studies by Hasso von Manteuffel, commander of *Grossdeutschland Panzer-Grenadier Division,* and Fridolin von Senger und Etterlin, the battle was precipitated when large Soviet forces struck German positions north of Iassy in an attempt to seize the city and advance deep into Romania.[27] The Germans identified the attacking force as **2d Tank Army** and cooperating **27th Army.** In three days of fighting, from 2–4 May, *LVII Panzer Corps* (principally *Grossdeutschland* and *24th Panzer Division*s) and *L Corps* defeated the Soviet force and destroyed over 350 Soviet tanks.

Soviet sources are silent on the battle. Scattered references appear in divisional histories concerning combat in Romania during this period, but only **2d Tank Army'**s history makes direct reference to this particular battle. It notes that in late March 1944, the tank army regrouped into **27th Army'**s sector with the mission of "attacking in the direction of Fokuri and Podul-Iloaei. Subsequently, the army was to strike a blow toward the city of Iassy and secure it."[28] In its narrative of subsequent operations, the history relates that the tank army attacked with **27th Army's 35th Rifle Corps,** and, although **3d Tank Corps** reached Targul-Frumos, it was thrown back by heavy German counterattacks. The account attributes the Soviet failure to a poor artillery preparation and German advance warning that the attack was to occur.

Historians are thus left with the question of whether the Soviet offensive was a major effort to penetrate into Romania or simply a local assault to improve the Soviet operational posture and opportunities for a renewed offensive in the future. The Germans maintain it was the former. This author has argued that it was the latter and was also associated with deception planning for future operations in Belorussia (to fix the future presence of **2d Tank Army** in Romania, while it was shortly moved elsewhere).[29] Only further release of Soviet archival materials will settle this long-standing debate.

Soviet (1st Belorussian Front's) Actions East of Warsaw in August–September 1944

No Eastern Front action has generated more heated controversy then Soviet operations east of Warsaw in August and September 1944, at the time of the Warsaw Uprising against the Germans by the Polish Home Army. Western historians have routinely blamed the Soviets for deliberately failing to assist the Poles, and in essence, aiding and abetting destruction of the Polish rebels by the German Army for political reasons. Soviet historians have countered that every attempt was made to provide assistance, but that operational considerations precluded such help. No complete single Soviet volume exists which recounts in detail these operations on the approaches to Warsaw. The historian is forced to reconstruct events by referring to a host of fragmentary sources. Ironically, German archival materials, in particular *2d Army* records and other materials (and probably the records of *9th Army,* captured by the Soviets and unavailable to Western historians), help to justify the Soviet argument.

Operational details about Soviet combat on the approaches to Warsaw can be reconstructed from fragmentary Soviet and German archival sources. On 28 July 1994, Gen. Major A. I. Radzievsky's **2d Tank Army,** which had been turned north from the Magnuszew region to strike at Warsaw, with three corps abreast, engaged the *73d Infantry Division* and the *Hermann Göring Parachute Panzer Division* 40 kilometers southeast of Warsaw. A race ensued between Radzievsky, who was seeking to seize the routes into Warsaw from the east, and the Germans, who were attempting to keep these routes open and maintain possession of Warsaw.[30] The nearest Soviet forces within supporting range of Radzievsky were **47th Army** and **11th Tank** and **2d Guards Cavalry Corps,** then fighting for possession of Seidlce, 50 kilometers to the east. On 29 July, Radzievsky dispatched his **8th Guards** and **3d Tank Corps** northward in an attempt to swing northeast of Warsaw and turn the German defender's left flank, while his **16th Tank Corps** continued to fight on the southeastern approaches to the city's suburbs.

Although **8th Guards Tank Corps** successfully fought to within 20 kilometers east of the city, **3d Tank Corps** ran into a series of successive panzer counterattacks orchestrated by Model, commander of *Army Group Center.* Beginning on 30 July, the *Hermann Göring* and *19th Panzer Divisions* struck the overextended and weakened tank corps north of Wolomin, 15 kilometers northeast of Warsaw.

Although the corps withstood three days of counterattacks, on 2 and 3 August, the *4th Panzer Division* and the *5th SS-Panzer Division "Wiking"* joined the fight. In three days of intense fighting, **3d Tank Corps** was severely mauled, and **8th Guards Tank Corps** was also severely pressed. By 5 August, **47th Army** forces had arrived in the region, and **2d Tank Army** was withdrawn for rest and refitting. The three rifle corps of **47th Army** were now stretched out along a front of 80 kilometers from south of Warsaw to Seidlce and were unable to renew the drive on Warsaw or to the Narew River. German communications lines eastward to *Army Group Center,* then fighting for its life north and west of Brest, had been damaged but not severed.

Meanwhile, on 1 August, the Polish Home Amy had launched an insurrection in the city. Although they seized large areas in downtown Warsaw, the insurgents failed to secure the four bridges over the Vistula and were unable to hold the eastern suburbs of the city (Praga). During the ensuing weeks, while the Warsaw uprising progressed and ultimately failed, the Soviets continued their drive against *Army Group Center* northeast of Warsaw. For whatever motive, **1st Belorussian Front** focused on holding firmly to the Magnuszew bridgehead, which was subjected to heavy German counterattacks throughout mid-August, and on driving forward across the Bug River to seize crossings over the Narew River necessary to facilitate future offensive operations.

Soviet **47th Army** remained the only major force opposite Warsaw until 20 August, when it was joined by the **1st Polish Army.** Soviet forces finally broke out across the Bug River on 3 September, closed up to the Narew River the following day, and fought their way into bridgeheads across the Narew on 6 September. On 13 September, lead elements of two Polish divisions assaulted across the Vistula River into Warsaw, but made little progress and were evacuated back across the river on 23 September.[31]

Political considerations and motivations aside, an objective consideration of combat in the region indicates that, prior to early September, German resistance was sufficient to halt any Soviet assistance to the Poles in Warsaw, were it intended. Thereafter, it would have required a major reorientation of military efforts from Magnuszew in the south or, more realistically, from the Bug and Narew River axis in the north, in order to muster sufficient force to break into Warsaw. And once broken into, Warsaw would have been a costly city to clear of Germans and an unsuitable location from which to launch a new offensive.

This skeletal portrayal of events outside of Warsaw demonstrates that much more needs to be revealed and written about these operations. It is certain that additional German sources exist upon which to base an expanded account. It is equally certain that extensive documentation remains in Soviet archival holdings. Release and use of this information can help answer and lay to rest this burning historical controversy.

Soviet Attempts to Exploit Offensive Success in Fall 1944

As was the case in spring 1944, there were many opportunities accorded to Soviet forces to exploit success in the wake of the Belorussian and associated strategic operations in late summer and fall 1944. The most prominent of these, as evidenced from German archival sources, occurred in October 1944, hard on the heels of the Soviet Memel operation, during which Soviet forces drove from the Siauliai region to the shores of the Baltic Sea. Immediately after the end of the Memel operation, multiple Soviet armies, subordinate to Chemiakhovsky's **3d Belorussian Front,** attempted to penetrate deep into East Prussia along the Gumbinnen axis.

The Gumbinnen or Goldap Operation (16–27 October 1944)

German documents cover this operation in considerable detail and focus, in particular, mobile operations by **2d Guards Tank Corps** south of Gumbinnen.[32] Soviet accounts are restricted to a single article and several passages from the memoirs of participants and unit histories.[33]

According to these sources, the *Stavka* authorized Chemiakhovsky to exploit the success achieved in the Memel operation by striking into the Prussian heartland along the Gumbinnen-Königsberg axis. The front commander planned to penetrate German defenses with **5th** and **11th Guards Armies** and then exploit with **2d Guards Tank Corps** and second echelon (and fresh) **28th Army. 31st** and **39th Armies** on the flanks would support the assault. On 16 October, Colonel General N. I. Krylov's **5th** and Colonel General K. N. Galitsky's **11th Guards Armies** went into action and drove 11 kilometers into the German defenses. The following day, **31st** and **39th Armies** joined the assault, and Galitsky's army crossed the East Prussian border of Germany. German resistance was fierce, and German fortified lines were so formidable that it took four days for Chemiakhovsky to penetrate the tactical defenses. The second defense line, along the German border, was so strong that Cherniakhovsky committed his tank corps to overcome it. Together, on 20 October, **11th Guards Army** and **2d Guards Tank Corps** finally ruptured the defense and approached the outskirts of Gumbinnen. The next day, Cherniakhovsky committed Lieutenant General A. A. Luchinsky's **28th Army** to battle, but the entire forces' advance faltered in the Stallupinen Defensive Region as heavy German panzer reinforcements arrived to stiffen the defense. Fighting continued until 27 October as the flank Soviet armies closed up with **11th Guards Army**'s forward positions. At a cost of heavy casualties (by German count), Soviet forces had advanced from 50–100 kilometers into East Prussia and learned from experience what extensive preparations would be required in the future to conquer Germany's East Prussian bastion.

The Gumbinnen operation stands as an example of an operation that had considerable impact on the manner in which Soviet forces would operate in the future. With the earlier Targul-Frumos operation and other unmentioned cases, it also raises serious questions about ultimate Soviet strategic aims in the waning stages of significant strategic operations. Again, accounts of the operation would be more thorough and conclusions more valid if the operation could be recounted and evaluated from Soviet as well as German sources.

Conclusions

What has been presented here is a sample of gaps in the operational history of the German-Soviet War. While the sample identifies many significant gaps, it is the product of only one historian's work, and even this historian can list many others. To the list must be added the many cases used by the modern German Army in its officers' education, to include the battles along the Chir (December 1942) and in the Donbas (February 1943), the various Nikopol battles, and many others, all of which rest on the basis of only one-sided German accounts. Other neglected areas span the entire war and include such topics as the encirclement and destruction of **Soviet 6th** and **12th Armies** at Uman, operations on the Kharkov and Kursk axes in late summer and fall of 1941, plans for offensive action in the north in winter 1943 (by *Group Khozin*), operations in the Staraia-Russa-Nevel sector in the autumn of 1943, and operations to reduce *Army Group North* after its isolation in Kurland in October 1944.

Investigation of all of these issues and others will cast more accurate light on the war and will help dispel the many myths that the war has produced, myths which have and will continue to victimize the Soviet (Russian) Army and Soviet (Russian) historiography. In the final analysis, the old axiom remains correct – that it is better to relate one's own history than to have someone else relate it.

Notes

1. For example, see Viktor Suvorov (ne Rezin), *Ledokol* [Icebreaker] and *Den-M* [M-Day], whose preposterous claims about blame for the war pervert history for political purposes and profit.

2. See, for example, such superb superb military analyses as those done by. D. M. Proektor on the Dukla Pass operation; A. A. Sidorenko on the Mogilev operation; V. Matsulenko on the Iassy-Kishinev operation and on a host of specialized themes; and equally candid and detailed memoirs by Moskalenko, Galitsky, Bagramian, Solomatin, Katukov, Batov, and many others. The groundbreaking and detailed studies of John Erickson raised the veil on Eastern Front operations for Western readers.

3. For example, see G. Kuleshov, *"Na Dneprovskom rubezhe"* [On the Dnepr line], *Voenno-istoricheskii zhurnal.* 6 (June 1966): 16–28 (hereafter cited as *VIZh*) and V. Bytkov. *"Kontrudar 5-iu mekhanizirovannoiu korpusa na lelelskom napravlenii"* [The counterstroke of 5th Mechanized Corps on the Lepel axis]. *VIZh*, 9 (September 1971): 60–65.

4. For example, see V. Shevchuk, *"Deistviia operativnykh grupp voisk v Smolenskom srazhenii (10 iiulia–10 sentiabriia 1941 g.)"* [The actions of operational groups of forces in the Battle of Smolensk]. *VIZh,* 12 (December 1979): 10–14.

5. A. V. Vladimirsky, *Na kievskom napravlenii* [On the Kiev axis]. (Moscow: Voenizdat, 1989).

6. A. A. Volko, *Nezavershennye frontovye nastupatelnye operatsii pervykh kampanii Velikoi Otechestvennoi voiny* [Incomplete front offensive operations of the initial campaigns of the Great Patriotic War]. (Moscow: Aviar, 1992).

7. B. Panov, N. Naumov, *"Vosstanovlenie strategicheskogo fronta na Zapadnom napravlenii (iiul 1941 g.)"* [Restoration of the strategic front on the Western axis (June 1941)]. *VIZh*, 8 (August 1976): 15–23.

8. For example, see numerous short articles such as E. Klimchuk, *"Vtoraia udarnaia i Vlasov,"* [2d Shock and Vlasov], *Sovetskii voin* [Soviet soldier], 20: 1989, 76–81; and V. A. Chernukhin, *"Na liubanskom napravlanii"* [On the Liuban axis]. *VIZh*, 8 (August 1992): 43–45. Stanislav Gagarin has also published a novel about the operation *Miasnoi Bor*, which has been serialized in *VIZh*.

9. For details, see David M. Glantz, *A History of Soviet Airborne Forces* (London: Frank Cass, 1994), 231–262.

10. A. Vasilevsky, *"Nekotorye voprosy rukovodstva vooruzhennoi borboi letom 1942 goda"* (Some questions concerning the direction of armed struggle in the summer of 1942]. *VIZh*, 8 (August 1965): 3–10; M. Kazakov, *"Na voronezhskom napravlenii letom 1942 goda"*(On the Voronezh axis in the summer of 1942]. *VIZh*, 10 (October 1964): 27–44; Kh. Bagramian, *Tak shli mv k pobeda* [As we went on to victory]. (Moscow: Voenizdat, 1977): 48–140; and K. S. Moskalenko, *Na iugo-zapadnom napravlenii* [On the southwestern axis]. (Moscow: "Nauka," 1969): 133–218. Of course, the best source is the period war experience volume, *"Opisanie operatsii voisk iugo-zapadnogo fronta na Kharkovskom napravlenii v mae 1942 goda"* [An account of the operations of

Southwestern Front forces on the Kharkov axis in May 1942] in *Sbornik voenno-istoricheskikh materialov Velikoi Otechestvennoi voiny* [Collection of military-historical materials of the Great Patriotic War]. 5 (Moscow: Voenizdat, 1951). Hereafter sited as *SVIMVOV*.

11. M. I. Kazakov, *"Boevye deistviia voisk Brianskogo i Voronezhskogo frontov letom 1942 na voronezhskom napralanii"* [Combat operations of Briansk and Voronezh Front forces on the Voronezh axis in summer 1942] in *SVIMVOV*, 15: 115–116.

12. G. Zhukov, *Reminiscences and Reflections*, (Moscow: Progress, 1985): 129–133.

13. M. D. Solomalin. *Krasnogradtsy* [The men of Krasnograd]. (Moscow: Voenizdat, 1963) 11–44.

14. M. E. Katukov, *Na ostrie glavnogo udara* [At the point of the main attack]. (Moscow: Voenizdat, 1976) 182–184.

15. A. Kh. Babadzhanian, *Dorogy pobedy* [Roads of victory]. (Moscow: Voenizdat, 1981) 99.

16. *Sovietskaia kavaleriia* [Soviet cavalry]. (Moscow: Voenizdat, 1984), 216.

17. For complete details, see *Anlage 5 zum Tatigkeitsbericht der Abteilung Ic/AO* [*Annex 5 to Activity Report of the Intelligence Staff Section/Army Headquarters*] in *AOK 9 (9th Army) 27970/6*, dated 1 July–31 December 1942, NAM T-312, Roll 304. These *Anlagen* contain full reports on the offensive with a complete Soviet order of battle and full assessments of the strengths and estimated losses of participating Soviet units. For example, **1st Mechanized Corps,** reinforced by the **47th** and **48th Mechanized Brigades,** had an initial strength of about 300 tanks and lost 85 percent of its armor in the operation.

18. For general officer losses, see A. A. Maslov, "Soviet general officer losses in the 1st period of the Great Patriotic War," *The Journal of Slavic Military Studies*, Vol. 7: 3 (September 1994).

19. See A. G ershov, *Osvobozhdenie Donbassa* [Liberation of the Donbas]. (Moscow Voenizdat, 1973); V. Morozov, *"Pochemu ne sovershalos nastuplenie v Donbasse vesnoi 1943 goda"* [Why was the offensive in the Donbas not completed in the spring of 1943?]. *VIZh,* 3 (March 1963): 16–33; and a variety of unit histories such as those of **4th Guards Tank Corps** and the **195th** and **35th Guards Rifle Divisions.**

20. See also the unit histories of **11th Tank Corps** and the **69th, 102d, 194th, 354th Rifle Divisions** and **1st Guards Motorized Rifle Division.** The best single source on planning for the operation is K. Rokossovsky, *Soldatskii dolg* [A soldier's duty]. (Moscow: Voenizdat).

21. See, for example, "Situation maps and overlays (1: 300,000), prepared by the 2d Army, Intelligence Officer (Ic/ AO), December 1942–July 1943." *AOK 2 (2d Army) 31811/23*, NAM T -312, Roll 1223 and a series of *"Chefkarten and Anlagen,"* Pz *AOK 2. Ia* (2d Panzer Army Operations Staff Section), NAM T-313, Roll 171.

22. G. F. Krivosheev, *Grif sekretnosti sniat: poteri vooruzhennykh sil SSSR v voinakh. boevykh deistviakh. i voennykh konfliktakh* [Classification secret removed: losses of the USSR's armed forces in wars, combat actions, and military conflicts]. (Moscow: Voenizdat, 1993). This is but one of many gaps in this otherwise useful and enlightening book.

23. I. Glebov, *"Manevr voisk v Chernigovsko-Pripiatskoi i Gomelsko-Rechitskoi nastupatel nykh operatsiakh"* [Maneuver of forces in the Chemigov-Pripiat and Gomel-Rechitsa offensive operations]. *VIZh,* 1 (January 1976): 13.

24. K. N. Galilsky, *Gody surovykh ispytanii 1941–1944* [Years of rigorous education 1941-1944], (Moscow: "Nauka," 1973). 347–348; and M. Absaliamov, *"Iz opyta vzaimodeistviia vozdushnykh dsantov s partisanami v Velikoi Otechestvennoi voine"* [From

the experience of the cooperation of airborne forces with partisans in the Great Patriotic War]. *VIZh*, 11 (November 1964): 104–108.

25. M. A. Gareev, *"Prichny i uroki neudachnykh nastupatelnykh operatsii Zapadnogo fronta zimoi 1943/44 goda"* [The causes and lessons of unsuccessful Western Front operations in winter 1943/44]. *Voennaia mysl* [Military Thought], 2 (February 1994): 50–58; and M. A. Gareev, *"O neudachnykh nastupatelnykh operatsiakh sovetskikh voisk v Velikoi Otechestvennoi voine. Po neopublikovannym dokumentam GKO"* [About unsuccessful offensive operations of Soviet forces in the Great Patriotic War. According to unpublished GKO documents]. *Novaia i noveishaia istoriia* [New and newer history]. 1 (January 1994): 3–29. The two superb studies by Gareev exemplify what must be done to fill in the historical gaps in the history of the war.

26. In particular, see the operational and intelligence records of *3d Panzer Army* and *4th Army*. *9th Army* records, which were captured by the Soviets and do not exist in the West, also should provide details on these failed Soviet operations. See also such excellent German unit histories as A. D. von Plato, *Die Geschichte der 5. Panzerdivision 1938 bis 1942* [The history of 5th Panzer Division, 1938–1945]. (Regensburg: Walhalla u. Praetoria, 1978).

27. For details, see Manteuffel, *The Battle of Targul-Frumos* (unpublished manuscript and briefing, 1948); and Senger und Etterlin, *Der Gegenschlag* [The encounter battle], n.p., n.d., which covers all of these popular German case studies.

28. F. I. Vysolsky, M. E. Makukhin, F. M, Sarychev, M. K. Shaposhnikov, *Gvareiskaia tankovaia* [Guards tank]. (Moscow: Voenizdat, 1963), 101–106.

29. David M. Glantz, *Soviet Military Deception in the Second World War* (London: Frank Cass, 1989), 350–356.

30. Among the few sources on this operation are A. Radzievsky, *"Na puti k Varshave"* [On the path to Warsaw]. *VIZh*, 10 (October 1971): 68–77; and Iu. V. Ivanov, I. N. Kosenko, *"Kto kogo predar."* [Who Betrayed Whom], VIZh, No. 3 (March 1993), 16-24.

31. R. Nazarevich, *"Varshavskoe vostanie 1944 g.,"* *Novaia i noveishaia istoriia.* 2 (February 1989): 186–210.

32. See a particularly detailed account in *3d Panzer Army* records.

33. M. Alekseev, *"Nachalo boev v Vostochnoi Prussii"* [The beginning of combat in Belorussia]. *VIZh*, 10 (October 1964): 11–22; Krivosheev, 227, provides casualty figures for what he calls the Goldap operation.

Selected Bibliography

Adair, Paul. *Hitler's Greatest Defeat*. London: Arms and Armour, 1994.

Anders, Wladyslaw. *Hitler's Defeat in Russia*. Chicago: Regnery, 1953.

— — —. *Russian Volunteers in Hitler's Army*. Bayside, NY: Axis Europa, 1998.

Andreas-Friedrich, Ruth. *Battleground Berlin: Diaries, 1945–48*. New York: Paragon House, 1990.

Andronnikov, N. G., A. S. Galitsan, M. M. Kiryan, Yu. G. Perechnev, and Yu V. Plotnikov. *Velikaya Otechestvennaya Voina 1941–1945. Slovar-Spravoynik*. (The Great Patriotic War, 1941–1945. Dictionary-reference). Moscow: Political Literature, 1983.

Argyle, Christopher. *Chronology of World War II*. New York: Exeter, 1980.

Armstrong, John A. *Ukrainian Nationalism, 1939–1945*. New York: Columbia Univ. Press, 1955.

Armstrong, John, ed. *Soviet Partisans in World War II*. Madison: Univ. of Wisconsin Press, 1964.

Armstrong, Richard N. *Red Armor Combat Orders: Combat Regulations for Tank and Mechanized Forces 1944*. Essex: Frank Cass, 1991.

— — —. *Red Army Tank Commanders: The Armored Guards*. Atglen, PA: Schiffer, 1994.

— — —. *Soviet Operational Deception: The Red Cloak*. Ft. Leavenworth: Command and General Staff College, 1988.

Axell, Albert. *Stalin's War: Through the Eyes of His Commanders*. London: Arms and Armour, 1997.

Axworthy, Mark, et al. *Third Axis Fourth Ally: Rumanian Armed Forces in the European War*. London: Arms and Armour, 1995.

Bahm, Karl. *Berlin 1945: The Final Reckoning*. Osceola, WI: Motorbooks, 2002.

Barbier, M. K. *Kursk: The Greatest Tank Battle, 1943*. Osceola, WI: Motorbooks, 2002.

Bartov, Omer. *Eastern Front, 1941–1945: German Troops and the Barbarization of Warfare*. New York: St. Martin's, 1996.

Beevor, Antony. *The Fall of Berlin, 1945*. New York: Viking, 2002.

GPO = U.S. Government Printing Office.

— — —. *Stalingrad: The Fateful Siege: 1942–1943.* New York: Viking, 1998.

Bergstrom, C., and A. Mikhailov. *Black Cross, Red Star: The Air War over the Eastern Front,* Vol. 1. Pacifica, CA: Pacifica Military History, 2000.

— — —. *Black Cross, Red Star: The Air War over the Eastern Front,* Vol. 2. Pacifica, CA: Pacifica Military History, 2001.

Bernad, Denes. *Rumanian Air Force: The Prime Decade, 1938–1947.* Carrollton, TX: Squadron/Signal, 1999.

Bialer, Seweryn, ed. *Stalin and His Generals.* New York: Pegasus, 1969.

Bidermann, Herbert. *In Deadly Combat: A German Soldier's Memoir of the Eastern Front.* Lawrence: Univ. Press of Kansas, 2000.

Boatner, III, Mark M. *The Biographical Dictionary of World War II.* Novato, CA: Presidio, 1996.

Boog, Horst, et al. *Germany and the Second World War,* Vol. 4, *Attack on the Soviet Union.* Oxford: Clarendon, 1999.

Buchner, Alex. *Ostfront 1944: German Defensive Battles on the Russian Front, 1944.* West Chester, PA: Schiffer, 1991.

Carell, Paul. *Hitler Moves East, 1941–1943.* New York: Bantam, 1965.

— — —. *Scorched Earth: The Russo-German War, 1943–1944.* London: Harrap, 1970.

— — —. *Stalingrad: Defeat of the German 6th Army.* Atglen, PA: Schiffer, 1993.

Carruthers, Bob, and John Erickson. *Russian Front, 1941–1945.* London: Cassell, 2000.

Chaney, Jr., Otto Preston. *Zhukov.* Norman: Oklahoma Univ. Press, 1971.

Chew, Allen F. *Fighting the Russians in Winter: Three Case Studies.* Leavenworth Paper. Washington, D.C.: GPO, 1981.

Chuikov, Vasili. *Battle for Stalingrad.* New York: Holt, Rinehart and Winston, 1964.

— — —. *Fall of Berlin.* New York: Holt, Rinehart and Winston, 1967.

Clark, Alan. *Barbarossa: The Russian-German Conflict, 1941–45.* New York: William Morrow, 1965.

Columbia University War Documents Project Staff. *Soviet Partisan Movement in WW II: Summary.* Maxwell AFB, 1954.

Conversino, Mark J. *Fighting with the Soviets: The Failure of Operation Frantic.* Lawrence: Univ. Press of Kansas, 1998.

Cooper, Matthew. *The German Air Force, 1933–1945: An Anatomy of Failure.* New York: Jane's, 1981.

— — —. *The Nazi War Against Soviet Partisans, 1941–1944*. New York: Stein and Day, 1979.

Corti, Eugenio. *Few Returned: Twenty-Eight Days on the Russian Front*. Univ. of Missouri Press, 1997.

Crofoot, Craig. *Order of Battle of the Soviet Armed Forces*, Vol. 1, Part 1. West Chester, OH: Nafziger Collection, 2001.

— — —. *Order of Battle of the Soviet Armed Forces*, Vol. 1, 22 June 1941. Madison, WI: Craig M. Crofoot, 2000.

Cross, Robin. *Citadel: The Battle of Kursk*. New York: Sarpedon, 1993.

Dallin, Alexander. *German Rule in Russia, 1941–1945: A Study of Occupation Policies*. London: Macmillan, 1957.

Drum, Karl. *Airpower and Russian Partisan Warfare*. New York: Arno, 1962.

Duffy, Christopher. *Red Storm on the Reich*. New York: Atheneum, 1991.

Dunn, Walter S. *Hitler's Nemesis: The Red Army, 1930–1945*. Westport, CT: Praeger, 1994.

— — —. *Kursk: Hitler's Gamble*. Westport, CT: Praeger, 1997.

— — —. *Soviet Blitzkrieg: The Battle for White Russia, 1944*. Boulder, CO: Lynne Rienner, 2000.

Dupuy, T. N., ed. *Historical Scenarios of Soviet Breakthrough Efforts in WWII*. McLean, VA: NOVA, 1971.

Dupuy, T. N. and Paul Martell. *Great Battles of the Eastern Front: Soviet German War, 1941–1945*. Indianapolis: Bobbs-Merrill, 1982.

Elting, John R. *Battles for Scandinavia*. Time-Life World War II series. Alexandria, VA: Time-Life Books, 1981.

Erfurth, Waldemar. *Der Finnische Krieg, 1941–1944*. Wiesbaden Germany: Limes Verlag, 1977.

Erickson, John (commentary). *Main Front: Soviet Leaders Look Back on World War II*. London: Brassey's, 1987.

Erickson, John. *The Road to Berlin*. New York: Harper and Row, 1983.

— — —. *The Road to Stalingrad*. New York: Harper and Row, 1975.

— — —. *The Soviet High Command*. London: Frank Cass, 2001.

Erickson, John, and David Dilks. *Barbarossa: The Axis and the Allies*. Edinburgh: Edinburgh Univ. Press, 1994.

Esteban-Infantes, Emilio. *Blaue Division: Spaniens Freiwillige an der Ostfront* (The Blue Division: Spain's volunteers on the Eastern Front). Leoni: Druffel, 1958.

Fowler, Will. *Eastern Front: The Unpublished Photographs, 1941–1945*. Osceola, WI: Motorbooks, 2001.

Fugate, Bryan. *Operation Barbarossa*. Novato, CA: Presidio, 1984.

Gebhardt, James. *The Petsamo-Kirkenes Operation: Soviet Breakthrough and Pursuit in the Arctic, October 1944.* Leavenworth Papers No. 17. Washington, D.C.: GPO, 1989.

Gellerman, Günter. *Die Armee Wenck – Hitlers letzte Hoffnung* (Army Wenck – Hitler's last hope). Koblenz: Bernard & Graefe, 1983.

Gerbet, Klaus, ed. *Generalfeldmarschall Fedor von Bock: The War Diary, 1939–1945.* Atglen, PA: Schiffer, 1996.

Geust, Carl-Fredrik. *Under the Red Star.* Shrewsbury: Airlife, 1995.

Glantz, David M. *Atlas and Survey: Prelude to Kursk.* Carlisle, PA: David M. Glantz, 1998.

— — —. *Atlas of Operation Blau, 28 June–18 November 1942.* Carlisle, PA: Glantz, 1998.

— — —. *Atlas of the Battle of Kursk.* Carlisle, PA: Glantz, 1997.

— — —. *Atlas of the Battle of Leningrad: Breaking the Blockade and Liberation.* Carlisle, PA: Glantz, 2001.

— — —. *Atlas of the Battle of Leningrad: Soviet Defense and the Blockade.* Carlisle, PA: Glantz, 2001.

— — —. *Atlas of the Battle of Moscow,* Vol. 2, *The Soviet Offensive.* Carlisle, PA: Glantz, 1998.

— — —. *Atlas of the Battle of Smolensk, 7 July–10 September 1941.* Carlisle, PA: Glantz, 2001.

— — —. *Atlas of the L'vov-Sandomiersz Offensive, 13 July–29 August 1944.* Carlisle, PA: Glantz, 2001.

— — —. *Atlas of the War on the Eastern Front, 1941–1945.* Carlisle, PA: Glantz, 1996.

— — —. *Battle for Smolensk, 7 July–10 September 1941.* Carlisle, PA: Glantz, 2001.

— — —. *Barbarossa: Hitler's Invasion of Russia, 1941.* Stroud, England: Tempus, 2001.

— — —. *Forgotten Battles of the German-Soviet War,* Vol. 1. Carlisle, PA: Glantz, 1999.

— — —. *Forgotten Battles of the German-Soviet War,* Vol. 2. Carlisle, PA: Glantz, 1999.

— — —. *Forgotten Battles of the German-Soviet War,* Vol. 3. Carlisle, PA: Glantz, 1999.

— — —. *Forgotten Battles of the German-Soviet War,* Vol. 4. Carlisle, PA: Glantz, 1999.

— — —. *Forgotten Battles of the German-Soviet War.* Vol. 5. Part 1. Carlisle, PA: Glantz, 2000.

— — —. *Forgotten Battles of the German-Soviet W ar.* Vol. 5. Part 2. Carlisle, PA: Glantz, 2000.

———. *From the Don to the Dnepr: Soviet Offensive Operations.* Essex: Frank Cass, 1991.

———. *The History of Soviet Airborne Forces.* Portland, OR: Frank Cass, 1994.

———. *The Initial Period of War on the Eastern Front: June–August 1941.* Portland, OR: Frank Cass, 1993.

———. *Kharkov 1942.* Hersham, UK: Ian Allan, 2002.

———. *Kharkov 1942: Anatomy of a Military Disaster.* Rockville Centre: Sarpedon, 1998.

———. *L'vov-Sandomiersz: The Soviet General Staff Study.* Carlisle, PA: Glantz, 1998.

———. *The Military Strategy of the Soviet Union.* Essex: Cass, 1993.

———. *Operation Mars: Marshal Zhukov's Greatest Defeat.* Carlisle, PA: Glantz, 1998.

———. *Red Army in 1943: Central Command and Control Organs and Leaders.* Carlisle, PA: Glantz, 1999.

———. *Red Army in 1943: Strength, Organization, and Equipment.* Carlisle, PA: Glantz, 1999.

———. *The Role of Intelligence in Soviet Military Strategy in World War II.* Novato, CA: Presidio, 1990.

———. *The Siege of Leningrad.* Staplehurst, UK: Spellmount, 2001.

———. *The Soviet Airborne Experience.* Ft. Leavenworth: U.S. Army Command and General Staff College, 1984.

———. *Soviet Defensive Tactics at Kursk.* Ft. Leavenworth: U.S. Army Command and General Staff College, 1986.

———. *Soviet Documents on the Use of War Experience,* Vol. 2. *Winter Campaign, 1941–1942.* Essex: Frank Cass, 1991.

———. *Soviet Documents on the Use of War Experience,* Vol. 3. *Military Operations, 1941 and 1942.* Essex: Frank Cass, 1993.

———. *Soviet-German War 1941–1945: Myths and Realities: A Survey Essay.* Carlisle, PA: Glantz, 2002.

———. *Soviet Military Deception in the Second World War.* Essex: Frank Cass, 1989.

———. *Soviet Military Intelligence in War.* Essex: Frank Cass, 1990.

———. *Soviet Military Operational Art: In Pursuit of Deep Battle.* Essex: Frank Cass, 1991.

———. *Stumbling Colossus: The Red Army on the Eve of World War.* Lawrence: Univ. Press of Kansas, 1998.

———. *Zhukov's Greatest Defeat: The Red Army's Epic Disaster in Operation MARS, 1942.* Lawrence: Univ. Press of Kansas, 1999.

Glantz, David M., and Jonathan House. *The Battle of Kursk.* Lawrence: Univ. Press of Kansas, 1999.

————. *When Titans Clashed: How the Red Army Stopped Hitler.* Lawrence: Univ. Press of Kansas, 1996.

Glantz, David M., and H. Orenstein. *Battle for Kursk 1943: The Soviet General Staff Study.* London: Frank Cass, 1999.

————. *The Battle for Lvov, July 1944: The Soviet General Staff Study.* London: Frank Cass.

————. *Belorussia 1944: The Soviet General Staff Study.* London: Frank Cass, 2001.

————. *Kursk 1943: The Soviet General Staff Study.* Carlisle, PA: Glantz, 1997.

Goerlitz, Walter. *Paulus and Stalingrad.* New York: Citadel, 1963.

Golley, John. *Hurricanes over Murmansk.* Wellingborough: Patrick Stephens, 1987.

Goralski, Robert. *World War II Almanac, 1931–1945.* New York: G. P. Putnam's Sons, 1981.

Gorodetsky, G., and A. Chubarian, eds. *The Soviet Union and the Outbreak of War, 1939–1941.* London: Frank Cass, 2001.

Gorodetsky, Gabriel. *Grand Delusion: Stalin and the German Invasion of Russia.* New Haven, CT: Yale Univ. Press, 1999.

Goure, Leon. *The Siege of Leningrad.* Palo Alto, CA: Stanford Univ. Press, 1962.

Grenkevich, Leonid D. *The Soviet Partisan Movement, 1941–1944.* London: Frank Cass, 1999.

Griehl, Manfred. *Luftwaffe at War. Fighters Over Russia.* Mechanicsburg, PA: Stackpole, 1997.

————. *Luftwaffe at War. German Bombers Over Russia.* Mechanicsburg, PA: Stackpole, 2000.

Grossjohann, Georg. *Five Years, Four Fronts: The War Years of Georg Grossjohann.* Bedford, PA: Aberjona, 1999.

Guderian, Heinz. *Panzer Leader.* London: Futura, 1952.

Gunter, Georg. *Last Laurels: The German Defence of Upper Silesia, Jan–May 1945.* London: Helion, 2002.

Harrison, Mark. *Accounting for War: Soviet Production, Employment and the Defence Burden, 1940–45.* Cambridge: Cambridge Univ. Press, 1996.

Haupt, Werner. *1945: Das Ende im Osten* (The end in the east). Dorheim/Hessen: Podzun, 1970.

————. *Army Group Center: The Wehrmacht in Russia.* Atglen, PA: Schiffer, 1997.

————. *Army Group North: The Wehrmacht in Russia.* Atglen, PA: Schiffer, 1997.

———. *Army Group South: The Wehrmacht in Russia*. Atglen, PA: Schiffer, 1998.

———. *Assault on Moscow, 1941: The Offensive, the Battle, the Retreat*. Atglen, PA: Schiffer, 1996.

———. *Kurland, die Vergessenen Heeresgruppe: 1944/45* (Kurland, the forgotten army group). Friedburg: Podzun-Pallas, 1979.

———. *Kurland: Die Letzte Front — Schicksal für Zwei Armeen* (Kurland: The last front — destiny for two armies). Bad Neuheim: Podzun, 1964.

Haupt, Werner, and Horst Scheibert. *Die Grosse Offensive, 1942: Ziel Stalingrad* (The great offensive, 1942: Objective Stalingrad). Dorheim: Podzun, n.d.

Hays, Otis. *Alaska-Siberia Connection: The World War II Air Route*. College Station: Texas A&M Univ. Press, 1996.

Hayward, Joel S. A. *Stopped at Stalingrad: The Luftwaffe and Hitler's Defeat in the East*. Lawrence: Univ. Press of Kansas, 1998.

Hempel, Andrew. *Poland in World War II: An Illustrated Military History*. New York: Hippocrene, 2000.

Herring, George C. *Aid to Russia, 1941–1946*. New York: Columbia Univ. Press, 1973.

Higgins, Trumbull. *Hitler and Russia: The Third Reich in a Two-Front War, 1937–1943*. New York: Macmillan, 1966.

Hlihor, Constantin, and Ioan Scurtu. *Red Army in Romania*. Yassy: Center for Romanian Studies, 2000.

Hoeffding, Oleg. *German Air Attacks Against Industry and Railroads in Russia*. Santa Monica: Rand, 1970.

Holztraeger, Hans. *In a Raging Inferno: Combat Units of the Hitler Youth, 1944–45*. Solihull, England: Helion, 2000.

Hoyt, Edwin P. *199 Days: The Battle for Stalingrad*. New York: Doherty, 1993.

Institute of Military History, USSR Ministry of Defense. *Voennyi Entsiklopedicheskii Slovar* (Military encyclopedic dictionary). Moscow: Military, 1983.

Jackson, Robert. *Red Falcons: Soviet Air Force in Action, 1919–1969*. Brighton: Clifton, 1970.

Jones, Robert H. *Roads to Russia: United States Lend-Lease to the Soviet Union*. Norman: Univ. of Oklahoma Press, 1969.

Jukes, Geoffrey. *Hitler's Stalingrad Decisions*. Berkeley: Univ. of California Press, 1985.

Kershaw, Robert J., *War Without Garlands: Operation Barbarossa*. Rockville Centre: Sarpedon, 2000.

Kleinfeld, Gerald R., and Lewis A. Tambs. *Hitler's Spanish Legion: The Blue Division in Russia*. Carbondale: Southern Illinois Univ. Press, 1979.

Kliment, Charles, and B. Nakladal. *Germany's First Ally: Armed Forces of the Slovak State, 1939–45*. Atglen, PA: Schiffer, 1998.

Kozlov, Army General M. M., ed. *Velikaya Otechestvennaya Voina, 1941–1945. Entsiklopediya*. (Encyclopedia of the Great Patriotic War, 1941–1945). Moscow: Soviet Encyclopedia, 1985.

Krivosheev, G. F. *Soviet Casualties and Combat Losses in the Twentieth Century*. London: Greenhill, 1997.

Krylov, Marshal N. *Glory Eternal: Defense of Odessa. 1941*. Moscow: Progress, 1972.

Kurowski, Franz. *Brandenburgers: Global Mission*. Winnipeg: Fedorowicz, 1997.

———. *Bridgehead Kurland*. Winnipeg: Fedorowicz, 2002.

———. *Deadlock Before Moscow: Army Group Center, 1942–1943*. West Chester, PA: Schiffer, 1992.

———. *Hitler's Last Bastion: The Final Battles for the Reich, 1944–1945*. Atglen, PA: Schiffer, 1998.

Kuusela, Kari. *Panzers in Finland, 1941–1944*. Helsinki: Wiking-Divisioona Oy, 2000.

Larionov, V. V., et.al. *Evolyutsia Voennogo Iskusstvo: Etapy, Tendentsii, Printsipy* (Evolution of military art: Stages, trends, and principles). Moscow: Military, 1987.

Le Tissier, Tony. *Battle of Berlin, 1945*. New York: St. Martin's, 1988.

———. *Race for the Reichstag: The 1945 Battle for Berlin*. London: Frank Cass, 2000.

———. *With Our Backs to Berlin*. Stroud, England: Sutton, 2001.

———. *Zhukov at the Oder: The Decisive Battle for Berlin*. Westport: Praeger, 1996.

Lepre, George. *Himmler's Bosnian Division: The Waffen-SS Handschar Division*. Atglen, PA: Schiffer, 1997.

Liddell Hart, B. H. *The German Generals Talk*. New York: William Morrow, 1968.

Logusz, Michael O. *Galicia Division: The Waffen-SS 14th Grenadier Division, 1943–45*. Atglen, PA: Schiffer, 1997.

Loza, Dmitriy. *Fighting for the Soviet Motherland*. Lincoln: Univ. of Nebraska Press, 1998.

Loza, Dmitriy. *Commanding the Red Army's Sherman Tanks: The World War II Memoirs of Hero of the Soviet Union Dmitriy Loza*. Lincoln: Univ. of Nebraska Press, 1996.

Loza, Dmitriy. *Attack of the Airacobras: Soviet Aces, American P-39s, and the Air War Against Germany*. Lawrence: Univ. Press of Kansas, 2001.

MacLean, French L. *Quiet Flows the Rhine: German General Officer Casualties in World War II*. Winnipeg: Fedorowicz, 1996.

Main Administration of Cadres, USSR Ministry of Defense. *Komandovaniye Korpusnogo i Divisionogo Zvena Sovetskikh Vooruzhennikh Sil Perioda Belikoi Otechestevennoi Voiny 1941–1945* (Command of corps and division units of the Soviet Armed Forces during the Great Patriotic War, 1941–1945). Moscow: Frunze Military Academy, 1964.

Mannerheim, Carl. *Memoirs of Marshal Mannerheim*. New York: E. P. Dutton, 1954.

March, Cyril, ed. *The Rise and Fall of the German Air Force, 1933–1945*. New York: St. Martin's, 1983.

Maslov, A. A. *Fallen Soviet Generals: Soviet General Officers Killed in Battle 1941–1945*. Essex: Frank Cass, 1998.

Maslov, Aleksander A. *Captured Soviet Generals*. London: Frank Cass, 2001.

Meretskov, Marshal K. A. *Serving the People*. Moscow: Progress, 1971.

Ministero della Difensa. Italian Official History. *Le Operazioni delle Unita Italiane al Fronte Russo, 1941–43*. Roma: Officio Storico, 1977.

Mitcham, Jr., Samuel W. *Crumbling Empire: The German Defeat in the East, 1944*. Westport, CT: Greenwood/Praeger, 2001.

Moynahan, Brian. *Claws of the Bear: A History of Soviet Armed Forces*. London: Hutchinson, 1989.

Muller, Richard. *The German Air War in Russia*. Baltimore: Nautical and Aviation Pub., 1992.

Muller, Rolf-Dieter. *Hitler's War in the East, 1941–1945: A Critical Assessment*. Providence, RI: Berghahn, 1997.

Munoz, Antonio J. *Hitler's Eastern Legions*, Vol. 1, *The Baltic Schutzmannschaft*. Bayside, NY: Axis Europa.

———. *The Kaminski Brigade: A History*. Bayside, NY: Axis Europa.

Murray, Williamson. *Strategy for Defeat: Luftwaffe, 1933–1945*. Maxwell AFB, AL: Air Univ. Press, 1983.

Nash, Douglas E. *Hell's Gate: The Battle of the Cherkassy Pocket, January to February 1944*. Southbury, CT: RZM, 2002.

Newton, Steven H. *Retreat from Leningrad: Army Group North, 1944/1945*. Atglen, PA: Schiffer, 1995.

Niehorster, Leo W. G. *The Royal Hungarian Army, 1920–1945*. Bayside, NY: Axis Europa, 1998.

Niepold, Gerd. *The Battle for White Russia: The Destruction of Army Group Centre, June 1944.* London: Brassey's, 1987.

Nipe, George, and Remy Spezzano. *Platz der Leibstandarte: The SS Panzer-Grenadier Division LSSAH and the Battle of Kharkov.* Southbury, CT: RZM, 2001.

Panov, B .V., et. al. *Istoriya Voennogo Iskusstvo* (History of military art). Textbook for military academies of the USSR. Moscow: Military, 1984.

Parrish, Michael, ed. *Battle for Moscow: The 1942 Soviet General Staff Study.* London: Brassey's, 1989.

Pavlov, Dmitri. *Leningrad, 1941: The Blockade.* Chicago: Univ. of Chicago Press, 1965.

Perro, Oskars. *Fortress Cholm.* Winnipeg: Fedorowicz, 1992.

Piekalkiewicz, Janusz. *Moscow, 1941: The Frozen Offensive.* Novato, CA: Presidio, 1981.

— — —. *Operation Citadel: Kursk and Orel.* Novato, CA: Presidio, 1987.

Pierik, Perry. *From Leningrad to Berlin: Dutch Volunteers in the Service of the German Waffen-SS, 1941–45.* Soesterberg, Netherlands: Aspekt, 2001.

— — —. *Hungary 1944–1945: The Forgotten Tragedy.* Nieuwegein, Netherlands: Aspekt, 1996.

Plocher, Hermann. *The German Air Force Versus Russia 1941.* New York: Arno, 1968.

— — —. *The German Air Force Versus Russia 1942.* New York: Arno, 1968.

— — —. *The German Air Force Versus Russia 1943.* New York: Arno, 1967.

Price, Alfred. *The Last Year of the Luftwaffe.* London: Arms and Armour, 1991.

Rauss, Erhard, and Oldwig Natzmer. *Anvil of War: German Generalship on the Eastern Front.* Mechanicsburg: Stackpole, 1994.

Restayn, Jean. *Kharkov.* Winnipeg: Fedorowicz, 2000.

Reynolds, Michael. *Men of Steel: I SS Panzer Corps: The Ardennes and Eastern Front.* New York: Sarpedon, 1999.

Ripley, Tim. *Spearhead No. 2. Grossdeutschland: Guderian's Eastern Front Elite.* Havertown, PA: Casemate, 2001.

Rotundo, Louis, ed. *Battle for Stalingrad: The 1943 Soviet General Staff Study.* London: Pergamon-Brassey's, 1989.

Ryan, Cornelius. *The Last Battle.* New York: Simon and Schuster, 1966.

Salisbury, Harrison. *The 900 Days: The Siege of Stalingrad.* New York: Harper and Row, 1969.

Sarhidai, Gyula, et al. *Hungarian Eagles: The Hungarian Air Force, 1920–1945.* Aldershot, UK: Hikoki, 1997.

Sarin, Oleg, and Lev Dvoretsky. *Alien Wars: The Soviet Union's Aggressions Against the World.* Novato, CA: Presidio, 1996.

Sasso, Claude R. *Soviet Night Operations in World War II.* Leavenworth Paper. Washington, D.C.: GPO, 1982.

Schmitz, Peter, and Klaus-Jürgen Thies. *Die Truppenkennzeichen der Verbände und Einheiten der deutschen Wehrmacht und Waffen-SS und ihre Einsätze im Zweiten Weltkrieg 1939–1945.* (The insignia of organizations and units of the German armed forces and Waffen-SS and their operations in WWII). Osnabrück, Germany, 1987. Five volumes pertain, namely

Vol. 1, *Das Heer* (The Army);

Vol. 2, *Die Kriegsmarine, Luftwaffe, and Waffen-SS* (The Navy, Air Force, and Waffen-SS); and

Vols. 3, 4, and 5, with additional information not in the first two.

Schroter, Heinz. *Stalingrad: The Battle That Changed the World.* New York: Dutton, 1958.

Schulte, Theo J. *German Army and Nazi Policies in Occupied Russia.* Oxford: Berg, 1989.

Seaton, Albert. *The Battle for Moscow.* New York: Stein and Day, 1971.

– – –. *The Fall of Fortress Europe, 1943–1945.* London: Batsford, 1981.

– – –. *Russo-German War, 1941–45.* New York: Praeger, 1971.

– – –. *Stalin as Military Commander.* New York: Praeger, 1976.

Sharp, Charles C. *Soviet Infantry Tactics in World War II.* West Chester, OH: Nafziger Collection, 1998.

Shores, Christopher. *Duel for the Sky: Ten Crucial Air Battles of World War II.* London: Grub Street, 1999.

Shtemenko, Army General A. M. *The Soviet General Staff at War, 1941–1945.* Moscow: Progress, 1975.

Silgalis, Arthur. *Latvian Legion.* San Jose, CA: Bender, 1986.

Spaeter. *History of Panzerkorps Grossdeutschland,* Vol. 3. Winnipeg: Fedorowicz, 2000.

Spahr, William J. *Stalin's Lieutenants: A Study of Command Under Duress.* Novato, CA: Presidio, 1997.

– – –. *Zhukov: The Rise and Fall of a Great Captain.* Novato, CA: Presidio, 1994.

Strawson, John. *The Battle for Berlin.* New York: Scribners, 1974.

Temkin, Gabriel. *My Just War: The Memoir of a Jewish Red Army Soldier in WWII.* Novato, CA: Presidio, 1998.

Tieke, Wilhelm. *The Caucasus and the Oil: The German-Soviet War in the Caucasus, 1942–1943.* Winnipeg: Fedorowicz, 1995.

Tieke, Wilhelm. *Tragedy of the Faithful: A History of III SS-Panzerkorps.* Winnipeg: Fedorowicz, 2001.

Toland, John. *The Last 100 Days: The Tumultuous and Controversial Story of the Final Days of World War II in Europe.* New York: Bantam, 1966.

Treptow, Kurt W., ed. *Romania and World War II.* Yassy: Center for Romanian Studies, 1996.

Tsouras, Peter G. *The Great Patriotic War: The Illustrated History.* London: Greenhill, 1993.

Tsouras, Peter G., ed. *Fighting in Hell: The German Ordeal on the Eastern Front.* London: Greenhill, 1995.

— — —. *Panzers on the Eastern Front: General Erhard Raus and His Panzer Divisions in Russia, 1941–1945.* Mechanicsburg, PA: Stackpole, 2002.

Turney, Alfred. *Disaster at Moscow: Von Bock's Campaigns 1941–1942.* Albuquerque: Univ. of New Mexico Press, 1970.

Tyushkevich, S. A. *Soviet Armed Forces: History of Their Organizational Development.* Washington, D.C: GPO, 1978.

U.S. Army. *Combat in Russian Forests and Swamps.* Washington, D.C.: GPO, 1982.

U.S. Army. *Effects of Climate on Combat in European Russia.* Washington, D.C.: GPO, 1952.

U.S. Army. *German Defensive Tactics Against Russian Breakthroughs.* Washington, D.C.: GPO, 1955.

U.S. Army. *Military Improvisations During the Russian Campaign.* Washington, D.C.: GPO, 1983.

U.S. Army. *Russian Combat Methods in World War II.* Washington, D.C.: GPO, 1950.

U.S. Army. *Small Unit Actions During the German Campaign in Russia.* Washington, D.C.: GPO, 1953.

U.S. Army. *Terrain Factors in the Russian Campaign.* Washington, D.C.: GPO, 1982.

U.S. War Department. Technical Manual TM-E 30-451, *Handbook on German Military Forces.* Washington, D.C.: GPO, 1945.

Vasilevskii, Marshal A. M. *A Lifelong Cause.* Moscow: Progress, 1981.

von Manstein, Erich. *Lost Victories.* Novato, CA: Presidio, 1982.

von Mellenthin, F. W. *Panzer Battles.* Norman: Univ. of Oklahoma Press, 2001.

von Senger und Etterlin, Frido. *Neither Hope nor Fear.* Novato, CA: Presidio, 1989.

Wagener, Carl. *Heeresgruppe Sud: Der Kampf im Suden der Ostfront, 1941-1945.* Dorheim: Friedberg Pozdun, n.d.

War Department. *Soviet Tactical Doctrine in WWII.* Pisgah, OH: Nafziger Collection, 1997.

Whaley, Barton. *Codeword Barbarossa.* Cambridge, MA: MIT Press, 1973.

Williamson, Gordon. *The Blood Soaked Soil: The Battles of the Waffen SS.* Osceola, WI: Motorbooks, 1995.

Wray, Timothy A. *Standing Fast: German Defensive Doctrine on the Russian Front During World War II: Prewar to 1943.* Leavenworth Paper. Washington, D.C.: GPO, 1986.

Yerger, Mark C. *Riding East: The SS Cavalry Brigade in Poland and Russia, 1939–42.* Atglen, PA: Schiffer, 1996.

Zaloga, Steven. *Bagration 1944: The Destruction of Army Group Center.* London: Osprey, 1996.

Zaloga, Steven J. and Leland Ness. *Red Army Handbook, 1939–1945.* Thrupp, England: Sutton, 1998.

Zapantis, Andrew. *Hitler's Balkan Campaign and the Invasion of the USSR.* Boulder, CO: East European Monographs, 1987.

Zetterling, Niklas, and A. Frankson. *Kursk 1943: A Statistical Analysis.* London: Frank Cass, 2000.

Zhukov, G. I. *Marshal Zhukov's Greatest Battles.* New York: Harper, 1969.

— — —. *Memoirs of Marshal Zhukov.* New York: Delacorte, 1971.

Zhukov, G., et al. *Battles Hitler Lost and the Soviet Marshals Who Won Them.* New York: Richardson, 1986.

Ziemke, Earl. *German Northern Theater of Operations, 1940–1945.* Washington, D.C.: GPO, 1959.

— — —. *Stalingrad to Berlin.* Washington, D.C.: GPO, 1966.

Ziemke, Earl, and Magna Bauer. *Moscow to Stalingrad: Decision in the East.* Washington, D.C.: GPO, 1987.

The National Archives, National Archives and Records Service, General Services Administration

Guides to German Records Microfilmed at Alexandria, Virginia. Assembled during the process of microfilming millions of pages of German military unit documents in the 1960s and 70s, these finding aids include detailed overviews of operations that are useful departure points for more thorough study. These formed the basis for many of

the German unit operations summaries included in this encyclopedia, although all were supplemented by information gained from
further research. It should be noted that operations elsewhere, that
is, besides the Eastern Front, are also included in these guides, and
more detail is included for such operations than the scope of this
book allowed.

Guide No. 14, *Armies* (Part I), 1959
Guide No. 40, *Army Groups* (Part I), 1964
Guide No. 41, *Divisions* (Part I), 1964
Guide No. 42, *Armies* (Part II), 1964
Guide No. 43, *Armies* (Part III), 1964
Guide No. 44, *Armies* (Part IV), 1964
Guide No. 45, *Divisions* (Part II), 1964
Guide No. 46, *Corps* (Part I), 1965
Guide No. 47, *Armies* (Part V), 1965
Guide No. 48, *Armies* (Part VI), 1965
Guide No. 49, *Armies* (Part VII), 1965
Guide No. 51, *Panzer Armies* (Part I), 1965
Guide No. 52, *Army Groups* (Part II), 1966
Guide No. 53, *Panzer Armies* (Part II), 1966
Guide No. 54, *Armies* (Part VIII), 1966
Guide No. 55, *Corps* (Part II), 1967
Guide No. 56, *Armies* (Part IX), 1968
Guide No. 58, *Corps* (Part III), 1968
Guide No. 59, *Corps* (Part IV), 1968
Guide No. 60, *Corps* (Part V), 1969
Guide No. 61, *Corps* (Part VI), 1969
Guide No. 62, *Corps* (Part VII), 1970
Guide No. 63, *Division* (Part III), 1970
Guide No. 64, *Divisions* (Part IV), 1970
Guide No. 65, *Divisions* (Part V), 1970
Guide No. 66, *Divisions* (Part VI), 1972
Guide No. 67, *Divisions* (Part VII), 1974
Guide No. 68, *Divisions* (Part VIII), 1974
Guide No. 69, *Divisions* (Part IX), 1974
Guide No. 70, *Divisions* (Part X), 1975
Guide No. 71, *Divisions* (Part XI), 1976
Guide No. 72, *Divisions* (Part XII), 1976
Guide No. 73, *Divisions* (Part XIII), 1976
Guide No. 74, *Divisions* (Part XIV), 1977

Websites

Although there is a great deal of nonsense on the Internet, there are also some very fine sites with reliable information. The following were useful for this book, and are recommended. In instances in which the title may not be self-explanatory, the relevance for readers of this book is briefly explained in each entry.

Ammentorp, Steen. *The Generals of World War II.*
URL: http://www.generals.dk/Main.htm
Grecu, Dan-Simion. *The Romanian Royal Army.*
URL: http://www.geocities.com/dangrecu/
Gustin, Emmanuel. *Military Aircraft Database.* (Outstanding collection of detailed data on twentieth-century combat aircraft.)
URL: http://www.csd.uwo.ca/~pettypi/elevon/
gustin_military/db/index.html
Düfel, Andreas. *Die Träger des Ritterkreuzes des Eisernen Kreuzes, 1939-45* ("The Bearers of The Knight's Cross of the Iron Cross, 1939-45"). Useful biographical material.
URL: http://www.das-ritterkreuz.de/
Exton, Brett. *Island Farm Prisoner of War Camp: Bridgend.* (Includes extensive biographical information about German officers incarcerated there during and after the war.)
URL: http://www.islandfarm.fsnet.co.uk/index.html
Fitzgibbon, Rob. *Waffen-SS Order of Battle.* (Comprehensive organizational information on Waffen-SS units.)
URL: http://www.wssob.com/
German Historical Museum, Berlin, Website. (Use the internal/local search engine to locate subject information, especially biographies of key personnel.)
URL: http://www.dhm.de/
Hovi, Henri Matti. *Puolustusvoimat* (The Finnish Army) *in World War II.*
URL: http://personal.inet.fi/private/hovi.pages/sa-int/
Mirams, David Paterson. *Katyn Forest Massacre.*
URL: http://www.katyn.org.au/
Niehorster, Leo. *World War II Armed Forces: Orders of Battle and Organizations.*
URL: http://freeport-tech.com/wwii/index.htm
Noomen, E.J., and Adroom Software. *Graves of World War II Personalities.*
URL: http://www.xs4all.nl/~ejnoomen/wwgrave.html

Nitu, Victor. *The Romanian Army in World War II.*
   URL: http://www.wwii.home.ro/

Parada, George, et al. Achtung Panzer! (Comprehensive site including vehicle data, biographical sketches, photos, articles on tactics,
   and more.)
   URL: http://www.achtungpanzer.com/

Pipes, Jason. *The German Armed Forces, 1919-1945.* (Extremely exten-
   sive and detailed information about the German armed forces in
   WWII.)
   URL: www.feldgrau.com

Pusca, Dragos. *The Dutch Helmet: The Romanian Army in the Second
   World War.*
   URL: http://www.armata.home.ro/index.htm

Potapov, Valeriy, et al. *The Russian Battlefield.* (Highly authentic and
   especially insightful articles, photos of equipment, and combat
   operations; data on armored vehicles and field artillery; memoirs;
   and information on Lend-Lease activities and its importance.)
   URL: http://www.battlefield.ru/

Wendel, Marcus. *Third Reich Factbook.*
   URL: http://www.skalman.nu/third-reich/

— — —. *Soviet Union Factbook: The Great Patriotic War.*
   URL: http://www.skalman.nu/soviet/ww2.htm

Zuljan, Ralph. OnWar.com Website: *Tanks of WWII* Section. (Highly
   comprehensive data summaries of a wide range of WWII armored
   fighting vehicles.)
   URL: http://www.onwar.com/tanks/index.htm